‖‖‖‖‖‖‖‖‖‖‖‖‖‖‖‖
W9-BNN-859

CLIFFS

PRAXIS II

National Teacher Examinations

Core Battery

PREPARATION GUIDE

by

Jerry Bobrow, Ph.D.
Harold Nathan, Ph.D.
Stephen Fisher, M.A.
William A. Covino, Ph.D.
Peter Z Orton, M.Ed.
Bill Bobrow, M.A.
Loraine Weber, M.A.

Series Editor

Jerry Bobrow, Ph.D.

Consultants

Rich Michaels, M.A.
Wendy R. Taub, M.A.
Dolores Y. Fitchman, M.Ed.
Merritt L. Weisinger, J.D.

Cliffs Notes
INCORPORATED
LINCOLN, NEBRASKA   68501

ACKNOWLEDGMENTS

I would like to thank the following people for their invaluable assistance in editing, proofreading, and typing the manuscript: Editor Michele Spence of Cliffs Notes; my typist, Charlene Harris; and my coordinating assistant, Stacey Baum. I would also like to give special thanks to my wife, Susan Bobrow; my daughter, Jennifer Lynn; and my son, Adam Michael, for their patience and understanding while I was buried in the manuscript.

Jerry Bobrow

Cover photograph by Nick Vedros, Vedros & Associates / Tony Stone Images

The Cliffs Notes logo, the names "Cliffs" and "Cliffs Notes," and the black and yellow diagonal-stripe cover design are all registered trademarks belonging to Cliffs Notes, Inc., and may not be used in whole or in part without written permission.

ISBN 0-8220-2058-0

FOURTH EDITION

© Copyright 1989 by Jerry Bobrow

Previous editions © Copyright 1987, 1984, 1981 by Jerry Bobrow

All Rights Reserved

Printed in U.S.A.

CONTENTS

Preface x

Study Guide Checklist xi

PART I: INTRODUCTION

RECENT FORMAT OF THE NATIONAL TEACHER EXAMINATIONS—CORE
BATTERY 3

GENERAL DESCRIPTION.. 4

QUESTIONS COMMONLY ASKED ABOUT THE NTE.............................. 5

TAKING THE NTE: TWO SUCCESSFUL OVERALL APPROACHES 7

PART II: ANALYSIS OF EXAM AREAS

Ability Tested • Basic Skills Necessary • Directions
Analysis • Suggested Approach with Samples

INTRODUCTION TO THE TEST OF COMMUNICATION SKILLS.................... 11

Listening 11

Part A: Questions and Statements.................................. 11

Part B: Conversations 14

Part C: Talks 15

Reading 17

General Procedure for Answering Reading Questions................. 20

Five Key Questions for Understanding and Interpreting What
You Read 21

Writing—Multiple Choice 22

Part A: Usage... 22

Part B: Sentence Correction 23

Writing—Essay 32

Sample A: Prewriting Methods and Essays 34

iii

Topic 34
Clustering.. 34
The "Story" Formula... 35
The Finished Essay 35
Outlining 36
Additional Finished Essays for Sample A 37
Sample B: Prewriting Methods and Essays........................... 40
Topic 40
Clustering.. 40
The Finished Essay 41
The "Why" Essay 42
Poor Essays—What Not to Do.. 43
Sample A.. 43
Sample B 43
Important Terms Used in Essay Questions 44
Examples.. 45
Practice Essay Topics 45
Practice Essay Checklist... 47
INTRODUCTION TO THE TEST OF GENERAL KNOWLEDGE 48
Social Studies... 48
Mathematics 52
Mark Key Words 53
Pull out Information 55
Plug in Numbers 56
Work from the Answers.. 56
Approximate 58
Make Comparisons 59
Mark Diagrams... 59
Draw Diagrams... 63
Procedure Problems 66
Other Sources of Data—Graphs 67
Tips for Working Math Problems 72
Literature and Fine Arts... 73
Science 76
INTRODUCTION TO THE TEST OF PROFESSIONAL KNOWLEDGE 79

PART III: ASSESSMENT MINI-TEST

ANSWER SHEET FOR THE MINI-TEST 85

MINI-TEST
Test of Communication Skills 87
Section I: Listening 87

Questions, Statements, Conversations, and Talks—Script 87
    Part A: Questions and Statements 87
    Part B: Conversations 88
    Part C: Talks 88
    Answer Choices 91
    Part A: Questions and Statements 91
    Part B: Conversations 92
    Part C: Talks 92
  Section II: Reading 94
  Section III: Writing—Multiple Choice 98
    Part A: Usage 98
    Part B: Sentence Correction 99
  Section IV: Writing—Essay 101
Test of General Knowledge 102
  Section I: Social Studies 102
  Section II: Mathematics 105
  Section III: Literature and Fine Arts 107
  Section IV: Science 109
Test of Professional Knowledge 111
Answer Key for the Mini-Test 116
Scoring the Mini-Test 117
Analyzing Your Test Results 117
Mini-Test General Analysis Sheet 118
Analysis—Tally Sheet for Questions Missed 119
Mini-Test Essay Checklist 120

COMPLETE ANSWERS AND EXPLANATIONS FOR THE MINI-TEST

Test of Communication Skills 121
  Section I: Listening 121
    Part A: Questions and Statements 121
    Part B: Conversations 121
    Part C: Talks 122
  Section II: Reading 122
  Section III: Writing—Multiple Choice 123
    Part A: Usage 123
    Part B: Sentence Correction 124
Test of General Knowledge 125
  Section I: Social Studies 125
  Section II: Mathematics 126
  Section III: Literature and Fine Arts 127
  Section IV: Science 128
Test of Professional Knowledge 130

PART IV: SUBJECT AREA REVIEWS

ENGLISH REVIEW
Punctuation 135
Grammar, Usage, and Sentence Structure 140
SOCIAL STUDIES REVIEW
Charts and Graphs 149
Area Review Outlines and Glossaries.. 155
U.S. History Outline 155
Political Science-Government Outline 159
Behavioral Sciences Outline 162
Economics Outline 165
Geography Outline.. 169
Glossary of Terms in U.S. History 172
Glossary of Terms in Political Science-Government................... 179
MATHEMATICS REVIEW
Symbols, Terminology, Formulas, and General Mathematical
Information 186
Common Math Symbols and Terms.. 186
Math Formulas 187
Important Equivalents 188
Measures 188
Math Words and Phrases 189
Mathematical Properties and Basic Statistics............................. 190
Arithmetic... 192
Arithmetic Diagnostic Test 192
Arithmetic Review 194
Algebra.. 209
Algebra Diagnostic Test 209
Algebra Review.. 210
Geometry... 215
Geometry Diagnostic Test 215
Geometry Review... 221
LITERATURE AND FINE ARTS REVIEW
Glossary of Terms in Literature 237
Glossary of Terms in Art 238
Styles of Western Art 239
Glossary of Terms in Music.. 239
SCIENCE REVIEW
Biology Review... 241
Basic Concepts 241

Glossary of Terms in Biology.. 244
Geology Review 249
  Basic Concepts 249
  Glossary of Terms in Geology and Meteorology 254
Chemistry Review.. 257
  Basic Concepts 257
  Glossary of Terms in Chemistry... 264
Physics Review.. 267
  Basic Concepts 267
  Glossary of Terms in Physics and Astronomy....................... 278
PROFESSIONAL KNOWLEDGE REVIEW
  Survey of Important People and Ideas in Education.............. 282

PART IV: PRACTICE-REVIEW-ANALYZE-PRACTICE
Two Full-Length Practice Tests

PRACTICE TEST 1
  Answer Sheet for Practice Test 1.. 296
  Test of Communication Skills 299
    Section I: Listening... 299
      Questions, Statements, Conversations, and Talks—Script....... 299
        Part A: Questions and Statements................................ 299
        Part B: Conversations 300
        Part C: Talks... 301
      Answer Choices... 305
        Part A: Questions and Statements................................ 305
        Part B: Conversations 306
        Part C: Talks... 307
    Section II: Reading... 310
    Section III: Writing—Multiple Choice................................ 321
      Part A: Usage... 321
      Part B: Sentence Correction 324
    Section IV: Writing—Essay 330
  Test of General Knowledge... 331
    Section I: Social Studies 331
    Section II: Mathematics 341
    Section III: Literature and Fine Arts.................................. 346
    Section IV: Science 361
  Test of Professional Knowledge.. 368
    Section I.. 368
    Section II... 376
    Section III 384

Section IV 392
Answer Key for Practice Test 1 400
Scoring Practice Test 1 403
Analyzing Your Test Results................................ 403
Practice Test 1 General Analysis Sheet 404
Analysis—Tally Sheet for Questions Missed 405
Practice Test 1 Essay Checklist........................... 406

COMPLETE ANSWERS AND EXPLANATIONS FOR PRACTICE TEST 1
Test of Communication Skills 407
   Section I: Listening....................................... 407
      Part A: Questions and Statements.............. 407
      Part B: Conversations 408
      Part C: Talks... 409
   Section II: Reading.. 410
   Section III: Writing—Multiple Choice............. 412
      Part A: Usage.. 412
      Part B: Sentence Correction 415
Test of General Knowledge................................. 418
   Section I: Social Studies 418
   Section II: Mathematics 422
   Section III: Literature and Fine Arts 427
   Section IV: Science 430
Test of Professional Knowledge.......................... 434
   Section I 434
   Section II... 437
   Section III 441
   Section IV 445

PRACTICE TEST 2
Answer Sheet for Practice Test 2 452
Test of Communication Skills 455
   Section I: Listening....................................... 455
      Questions, Statements, Conversations, and Talks—Script 455
      Part A: Questions and Statements.............. 455
      Part B: Conversations 456
      Part C: Talks... 457
      Answer Choices....................................... 461
      Part A: Questions and Statements.............. 461
      Part B: Conversations 462
      Part C: Talks... 463
   Section II: Reading.. 465
   Section III: Writing—Multiple Choice............. 476
      Part A: Usage.. 476

Part B: Sentence Correction 479
Section IV: Writing—Essay 485
Test of General Knowledge................................ 486
Section I: Social Studies 486
Section II: Mathematics 496
Section III: Literature and Fine Arts 501
Section IV: Science 515
Test of Professional Knowledge........................ 522
Section I 522
Section II................................ 529
Section III 536
Section IV 543
Answer Key for Practice Test 2......................... 551
Scoring Practice Test 2 554
Analyzing Your Test Results................. 554
Practice Test 2 General Analysis Sheet 555
Analysis—Tally Sheet for Questions Missed 556
Practice Test 2 Essay Checklist......................... 557

COMPLETE ANSWERS AND EXPLANATIONS FOR PRACTICE TEST 2
Test of Communication Skills 559
Section I: Listening......................... 559
Part A: Questions and Statements.................... 559
Part B: Conversations 560
Part C: Talks......................... 560
Section II: Reading......................... 562
Section III: Writing—Multiple Choice......................... 564
Part A: Usage......................... 564
Part B: Sentence Correction 566
Test of General Knowledge................................ 570
Section I: Social Studies 570
Section II: Mathematics 574
Section III: Literature and Fine Arts 579
Section IV: Science 583
Test of Professional Knowledge......................... 587
Section I 587
Section II................................ 590
Section III 593
Section IV 596
Final Preparation: "The Final Touches"............................... 601

PREFACE

We know that getting a good score on the NTE is important to you! And because the NTE covers information in a wide range of subjects, thorough preparation is the key to doing your best. This makes your study time more valuable than ever; it must be used most effectively. With this in mind, this Cliffs NTE Preparation Guide was developed by leading experts and instructors in the field of test preparation. This guide is thorough, direct, concise, and easy to use. It is the most comprehensive, up-to-date test preparation guide available today. The materials, techniques, and strategies presented here have been carefully researched, tested, and evaluated and are presently used at NTE preparation programs at many leading colleges and universities.

This guide is divided into five parts:

Part I: Introduction—a general description of the exam, recent format, questions commonly asked, and a basic overall strategy.

Part II: Analysis of Exam Areas—focuses on ability tested, basic skills necessary, directions, analysis, suggested approaches with samples, and additional tips.

Part III: Assessment—a short Mini-Test to familiarize you with the various tests and to assess your strengths and weaknesses.

Part IV: Subject Area Reviews—intensive reviews in English, social studies, mathematics, literature, fine arts, science, and professional knowledge.

Part V: Practice-Review-Analyze-Practice—two complete full-length practice tests with answers and *in-depth explanations*.

The Mini-Test and each practice test are followed by analysis charts to assist you in evaluating your progress.

This guide is not meant to substitute for comprehensive courses, but if you follow the Study Guide Checklist and study regularly, you will get the best NTE test preparation possible.

STUDY GUIDE CHECKLIST

_____ 1. Read the NTE information materials available at the Testing Office, Counseling Center, or your undergraduate institutions.

_____ 2. Become familiar with the Test Format, page 3.

_____ 3. Read the General Description and Questions Commonly Asked about the NTE Core Battery, starting on page 4.

_____ 4. Learn the techniques of Two Successful Overall Approaches, page 7.

_____ 5. Carefully read Part II, Analysis of Exam Areas, starting on page 11.

_____ 6. Take the Mini-Test Assessment, starting on page 85.

_____ 7. Check your answers and analyze your results, starting on page 116.

_____ 8. Fill out the Tally Sheet for Questions Missed to pinpoint your mistakes, page 119.

_____ 9. Review English, starting on page 135.

_____ 10. Review social studies, starting on page 149.

_____ 11. Review mathematics, starting on page 186.

_____ 12. Review literature and fine arts, starting on page 237.

_____ 13. Review science, starting on page 241.

_____ 14. Review professional knowledge, starting on page 282.

_____ 15. Strictly observing time allotments, take Practice Test 1, starting on page 296.

_____ 16. Check your answers and analyze your Practice Test 1 results, starting on page 400.

_____ 17. Fill out the Tally Sheet for Questions Missed to pinpoint your mistakes, page 405.

_____ 18. Study ALL the Answers and Explanations to Practice Test 1, starting on page 407.

_____ 19. Review weak areas as necessary.

_____ 20. Strictly observing time allotments, take Practice Test 2, beginning on page 452.

_____ 21. Check your answers and analyze your Practice Test 2 results, starting on page 551.

_____ 22. Fill out the Tally Sheet for Questions Missed to pinpoint your mistakes, page 556.

_____ 23. Study ALL the Answers and Explanations to Practice Test 2, starting on page 559.

_____ 24. Review weak areas.

_____ 25. Review Analysis of Exam Areas, starting on page 11.

_____ 26. Carefully read Final Preparation: "The Final Touches," page 601.

PART I: Introduction

RECENT FORMAT OF THE
NATIONAL TEACHER EXAMINATIONS—
CORE BATTERY

	Minutes	Approximate Number of Questions
TEST OF COMMUNICATION SKILLS		
Section I: Listening	30	30
Section II: Reading	30	30
Section III: Writing—Multiple Choice	30	45
Section IV: Writing—Essay	30	1 Essay
TOTAL	120	105 Questions 1 Essay

	Minutes	Approximate Number of Questions
TEST OF GENERAL KNOWLEDGE		
Section I: Social Studies	30	30
Section II: Mathematics	30	25
Section III: Literature and Fine Arts	30	35
Section IV: Science	30	30
TOTAL	120	120

	Minutes	Approximate Number of Questions
TEST OF PROFESSIONAL KNOWLEDGE		
Sections I, II, III, and IV	30 Each	30 Each
TOTAL	120	120

Approximate Total Time: 360 Minutes (6 Hours)
Approximate Total Questions: 345 Plus One Essay

Note: The order in which the *tests* or *sections* appear may vary, as there are several different forms of the NTE.

GENERAL DESCRIPTION

The NTE Core Battery is 6 hours long and is composed of three two-hour tests, each having four sections. The first test (although not necessarily given first) is the **Test of Communication Skills.** It is 2 hours long and contains about 105 questions, plus one essay topic. It is divided into 4 sections, each 30 minutes long, as follows:

Listening—about 30 questions, requires the ability to understand spoken messages quickly and accurately

Reading—about 30 questions, requires the ability to read and answer questions based on short written passages

Writing—Multiple Choice—about 45 questions, requires the ability to detect and correct errors in standard written English

Writing—Essay—requires the ability to plan and write a well-organized, careful essay on an assigned topic

The second test is the **Test of General Knowledge.** It is 2 hours long and contains about 120 questions. It is divided into 4 sections, each 30 minutes long, as follows:

Social Studies—about 30 questions, requires a competence in a broad range of social studies areas as well as the ability to interpret and analyze data

Mathematics—about 25 questions, requires a cumulative knowledge of math in order to solve problems of a type any teacher may need for the classroom

Literature and Fine Arts—about 35 questions, requires a basic knowledge of major works and basic elements of literature and fine arts

Science—about 30 questions, requires an understanding of major principles, theories, and methods in the area of science.

The third test is the **Test of Professional Knowledge.** It is 2 hours long and divided into 4 sections. Each section is 30 minutes in length and contains approximately 30 questions. All parts of this test draw on the knowledge that is considered essential for a beginning teacher. Areas such as planning instruction, implementing instruction, evaluating students' work, appropriate professional behavior, and legal implications in the classroom are some of the fields covered.

QUESTIONS COMMONLY ASKED ABOUT THE NTE

Q: WHO ADMINISTERS THE NTE?

A: Educational Testing Service (ETS) administers the NTE and conducts the NTE program for the NTE Policy Council, which consists of twelve representatives of state departments of education, school districts, and teacher training institutions.

Q: WHAT ARE THE NTE CORE BATTERY TESTS?

A: The NTE Core Battery consists of 3 tests: the Test of Communication Skills, the Test of General Knowledge, and the Test of Professional Knowledge. Each of these tests is 2 hours long and consists of 4 separate sections.

Q: WHAT ARE THE AREA EXAMINATIONS?

A: The NTE Area Examinations include twenty-five separate exams on specific subjects and fields of specialization. Each area exam is two hours long.

Q: HOW IS THE NTE SCORE USED?

A: The NTE score is used in a variety of ways: By state departments of education for certification, by local school districts to evaluate prospective teachers, by institutions to measure the preparation of their students, and by other agencies concerned with education. As each sets its own minimum standards and requirements, you should contact the appropriate institution, district, or agency.

Q: HOW IS THE NTE CORE BATTERY SCORED?

A: Each of the 3 Core Battery tests is scored from 600 to 690, with the following average scores (approximations): Communications Skills 659, General Knowledge 656, and Professional Knowledge 656.

Q: WHEN AND WHERE IS THE NTE ADMINISTERED?

A: The NTE is administered three times a year in November, February, and June. These administrations are usually on Saturday mornings. Check your NTE Bulletin of Information for precise dates and locations. The bulletin is generally available at the Testing Office, Counseling Center, or your undergraduate institutions.

Q: HOW AND WHEN SHOULD I REGISTER?

A: To register for the NTE, complete all items on both sides of the registration form inserted in the center of the NTE Bulletin of Information. Check the appropriate closing dates for registration listed on the back of the bulletin. Registration usually closes approximately five weeks before the test date.

Q: Is walk-in registration provided?
A: Yes, on a limited basis. If you are unable to meet regular registration deadlines, you may attempt to register on the day of the test (an additional fee is required). You will be seated only if space remains after those preregistered have been seated.

Q: Are there any special arrangements for taking the tests?
A: Yes, basically three: (1) Special Monday test dates are possible in case of religious circumstances that conflict with the regular test date. (2) Special supplementary test centers may be requested under special conditions. (3) Handicapped individuals may also request special arrangements. If you are in need of any special arrangements, contact ETS well before the testing date.

Q: Can I take the test more than once?
A: Yes. You may take the exam as often as you wish.

Q: What materials may I bring to the NTE?
A: Bring your registration form, positive identification, a watch, three or four sharpened Number 2 pencils, and a good eraser. You may *not* bring scratch paper, calculators, or books. You may do your figuring in the space provided in the test booklet.

Q: How should I prepare for the NTE?
A: Because the NTE covers a broad range of topics and asks for specific information, subject area reviews will be helpful. Understanding and practicing test-taking strategies and techniques will also be especially valuable. Both subject matter reviews and strategies are fully covered in this book. Reading the daily newspaper and well-known magazines would also be of use.

Q: Should I guess on the NTE Core Battery?
A: Yes! Since there is no penalty for wrong answers (a wrong answer is worth the same as no answer), guess if you have to. If possible, first try to eliminate some of the choices to increase your chances of guessing the correct answer. But don't leave any blanks.

Q: Can I get more information?
A: Yes. If you require information which is not available in this book, write to National Teacher Examinations, Princeton Office, Educational Testing Service, Rosedale Road, Princeton, New Jersey 08541. Or telephone: (609) 921-9000.

TAKING THE NTE:
TWO SUCCESSFUL OVERALL APPROACHES

I. The "Plus-Minus" System

Many who take the NTE don't get their best possible score because they spend too much time on difficult questions, leaving insufficient time to answer the easy questions. Don't let this happen to you. Since every question within each section is worth the same amount, use the following system.

1. Answer easy questions immediately.

2. When you come to a question that seems "impossible" to answer, mark a large minus sign ("−") next to it on your test booklet.

3. Then mark a "guess" answer on your answer sheet and move on to the next question.

4. When you come to a question that seems solvable but appears too time consuming, mark a large plus sign ("+") next to that question in your test booklet and register a guess answer on your answer sheet. Then move on to the next question.

Since your time allotment is approximately one minute per question, a "time-consuming" question is a question that you estimate will take you more than several minutes to answer. But don't waste time deciding whether a question is a "+" or a "−." Act quickly, as the intent of this strategy is, in fact, to save you valuable time.

After working all the easy questions, your booklet should look something like this:

              1.
         + 2.
              3.
         − 4.
         + 5.
            etc.

5. After working all the problems you can do immediately in that section (the easy ones), go back and work your "+" problems. Change your "guess" on your answer sheet, if necessary, for those problems you are able to work.

7

6. If you finish working your "+" problems and still have time left, you can either

(A) attempt those "−" questions—the ones that you considered "impossible." Sometimes a problem later in that section will "trigger" your memory and you'll be able to go back and answer one of the earlier "impossible" problems.

or

(B) don't bother with those "impossible" questions. Rather, spend your time reviewing your work to be sure you didn't make any careless mistakes on the questions you thought were easy to answer.

REMEMBER: You do not have to erase the pluses and minuses you made on your *question booklet*. And be sure to fill in all your answer spaces—if necessary, with a guess. As there is no penalty for wrong answers, it makes no sense to leave an answer space blank. And, of course, remember that you may work only in one section of the test at a time.

II. The Elimination Strategy

Take advantage of being allowed to mark in your testing booklet. As you eliminate an answer choice from consideration, make sure to *mark it out in your question booklet* as follows:

(A)
?(B)
(C)
(D)
?(E)

Notice that some choices are marked with question marks, signifying that they may be possible answers. This technique will help you avoid reconsidering those choices you have already eliminated. It will also help you narrow down your possible answers.

Again, these marks you make on your testing booklet do not need to be erased.

PART II: Analysis of Exam Areas

This section is designed to introduce you to each NTE area by carefully reviewing the

1. Ability Tested
2. Basic Skills Necessary
3. Directions
4. Analysis
5. Suggested Approach with Samples

This section emphasizes important test-taking techniques and strategies and how to apply them to a variety of question types.

INTRODUCTION TO THE TEST OF COMMUNICATION SKILLS

The Test of Communication Skills is 2 hours long and contains 4 sections, each 30 minutes in length. These sections include Listening, Reading, Writing—Multiple Choice, and Writing—Essay.

LISTENING

The Listening section of the Test of Communication Skills consists of four types of questions, totaling approximately 30. You are required to answer short questions, understand short statements, answer questions based on a conversation, and answer questions based on a short talk. All material except the answer choices will be heard rather than read. Note that some questions, conversations, and talks may include voices with a non-American accent or with an American regional dialect.

PART A: QUESTIONS AND STATEMENTS

Ability Tested

This section tests your ability to listen carefully and to identify the key terms and essential information in questions and statements.

Basic Skills Necessary

This section requires a well-developed skill for extracting relevant information from spoken words. This is the skill attentive students develop in classes and effective teachers practice as they listen to their students' questions and statements.

Directions

You will be faced with two kinds of problems. You must either answer a short question or understand a brief statement. Each question and each statement will be spoken one time. After you hear a question, you will read four answer choices; select the correct answer. After you hear a statement, you will read four sentences; select the sentence closest to the meaning of the statement or supported by the statement.

Analysis

1. Listen carefully to the spoken questions and statements. In most cases they will be very brief, and you must focus on their meaning quickly and accurately. The spoken questions and statements will not be repeated.
2. The correctness of an answer to a question depends not upon the content of the answer but rather upon whether the answer is recognizable as a reasonable response to the particular question.
3. A correct response to a statement will be either a *rephrasing* of information in the statement or a *conclusion* that is supported by the statement.

Suggested Approach with Samples

1. When you are asked a question, pay particular attention to key words that restrict the answer. Such key words are *who, what, when, where, why,* and *how.*

    You will hear
    Speaker: Who are you bringing to the party tonight?

    You will read
    (A) We will arrive about 8 o'clock.
    (B) We will bring dessert and some wine.
    (C) My mother will probably drive us over.
    (D) One of my old boyfriends will be with me.

    Only (D) answers the question *who*; each of the other choices refers to *when* (A), *what* (B), and *how* (C) and are therefore incorrect.

2. Other key terms, which may be either expressed or implied by the question, are *how much, how little, how long,* and *if (whether).*

    You will hear
    Speaker: Will it rain tomorrow?

    You will read
    (A) No one expected rain last week.
    (B) Showers will begin falling by the afternoon.
    (C) Yesterday it rained all morning.
    (D) A storm is traveling down from the north.

    The question asks *if* it will rain without using that term directly, and the only choice that tells whether it will rain is (B).

3. When you hear a statement, try to mentally rephrase it in your own words and be aware of any conclusions it immediately suggests.

You will hear

Speaker: Even though the weather was clear, it was too cold for us to picnic at the park.

You will read

(A) The picnic was clearly held at the park.
(B) We did not picnic at the park.
(C) The picnic was set for Sunday.
(D) We were hoping it would snow at the picnic.

Choice (B) is a rephrasing of the final part of the spoken sentence. Since *it was too cold for us to picnic at the park*, obviously we did not picnic at the park.

4. The correct answer choice following a statement may restate part or all of the statement.

You will hear

Speaker: On graduation day, the business majors will graduate at 11 A.M. and all other majors will graduate at 2 P.M.

You will read

(A) Business majors outnumber all other majors.
(B) All graduation ceremonies will be held in the same place.
(C) Business majors will graduate earlier than other majors.
(D) The graduation of business majors will last three hours.

Choice (C) is close to the meaning of the original statement, retaining the meaning of the statement without including the details.

5. The correct answer choice following a statement may give a conclusion supported by the statement. Always prefer a *necessary* conclusion to an *unsupported* conclusion or an *irrelevant* conclusion.

You will hear

Speaker: Most families today include only two children and are smaller than families of the past.

You will read

(A) Many of today's children attend college.
(B) Children were not as expensive to raise in the past.
(C) Parents of the past were not content with two children.
(D) Families of the past included more than two children.

We must conclude that families of the past included more than two children (D). The conclusions expressed in (B) and (C) are *unsupported*;

they need additional information not provided by the statement, and (A) is irrelevant to the statement.

PART B: CONVERSATIONS

Ability Tested

This section tests your ability to listen carefully to conversations and to draw conclusions about the situation and the attitudes of the speakers.

Basic Skills Necessary

This section requires a well-developed skill for drawing accurate conclusions about the expressed and implied content of conversation. Practice in group discussions sharpens this skill.

Directions

You will hear short conversations between two speakers. After each conversation, a third speaker will ask questions about what the two were discussing. The conversations and each question will be spoken only once. After you hear each question, choose the best of four possible answers.

Analysis

Listen carefully to each conversation, paying attention to the speakers' intonation as well as the content of their statements.

Suggested Approach with Samples

As you listen to each conversation, mentally create a *context of situation* and speaker *attitudes*. Alongside the following conversation, in parentheses, are the sorts of mental notes you might make.

Conversation	Mental Notes
Man: Can you raise enough money to pay for the football team's uniforms?	(A football team needs uniforms, and a purchaser needs money.)
Woman: The community is behind the team, so I suggest we request funds at a town meeting.	(Supportive community members might pay for the uniforms.)
Man: But remember, we asked for travel money for the basketball team at the last town meeting.	(The community might not give money again. The man is skeptical about the woman's idea.)

With these mental notes, you are prepared to listen to the questions.

1. You will hear
   Speaker: What does the man conclude about community funding of the team uniforms?

   You will read
   (A) The community will not attend a town meeting.
   (B) The community might not pay for the uniforms.
   (C) The community prefers the basketball team.
   (D) The football team should move to another community.

2. You will hear
   Speaker: What is the community's general attitude toward the football team?

   You will read
   (A) hostile   (C) supportive
   (B) apathetic   (D) resentful

   Your mental notes should lead you to choose (B) as the answer to question 1; you will recall that the man is skeptical about getting further financial support from the community. For question 2, the answer is (C); the woman makes clear that, in general, the community is supportive. Paying attention to the context of situation and speaker attitudes, you should be able to address such questions with confidence and clarity.

PART C: TALKS

Ability Tested

This section tests your ability to extract essential information and main ideas from brief talks.

Basic Skills Necessary

This section requires a well-developed skill for maintaining concentration while listening. Attentive students develop this skill through careful attention to classroom lectures, and teachers practice this skill as they monitor their own students' oral presentations.

Directions

You will hear several short talks, each followed by questions. When you hear a question, choose the best answer of the four printed in your test booklet. Remember that the talks and questions will be spoken only once, so you must listen carefully while you attempt to understand and remember what the speaker says.

Analysis

Distraction is especially dangerous in this part of the test. Maintain concentration on the talk so that you do not miss important information.

Suggested Approach with Sample

1. Pay particular attention to introductory and concluding remarks, which often state and reinforce the main topic of the talk.

Talk

Students learn better when they feel that the subject matter is relevant to their personal lives. When teaching reading, we should introduce stories about boys and girls much like our own students, boys and girls with similar desires and problems. When teaching math, we should continually illustrate the ways in which arithmetic, algebra, and geometry are used in the real, everyday world. Students who feel that what they are learning will enrich their lives outside the classroom will be more willing to learn and more excited about it.

Note that the first sentence and the last sentence repeat the main point and that the middle of the talk offers supporting details and reasons.

2. When reading answer choices, eliminate those which are *contradictory* or *irrelevant* to the passage. Consider the following question based on the above talk.

You will hear
Speaker: What is the speaker encouraging listeners to do?

You will read
(A) make students learn reading and math
(B) use parents as classroom aides
(C) connect subject matter with the lives of their students
(D) expose students to unfamiliar situations

Choice (C) reiterates the main point of the talk, but choices (A) and (D) *contradict* the speaker's stress that subject matter should be relevant and interesting to the students, and choice (B) is *irrelevant*. (C) is the best choice. Paying attention to main points and eliminating irrelevant and contradictory choices are essential strategies on this part of the test.

READING

The Reading section consists of about 30 questions and is 30 minutes long. It contains passages of approximately 200 words, shorter passages of approximately 100 words, short statements of one or more sentences, and possibly graphic materials such as tables and charts. Each passage or statement is followed by questions based on its content.

Ability Tested

This section tests your ability to understand the content of the passages and any of the following: its main idea, supporting ideas, specific details, author's purpose, authors assumptions, author's tone, strengths and weaknesses of the author's argument, inferences drawn from the passage, relationship of the passage to its intended audience, supporting evidence in the passage, etc.

Basic Skills Necessary

Understanding, interpreting, and analyzing passages are the important skills for this section. The technique of *actively* reading and marking a passage is also helpful.

Directions

Questions follow each of the passages below. Using only the stated or implied information in each passage, answer the questions.

Analysis

1. Answer all the questions for one passage before moving on to the next one. If you don't know the answer, take an educated guess or skip it.
2. Use only the information given or implied in a passage. Do not consider outside information, even if it seems more accurate than the given information.

Suggested Approach with Short Sample Passages

Two strategies that will improve your reading comprehension are *prereading the questions* and *marking the passage*. Readers who use these strategies tend to score much higher on reading tests than readers who don't.

Prereading the Question. Before reading the passage, read each question (but don't spend time reading all the multiple-choice answers) and circle the most important word or phrase.

Sample

The author's argument in favor of freedom of speech may be summarized in which of the following ways?
(A) If every speaker is not free, no speaker is.
(B) Speech keeps us free from the animal kingdom.
(C) As we think, so we speak.
(D) The Bill of Rights ensures free speech.
(E) Lunatic speeches are not free speeches.

The most *important* part is usually the most concrete and specific one. In this case, you might circle *freedom of speech.* The question parts that you circle will be those you'll tend to remember when you read the passage. In this case, you would be likely to notice and pay close attention to *freedom of speech* when it occurs in the passage. Thus, prereading allows you to focus on the parts of the passage that contain the answers.

Marking the passage. After prereading the questions, read and mark the passage. *Always mark those spots that contain information relevant to the questions you've read. In addition, you should mark other important ideas and details.* More specific advice on marking, in reference to specific subareas of reading skills, follows. In general though, *remember not to overmark;* never make more than a few marks per paragraph in order to make those parts that you mark stand out.

Passage

*By the time a child starts school, he has mastered the major part of the rules of his grammar. He has managed to accomplish this remarkable feat in such a short time by experimenting with and generalizing the rules all by himself. Each child, in effect, rediscovers language in the first few years of his life.

*When it comes to vocabulary growth, it is a different story. Unlike grammar, the chief means through which a vocabulary is learned is memorization. *And some poeple have a hard time learning and remembering new words.

*Indicates portions of the passage which refer directly to a question you've skimmed. Also marked are main points and key terms.

1. A child has mastered many rules of grammar by about the age of
   (A) 3   (B) 5   (C) 8   (D) 10   (E) 18

The first sentence of the passage contains several words from this question, so it is likely to contain the correct answer. *By the time a child starts school* tells us that the answer is 5. Before choosing (B), you should look at all the answers and cross out those which seem incorrect.

2. Although vocabulary growth involves memorization and grammar learning doesn't, we may conclude that both vocabulary and grammar make use of

(A) memorization
(B) study skills
(C) words

(D) children
(E) teachers

The question asks you to simply use your common sense. Choice (A) is incorrect; it contradicts both the passage and the question. Choices (D) and (E) make no sense. (B) is a possibility, but (C) is better because grammar learning in young children does not necessarily involve study skills but does involve words.

3. The last sentence in the passage implies that

(A) some people have little difficulty learning and remembering new words
(B) some people have a hard time remembering new words
(C) grammar does not involve remembering words
(D) old words are not often remembered
(E) learning and remembering are kinds of growth

Implies tells us that the answer is something suggested but not explicitly stated in the passage. Choice (B) is explicitly stated in the passage, so it may be eliminated. But (B) implies the opposite: if *some* people have a hard time, it must be true that *some* people don't. (A) is therefore the correct choice. Choices (C), (D), and (E) are altogether apart from the meaning of the last sentence.

Passage

The development of a scientific method for arriving at truth concerning natural phenomena was furthered by Roger Bacon (1214–1294). He was a pupil of Grosseteste, a Franciscan monk, and a teacher at Oxford. He began as a lecturer on the works of Aristotle but came to the conclusion that educational policies in the schools of his time were very much in need of reform. To bring it about he devoted his time to the study of science, including both mathematics and the empirical sciences which make use of the experimental methods. He was a reformer in the field of education and a philosopher whose work anticipated in no small degree that of the more famous Francis Bacon.

1. Educational reforms brought about by Roger Bacon were most likely based upon
   (A) his strict religious upbringing
   (B) Franciscan theories
   (C) procedures used in mathematics and science
   (D) the work of Francis Bacon
   (E) the works of Aristotle

Having skimmed this question, you should probably have circled *educational reforms* and *based upon* and then paid attention to (and perhaps marked) that portion of the passage discussing the foundation/causes for Roger Bacon's instituting educational reform. Choices (A) and (B) do not have ample evidence in the passage to support either being the correct answer. Choice (D) is incorrect; Francis Bacon, according to the passage, came *after* Roger Bacon. Choice (E) is also unsupported; it would require speculating beyond the facts in the paragraph. Choice (C) is explicitly stated in the passage—*To bring it about he devoted his time to the study of science, including both mathematics and the empirical sciences which make use of the experimental methods.* Well supported as it is, (C) is the best answer.

2. From the information in the passage, we must conclude that Roger Bacon was
   (A) a hardened radical   (D) a cynical critic
   (B) an upset pessimist   (E) a hard-working progressive
   (C) a cockeyed optimist

Skimming this question is not very helpful; it does not point specifically to any information in the passage. Questions of this sort usually assess your overall understanding of the meaning, style, tone, or point of view of the passage. In this case, you should have recognized that Roger Bacon was *progressive*, as he made reforms in both education and philosophy, and that he was also hard-working, having been a pupil of a Franciscan monk and a teacher at Oxford, finally devoting time to the study of science in order to effect change in the schools. Choice (E) is correct. The other choices are unsupported by the passage.

General Procedure for Answering Reading Questions

1. *Skim the questions,* circling the word or phrase that stands out in each question. *Don't* read the answer choices.
2. *Read and mark the passage,* paying special attention to information relevant to the questions you've skimmed.

3. *Answer the questions.* Base your answers *only on the material given in the passage.* Assume that the information in each passage is accurate. The questions test your understanding of the passage alone; they do *not* test the historical background of the passage, the biography of the author, or previous familiarity with the work from which the passage is taken.

Five Key Questions for Understanding and Interpreting What You Read

Main Idea

What is the main idea of the passage? After reading any passage, try summarizing it in a brief sentence. To practice this very important skill, read the editorials in your local paper each day and write a brief sentence summarizing each one.

Details

What details support the main idea? Usually such details are facts, statistics, experiences, etc., that strengthen your understanding of and agreement with the main idea.

Purpose

What is the purpose of the passage? Ask yourself what the author is trying to accomplish. The four general purposes are (1) to narrate (to tell a story), (2) to describe, (3) to inform, and (4) to persuade.

Style and Tone

Are the style and tone of the passage objective or subjective? In other words, is the author presenting things factually or from a personal point of view? If an author is subjective, you might want to pin down the nature of the subjectivity. Ask yourself, is the author optimistic? pessimistic? angry? humorous? serious?

Difficult or Unusual Words

What are the difficult or unusual words in the passage? Readers who do not *mark* words that are difficult or used in an unusual way in a passage often forget that the words occurred at all and have difficulty locating them if this becomes necessary. By calling your attention to difficult or unusual words, you increase your changes of defining them by understanding their meaning in context.

WRITING—MULTIPLE CHOICE

The Writing—Multiple Choice section contains about 45 questions and is 30 minutes in length. It consists of two types of questions—Usage and Sentence Correction.

Ability Tested

You will be required to recognize errors in standard written English. These include errors in grammar, sentence structure, punctuation, wordiness, and word choice.

Basic Skills Necessary

Knowledge of some basic grammar will help in this section. Review the rules of correctness that have been emphasized in your high school and college English classes. A summary of some of the more important rules follows.

PART A: USAGE

Directions

Some of the sentences are correct. Others contain problems in grammar, usage, idiom, and diction (word choice). There is not more than one error in any sentence.

If there is an error, it will be underlined and lettered. Find the one underlined part that must be changed to make the sentence correct, and choose the corresponding letter on your answer sheet. Mark (E) if the sentence contains no error.

Analysis

You are looking for errors in standard written English, the kind of English used in most textbooks. Do not evaluate a sentence in terms of the spoken English we all use.

When deciding whether an underlined portion is correct or not, assume that *all other parts of the sentence are correct.*

PART B: SENTENCE CORRECTION

Directions

Some part of each sentence is underlined; sometimes the whole sentence is underlined. Five choices for rephrasing the underlined part follow each sentence; the first choice (A) repeats the original, and the other four are different. If choice (A) seems better than the alternatives, choose answer (A); if not, choose one of the others.

For each sentence, consider the requirements of standard written English. Your choice should be a correct and effective expression, not awkward or ambiguous. Focus on grammar, sentence structure, punctuation, wordiness, and word choice. If a choice changes the meaning of the original sentence, do not select it.

Analysis

Several alternatives to an underlined portion may be correct; you are to pick the *best* (most clear and exact) one.

Any alternative which changes the meaning of the sentence should not be chosen, no matter how clear or correct it is.

Suggested Approach with Samples:

1. *Wordiness.* Be alert to unnecessary or repetitious elements in sentences. Ask yourself whether any of the underlined portion may be eliminated without damaging the meaning of the sentence.

EXAMPLE A—USAGE

Although a well-balanced diet is necessary for good health,
          A   B

exercise is the essential factor that is crucial in maintaining
      C   D

fitness. No error
       E

When checking a sentence for wordiness, pay special attention to phrases beginning with *which, that,* or *who;* sometimes these pronouns introduce an unnecessary or extraneous piece of information. In the sentence above, choice (D) contains the word *crucial;* this word is unnecessary because it repeats the meaning of *essential.* The phrase *that is crucial in maintaining* could be replaced with *in maintaining*, thus eliminating wordiness.

EXAMPLE B—SENTENCE CORRECTION

Because of our work with handicapped people who suffer from disabilities, Tom and I received a hearty round of applause from the local Rotary Club.

(A) Because of our work with handicapped people who suffer from disabilities
(B) Because of our work with handicapped people who suffer from various disabilities
(C) Because of our work with locally handicapped people
(D) Because of our work with handicapped people
(E) Because of our work with the handicapped and disabled

Remember that wordy phrases often begin with *which, that,* or *who.* With this in mind, you should notice that the phrase *who suffer from disabilities* unnecessarily repeats the meaning of *handicapped.* Choice (D) removes this repetitious phrase. All other choices add unnecessary information or change the meaning of the sentence.

2. *Word Order.* Words that refer to each other should be clearly connected in a sentence.

EXAMPLE A—USAGE

Either I'll prepare my lesson plan today or tomorrow morning; in
                A   B

either case I'll be ready for tomorrow afternoon's class. No error
         C   D   E

The word *either* is meant to refer to *today or tomorrow morning,* but as it stands, *either* is too far away from the words it modifies. To improve this sentence, choice (A) should be changed so that *either* occurs immediately before *today.*

EXAMPLE B—SENTENCE CORRECTION

Although he holds a Ph.D. in history, Andy has not secured a teaching job, and so he sells reference books to provide himself with an income, such as encyclopedias.

(A) to provide himself with an income, such as encyclopedias.
(B) in order to provide himself with an income, such as encyclopedias.
(C) , such as encyclopedias, to provide himself with an income.
(D) , such as encyclopedias, in order to provide himself with an income.
(E) to provide himself income.

Such as encyclopedias is meant to modify *reference books* but does not do so clearly because it occurs at the end of the sentence. Choice (C) places *such as encyclopedias* next to *reference books*, so the connection is clear. Choice (D) is not the best choice because it unnecessarily adds the phrase *in order*.

The words *who, which,* and *that* are sometimes used to introduce misplaced modifiers:

Unclear: I ate some food at the party *that was stale.*
Clear: I ate some food *that was stale* at the party.

Unclear: Sharpshooter Smith is the owner of a monkey *who is a big-game hunter.*
Clear: Sharpshooter Smith, *who is a big-game hunter,* is the owner of a monkey.

Unclear: He read a poem to the class, *which happens to be one of his favorites.*
Clear: He read a poem, *which happens to be one of his favorites,* to the class.

3. *Word Usage—A Short Glossary*

● *Between, Among.* Use *between* with two people or objects and *among* with more than two:

We divided the cake *between* the two of us.
We divided the cake *among* the three of us.

● *Different than, Different from.* The preferred expression is *different from.*

● *Fewer-Less, Amount-Number.* Use *fewer* with quantities that are countable: *We expected* fewer *than twenty* people *at the party.* Use *less* for quantities that are not counted: *We harvested* less grain *today because of the bad weather.* Also use *less* with abstract terms: *She showed* less interest *in economics than in history.* Use *number* with things that are countable and *amount* with uncountable quantities: *A* number *of students worked past the allotted* amount *of time.*

● *Inferior than.* The correct expression is *inferior to.*

● *Like, As.* Generally, *as* is a more acceptable conjunction than is *like.*

Unacceptable: It looks *like* it will rain.
Acceptable: It looks *as if* it will rain.

● *Most, Almost. Almost* is the more acceptable expression.

Unacceptable: I am most always on time.
Acceptable: I am almost always on time.

• *Nowhere near, Not nearly.* The more acceptable expression is *not nearly.*

• *Off of.* The *of* is not acceptable. Write *He took the hat off his head*, not *He took the hat off of his head.*

• *On the part of.* This phrase is usually wordy and unnecessary.

Wordy: There has been general agreement on the part of the Republicans.
Better: There has been general agreement among Republicans.

• *Reason is because.* The more acceptable phrase is *the reason is that.*

• *Scarcely than. Scarcely* should be used with *when,* and *no sooner* should be used with *than.*

Incorrect: I had *scarcely* arrived *than* the party suddenly ended.
Correct: I had *scarcely* arrived *when* the party suddenly ended.
Correct: I had *no sooner* arrived *than* the party suddenly ended.

• *Where . . . at, to.*

Incorrect: Where were they *at*? Where are they going *to*?
Correct: Where were they? Where are they going?

4. *Pronouns.* Focus upon words like *he, him, she, her, we, us, they, them, who, whom, whoever, whomever, you, it, which,* or *that.*

EXAMPLE A—USAGE

We rewarded the workers whom, according to the manager, had done
                        ‾‾‾‾   ‾‾   ‾‾‾‾‾‾‾‾
                         A   B   C
the most imaginative job. No error
        ‾‾‾‾‾‾‾‾‾‾‾‾‾‾‾ ‾‾‾‾‾‾‾‾
             D   E

It is possible that *whom* is an error just because it's a pronoun, and pronouns are error-prone. Try replacing *whom* with either *him* or *them: them . . . had done the most imaginative job.* This sounds wrong, a clue that *whom* is wrong. To test whether *who* is correct instead, try substituting *he* or *they: they . . . had done the most imaginative job.* This sounds right. Remember, if *him* or *them* sounds right when substituted, *whom* is correct; if *he* or *they* sounds right when substituted, *who* is correct.

Example B—Sentence Correction

The Rotary Club applauded Tom and I for our work helping the handicapped in town find secure jobs.
(A) The Rotary Club applauded Tom and I
(B) The Rotary Club applauded I and Tom
(C) The Rotary Club applauded me and Tom
(D) The Rotary Club applauded Tom and me
(E) The Rotary Club applauded both of us

Focus on *I,* because it's a pronoun. To test whether *I* is correct, remove *Tom and.* The result is, *The Rotary Club applauded . . . I. Me* would sound better, and in fact (D) is the correct choice. (E) changes the meaning of the sentence.

5. *Subject-Verb Agreement*

Example A—Usage

Here on the table is an apple and three pears. No error
  A   B   C   D   E

Focus on the verb (*is*) and ask yourself what the subject is. In this sentence, the subject (*an apple and three pears*) *follows* the verb. Since the subject is plural, the verb must be plural—*are* instead of *is.*

Example B—Sentence Correction

The trunk containing costumes, makeup, and props were left at the stage entrance of the theater.
(A) costumes, makeup, and props were left
(B) costumes, makeup, and props were all left
(C) costumes, makeup, and props was left
(D) costumes, makeup, and props to be left
(E) costumes, makeup, and props left

The verb is *were left.* Since the subject is singular (*trunk*) the verb must be singular—*was* instead of *were.* Don't assume that the subject immediately precedes the verb; in this case, the subject and verb are some distance apart.

6. *Faulty Parallelism.* Look for a series of items separated by commas and make sure each item has the same *form.*

EXAMPLE A—USAGE

He liked swimming, weight lifting, and to run. No error
   A   B   C   D   E

To run is incorrect; it should be an *—ing* word like the other items.

EXAMPLE B—SENTENCE CORRECTION

To strive, to seek, to find, and not yielding are the heroic goals of Ulysses
in Tennyson's famous poem.
(A) To strive, to seek, to find, and not yielding
(B) To strive, to seek, to find, and to yield
(C) To strive, to seek, to find, and not to yield
(D) To strive, to seek, to find, and yet to yield
(E) Striving, seeking, finding, and yielding

Not yielding is incorrect; it should have the *to* _____ form of the other
items. (C) is the best choice; (B), (E), and (D) are correct, but they change
the meaning of the sentence.

7. Another *verb error* happens when the verb tense (past, present, future)
is inconsistent. If there are two verbs in the sentence, make sure the verb
tense of each is appropriate.

EXAMPLE A—USAGE

He walked for miles and finally sees a sign of civilization. No error
           A   B   C   D   E

Walked describes the past; *sees* describes the present. *Sees* should be
changed to *saw* so that the whole sentence describes the past.

EXAMPLE B—SENTENCE CORRECTION

If he would have worked harder, he could have gone to the movies.
(A) If he would have worked   (D) If he had worked
(B) If he worked   (E) After working
(C) Working

In general, if a sentence contains two *would haves*, two *should haves*, two
could haves, or any combination of these terms (in this case *would have* and
could have), one of the verbs should be changed to *had,* to indicate that one of
the actions (working) occurred earlier than the other (going to the movies).
(D) is correct.

8. Sometimes a sentence contains an *error in idiom;* that is, it employs a word or phrase that is incorrect simply because it has not been established as standard usage. Such errors just don't "sound right."

EXAMPLE A—USAGE

The young man <u>had been</u> <u>addicted of</u> drugs <u>ever since</u> his <u>thirteenth</u>
              A   B   C   D

birthday. <u>No error</u>
         E

Addicted of is unidiomatic; the correct expression is *addicted to.* Idiomatic expressions are widely accepted and familiar to native speakers and writers. If a phrase in a sentence strikes you as unfamiliar or strange, it may be an idiom error. Idiom errors often involve "little" words like *of, over, in, at, to, by , with,* and *from.* For instance, *try to* is idiomatic; *try and* is not.

EXAMPLE B—SENTENCE CORRECTION

The new recruits <u>are liable from making tactical errors</u>, but we do hope that their mistakes will disappear after a few weeks.

(A) are liable from making tactical errors
(B) are liable from making tactical mistakes
(C) are liable to make tactical errors
(D) are liable to make tactical mistakes
(E) are liable about making tactical errors

The correct answer is (C). *Liable from making* is not idiomatic; that is, it doesn't sound right to most native English speakers. *Liable to make* is idiomatically correct.

9. *Adjective or adverb misuse* constitutes another type of error.

EXAMPLE A—USAGE

The mechanic <u>repaired</u> <u>my</u> engine and <u>installed</u> a new clutch very
              A   B   C

quick. <u>No error</u>
 D   E

Adjectives describe *things,* and adverbs describe *actions.* In this case, *actions* are being described (repairing and installing), so the word that describes these actions should be an adverb, *quickly* instead of *quick.* As you might notice, adverbs often end with *-ly.* The correct use of the adjective *quick* in a sentence occurs in this example: *The quick work of the mechanic pleased me very much.* In this case, a *thing* is being described (work), so an adjective is appropriate.

EXAMPLE B—SENTENCE CORRECTION

Adam and Eve walked slow out of paradise, hanging their heads in sorrow and wondering about the future.
- (A) Adam and Eve walked slow out of paradise
- (B) Adam and Eve walked slowly out of paradise
- (C) Adam and Eve walked slowly out to paradise
- (D) Adam and Eve walked real slow out of paradise
- (E) Adam and Eve walked slowly out in paradise

The correct choice is (B). *Slow* is an adjective, and since it is meant to describe an action (walking), it must be changed to an adverb, *slowly.* Although (C) and (E) contain *slowly,* they change the meaning of the original sentence.

10. One type of error that affects a whole phrase rather than just one word is a *dangling element error.*

EXAMPLE A—USAGE

Stumbling around, the light switch was nowhere to be found.   No error
        A   B   C   D   E

The sentence seems to say that the light switch is *stumbling around.* In order to change this absurd and humorous meaning, you would need to insert *I realized that* so that the sentence reads, *Stumbling around, I realized that . . .* Otherwise, *stumbling around* dangles, not referring clearly to any other element in the sentence.

EXAMPLE B—SENTENCE CORRECTION

Struggling with every word, the essay was completed by John at the expense of several hours sleep.
- (A) the essay was completed by John
- (B) John completed the essay
- (C) the essay John completed
- (D) the essay completed itself
- (E) the essay itself was completed

The sentence seems to say that the essay did the struggling! (B) eliminates this problem, clearly associating *John* with the opening phrase about struggling.

11. A sentence may contain a *comparison error.*

EXAMPLE A—USAGE

After deliberating for hours, the judges could not decide who was
<u> </u>   A   B   C
the greatest of the two boxers. No error
    D   E

When only two things are being compared, in this case two boxers, *-er* words (*greater, taller, more beautiful*) should be used. *Est* words like *greatest* are used only when more than two things are being compared: *He was the greatest contender in the history of boxing.*

EXAMPLE B—SENTENCE CORRECTION

She wished that her career were as glamorous as the other women.
(A) as glamorous as the other women.
(B) as glamorous as those other women.
(C) as glamorous than those other women.
(D) as glamorous as those of the other women.
(E) as glamorous as those of the other women's.

This is a more subtle type of correction error. In this sentence, two very different, *in*comparable items are being compared: *her career* is compared to *the other women.* A clearer and more sensible sentence would compare *her career* to *the careers of the other women,* or to *those of the other women.* Therefore, (D) is the best choice.

12. A sentence may contain a *punctuation error.*

EXAMPLE A—USAGE

Daily President Lincoln met with the constituents lined up
<u> </u>   A   B   C
outside his office door. No error
     D   E

An introductory word or phrase should be followed by a comma. In this case, the comma should follow *daily.*

EXAMPLE B—SENTENCE CORRECTION

Lord Byron was called immoral by many of his <u>contemporaries; his</u>
<u>longest poem, *Don Juan,* contributed to this infamous reputation.</u>
(A) contemporaries; his longest poem, *Don Juan,* contributed to this
infamous reputation.
(B) contemporaries, as his longest poem, *Don Juan,* shows.
(C) contemporaries, his longest poem, *Don Juan,* contributed to this
infamous reputation.
(D) contemporaries who read his longest poem, *Don Juan.*
(E) contemporaries reading his longest poem.

The original sentence is correct. A semicolon may be used to punctuate two
related statements, each of which is itself a complete sentence.

WRITING—ESSAY

The writing section of the NTE is 30 minutes in length and contains one
essay question. You are asked to draw upon your personal experience and
observations for information, examples, and generalizations to be used in
your writing.

Ability Tested

The writing section of this exam tests your ability to read a topic carefully,
to organize your ideas before you write, and to write with clarity and
precision.

Basic Skills Necessary

This section requires a basic college level writing background. Papers are
scored on the writer's ability to perform the following: development and
organization of ideas with supporting evidence or specific examples; understanding of the essay's intended audience (for example, a speech urging
members of the Board of Education to vote a certain way); comprehension of
the assigned task; skillful use of language; and correctness of mechanics,
usage, and paragraphing.

Directions

In this section, you will have 30 minutes to plan and write one essay for the
topic given. You may use the bottom of this page to organize and plan your

essay before you begin writing. You should plan your time wisely. Read the topic carefully to make sure that you are properly addressing the issue or situation. YOU MUST WRITE ON THE SPECIFIED TOPIC. AN ESSAY ON ANOTHER TOPIC WILL NOT BE ACCEPTABLE.

The essay question included in this section is designed to give you an opportunity to write clearly and effectively. Use specific examples whenever appropriate to aid in supporting your ideas. Keep in mind that the quality of your writing is much more important than the quantity.

Your essay is to be written on the special answer sheets provided. No other paper may be used. Your writing should be neat and legible. Because you have only a limited amount of space in which to write, please do NOT skip lines, do NOT write excessively large, and do NOT leave wide margins.

Remember, use the bottom of this page for any organizational notes you may wish to make.

Analysis of Directions

On the written essay portion of the NTE you will have 30 minutes to write on the assigned topic.

You will have space for prewriting. It is recommended that you use this space to organize your thoughts. Double-check to determine how much space you have in which to write your essay. At present, the test provides two blank sides of lined $8\frac{1}{2}''$ by $11''$ paper per essay.

Some General Tips

1. Read the topic twice—three times if necessary—before writing. Circle key words. This will help you focus on the assigned task.
2. Use a form of "prewriting" *before* you begin writing your actual essay. Prewriting may consist of outlining, brainstorming, clustering, etc.
3. Spend about five minutes organizing your thoughts before you begin writing. A poorly written essay is often the result of inadequate planning.
4. Don't let spelling slow down your writing. That is, keep the flow of your writing going; then come back later to correct spelling errors.
5. If possible, leave several minutes at the end to reread and edit/correct your essay. Don't make extensive changes when you reread; just correct spelling errors and other minor flaws.
6. Don't use excessively large writing, don't leave wide margins, and don't skip any lines.
7. Double-check your time allotment and the amount of space you have in which to write each essay.

SAMPLE A: PREWRITING METHODS AND ESSAYS

Topic

Some students can look back on their years in school and pinpoint one particular course or one particular teacher most instrumental in shaping their lives.

Reflect on your own school years and focus on one such instructor or course. Describe the conditions or qualities that made that particular experience or teacher special.

Clustering

Use prewriting (clustering) as a way of organizing your thoughts before you write. After you choose a topic, write it down on the prewriting area and draw a circle around that topic:

For a few moments, think of all the elements of that topic and connect them to the central topic cluster:

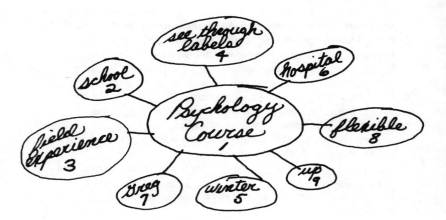

You can then number the parts of the cluster to give an order to your thoughts. You do not have to use all of the elements of your cluster. Clustering provides a way to put all of your thoughts down on paper before you write so you can quickly see the structure of the whole paper.

The "Story Formula"

One good way to approach a question that asks you to describe one experience is through the use of the "story formula." The story formula consists of

A. Setting—where the story took place
B. Main characters—who were the people in the story
C. Plot—the problem in the story or the crisis to be overcome
D. Climax—the turning point in the story
E. Resolution—the ending or how you are now as a result of the experience

So, in the sample essay—

Paragraph 1—introduce the setting and the main characters in the story
Paragraph 2—introduce the plot   ⎱
Paragraph 3—introduce the climax   ⎰ number of paragraphs may vary
Final paragraph—introduce the resolution

The story formula allows you to describe one experience in detail using clear transitions while keeping a unifying theme throughout your essay.

The Finished Essay

Here's the finished essay in "story formula," the writer having first used clustering to organize the essay's elements.

Ten years ago, I was twenty-one and a junior at California State University at Long Beach. My schooling had been quite traditional and because of this I regarded my college experience as a necessary means to an end and rarely educational. Shortly after I began my second semester in the Education Department, however, I took a course in abnormal psychology that became most instrumental in shaping my life.

On a cold blustery winter day, as I drove to my part-time job at the neuropsychiatric hospital, I had a nagging feeling that the psychology class I enrolled in was slowly changing my point of view. As I drove onto the damp parking lot and walked in the doorway to the children's unit, my professor's words haunted me: "The challenge of the new psychology is to look beyond the 'labels' given to people and to see for oneself the human being that is there." I mulled over in my mind whether this day would bring me any closer to that goal.

That day a new patient arrived. He was a four-year-old child pinned tightly with the label of "autistic." His name was Gregory, and in him I saw immediately all that I had previously only read about. He had all of the usual behaviors of a child who was autistic. He would not respond to touch or affection, engaged in constant finger flicking and hand gazing, and seemed to withdraw into his own world.

In the days that passed I spent much time with Gregory, involving him in whatever I was doing, always maintaining some physical contact with him. It was not until the fourteenth day that I dropped my ever-so-precious label.

Gregory and I frequently engaged in games, but his favorite game was entitled "Up." In this game I was to lift Gregory into the air as he gleefully shouted out, "up, up!" After several times my arms grew weary, and instead of putting him down, I held Gregory in my arms. There we stood in an embrace of trust—an opening to a place beyond his label. Tears flowed freely from my eyes as he calmly touched each one with his fingers, smiling as their wetness served to cement our relationship. Somehow, in that moment, all of what I had read mattered little compared to what I now knew. As my professor had warned us in class, "The labels only serve to make things easy—it is up to you to discover the truth."

Each day I went to the neuropsychiatric institute filled with a joy I had never known, yet in one sharp moment it was all shattered. On December 26, 1972, Gregory was transferred to a state mental institution. Over the advice of the staff and the doctors, Gregory was taken to a place where he would wear his label forever.

The next few weeks at the hospital seemed empty to me. A challenge by a professor to see through the labels and the willingness and trust of a four-year-old child enabled me to learn a lesson that I shall never forget. For the first time a college course provided me with a real learning experience; all of the coursework that I had taken never touched me as deeply as this one course.

Outlining

Another way of prewriting is outlining. A simple outline for Sample A could go something like this:

Course: Music 101—Introduction to Mozart

I. Caused me to change my major
  A. Hated economics but never knew it
  B. Music raised my spirits—new outlook on life
II. Broadened my life
  A. Began attending concerts—became more social
  B. Got out of the house
  C. Appreciation for a new art form—now more open about other things as well
III. Developed new skills
  A. Learned how to listen better
  B. Began learning to play French horn
    1. Made new friends in Community Orchestra
    2. Met my present husband who played first-chair French horn in Community Orchestra

Organizing an outline like the one above (it need not be this formal) will help you write a well-structured, well-planned essay. You can readily see that constructing a good essay from the outline above would be a fairly simple task.

Whatever way you prewrite—cluster, outline, etc.—the important thing is that you think and plan before you actually begin writing your essay.

Additional Finished Essays for Sample A

Following are two more attempts for Sample A. Both essays are evaluated in detail (comments run alongside each paragraph). Analyze each essay's strengths or weaknesses.

ESSAY 1

1. Orienting the reader to the writer's background and experience.

2. Designating the points which he or she will discuss; focusing the essay.

3. Restricting the discussion appropriately.

By the time I was a junior in college, I had developed criteria for good teaching and bad teaching, criteria based on my experiences during those first two college years. The good teachers were always (1) models of enthusiasm and curiosity about their subject, (2) interested in students' fulfilling their own potential and not trying to please the instructor, and (3) friendly as well as scholarly. Of the few good teachers I enjoyed, Bob Lincoln (a professor of English) was the best.

4. Vivid portrait of bad teacher and the effects of bad teaching.

5. Balanced, contrasting sentence addressing point (1) from first paragraph. Able to control syntax, reference to specific details, orderly phrasing.

6. Thesis sentence, highlighting the significance of this paragraph.

7. Effective transition (*but*), reference to point (2).

8. Clear, brief sentence; interesting contrast with longer ones.

9. Specific supporting details, logical parallel structure.

10. Summary sentence, reinforcing the overall point of the paragraph.

11. Reference to point (3) of the opening paragraph.

12. Specific supporting detail.

13. Additional information, fluency, and humor; clearly states the significance of the experience and its relationship to the general topic.

Four times a week, sluggish and yawning from listening to my classics professor drone endlessly in a muffled monotone about Zeus and the Olympians, I slumped into Dr. Lincoln's class on the Victorian novel. And always he would lift my spirits with his own spirited approach; his was a remarkable talent for making connections between the experiences of Jane Eyre, Becky Sharp, and Adam Bede, and very modern problems of repression, alienation, and greed. He showed that good teachers make their subjects part of their own life and time and that literature can help us understand ourselves.

But Dr. Lincoln never imposed his viewpoints on us. The importance of the literature was ours to decide. We kept journals in which we wrote about how instances in the novels were like those in our own experience, and by sharing those responses in class we learned how many different viewpoints a novel can provoke and learned to respect each other's differences. All this came about because Dr. Lincoln was more interested in what the subject meant to us than what it meant to him.

His attention to our learning didn't stop at the end of a class meeting. Always willing to make himself available for further discussion, Dr. Lincoln even invited us to his home at times. These uncommon occasions, sharing the professor's "natural habitat," helped us to learn that teachers are people, too, and that the best teachers are those who transform their students into a community, not just a bunch of anonymous paper pushers.

14. Ties the past into the present gracefully.

15. Summary conclusion that does more than simply restate what has already been said.

Each day of my own training in education and practice in teaching, I try to remember what Dr. Lincoln taught me. Good teaching takes energy, commitment, and good humor; it is a product of people, not merely of books and papers.

ESSAY 2

1. Fragment sentence, which states information irrelevant to the topic and already known to the audience.

2. Faulty parallelism, subject-verb disagreement, missing verb, vague sentence structure and diction.

3. Seemingly irrelevant point. Paragraph as a whole lacks focus and clarity.

4. Faulty logic.

5. Example of unclear relevance, ungrammatical verb, adjective-adverb confusion

6. Vague pronoun reference, vague sentence in general. Paragraph lacks a clear thesis.

7. Run-on sentences, full of vague cliches, missing verb preceding *in*, spelling error; in general a crazy quilt of undeveloped ideas.

8. Faulty logic, missing question mark, misspelling.

9. Vague sentence.

As a person who would like to be a full-time teacher and who is right now student teaching until I pass my courses and this test, so that I can apply for promising positions. I can say that my best teachers throughout elementary, secondary school and higher was always on my side and very much a sense of humor. As long as we had the assignment read, he would discuss it with us.

Good teaching makes you want to know more, especially for tests since they are how we learn. I remember one day I have studied extremely complete, and then the test was not what I expected. This is what I mean by good teaching.

And then another time I enjoyed the class so much that when it came time to "show what you know" I was ready, willing and able, with so many of the lectures in an interesting fashion, to show me that if the teacher likes his job, than there is nothing to worry about.

How many times have you looked for the teacher and he doesn't answer the phone or even make an effort to be their. Giving of yourself is when you take extra time to make sure that students know how they got the answers.

10. Restatement of part of the question, disguised attempt to focus the conclusion, inappropriate verb (*doing*).

11. Vague pronoun reference.

The conditions or qualities that made the particular experience special, in conclusion, were what I find myself doing whenever I think about teaching and try to do something out of the ordinary. And it works.

In general, the response is disunified, lacks relevant and specific details, does not address only *one* instructor or experience, lacks planning and organization, and displays a number of mechanical errors.

SAMPLE B: PREWRITING METHODS AND ESSAYS

Topic

A recent movement in education has been called "Back to Basics." Its proponents argue that the curriculum should concentrate only on reading, writing, and mathematics skills and completely ignore such courses as sociology, art appreciation, and drama.

Imagine that you are a school principal faced with the task of making policy for your school. Present your argument(s) either for or against "Back to Basics."

Clustering

Using the clustering technique for prewriting, this is what the cluster for Sample B might look like.

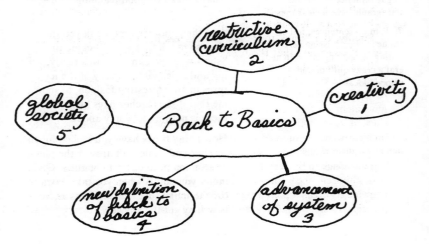

The Finished Essay

As principal of your school, I have seen many educational movements come and go. Some are worthy of the attention given to them, and others should be ignored because of their devastating effect on the educational system. One such movement that falls into the latter category is the "Back to Basics" movement. Its proponents argue that education should concentrate on reading, writing, and mathematics skills and completely ignore such courses as drama, art appreciation, and sociology. I am against the "Back to Basics" movement because it inhibits creativity, fails to recognize the importance of the arts, and restricts the curriculum.

The enhancement of creative thinking is primal to the advancement of any educational system. To create, to invent, or to discover, one needs not only to have freedom of thought but the exposure and application of that creativity to all areas of the curriculum. To concentrate on only reading, writing, and mathematics would restrict thinking to a narrow focus. The future needs thinkers who can create in the widest spectrum so as to be able to meet the challenge of a global society.

The "Back to Basics" proponents also fail to see that a restrictive curriculum of only mathematics, reading, and writing fails to support the many great advancements made in our culture by those whose first exposures to art, drama, or sociology took place in the schools. The great artists who have changed the way people see; the great dramatists who have told their stories worldwide; and the great sociologists who have helped us to understand social relations, organizations, and changes in our culture have all been products of an education that included the arts as basic to a well-rounded education.

Finally, the "Back to Basics" supporters fail to see in their narrow view of education that the basics *include* art, drama, and sociology as well as music, dance, and computer literacy. "Basics," by definition, means that knowledge which is needed by children in our society in order to compete and simply survive in that society. The "Back to Basics" movement is an attempt to take education back to a time that has long since passed. The narrow focus of the movement also overlooks the integrative value of reading, writing, and mathematics throughout all curriculum areas and especially in the arts.

The "Back to Basics" issue is a sad attempt to restrict the information that children need for their future. It will stifle creativity in those knowledge areas upon which our society is dependent. So, as your principal, I hope that you on the school board continue to support an education for the future—an education that defines the "basics" as those curriculum areas beyond the courses of reading, writing, and mathematics. We must meet the future with an education that *includes* art, drama, and sociology.

The "Why" Essay

One good way to approach a question which asks you to explain, analyze, or evaluate is to use a "why" essay format. A "why" essay is built around a thesis sentence. The thesis sentence begins with your opinion, followed by the word *because* and then a list of the most important reasons why the opinion is valid, reasonable, or well founded. For example, in the Sample B essay the thesis statement is:

I am against the "Back to Basics" movement because it inhibits creativity, fails to recognize the importance of the arts, and restricts the curriculum.

The thesis statement comes at the end of the introductory paragraph followed by paragraphs that explain each of your reasons. Finally the paper ends with a summary of the reasons and a restatement of the thesis sentence.

The "why essay" format could look like this in outline form:

Paragraph	"Why Essay" Format	Sample B Examples by Paragraph
1	Introduction—Thesis Sentence	Paragraph 1
2	Reason 1	Paragraph 2
3	Reason 2	Paragraph 3
4	Reason 3	Paragraph 4
5	Conclusion	Paragraph 5

Each paragraph should contain approximately three to five sentences. The introduction invites the reader to read on. Your reasons (three are often sufficient) that follow should give examples or evidence to support each reason. Your concluding paragraph summarizes your reasons and restates the thesis statement.

POOR ESSAYS—WHAT NOT TO DO

Sample A

One course I had in college which was instrumental in shaping my life was a college speech course. I was not a talkative person. During classroom discussions, my teacher made me participate and that was something I had not done in a long time.

This particular subject was a coed class and I had to discuss the current issues of today. There were only three females in a class of forty men.

After the semester was over, I was quite a different person than before the speech class.

I am now employed by the Over the Rainbow School District as a kindorgotten teacher in an area where people don't speak good. I feel happy to see the children grow up with the kind of experiences I can give them.

Analysis

This Sample A essay contains major faults in the writing. The essay lacks unity, focus, and a clear description of one experience.

The paper has only a brief description that gives the reader a hint of the setting and early experiences.

The paper rushes to the conclusion (resolution) without giving the reader an experience that caused a change. Simply enrolling in a class does not cause one to change. The writer left out a description of any experience that caused this change.

The paper lacks a unified, clear focus without a described experience and fails to go beyond a general discussion. The final sentence doesn't seem to fit because we still don't know why this course was special and how it helped this person in his or her job as a teacher.

The paper also contains many flaws in grammar and usage.

Sample B

Back to Basics is wrong for the schools. I don't like it. For one thing what are we going to do with all of the extra teachers when they fire all of the others. I will probably lose my job cause I have only been teaching for four years.

People get bored with the same thing day after day and the children will come to hate school and that is not good. I love to teach art and drama in my classroom. I have not taught sociology yet though. I know the children in my class could not stand to have only reading, writing, and mathematics. All the time without ever a break. Behavior problems would increase because the children would be so board that I would have to be very strict to have any control. Those people in the back to basics movement probably have never taught and are just mad at schools because they have to pay taxes to the schools and they are mad. Being a teacher I don't like the back to basics movement and don't want to see it.

Analysis

This Sample B essay has major flaws in its organization, development, and grammar. It does not have a clear beginning, middle, and end. Nowhere in the paper is there a clear thesis statement; reasons are merely scattered throughout the paper.

In this paper the author fails to choose the two or three most important reasons and develop them fully, giving examples or evidence. The sentence beginning "Behavior problems . . ." hints at a possible example; yet this thought is not well developed with examples or evidence.

The paper contains many basic grammar and usage errors.

IMPORTANT TERMS USED IN ESSAY QUESTIONS

Pay close attention to how the essay question is phrased. Are you asked to compare and contrast? Or simply to describe? It is very important to focus on the exact assigned task; if you don't answer the question asked, you will receive little credit for your work. Some terms to look for:

Describe: Requires the use of adjectives, adverbs, and descriptive type phrases. You are trying to "paint a mental picture" for your reader.

Compare: Requires analyzing similarities and differences between two or more items.

Explain: Requires reasons substantiating an opinion or strengthening an argument. Answers the question "why?"

Contrast: Requires setting up a comparison between items, usually focusing on their differences.

Discuss: Usually allows a more open-ended approach, enabling the writer a broader range of possibilities of approach.

Argue (or Present a Point of View): Requires the writer to take only one point of view (either pro or con) and substantiate the position. Don't be concerned about taking the "right" or "wrong" position. That doesn't matter. What matters is, whichever position you take, that it be soundly and clearly supported.

Examples

In most essay questions, regardless of "type" ("compare" or "describe" or "explain"), you will need to use *examples* to support your thoughts. Thinking in terms of examples will also be helpful in planning your writing.

Compare and Contrast

Compare a time in your life when a teacher helped you and a time when a teacher hindered you. Explain *which* teacher you learned the most from as a result of these experiences.

When writing an essay on a question that asks you to compare or contrast two things, you can use this framework as a basic outline for your paper:

Paragraph 1: Introduction
1. Introduce reader to topic.
2. Restate question and tell opinion and reasons. (thesis)

Paragraph 2
1. Describe one teacher and his or her attributes.
2. Tell how the teacher helped you.
3. Include your feelings about the experience.

Paragraph 3
1. Describe second teacher and his or her attributes.
2. Tell how this teacher hindered you.
3. Include your feelings about the experience.

Paragraph 4: Conclusion
1. Tell how and why one teacher was the better one for you.
2. Restate thesis.

PRACTICE ESSAY TOPICS

Following are topics you may use for practice. Allow 30 minutes to plan and write each essay. Give yourself about a half-page to organize your notes and two sides of lined 8½" x 11" paper to write the actual essay. Then, upon completion of each essay, evaluate, or have a friend evaluate, your writing using the checklist provided.

Topic 1

Every year more and more computers are finding their way into the classroom. Discuss and explain your opinions on the growing use of computer-assisted instruction in the classroom.

Topic 2

Some have argued that imagination is not as important as perspiration. Take one side of the argument and present your own personal feelings on the matter.

Topic 3

We meet many people in the course of our lifetimes. Choose one particular person you would call the most unforgettable and describe why he or she is so unforgettable.

Topic 4

Many recent high school graduates discover that, despite possessing a high school diploma, they have no specific skills to enable them to obtain employment. Explain your feelings about introducing a "vocational skills program" as an alternative choice to the academic high school curriculum.

Topic 5

Recent educational experiments have included ungraded classrooms which consist of students grouped by level of achievement rather than by age. Imagine that such an "ungraded classroom" system is suggested for your school. Write a strong argument (either pro or con) to be read at the next meeting of the Board of Education.

Topic 6

Our lives have high points and low points. Choose one particular high point or low point and describe why it had such impact on you.

Topic 7

Some educators believe that the most important trait a teacher can have is self-acceptance. It allows the teacher to better relate to his or her students, to better deal with student problems, and to better provide a positive and constructive role model.

Present your arguments in agreement with this statement, or, if you disagree, present your viewpoints as to what you believe *is* the most important quality for a teacher to have.

Topic 8

What particular experience had the greatest impact on your decision to enter education? Explain why that particular experience was so important.

Topic 9

Some American public schools have removed the "A" to "F" grading system and substituted "Pass-Fail" grading with the instructor adding a written statement about the student's progress. Comment on the pros or cons of such a system.

Topic 10

Reflect upon a good friend and select the one character trait that you feel to be the most important. Describe and explain why that particular trait is more important than any other.

PRACTICE ESSAY CHECKLIST

Diagnosis/Prescription for Timed Writing Exercise

A good essay will:

_____ address the assignment
        be well focused
_____ be well organized
        smooth transition between paragraphs
        coherent, unified
_____ be well developed
        contain specific examples to support points
_____ be grammatically sound (only minor flaws)
        correct sentence structure
        correct punctuation
        use of standard written English
_____ use language skillfully
        variety of sentence types
        variety of words
_____ be legible
        clear handwriting
        neat

INTRODUCTION TO THE TEST OF GENERAL KNOWLEDGE

The Test of General Knowledge is 2 hours long and contains 4 sections, each 30 minutes in length. These sections include Social Studies, Mathematics, Literature and Fine Arts, and Science.

SOCIAL STUDIES

This section contains approximately 30 questions and is 30 minutes in length.

Ability Tested

This section tests your knowledge and understanding of fundamental areas of social studies. The questions deal with general themes rather than recall of specific or isolated facts.

Basic Skills Necessary

The basic skills necessary to be successful on this section include

1. An understanding of the various social sciences included in college-level survey courses.

2. The ability to draw conclusions based on various materials (charts, graphs, tables, narrations, maps, political cartoons).

3. A general knowledge of the important issues, ideas and problems in the following areas:
   U.S. history—social, political, cultural, and economic problems, movements, and institutions
   Societal/cultural characteristics—values, organizations, patterns, similarities, and differences
   Culture's effect on individuals—prejudice, stereotyping, socialization
   Economic issues and processes—on individuals and institutions
   Geographical issues—features, characteristics affecting individuals and society
   Social science methodology—tools and resources to understand society
   Evolution—as it relates to present human cultures and institutions
   Behavior—individual, groups, institutions, and their interrelationships

Directions

Following each of the questions or statements, select the choice that best answers the question or completes the statement.

Analysis

Keep in mind that you are asked for the *best* of the five choices, which may not always be the ideal choice. Mark key words and phrases as you read each question; make certain you understand what you are being asked.

The questions on the Social Studies section of the test focus on important ideas, facts, principles, theories, and methods of social studies. A general review of the highlights and basic ideas of each area of social studies will be helpful, but the questions are of such a general nature that intensive, detailed review is unnecessary. Understanding of test-taking strategies for multiple-choice questions is essential.

Suggested Approach with Samples

In answering questions based on short reading passages or quotes, it is advisable to look for the following key points. Are there conflicting theories? Is the historical time period evident? Are causes and results apparent? Are ideas or concepts presented?

In answering questions based on nonnarrative material, pay particular attention to the type of answer called for (general knowledge, application, etc.). The following sample questions and analyses provide a preview of the content and format of the sample tests.

1. At the beginning of the Civil War, President Lincoln regarded as his greatest goal the
   (A) restoration of the Union
   (B) freeing of the slaves
   (C) conciliation of the South at all costs
   (D) maintaining of cordial relations with Great Britain
   (E) appointing of a Cabinet that represented abolitionist interests

The correct answer is (A). The question must be answered on the basis of your background in American history. The question asks for Lincoln's most important goal (objective). It is important to note that the question is based on a specific time period—the beginning of the Civil War (1861). Choices (B) and (D) are goals that Lincoln might have had. However, they were not his most important goals. Choice (C) is an incorrect statement. The reader should be aware that if Lincoln wanted to prevent the war at any cost, we probably would not have had a Civil War. Lincoln is considered one of the nation's most outstanding Presidents precisely because he preserved the Union. Although Lincoln personally abhorred slavery, in 1861 the abolition of slavery was secondary to his main objective—saving the Union. The reader should also be aware that goals can change as conditions change. Therefore, at the end of the Civil War (1865), one of Lincoln's most important goals was a "generous" plan of Reconstruction of the defeated South.

2. Of the following, who would be most affected by continued inflation?

   (A) a worker who has been laid off
   (B) a person who has a large debt
   (C) a government worker who had his salary frozen
   (D) a farmer who must pay higher prices for feed
   (E) a retired person on a fixed income

The correct answer is (E). Inflation by definition is a continual increase in prices without proportionate increases in the quality of goods and services. In other words, the amount of money entering the market is greater than the amount of goods in the marketplace, and thus inflation is expressed in terms of higher prices. If the dollar loses 30% of its purchasing power, the value of savings accounts, pensions, bank deposits, etc., will be correspondingly 30% less. All income on a fixed level (such as pensions) is therefore most affected by inflation. People who have a job based on a contract are similarly affected, but unlike retired people on pensions, new contracts can be negotiated to offset inflation factors. A union worker who has been laid off can be reemployed when economic conditions improve; a person who has a large debt might welcome inflation, since the debt would be paid back in inflated dollars (the original amount borrowed was worth more in purchasing power than the amount subsequently paid back); a "frozen salary" is usually a temporary situation and, as in choice (A), subsequent salary raises can be adjusted to counter inflation; a farmer who must pay higher prices for feed can pass on the increased prices to the consumer. A retired person on a fixed income is usually too old to successfully reenter the job market, and therefore his income is continually eaten away by inflation.

Some Extra Tips

Many questions may deal with graphs, maps, or political cartoons. The graphs are carefully discussed in the beginning of the social studies review, but here are a few tips about political cartoons and maps.

Political Cartoons

A political cartoon represents a caricature of people, places, or things that is used to symbolize or satirize some subject of popular interest. To understand a political cartoon one must be able

1. to evaluate and critically interpret the current event capsulized in the cartoon.
2. to become familiar with the symbols used in political cartoons. For instance, the "donkey" represents the Democratic Party; the "elephant" is a symbol of the Republican Party; the "dove" is a symbol of peace; the "hawk" is a symbol of war; and "Washington, D.C." and "Uncle Sam" are symbols of the United States government.
3. to determine the point of view of the political cartoonist. What is the cartoonist trying to say? Remember, most good political cartoonists are often critics commenting on the social issues that confront the United States and the world.
4. to understand the significance of the statement that accompanies the political cartoon; this is often a clue to the cartoonist's attitude.

Geographic Factors to Be Considered in Maps

1. Location of the event
2. Size of the area involved
3. Geographic relationship of the area to other concerned places
4. Important water areas
5. Means of access to the area
6. Physical factors such as mountains and plains
7. Natural resources that play a part
8. Soil, climate, and rainfall

Human Factors to Be Considered in Maps

1. Industries of the area
2. Trade and other relations with the outside world
3. Available means of transportation
4. Size and location of population
5. Large cities concerned in the event
6. Racial, religious, and other factors involved
7. Developments from history

Remember to carefully review chart and graph reading beginning on page 149.

MATHEMATICS

The mathematics section of the test is 30 minutes long and usually contains 25 questions. The questions are selected from different areas of mathematics (for instance: measurement, ratio, percent, diagram reading, and interpreting formulas). Complex computation is not required, and most of the terms used are general, commonly encountered mathematical expressions (for instance: area, perimeter, integer, and prime number).

Ability Tested

This part of the exam tests your ability to use your cumulative knowledge of mathematics and your reasoning ability. Computation is minimal; you are not required to have memorized many specific formulas or equations. A general working understanding of math concepts that *any* teacher may need is most important—averaging grades, reading charts and graphs, understanding diagrams that could appear in class, interpreting test results, etc.

Basic Skills Necessary

A cumulative knowledge of mathematics is necessary for this section of the NTE—from elementary grades through at least one year in high school, and possibly one year in college. Thus, no single course specifically prepares examinees for this part of the test.

Directions

In the questions or incomplete statements below, select the one *best* answer or completion of the five choices given.

Analysis of Directions

You have 30 minutes to do 25 problems. This averages to approximately one minute per problem. Keep that in mind as you attack each problem. Even if you know you can work a problem but that it will take you far, far longer than one minute, you should skip it and return to it later if you have time. Remember, you want to do all the easy, quick problems first, before spending valuable time on the others.

There is no penalty for guessing, so you should not leave any blanks. If you do not know the answer to a problem but you can size it up to get a general range for your answer, you may be able to eliminate one or more of the answer choices. This will increase your odds of guessing the correct answer. But even if you cannot eliminate any of the possible choices, take a guess because there is no penalty for wrong answers.

Above all, be sure that your answers on your answer sheet correspond to the proper numbers on your question sheet. Placing one answer in the incorrect number on the answer sheet could possibly shift *all* your answers to the incorrect spots. Be careful of this!

SUGGESTED APPROACH WITH SAMPLES

Here are a number of different approaches which can be helpful in attacking many types of mathematics problems. Of course, these strategies will not work on *all* the problems, but if you become familiar with them, you'll find they'll be helpful in answering quite a few questions.

Mark Key Words

Circling and/or underlining key words in each question is an effective test-taking technique. Many times you may be misled because you may overlook a key word in a problem. By circling or underlining these key words, you'll help yourself focus on what you are being asked to find. Remember, you are allowed to mark and write on your testing booklet. Take advantage of this opportunity. *For example:*

1. In the following number, which digit is in the thousandths place?

$$6574.12398$$

(A) 5   (B) 7   (C) 2   (D) 3   (E) 9

The key words here is *thousandths*. By circling it you will be paying closer attention to it. This is the kind of question which, under time pressure and testing pressure, may often be misread. It may be easily misread as *thousands* place. Hopefully your circling the important words will minimize the possibility of misreading. Your completed question may look like this after you mark the important words or terms:

1. Which(digit)is in the(thousandths)place?

$$6574.12③98$$

(A) 5   (B) 7   (C) 2   (D) 3   (E) 9

Here's another example:

2. If 3 yards of ribbon cost $2.97, what is the price per foot?
    (A) $.99   (B) $8.91   (C) $2.94   (D) $.33   (E) $3.00

The key word here is *foot*. Dividing $2.97 by 3 will tell you only the price per *yard*. Notice that $.99 is one of the choices, (A). You must still divide by 3 (since there are 3 feet per yard) to find the cost per foot, $.99 divided by 3 is $.33, which is choice (D). Therefore it would be very helpful to circle the words *price per foot* in the problem.

And another example:

3. If $3x + 1 = 16$, what is the value of $x - 4$?
    (A) 16   (B) 5   (C) 19   (D) 1   (E) −1

The key here is *find the value of x − 4*. Therefore circle *x − 4*. Note that solving the original equation will tell only the value of x:

$$3x + 1 = 16$$
$$3x = 15$$
$$x = 5$$

Here again notice that 5 is one of the choices, (B). But the question asks for the value of $x - 4$, not just x. To continue, replace x with 5 and solve:

$$x - 4 =$$
$$5 - 4 = 1$$

The correct answer choice is (D).

And one more example:

4. Together a bat and ball cost $1.25. The bat costs $.25 more than the ball. What is the cost of the bat?
    (A) $1.00   (B) $.25   (C) $.75   (D) $.50   (E) $1.25

The key words here are *cost of the bat*, so circle those words. If we solve this algebraically:

x = ball
x + .25 = bat (cost $.25 more than the ball)
Together they cost $1.25

$$(x + .25) + x = 1.25$$
$$2x + .25 = 1.25$$
$$2x = 1.00$$
$$x = .50$$

But this is the cost of the *ball*. Notice that $.50 is one of the choices, (D). Since x = .50, then x + .25 = .75. Therefore, the bat costs $.75, which is choice (C). *Always answer the question that is being asked.* Circling the key word or words will help you do that.

Pull out Information

Pulling information out of the wording of a word problem can make the problem more workable for you. Pull out the given facts and identify which of those facts will help you to work the problem. Not all facts will always be needed to work out the problem. *For example:*

1. Bill is 10 years older than his sister. If Bill was 25 years of age in 1983, in what year could he have been born?
   (A) 1948   (B) 1953   (C) 1958   (D) 1963   (E) 1968

The key words here are *in what year* and *could he have been born*. Thus the solution is simple: 1983 − 25 = 1958, answer (C). Notice that you pulled out the information *25 years of age* and *in 1983*. The fact about Bill's age in comparison to his sister's age was not needed, however, and was not pulled out.

Another example:

2. John is 18 years old. He works for his father for ¾ of the year, and he works for his brother for the rest of the year. What is the ratio of the time John spends working for his brother to the time he spends working for his father per year?
   (A) ¼   (B) ⅓   (C) ¾   (D) ⁴⁄₃   (E) ⁴⁄₁

The key word *rest* points to the answer:

$1 - \frac{3}{4} =$

$\frac{4}{4} - \frac{3}{4} = \frac{1}{4}$ (the part of the year John works for his brother)

Also, a key idea is the way in which the ratio is to be written. The problem becomes that of finding the ratio of ¼ to ¾.

$$\frac{1/4}{3/4} = \frac{1}{4} \div \frac{3}{4} = \frac{1}{4} \times \frac{4}{3} = \frac{1}{3}$$

Therefore the answer is choice (B). Note that here John's age is not needed to solve the problem.

Sometimes you may not have sufficient information to solve the problem. *For instance:*

3. A woman purchased several skirts at $15 each plus one more for $12.
What was the average price of each skirt?

   (A) $12   (D) $15
   (B) $13   (E) not enough information
   (C) $14

To calculate an average, you must have the total amount and then divide by
the number of items. The difficulty here, however, is that *several skirts at
$15* does not specify exactly *how many* skirts were purchased at $15 each.
Does *several* mean two? Or does it mean three? *Several* is not a precise
mathematical term. Therefore there is not enough information to pull out to
calculate an average. The answer is (E).

Plug in Numbers

When a problem involving variables (unknowns, or letters) seems difficult
and confusing, simply replace those variables with numbers. Simple numbers
will make the arithmetic easier for you to do. Usually problems using
numbers are easier to understand. Be sure to make logical substitutions. Use
a positive number, a negative number, or zero when applicable to get the full
picture. *For example:*

1. If x is a positive integer in the equation $2x = y$, then y must be
   (A) a positive even integer
   (B) a negative even integer
   (C) zero
   (D) a positive odd integer
   (E) a negative odd integer

At first glance this problem appears quite complex. But let's plug in some
numbers and see what happens. For instance, first plug in 1 (the simplest
positive integer) for x:

$$2x = y$$
$$2(1) = y$$
$$2 = y$$

Now try 2:

$$2x = y$$
$$2(2) = y$$
$$4 = y$$

Try it again. No matter what positive integer is plugged in for x, y will always
be positive and even. Therefore the answer is (A).

Another example:

2. If a, b, and c are all positive whole numbers greater than 1 such that a < b < c, which of the following is the largest quantity?

(A) a(b + c)   (D) they are all equal
(B) ab + c   (E) cannot be determined
(C) ac + b

Substitute 2, 3, and 4 for a, b, and c, respectively.

a(b + c) =	ab + c =	ac + b =
2(3 + 4) =	2(3) + 4 =	2(4) + 3 =
2(7) = 14	6 + 4 = 10	8 + 3 = 11

Since 2, 3, and 4 meet the conditions stated in the problem and choice (A) produces the largest numerical value, it will consistently be the largest quantity. Therefore, a(b + c) is the correct answer, (A).

Work from the Answers

At times the solution to a problem will be obvious to you. At other times it may be helpful to work from the answers. If a direct approach is not obvious to you, try working from the answers. This technique is even more efficient when some of the answer choices are easily eliminated. *For example:*

1. Barney can mow the lawn in 5 hours, and Fred can mow the lawn in 4 hours. How long will it take them to mow the lawn together?

(A) 5 hours   (D) 4½ hours
(B) 4 hours   (E) 2⅘ hours
(C) 8 hours

You may never have worked a problem like this, or perhaps you have worked one but do not remember the procedure required to find the answer. If this is the case, try working from the answers. Since Fred can now mow the lawn in 4 hours by himself, it will take less than 4 hours if Barney helps him. Therefore choices (A), (B), (C), and (D) are ridiculous. Thus the correct answer—by working from the answers and eliminating the incorrect ones—is (E).

Another example:

2. Find the counting number that is less than 15 and when divided by 3 has a remainder of 1, but when divided by 4 has a remainder of 2.

(A) 12   (B) 13   (C) 8   (D) 5   (E) 10

By working from the answers, you can eliminate wrong answer choices. For instance, (A) and (C) can be immediately eliminated because they are divisible by 4, leaving no remainder. Choices (B) and (D) can also be eliminated because they leave a remainder of 1 when divided by 4. Therefore the correct answer is (E): 10 leaves a remainder of 1 when divided by 3 and a remainder of 2 when divided by 4.

Approximate

If a problem involves calculations with numbers that seem tedious and time consuming, round off or approximate those numbers. Replace those numbers with whole numbers that are easier to work with. Find the answer choice that is closest to your approximated answer. *For example:*

1. The value for $(.889 \times 55)/9.97$ to the nearest tenth is
   (A) 49.1   (B) 4.9   (C) 4.63   (D) .5   (E) 17.7

Before starting any computations, take a glance at the answers to see how far apart they are. Notice that the only close answers are (B) and (C), but (C) is not a possible choice, since it is to the nearest hundredth, not tenth. Now making some quick approximations, $.889 \approx 1$ and $9.97 \approx 10$, leaving the problem in this form:

$$\frac{1 \times 55}{10} = \frac{55}{10} = 5.5$$

The closest answer is (B); therefore it is the correct answer. Notice that choices (A) and (D) are not reasonable.

Or:

2. The value of $\sqrt{7194/187}$ is approximately
   (A) 6   (B) 18   (C) 72   (D) 35   (E) 9

Round off both numbers to the hundreds place. The problem then becomes:

$$\sqrt{\frac{7200}{200}}$$

This is much easier to work. By dividing, the problem now becomes:

$$\sqrt{36} =$$

$$= 6$$

The closest answer choice is the exact value of choice (A).

Make Comparisons

At times, questions will require you to compare the sizes of several decimals, or of several fractions. If decimals are being compared, make sure that the numbers being compared have the same number of digits. (Remember: Zeros to the far right of a decimal point can be inserted or eliminated without changing the value of the number.)

For example:

1. Put these in order from smallest to largest: .6, .16, .66⅔, .58

    (A) .6, .16, .66⅔, .58   (D) .66⅔, .6, .58, .16
    (B) .58, .16, .6, .66⅔   (E) .58, .6, .66⅔, .16
    (C) .16, .58, .6, .66⅔

Rewrite .6 as .60; therefore all of the decimals now have the same number of digits: .60, .16, .66⅔, .58. Treating these as though the decimal point were not there (this can be done only when all the numbers have the same number of digits to the right of the decimal), the order is as follows: .16, .58, .60, .66⅔. The correct answer is (C). Remember to circle *smallest to largest* in the question.

2. Put these in order from smallest to largest: ⅝, ¾, ⅔

    (A) ⅔, ¾, ⅝   (D) ¾, ⅝, ⅔
    (B) ⅔, ⅝, ¾   (E) ¾, ⅔, ⅝
    (C) ⅝, ⅔, ¾

Using common denominators, we find: $⅝ = \frac{15}{24}$, $¾ = \frac{18}{24}$, and $⅔ = \frac{16}{24}$.

Therefore the order becomes: ⅝, ⅔, ¾.

Using decimal equivalents: $5/8 = .625$
$$3/4 = .75 \text{ or } .750$$
$$2/3 = .66⅔ \text{ or } .666⅔$$

The order again becomes: ⅝, ⅔, ¾. The answer is (C).

Mark Diagrams

When a figure is included with the problem, mark the given facts on the diagram. This will help you visualize all the facts that have been given. *For example:*

1. If each square in the figure
   has a side of length 1,
   what is the perimeter?
   (A) 12
   (B) 14
   (C) 8
   (D) 20
   (E) 16

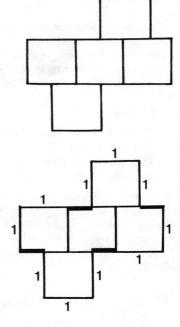

Mark the known facts:

We now have a calculation for the perimeter: 10 *plus* the darkened parts.
Now look carefully at the top two darkened parts. They will add up to 1.
(Notice how the top square may slide over to illustrate that fact.)

These together total 1

The same is true for the bottom
darkened parts. They will add to 1.
Thus, the total perimeter is 10 + 2,
or 12, choice (A).

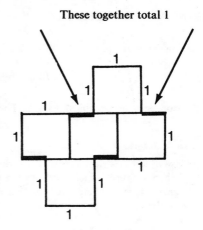

△ ABC is isosceles
$\overline{AB} = \overline{AC}$

2. The perimeter of the isosceles triangle is 42″. The two equal sides are each three times as long as the third side. What are the lengths of each side?
    (A) 21, 21, 21   (D) 18, 18, 6
    (B) 6, 6, 18   (E) 4, 19, 19
    (C) 18, 21, 3

Mark the equal sides $\overline{AB}$ and $\overline{AC}$ are each three
on the diagram: times as long as $\overline{BC}$:

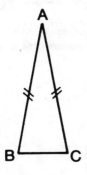   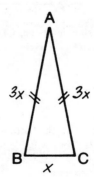

The equation for perimeter is:

$$3x + 3x + x = 42$$
$$7x = 42$$
$$x = 6$$

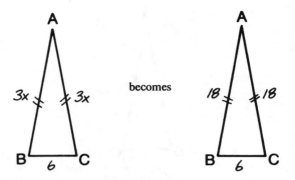

The answer is (D). NOTE: This problem could have been solved by working from the answers given.

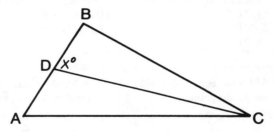

3. In the triangle above, CD is an angle bisector, angle ACD is 30°, and angle ABC is a right angle. What is the measurement of angle x in degrees?

(A) 60°   (D) 180°
(B) 30°   (E) 75°
(C) 45°

You should have read the problem and marked as follows:

In the triangle above, CD is an angle bisector (STOP AND MARK IN THE DRAWING), angle ACD is 30° (STOP AND MARK IN THE DRAWING), and angle ABC is a right angle (STOP AND MARK IN THE DRAWING). What is the measurement of angle x in degrees? (STOP AND MARK IN OR CIRCLE WHAT YOU ARE LOOKING FOR IN THE DRAWING.)

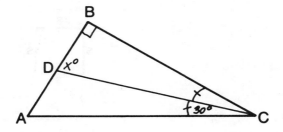

Now with the drawing marked in, it is evident that, since angle ACD is 30°, then angle BCD is also 30° because they are formed by an angle bisector (divides an angle into two equal parts). Since angle ABC is 90° (right angle) and BCD is 30°, then angle x is 60° because there are 180° in a triangle, 180 − (90 + 30) = 60. The correct answer is (A). ALWAYS MARK IN DIAGRAMS AS YOU READ DESCRIPTIONS AND INFORMATION ABOUT THEM. THIS INCLUDES WHAT YOU ARE LOOKING FOR.

Draw Diagrams

Drawing diagrams to meet the conditions set by the word problem can often make the problem easier for you to work. Being able to "see" the facts is more helpful than just reading the words. *For example:*

1. If all sides of a square are doubled, the area of that square is
   (A) doubled
   (B) tripled
   (C) multiplied by 4
   (D) remains the same
   (E) not enough information to tell

One way to solve this problem is to draw a square and then double all its sides. Then compare the two areas:

your first diagram

doubling every side

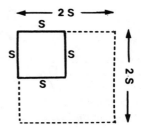

Notice that the total area of the new square will now be four times the original square. The correct answer is (C).

2. A hiking team begins at camp and hikes 5 miles north, then 8 miles west, then 6 miles south, then 9 miles east. In what direction must they now travel in order to return to camp?
   (A) north
   (B) northeast
   (C) northwest
   (D) west
   (E) They already are at camp.

For this question, your diagram would look something like this:

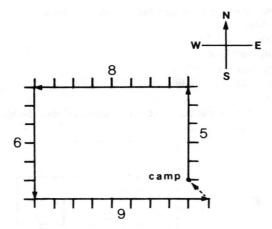

Thus they must travel northwest (C) to return to camp. Note that in this case it is important to draw your diagram very accurately.

3. What is the probability of throwing two dice in one toss so that they total 11?

   (A) 1/6   (B) 1/11   (C) 1/18   (D) 1/20   (E) 1/36

Following are listed, for your information, the total possibilities. But you would NOT want to construct a chart of this length to answer a question because it is too time consuming. You could, instead, simply list all the possible combinations resulting in 11 (5 + 6 and 6 + 5) and realize that the total possibilities are 36 (6 × 6).

TOTAL POSSIBILITIES

First Die	Second Die	First Die	Second Die
1	1	4	1
1	2	4	2
1	3	4	3
1	4	4	4
1	5	4	5
1	6	4	6
2	1	5	1
2	2	5	2
2	3	5	3
2	4	5	4
2	5	5	5
2	6	5	6
3	1	6	1
3	2	6	2
3	3	6	3
3	4	6	4
3	5	6	5
3	6	6	6

These are all the possibilities. Notice that only two possibilities (those circled) will total 11. Thus the probability equals

$$\frac{\text{possibilities totaling 11}}{\text{total possibilities}} = \frac{2}{36} = \frac{1}{18}$$

Answer (C) is correct.

Procedure Problems

Some problems may not ask you to solve and find a correct numerical answer. Rather, you may be asked *how to work* the problem. *For instance:*

1. To find the area of the following figure, a student would use which formula?

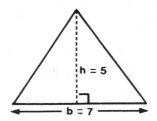

     I. area = base times height
    II. area = ½ times base times height
   III. area = one side squared

  (A) I   (B) II   (C) III   (D) I and II   (E) I and III

Notice that it is not necessary to use any of the numerical values given in the diagram. You are to simply answer how the problem is to be worked. In such cases don't bother working the problem; it is merely a waste of time. The correct answer is **(B) II.**

Or:

2. 51 × 6 could be quickly mentally calculated by
  (A) 50 × 6 + 1
  (B) 51 + 51 + 51 + 51 + 51 + 51
  (C) (50 × 6) + (1 × 6)
  (D) (50 × 6) + 1/6
  (E) adding fifty-one sixes

Answer (C) is correct. The quickest method of calculating 51 × 6 is to first multiply 50 × 6 (resulting in 300), then multiplying 1 × 6 (resulting in 6), and adding them together (300 + 6 = 306). Answer choices (B) and (E) will give the correct answer as well (306) but neither is the best way to *quickly* calculate the answer.

Sometimes, however, actually working the problem can be helpful. *For instance:*

3. The fastest method to solve 7/48 × 6/7 = would be to
   (A) invert the second fraction and then multiply
   (B) multiply each column across and then reduce to lowest terms
   (C) find the common denominator and then multiply across
   (D) divide 7 into numerator and denominator, divide 6 into numerator and denominator, and then multiply across
   (E) reduce the first fraction to lowest terms and then multiply across

In this problem, the way to determine the fastest procedure may be to actually work the problem as you would if you were working toward an answer. Then see if that procedure is listed among the choices. You should then compare it to the other methods listed. Is one of the other *correct* methods faster than the one you used? If so, select the fastest.

These types of problems are not constructed to test your knowledge of *obscure* tricks in solving mathematical equations. Rather they test your knowledge of common procedures used in standard mathematical equations. Thus the fastest way to solve this problem would be to first divide 7 into the numerator and denominator:

$$\frac{\cancel{7}^{1}}{48} \times \frac{6}{\cancel{7}_{1}} =$$

Then divide 6 into the numerator and denominator:

$$\frac{\cancel{7}^{1}}{\cancel{48}_{8}} \times \frac{\cancel{6}^{1}}{\cancel{7}_{1}} =$$

Then multiply across:

$$\frac{\cancel{7}^{1}}{\cancel{48}_{8}} \times \frac{\cancel{6}^{1}}{\cancel{7}_{1}} = \frac{1}{8}$$

The correct answer is (D).

Other Sources of Data—Graphs

Certain problems will be based on graphs that are included in the test. You will need to be able to read and interpret the data on each graph as well as do some arithmetic with this data.

In working with graphs, spend a few moments to understand the title of each graph, as well as what the numbers on the graph are representing.

● Ask yourself if you can (1) read numbers and facts given on the graph and (2) understand what amount those numbers represent.

● There are three main types of graphs. They are (1) circle graphs, (2) bar graphs, and (3) line graphs.

- The amounts in decimal or fractional form on a circle graph will always total one whole. The amounts in percentage form on a circle graph will always total 100%.

- The amounts written as money, or in numerical form, on a circle graph will always add up to the total amount being referred to.

- Be sure to thoroughly read the paragraph under a graph if there is one and to interpret a legend if one is included.

- On bar or line graphs it is sometimes helpful to use the edge of your answer sheet as a straightedge. This will help you line up points on the graph with their numerical value on the graph scale. Also, look for trends such as increases, decreases, sudden low points, or sudden high points.

Questions 1, 2, and 3 refer to the following circle graph (pie chart).

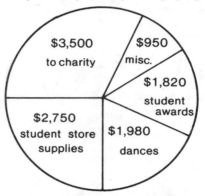

**How the Kettle School Distributed
Its Fund-Raising Earnings in 1979
(1979 fund-raising earnings totaled $11,000)**

1. The amount of money given to charity in 1979 was approximately what percent of the total amount earned?
   (A) 50%   (B) 34%   (C) 82%   (D) 45%   (E) 18%

2. Last year, 1978, the Kettle School spent 40% of its earnings on student store supplies. This percent exceeds the 1979 figure by how much?
   (A) 10%   (B) 30%   (C) 15%   (D) 85%   (E) 0%

3. If the Kettle School spends the same percentage on dances every year, how much will they spend in 1980 if their earnings are $15,000?
   (A) $4,000   (B) $2,700   (C) $15,000   (D) $11,000
   (E) $270

Answers to questions 1, 2, and 3

1. The answer is (B). Set up a simple ratio:

$$\frac{\text{money to charity}}{\text{total}} = \frac{\$3,500}{\$11,000} \approx \frac{1}{3} = 33\frac{1}{3}\%$$

2. The answer is (C).

$$\frac{\text{student store supplies in 1979}}{\text{total}} = \frac{\$2,750}{\$11,000} = 25\% \qquad 40\% - 25\% = 15\%$$

3. The answer is (B).

$$\text{This year } \frac{\$1,980}{\$11,000} = 18\%$$

So 18% of $15,000 next year = $2,700

Questions 4, 5, and 6 refer to the following circle graph (pie chart).

How John Spends His Monthly Paycheck

4. If John receives $100 per paycheck, how much money does he put in the bank?

   (A) $35 (B) $20 (C) $80 (D) $100 (E) $2

5. John spends more than twice as much on _____ as he does on school supplies.

   (A) car and bike repair   (D) miscellaneous items
   (B) his hobby   (E) cannot be determined
   (C) entertainment

6. The ratio of the amount of money John spends on his hobby to the amount he puts in the bank is

(A) ½   (B) ⅔   (C) ¾   (D) ⅝   (E) ⅙

Answers to questions 4, 5, and 6

4. The answer is (B). 20% of $100 = .2(100) = $20.00.

5. The answer is (C). School supplies are 10%. The only amount more than twice 10% (or 20%) is 25% (entertainment).

6. The answer is (C). Set up the ratio:

$$\frac{\text{amount to hobby}}{\text{amount to bank}} = \frac{15}{20} = \frac{3}{4}$$

Questions 7, 8, and 9 refer to the following bar graph.

Shares of Stock X Owned by Five Major Corporations

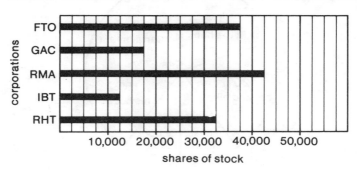

7. The number of shares owned by RHT exceeds the number of shares owned by GAC by

(A) 32,500   (D) 20,000
(B) 15,000   (E) 10,000
(C) 17,500

8. The number of shares of stock owned by IBT is approximately what percent of that owned by FTO?

(A) 50%   (B) 33%   (C) 18%   (D) 42%   (E) 25%

9. The number of shares of stock owned by RMA exceeds which other corporations' by more than 20,000?

(A) GAC and IBT   (D) IBT and FTO
(B) FTO and RHT   (E) IBT and RHT
(C) GAC and FTO

Answers to questions 7, 8, and 9

7. The answer is (B).

$$
\begin{array}{r}
32{,}500 \text{ RHT} \\
- \ 17{,}500 \text{ GAC} \\
\hline
15{,}000
\end{array}
$$

8. The answer is (B). 12,500 is what percent of 37,500?

$$\frac{12{,}500}{37{,}500} = \frac{1}{3} \simeq 33\%$$

9. The answer is (A).

$$
\begin{array}{r}
42{,}500 \text{ RMA} \\
- \ 17{,}500 \text{ GAC} \\
\hline
25{,}000
\end{array}
\qquad
\begin{array}{r}
42{,}500 \text{ RMA} \\
- \ 12{,}500 \text{ IBT} \\
\hline
30{,}000
\end{array}
$$

Questions 10, 11, and 12 are based on the following graph.

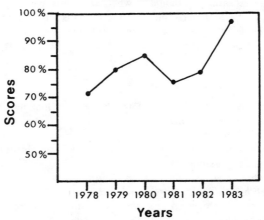

**Average Score (Statewide)
On Student Aptitude Test
1978–1983**

10. Between which two years was the greatest rise in average test scores?

(A) 1978 and 1979   (D) 1981 and 1982
(B) 1979 and 1980   (E) 1982 and 1983
(C) 1980 and 1981

11. In which year was the average score approximately 85%?

(A) 1978   (B) 1979   (C) 1980   (D) 1981   (E) 1982

12. Approximately what was the highest score achieved statewide on the test?

(A) 80%   (D) 97%
(B) 85%   (E) cannot be determined
(C) 90%

Answers to questions 10, 11, and 12

10. **(E)** The most efficient way to compute greatest rise is to locate the *steepest* upward slope on the chart. Note that the steepest climb is between 1982 and 1983. Therefore choice (E) indicates the greatest rise in average test scores.

11. **(C)** According to the graph, the average test score was approximately 85% in 1980 (C). In such cases when you must read the graph for a precise measurement, it may be helpful to use your answer sheet as a straightedge to more accurately compare points with the grid marks along the side.

12. **(E)** The first thing you should do when confronted with a graph or chart is read its title to understand what the graph is telling you. In this case the graph is relating information about *average scores*. It tells you nothing about the *highest* score achieved. Thus (E) is the correct answer.

Tips for Working Math Problems

1. Read the question carefully, circling what you are looking for.
2. Pull out important information.
3. Draw, sketch, or mark in diagrams.
4. If you know a simple method, or formula, work the problem out as simply and quickly as possible.
5. If you do not know a simple method, or formula,
   (a) try eliminating some unreasonable choices.
   (b) work from the answers or substitute in numbers if appropriate.
   (c) try approximating to clarify thinking and simplify work.
6. Always make sure that your answer is reasonable.

LITERATURE AND FINE ARTS

This section contains about 35 questions and is 30 minutes in length.

Ability Tested

The questions evaluate your skill at accurate observation, interpretation, and comprehension of works from the humanities. The test questions refer to passages from literature and photographs of artworks.

Basic Skills Necessary

Some understanding of obvious techniques employed by authors and artists, as well as an understanding of the content and implications of a given work, will be required. These questions are intended to cover general principles and broad themes and test analytical skill rather than quiz you on recall of specific, isolated facts. Questions will usually provide a specific example and then ask about its

Standout features
Comparison to some other "real world" example
Obvious detail
General, apparent theme
Meaning, if any
Content
Representation

The questions concern literature, the graphic arts, and music and stress the ability for artistic appreciation expected of a teacher. Although you may be asked a question or two that requires your knowledge of a commonplace and well-known fact, you should prepare yourself by practicing thoughtful evaluation of literature and art, not by memorizing information.

The literature questions refer to plays, poems, novels, essays, and short stories and presuppose that you have become somewhat familiar with reading such material in college literature courses. You will not need to identify characters, plots, titles, authors, and so forth but will need to draw logical, intelligent conclusions about the material presented. The fine arts questions refer to paintings, sculptures, pieces of architecture, photographs, films, and music. Many of these questions provide you with a photograph of an art work and ask you to interpret what you see or recognize important details or techniques. You may also be asked to draw conclusions from statements about music.

Directions

Each of the following questions or incomplete statements is followed by five possible answers or completions. Select the answer or completion that is best in each case.

Analysis

More than one answer choice may seem like a good one; be careful to read all answer choices and eliminate all but the *best* choice. Remember that the best choice must be supported by the expressed or implied information in the literature or artwork you are asked to evaluate. Do not apply outside information unless the nature of the question clearly requires you to do so.

Suggested Approach with Samples

Questions 1 and 2 refer to the following excerpt from a Shakespearean sonnet.

> Full many a glorious morning have I seen
> Flatter the mountain-tops with sovereign eye,
> Kissing with golden face the meadows green,
> Gilding pale streams with heavenly alchemy;

1. The poet probably intended *alchemy* to rhyme with which of the following words?

    (A) heavenly   (D) seen
    (B) balcony   (E) green
    (C) eye

2. *Sovereign eye* is probably a figurative reference to which of the following objects in nature?

    (A) the mountain-tops   (D) the sun
    (B) the eye of the poet   (E) the moon
    (C) the eye of a king

First, a few general comments on the strategy you should adopt here and throughout this section of the test. Before reading a given literary passage or examining an artwork, *read the question(s)*. The questions will indicate what parts or aspects of the work you should focus on, and prereading will save you the time of reconsidering the work. Also, do not be disconcerted if you are unfamiliar with the literature or artwork; familiarity with the particular work is almost never necessary for answering questions correctly. For instance, in this case particular familiarity with Shakespeare's sonnets is not necessary, but previous experience in reading and understanding poetry is.

1. (C) Having preread the question, you should be especially attentive to the rhyme scheme. Note that lines 1 and 3 rhyme with one another. This fact suggests that every other line rhymes and that lines 2 and 4 were intended to rhyme with one another. In other words, *alchemy* was intended to rhyme with *eye.* This choice is reinforced if we recall that pronunciation was more flexible and less standardized in Shakespeare's day, thus allowing for a pronunciation of *alchemy* which doesn't seem "right" to us now.

2. (D) The question tells you that the correct answer will be an object in nature; you should immediately eliminate choices (B) and (C). The poem speaks of *morning* and of a *sovereign eye* above the *mountain-tops;* the time of day and the distinction between *sovereign eye* and *mountain-tops* should lead you to eliminate choices (A) and (E). The correct choice, (D), is a reasonable, literal (direct) expression for the figurative (indirect), poetic term *sovereign.* Note that the best answer was attainable through a process of elimination; such a process of elimination will work well in many cases.

3. The attitude expressed in the picture at the right is best described as
   (A) zaniness
   (B) anger
   (C) thoughtfulness
   (D) playfulness
   (E) indecision

3. (C) After prereading the question, pay particular attention to the expression of the man in the picture. Notice that his face is quiet and serene, not betraying any extreme emotions such as zaniness or anger. His expression

is serious and neutral, signifying neither playfulness nor indecision. The best answer is that which reflects a calm, inward attitude appropriate to a placid expression—thoughtfulness.

In most cases, what you are asked to observe in a work will be fairly obvious rather than subtle. Some test takers make the grave mistake of presuming that they should look for "hidden meanings" or "tricks" as they analyze works and answer questions. This attitude will lead you to overanalyze and jump to incorrect conclusions. Always prefer fairly obvious, straightforward answer choices, even in lengthy questions, and try to inspect the work carefully but without unwarranted anxiety.

SCIENCE

The Science section contains about 30 questions and is 30 minutes in length.

Ability Tested

This section tests your knowledge and understanding of fundamental areas of scientific concern and interest. The questions deal with general themes rather than recall of specific or isolated facts.

Basic Skills Necessary

General knowledge of the following scientific areas is required.

Energy—relationships among living and nonliving things
Life forms—their general functions and structures
Natural processes—variety among organisms, changes through the ages
Relationships—between living organisms and the environment
The earth—its components, its changes, its origins
Matter—atomic composition and properties of substances
Forces—gravitational, nuclear, electromagnetic, etc.
Scientific method—laws of science, technology, scientific observation and experimentation
Science and values—nutrition, ecology, life enhancement through scientific advancement

Directions

Each of the Science questions is followed by five suggested answers. Select the best answer for each question.

Analysis

The questions on the Science section of the test focus on important ideas, facts, principles, theories, and methods of science. A general review of the highlights and basic terminology of each area of scientific study (for example, chemistry, physics, geology) will be helpful, but the questions are of such a general nature that intensive, detailed review is unnecessary. Understanding of test-taking strategies for multiple-choice questions is essential.

Suggested Approach with Samples

Some questions will deal with modern science in your daily life.

1. Tampering with over-the-counter, nonprescription drugs has become a major national problem. Of the following, the best way that consumers could protect themselves from this type of tampered-with product would be by
   (A) buying these products at a respectable neighborhood pharmacy
   (B) examining the list of ingredients on the label
   (C) writing to the Food and Drug Administration asking about the products that are most likely to be tampered with
   (D) checking the package to see if the seam seal is damaged or broken
   (E) checking the expiration date of the product

The *best* answer is (D). Because of recent tampering, many of these drugs are now seam sealed specifically to prevent unnoticed tampering. Choice (A), buying these products at a respectable neighborhood pharmacy, may sound safe but is still no guarantee. Choice (C), writing to the Food and Drug Administration, could also be helpful but is not the best protection. Choices (B) and (E) would not necessarily be helpful.

Some questions will ask about specific knowledge in the field of science. Sometimes these questions are best attacked by eliminating wrong choices.

2. Which substance is *not* gaseous at normal temperature and pressure?
   (A) ammonia   (D) nitrogen
   (B) chlorine   (E) sulfur
   (C) methane

You may know that sulfur is a yellow solid, so (E) is the correct choice. Let's assume, however, that you're not sure about sulfur. You can answer the question by crossing out false choices. Ammonia is a pungent gas, familiar in cleaning solutions. Chlorine is a green, poisonous gas employed as a weapon in World War I. Methane is a marsh gas, a combustible natural gas from decay. Nitrogen is the principal component of air. Knowing any of those four facts enables you to make an educated guess. Remember to keep working and do not ponder difficult questions too long.

Some questions will ask you to apply common sense reasoning and/or draw inferences from your knowledge of modern science and scientific principles.

3. When the moon is at crescent phase, it must be
   (A) inside the earth's orbit
   (B) outside the earth's orbit
   (C) rising as the sun sets
   (D) setting
   (E) undergoing an eclipse

You are not expected to have memorized the answer to that *difficult* question. You can figure it out by considering the relative positions of the earth, moon, and sun. The half of the moon facing the sun is illuminated. Where, then, must the observer be to perceive less than half (a crescent) of the bright half? The answer is (A). When the moon is within the earth's orbit, less than half of it is illuminated from our viewpoint. Outside the earth's orbit, over half of it would appear bright, called a gibbous phase. The moon would appear full if it rose as the sun set. A lunar eclipse is a different phenomenon.

INTRODUCTION TO THE TEST OF PROFESSIONAL KNOWLEDGE

The Test of Professional Knowledge contains 4 sections, each thirty minutes in length. Each section contains approximately 30 questions.

Ability Tested

This exam tests your ability to use theoretical and practical knowledge in dealing with the procedures necessary for effective teaching. It tests your ability to understand classroom situations in terms of goals, behavior, and guidelines. The exam questions cover a wide range, focusing particularly on

Classroom management and methodology
Learning theory
Planning curriculum
Implementing curriculum
Evaluating student achievement and instructional effectiveness
Professional behavior
Rights of students and of teachers
Special and alternative education
Community relations
Extracurricular influences

Basic Skills Necessary

The basic skills necessary are an understanding of educational survey courses in history, psychology, philosophy, and sociology of education along with the ability to apply that knowledge in classroom teaching and management. The use of common-sense reasoning with an understanding of motivation and learning theory, along with the knowledge of the role of the teacher, principal, and other school officials, is also necessary.

Directions

You will be required to identify and react to information relative to the history and philosophy of education and effective classroom techniques.

Following each of the questions or statements, select the choice that best answers the question or completes the statement.

Analysis

Keep in mind that you are asked for the *best* of five choices, which may not always be the *ideal* choice.

Mark key words and phrases as you read each question; make certain you understand what you are being asked.

Use common-sense reasoning in selecting your choice.

Suggested Approach with Samples

Some questions will deal with classroom or school-related situations. In answering situation-type questions, pay special attention to the complete situation and the established criteria. Use common-sense reasoning in arriving at your final choice. *Sample:*

1. A seventh-grade teacher puts a list of three countries on the board. The teacher informs the students that through a popular vote the class will decide the country to be studied next. The class, in a close vote, decides on Ireland. Before starting the lesson what would be the *most* appropriate measure to assess the students' background on Ireland?

    (A) Initiate a class discussion that centers on the culture and people of Ireland.
    (B) Administer a pretest.
    (C) Determine appropriate behavioral objectives.
    (D) Assess the cognitive learning that must take place.
    (E) Ask if any students have been to Ireland and have them share their experience with the class.

The best answer is choice (B). The question calls for the *most* appropriate measure, *before* starting a lesson, to assess student background on Ireland. A pretest is the only choice that specifically answers the criterion established in the question. A pretest would be the most effective measure to determine what students already know about a specific subject. In answering situation-type questions, pay special attention to the established criteria. It should be apparent that determining appropriate behavioral objectives (C) would be the first step in planning for a successful unit; however, objectives would not provide specific information on students' prior knowledge of a subject area. Note that the results of the pretest could be used to evaluate explicit objectives already determined to be appropriate for the unit. Choice (D), assessment of desired cognitive learning, would also be a preliminary step in preparing for a successful unit; choices (A) and (E) are obviously not the most appropriate methods to assess prior knowledge.

Some questions will require specific knowledge related to a certain area of education. By using your general knowledge, you can often arrive at the correct answer by eliminating the wrong choices first. *Sample:*

2. The American normal school deserves the principal credit for
    (A) encouraging education in agriculture and the mechanical arts
    (B) establishing the ideal that elementary and secondary teaching deserved to be characterized as "professional"
    (C) designing education programs to prepare students for the ministry
    (D) expanding the college and university curriculum
    (E) initiating teacher-education programs that consisted of a four-year, liberal-arts education, followed by a fifth year of professional training

The best answer is choice (B). This question can be answered on the basis of specific knowledge related to the historical development of American public education. Normal schools, even in the early twentieth century, were associated with teacher training. The American normal schools, originally established in the late 1820s, responded to the need for *professional education* by offering courses in teaching methods, discipline, and the management of children.

A general knowledge of educational time periods, however, can also be effective in selecting the best answer. For instance, choice (A) can be eliminated, since education in agriculture and mechanical arts was embodied in the land-grant colleges provided for in the Morrill Act (1862); choice (C) should be quickly eliminated, since education to prepare students for the ministry was primarily associated with Puritan New England in the seventeenth and eighteenth centuries. By simply knowing that the American normal school was established in the middle nineteenth century one could eliminate choice (E), since it was not until the twentieth century that some professional-education schools required five years of college. Through a process of elimination, the correct answer can be narrowed to choices (B) and (D). By realizing that the development of the university movement was historically centered in private institutions, one could assume that the American normal school was probably not associated with expanding the university curriculum. Therefore, through a process of elimination, and a general knowledge of the historical development of American public education, one could arrive at the best answer—choice (B). *Remember,* if you can eliminate one or more choices, the chances of correctly answering the question are greatly increased.

Some questions will require the use of general knowledge, acquired in an education class or through practical experience. Make sure that the answer specifically addresses the issue that underlies the situation. *Sample:*

3. Ms. Benson asked her sixth-grade class if they would volunteer to take a practice test that she planned to administer to her Sunday-school class. The test included interpreting specific passages from the Bible. Ms. Benson did not coerce any students to participate in the project and even used the lunch period to administer the test. The school administrator should

(A) inform Ms. Benson that she showed good judgment in allowing the test to be voluntary

(B) inform Ms. Benson that she would have violated the law if the project had taken place during an academic period

(C) inform Ms. Benson that her actions are in violation of the First Amendment of the Constitution

(D) contact the parents of the children involved and apologize for Ms. Benson's actions

(E) contact the Sunday school and inform them of Ms. Benson's actions

   The best answer is choice (C). A general knowledge of current school law is necessary to answer this question. The schools have a responsibility to teach students about their First Amendment freedoms. To effectively accomplish this goal, teachers must be aware of the legal framework in which the schools must operate. Ms. Benson's actions are in violation of the principle of separation of church and state embodied in the First Amendment. The First Amendment prohibits public agencies from aiding or opposing religion. Bible reading is prohibited in public schools even if it is done without comment and even if students have the option of being excused from the exercise. Choices (A) and (B) would indicate that the building supervisor was not aware of the legal ramifications of Ms. Benson's actions. Choices (D) and (E) are possible answers, but they do not specifically address the constitutional issue that underlies the situation.

PART III: Assessment Mini-Test

The Mini-Test that follows is designed to introduce you to the NTE Core Battery and to assess your strengths and weaknesses. This assessment includes complete answers and explanations. These questions are not taken directly from the actual NTE. The actual NTE is copyrighted and may not be duplicated.

This Mini-Test is a fraction of the length of the actual exam. Follow these time allotments for each test:

Test of Communication Skills
Section I: Listening (17 Minutes, 16 Questions)
Section II: Reading (12 Minutes, 10 Questions)
Section III: Writing—Multiple Choice (10 Minutes, 11 Questions)
Section IV: Writing—Essay (30 Minutes, 1 Essay)

Test of General Knowledge
Section I: Social Studies (6 Minutes, 6 Questions)
Section II: Mathematics (7 Minutes, 6 Questions)
Section III: Literature and Fine Arts (5 Minutes, 7 Questions)
Section IV: Science (6 Minutes, 7 Questions)

Test of Professional Knowledge (20 Minutes, 20 Questions)

ANSWER SHEET FOR THE MINI-TEST
(Remove This Sheet and Use It to Mark Your Answers)

TEST OF COMMUNICATION SKILLS

SECTION I	SECTION II	SECTION III

SECTION I

1 Ⓐ Ⓑ Ⓒ Ⓓ
2 Ⓐ Ⓑ Ⓒ Ⓓ
3 Ⓐ Ⓑ Ⓒ Ⓓ
4 Ⓐ Ⓑ Ⓒ Ⓓ
5 Ⓐ Ⓑ Ⓒ Ⓓ
6 Ⓐ Ⓑ Ⓒ Ⓓ
7 Ⓐ Ⓑ Ⓒ Ⓓ
8 Ⓐ Ⓑ Ⓒ Ⓓ
9 Ⓐ Ⓑ Ⓒ Ⓓ
10 Ⓐ Ⓑ Ⓒ Ⓓ
11 Ⓐ Ⓑ Ⓒ Ⓓ
12 Ⓐ Ⓑ Ⓒ Ⓓ
13 Ⓐ Ⓑ Ⓒ Ⓓ
14 Ⓐ Ⓑ Ⓒ Ⓓ
15 Ⓐ Ⓑ Ⓒ Ⓓ
16 Ⓐ Ⓑ Ⓒ Ⓓ

SECTION II

1 Ⓐ Ⓑ Ⓒ Ⓓ Ⓔ
2 Ⓐ Ⓑ Ⓒ Ⓓ Ⓔ
3 Ⓐ Ⓑ Ⓒ Ⓓ Ⓔ
4 Ⓐ Ⓑ Ⓒ Ⓓ Ⓔ
5 Ⓐ Ⓑ Ⓒ Ⓓ Ⓔ
6 Ⓐ Ⓑ Ⓒ Ⓓ Ⓔ
7 Ⓐ Ⓑ Ⓒ Ⓓ Ⓔ
8 Ⓐ Ⓑ Ⓒ Ⓓ Ⓔ
9 Ⓐ Ⓑ Ⓒ Ⓓ Ⓔ
10 Ⓐ Ⓑ Ⓒ Ⓓ Ⓔ

SECTION III

1 Ⓐ Ⓑ Ⓒ Ⓓ Ⓔ
2 Ⓐ Ⓑ Ⓒ Ⓓ Ⓔ
3 Ⓐ Ⓑ Ⓒ Ⓓ Ⓔ
4 Ⓐ Ⓑ Ⓒ Ⓓ Ⓔ
5 Ⓐ Ⓑ Ⓒ Ⓓ Ⓔ
6 Ⓐ Ⓑ Ⓒ Ⓓ Ⓔ
7 Ⓐ Ⓑ Ⓒ Ⓓ Ⓔ
8 Ⓐ Ⓑ Ⓒ Ⓓ Ⓔ
9 Ⓐ Ⓑ Ⓒ Ⓓ Ⓔ
10 Ⓐ Ⓑ Ⓒ Ⓓ Ⓔ
11 Ⓐ Ⓑ Ⓒ Ⓓ Ⓔ

CUT HERE

86

ANSWER SHEET FOR THE MINI-TEST
(Remove This Sheet and Use It to Mark Your Answers)

TEST OF GENERAL KNOWLEDGE

SECTION I

1 Ⓐ Ⓑ Ⓒ Ⓓ Ⓔ
2 Ⓐ Ⓑ Ⓒ Ⓓ Ⓔ
3 Ⓐ Ⓑ Ⓒ Ⓓ Ⓔ
4 Ⓐ Ⓑ Ⓒ Ⓓ Ⓔ
5 Ⓐ Ⓑ Ⓒ Ⓓ Ⓔ
6 Ⓐ Ⓑ Ⓒ Ⓓ Ⓔ

SECTION II

1 Ⓐ Ⓑ Ⓒ Ⓓ Ⓔ
2 Ⓐ Ⓑ Ⓒ Ⓓ Ⓔ
3 Ⓐ Ⓑ Ⓒ Ⓓ Ⓔ
4 Ⓐ Ⓑ Ⓒ Ⓓ Ⓔ
5 Ⓐ Ⓑ Ⓒ Ⓓ Ⓔ
6 Ⓐ Ⓑ Ⓒ Ⓓ Ⓔ

SECTION III

1 Ⓐ Ⓑ Ⓒ Ⓓ Ⓔ
2 Ⓐ Ⓑ Ⓒ Ⓓ Ⓔ
3 Ⓐ Ⓑ Ⓒ Ⓓ Ⓔ
4 Ⓐ Ⓑ Ⓒ Ⓓ Ⓔ
5 Ⓐ Ⓑ Ⓒ Ⓓ Ⓔ
6 Ⓐ Ⓑ Ⓒ Ⓓ Ⓔ
7 Ⓐ Ⓑ Ⓒ Ⓓ Ⓔ

SECTION IV

1 Ⓐ Ⓑ Ⓒ Ⓓ Ⓔ
2 Ⓐ Ⓑ Ⓒ Ⓓ Ⓔ
3 Ⓐ Ⓑ Ⓒ Ⓓ Ⓔ
4 Ⓐ Ⓑ Ⓒ Ⓓ Ⓔ
5 Ⓐ Ⓑ Ⓒ Ⓓ Ⓔ
6 Ⓐ Ⓑ Ⓒ Ⓓ Ⓔ
7 Ⓐ Ⓑ Ⓒ Ⓓ Ⓔ

TEST OF PROFESSIONAL KNOWLEDGE

1 Ⓐ Ⓑ Ⓒ Ⓓ Ⓔ
2 Ⓐ Ⓑ Ⓒ Ⓓ Ⓔ
3 Ⓐ Ⓑ Ⓒ Ⓓ Ⓔ
4 Ⓐ Ⓑ Ⓒ Ⓓ Ⓔ
5 Ⓐ Ⓑ Ⓒ Ⓓ Ⓔ
6 Ⓐ Ⓑ Ⓒ Ⓓ Ⓔ
7 Ⓐ Ⓑ Ⓒ Ⓓ Ⓔ
8 Ⓐ Ⓑ Ⓒ Ⓓ Ⓔ
9 Ⓐ Ⓑ Ⓒ Ⓓ Ⓔ
10 Ⓐ Ⓑ Ⓒ Ⓓ Ⓔ

11 Ⓐ Ⓑ Ⓒ Ⓓ Ⓔ
12 Ⓐ Ⓑ Ⓒ Ⓓ Ⓔ
13 Ⓐ Ⓑ Ⓒ Ⓓ Ⓔ
14 Ⓐ Ⓑ Ⓒ Ⓓ Ⓔ
15 Ⓐ Ⓑ Ⓒ Ⓓ Ⓔ
16 Ⓐ Ⓑ Ⓒ Ⓓ Ⓔ
17 Ⓐ Ⓑ Ⓒ Ⓓ Ⓔ
18 Ⓐ Ⓑ Ⓒ Ⓓ Ⓔ
19 Ⓐ Ⓑ Ⓒ Ⓓ Ⓔ
20 Ⓐ Ⓑ Ⓒ Ⓓ Ⓔ

CUT HERE

MINI-TEST

TEST OF COMMUNICATION SKILLS

SECTION I: LISTENING

Time: 17 Minutes for Three Parts
16 Questions

Cut out pages 87 through 89 as shown and give them to a friend to read aloud to you. (In the actual exam, a tape recorder will be used.) These pages contain the script of the listening questions, statements, conversations, and talks for the Mini-Test, Parts A, B, and C. Ask the reader to allow 10 to 15 seconds after each question for you to mark your answer. Turn to page 91 where you will find the answer choices for each of the questions. Read the directions before beginning each part of Section I.

Questions, Statements, Conversations, and Talks—Script

Part A: Questions and Statements

1. Computer science is becoming a required course in many high schools but was unheard-of as part of the curriculum ten years ago.

2. When did you agree to become chairperson of the committee?

3. Sometimes children cannot concentrate on schoolwork when their diet (especially breakfast) lacks protein.

4. The testing service that designs the teachers' test also designs tests that certify auto mechanics.

5. Why has the picnic been rescheduled for next Saturday?

6. Many readers like novels better than most poetry because novels have a plot.

CUT HERE

Part B: Conversations

Questions 7 and 8 are based on the following conversation.

Woman: You arrive here at school each day looking very fatigued.

Child: I get up early to deliver papers at 4:00 A.M.

Woman: Well, I suggest that you give up your paper route so you can get more sleep at home.

7. How does the woman feel about sleeping?

8. What does the woman assume about the paper route?

Questions 9 and 10 are based on the following conversation.

Man 1: I'll be teaching math instead of English next semester, unless you agree to teach six periods.

Man 2: I wouldn't mind teaching an extra class, but if I do, the administration will have another excuse not to hire a math teacher. We need another full-timer.

Man 1: They have a good excuse already. Three of us English teachers minored in math.

9. What does the English teacher imply with his final remark?

10. What can we conclude about a six-period teaching load?

Part C: Talks

Questions 11, 12, and 13 refer to the following talk.

Human nature is essentially selfish. People are looking out for their own interests, even though they may pretend to be more interested in the welfare of other people. Furthermore, people are ruled by their passions and their feelings rather than by reason. A government, in order to be successful, must recognize that this is true and adopt policies accordingly. This means that it is far more important to make people think you are acting in their interest than it is to do so in fact. For this purpose, rulers of states should not hesitate to use *deception* in order to achieve the ends which they desire. Furthermore, because fear is a stronger motive than love, it is *better for a ruler to be feared than to be loved.*

11. What is the speaker's attitude toward human nature?

12. Why, according to the speaker, should rulers make their subjects fearful?

13. What is the main topic of this talk?

CUT HERE

Questions 14, 15, and 16 refer to the following talk.

Our schools encourage students to believe that knowledge is power. But how can the students believe this when it is quite clear that in the world outside school, knowledge is not power. The presidents of major corporations are rumored to be illiterate, but they are rich and powerful. The chiefs of organized crime are certainly not distinguished university graduates, but they are rich and powerful. Where are those who love and pursue knowledge? They are teaching in our schools and colleges, earning low pay and subject to ever-increasing cuts in education. If teachers are not granted greater economic and social power, in the form of higher salaries and greater job security, our students will continue to believe that knowledge gets people nowhere. The present bill before the legislature grants money for more classroom materials and for the renovation of our older schools but grants no salary raises to teachers. We must contact our legislators and urge them to vote against this bill and any bill that continues to treat teachers and the knowledge they represent as second-class citizens.

14. According to the speaker, what should be done about the salaries of teachers?

15. According to the speaker, what often goes along with power?

16. What is the speaker urging the listeners to do?

CUT HERE

Answer Choices

Part A: *Questions and Statements*

DIRECTIONS

You will be faced with two kinds of problems. You must either answer a short question or understand a brief statement. Each question and each statement will be spoken one time. After you hear a question, you will read four answer choices; select the correct answer. After you hear a statement, you will read four sentences; select the sentence closest to the meaning of the statement or supported by the statement.

1. (A) High school requirements force students to buy home computers.
   (B) Educators don't recognize the value of computer science.
   (C) Computer science is too difficult to introduce before high school.
   (D) Computer science did not exist in the schools ten years ago.

2. (A) I was forced to accept the position.
   (B) When I last served on this committee, I became discouraged.
   (C) I accepted the position last January.
   (D) When the job becomes too difficult, I will resign.

3. (A) Protein contributes to better concentration.
   (B) Many children concentrate more on their diet than on schoolwork.
   (C) An unbalanced diet does not affect adults.
   (D) The more children concentrate, the better they feel.

4. (A) The teachers' test is designed by people who understand only cars.
   (B) The testing service designs more than one test.
   (C) Auto mechanics should know what teachers know.
   (D) Some certified auto mechanics are teachers.

5. (A) It was rescheduled last week by the committee.
   (B) Many don't want to hold a picnic at all.
   (C) Last Saturday was a fine day for a picnic.
   (D) Most who would like to come are free only next Saturday.

6. (A) Most novels tell a story.
   (B) Novelists cannot also write poetry.
   (C) Novels are easily discussed in informal conversation.
   (D) A poem is always harder to read than a novel.

PROCEED DIRECTLY TO PART B.

Part B: Conversations

DIRECTIONS

You will hear short conversations between two speakers. After each conversation, a third speaker will ask questions about what the two were discussing. The conversations and each question will be spoken only once. After you hear each question, choose the best of the four possible answers.

7. (A) It is important for the child.
   (B) The paper route is more important.
   (C) The woman is very sleepy.
   (D) It should be done in school.

8. (A) It is unfair.
   (B) It is unnecessary.
   (C) It is unprofitable.
   (D) It is unaffecting.

9. (A) The math teacher's opinion is not valid.
   (B) The administration will rely on English teachers to teach math.
   (C) All English teachers are good math teachers.
   (D) He will not welcome a full-time math teacher.

10. (A) It is not normal.
    (B) It is impossible.
    (C) It is irresponsible.
    (D) It is preferred by the math teacher.

PROCEED DIRECTLY TO PART C.

Part C: Talks

DIRECTIONS

You will hear several short talks, each followed by questions. When you hear a question, choose the best answer of the four printed in your test booklet. Remember that the talks and questions will be spoken only once, so you must listen carefully while you attempt to understand and remember what the speaker says.

11. (A) cynical
    (B) optimistic
    (C) hopeful
    (D) loving

12. (A) Feared rulers can teach people to love them.
    (B) People who fear a ruler love a ruler.
    (C) People will more likely respond to fear than love.
    (D) People love being afraid.

13. (A) human nature and government
    (B) ruling through love
    (C) human reason
    (D) the causes of selfishness

14. (A) They should equal those of corporate presidents.
    (B) They should be reported to students.
    (C) They should be cut by the legislature.
    (D) They should be raised.

15. (A) knowledge
    (B) material wealth
    (C) honesty
    (D) dishonesty

16. (A) speak to their students
    (B) pursue knowledge
    (C) oppose an education bill
    (D) raise the salaries of teachers

STOP: IF YOU FINISH BEFORE TIME IS CALLED, CHECK YOUR WORK ON THIS SECTION ONLY. DO NOT WORK ON ANY OTHER SECTION IN THE TEST.

SECTION II: READING

Time: 12 Minutes
10 Questions

DIRECTIONS

A question or number of questions follow each of the statements or passages in this section. Using only the *stated* or *implied* information given in the statement or passage, answer the question or questions by choosing the *best* answer from among the five choices given.

It is an important guideline to avoid discussing other students during a parent-teacher conference. Such comments often result in an emotional reaction by the parent and can interfere with the purpose of the conference.

1. Which of the following facts, if true, would most strengthen the argument of the passage?
   (A) The discussion of other students gives many parents a comfortable sense that the teacher understands the whole classroom "scene."
   (B) Most parents avoid taking the trouble to attend a conference.
   (C) The child's relationship with other students is most often the cause of problems that necessitate a conference.
   (D) Researchers witnessing parent-teacher conferences have verified that parents become angry in 90% of the conferences in which other students are discussed.
   (E) Emotional reactions by parents must be understood as the parents' legitimate expression of deeply felt concerns.

A test is valid if it measures what it is intended to measure. A test is reliable if it is consistent. Therefore, a test may be consistent even though it does not measure what it is intended to measure.

2. The author's primary purpose in this passage is to
   (A) contribute to recent research in testing validity and reliability
   (B) question whether we should use the terms *valid* and *reliable* to describe tests
   (C) insist that all tests must be both valid and reliable
   (D) call for the abolition of invalid tests
   (E) explain the difference between validity and reliability

Teacher salaries account for approximately seventy percent of a school budget. Any major proposal designed to reduce educational expenditures will ultimately necessitate a cut in teaching staff.

3. Neighborhood High School is staffed by fifty teachers, and its administration has just ordered a reduction in educational expenditures. According to the above passage, which of the following will be one result of the reduction?

(A) a reduction in both administrative and teaching salaries
(B) a teaching staff dependent on fewer educational materials
(C) a teaching staff of fewer than fifty teachers
(D) a teaching staff of only fifteen teachers
(E) a substantial change in the quality of education

Twenty years ago, most television programs were shown in black and white. These days, the brightly colored clothes most of us wear signal that the medium has changed.

4. The author implies which of the following in the above passage?

(A) Twenty years ago, people wore only black and white clothes.
(B) Most people no longer will tolerate black and white television.
(C) There is only a slight relationship between our self-image and the images we see on television.
(D) Color television is significantly responsible for our preference for brightly colored clothes.
(E) Clothing technology, like television, was relatively primitive twenty years ago.

The political party is a voluntary association of voters whose purpose in a democracy is to control the policies of government by electing to public office persons of its membership.

5. The above passage would be most likely to appear in which of the following?

(A) an introductory text on political science
(B) a general interest magazine
(C) a manual of rules for legislators
(D) a piece of campaign literature
(E) a brief essay discussing the president's most recent news conference

Questions 6 and 7 refer to the following passage.

Charles Darwin was both a naturalist and a scientist. Darwin's *Origin of Species* (1859) was based on twenty-five years of research in testing and checking his theory of evolution. "Darwinism" had a profound effect on the natural sciences, the social sciences, and the humanities. Churchmen who feared for the survival of religious institutions rushed to attack him. However Darwin never attempted to apply his laws of evolution to human society. It was the social Darwinists who expanded the theory of evolution to include society as a whole. The social Darwinists viewed society as a "struggle for existence" with only the "fittest" members of society able to survive. They espoused basically a racist and elitist doctrine. Some people were naturally superior to others; it was in the "nature of things" for big business to take over "less fit," smaller concerns.

6. The final sentence of the passage beginning *Some people...* is the author's attempt to
   (A) discredit Charles Darwin's theory
   (B) voice his or her own point of view
   (C) summarize one point of view
   (D) give social Darwinism a fair shake
   (E) explain the modern prominence of big business

7. The author's primary purpose in this passage is to
   (A) warn of the dangers of having one's ideas abused
   (B) show that Darwin was unconcerned with human society
   (C) defend Darwin against modern charges of racism and elitism
   (D) explain how Darwin's theory was applied to society
   (E) give an example of Darwinian evolution

Questions 8 through 10 refer to the following passage.

He who lets the world, or his own portion of it, choose his plan of life for him has no need of any other faculty than the ape-like one of imitation. He who chooses his plan for himself employs all his faculties. He must use observation to see, reasoning and judgment to foresee, activity to gather materials for decision, discrimination to decide, and when he has decided, firmness and self-control to hold to his decision. And these qualities he requires and exercises exactly in proportion as the part of his conduct which he determines according to his own judgment and feelings is a large one. It is possible that he might be guided in some good path, and kept out of harm's way, without any of these things. But what will be his comparative worth as a human being? It really is of importance, not only what men do, but also what manner of men they are that do it. Among the works of man, which human life is rightly employed in perfecting and beautifying, the first in importance surely is man himself. Supposing it were possible to get houses built, corn grown, battles fought, causes tried, and even churches erected and prayers said, by machinery—by automatons in human form—it would be a considerable loss to exchange for these automatons even the men and women who at present inhabit the more civilized parts of the world, and who assuredly are but starved specimens of what nature can and will produce. Human nature is not a machine to be built after a model, and set to do exactly the work prescribed for it, but a tree, which requires to grow and develop itself on all sides, according to the tendency of the inward forces which make it a living thing.

8. One major distinction in this passage is between
   (A) automatons and machines
   (B) people and machines
   (C) beauty and perfection
   (D) apes and machines
   (E) growing food and fighting battles

9. Which of the following groups best represents the type of person that the author calls an *automaton?*
   (A) comedians
   (B) botanists
   (C) workers on an assembly line
   (D) a team of physicians in surgery
   (E) students who consistently ask challenging questions

10. Which of the following is an unstated assumption of the passage?
   (A) Mankind will probably never improve.
   (B) The essence of people themselves is more important than what people do.
   (C) It is desirable to let modern technology do some of our more unpleasant tasks.
   (D) Some people in the world do not select their own life plans.
   (E) What man produces is really no different than man himself.

STOP: IF YOU FINISH BEFORE TIME IS CALLED, CHECK YOUR WORK ON THIS SECTION ONLY. DO NOT WORK ON ANY OTHER SECTION IN THE TEST.

SECTION III: WRITING—MULTIPLE CHOICE

Time: 10 Minutes for Both Parts
11 Questions

Part A: Usage

DIRECTIONS

Some of the following sentences are correct. Others contain problems in grammar, usage, sentence construction, punctuation, and wordiness. There is not more than one error in any sentence. If there is an error, it will be underlined and lettered. Find the one underlined part that must be changed to make the sentence correct and choose the corresponding letter on your answer sheet. Mark (E) if the sentence contains no error.

1. When one wishes to be polite, they must refrain from eating food with
      A   B   C
   the hands when a knife and fork have been provided. No error
             D   E

2. During the examination, two of the three hours will be allotted
                      A   B
   for writing; the third hour would be for editing your work. No error
       C   D   E

3. Working at a full-time job, helping to support a family, and
          A   B
   a college education added up to a tremendous burden for Tom. No error
         C   D   E

4. Unmoved by neither the arguments for nor the arguments against rent
      A   B   C
   control, the citizens' committee adjourned to gather further
             D
   information about the issue. No error
                  E

5. Cognizant and interested in all the opinions of his constituency,
           A   B
   Senator Gadabout admired his own reputation as a man of the people.
                C   D
   No error
    E

PROCEED DIRECTLY TO THE SENTENCE CORRECTION QUESTIONS.

Part B: Sentence Correction

DIRECTIONS

Some part of each sentence below is underlined; sometimes the whole sentence is underlined. Five choices for rephrasing the underlined part follow each sentence; the first choice (A) repeats the original, and the other four are different. If choice (A) seems better than the alternatives, choose answer (A); if not, choose one of the others.

For each sentence, consider the requirements of standard written English. Your choice should be a correct and effective expression, not awkward or ambiguous. Focus on grammar, sentence structure, punctuation, wordiness, and word choice. If a choice changes the meaning of the original sentence, do not select it.

6. The President is an expert <u>speechmaker, therefore his public addresses</u> are particularly effective.
   (A) speechmaker, therefore his public addresses
   (B) speechmaker therefore his public addresses
   (C) speechmaker; therefore his public addresses
   (D) speechmaker; therefore his publicity addresses
   (E) speechmaker there for his public addresses

7. <u>Although he was nowhere near the finish line,</u> the exhausted young long distance runner stopped to rest while the rest of the athletes passed him by.
   (A) Although he was nowhere near the finish line
   (B) Although he neared the finish line
   (C) Nearing the finish line
   (D) Although he was not near the finish line
   (E) Not nearing the finish line

8. <u>Whether the civic leaders can pass a tax reduction bill,</u> the citizens will continue to protest the ever-rising cost of government.
   (A) Whether the civic leaders can pass a tax reduction bill
   (B) Whether or not passing a tax reduction bill
   (C) Whether or not the civic leaders can pass a tax reduction bill
   (D) Whether passing a tax reduction bill by the civic leaders or not
   (E) Whether, the civic leaders or not can pass a tax reduction bill

9. Unable to perform real well during the Superbowl, the quarterback nevertheless was able to lead the team to a 12–10 victory.
   (A) Unable to perform real well
   (B) Unable to perform well
   (C) Unable to really perform
   (D) Unable to perform
   (E) Unable to perform good

10. At 6 A.M. in the morning we hiked up the icy mountain trail to witness the magnificent sunrise in the snowcapped High Sierras.
    (A) At 6 A.M. in the morning
    (B) At 6 A.M. in the morning;
    (C) At 6 A.M.
    (D) In the morning
    (E) At 6 A.M. in the early morning

11. To be responsive to the diverse needs of their students, teachers need not one but several approaches for teaching the same skill.
    (A) teachers need not one but several approaches
    (B) teachers need several, not only one, approaches
    (C) there should be several approaches not just one
    (D) there should be not one but several approaches
    (E) not only one but several approaches is needed by teachers

STOP. IF YOU FINISH BEFORE TIME IS UP, CHECK YOUR WORK ON THIS SECTION ONLY. DO NOT WORK ON ANY OTHER SECTION OF THE TEST. YOU MAY RETURN TO THE USAGE QUESTIONS IF TIME PERMITS.

SECTION IV: WRITING—ESSAY

Time: 30 Minutes
1 Essay

DIRECTIONS

In this section, you will have 30 minutes to plan and write one essay. You may use the bottom of this page to organize and plan your essay before you begin writing. You should plan your time wisely. Read the topic carefully to make sure that you are properly addressing the issue or situation. YOU MUST WRITE ON THE SPECIFIED TOPIC. AN ESSAY ON ANOTHER TOPIC WILL NOT BE ACCEPTABLE.

The essay question included in this section is designed to give you an opportunity to write clearly and effectively. Use specific examples whenever appropriate to aid in supporting your ideas. Keep in mind that the quality of your writing is much more important than the quantity.

Your essay is to be written on the special answer sheets provided. No other paper may be used. Your writing should be neat and legible. Because you have only a limited amount of space in which to write, please do NOT skip lines, do NOT write excessively large, and do NOT leave wide margins.

Remember, use the bottom of this page for any organizational notes you may wish to make.

___

Topic

Describe a particular time in your life when you had difficulty making an important decision.

___

FOR YOUR ESSAY, USE TWO SIDES OF AN 8½" BY 11" LINED SHEET OF PAPER.

TEST OF GENERAL KNOWLEDGE

SECTION I: SOCIAL STUDIES

Time: 6 Minutes
6 Questions

DIRECTIONS

Following each of the questions or statements below, select the choice that best answers the question or completes the statement.

1. The French and Indian War resembled the American Revolution in that it
   - (A) was part of a larger world conflict
   - (B) was an expression of colonial resentment against England
   - (C) resulted in a British defeat
   - (D) was without important territorial results
   - (E) resulted in English control over colonial manufacturing

2. Following the election of 1980, President Reagan stated that a basic aim of his administration would be to turn over many of the national government's domestic responsibilities to the states. In effect, President Reagan was attempting to reverse a philosophy rooted in the premise that it is the federal government's business to protect and secure the public welfare through social and economic means.

   Which of the following terms best describes President Reagan's approach to government?

   - (A) Bureaucracy
   - (B) Affirmative Action
   - (C) Nationalistic Centralization
   - (D) Revenue Sharing
   - (E) New Federalism

3. A family emphasizing marriage ties and consisting simply of husband, wife, and children is called
   - (A) matriarchal
   - (B) nuclear
   - (C) egalitarian
   - (D) patriarchal
   - (E) extended

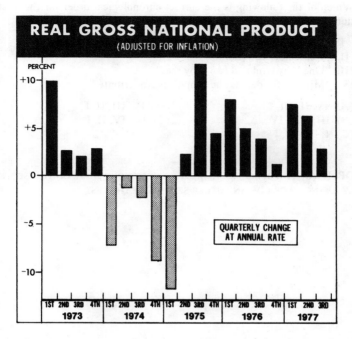

4. Based on the information in the chart above, which of the following is a true statement?
   (A) The nation's greatest period of no growth was in 1977.
   (B) The nation's greatest period of growth was experienced in the first quarter of 1975.
   (C) The nation's economic growth rate showed a slight increase in the third quarter of 1976.
   (D) The nation's greatest period of growth was in 1974.
   (E) The greatest change in gross national product occurred in 1975.

5. In order to market a new "wonder drug" that supposedly has the potential to act as a cure for throat cancer, the makers of the product must first get approval from which government agency before the product can be marketed in the United States?
   (A) U.S. Congress
   (B) American Medical Association
   (C) Consumer Protection Agency
   (D) American Cancer Society
   (E) Food and Drug Administration

6. Which of the following is the correct chronological order for the quotations associated with U.S. history listed below?

   I. "Walk softly and carry a big stick."
   II. "Remember the Alamo."
   III. "One if by land and two if by sea."
   IV. "Millions for defense but not a cent for tribute."

   (A) IV, II, III, I   (D) IV, III, II, I
   (B) III, II, I, IV   (E) III, IV, II, I
   (C) I, III, IV, I

STOP. IF YOU FINISH BEFORE TIME IS UP, CHECK YOUR WORK ON THIS SECTION ONLY. DO NOT WORK ON ANY OTHER SECTION OF THE TEST.

SECTION II: MATHEMATICS

Time: 7 Minutes
6 Questions

DIRECTIONS

Each of the mathematics questions or problems below is followed by five suggested answers. Select the best answer for each question.

1. The fraction $\frac{3}{11}$ is within the range of each of the following pairs *except*
   (A) 0 and 1   (D) $-\frac{1}{2}$ and $\frac{1}{2}$
   (B) 0.11 and 0.53   (E) -1 and 1
   (C) 0.3 and 0.7

2. A rectangle has a length of 8 inches and a perimeter of 26 inches. What is its approximate area in *square feet*?
   (A) 0.13   (B) 0.28   (C) 5   (D) 13.2   (E) 40

3. A car that gets 25 miles per gallon has a maximum driving range of 350 miles. What would be the highest possible charge for filling the tank with gasoline selling for $1.34 a gallon?
   (A) $10.45   (B) $13.40   (C) $14   (D) $18.76   (E) $26.80

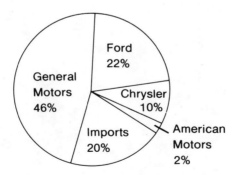

4. The pie diagram above shows company shares of the American automobile market during a recent year when sales totaled 11.8 million cars. How many million more cars did General Motors sell than all its domestic competitors together?
   (A) 1.4   (B) 1.7   (C) 3.8   (D) 4.6   (E) 14

5. The scores on a history test were 52, 89, 65, 68, and 70. By how much did the mean score exceed the median score?
   (A) 0.8   (B) 1.5   (C) 2.3   (D) 2.9   (E) 3.8

6. A color television set is marked down 20% to $320. Which of the following equations could be used to determine its original price, P?
   (A) $320 − .20 = P
   (B) .20P = $320
   (C) P = $320 + .20
   (D) .80P + .20P = $320
   (E) .80P = $320

STOP. IF YOU FINISH BEFORE TIME IS UP, CHECK YOUR WORK ON THIS SECTION ONLY. DO NOT WORK ON ANY OTHER SECTION OF THE TEST.

SECTION III: LITERATURE AND FINE ARTS

Time: 5 Minutes
7 Questions

DIRECTIONS

Each of the following questions or incomplete statements is followed by
five possible answers or completions. Select the answer or completion that is
best in each case.

1. The story "Metamorphosis" by Franz Kafka begins with the sentence:
   "As Gregor Samsa awoke one morning from uneasy dreams he found
   himself transformed in his bed into a gigantic insect." That sentence
   affects the reader by creating a sense of
   (A) hope   (D) paradox
   (B) joy   (E) shock
   (C) mischief

2. Many European cathedrals
   are decorated with small,
   carved monsters known as
   (A) fortresses
   (B) buttresses
   (C) gargoyles
   (D) minuets
   (E) unicorns

3. The *Portrait of a Lady in
   Yellow* (right) would
   provide a fine example of
   all of the following *except*
   (A) feminine gentility
   (B) a human profile
   (C) precise brushwork
   (D) abstract art
   (E) symmetrical
       ornamentation

> How weary, stale, flat, and unprofitable
> Seem to me all the uses of the world.

4. The attitude expressed in the lines above is which of the following?
   (A) resigned loyalty   (D) absolute disdain
   (B) curious precision   (E) partial hopefulness
   (C) unqualified surrender

It is all there on the stage: opulent costumes and stage sets, soaring arias, grand orchestral crescendos, and the suspense and delight of high drama.

5. Which of the following arts is described in the passage above?
   (A) musical comedy   (D) film
   (B) opera   (E) ballet
   (C) Greek tragedy

Manuel drank his brandy. He felt sleepy himself. It was too hot to go out into the town. Besides there was nothing to do. He wanted to see Zurito. He would go to sleep while he waited.

6. Which of the following terms best describes the style of the passage above?
   (A) ornate   (D) simple
   (B) complex   (E) obscure
   (C) foreign

> No coward soul is mine,
> No trembler in the world's storm-troubled sphere:
> I see Heaven's glories shine,
> And faith shines equal, arming me from fear.

7. In the preceding lines of poetry by Emily Brontë, the word *arming* means
   (A) guarding   (D) shaking
   (B) pushing   (E) taking
   (C) reaching

STOP. IF YOU FINISH BEFORE TIME IS UP, CHECK YOUR WORK ON THIS SECTION ONLY. DO NOT WORK ON ANY OTHER SECTION OF THE TEST.

SECTION IV: SCIENCE

Time: 6 Minutes
7 Questions

DIRECTIONS

Each of the Science questions is followed by five suggested answers. Select the best answer for each question.

1. Which of the following organs is *not* part of the circulatory system?
   - (A) aorta
   - (B) capillary
   - (C) heart
   - (D) trachea
   - (E) vein

2. Litmus paper dipped into an aqueous solution would detect the presence of
   - (A) alcohol
   - (B) acid
   - (C) colloids
   - (D) oxygen
   - (E) sugar

3. A light-year is a unit of
   - (A) distance
   - (B) energy
   - (C) illumination
   - (D) temperature
   - (E) time

4. All of the following processes directly affect the concentration of carbon dioxide in the atmosphere *except*
   - (A) combustion of oil
   - (B) decay of forest waste
   - (C) photosynthesis of plants
   - (D) respiration of animals
   - (E) rusting of iron

5. An instrument used to record earthquakes is called a
   - (A) barometer
   - (B) bathyscaphe
   - (C) microscope
   - (D) seismograph
   - (E) spectrometer

6. An eagle, an elephant, a frog, and a shark are all
   - (A) amphibians
   - (B) carnivores
   - (C) mammals
   - (D) terrestrial
   - (E) vertebrates

7. Were we to perform an experiment measuring the time for pieces of aluminum and copper to fall equal distances in a vacuum, we should observe that

(A) the aluminum falls sooner
(B) the copper falls sooner
(C) the larger piece falls sooner
(D) the rounder piece falls sooner
(E) the pieces fall in equal times

STOP. IF YOU FINISH BEFORE TIME IS UP, CHECK YOUR WORK ON THIS SECTION ONLY. DO NOT WORK ON ANY OTHER SECTION OF THE TEST.

TEST OF PROFESSIONAL KNOWLEDGE

Time: 20 Minutes
20 Questions

DIRECTIONS

Following each of the questions or statements below, select the choice that best answers the question or completes the statement.

1. Which of the following would best illustrate the failure of the schools to "educate for political awareness"?
   (A) One out of every three people refuses to answer a survey requesting information on political behavior.
   (B) A dramatic rise occurs in the number of underground high school newspapers.
   (C) Two-fifths of all eligible citizens didn't vote in the last presidential election.
   (D) Only a minority of students participated in student government.
   (E) Thirty-three percent of all eligible voters registered as independents.

2. Which of the following is the most appropriate instructional strategy for developing comprehension and solving problems?
   (A) programmed instruction
   (B) observation
   (C) independent study
   (D) Socratic questioning
   (E) field trips

3. If a third-grade student cannot sustain the locomotor movement of skipping for a distance of fifty feet, the best method to improve this skill would be to
   (A) refer the student to the school psychologist for special testing
   (B) individualize the instruction by breaking down the pattern and reinforcing the components
   (C) have the student practice the skill until it can be done correctly
   (D) isolate the student from the class so that when practicing skipping, the individual's self-image would not suffer
   (E) offer a reward to the student for attempting to improve skipping skills

4. Which of the following is generally considered the most desirable first step before using a filmstrip in the classroom?
   (A) determining if the audiovisual equipment is working properly
   (B) providing readiness for viewing by establishing purposes, goals, and questions
   (C) providing good viewing standards for classroom behavior
   (D) previewing the material to determine content
   (E) utilizing the material to reinforce previous learning

5. Prior to the Civil War, the education of blacks in the South was
   (A) the responsibility of the individual plantation owner
   (B) limited to free blacks
   (C) comparable to the education of blacks in the North
   (D) legislatively prohibited for both free and slave blacks
   (E) organized on the basis of separate school facilities

6. Which of the following educational theorists advocated the use of counseling groups composed of students and the elimination of traditional A through F grades as a method to reduce failure in the schools?
   (A) Glazer   (D) Piaget
   (B) Rickover   (E) Ginot
   (C) Bruner

7. Harry is an eight-year-old boy who often seeks the teacher's attention. He pounds his desk one afternoon before recess but is ignored by Ms. Smith, the teacher. The most educationally sound reason for Ms. Smith to pretend that she isn't aware of the pounding is because
   (A) she does not want to reward undesirable behavior
   (B) recess will soon end the problem
   (C) she wants Harry's classmates to quiet him
   (D) she feels Harry will be happier if he expresses himself
   (E) she is waiting for recess to scold Harry

8. A disciplinary measure imposed by a teacher on a student should
   (A) be severe enough that the child will not misbehave again
   (B) always be done in consultation with parents
   (C) always be done in consultation with the principal
   (D) take into consideration the offense and motive of the student
   (E) be immediate

9. Which of the following best describes the use of students' reports in teaching skill objectives?
   (A) Reports allow students to show that their time has been used effectively.
   (B) Students who make neatly organized reports have developed the skill of synthesizing information.
   (C) Reports allow students to use their own interests in developing writing skills.
   (D) Research is the most important skill developed in written or oral reports.
   (E) The skills of researching and organizing material from several sources and presenting it in pictorial, oral, written, and graphic form can be developed.

10. A good example of a cognitive objective is
    (A) to understand one's own religious values
    (B) to be able to identify the ten major goods and services produced in the United States
    (C) to be aware of the ten pieces of art that have shaped history
    (D) to develop feelings of adequacy in beginning a new task
    (E) to make judgments on the basis of general principles

11. After correcting his seventh-grade class's math tests, Mr. Robbins decides to group them before giving them a letter grade. If the most frequent scores on the test fall evenly into two categories, then his distribution is said to be
    (A) normal   (D) dual
    (B) bilateral   (E) biserial
    (C) bimodal

12. One of the major advantages in using the arithmetic mean in computing scores is that it
    (A) is simple to compute
    (B) is used more commonly than other measures
    (C) is more stable then the median
    (D) is less stable than the mode
    (E) discriminates between the lowest and highest scores

13. All of the following are important features of the open classroom except
    (A) students learning from each other
    (B) individualized instruction
    (C) small-group instruction
    (D) sex-role stereotypes
    (E) students making choices

14. According to John Dewey, the primary function of the school should be to
    (A) teach reading and computation skills
    (B) prepare students for proper living within society
    (C) train students for occupational success
    (D) teach the communication skills of writing, speaking, and reading
    (E) channel students' skills into appropriate employment

15. Some pupils in regular elementary classes find it difficult, if not impossible, to safely and successfully participate in regular physical education. All of the following are primary reasons to recommend a student for an adapted physical education program *except*
    (A) orthopedic conditions
    (B) low self-esteem
    (C) poor coordination
    (D) sensory problems
    (E) physical handicaps

16. Teaching machines are an example of
    (A) simulated instruction   (D) inquiry instruction
    (B) empirical instruction   (E) experiential learning
    (C) programmed instruction

17. A new fourth-grade transfer student reads *now* for *won*, *d* for *b*, *97* for *79*, and has difficulty learning. He can answer questions orally but can't write them down. The teacher should immediately suspect
    (A) visual-motor disability
    (B) association disability
    (C) emotional-trauma disability
    (D) auditory-decoding disability
    (E) vocal-encoding disability

18. Anwar, a seventh-grade student in a public elementary school, refuses to stand during the Pledge of Allegiance. Instead he remains quietly seated until the flag salute has been completed. Legally, the teacher
    (A) may compel the student to stand, but not compel the student to recite the Pledge of Allegiance
    (B) may suspend the student from the class for insubordination
    (C) must accept the fact that the student refuses to stand for the Pledge of Allegiance
    (D) may compel the student to both stand and recite the Pledge
    (E) must report the incident to the building supervisor immediately

Check (X) only for the statements that express your feeling toward social studies.

1. _____ I feel social studies is boring and not relevant.
2. _____ Working with maps and charts is fun.
3. _____ I like social studies because the stories are interesting.
4. _____ Social studies is a necessary subject, even though it's not very interesting.

19. The above questions would be representative of which of the following types of test?
   (A) Test of Basic Social Studies Readiness
   (B) Behavior Modeling Test
   (C) Diagnostic Inventories Test
   (D) Evaluation of Attitudes Test
   (E) Fundamentals and Reasoning Test

20. During a sixth-grade English class, the teacher has individual students read aloud while the rest of the class silently reads the identical material. Which of the following would be the most valid criticism of this procedure?
   (A) Current educational theory discredits silent reading.
   (B) Students with learning disorders will be subject to undue ridicule.
   (C) Individualization of instruction is not possible.
   (D) Oral reading can reinforce poor reading habits.
   (E) Oral reading is effective only when the students are interested in the reading material.

STOP. IF YOU FINISH BEFORE TIME IS UP, CHECK YOUR WORK ON THIS SECTION ONLY. DO NOT WORK ON ANY OTHER SECTION OF THE TEST.

ANSWER KEY FOR THE MINI-TEST

Test of Communication Skills

Section I: Listening

Part A Questions and Statements	Part B Conversations	Part C Talks
1. (D)	7. (A)	11. (A)
2. (C)	8. (B)	12. (C)
3. (A)	9. (B)	13. (A)
4. (B)	10. (A)	14. (D)
5. (D)		15. (B)
6. (A)		16. (C)

Section II: Reading		*Section III: Writing—Multiple Choice*	
1. (D)	6. (C)	**Part A: Usage**	**Part B: Sentence Correction**
2. (E)	7. (D)	1. (B)	6. (C)
3. (C)	8. (B)	2. (D)	7. (D)
4. (D)	9. (C)	3. (C)	8. (C)
5. (A)	10. (D)	4. (A)	9. (B)
		5. (A)	10. (C)
			11. (A)

Test of General Knowledge

Section I: Social Studies		*Section II: Mathematics*	
1. (A)	4. (E)	1. (C)	4. (A)
2. (E)	5. (E)	2. (B)	5. (A)
3. (B)	6. (E)	3. (D)	6. (E)

Section III: Literature and Fine Arts		*Section IV: Science*	
1. (E)	5. (B)	1. (D)	5. (D)
2. (C)	6. (D)	2. (B)	6. (E)
3. (D)	7. (A)	3. (A)	7. (E)
4. (D)		4. (E)	

Test of Professional Knowledge

1. (C)	11. (C)
2. (D)	12. (C)
3. (B)	13. (D)
4. (D)	14. (B)
5. (D)	15. (B)
6. (A)	16. (C)
7. (A)	17. (A)
8. (D)	18. (C)
9. (E)	19. (D)
10. (B)	20. (C)

SCORING THE MINI-TEST

To score the Mini-Test, total the number of correct responses for each of the three tests separately. Do not subtract any points for questions attempted but missed, as there is no penalty for guessing. The score for each test is then scaled from 600 to 690.

ANALYZING YOUR TEST RESULTS

The charts on the following pages should be used to carefully analyze your results and spot your strengths and weaknesses. The complete process of analyzing each subject area and each individual question should be completed for this Mini-Test and for each Practice Test. These results should be reexamined for trends in types of error (repeated errors) or poor results in specific subject areas. THIS REEXAMINATION AND ANALYSIS IS OF TREMENDOUS IMPORTANCE FOR EFFECTIVE TEST PREPARATION.

MINI-TEST GENERAL ANALYSIS SHEET

Test of Communication Skills

	Possible	Completed	Right	Wrong
Section I: Listening	16			
Section II: Reading	10			
Section III: Writing—Multiple Choice	11			
COMMUNICATION SKILLS TOTALS	37			

Test of General Knowledge

Section I: Social Studies	6			
Section II: Mathematics	6			
Section III: Literature and Fine Arts	7			
Section IV: Science	7			
GENERAL KNOWLEDGE TOTALS	26			

Test of Professional Knowledge

PROFESSIONAL KNOWLEDGE TOTALS	20			

ANALYSIS—TALLY SHEET FOR QUESTIONS MISSED

One of the most important parts of test preparation is analyzing WHY you missed a question so that you can reduce the number of mistakes. Now that you have taken the Mini-Test and corrected your answers, carefully tally your mistakes by marking in the proper column.

	REASON FOR MISTAKE		
Total Missed	Simple Mistake	Misread Problem	Lack of Knowledge

Test of Communication Skills

	Total Missed	Simple Mistake	Misread Problem	Lack of Knowledge
Section I: Listening				
Section II: Reading				
Section III: Writing—Multiple Choice				
COMMUNICATION SKILLS TOTALS				

Test of General Knowledge

	Total Missed	Simple Mistake	Misread Problem	Lack of Knowledge
Section I: Social Studies				
Section II: Mathematics				
Section III: Literature and Fine Arts				
Section IV: Science				
GENERAL KNOWLEDGE TOTALS				

Test of Professional Knowledge

	Total Missed	Simple Mistake	Misread Problem	Lack of Knowledge
PROFESSIONAL KNOWLEDGE TOTALS				

MINI-TEST ESSAY CHECKLIST

Diagnosis/Prescription for Timed Writing Exercise

A good essay will:

_____ address the assignment
               be well focused
_____ be well organized
               smooth transitions between paragraphs
               coherent, unified
_____ be well developed
               contain specific examples to support points
_____ be grammatically sound (only minor flaws)
               correct sentence structure
               correct punctuation
               use of standard written English
_____ use language skillfully
               variety of sentence types
               variety of words
_____ be legible
               clear handwriting
               neat

COMPLETE ANSWERS AND EXPLANATIONS FOR THE MINI-TEST

TEST OF COMMUNICATION SKILLS

SECTION I: LISTENING

Part A: Questions and Statements

1. (D) This choice rephrases part of the information given explicitly in the statement. Choice (B) contradicts the statement, and (A) and (C) draw unsupported conclusions.

2. (C) Although two choices include the word *when*, neither (B) nor (D) refer to the *time of agreement* that is asked about in the question.

3. (A) The statement connects lack of concentration with lack of protein and leads to the conclusion that protein contributes to concentration. None of the other conclusions necessarily follows from the statement.

4. (B) The statement tells us that the testing service designs two different tests; therefore we can conclude that the service designs more than one test.

5. (D) Only choice (D) answers the question *why* relative to the rescheduling of the picnic.

6. (A) Choice (A) rephrases part of the explicit information given in the statement: *Novels have a plot* is another way of saying *novels tell a story*.

Part B: Conversations

7. (A) The woman's suggestion that the child get more sleep at home suggests that she thinks it is important.

8. (B) The woman does not refer to the fairness or the profitability of the paper route and does not conclude that it is unaffecting (she sees that it does affect the child). Her suggestion that the child give up the route rests on the assumption that it can be given up, that it is unnecessary.

9. (B) Man 1 identifies himself as an English teacher who will be teaching math and in his final remark says that other English teachers minored in math as well, thus implying the connection between English teachers and the teaching of math.

121

10. (A) Man 2 suggests that the six-period load contains an extra class; that is not normal.

Part C: Talks

11. (A) The other choices are all positive, and the speaker here certainly does not take a positive view of human nature. The talk begins: *Human nature is essentially selfish.*

12. (C) Both choices (A) and (B) emphasize love, contradicting the author's cynical viewpoint. Choice (D) is not supported by the talk. The speaker says that *fear is a stronger motive than love,* suggesting that it is more likely to evoke a response.

13. (A) This is a discussion of rulers and governments based on the author's conception of human nature. None of the other choices is treated in the talk.

14. (D) The speaker explicitly urges *higher salaries and greater job security.* Choice (C) contradicts the opinion of the speaker, and (A) and (B) are points not covered in the talk.

15. (B) The speaker repeatedly associates power with riches, twice using the phrase *rich and powerful* and stressing the connection between power for teachers and higher salaries.

16. (C) The speaker urges listeners to *contact . . . legislators* and to voice their opposition to a bill that does not raise teachers' salaries. Though the speaker favors the raising of teachers' salaries, the speech does not directly urge the *listeners* to raise those salaries (D), as only the legislators can do that.

SECTION II: READING

1. (D) The passage states that discussion of other students has a negative effect on parents and on the conference; the fact expressed in choice (D) directly validates this assertion.

2. (E) Each of the other choices introduces information well beyond the scope of the passage.

3. (C) The passage says that budget cuts result in teaching staff cuts; choices (C) and (D) mention a staff cut, but (D) is a weak answer because it is overly specific and not necessarily true.

4. (D) The author sketches parallel changes in television and clothes, implying that the medium (TV) is responsible for changing taste in clothes.

5. (A) The definition of a political party belongs in a text which explains such organizations and systems—namely, an introductory text on political science.

6. (C) The final sentence summarizes the *racist and elitist doctrine* mentioned in the sentence which precedes it.

7. (D) The fourth sentence of the passage focuses on the relevance of Darwin's theory to human society, and the bulk of the passage develops this connection.

8. (B) The author says that *human nature is not a machine* and stresses this point throughout the passage.

9. (C) One way in which the author describes an automaton is a human machine *set to do exactly the work prescribed for it*. This description corresponds most closely to workers on an assembly line.

10. (D) The author develops arguments in favor of *he who chooses his plan for himself;* therefore, the author must assume that there are those who need to hear this argument—namely, those who do not select their own life plans.

SECTION III: WRITING—MULTIPLE CHOICE

Part A: Usage

1. (B) *They* is meant to refer to *one;* since *one* is singular, *they* (a plural) is incorrect. The correct pronoun is *one* or *he or she*.

2. (D) The second verb, *would be*, must be the same tense as the first verb, *will be*. So *would be* must be changed to *will be*.

3. (C) An error in parallelism occurs with *a college education*, which may be corrected by adding an *-ing* word, *completing*. So the correct, parallel phrase is *completing a college education*.

4. (A) *Unmoved* makes the sentence a confusing double negative; *moved* is correct usage.

5. (A) *Cognizant . . . in* is nonstandard; *cognizant of* is correct, so (A) should read *Cognizant of and interested in*.

Part B: Sentence Correction

6. (C) When words such as *therefore* and *however* are used as conjunctions, each should be preceded by a semicolon.

7. (D) *Nowhere near* is nonstandard usage. Choice (D) corrects this error by supplying *not near*, which is appropriate for standard written English.

8. (C) *Whether* as used in this sentence makes no sense; *whether or not* does. Choice (B) shifts the meaning of the original sentence slightly, while choice (D) changes the meaning.

9. (B) *Real* is an adjective. To modify the adverb *well*, another adverb would be required. However, the word *well* alone carries the intended meaning without redundancy. Choice (D) changes the meaning of the original sentence.

10. (C) *In the morning* is unnecessary repetition of the meaning of *A.M.* Choice (D) is not as specific as the original sentence.

11. (A) This sentence is correct as it stands. Choice (B) unnecessarily shifts the word order. Choices (C) and (D) take *teachers* out of the sentence, creating possible ambiguity. Choice (E) is awkward and introduces an error in grammar.

TEST OF GENERAL KNOWLEDGE

SECTION I: SOCIAL STUDIES

1. (A) Both the French and Indian War and the American Revolution were part of larger world conflicts fought between England and France for economic and military control over Europe. The French and Indian War and its counterpart in Europe, the Seven Years' War (1756–63), resulted in a decisive territorial defeat for the French. When France and the United States signed the French Alliance (1778), the American Revolution was also transformed into a worldwide conflict. The French and Indian War and the American Revolution began in colonial America, but the scope of the fighting spread to Europe, making them global conflicts.

2. (E) The statement refers to the "New Federalism." Traditionally, Federalism invoked a division of government power between national and state governments. However, since the Depression, the federal government has increasingly expanded its power over state and local authority. President Reagan envisioned a progressively decentralized federal structure, with the states, through their own tax base, determining "necessary" programs. The responsibility for funding many social welfare programs would be determined by individual states. In effect, the New Federalism simply shifts the burden for welfare and social programs from the federal to the state governments.

3. (B) A nuclear family consists of husband, wife, and children. The nuclear family emphasizes marriage ties and is very common in industrialized nations. Choice (E) identifies a family structure made up of persons related by common lineage and blood ties. It typically involves more individuals than the single nuclear family. In societies dominated by a rural economy, the extended family is quite common.

4. (E) You are looking for the one true statement. The GNP is the total value of goods and services produced in the United States. The greatest change in the GNP occurred in 1975. The first quarter of 1975 showed approximately a negative 13% growth rate; by the third quarter (1975) the GNP had improved to approximately a positive 12% growth rate. Although there was an erosion in the growth rate in the fourth quarter of 1975, the greatest change in the GNP did occur in that year.

5. (E) The Food and Drug Administration was set up in 1906 to enforce federal laws to ensure the "purity, safety, and truthful labeling of foods, drugs, and cosmetics." The American Medical Association, Consumer Protection, and the U.S. Congress can offer input about a particular drug, but the FDA is responsible for the testing of new products to determine their safety and effectiveness. FDA approval is necessary before a new drug can be marketed in the United States. The FDA can also ban a drug currently on the market.

6. (E) "One if by land . . ." was said by Paul Revere in 1775 in response to the potential British invasion at Lexington and Concord. "Millions for defense . . ." was said in 1798. The United States refused to pay "tribute" to prevent French harrassment of U.S. shipping on the open seas. The quotation was in response to the famous "XYZ Affair." "Remember the Alamo" was popularized following the massacre at the Alamo in 1836. And the "Big Stick" policy was first formulated by Theodore Roosevelt in 1904 as part of the "Roosevelt Corollary" to the Monroe Doctrine.

SECTION II: MATHEMATICS

1. (C) For four of the answer choices—(A), (B), (D), and (E)—the lower number of the pair is less than 3/11, and the higher number is greater than 3/11. However, in choice (C), both the numbers are greater than 3/11. Since 0.3 = 3/10, you can compare the two fractions by obtaining a common denominator.

$$\frac{3}{11} = \frac{30}{110} \quad \text{and} \quad \frac{3}{10} = \frac{33}{110}$$

Hence, 3/11 is less than 3/10.

2. (B) To find the area from the formula A = lw you must know the length and the width. The length is given and the width may be calculated from the perimeter.

$$P = 2l \times 2w$$
$$26 = 2(8) \times 2w$$
$$26 = 16 + 2w$$
$$26 - 16 = 2w$$
$$10 = 2w$$
$$5 = w$$
$$A = lw = 8 \times 5 = 40 \text{ sq in}$$

Since a square foot has 12 × 12 = 144 square inches, the area of the rectangle in square feet is 40/144 = 0.2778.

3. (D) The tank has a capacity of 350/25 = 14 gallons. The charge for 14 gallons of gasoline would be 14 × $1.34 = $18.76.

4. (A) The *domestic* rivals of General Motors are Ford, Chrysler, and American Motors. Those three companies share 22 + 10 + 2 = 34 percent of the market, 12 percent less than General Motors. So General Motors sold 0.12 × 11.8 million = 1.416 million more cars.

5. (A) The mean (or average) score is the sum of the scores divided by the number of scores:

$$\frac{52 + 89 + 65 + 68 + 70}{5} = 68.8$$

The median score is the middle score when they are listed in an increasing sequence: 52, 65, 68, 70, and 89. The median is 68. So the mean exceeds the median by 68.8 − 68 = 0.8.

6. (E) If the color television is marked down 20%, then its current price is 80% of its original price. Thus, .80P = $320.

SECTION III: LITERATURE AND FINE ARTS

1. (E) The sentence seems quite ordinary until the last two words, *gigantic insect*. The shock to the reader's sense of fitness is so severe that the consequence of the dilemma is read with morbid curiosity. Many of Franz Kafka's stories involve the psychology of the macabre. His characters become entangled in disturbing, nightmarish events.

2. (C) A gargoyle is a grotesque animal or human figure that decorates old stone buildings; usually it serves as a rainspout. A buttress (B) is a support for a wall. A minuet (D) is a dance. Unicorns (E) are mythical horselike beasts bearing single horns.

3. (D) The lady in yellow was painted in Florence, Italy, during the Renaissance, probably by Alessio Baldovinetti. Note the precise brushwork in the profile, especially in the hair, and the symmetrical ornamentation of the sleeve. The work is humanistic and is not an example of abstract art.

4. (D) The speaker's attitude is obviously negative; therefore all positive or neutral choices should be eliminated: (A), (B), and (D). In the lines, the speaker does not explicitly or implicitly surrender but does express absolute disdain (dislike) for the world.

5. (B) *Aria* is a term associated only with opera, but even without knowledge of this term, you could eliminate incorrect choices: (A) contradicts *high drama;* (C) contradicts the mention of music; (D) contradicts the mention of the stage; and (E) must be eliminated because the passage does not mention dance.

6. (D) The passage is written in short, simple sentences, using commonplace diction. The author (whose identity need not be known to answer the question) is Ernest Hemingway.

7. (A) The poem asserts that she is brave because faith guards her from fear. It is essential that you use the given passage to answer this type of interpretive question rather than rely on your prior knowledge.

SECTION IV: SCIENCE

1. (D) The trachea is part of the human respiratory system, being the windpipe between the mouth and the lungs. The basic human circulatory system is heart to artery to capillary to vein to heart. The aorta is the large artery from the left ventricle of the heart.

2. (B) Litmus paper is a pH indicator, turning blue in bases and red in acids. Two other well-known indicators are methyl red (for acids only) and phenolphthalein (for bases only).

3. (A) A light-year is the distance light travels in one year. Since the speed of light is 186,000 miles per second, a light-year is about six trillion miles. This is a convenient unit for describing the immensity of interstellar space. The star nearest to the sun is four light-years away.

4. (E) Iron rusts by combining with the oxygen from the air. Combustion, decay, and respiration all involve the oxidation of organic (carbon-rich) matter, so these processes consume oxygen and produce CO_2. Photosynthesis in plants is the reverse, absorbing CO_2 and yielding oxygen.

5. (D) Seismographs are instruments that detect earth movements, and the graphic record is called a seismogram. Barometers measure air pressure. A bathyscaphe is a vessel used for deep-sea diving. A spectrometer detects the presence of specific chemical elements from their characteristic optical spectra.

6. (E) All four animals have backbones and belong to the phylum of chordates. Amphibians are vertebrates that live both in water and on land; the frog is an example. Mammals are vertebrates that are warm-blooded and

suckle their young; the elephant is a mammal. Carnivores are meat-eating mammals, like the dog and cat. Terrestrial organisms live on land, but the shark is marine.

7. (E) Since the experiment would be performed in a vacuum, there would be no air friction. Any material would accelerate at a uniform 32 ft/sec^2. Objects would fall equal distances in equal times. Recall Galileo dropping large and small lead balls from the Leaning Tower of Pisa.

TEST OF PROFESSIONAL KNOWLEDGE

1. (C) The question specifically calls for the best example of the failure to educate for political awareness. A primary function of the public school system is to develop an understanding and appreciation of the American democratic process—a process that depends on the participation of an informed and involved electorate. When approximately forty percent of the eligible voters don't even bother to vote in most presidential elections, it is evident that education for political awareness is basically a failure. Choice (B) could actually reflect political awareness. Choice (D) is too limited in scope to be an acceptable answer. Registering to vote (E) indicates a degree of involvement.

2. (D) The question deals with a specific criteria—an instructional strategy for developing comprehension and solving problems. Socratic questioning is the best answer since it may be used to challenge social and personal values. It also develops decision-making skills through question-and-answer techniques. Choices (A), (B), (C), and (E) are strategies for gathering data.

3. (B) Breaking down an activity into its component parts facilitates learning. Individualized instruction will provide the maximum opportunity to improve locomotor skills. Choice (C) is incorrect, since practice is not clearly defined. Choice (D) is incorrect, since this could result in reinforcing a negative self-image.

4. (D) Previewing enables a teacher to (1) determine content, (2) evaluate the content on the basis of the specific learning ability of the class, and (3) determine if the material is appropriate for the class activity. Choice (A) would be accomplished during the preview session. Once content is determined, the other responses can be implemented.

5. (D) The South, prior to the Civil War, enacted legislation to prohibit the education of all blacks. Many northern states at this time had established separate facilities for the education of blacks. The principle of "separate but equal" was established in law by *Roberts* v. *City of Boston* (1849).

6. (A) William Glazer's controversial book *Schools Without Failure* (1969) maintained that "faulty" education was the primary cause of school failure. Glazer's thesis was that students should never be labeled as failures or led to believe they are failures as a result of any grading system.

7. (A) She does not want to reward undesirable behavior. This is the only answer that takes a motivation into consideration and attempts to remedy a

problem. The motivation implied in choice (A) is that Harry wants attention; the remedy is to ignore Harry. Choices (B), (C), (D), and (E) are not adequate, since they show no understanding of a motivation for the problem.

8. (D) The teacher should take into consideration the offense and the motive of the student. Choices (B) and (C) are incorrect, since most disciplinary measures are too trivial to involve others. Choice (D) is the most reasonable response and most comprehensive answer.

9. (E) The skills of researching and organizing material from several sources and presenting it in pictorial, oral, written, and graphic form can be developed. Choice (A) does not address skill development, and the other choices are not as comprehensive as is (E).

10. (B) Cognitive objectives are based on factual information. Choice (B), to be able to identify the ten major goods and services produced in the United States, is the only answer that can be measured. If choice (C) were to use the word *list* in place of *be aware of*, it would be a possibility.

11. (C) This distribution is said to be bimodal. The score or measure that appears most often in a distribution is the mode. When two scores are the most frequent, the distribution is bimodal.

12. (C) The arithmetic mean is computed by adding the scores and dividing by the number of scores. This makes the arithmetic mean very stable, as it takes each score into account. (B) is probably true; the arithmetic mean is more commonly used than other measures, but this is not a direct advantage unless you are comparing with others.

13. (D) Sex-role stereotypes are not a feature of open classrooms. In fact, open-classroom theory encourages teachers to avoid sex-role stereotyping. Boys and girls are all encouraged to participate in all activities, regardless of sex.

14. (B) While John Dewey advocated teaching reading, writing, speaking, and computation skills, these were merely means toward an end. Dewey's primary objective was to create a better society. Schools, then, were the means to train children to live properly within that society and thus be the fundamental elements of progress.

15. (B) Low self-esteem is not, in itself, a criteria for placing a student in an adapted physical education program. Adapted physical education provides an appropriate education for handicapped children. The criteria used for placement in such programs is based on diagnostic testing to determine the child's level of function. Adapted physical education is a division of

special education and is funded by both the state and federal government. To be eligible for an adapted physical education program, the following conditions must be met: (1) a written referral must be completed which describes the behavior manifested by the student; (2) a school appraisal team must determine if the student meets program requirements; (3) the parent or legal guardian must sign a special education form admitting the child to the program.

16. (C) Teaching machines use a series of questions and answers that the student may use to progress at his or her own speed. This is called programmed instruction.

17. (A) Observable classroom behavior for students who have visual-motor disability (auditory learners) includes reversals and inversion of numbers. Early identification of learning problems is essential if students with perceptual difficulty are to maximize their learning potential.

18. (C) The U.S. Supreme Court, in *West Virginia State Board of Education* v. *Barnette,* recognized that students may not be compelled to salute the American flag. The court further ruled that requiring students to stand during the Pledge is unconstitutional.

19. (D) An Evaluation of Attitudes Test helps the teacher establish whether a particular student has a preconceived positive or negative attitude about a subject. An attitudes test can also be used to provide data for pupil guidance.

20. (C) In the example, the rigid restraints placed on the exercise makes individualization of instruction impossible. Individualized reading instruction allows the student to choose appropriate reading material and to proceed at his/her own reading rate. Also, the individualized approach effectively integrates reading into other language arts areas (writing, spelling, speaking). The use of oral reading as one factor in an integrated reading program is educationally sound.

PART IV: Subject Area Reviews

This section reviews the major facts and concepts used on the NTE. Covered are English, social studies, mathematics, literature, fine arts, science, and professional knowledge.

Your review will be most effective if you keep the following advice in mind:

> *Short* review sessions provide the best preparation; lengthy cram sessions are exhausting and ineffective.

> Allow five or six weeks to prepare for the test, spending about an hour five days a week working on practice tests and reviewing facts and concepts. *Do not try to memorize this material.*

> To complement your review, read widely in newspapers and national news magazines to gain familiarity with topics of current interest that may appear on the NTE.

PART IV: Subject Area Reviews

ENGLISH REVIEW

The following pages review the major concepts, rules, and most common errors covered in the NTE Test of Communication Skills, Writing sections. This review also includes many helpful study techniques.

Before reading the review in full, skim through it and read the headings of each section. Then read first those sections that are most important to you, the sections that cover your personal "trouble spots." After you read a section, close the book and try to write a brief summary of what you've read to check your understanding.

PUNCTUATION

Instances of incorrect or omitted punctuation appear on the NTE in the multiple-choice Writing section. The most important marks of punctuation tested are the comma (,) and semicolon (;). Typically, the NTE tests *obvious* and *basic* punctuation skills rather than subjective, stylistic uses of the comma or semicolon.

The Comma

Use a comma

- before words like *and, or, but, so, for,* and *yet* that join two or more complete sentences (each with a subject and verb and able to stand alone and make sense) into a compound sentence:

  The horrifying aftermath of the fire was reported on all the news stations, and the arson squad worked diligently to uncover the cause of the tragedy.

  Linguists expect to find primitive languages simple and uncomplicated, but they find instead that early language systems were strikingly elaborate and complex.

  NOTE: To punctuate a compound sentence when the two or more clauses themselves contain commas, a semicolon is sometimes needed. See the review section on the semicolon for further explanation.

- to set off interrupting or introductory words or phrases:

  Safe in the house, we watched the rain fall outside.
  Regrettably, many of my friends will not attend the party.

Tom, *after all,* is one of twelve children.

Your home is in Lincoln, Nebraska, *isn't it?*

One must, *of course,* save a great deal of money before one goes into business for oneself.

- to separate a series of words or word groups:

The threat of runaway inflation, the heightened tension regarding foreign affairs, and the lack of quality education in many schools are issues that will be addressed in political campaigns for years to come.

- to set off nonessential clauses and phrases that are descriptive but not needed to get across the basic meaning of the sentence:

Truman, who tried to continue Roosevelt's conciliatory approach to the Soviet Union, adopted a much tougher policy toward the Russians by 1946.

The clause *who tried ... Union* is not necessary. Truman's name is sufficient and the clause is merely descriptive not definitional. The clause is then nonessential and therefore set off by commas.

My wealthy Aunt Em, exceeding the trait of being economical, is so parsimonious she washes paper plates to be used again.

The phrase *exceeding the trait of being economical* is set off by commas because it is extra information and descriptive, not essential and definitional.

Remember, clauses and phrases that *are* essential and definitional are *not* set off by commas.

Any teacher who ignores the varying and individual skill levels of his or her students is apt to devise lesson plans either too elementary or too advanced for effective sequential learning of new skills.

The clause *who ignores the varying ... students* is essential; without it the reader might wonder *which* teachers. Because it defines precisely which teachers, it is not set off by commas.

Nothing was allowed to be published in Iron Curtain countries except material that had secured the approval of the Communist Party.

The clause *that had secured ... party* is essential here and is therefore not set off by commas. Without this clause the sentence meaning would be quite ambiguous. Again, the reader would not know *which* material because the definitional clause is necessary here.

- to set off appositives (second nouns or noun equivalents that give additional information about a preceding noun):

    Mr. Johnson, a teacher, ran for Chairman of the School Board.
    Robert's wife, Marsha, played the harp.

    When the second noun is needed to identify and to distinguish the first noun from others of its kind, the second noun is not set off with commas:

    The word *tenacious* was misspelled.
    My daughter Wendy loves to swim more than her sister does.

    Since there are two daughters, *Wendy* is essential to distinguish which daughter loves to swim, and the word is therefore not set off by commas.

- after introductory clauses or phrases:

    Although the thirteen-year-old boys grew restive under the new discipline policy, the girls seemed unperturbed by it.
    When finishing an essay, do not end with an apology for not having said anything or with an indignant statement about the unfair allotment of time.

    The following are some situations in which commas should *not* be used. Some of these sentence constructions may appear on the NTE.

Do NOT use a comma

- to separate a subject and its verb or a verb and its complement:

    Requiring the study of grammar in our secondary English classes, is, somewhat controversial.

    The first comma unnecessarily separates *requiring* and *is* (subject and verb); the second separates *is* and *somewhat controversial* (verb and its complement).

- to separate a verb from its object:

    Dolly Parton combines, a buxom blonde appearance, a homespun country-western sense of humor, and a dynamic vocal range.

    In this sentence the first comma separates *combines* (verb) from *appearance . . . sense . . . range* and splits the verb from the objects.

- to connect independent sentences without also using conjunctions such as *but, and, or, so, for,* and *yet.*

At the last school board meeting, an irate school administrator argued that principals should be given the right to suspend appropriate students if necessary to enforce board policies, that right was conceded.

Both a comma and *and* are needed after *policies* to connect the two independent sentences correctly. A semicolon would also be correct here. See the review section dealing with semicolons for more information.

• to set off essential modifying information from the word modified:

A steadily increasing incidence of school vandalism is an appalling reality, characteristic of the inner-city neighborhoods, in many metropolitan areas.

The two commas in this sentence are unnecessary and separate modifying phrases from the two words they modify.

NOTE: To avoid some of the punctuation errors involving either misuse of or omission of commas try reading the sentence out loud (in a whisper) to yourself. Often your ear will catch an error your eye might overlook. Read over the examples in the section headed "Do *not* use a comma," and you will *hear*, in most cases, the correct punctuation.

The Semicolon

Use a semicolon

• to separate two complete sentences when they are not joined by words like *and, but, for, or, nor,* or *yet:*

The winter was exceptionally cold; once again fuel shortages plagued the northeastern cities.
Long awaited relief from the six-month drought was in sight; the barometric pressure readings indicated a rainstorm was on its way.

A common error in punctuation is to connect sentences such as the two above with a comma only. One way of avoiding this error is to read the sentences out loud. A long pause between the two sentences indicates the need for a semicolon. Also, remember that two independent sentences may be punctuated as separate sentences with periods at the end of each or as two connected sentences punctuated with a semicolon (;) alone or with a comma and a conjunction (, and) (, but) (, or).

• before words like *however, therefore, moreover, then,* and *consequently* when they are used to link two complete sentences:

It was raining outside; *however* we felt quite warm and dry inside the house.

I feel happy about my new job; *consequently* I work quickly and efficiently.

My friend spends afternoon hours watching TV talk shows; *then* he watches situation comedies all evening.

• before words like *and, but, for, or, nor,* and *yet* that join two complete sentences of a compound sentence if either of the two sentences contains a comma:

Kim, my sister, could not take time off from work in August; but she took her vacation in September to travel to Canada, where she camped for two weeks.

The Colon

Use a colon

• to formally introduce a statement, a quotation, or a series of terms:

Introducing a statement—The members of the community all hold the following belief: We should all love our neighbors.
Introducing a quotation—John F. Kennedy is remembered for these words: "Ask not what your country can do for you; ask what you can do for your country."
Introducing a series—The most familiar punctuation devices are these: the period, the comma, the semicolon, the colon, and the question mark.

Playing the Punctuation Game: Some Extra Practice

In addition to the practice this book provides, you can strengthen your punctuation skill by doing the following. Have a friend recopy for you a long newspaper or magazine article or editorial, leaving out all the punctuation marks. Then your task becomes putting the punctuation marks back in. Use the original article to check your choices. In current magazine and newspaper articles there may be a wide range of uses of some marks of punctuation, especially the comma. Your practice time playing the "Punctuation Game" is well spent, however, because you have practiced looking for the appropriate places for punctuation. Practicing this editing skill will help you on the NTE.

GRAMMAR, USAGE, AND SENTENCE STRUCTURE

Pronouns

- Use *I, he, she, we,* and *they* in place of the *subject* of a sentence. (The subject is the *doer.*):

  Bill wrote a sentence.
  He wrote a sentence.
  I wrote a sentence.
  Susan was late for work.
  She was late for work.
  My family always takes a summer vacation.
  We always take a summer vacation.
  Jerry's family always takes a summer vacation.
  They always take a summer vacation.

- Use *me, him, her, us,* and *them* in place of the *object* of a sentence. (The object is the *receiver.*):

  Bill greeted *Jerry.*
  Bill greeted *him.*
  Bill greeted *me.*
  The boss fired *Susan.*
  The boss fired *her.*
  Camille helped *Christopher and me* pack our suitcases.
  Camille helped *us* pack our suitcases.
  The lifeguard saved *three people* from drowning.
  The lifeguard saved *them* from drowning.

- Use *who* as a *subject* (a *doer*):

  Who knocked at the door?
  Do you know *who knocked* at the door?
  No doubt it was a neighbor *who,* a few minutes ago, *knocked* at the door.

- Use *whom* as an *object* (a *receiver*):

  To whom were you *speaking*?
  Your line was busy, and I wondered *to whom* you were *speaking.*
  I'm the person *whom* you *telephoned* yesterday.

PRONOUN REVIEW CHART
PERSONAL PRONOUNS

	Nominative (subject)		Objective (object)		Possessive (ownership)	
	singular	*plural*	*singular*	*plural*	*singular*	*plural*
First Person	I	we	me	us	my mine	our ours
Second Person	you	you	you	you	your yours	your yours
Third Person	he she it	they	him her it	them	his her, hers its	their theirs

RELATIVE PRONOUNS

Nominative (subject)	Objective (object)	Possessive (ownership)
who (persons) which (things) that (things and persons)	whom	whose

Verb Tense

- Most verbs are regular. For these verbs add *-ed* to talk about the past and *will* or *shall* to talk about the future.

> *Past:* I *walked* yesterday.
> *Present:* I *walk* today.
> *Future:* I *will walk* tomorrow.

One way to practice the basic forms of regular verbs is to recite the *past tense* and *past participle* when you are given only the *present tense*. Here are some examples:

Present	*Past (-ed)*
I *talk* today.	I *talked* yesterday.
I *help* you today.	I *helped* you yesterday.
I *close* shop early today.	I *closed* shop early yesterday.

Past Participle (-ed)

I have *talked* on many occasions.

I have *helped* you often.

I have *closed* shop early for a week.

• Some verbs are *irregular* and require special constructions to express the past and past participle. Here are some of the most troublesome irregular verbs:

Present	Past	Past Participle
begin	began	begun
burst	burst	burst
do	did	done
drown	drowned	drowned
go	went	gone
hang (to execute)	hanged	hanged
hang (to suspend)	hung	hung
lay (to put in place)	laid	laid
lie (to rest)	lay	lain
set (to place in position)	set	set
sit (to be seated)	sat	sat
shine (to provide light)	shone	shone
shine (to polish)	shined	shined
raise (to lift up)	raised	raised
rise (to get up)	rose	risen
swim	swam	swum
swing	swung	swung

Subject-Verb Agreement

• If a subject is plural, the verb must be plural; if a subject is singular, the verb must be singular. The following sentence is incorrect:

Here on the table *is* an *apple and three pears*.

Focus on the verb (*is*) and then locate the subject. In this sentence, the subject (*an apple and three pears*) *follows* the verb. Since the subject is plural, the verb must be plural, and the sentence should say:

Here on the table *are* an apple and three pears.

Here is another example that is incorrect:

The man, along with his friends and neighbors, support the home-town candidate.

The verb is *support*. Since the subject is singular (*man*), the verb must be singular—*supports* instead of *support*. Notice that in this case many words separate the subject from the verb; subject and verb will not always be close to one another.

Adjectives and Adverbs

● Adjectives describe nouns:

Holidays are *happy* occasions. (*Happy* describes *occasions*.)
His was a *narrow* escape. (*Narrow* describes *escape*.)
Jesse Owens was a *successful* athlete. (*Successful* describes *athlete*.)

● Adverbs describe verbs:

We all sang *happily*. (*Happily* describes *sang*.)
He *narrowly* missed an oncoming car. (*Narrowly* describes *missed*.)
Jesse Owens *successfully* completed the race. (*Successfully* describes *completed*.)

● Making comparisons—Adjectives normally add *-er* or *-est* to make comparisons.

Use *-er* to compare two items: Cindy was the great*er* of the two athletes.
Sometimes use *more* to compare two items: Christopher was the *more* handsome of the twins.
Use *-est* to compare more than two items: Cindy was the great*est* athlete on the team.
Sometimes use *most* to compare more than two items: Christopher was the *most* handsome member of the family.

Adverbs normally use *more* or *most* to make comparisons:

Bob ran *more* quickly today than he did yesterday.
Bob runs *most* quickly in the early morning.

NOTE: The first sentence compares only two items, today and yesterday, and so it requires *more*. The second sentence compares one time (early morning) with many other possible times, and so it requires *most*.

● Use an adjective after a verb that expresses being, feeling, tasting, or smelling.

Harry seems happy. (not <u>happily</u>)
Bill feels bad. (not <u>badly</u>)
The candy tastes sweet. (not <u>sweetly</u>)
The flowers smell sweet. (not <u>sweetly</u>)

Idiom

To native English speakers, certain expressions "sound right" because they are so commonly used. Such expressions are called "idiomatic" and are correct simply because they are so widely accepted. Here is a list of examples:

Idiomatic	Unidiomatic
addicted *to*	addicted *from*
angry *with*	angry *at*
capable *of*	capable *to*
different *from*	different *than*
identical *with*	identical *to*
obedient *to*	obedient *in*
on *the* whole	on *a* whole

Remember that the standard of correctness is standard written English. Be alert to idiomatic expressions not acceptable or characteristic of standard *written* English.

Double Negatives

To use a double negative is incorrect in standard written English. When words like *hardly, scarcely,* and *barely,* considered "negative" words, are used along with other negative words such as *not, no, none, never,* and *nothing* in the same sentence to express the same negative meaning twice, a "double negative" occurs. For example:

The puppy *didn't* have *no one* to love.

The notion that there is not anyone to love is expressed twice—once by the *didn't* (did + not) and once by *no one.*

After a hard day's work, Susan *can't hardly* stay awake.

Susan's not being able to stay awake is expressed twice—once with the *can't* (can + not) and again with *hardly.* Here are some other examples of "double negatives":

You *don't* have *scarcely* anything to worry about.
The fans *can't hardly* wait for the concert to begin.

NOTE: Merely the occurrence of two negative words in the same sentence does not result in a "double negative" as in the following example:

I had *no* time available on weekends, so I decided I would *not* take the part-time job offer.

The *no* and the *not* in this sentence express two different negatives and are therefore not considered "double negatives."

Either/Or—Neither/Nor

● Use *either* or *neither* to compare two items (*either* is sometimes used to compare more than two items):

Uncle Joe will arrive *either* today or tomorrow morning.
Neither of these two shirts fits me very well.

● Use *either* with *or:*

Uncle Joe will arrive *either* today *or* tomorrow.

● Use *neither* with *nor:*

Neither the white shirt *nor* the blue shirt fits me very well.

NOTE: *Nor* may not be used in a sentence without *neither.* The following sentence is incorrect. *No* rain *nor* snow had fallen for weeks. The sentence should read like this: *Neither* rain *nor* snow had fallen for weeks.

Exact Word Choice

Sometimes words that sound alike are confused with one another. Checking their dictionary meanings will help you to avoid their misuse. Here are some commonly confused words:

1. adapt/adept
2. capital/capitol
3. compile/comply
4. detain/retain
5. elicit/illicit
6. foreword/forward
7. human/humane
8. incite/insight
9. lay/lie
10. persecute/prosecute
11. precede/proceed
12. raise/rise
13. set/sit
14. their/there/they're
15. weather/whether

Special Problems

Fewer/Less

● *Fewer* is used with *countable* items:

There are *fewer people* in the room than I had expected.

● *Less* is used with *uncountable* items:

There has been *less rain* this year than in years past.

Many/Much

● *Many* is used with *countable* items:

There are *many people* at the meeting tonight.

● *Much* is used with *uncountable* items:

Frank spends too *much time* worrying about the future.

Sentence Fragments

A sentence fragment is an *incomplete* sentence that is written and punctuated as if it were a *complete* sentence. Here are some examples of sentence fragments.

Fragment: Although Fred must leave for work early each morning.
Problem: Although suggests another action that would make the sentence complete.
Complete Sentence: Although Fred must leave for work early each morning, *he never gets to bed before one A.M.*

Fragment: Hard study, a baseball game with friends, or just some sleep.
Problem: There is no subject (doer) and no verb (action).
Complete Sentence: Tim [subject] could not *decide* [verb] whether to devote his afternoon to hard study, a baseball game with friends, or just some sleep.

Fragment: People who sing loudly and happily in the shower.
Problem: People who signals the need for additional information, what the people who sing do.
Complete Sentence: People who sing loudly and happily in the shower *often start the day feeling optimistic.*

Wordiness

Saying the same thing twice is one common type of wordiness. Here are some examples with the repetitions italicized:

At 8 *A.M. in the morning* it *suddenly* started to rain *without warning.*
In this *modern world* of *today* there are hundreds of *millionaires with a great deal of money.*
Several *separate* and *distinct* programs signaled a new era of economic progress.
Students found the *lectures* Professor Smith gave while he was *speaking* difficult to *understand* and *comprehend.*

Parallelism

Items in a sentence are *parallel* when they have the same *form*. Here are three series of parallel items:

to join the army, to find a job, to enroll in college
joining the army, finding a job, enrolling in college
the army, a job, college

The following sentence *mixes forms,* an example of *faulty parallelism:*

Faulty: Once he turned eighteen, the young man's choices were *joining the army, to find a job, or college.*

Correct: Once he turned eighteen, the young man's choices were *the army, a job, or college.*

Sometimes faulty parallelism occurs in just two items instead of three:

Faulty: The youngster needed to choose between *playing* outdoors with friends and *to study* for a test.

Correct: The youngster needed to choose between *playing* outdoors with friends and *studying* for a test.

Misplaced Modifiers

A misplaced modifier occurs when a *description* does not clearly refer to the *item described:*

Faulty: Galloping across the finish line, *I* realized I had bet on the wrong horse.

The sentence structure indicates that *I* am doing the *galloping.*

Correct: As the winner galloped across the finish line, I realized I had bet on the wrong horse.

Here are some other misplaced modifiers. Notice that in each case the *description* does not clearly refer to the *item described.*

A *piano* [item described] is for sale by an *elderly woman* with *walnut legs* [description].
(The item described is not clearly connected with its description.)
To keep cool [description] during summer weather, my air conditioner ran constantly.
(The item described— a person—is omitted altogether.)

Corrections:

A *piano with walnut legs* is for sale by an elderly woman.

To keep cool during summer weather, *I* run my air conditioner constantly.

Comparisons

- As/than—*As* and *than* are often used to structure comparisons, sometimes incorrectly and incompletely:

      Correct combinations: as . . . as . . . than
                                  as . . . as
      Incorrect combinations: as . . . than

Correct sentences:

She is *as* pretty *as,* if not prettier *than,* any other girl.

Linda is *as* pretty *as* any of her sisters.

Incorrect sentences:

She is *as* pretty, if not prettier *than,* any other girl.

Linda is *as* pretty *than* any of her sisters.

SOCIAL STUDIES REVIEW

The following pages are designed to give you an intensive review of the major concepts used on the NTE Social Studies section. The social studies outlines provide introductions and explanations of the main ideas in each area. *Do not spend excessive time on any one part of the review.* If you are having difficulty understanding a concept, write a question mark in the margin and return later. Further reading may clarify the concept.

A glossary of important social studies terms associated with each of the major areas in the test is also included. *Do not attempt to memorize these lists;* rather, use the glossary together with the reviews to provide a mini-course approach to the social studies areas. When reviewing the terms, think about which terms are related or contrasted, like *tax* and *tariff*. Write your own comments after many of the terms; make helpful notes.

Begin your review with the following analysis and discussion of charts and graphs.

CHARTS AND GRAPHS

The NTE social studies section also makes use of many questions that are based on interpretations of charts and graphs. You will need to understand and derive information from the various types of graphic representations that are used to present facts and ideas, and promote a particular point of view.

In order to successfully answer questions based on charts and graphs, it is important to familiarize yourself with the data as presented. Unless specifically stated, use only the data as presented in the chart or graph. Remember that a chart or graph is a reference tool; therefore look for trends, fluctuations, or changing patterns that might appear in the presentation of the data.

Here are some helpful strategies for extracting accurate information from the graph or chart problems.

1. Skim the questions and quickly examine the whole graph before starting to work problems; this sort of prereading will tell you what to look for.
2. Use your answer sheet as a straightedge in order to align points on the graph with their corresponding number values.
3. Sometimes the answer to a question is available in supplementary information given with a graph (headings, scale factors, legends, etc.); be sure to read this information.
4. Look for the obvious: dramatic trends, high points, low points, etc. Obvious information often leads directly to an answer.

5. Graphs and charts list a number scale along one edge and individual categories along another edge. Bar graphs and line graphs show a relationship between two or more objects. Always try to determine the relationship between the columns in a graph or chart.
6. Bar graphs simply convert the data in a chart into separate bars or columns.
7. Bar graphs, line graphs, circle graphs, etc., are different methods to visually evaluate the same data.
8. A circle graph, or pie chart, shows the relationship between the whole circle (100%) and the various slices that represent portions of that 100%. The larger the slice, the higher the percentage.

The following sample questions and analyses will provide familiarity with a wide range of chart and graph types.

Questions 1, 2, and 3 are based on the following line graph.

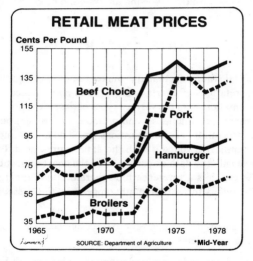

1. A pound of hamburger in 1975 cost approximately how much more than it did in 1970?
   (A) 20 cents   (D) 35 cents
   (B) 25 cents   (E) none of these
   (C) 30 cents

2. If a person purchased 20 pounds of beef choice in 1965, how much more money would it cost in 1978 to purchase the same amount of beef choice?
   (A) $12   (B) $16   (C) $28   (D) $80   (E) $140

3. Which of the following is an accurate statement based on the information provided in the chart?

(A) The figures for mid-year 1978 indicate a downward trend in retail meat prices.

(B) Pork prices increased more gradually than broiler prices.

(C) More hamburger was sold than beef choice.

(D) The figures for mid-year 1978 indicate a continued increase in retail meat prices.

(E) The overall price of retail meat declined in the 1970s.

Answer Analysis for Questions 1, 2, and 3

1. The correct answer is (A). A line graph shows the relationship between two or more factors. This question calls for comparing the price of hamburger in 1975 with the price of hamburger in 1970. You are asked to determine the approximate price increase during the stated period. To answer the question, one must differentiate among the four items listed on the chart. Note that the lower horizontal line indicates the time reference as stated in years 1965 to 1978, and each line extending from it represents a one-year increment. The vertical line on the far left indicates the price or cents per pound (35¢ to $1.55 per pound), and each line extending from it represents a 20¢ increment (35¢ to 55¢; 55¢ to 75¢, etc.). In 1975 hamburger sold for slightly more than 85¢ per pound. The price increase from 1970 to 1975 was approximately 20¢ per pound.

2. The correct answer is (A). In this question one is asked to determine how much *more* money 20 pounds of an item (beef choice) cost over a specified period of time. In 1965 beef choice cost approximately 80¢ a pound ($.80 × 20 = $16.00); in 1978 beef choice cost approximately $1.40 per pound ($1.40 × 20 = $28.00); the difference is $12.00 ($28.00 − $16.00 = $12.00).

3. The correct answer is (D). This question calls for an interpretation of the data to determine the *one* statement that is consistent with the information provided in the chart. Mid-year 1978 is shown by the continuation of the lines representing meat prices beyond the 1978 line. Notice that all lines represent an *upward* trend. Statement (A) is therefore inconsistent with the data in the chart. Statement (B) calls for comparing two items to determine which one showed the most consistent price over the entire period of the study. It should be apparent that pork prices, especially since 1971, increased more dramatically than broiler prices. There is not sufficient evidence in the chart to support statement (C). (*Do not* read information into the chart.) It should be obvious that statement (E) is incorrect. *All* meat items showed an increase in price over the 1970s. The only statement that is consistent with the data is

(D). All meat prices, as indicated by the mid-year 1978 prices, represented a continued increase in meat prices.

Questions 4 and 5 are based on the following chart.

MEDIAN EXPENDITURES FOR MONTHLY HOUSING EXPENSES

Metropolitan area	Mortgage payment	Real estate tax	Hazard Insurance	Utility cost	Total monthly expenses
Large					
Chicago	$291	$ 64	$ 14	$ 60	$429
Houston	291	48	26	74	439
Los Angeles	403	99	15	50	567
New York	291	111	25	70	497
San Francisco	445	99	20	50	614
Washington	388	85	14	91	578
All U.S. metropolitan areas with populations of 1.5 million or more	$299	$ 70	$ 13	$ 60	$442
All of the United States	$273	$ 54	$ 13	$ 60	$400

Median means half the houses have higher expenses and half have lower costs.

Source: U.S. League of Savings Associations.

4. Which metropolitan city was closest to the total monthly expenses for areas with populations of 1.5 million or more?
   (A) Chicago   (B) Houston   (C) New York   (D) Los Angeles
   (E) Washington

5. Which of the following statements can be inferred from information presented in the chart?
   (A) Los Angeles residents have larger incomes than residents in New York.
   (B) The median mortgage payment in Los Angeles is lower than in Washington.
   (C) It takes fewer housing dollars in the United States considered as a whole for total monthly expenses than it does in large metropolitan cities.
   (D) Hazard insurance is higher as the total monthly expenses increase.
   (E) It costs more for monthly expenses in Washington, San Francisco, and New York than anywhere else in the country.

Answer Analysis for Questions 4 and 5

   4. The correct answer is (B). The bottom left-hand corner of the table gives a definition for the term *median*. Remember to quickly scan all the data

presented in a graph or chart. First, this question calls for determining the total monthly expenses for all U.S. cities with a population of 1.5 million or more. The figure is stated as $442 per month (see the figures that represent total monthly expenses for all U.S. metropolitan areas with populations in excess of 1.5 million). Second, one must determine which metropolitan city is closest to the $442 monthly figure. The correct answer is Houston which has a total monthly expense of $439.

5. The correct answer is (C). This question calls for drawing a conclusion from information presented in the table. The information in statement (A) cannot be determined from the data in the table. (Don't assume information not presented in the chart or graph, even if the statement might be based on accepted fact.) Statement (B) can quickly be eliminated. The mortgage payment table shows that the Los Angeles average is $403 while the Washington average is $388. Statement (D) can be determined as false by looking at the hazard insurance column. Houston has the highest hazard insurance ($26) but is among the lowest large metropolitan cities in terms of total monthly expenses ($439). Statement (E) is incorrect, since Los Angeles has the third highest total monthly expenses ($567). Note that the monthly expense column is *not* in rank order—lowest to highest. The correct answer (C) can be supported by data presented in the chart. Notice that all cities with populations of 1.5 million or more have a total monthly expense figure of $442. "All of the United States" (the United States considered as a whole) has a total monthly expense of $400. This means that many small cities reduced the $442 total monthly figure. It therefore can be concluded that housing dollars would stretch further in smaller cities.

Question 6 is based on the following pie chart.

Distribution of Earned Degrees
By Field of Study, 1974-75

Bachelors	Masters	Doctors
945.9 Thousand = 100%	291.7 Thousand = 100%	36.1 Thousand = 100%

a. Social Sciences
b. Education

c. Natural Sciences
d. Humanities

e. Business, Accounting,
   and other

6. Which field of study showed the greatest percentage change in comparing bachelors degrees to doctors degrees?

(A) social sciences   (D) humanities
(B) education   (E) business, accounting, and other
(C) natural sciences

Answer Analysis for Question 6

6. The correct answer is (C). This question calls for comparing total percentage changes. If the question called for determining the negative percentage change (percentage loss) the correct answer would have been (E). (Business showed a 15% reduction in earned degrees.) To answer the question one can visually determine that choices (C) and (E) will show the greatest percentage change. Choice (C) showed a 20% change, while choice (E) showed a 15% change.

Question 7 is based on the following bar graph.

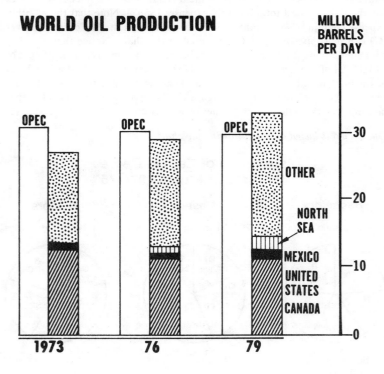

7. Since 1973 the rate of United States and Canadian oil production has
   (A) risen sharply
   (B) outpaced OPEC production
   (C) dropped dramatically
   (D) declined gradually
   (E) fluctuated sharply

Answer Analysis for Question 7

7. The correct answer is (D). This question calls for a conclusion based on the facts (data) presented in the graph. A visual analysis of the data would indicate that the production of U.S. and Canadian oil has declined *slightly* over the 1973–1979 period. The term OPEC refers to the Oil Producing Exporting Countries; Saudi Arabia, the leading producer of world oil, is the most significant member of OPEC. A further question might have asked in what year did OPEC oil production fall behind the total oil production of non-OPEC countries (1979).

AREA REVIEW OUTLINES AND GLOSSARIES

U.S. HISTORY OUTLINE—TWENTIETH CENTURY

I. SOCIETY RESHAPED

A. Immigrants were needed to work in an expanding industrial America.

1. The vast majority of the new immigrants came from eastern and southern Europe to escape religious, political, and economic persecution.
2. Immigrants retained much of their ethnic identity.

B. There were many common problems of urban life, such as sanitation, health, crime, and housing.

C. Reforms were initiated to enrich the lives of the American people.

1. Better treatment for the insane, the temperance movement, and the women's rights movement were important areas of reform.
2. The public school movement provided free public education.

II. THE DEVELOPMENT OF THE UNITED STATES AS A WORLD POWER: THE TWENTIETH CENTURY

A. **The new empire period was marked by territorial expansion.**
   1. Alaska and Hawaii were purchased to provide increased national security.
   2. The Spanish-American War (1898) resulted in the ceding of Puerto Rico, Guam, and the Philippines to the United States.
   3. The Panama Canal was built to protect the new global interests of the United States.

B. **U.S. foreign policy in Central America and South America was marked by new applications of the Monroe Doctrine.**

C. **U.S. relations with Japan and China were dictated by the need for trade and raw materials.**

D. **Events in Europe drew the United States into World War I.**
   1. The U.S. entry into World War I (1917) ended U.S. neutrality and dictated new alliances.
   2. The results of the war included Wilson's Fourteen Points and the failure of Congress to ratify the League of Nations.

E. **The end to the American economic boom period following World War I foreshadowed the Great Depression of 1929.**
   1. Among the basic causes of the Depression were the growth of monopolies, the unequal distribution of income, and overspeculation in the stock market.
   2. Franklin Roosevelt initiated the New Deal (1932–1938) which included government programs to provide jobs for the unemployed, the broadening of the scope of the federal government's activities and the expansion of the role of the Presidency.

F. **Events in Europe and Asia foreshadowed World War II.**
   1. Europe saw the rise of dictators in Russia, Germany, and Italy.
   2. Japanese aggression in Manchuria encouraged further military activity.
   3. The American foreign policy response was based on isolationism.

G. **The Japanese surprise attack on Pearl Harbor drew the United States into World War II.**
   1. The Allies won the war in Europe.
   2. The atomic bomb ended the war in the Pacific.

3. The results of the war included the occupation of Japan and Germany by the Allies, the economic recovery of Europe (the Marshall Plan), the development of the United Nations, and the emergence of Communism as a world threat.

III. CRISIS IN THE FIFTIES

A. **The Korean conflict (1950–1952) was a controversial United Nations attempt to stop Communist aggression.**

B. **The cold war dictated new foreign policy considerations.**

1. Russia established an "iron curtain" in Eastern Europe.
2. The United States developed a foreign policy based on the containment of Communism.

C. **The cold war affected American domestic policy.**

1. Senator Joseph McCarthy exploited the climate of fear following the Korean War.
2. The credibility of U.S. technological superiority was shattered by Sputnik.
3. The national frustration over Korea contributed to the nomination and election to the Presidency of Dwight D. Eisenhower (1952).
4. The United States protected its global interests by joining the North Atlantic Treaty Organization (NATO).

D. **The late 1950s was marked by a national concern with science, labor, and civil rights.**

IV. THE UNITED STATES SINCE 1960

A. **President John F. Kennedy's New Frontier pledged to resolve domestic and cold war problems.**

1. The Bay of Pigs invasion of Cuba (1961) proved to be a foreign policy fiasco.
2. The Cuban missile crisis (1962) almost led to a superpower conflict.
3. Russian-U.S. relations improved following the Cuban missile crisis.
4. The space program and civil rights legislation were both expanded.
5. The tragic circumstances of Kennedy's assassination left conflict and doubt.

B. President Lyndon Johnson's Great Society (1964) attempted to continue New Deal type programs.

1. Broad goals encompassed ending poverty, reducing pollution, regenerating urban life, and pursuing civil rights legislation.
2. The escalation in Vietnam shattered the dream of the Great Society.
3. Domestic turmoil and frustration over Vietnam contributed to the election of Richard Nixon as President (1968).

C. President Nixon attempted to unify the nation.

1. The tragedy of Vietnam ended in violence and disillusionment.
2. Inflation and recession became increasingly serious.
3. The Middle East became the second focus of diplomatic troubles with the Arab oil embargo following the Arab-Israeli War (1974).
4. Nixon established better relations with Russia and China.
5. Watergate (1974), a national tragedy, destroyed the credibility of the American government.

D. The post-Watergate era began in an uncertain climate.

1. President Gerald Ford's political future was damaged by the pardon of Nixon.
2. President Jimmy Carter captured the imagination of the people but his administration was plagued by serious problems.
   a. The energy crisis continued to affect the U.S. economy.
   b. Israel and Egypt signed a historic peace treaty but key problems were left unsolved.
   c. The need for alternate sources of energy became a national priority.
   d. Detente with Russia suffered serious setbacks.
   e. Inflation continued to be a major problem affecting the U.S. economy.

E. The Iranian hostage crisis (1980–1981) and Russia's invasion of Afghanistan (1980) created an American dilemma.

F. Carter and Ronald Reagan vied for the Presidency (1980).

1. John Anderson represented a third-party challenge.
2. Inflation, Afghanistan, Iran, and domestic problems spelled defeat for Carter.

G. Ronald Reagan received an overwhelming electoral mandate from the American people.

POLITICAL SCIENCE-GOVERNMENT OUTLINE

I. CLASSIFICATION ACCORDING TO THE RELATIONSHIP BE-TWEEN THE EXECUTIVE AND THE LEGISLATURE

A. Presidential government.

1. A distinctive feature of the executive is that it is elected independently of the legislature and holds office for a fixed period. Also, the executive has extensive power not subject to control by the legislature.
2. The term *presidential government* is descriptive of the system employed by the United States.

B. Cabinet or parliamentary government.

1. Policy-making executives are the Prime Minister and the Cabinet, all of whom are members of the legislature and dependent on support of the legislature for continuance in office.
2. Parliamentary government differs from the American system of *separation of powers* in that executive authority is dependent on the legislature.

II. CLASSIFICATION ACCORDING TO THE LOCATION OF POWER IN GOVERNMENT

A. Confederation.

1. Loose union of states in which the principal powers of government (perhaps *all* the real power) are retained by the individual member states.
2. Central government exists to perform a limited number of functions, such as national defense.
3. The United States was a confederation for eight years under the Articles of Confederation.

B. Federation

1. A federation, such as the United States, is a union of two or more local governments under one central government, *with both the central and the local governments exercising independent spheres of authority, either in theory or in practice.*
2. Encourages unity in matters of general concern, but autonomy (independent authority) in matters of local concern.

III. CLASSIFICATION ACCORDING TO THE DEGREE OF GOVERNMENTAL REGULATION OF THE LIVES OF INDIVIDUALS

A. **Anarchism holds that all government is evil, unnecessary, and undesirable.**

B. **Individualism advocates the restriction of governmental activities within narrow limits, leaving a broad area of freedom to the individual.**

C. **Socialism stands for relatively rapid and sweeping economic collectivism (government ownership).**

IV. CLASSIFICATION ACCORDING TO LIMITATION ON GOVERNMENTAL POWER

A. **Dictatorship.**

1. Government resting on the will of a single person or a small group of persons.
2. The welfare of the state is often held above the welfare of the individual.

B. **Democracy.**

1. Primary meaning is *government by the people.*
2. *Indirect* democracy implies government by the people's representatives, as in the United States.

V. THE CONSTITUTION OF THE UNITED STATES AS A RESTRAINT ON GOVERNMENTAL POWER

A. **National power: the separation principle.**

1. Powers are carefully separated and balanced among executive, legislative, and judicial branches to avoid centralization of powers and resultant tyranny.
2. The Presidential veto is an example of executive check on the legislative branch.
3. Control of expenditures is an example of legislative check on the executive branch.
4. The power to interpret the Constitution and laws is an example of check the judiciary holds over the President and Congress.

5. The power of enforcement of court decisions is a check of the executive over the judicial branch.

B. **Restraints on state power.**

1. Article I, Section 10.

   a. Forbids the states to enter treaties, coin money, subvert the national currency, or pass any law impairing the obligation of contracts, etc.

   b. Outlaws tariffs by states.

2. Supremacy of the Constitution, laws, and treaties of the United States.

3. The Fourteenth Amendment.

   a. Defines citizenship, providing supremacy of national citizenship over state citizenship.

   b. Restrains the states from depriving persons of life, liberty, or property without due process of law or denying persons the equal protection of laws.

4. The Fifteenth Amendment intended to give blacks the right to vote.

5. The Nineteenth Amendment forbids states to deny women the right to vote.

6. The Twenty-Fourth Amendment forbids states to collect poll tax as a prerequisite to voting in national elections.

7. The Twenty-Sixth Amendment allows 18-year-olds to vote in national elections.

VI. THE TWO-PARTY SYSTEM

A. **Traditions in American politics.**

1. During most of U.S. history, power has alternated between two major parties.

2. Minor parties do arise and influence national politics.

3. No minor party has ever elected a President.

4. Major parties sometimes disappear, but development of a new second party is the traditional pattern.

5. Minor parties sometimes elect congressmen.

6. Minor parties have occasionally dominated state and local politics.

B. **Advantages of a two-party system.**

1. Voters can be confronted with an either-or choice, thus simplifying decisions and political processes.

2. Electoral decisions are usually majority decisions, encouraging majority support for governmental policies.
3. Governmental stability is enhanced by a two-party system as opposed to a multiparty system.

BEHAVIORAL SCIENCES OUTLINE

I. ANTHROPOLOGY

A. **The scope of anthropology is concerned with all varieties of man and it considers men of all periods, beginning with the emergence of man and tracing his development until the present.** Anthropology is comparative (comparing differing cultures) and historical.

B. **The subfields of anthropology relate to each other.**

1. Physical anthropology studies man as a biological organism.
2. Cultural anthropology studies man's cultures.
3. Ethnology studies man and why cultures differ.
4. Archaeology and prehistory studies the ways of life of peoples of the past.
5. Anthropological linguistics studies the cultural development of language and communication.

C. **The concept of culture.**

1. Culture is the sum total of man's customs, practices, and beliefs, learned and shared by him as a member of a human group.
2. An item of behavior is referred to as a culture trait.
3. A group of related culture traits is called a culture complex.
4. Culture is not static and therefore is always changing.

D. **The evolution of culture traces the technological development of man.**

1. Technology is the study of the ways that a society employs to achieve a successful adaptation to the environment.
2. Subsistence technology is the study of the techniques of obtaining food.
3. Food producing or domestication includes the cultivation of plants and the keeping and breeding of animals.
4. Stock breeding combined with farming is called mixed subsistence.

E. **Economic systems were developed to distribute goods and services.**
   1. Reciprocity refers to giving and taking without the use of money.
   2. Redistribution is the accumulation of goods for the purpose of subsequent distribution.
   3. The development of market exchange occurs when surpluses of food are regularly produced.

F. **The development of social systems.**
   1. Egalitarian societies occur where there are as many positions of prestige in any given age-sex group as there are persons capable of filling them.
   2. Stratified societies are characterized by socially structured unequal access to economic resources.

G. **Kinship is based on descent, and it is associated with a set of privileges and obligations.**
   1. In most societies culture is transmitted through the kin group.
   2. Lineage is a kinship group whose members trace their descent from a common ancestor.
   3. Patterns of marital residence are often determined by kinship.
   4. Members of a society are bound together into ascending ranks through kinship.

H. **Political organizations are usually classified according to degree of centralization of authority and include tribes, states, and nations.**

I. **Religion is a universal phenomenon present in all cultures.**

J. **Culture dynamics in the modern world.**
   1. Culture borrowing results from the direct or indirect exposure to another culture.
   2. Diffusion is the process of borrowing.

II. SOCIOLOGY

A. **Sociologists study societies to obtain data, develop concepts, and formulate theories about human interaction.**
   1. A society is a group of persons who are organized in an orderly manner, share a distinct lifestyle, and think of themselves as united.

2. Society consists of a network or system of social relationships among individuals.
3. Status is a position an individual occupies in a group or society.
4. A role is the expectations of behavior (norms) for those who occupy a given status.
5. Societies can be basically divided into folk or modern.
   a. A folk society is small, generally based on agriculture, and today is found only in isolated areas.
   b. A modern society is large, generally based on advanced division of labor, and is rapidly changing.

B. **Sociologists, as well as anthropologists, study culture, since culture depends on human interaction.**

1. There is a culture for every society.
2. Culture can be classified as learned, taught, adaptive, shared, etc.
3. Only man is considered to have culture, since he alone is known capable of creating a language.
4. Values, attitudes, and norms of behavior are defined by the culture.

C. **The individual learns about the culture through the process of socialization.**

1. Disciplines, aspirations, skills, and roles are learned by the individual through socialization.
2. Socialization is deliberately carried out by such institutions as the school or family.
3. Socialization encourages a mold for personality development reflecting that culture's values.
4. Social deviance is behavior that differs a great deal from the given norm.
5. Social movements are deliberate efforts to produce change in society.
6. Groups are fundamental to the socialization process.
   a. Groups may be classified from primary (in which members feel close to one another) to secondary (in which members fell no strong ties to one another).
   b. The family is the most important primary group.
   c. Cooperation, competition, and conflict are part of group processes.
   d. The social nature of minority classification.

(1) Racial and ethnic group differences are closely related to respective class and status positions.

(2) A variety of groups can be classified as a minority in any given society.

(3) A group becomes a minority when it is defined as such.

(4) Prejudice and discrimination are learned behaviors and have limited the social and economic mobility of minorities.

7. Religion, government, and the economy are fundamental to the socialization process.

ECONOMICS OUTLINE

I. THE BACKGROUND OF ECONOMICS

A. **All civilized societies are organized to fulfill basic social needs.**

1. The institution of the family fulfills primary and basic needs.
2. Educational and religious institutions transmit the ideals and values of society.
3. Political institutions provide the means for enforcing rules and regulations.
4. Economic institutions provide a method to analyze the goods and services in a society.

B. **There are four basic universals of economics that are present in all types of economic organizations.**

How to allocate scarce resources among competing and alternative uses
How to distribute goods and services among the population
How to provide economic stability and security
How to provide continued economic growth

C. **The basis of economics is that society must make choices.**

1. Since there are not enough resources to satisfy all wants, there is a conflict between unlimited wants and limited resources.
2. Societal choices: what to produce, how to produce, and for whom to produce.

D. **Some basic economic principles that are fundamental to an understanding of economics.**
   1. Marginal costs: the costs of producing additional units of a good.
   2. Law of diminishing returns: the point at which the production of extra units results in decreased returns.
   3. Markets: bringing together persons who wish to exchange goods.

II. ECONOMIC ORGANIZATION

A. **The U.S. economy is based on concepts of modern capitalism.**
   1. Private ownership of property is fundamental to a capitalistic society.
   2. A competitive free-market, free-price system is necessary for capitalism to function efficiently.
   3. Modern capitalism can be divided into basic sectors.

SECTOR

Consumption	Characterized by freedom of consumer choice
Production	Characterized by freedom of enterprise
Financial	Composed of all banking and financial institutions
Government	Performs task of stabilizing the economy through monetary and fiscal policies

   4. Measuring economic variables provides a means of analyzing the economy.
      a. Wealth is a measurement of assets on hand at a given point in time.
      b. Income is the monetary return or other material benefits from currently produced goods and services.
      c. The purchasing power of the dollar has to do with its ability to command goods and services. Measuring changes in the value of the dollar is a key economic concept.
   5. Production is a source of wealth and income and involves the inflow and outflow of goods and services. The economic growth of the United States is measured by the Gross National Product (GNP) which is the value of all goods and services produced in a particular year.

B. **The underdeveloped areas of the world have shown limited economic growth.**

1. Two thirds of the world's population is economically deprived.
2. Restricted growth is the result of a combination of many factors.
    a. The quality of land, labor, and capital are key factors that determine economic growth.
    b. Less developed countries usually have high population densities.
    c. Low incomes retard economies by restricting the opportunity to consume goods.

III. THE ROLE OF GOVERNMENT IN THE U.S. ECONOMY

A. **The degree of government control and influence in our economy has steadily grown throughout history.**

1. Industrialization has created problems in labor-management relations that government seems to be able to handle best.
2. Urbanization has created problems in providing essential public services such as police and fire protection and sewage disposal.
3. Foreign policy commitments and military expenditures have had lasting effects on the role of government in the economy.
4. In our modern society people have simply demanded more of government.

B. **The major types of government activities in the economy include direct controls over the economy, ownership of production (for example, Hoover Dam), and welfare expenditures**

C. **The major economic impact of government activity comes from its spending, taxing, and public debt policies.**

1. The various types of taxes include direct, indirect, proportional, progressive, and regressive.
    a. Federal personal and corporate taxes are progressive.
    b. Most state and local taxes are proportional.
    c. Nearly all excise, sales, and property taxes are regressive.
2. Taxes may affect economic growth by reducing the purchasing power of income earnings and affecting the allocation of resources.
3. "Ability to pay" and "benefits received" are the cornerstones of the U.S. tax system.
    a. "Ability to pay" is a theory that bases taxation in accordance with income and wealth position.

b. "Benefits received" is a theory that bases taxation in accordance with the benefits received by the taxpayer; hunting and fishing fees are examples.

IV. CONSUMER CHOICE AND THE PRICE SYSTEM

A. **In the United States economic production is aimed at satisfying the desires of the consumer.**
   1. The utility of a product is the satisfaction one receives from consuming goods.
   2. Consumer behavior is determined by available money, priorities, and utilities.

B. **Basic to the price system are demand, supply, and equilibrium.**

C. **The government's role in the marketplace includes the enforcement of regulations, imposing taxes, and controlling prices.**
   1. Government actions can create shortages or surpluses.
   2. Government actions can restrict the price system.

V. THE LABOR MARKET

A. **The demand for labor is largely determined by the demand for the final product and the price of substitute factors.**

B. **The supply of labor is largely determined by population growth, immigration, and alternative lifestyles.**

C. **Changes in the labor market have brought about the formation and growth of large firms and labor unions.**
   1. Management usually seeks to maximize long-term profits.
   2. Labor unions attempt to obtain high wages, full employment, and job security.
   3. The conflict of goals between labor and management is usually resolved through collective bargaining.

VI. INTERNATIONAL TRADE AND FINANCE

A. **International economic relations involve the movement of goods, services, people, and capital across national political boundaries.**

B. The United States is the world's largest single exporter and importer.
1. The volume of U.S. imports is of vital significance to other countries' economies.
2. The volume of U.S. imports is closely related to the level of its national income; the higher the income, the greater its imports.

C. The balance of payments includes all the economic and financial transactions between one country and the rest of the world over a given period of time.
1. A favorable balance of trade results when exports are greater than imports.
2. An unfavorable balance of trade results when imports are greater than exports.

GEOGRAPHY OUTLINE

I. THE IMPORTANCE OF TODAY'S GEOGRAPHY

A. Peoples of the world are brought closer together by improved means of transportation and communication.

B. The division of the earth into separate nations has influenced the lives of people and the way in which they use the land.

C. The effects of geography on world conditions are readily seen in the politcal and social arena.
1. Russia's desire for defensible borders encouraged the domination of Eastern Europe following World War II.
2. The emergence of the Middle East as a political force was a result of the world's dependence on oil.

II. THE EFFECTS OF THE INCLINATION OF THE EARTH'S AXIS CAUSE SEASONAL CHANGES

A. The number of growing seasons a country has is influenced by both geography and climate.

B. The Tropics of Cancer and Capricorn are generally areas of warmer temperatures and climates.

C. The Arctic Circle and Antarctic Circle are generally areas of colder temperatures and climates.

III. **GLOBES AND MAPS ARE ESSENTIAL TOOLS OF GEOGRAPHY AND DEPICT MAN'S KNOWLEDGE OF THE EARTH AND ITS FEATURES**

A. **Maps are drawings which show where places are in relation to each other.**

   1. Information given on maps consists of the title, legend, scale, direction, longitude and latitude, etc.
   2. Longitude is an angular distance east and west of a given meridian measured in degrees.
   3. Latitude is distance measured in degrees north and south of the equator.
   4. The prime meridian is the reference point for measuring longitude.
   5. The time of the day or night at any place in the world is measured from the prime meridian.

B. **Map projections (Mercator, polar, orthographic, etc.) show some distortion of the earth's surface.**

C. **There are many types of maps including political (political divisions), physical (geographic features), relief (elevations and depressions), and special-purpose (products, vegetation, mining, population, etc.).**

D. **Globes are accurate representations of the earth and show relative size, shape, and distance.**

IV. **WEATHER AND CLIMATE**

A. **Weather is the day-by-day change in the earth's atmosphere, and climate is weather conditions over a long period of time.**

B. **Weather and climate are affected by many factors.**

   1. Air movements such as prevailing winds (westerlies, trade winds) affect climate.
   2. Local air movements such as land-sea breeze and valley-mountain breeze affect climate.
   3. Marine (sea) and continental (land) air masses affect weather and climate.
   4. Ocean currents and mountain barriers affect weather and climate.

V. GEOGRAPHERS DIVIDE THE EARTH INTO REGIONS IN
ORDER TO STUDY IT MORE ADEQUATELY

   A. The topography of land masses includes mountains, deserts, plains,
   plateaus, and valleys.

   B. The major bodies of water include oceans, seas, lakes, rivers, and
   gulfs.

   C. Vegetation is affected by land forms and water distribution.

VI. THE STUDY OF GEOGRAPHY ATTEMPTS TO ANALYZE
THE INTERRELATIONSHIP BETWEEN MAN AND HIS
ENVIRONMENT

   A. The distribution of the world's population is determined by such
   things as climatic regions, vegetation regions, soil, water systems,
   and resources.

   B. Unfavorable regions are generally those with extreme climatic
   conditions or limited natural resources.

   C. The relationship of man's environment to land use determines
   occupations, political organizations, econòmic prosperity, etc.

   D. Physical features often determine political boundaries.

   E. A knowledge of climate and topography are important in understanding land-use patterns.

   F. Environment influences economic, cultural, and political development.

VII. U.S. GEOGRAPHY: AN OVERVIEW

   A. The Gulf Stream, an Atlantic warm water current, warms the East
   Coast in winter and is responsible for excellent fishing.

   B. The southeastern Coastal Plain extends along the coast from New
   Jersey to Texas and is generally low land.

   C. The Piedmont (the foothills at the base of the Appalachian Mountains), the Appalachian Mountains, and the Cumberland and Alle-
   gheny plateaus are in the eastern region of the United States.

   D. In the northeast, the Appalachians meet the ocean, forming a rough,
   rocky coast.

E. West of the Appalachians the wind (prevailing westerlies) is an important influence on climate.

1. In the winter cold air from the northwest produces freezing temperatures.
2. In summer warm, moist southwesterly winds cause hot, humid weather.

F. Most of the interior is generally flat land.

1. The eastern half is called the interior lowlands.
2. The western half is called the Great Plains.

G. The Mississippi River drains the interior of the United States.

1. In this area most of the streams and rivers flow toward the Gulf of Mexico.
2. The Great Lakes are the largest bodies of water.

H. The crest of the Rockies is called the Continental Divide.

1. Rivers that begin east of the Continental Divide flow toward the Atlantic.
2. Western rivers flow toward the Pacific.

I . The land between the Rockies and the Sierra Nevadas is called the Great Basin.

J . The Sierra Nevadas and the Cascades form the western mountain ranges.

1. The western slope of the Sierra Nevadas borders the central valley of California.
2. On the eastern slope lie the coast ranges.

GLOSSARY OF TERMS IN U.S. HISTORY

ABOLITIONISTS: Individuals or organizations who wanted to abolish slavery; antislavery crusaders.

ALAMO: The historic battle in Texas in which the Mexican general Santa Anna stormed the Alamo and killed all its defenders; symbol of resisting overwhelming odds.

ALIEN AND SEDITION ACTS: Acts passed by the Federalist-dominated Congress; designed to suppress political opposition to John Adams's Presidency.

AMERICA FIRST: The principal isolationist lobby of the pre-World War II era that charged President Roosevelt with willfully leading the nation into war.

ANNEXATION: A policy of adding territory to an already established area or country; the United States annexed Texas in 1845.

BAY OF PIGS: The ill-conceived, American-backed invasion of Cuba in 1961 that ended in disaster.

BERLIN AIRLIFT: The Allied airlift that saved Berlin after Russia had blockaded the city in June 1948.

BERLIN WALL: The barbed wire and concrete barrier erected by the East Germans and Russians in August 1961 to halt the flow of refugees to West Germany.

BLACK CODES: Generally harsh laws passed by the Southern States to deal with the freed blacks during Reconstruction.

BLACK RECONSTRUCTION: The term referring to the role of blacks in the Reconstruction period.

BLOCKADE: A policy that restricts or prevents the passage of goods and supplies from reaching a destination; for example, blockading the Southern coastline during the Civil War.

BOYCOTT: A refusal to buy or trade certain products; an economic measure designed to produce a desired result.

BRICKER AMENDMENT: The constitutional amendment that came close to passage during the Eisenhower Presidency; it attempted to restrict the power of the President to conduct foreign relations by specifying that "a treaty or other international agreement shall become effective as internal law in the United States only through legislation by the Congress."

BROWN V. BOARD OF EDUCATION OF TOPEKA: The historic 1954 Supreme Court decision declaring that "separate educational facilities are inherently unequal."

CARPETBAGGERS: The name given to Northern whites who journeyed to the South after the Civil War and cooperated with Radical Reconstruction.

CATTLE KINGDOM: The area between the Missouri River and the Rocky Mountains where the cattle barons flourished in the 1870s and 1880s.

CHINESE EXCLUSION ACT: The 1882 act that barred Chinese from immigrating to the United States.

CIVIL RIGHTS ACTS: The 1866 law that forbade states to discriminate because of race or color; it was vetoed by President Andrew Johnson, and its major features were incorporated into the Fourteenth Amendment.

CIVIL RIGHTS ACT OF 1964: The civil rights measure that was sponsored by President Kennedy but was not passed until well after his death; it forbade discrimination in hotels, restaurants, and stores and provided for greater protection of black voting rights.

CLOSED SHOP: A policy that allows only members of a particular union to be hired by a business firm; nonunion labor is not eligible for employment.

COLD WAR: A "war of words"; a conflict that falls short of war.

COMMITTEE TO DEFEND AMERICA BY AIDING THE ALLIES: The group headed by William A. White that favored American aid to the Allies in order to stem Nazi aggression; its rival was the America First Committee.

COMPROMISE OF 1877: The deal made between Republicans and Southern Democrats by which the latter acquiesced in the election of Rutherford B. Hayes in return for certain favors.

COMSTOCK LODE: An incredibly rich vein of silver in Nevada.

CONGRESS OF INDUSTRIAL ORGANIZATIONS (CIO): The national labor organization established in 1938 that organized industrial workers.

CONTAINMENT POLICY: The policy initially adopted by President Truman by containing Communist expansion and aiding peoples resisting Communist subjugation.

CONTINENTAL DIVIDE: The mountain line that separates the rivers that flow east from those that flow west; Rocky Mountain chain.

COPPERHEADS: A derogatory term applied to northerners who sympathized with the South during the Civil War.

CRAFT UNION: An organization of workers that includes all members of a particular craft or skilled trade.

CREDIT MOBILIER: The dummy construction company set up to defraud the stockholders of the Union Pacific Railroad; it was a much-publicized scandal of the Grant era.

CUBAN MISSILE CRISIS: The diplomatic conflict between the United States and the Soviet Union that developed in 1962 when it was learned that Soviet missiles had been secretly installed in Cuba; President Kennedy demanded their removal and the Soviets backed down.

CUMBERLAND GAP: A pass through the Appalachian Mountains that enabled early settlers to move west.

DAWES ACT: The 1887 law that dissolved Indian tribes as legal entities and provided for the distribution of land to individuals.

DIXIECRATS: The name often applied to the States' Rights Party, a splinter group of Southern Democrats that ran J. Strom Thurmond for the Presidency in 1948.

DOLLAR DIPLOMACY: Pressure exerted by the Taft administration on foreign governments to accept American investments.

DUST BOWL: A term that refers to the extreme dust storms that stripped an area of most of its top soil; primarily centered in the Great Plains states of Oklahoma and Kansas.

EISENHOWER DOCTRINE: The 1957 foreign policy pronouncement that the United States would aid any Middle Eastern nation that requested help in retaining its independence.

EMANCIPATION: A term primarily associated with the freeing of black slaves; freeing of a person who is held in bondage.

EMBARGO: A government measure designed to prevent commerce with foreign countries; restrictions on trade that result in prohibiting ships from entering or leaving a port.

EMIGRATION: Leaving one country to settle in another country.

FAIR DEAL: The term given to the program of social reform announced by President Truman in September 1945.

FEDERAL HOUSING ADMINISTRATION: The agency created in 1934 to provide home-improvement and mortgage loans.

FEDERAL TRADE COMMISSION: The federal regulatory commission established in 1914 to eliminate unfair competition; although passed under Wilson, it embodied Theodore Roosevelt's idea of trust regulation.

FOURTEENTH AMENDMENT: An outgrowth of the vetoed Civil Rights Act of 1866; it has theoretically guaranteed the civil rights of blacks.

GENTLEMEN'S AGREEMENT: The series of notes between the United States and Japan (1907–08) whereby Japan agreed to cease issuing passports to laborers in return for Theodore Roosevelt's intervention in its dispute with the San Francisco school board.

GOOD NEIGHBOR POLICY: The term often applied to President Franklin D. Roosevelt's policy of improving relations between the United States and Latin America.

GREAT DEPRESSION: The depression that began with the stock market crash of 1929 and lasted throughout the 1930s.

GREAT PLAINS: The area of the United States that extends approximately from longitude 98° west to the Rockies and from Texas to Canada.

GREAT SOCIETY: The name given to the domestic reform program of the Lyndon Johnson administration.

GULF OF TONKIN RESOLUTION: The 1964 Senate resolution that authorized President Johnson to take military action against North Vietnam.

HIROSHIMA: The Japanese city on which the first atomic bomb was dropped by the United States on August 6, 1945.

INITIATIVE: The popular reform during the progressive era providing for initiation of legislation by petition.

INTERSTATE COMMERCE ACT: The 1887 law establishing the principle of federal regulation of railroads.

"IRON CURTAIN": The term used by Winston Churchill in a 1946 speech at Fulton, Missouri, describing the Soviet threat.

ISOLATIONISTS: Individuals who advocated the general withdrawal of the United States from world affairs; advocates of the neutrality legislation of the 1930s.

KELLOGG-BRIAND PACT: The multilateral treaty concluded in 1928 outlawing aggressive wars but permitting defensive wars.

KOREAN WAR: The war (1950–53) in which United Nations troops (largely American) defended South Korea against Communist aggression.

KU KLUX KLAN: The secret terrorist organization that flourished largely in the 1920s; its efforts were directed against Catholics, blacks, Jews, and foreigners.

LEND-LEASE ACT: The 1941 law authorizing the free loan of military equipment to the Allies.

LIBERATION POLICY: John Foster Dulles's aggressive approach to foreign policy which pledged America to free the captive nations of Eastern Europe.

MAINE: The battleship that exploded in Havana habor in 1898; although Spanish responsibility was never proven, "Remember the Maine" became the battle cry of the Spanish-American War.

MARSHALL PLAN: The postwar American program of economic assistance to Europe.

MEDICARE: The 1965 act providing medical aid for persons over 65 to be administered through the Social Security system. Congress had rejected it twice during the Kennedy administration, but finally passed it during the Johnson administration.

MUCKRAKERS: Reform-minded journalists who helped the progressives by publicizing unsavory conditions in America.

MUNICH CONFERENCE: The 1938 conference at which Britain and France agreed to allow Hitler to take the Sudetenland.

NATIONAL ASSOCIATION FOR THE ADVANCEMENT OF COLORED PEOPLE (NAACP): The group founded in 1909 to promote political and civic equality for blacks.

NATURALIZATION: A power of Congress to determine the rules and qualifications for foreigners (aliens) to become U.S. citizens.

NEUTRALITY LAWS: The three laws passed in 1935, 1936, and 1937 prohibiting Americans from sailing on belligerent ships and from selling arms or making loans to belligerents.

NEW DEAL: The term given to Franklin D. Roosevelt's domestic program.

NEW FREEDOM: Woodrow Wilson's program in the 1912 election calling for restoration of free competition by destroying the trusts.

NEW NATIONALISM: Theodore Roosevelt's program in the 1912 election advocating federal intervention in the nation's economic life and calling for regulation rather than dissolution of the trusts.

NONAGGRESSION: A policy that results in formal agreements among nations not to attack each other in case of war.

NORTH ATLANTIC TREATY ORGANIZATION (NATO): The organization created in 1949 by twelve nations (including the United States) which agreed that an attack on one would be considered an attack on all.

NUCLEAR TEST BAN TREATY: The 1963 treaty with the Soviet Union that forbade all nuclear testing in the air, in space, and under water.

NULLIFICATION: A process to prevent an undesirable law from going into effect; historically, refers to the refusal of South Carolina to accept the Tariff of 1832; in effect, a state refusal to enforce a federal law.

OFFICE OF ECONOMIC OPPORTUNITY: The agency established by the Economic Opportunity Act of 1964; almost $1 billion was appropriated to retrain the jobless poor to enable them to find gainful employment.

OPEN DOOR POLICY: The policy emerging from two "Open Door" notes. The first (1899) requested that the major powers accept the principle of equal trading rights in China for all nations. The second note, sent after the Boxer Rebellion, asked the cooperation of the major powers in preserving the territorial integrity of China.

PACIFISM: Opposition to war; advocating nonmilitary solutions to conflicts between nations; a refusal to participate in military conflict.

POPULISM: The political expression of late-nineteenth-century agrarian discontent that culminated in the candidacy of William Jennings Bryan for President in 1896.

PROGRESSIVISM: The middle-class movement at the beginning of the twentieth century that urged such reforms as the initiative, referendum, recall, secret ballot, direct primary, city manager form of government, and direct election of U.S. Senators.

PROHIBITION: The Eighteenth Amendment barring the sale, manufacture, or shipment of intoxicating beverages; it was passed in 1917, went into effect in 1920, and was repealed in 1933.

"QUARANTINE SPEECH": The speech made by President Roosevelt in October 1937 suggesting the use of economic sanctions against aggressor nations.

RADICAL RECONSTRUCTION: The term given to the harsh Reconstruction policies of the Radical Republicans.

REACTIONARY: Advocating prior political or social policies; resistant to change.

RECALL: The method by which officials could be removed from office by petition and vote, before the expiration of their terms of office.

RED SCARE: The anti-Communist vendetta of 1919–20.

REFERENDUM: The progressive reform measure at the state and local levels by which legislation was submitted directly to the voters for their approval or rejection.

ROOSEVELT COROLLARY: Theodore Roosevelt's peculiar interpretation of the Monroe Doctrine by which he justified U.S. intervention in Latin Amerian on the grounds that the United States could not permit European nations to intervene.

SANCTIONS: Policies designed to prevent the continuation of an undesirable action; restrictions on trade and commerce.

SCALAWAGS: The name given to Southern whites who cooperated with Radical Reconstruction.

SCHENCK CASE: The 1919 case in which the Supreme Court ruled that freedom of speech does not fully apply during wartime.

SCOPES TRIAL: The famous trial (1925) in which a high school teacher, John Scopes, was found guilty of violating a Tennessee law against the teaching of evolution. Acting for the defense, Clarence Darrow devastated the aging William Jennings Bryan, who supported the state's position, but the law remained on the books.

SECRET BALLOT: The progressive reform guaranteeing the voter a chance to cast his ballot secretly; it is also known as the Australian ballot.

SECTIONALISM: A philosophy favoring the interests of a smaller geographic area (section) instead of the interests of the nation; protection of one's self-interest.

SECURITIES AND EXCHANGE COMMISSION: The commission created in 1934 with authority to regulate the stock exchange.

SEDITION: Actions designed to initiate an insurrection (rebellion) against an existing government.

SELECTIVE SERVICE ACT: The act passed in 1940 (renewed in 1941) providing for the first peacetime conscription in the United States.

SHERMAN ANTITRUST ACT: The 1890 law that attempted to regulate trusts by outlawing all trusts and conspiracies in restraint of trade.

TEAPOT DOME SCANDAL: The widely publicized scandal of the Harding administration that involved the leasing of oil reserves by Secretary of the Interior Albert Fall to the Doheny and Sinclair oil interests in return for large bribes.

TERRITORY: An area of the United States that is governed by the Congress; territories, when they meet certain qualifications determined by Congress, are eligible for statehood.

TRUMAN DOCTRINE: The American pledge to aid free peoples to resist Communist subjugation; it was enunciated by President Truman in 1947 when Britain announced its inability to aid Greece and Turkey.

TRUST: The business mergers and combinations that were frequently in restraint of trade.

U-2 CRISIS: The crisis that developed in 1960 when an American spy plane was shot down over the Soviet Union on the eve of the Paris summit meeting; contrary to diplomatic practice, Eisenhower assumed full responsibility and Khrushchev walked out of the meeting.

UNCONDITIONAL SURRENDER: The terms for surrender demanded of both Germany and Japan by the Allies in World War II.

WORKMEN'S COMPENSATION ACT: The measure passed during the Wilson administration providing compensation for federal employees injured on the job.

YALTA CONFERENCE: The February 1945 meeting of Roosevelt, Churchill, and Stalin that settled the fate of Poland and provided for Russian entry into the war against Japan.

GLOSSARY OF TERMS IN POLITICAL SCIENCE-GOVERNMENT

BASIC TERMS

AMBASSADOR: One acting as an official representative of a government in its relations with foreign nations.

APPEAL: The right of an individual to ask a higher court to review a case in order to obtain a retrial or reversal of a decision.

APPELLATE JURISDICTION: The authority of a court to review a case already decided in a lower court.

BAIL: Money deposited with a court that allows a person to be released from jail; the accused pledges to appear in court at a specified time.

BALLOT: A printed list that contains the names of candidates running for public office; also the public issues to be decided by the voters.

BILL: A proposed law; a bill does not become a law until it goes through the necessary legislative steps.

CAPITALISM: An economic system based on private ownership, freedom of choice, and access to the means of production; characterized by a free-enterprise system.

CHECKS AND BALANCES: Division of the power of the government into three distinct branches so that each branch can check or limit the power of the other two branches; for example, the President can veto a bill passed by Congress.

CITIZEN: A member of a state or country who enjoys certain rights and privileges and is able to participate in the political process.

CIVIL RIGHTS: Political, economic, and social rights guaranteed by legal statute and custom; the Bill of Rights was designed to protect civil liberties.

CIVIL SERVICE: A system that bases employment on competitive testing; the first U.S. Civil Service Commission was established in 1883.

CLOSED PRIMARY: An election process in which only voters who are members of a particular party are allowed to vote for the party's candidates; for example, only Democrats are allowed to vote in the Democratic primary.

COMMUNISM: An economic system based on total government control of all sectors of the economy; the opposite of free enterprise.

CONCURRENT POWERS: Powers shared by the state and federal government; for example, the power to tax.

CONGRESS: The legislative branch of government; the House and Senate make up the legislative branch at the national level; Congress has the power to pass laws.

CONSTITUTION: A written plan of government listing the organization and the basic laws of the government.

DEMOCRACY: A government which is based on the direct involvement of the people in the governmental process; rule by the people, either directly or indirectly.

DICTATORSHIP: A government based on the rule of one person or a small group of people; characterized by an abuse of power.

DIRECT DEMOCRACY: Pure democracy; all people in a community decide on the laws or actions a government should take; rule by the people directly.

DUE PROCESS: The right of all people to the legal protection of a government; guaranteed legal protection.

EXECUTIVE BRANCH: The branch of government (federal, state, local) that is responsible for carrying out laws; the President is the Chief Executive for the United States.

FEDRERAL GOVERNMENT: The national government; the central government based in Washington, D.C.

FEDERALISM: A philosophy of government advocating division of power between the state and federal governments.

FEDERAL RESERVE SYSTEM: The central bank of the United States; regulates the banking needs of the national government.

FILIBUSTER: A method of delaying or preventing a vote on a bill before Congress; talking a bill to death.

GRAND JURY: A pretrial hearing in which a select group of people hears evidence in a case to determine if the evidence warrants bringing an accused person to trial.

HABEAS CORPUS: An official paper that requires that a person accused of a crime must be brought before a judge; prevents an unreasonable delay in obtaining a fair trial.

IMPLIED POWER: Powers not specifically stated in the Constitution; enables the Congress to make "all laws that are necessary and proper."

INITIATIVE: A process that enables people in a state to directly propose legislation.

JUDICIAL BRANCH: The branch of the federal government whose main responsibility is to interpret the law; the national court system.

JUDICIAL REVIEW: A term that refers to the power of the federal courts to interpret the Constitution and to declare acts of Congress unconstitutional.

LOBBYIST: A person or group that attempts to govern or control a particular area or case.

NATURALIZATION: A power of Congress to determine the rules and qualifications for foreigners (aliens) to become U.S. citizens.

OPEN PRIMARY: A primary election in which eligible voters can vote for the candidate of their choice; not based on party affiliation.

POCKET VETO: A Presidental power in which a bill automatically dies because the President does not return the bill to Congress; this power may be used only in the last ten days of a legislative session; if it is prior to the last ten days, the vetoed bill must be sent back to Congress where an override of the veto may be possible.

RECALL: A method that enables the people to remove government officials before their terms of office expire.

REFERENDUM: A method that allows legislation to be directly submitted to the voters for their consideration.

SEPARATION OF POWER: Division of the power of government into three distinct branches: legislative (makes laws), executive (enforces laws), and judicial (interprets laws).

KEY TERMS ASSOCIATED WITH CURRENT AMERICAN SOCIAL PROBLEMS

AFFLUENT SOCIETY: A term usually used in reference to the wealthy (affluent) members of society.

APPALACHIA: A term usually referring to a depressed area, or geographic area of poverty; as a region it includes parts of Alabama, Georgia, South Carolina, Tennessee, West Virginia, Kentucky, and Pennsylvania; referred to as a depressed area because of the large-scale unemployment and substandard living conditions of the permanently out-of-work coal miners who live there.

AUTOMATION: Replacing hand labor by a machine.

BACKLASH: A term usually referring to reactionary white views of advances made by minority groups in the areas of housing, voting, etc.

BOYCOTT: A refusal to buy or trade certain products; an economic measure designed to produce a desired result.

COLLECTIVE BARGAINING: Group bargaining; representatives of labor and management working together to work out a labor contract.

DE FACTO SEGREGATION: Segregation which exists as a result of economic or social restrictions, but not as a result of official government policies.

DE JURE SEGREGATION: Segregation as a result of legal statutes; for example, establishing school boundaries to exclude blacks.

DEPRESSED AREA: A region or era characterized by a high rate of unemployment and a low standard of living; a depressed area can be regional (Appalachia) or local (slum/ghetto).

DISCRIMINATION: a distinction made in favor of or against a person on the basis of the group, class, religion, etc., that a person belongs to, rather than on the basis of actual merit. (Compare *prejudice* and *racist*.)

GENERALIZATION: Consideration of a small segment of a particular class, religious group, etc., as an example of that entire class or group; formation of a general opinion or trend through the study of a large number of facts or statements.

GHETTO: Historically, an area where one particular minority group was *required* to live; today, in the United States, usually refers to an area of a city where blacks, Puerto Ricans, and other minority groups live, often as a result of restrictive social or economic conditions.

IMMIGRANT: A new arrival to a country; historically, immigrants moved to the inner-city areas where the rents were relatively cheap; today, most noticeable in New York where the inner city is heavily populated by Puerto Ricans.

INFLATION: An abnormal increase in money (currency) and credit beyond the proportion of available goods, resulting in a sharp and *continuous* rise in prices; a rise in prices that is not equated with a corresponding rise in production.

INFLATIONARY SPIRAL: A continuous increase in costs, wages, and prices.

INJUNCTION: A judicial process that allows *labor or management* to prevent a particular act from being carried out or continued; for example, the President invokes the Taft-Hartley Act (injunction) to prevent labor from continuing a strike, or management obtains a court order (injunction) preventing a labor union from boycotting a firm.

INNER CITY: A term that refers to the slum area of a large city; the city areas that were first developed and subsequently became the first depressed areas of the city; today, the inner city is populated by the older industrial elements of the city and by minority groups.

INSTITUTIONAL RACISM: The following of a policy by a government agency or a large business concern that restricts the economic mobility of a particular race, because of racial views.

INVISIBLE AMERICANS: A term that refers to the over eight million American poor—both black and white—who are rarely seen by the majority of Americans; that is, the conditions of the poor are rarely seen by the nonpoor.

PREJUDICE: An opinion, *usually formed without fact or reason,* that holds up a racial, religious, economic group, etc., to ridicule and hostile attitudes.

RACIST: One who holds that one race is superior to another race and that the superior race, therefore, has a right to rule others. *Racist views are not confined to any particular race.*

RELIEF: Money, food, or other help given to those in need by an agency of a state, local, or federal government.

SEGREGATION: A policy of separating the races.

SOCIAL SECURITY: A form of insurance that provides an income for use during old age; both the worker and employer contribute, as well as the federal government.

STEREOTYPE: To put into a mold that lacks any individuality; a standardized image that has special meaning and is held in common by a great many people; the American cowboy, Indian, and black are typical examples.

STRIKE: A suspension or stoppage of work by employees (*labor*) against employers (*management*) to achieve an objective or demands (better hours, wages, conditions of employment); to withdraw services to compel management to accept labor objectives.

SUBURBS: A town or population center lying outside the central city; usually considered to be occupied by the so-called white, middle-class American who wants to escape from the problems associated with the inner city and live with people who have the same racial background as he or she does.

TECHNOLOGICAL UNEMPLOYMENT: Unemployment in which people become unemployable because of technological (scientific) advances that have made their jobs obsolete (out of date).

TENEMENT: A term that refers to a multistory buliding, in the poorer areas of a city, that seems to be in a permanent state of decay.

URBAN RENEWAL: Rehabilitation of dilapidated city areas by demolishing, remodeling, or repairing existing structures.

WELFARE: Financial aid given by a government (state, local, or federal) or by private organizations, because of the recipient's extreme poverty, physical handicap, or advanced age.

KEY TERMS ASSOCIATED WITH THE AMERICAN POLITICAL PROCESS

ABSENTEE VOTING: Balloting by mail in advance of an election; permitted in many states for servicemen and voters who, because of travel, disability, etc., are unable to reach the polling place.

ALTERNATE: A person sent to a party convention to replace any delegate unable to serve.

BANDWAGON: A propanganda technique; delegates "get on the bandwagon" when they switch their support to the candidate who seems to be winning.

BOLT: To leave one party and support another.

BOOM: Growing support for a candidate.

BOSS: A politician who controls many votes and dictates party policies.

CAUCUS: A meeting of party members to choose delegates and committee members.

CONGRESSIONAL DISTRICT: A specific state area entitled to one member in the House of Representatives.

CONGRESSMAN AT LARGE: A representative chosen by an entire state, rather than by a district.

CREDENTIALS COMMITTEE: The convention group that decides which of two opposing delegates has the right to vote in convention.

DARK HORSE: An unexpected candidate who wins support for nomination in a political convention.

DRAFT: A popular move to persuade an unwilling candidate to run for office.

FAVORITE SON: A candidate nominated by his own state delegation; usually without much hope of success.

GENERAL ELECTION: An election for federal offices.

INCUMBENT: A person holding office.

INDEPENDENTS: Voters who do not hold formal membership in a political party.

LOGROLLING: Trading political favors.

LOWER HOUSE: The House of Representatives; the larger of two houses in any legislature.

MACHINE: A large organization and body of voters controlled by a "boss."

MAJORITY: More than half of the total number of votes.

NATIONAL COMMITTEE: A national political party organization, consisting of members from each major party.

PATRONAGE: The practice of awarding government jobs as a reward for successful party work.

PIVOTAL STATE: A state whose vote may decide a nomination or an election.

PLANK: One section of a program promised by a candidate or a party. Several planks make up the "platform."

PLEDGED DELEGATE: A delegate who has promised to support a certain candidate until it is certain that he or she cannot win.

PLURALITY: More votes than any other candidate.

POPULAR VOTE: The total number of ballots cast in an election.

PRECINCT: An election area; part of a ward.

PRIMARY: An election in which people choose candidates for their party ticket; primaries can also choose convention delegates and can be either open or closed.

REGISTRATION: The entering of a person's name as a qualified voter; required in many states.

SLATE: A list of candidates.

SLUSH FUND: A large campaign treasury; a term of contempt, since it implies a misuse of campaign monies.

SOLID SOUTH: States south of the Mason-Dixon line that usually vote Democratic.

SPLIT TICKET: A ballot in which a voter supports candidates of more than one party.

SPOILS: Rewards, such as jobs, for party workers who have helped to win an election.

STRAIGHT TICKET: A ballot cast for all candidates of one party.

STRAW VOTE: A test poll to forecast election results.

THIRD PARTY: A party strong enough to threaten the success of one of the major parties.

UNINSTRUCTED DELEGATE: A convention delegate who is free to vote for any candidate.

WARD: A voting area in town or city; several precincts.

WARD HEELER: A ward party worker who follows orders of the political "boss."

MATHEMATICS REVIEW

The following pages are designed to give you an intensive review of the basic skills used on the NTE Mathematics section. Arithmetic, algebra, geometry, axioms, properties of numbers, terms, and simple statistics are covered. Before you begin the diagnostic review tests, it would be wise to become familiar with basic mathematics terminology, formulas, and general mathematical information, a review of which begins below. Then proceed to the arithmetic diagnostic test, which you should take to spot your weak areas. Then use the arithmetic review that follows to strengthen those areas.

After reviewing the arithmetic, take the algebra diagnostic test and once again use the review that follows to strengthen your weak areas. Next, take the geometry diagnostic test and carefully read the complete geometry review.

Even if you are strong in arithmetic, algebra, and geometry, you may wish to skim the topic headings in each area to refresh your memory of important concepts. If you are weak in math, you should read through the complete review. *Note, however, that recent NTEs have emphasized arithmetic more than they have algebra and geometry. Therefore, you should spend the major portion of your review time on sharpening your arithmetic skills and knowledge of terms and concepts.*

SYMBOLS, TERMINOLOGY, FORMULAS, AND GENERAL MATHEMATICAL INFORMATION

COMMON MATH SYMBOLS AND TERMS

Symbol References:

$=$ is equal to	$\geq$ is greater than or equal to
$\neq$ is not equal to	$\leq$ is less than or equal to
$>$ is greater than	$\parallel$ is parallel to
$<$ is less than	$\perp$ is perpendicular to

Natural numbers—the counting numbers: 1, 2, 3, . . .
Whole numbers—the counting numbers beginning with zero: 0, 1, 2, 3, . . .

Integers—positive and negative whole numbers and zero: . . . -3, -2, -1, 0, 1, 2, . . .

Odd numbers—numbers not divisible by 2: 1, 3, 5, 7, . . .

Even numbers—numbers divisible by 2: 0, 2, 4, 6, . . .

Prime number—number divisible by only 1 and itself: 2, 3, 5, 7, 11, 13, . . .

Composite number—number divisible by more than just 1 and itself: 4, 6, 8, 9, 10, 12, 14, 15, . . .

Squares—the result when numbers are multiplied by themselves, $(2 \cdot 2 = 4)$ $(3 \cdot 3 = 9)$: 1, 4, 9, 16, 25, 36, . . .

Cubes—the result when numbers are multiplied by themselves twice, $(2 \cdot 2 \cdot 2 = 8)$, $(3 \cdot 3 \cdot 3 = 27)$: 1, 8, 27, . . .

MATH FORMULAS

Triangle	Perimeter $= s_1 + s_2 + s_3$ Area $= \frac{1}{2}bh$
Square	Perimeter $= 4s$ Area $= s \cdot s$, or s^2
Rectangle	Perimeter $= 2(b + h)$, or $2b + 2h$ Area $= bh$, or lw
Parallelogram	Perimeter $= 2(l + w)$, or $2l + 2w$ Area $= bh$
Trapezoid	Perimeter $= b_1 + b_2 + s_1 + s_2$ Area $= \frac{1}{2}h(b_1 + b_2)$, or $h\left(\dfrac{b_1 + b_2}{2}\right)$
Circle	Circumference $= 2\pi r$, or πd Area $= \pi r^2$

Pythagorean theorem (for right triangles) $a^2 + b^2 = c^2$

The sum of the squares of the legs of a right triangle equals the square of the hypotenuse.

Cube	Volume $= s \cdot s \cdot s = s^3$ Surface area $= s \cdot s \cdot 6$
Rectangular Prism	Volume $= l \cdot w \cdot h$ Surface area $= 2(lw) + 2(lh) + 2(wh)$

IMPORTANT EQUIVALENTS

$\frac{1}{100} = .01 = 1\%$

$\frac{1}{10} = .1 = 10\%$

$\frac{1}{5} = \frac{2}{10} = .2 = .20 = 20\%$

$\frac{3}{10} = .3 = .30 = 30\%$

$\frac{2}{5} = \frac{4}{10} = .4 = .40 = 40\%$

$\frac{1}{2} = \frac{5}{10} = .5 = .50 = 50\%$

$\frac{3}{5} = \frac{6}{10} = .6 = .60 = 60\%$

$\frac{7}{10} = .7 = .70 = 70\%$

$\frac{4}{5} = \frac{8}{10} = .8 = .80 = 80\%$

$\frac{9}{10} = .9 = .90 = 90\%$

$\frac{1}{4} = \frac{25}{100} = .25 = 25\%$

$\frac{3}{4} = \frac{75}{100} = .75 = 75\%$

$\frac{1}{3} = .33\frac{1}{3} = 33\frac{1}{3}\%$

$\frac{2}{3} = .66\frac{2}{3} = 66\frac{2}{3}\%$

$\frac{1}{8} = .125 = .12\frac{1}{2} = 12\frac{1}{2}\%$

$\frac{3}{8} = .375 = .37\frac{1}{2} = 37\frac{1}{2}\%$

$\frac{5}{8} = .625 = .62\frac{1}{2} = 62\frac{1}{2}\%$

$\frac{7}{8} = .875 = .87\frac{1}{2} = 87\frac{1}{2}\%$

$\frac{1}{6} = .16\frac{2}{3} = 16\frac{2}{3}\%$

$\frac{5}{6} = .83\frac{1}{3} = 83\frac{1}{3}\%$

$1 = 1.00 = 100\%$

$2 = 2.00 = 200\%$

$3\frac{1}{2} = 3.5 = 3.50 = 350\%$

MEASURES

Customary System, or English System

Length
12 inches (in) = 1 foot (ft)
3 feet = 1 yard (yd)
36 inches = 1 yard
1,760 yards = 1 mile (mi)
5,280 feet = 1 mile

Area
144 square inches (sq in) = 1 square foot (sq ft)
9 square feet = 1 square yard (sq yd)

Weight
16 ounces (oz) = 1 pound (lb)
2000 pounds = 1 ton (T)

Capacity
2 cups = 1 pint (pt)
2 pints = 1 quart (qt)
4 quarts = 1 gallon (gal)
4 pecks = 1 bushel

Time
365 days = 1 year
52 weeks = 1 year
10 years = 1 decade
100 years = 1 century

Metric System, or The International System of Units
(SI, Le Système International d'Unités)

Length—meter
Kilometer (km) = 1000 meters (m)
Hectometer (hm) = 100 meters
Dekameter (dam) = 10 meters

Meter
10 decimeters (dm) = 1 meter
100 centimeters (cm) = 1 meter
1000 millimeters (mm) = 1 meter

Volume—liter
Common measures
1000 milliliters (ml, or mL) = 1 liter (l, or L)
1000 liters = 1 kiloliter (kl, or kL)

Mass—gram
Common measures
1000 milligrams (mg) = 1 gram (g)
1000 grams = 1 kilogram (kg)
1000 kilograms = 1 metric ton (t)

Some Approximations
Meter is a little more than a yard
Kilometer is about .6 mile
Kilogram is about 2.2 pounds
Liter is slightly more than a quart

MATH WORDS AND PHRASES

Words that signal an operation:

ADDITION	*MULTIPLICATION*
● Sum	● Of
● Total	● Product
● Plus	● Times
● Increase	● At (Sometimes)
● More than	● Total (Sometimes)
● Greater than	

SUBTRACTION	*DIVISION*
• Difference	• Quotient
• Less	• Divisor
• Decreased	• Dividend
• Reduced	• Ratio
• Fewer	• Parts
• Have left	

MATHEMATICAL PROPERTIES AND BASIC STATISTICS

Some Properties (Axioms) of Addition

• *Commutative* means that the *order* does not make any difference.

$$2 + 3 = 3 + 2$$
$$a + b = b + a$$

NOTE: Commutative does *not* hold for subtraction.

$$3 - 1 \neq 1 - 3$$
$$a - b \neq b - a$$

• *Associative* means that the *grouping* does not make any difference.

$$(2 + 3) + 4 = 2 + (3 + 4)$$
$$(a + b) + c = a + (b + c)$$

The grouping has changed (parentheses moved), but the sides are still equal.

NOTE: Associative does *not* hold for subtraction.

$$4 - (3 - 1) \neq (4 - 3) - 1$$
$$a - (b - c) \neq (a - b) - c$$

• The *identity element* for addition is 0. Any number added to 0 gives the original number.

$$3 + 0 = 3$$
$$a + 0 = a$$

• The *additive inverse* is the opposite (negative) of the number. Any number plus its additive inverse equals 0 (the identity).

$$3 + (-3) = 0; \text{ therefore 3 and } -3 \text{ are inverses}$$
$$-2 + 2 = 0; \text{ therefore } -2 \text{ and 2 are inverses}$$
$$a + (-a) = 0; \text{ therefore a and } -a \text{ are inverses}$$

Some Properties (Axioms) of Multiplication

- *Commutative* means that the *order* does not make any difference.

$$2 \times 3 = 3 \times 2$$
$$a \times b = b \times a$$

NOTE: Commutative does *not* hold for division.

$$2 \div 4 \neq 4 \div 2$$

- *Associative* means that the *grouping* does not make any difference.

$$(2 \times 3) \times 4 = 2 \times (3 \times 4)$$
$$(a \times b) \times c = a \times (b \times c)$$

The grouping has changed (parentheses moved), but the sides are still equal.

NOTE: Associative does *not* hold for division.

$$(8 \div 4) \div 2 \neq 8 \div (4 \div 2)$$

- The *identity element* for multiplication is 1. Any number multiplied by 1 gives the original number.

$$3 \times 1 = 3$$
$$a \times 1 = a$$

- The *multiplicative inverse* is the reciprocal of the number. Any number multiplied by its reciprocal equals 1.

$$2 \times \tfrac{1}{2} = 1; \text{ therefore 2 and } \tfrac{1}{2} \text{ are inverses}$$
$$a \times 1/a = 1; \text{ therefore a and } 1/a \text{ are inverses}$$

A Property of Two Operations

- The *distributive property* is the process of distributing the number on the outside of the parentheses to each number on the inside.

$$2(3 + 4) = 2(3) + 2(4)$$
$$a(b + c) = a(b) + a(c)$$

NOTE: You cannot use the distributive property with only one operation.

$$3(4 \times 5 \times 6) \neq 3(4) \times 3(5) \times 3(6)$$
$$a(bcd) \neq a(b) \times a(c) \times a(d) \text{ or } (ab)\,(ac)\,(ad)$$

Some Basic Terms in Statistics

- To find the arithmetic *mean,* or average, simply total the numbers and divide by the number of numbers.

  Find the arithmetic mean of 3, 5, 6, 7, and 9. The total is: $3 + 5 + 6 + 7 + 9 = 30$. Then divide 30 by 5, giving a mean, or average, of 6.

- To find the *mode,* look for the most frequently occurring score or measure.

  Find the mode of these scores: 3, 5, 5, 5, 6, 7. The mode is 5, since it appears most. If there are two modes, distribution of scores is called *bimodal.*

- To find the *median,* arrange the scores or numbers in order by size. Then find the middle score or number.

  Find the median of these scores: 2, 5, 7, 3, 6. First arrange them in order by size: 7, 6, 5, 3, 2. The middle score is 5; therefore the median is 5. If the number of scores is even, take the average of the two middle scores. Find the median of these scores: 2, 5, 7, 4, 3, 6. First arrange them in order by size: 7, 6, 5, 4, 3, 2. The two middle numbers are 4 and 5; therefore the median is $4\frac{1}{2}$.

- The *range* of a group of scores or numbers is calculated by subtracting the smallest from the largest.

  Find the range of the scores 3, 2, 7, 9, 12. The range is $12 - 2 = 10$.

ARITHMETIC

ARITHMETIC DIAGNOSTIC TEST

Questions

1. $6 = ?/4$

2. Change $5\frac{3}{4}$ to an improper fraction.

3. Change $\frac{32}{6}$ to a whole number or mixed number in lowest terms.

4. $\frac{2}{5} + \frac{3}{5} =$

5. $\frac{1}{3} + \frac{1}{4} + \frac{1}{2} =$

6. $1\frac{3}{8} + 2\frac{5}{6} =$

7. $7/9 - 5/9 =$

8. $11 - 2/3 =$

9. $6\frac{1}{4} - 3\frac{3}{4} =$

10. $\frac{1}{6} \times \frac{1}{6} =$

11. $2\frac{3}{8} \times 1\frac{5}{6} =$

12. $\frac{1}{4} \div \frac{3}{2} =$

13. $2\frac{3}{7} \div 1\frac{1}{4} =$

14. $.07 + 1.2 + .471 =$

15. $.45 - .003 =$

16. $\$78.24 - \$31.68 =$

17. $.5 \times .5 =$

18. $8.001 \times 2.3 =$

19. $.7\overline{)\,.147}$

20. $.002\overline{)\,12}$

21. $\frac{1}{3}$ of $\$7.20 =$

22. Circle the larger number: 7.9 or 4.35

23. 39 out of 100 means:

24. Change 4% to a decimal.

25. 46% of 58 =

26. Change .009 to a percent.

27. Change 12.5% to a fraction.

28. Change $\frac{3}{8}$ to a percent.

29. Is 93 prime?

30. What is the percent increase of a rise in temperature from 80° to 100°?

31. Average 0, 8, and 10

32. $8^2 =$

33. Approximate $\sqrt{30}$

Answers

1. 24	18. 18.4023
2. $^{23}/_4$	19. .21
3. $5^2/_6$ or $5^1/_3$	20. 6,000
4. $^5/_5$ or 1	21. $2.40
5. $^{13}/_{12}$ or $1^1/_{12}$	22. 7.9
6. $4^5/_{24}$	23. 39% or $^{39}/_{100}$
7. $^2/_9$	24. .04
8. $10^1/_3$	25. 26.68
9. $2^2/_4$ or $2^1/_2$	26. .9% or $^9/_{10}$%
10. $^1/_{36}$	27. $^{125}/_{1000}$ or $^1/_8$
11. $^{209}/_{48}$ or $4^{17}/_{48}$	28. 37.5% or $37^1/_2$%
12. $^1/_6$	29. No
13. $^{68}/_{35}$ or $1^{33}/_{35}$	30. 25%
14. 1.741	31. 6
15. .447	32. 64
16. $46.56	33. 5.5 or $5^1/_2$
17. .25	

ARITHMETIC REVIEW

Rounding Off

To round off any number:

1. Underline the place value to which you're rounding off.
2. Look to the immediate right (one place) of your underlined place value.
3. Identify the number (the one to the right). If it is 5 or higher, round your underlined place value up 1. If the number (the one to the right) is 4 or less, leave your underlined place value as it is and change all the other numbers to its right to zeros. *For example:*

Round to the nearest thousands:

345,678   becomes 346,000
928,499   becomes 928,000

This works with decimals as well. Round to the nearest hundredth:

3.4678   becomes 3.47
298,435.083   becomes 298,435.08

Place Value

Each position in any number has *place value*. For instance, in the number 485, 4 is in the hundreds place, 8 is in the tens place, and 5 is in the ones place. Thus, place value is as follows:

3 , 0 9 2 , 3 4 5 , 8 7 6   4 3 6 2 9 7 0 2   etc.

billions · hundred millions · ten millions · millions · hundred thousands · ten thousands · thousands · hundreds · tens · ones · tenths · hundredths · thousandths · ten-thousandths · hundred-thousandths · millionths · ten-millionths · hundred-millionths

Fractions

Fractions consist of two numbers: a *numerator* (which is above the line) and a *denominator* (which is below the line).

$\dfrac{1\ \text{numerator}}{2\ \text{denominator}}$ or   numerator ½ denominator

The denominator lets us know the number of equal parts into which something is divided. The numerator tells us how many of these equal parts are contained in the fraction. Thus, if the fraction is ⅗ of a pie, then the denominator 5 tells us that the pie has been divided into 5 equal parts, of which 3 (numerator) are in the fraction.

Sometimes it helps to think of the dividing line (in the middle of a fraction) as meaning "out of." In other words, ⅗ would also mean 3 "out of" 5 equal pieces from the whole pie.

Common Fractions and Improper Fractions

A fraction like ³/₅, where the numerator is smaller than the denominator, is less than one. This kind of fraction is called a *common fraction*. But sometimes a fraction may be more than one. This is when the numerator is larger than the denominator. Thus, ¹²/₇ is more than one. This is called an *improper fraction*.

Mixed Numbers

When a term contains both a whole number (such as 3, 8, 25, etc.) and a fraction (such as ½, ¼, ¾, etc.), it is called a *mixed number*. For instance, 5¼ and 290¾ are both mixed numbers.

To change an improper fraction to a mixed number, you divide the denominator into the numerator. *For example:*

$$\frac{18}{5} = 3\tfrac{3}{5} \qquad 5\overline{)\,18\,} \begin{array}{r} 3 \\ \hline 18 \\ \underline{15} \\ 3 \end{array}$$

To change a mixed number to an improper fraction, you multiply the denominator times the whole number, add in the numerator, and put the total over the original denominator. *For example:*

$$4\tfrac{1}{2} = \tfrac{9}{2} \qquad 2 \times 4 + 1 = 9$$

Reducing Fractions

A fraction must be reduced to *lowest terms*. This is done by dividing both the numerator and denominator by the largest number that will divide evenly into both. For example, ¹⁴/₁₆ is reduced by dividing both terms by 2, thus giving us ⅞. Likewise, ²⁰/₂₅ is reduced to ⅘ by dividing both numerator and denominator by 5.

Adding Fractions

To add fractions, you must first change all denominators to their *lowest common denominator* (LCD)—the lowest number that can be divided evenly by all the denominators in the problem. When you have all the denominators the same, you may add fractions by simply adding the numerators (the denominator remains the same). *For example:*

$$\frac{3}{8} = \frac{3}{8}$$
$$+ \frac{1}{2} = \frac{4}{8} \leftarrow \begin{cases} \text{one-half is} \\ \text{changed to} \\ \text{four-eighths} \end{cases}$$
$$\frac{7}{8}$$

$$\frac{1}{4} = \frac{3}{12} \searrow \begin{cases} \text{change both} \\ \text{fractions to} \\ \text{LCD of 12} \end{cases}$$
$$+ \frac{1}{3} = \frac{4}{12} \nearrow$$
$$\frac{7}{12}$$

In the first example, we changed the $\frac{1}{2}$ to $\frac{4}{8}$ because 8 is the lowest common denominator, and then we added the numerators 3 and 4 to get $\frac{7}{8}$.

In the second example, we had to change both fractions to get the lowest common denominator of 12, and then we added the numerators to get $\frac{7}{12}$. Of course, if the denominators are already the same, just add the numerators. *For example:*

$$\frac{6}{11} + \frac{3}{11} = \frac{9}{11}$$

Adding Mixed Numbers

To add mixed numbers, the same rule (find the LCD) applies, but make sure that you always add the whole numbers to get your final answer. *For example:*

$$2\frac{1}{2} = 2\frac{2}{4} \leftarrow \begin{cases} \text{one-half is changed} \\ \text{to two-fourths} \end{cases}$$
$$+ 3\frac{1}{4} = 3\frac{1}{4}$$
$$5\frac{3}{4} \quad \begin{cases} \text{remember to add the} \\ \text{whole numbers} \end{cases}$$

Subtracting Fractions

To subtract fractions, the same rule (find the LCD) applies, except that you subtract the numerators. *For example:*

$$\frac{7}{8} = \frac{7}{8}$$
$$- \frac{1}{4} = \frac{2}{8}$$
$$\frac{5}{8}$$

$$\frac{3}{4} = \frac{9}{12}$$
$$- \frac{1}{3} = \frac{4}{12}$$
$$\frac{5}{12}$$

Subtracting Mixed Numbers

When you subtract mixed numbers, sometimes you may have to "borrow" from the whole number, just like you sometimes borrow from the next column when subtracting ordinary numbers. *For example:*

$$\begin{array}{r} 4\ \ 11 \\ 6\cancel{5}\cancel{1} \\ -\ 129 \\ \hline 522 \end{array} \qquad \begin{array}{r} 3\%_6 \\ \cancel{4}^1\!/_6 \\ -\ 2\%_6 \\ \hline 1\%_6 = 1\%_3 \end{array}$$

you borrowed 1
from the 10's
column

you borrowed one in
the form %_6 from
the 1's column

To subtract a mixed number from a whole number, you have to "borrow" from the whole number. *For example:*

$$\begin{array}{r} 6\ \ = 5\%_5 \\ -\ 3\%_5 = 3\%_5 \\ \hline 2\%_5 \end{array}$$

borrow one in the form of %_5 from the 6

remember to subtract the remaining whole numbers

Multiplying Fractions

Simply multiply the numerators, then multiply the denominators. Reduce to lowest terms if necessary. *For example:*

$$\%_3 \times \%_{12} = {}^{10}\!/_{36} \qquad \text{reduce } {}^{10}\!/_{36} \text{ to } \%_{18}$$

This answer had to be reduced as it wasn't in lowest terms.

Canceling when multiplying fractions: You could first have "canceled." That would have eliminated the need to reduce your answer. To cancel, find a number that divides evenly into one numerator and one denominator. In this case, 2 will divide evenly into 2 in the numerator (it goes in one time) and 12 in the denominator (it goes in 6 times). *Thus:*

$$\frac{\overset{1}{\cancel{2}}}{3} \times \frac{5}{\underset{6}{\cancel{12}}} =$$

Now that you've canceled, you can multiply out as you did before.

$$\frac{\overset{1}{\cancel{2}}}{3} \times \frac{5}{\underset{6}{\cancel{12}}} = \frac{5}{18}$$

Remember, you may cancel only when *multiplying* fractions.

Multiplying Mixed Numbers

To multiply mixed numbers, first change any mixed number to an improper fraction. Then multiply as previously shown. To change mixed numbers to improper fractions:

1. multiply the whole number by the denominator of the fraction
2. add this to the numerator of the fraction
3. this is now your numerator
4. the denominator remains the same

$$3\tfrac{1}{3} \times 2\tfrac{1}{4} = \tfrac{10}{3} \times \tfrac{9}{4} = \tfrac{90}{12} = 7\tfrac{6}{12} = 7\tfrac{1}{2}$$

Then change the answer, if in improper fraction form, back to a mixed number and reduce if necessary.

Dividing Fractions

To divide fractions, invert (turn upside down) the second fraction and multiply. Then reduce if necessary. *For example:*

$$\frac{1}{6} \div \frac{1}{5} = \frac{1}{6} \times \frac{5}{1} = \frac{5}{6} \qquad \frac{1}{6} \div \frac{1}{3} = \frac{1}{6} \times \frac{3}{1} = \frac{3}{6} = \frac{1}{2}$$

Simplifying Fractions

If either numerator or denominator consists of several numbers, these numbers must be combined into one number. Then reduce if necessary. *For example:*

$$\frac{28 + 14}{26 + 17} = \frac{42}{43} \quad \text{or}$$

$$\frac{\dfrac{1}{4} + \dfrac{1}{2}}{\dfrac{1}{3} + \dfrac{1}{4}} = \frac{\dfrac{1}{4} + \dfrac{2}{4}}{\dfrac{4}{12} + \dfrac{3}{12}} = \frac{\dfrac{3}{4}}{\dfrac{7}{12}} = \frac{3}{4} \times \frac{12}{7} = \frac{36}{28} = \frac{9}{7} = 1\frac{2}{7}$$

Decimals

Fractions may also be written in decimal form by using a symbol called a *decimal point*. All numbers to the left of the decimal point are whole numbers. All numbers to the right of the decimal point are fractions with denominators of only 10, 100, 1,000, 10,000, etc., as follows:

$$.6 = \frac{6}{10} = \frac{3}{5}$$

$$.7 = \frac{7}{10}$$

$$.07 = \frac{7}{100}$$

$$.007 = \frac{7}{1000}$$

$$.0007 = \frac{7}{10,000}$$

$$.00007 = \frac{7}{100,000}$$

$$.25 = \frac{25}{100} = \frac{1}{4}$$

Adding and Subtracting Decimals

To add or subtract decimals, just line up the decimal points and then add or subtract in the same manner you would add or subtract regular numbers. *For example:*

$$23.6 + 1.75 + 300.002 = \begin{array}{r} 23.6 \\ 1.75 \\ 300.002 \\ \hline 325.352 \end{array}$$

Adding in zeros can make the problem easier to work:

$$\begin{array}{r} 23.600 \\ 1.750 \\ 300.002 \\ \hline 325.352 \end{array}$$

and

$$54.26 - 1.1 = \begin{array}{r} 54.26 \\ -\ 1.10 \\ \hline 53.16 \end{array}$$

and

$$78.9 - 37.43 = \begin{array}{r} \overset{8}{78.\cancel{9}{}^{1}0} \\ -\ 37.4\ 3 \\ \hline 41.4\ 7 \end{array}$$

Whole numbers can have decimal points to their right. *For example:*

$$17 - 8.43 = \begin{array}{r} \overset{6\ \ 9}{1\cancel{7}.\cancel{0}{}^{1}0} \\ -\ 8.4\ 3 \\ \hline 8.5\ 7 \end{array}$$

Multiplying Decimals

To multiply decimals, just multiply as usual. Then count the total number of digits above the line which are to the right of all decimal points. Place your decimal point in your answer so there is the same number of digits to the right of it as there was above the line. *For example:*

$$
\begin{array}{r}
40.012 \leftarrow 3 \text{ digits} \\
\times \quad 3.1 \leftarrow 1 \text{ digit} \\
\hline
40012 \\
120036 \\
\hline
124.0372 \leftarrow 4 \text{ digits}
\end{array}
$$

total of 4 digits above the line
that are to the right of the decimal point

decimal point placed so there is
same number of digits to the right
of the decimal point

Dividing Decimals

Dividing decimals is the same as dividing other numbers, except that if the divisor (the number you're dividing by) has a decimal, move it to the right as many places as necessary until it is a whole number. Then move the decimal point in the dividend (the number being divided into) the same number of places. Sometimes you may have to add zeros to the dividend (the number inside the division sign).

$$
1.25\overline{)5.} = 125\overline{)500.}^{4.} \qquad \text{or} \qquad 0.002\overline{)26.} = 2\overline{)26000.}^{13000.}
$$

Changing Decimals to Percents

To change decimals to percents:

1. move the decimal point two places to the right and
2. insert a percent sign

$$.75 = 75\% \qquad .05 = 5\%$$

Changing Percents to Decimals

To change percents to decimals:

1. eliminate the percent sign and
2. move the decimal point two places to the left (sometimes adding zeros will be necessary)

$$75\% = .75 \qquad 5\% = .05$$
$$23\% = .23 \qquad .2\% = .002$$

Changing Fractions to Percents

To change a fraction to a percent:

1. multiply by 100 and
2. insert a percent sign

$$1/2 = 1/2 \times 100 = 100/2 = 50\%$$
$$2/5 = 2/5 \times 100 = 200/5 = 40\%$$

Changing Percents to Fractions

To change percents to fractions:

1. divide the percent by 100,
2. eliminate the percent sign, and
3. reduce if necessary

$$60\% = 60/100 = 3/5 \qquad 13\% = 13/100$$

Changing Fractions to Decimals

To change a fraction to a decimal simply do what the operation says. In other words, $^{13}/_{20}$ means 13 divided by 20. So do just that (insert decimal points and zeros accordingly):

$$20\overline{)13.00}^{.65} = .65 \qquad 5/8 = 8\overline{)5.000}^{.625} = .625$$

Changing Decimals to Fractions

To change a decimal to a fraction:

1. move the decimal point two places to the right,
2. put that number over 100, and
3. reduce if necessary

$$.65 = 65/100 = 13/20$$
$$.05 = 5/100 = 1/20$$
$$.75 = 75/100 = 3/4$$

Read it: .8
Write it: 8/10
Reduce it: 4/5

Finding Percent of a Number

To determine percent of a number, change the percent to a fraction or decimal (whichever is easier for you) and multiply. Remember, the word "of" means multiply.

What is 20% of 80?

$20/100 \times 80 = 1600/100 = 16$ or $.20 \times 80 = 16.00 = 16$

What is 12% of 50?

$12/100 \times 50 = 600/100 = 6$ or $.12 \times 50 = 6.00 = 6$

What is 1/2% of 18?

$\dfrac{1/2}{100} \times 18 = 1/200 \times 18 = 18/200 = 9/100$ or $.005 \times 18 = .09$

Other Applications of Percent

Turn the question word-for-word into an equation. For "what" substitute the letter x; for "is" substitute an *equal sign;* for "of" substitute a *multiplication sign.* Change percents to decimals or fractions, whichever you find easier. Then solve the equation.

18 is what percent of 90?

$$18 = x(90)$$
$$18/90 = x$$
$$1/5 = x$$
$$20\% = x$$

10 is 50% of what number?

$$10 = .50(x)$$
$$10/.50 = x$$
$$20 = x$$

What is 15% of 60?

$$x = 15/100 \times 60 = 90/10 = 9$$
$$\text{or} \quad .15(60) = 9$$

Finding Percentage Increase or Percentage Decrease

To find the *percentage change* (increase or decrease), use this formula:

$$\frac{\text{change}}{\text{starting point}} \times 100 = \text{percentage change}$$

For example:

What is the percentage decrease of a $500 item on sale for $400?

Change: 500 − 400 = 100

$$\frac{\text{change}}{\text{starting point}} \times 100 = \frac{100}{500} \times 100 = \frac{1}{5} \times 100 = 20\% \text{ decrease}$$

What is the percentage increase of Jon's salary if it went from $150 a month to $200 a month?

Change: 200 − 150 = 50

$$\frac{\text{change}}{\text{starting point}} \times 100 = \frac{50}{150} \times 100 = \frac{1}{3} \times 100 = 33\frac{1}{3}\% \text{ increase}$$

Prime Numbers

A *prime number* is a number that can be evenly divided by only itself and one. For example, 19 is a prime number because it can be evenly divided only by 19 and 1, but 21 is not a prime number because 21 can be evenly divided by other numbers (3 and 7).

The only even prime number is 2; thereafter any even number may be divided evenly by 2. Zero and one are *not* prime numbers. The first ten prime numbers are 2, 3, 5, 7, 11, 13, 17, 19, 23, and 29.

Arithmetic Mean, or Average

To find the *average* of a group of numbers:
1. add them up and
2. divide by the number of items you added

For example:

What is the average of 10, 20, 35, 40, and 45?

$$10 + 20 + 35 + 40 + 45 = 150$$
$$150 \div 5 = 30$$
The average is 30

What is the average of 0, 12, 18, 20, 31, and 45?

$$0 + 12 + 18 + 20 + 31 + 45 = 126$$
$$126 \div 6 = 21$$
The average is 21

What is the average of 25, 27, 27, and 27?

$$25 + 27 + 27 + 27 = 106$$
$$106 \div 4 = 26\frac{1}{2}$$
The average is $26\frac{1}{2}$

Median

A *median* is simply the middle number of a list of numbers after it has been written in order. (If the list contains an even number of items, average the two middle numbers to get the median.) For example, in the following list—3, 4, 6, 9, 21, 24, 56—the number 9 is the median.

Mode

The *mode* is simply the number most frequently listed in a group of numbers. For example, in the following group—5, 9, 7, 3, 9, 4, 6, 9, 7, 9, 2—the mode is 9 because it appears more often than any other number.

Squares and Square Roots

To *square* a number just multiply it by itself. For example, 6 squared (written 6^2) is 6 × 6 or 36. 36 is called a perfect square (the square of a whole number). Any exponent means multiply by itself that many times. *For example:*

$$5^3 = 5 \times 5 \times 5 = 125$$
$$8^2 = 8 \times 8 = 64$$

Remember, $x^1 = x$ and $x^0 = 1$ when x is any number (other than 0).

Following is a list of perfect squares:

$0^2 = 0$	$5^2 = 25$	$9^2 = 81$
$1^2 = 1$	$6^2 = 36$	$10^2 = 100$
$2^2 = 4$	$7^2 = 49$	$11^2 = 121$
$3^2 = 9$	$8^2 = 64$	$12^2 = 144$ etc.
$4^2 = 16$		

Square roots of nonperfect squares can be approximated. Two approximations you may wish to remember are:

$$\sqrt{2} \approx 1.4$$
$$\sqrt{3} \approx 1.7$$

To find the *square root* of a number, you want to find some number that when multiplied by itself gives you the original number. In other words, to find the square root of 25 you want to find the number that when multiplied by itself gives you 25. The square root of 25, then, is 5. The symbol for square root is $\sqrt{\ }$. Following is a list of perfect (whole number) square roots:

$$\sqrt{0} = 0 \qquad \sqrt{16} = 4 \qquad \sqrt{64} = 8$$
$$\sqrt{1} = 1 \qquad \sqrt{25} = 5 \qquad \sqrt{81} = 9$$
$$\sqrt{4} = 2 \qquad \sqrt{36} = 6 \qquad \sqrt{100} = 10 \quad \text{etc.}$$
$$\sqrt{9} = 3 \qquad \sqrt{49} = 7$$

Square Root Rules

Two numbers multiplied under a radical (square root) sign equal the product of the two square roots. *For example:*

$$\sqrt{(4)(25)} = \sqrt{4} \times \sqrt{25} = 2 \times 5 = 10 \text{ or } \sqrt{100} = 10$$

and likewise with division:

$$\sqrt{\frac{64}{4}} = \frac{\sqrt{64}}{\sqrt{4}} = \frac{8}{2} = 4 \text{ or } \sqrt{16} = 4$$

Addition and subtraction, however, are different. The numbers must be combined under the radical before any computation of square roots may be done. *For example:*

$$\sqrt{10 + 6} = \sqrt{16} = 4 \qquad (\sqrt{10 + 6} \text{ does } not \text{ equal } [\neq] \; \sqrt{10} + \sqrt{6})$$

or $\sqrt{93 - 12} = \sqrt{81} = 9$

Approximating Square Roots

To find a square root which will not be a whole number, you should approximate. *For example:*

Approximate $\sqrt{57}$

Because $\sqrt{57}$ is between $\sqrt{49}$ and $\sqrt{64}$, it will fall somewhere between 7 and 8. And because 57 is just about halfway between 49 and 64, $\sqrt{57}$ is therefore approximately $7\frac{1}{2}$.

Approximate $\sqrt{83}$

$$\sqrt{81} < \sqrt{83} < \sqrt{100}$$
$$9 \qquad\qquad\quad 10$$

Since $\sqrt{83}$ is slightly more than $\sqrt{81}$ (whose square root is 9), then $\sqrt{83}$ is a little more than 9. Since 83 is only two steps up from the nearest perfect square (81) and 17 steps to the next perfect square (100), then 83 is $\frac{2}{19}$ of the way to 100.

$$\tfrac{2}{19} \simeq \tfrac{2}{20} = \tfrac{1}{10} = .1$$

Therefore: $\sqrt{83} \simeq 9.1$

Simplifying Square Roots

To simplify numbers under a radical (square root sign):

1. factor the number to two numbers, one (or more) of which is a perfect square,
2. then take the square root of the perfect square(s), and
3. leave the others under the $\sqrt{}$

Simplify $\sqrt{75}$

$$\sqrt{75} = \sqrt{25 \times 3} = \sqrt{25} \times \sqrt{3} = 5\sqrt{3}$$

Simplify $\sqrt{200}$

$$\sqrt{200} = \sqrt{100 \times 2} = \sqrt{100} \times \sqrt{2} = 10\sqrt{2}$$

Simplify $\sqrt{900}$

$$\sqrt{900} = \sqrt{100 \times 9} = \sqrt{100} \times \sqrt{9} = 10 \times 3 = 30$$

Signed Numbers (Positive Numbers and Negative Numbers)

On a number line, numbers to the right of 0 are positive. Numbers to the left of 0 are negative, as follows:

Given any two numbers on a number line, the one on the right is always larger, regardless of its sign (positive or negative).

Addition of Signed Numbers

When adding two numbers with the same sign (either both positive or both negative), add the numbers and keep the same sign. *For example:*

$$\begin{array}{r} +5 \\ +\ +7 \\ \hline +12 \end{array} \qquad \begin{array}{r} -8 \\ +\ -3 \\ \hline -11 \end{array}$$

When adding two numbers with different signs (one positive and one negative), subtract the numbers and keep the sign from the larger one. *For example:*

$$
\begin{array}{r}
+5 \\
+ \ -7 \\
\hline
-2
\end{array}
\qquad
\begin{array}{r}
-59 \\
+ \ +72 \\
\hline
+13
\end{array}
$$

Subtraction of Signed Numbers

To subtract positive and/or negative numbers, just change the sign of the number being subtracted and then add. *For example:*

$$
\begin{array}{r}
+12 \\
- \ +4 \\
\hline
\end{array}
\quad
\begin{array}{r}
+12 \\
+ \ -4 \\
\hline
+8
\end{array}
\quad
\begin{array}{r}
-19 \\
- \ +6 \\
\hline
\end{array}
\quad
\begin{array}{r}
-19 \\
+ \ -6 \\
\hline
-25
\end{array}
$$

$$
\begin{array}{r}
-14 \\
- \ -4 \\
\hline
\end{array}
\quad
\begin{array}{r}
-14 \\
+ \ +4 \\
\hline
-10
\end{array}
\quad
\begin{array}{r}
+20 \\
- \ -3 \\
\hline
\end{array}
\quad
\begin{array}{r}
+20 \\
+ \ +3 \\
\hline
+23
\end{array}
$$

Multiplying and Dividing Signed Numbers

To multiply or divide signed numbers, treat them just like regular numbers but remember this rule: An odd number of negative signs will produce a negative answer. An even number of negative signs will produce a positive answer. *For example:*

$$(-3)(+8)(-5)(-1)(-2) = +240$$

$$(-3)(+8)(-1)(-2) = -48$$

$$\frac{-64}{-2} = +32$$

$$\frac{-64}{2} = -32$$

Parentheses

Parentheses are used to group numbers. Everything inside parentheses must be done before any other operations. *For example:*

$$50(2 + 6) = 50(8) = 400$$

When a parenthesis is preceded by a minus sign, change the minus to a plus by changing all the signs in front of each term inside the parentheses. Then remove the parentheses. *For example:*

$$6 - (-3 + a - 2b + c) =$$
$$6 + (+3 - a + 2b - c) =$$
$$6 + 3 - a + 2b - c = 9 - a + 2b - c$$

Order of Operations

If multiplication, division, powers, addition, parentheses, etc., are all contained in one problem, the order of operations is as follows:

1. parentheses
2. powers and square roots
3. multiplication ⎫ whichever comes first, left to right
4. division   ⎭
5. addition   ⎫ whichever comes first, left to right
6. subtraction ⎭

For example:

$$10 - 3 \times 6 + 10^2 + (6 + 1) \times 4 =$$
$$10 - 3 \times 6 + 10^2 + (7) \times 4 = \quad \text{(parentheses first)}$$
$$10 - 3 \times 6 + 100 + (7) \times 4 = \quad \text{(powers next)}$$
$$10 - 18 + 100 + 28 = \quad \text{(multiplication)}$$
$$-8 + 100 + 28 = \quad \text{(addition/subtraction, left to right)}$$
$$92 + 28 = 120$$

An easy way to remember the order of operations *after parentheses* is: Please My Dear Aunt Sarah (Powers, Multiplication, Division, Addition, Subtraction).

ALGEBRA

ALGEBRA DIAGNOSTIC TEST

Questions

1. Solve for x: $x + 5 = 17$

2. Solve for x: $4x + 9 = 21$

3. Solve for x: $5x + 7 = 3x - 9$

4. Solve for x: $mx - n = y$

5. Solve for x: $\dfrac{r}{x} = \dfrac{s}{t}$

6. Solve for y: $\dfrac{3}{7} = \dfrac{y}{8}$

7. Evaluate: $3x^2 + 5y + 7$ if $x = -2$ and $y = 3$

8. Simplify: $8xy^2 + 3xy + 4xy^2 - 2xy =$

9. Simplify: $6x^2(4x^3y) =$

10. Simplify: $(5x + 2z) + (3x - 4z) =$

11. Simplify: $(4x - 7z) - (3x - 4z) =$

12. Factor: $36y^2 - 24y$

13. Solve for x: $2x + 3 \le 11$

14. Solve for x: $3x + 4 \ge 5x - 8$

Answers

1. $x = 12$

2. $x = 3$

3. $x = -8$

4. $x = (y + n)/m$

5. $x = \dfrac{rt}{s}$

6. $y = {}^{24}/_7$ or $3\frac{3}{7}$

7. 34

8. $12xy^2 + xy$

9. $24x^5y$

10. $8x - 2z$

11. $x - 3z$

12. $12y(3y - 2)$

13. $x \le 4$

14. $x \le 6$

ALGEBRA REVIEW

Equations

An *equation* is a relationship between numbers and/or symbols. It helps to remember that an equation is like a balance scale, with the equal sign (=) being the fulcrum, or center. Thus, if you do the *same thing to both sides* of the equal sign (say, add 5 to each side), the equation will still be balanced. To solve the equation $x - 5 = 23$, you must get x by itself on one side; therefore, add 5 to both sides:

$$x - 5 = 23$$
$$\underline{+ 5 + 5}$$
$$x \quad = 28$$

In the same manner, you may subtract, multiply, or divide *both* sides of an equation by the same (nonzero) number, and the equation will not change. Sometimes you may have to use more than one step to solve for an unknown. *For example:*

$$3x + 4 = 19$$

Subtract 4 from both sides to get the 3x by itself on one side:

$$3x + 4 = 19$$
$$\underline{- 4 - 4}$$
$$3x \quad = 15$$

Then divide both sides by 3 to get x:

$$\frac{3x}{3} = \frac{15}{3}$$

$$x = 5$$

Remember: Solving an equation is using opposite operations, until the letter is on a side by itself (for addition, subtract; for multiplication, divide, etc.).

Understood Multiplying

When two or more letters, or a number and letters, are written next to each other, they are understood to be *multiplied*. Thus 8x means 8 times x. Or ab means a times b. Or 18ab means 18 times a times b.

Parentheses also represent multiplication. Thus (a)b means a times b. A raised dot also means multiplication. Thus 6·5 means 6 times 5.

Literal Equations

Literal equations have no numbers, only symbols (letters). *For example:*

$$\text{Solve for Q: } QP - X = Y$$

First add X to both sides:

$$QP - X = Y$$
$$\underline{+ X \quad + X}$$
$$QP \quad = Y + X$$

Then divide both sides by P: $\dfrac{QP}{P} = \dfrac{Y + X}{P}$

$$Q = \dfrac{Y + X}{P}$$

Again opposite operations were used to isolate Q.

Cross Multiplying

Solve for x: $\dfrac{b}{x} = \dfrac{p}{q}$

To solve this equation quickly, you cross multiply. To cross multiply:

1. bring the denominators up next to the opposite side numerators and
2. multiply

$$\dfrac{b}{x} = \dfrac{p}{q}$$

$$bq = px$$

Then divide both sides by p to get x alone:

$$\dfrac{bq}{p} = \dfrac{px}{p}$$

$$\dfrac{bq}{p} = x \text{ or } x = \dfrac{bq}{p}$$

Cross multiplying can be used only when the format is: 2 fractions separated by an equal sign.

Proportions

Proportions are written as two fractions equal to each other.

Solve this proportion for x: $\dfrac{p}{q} = \dfrac{x}{y}$

This is read "p is to q as x is to y." Cross multiply and solve:

$$py = xq$$

$$\dfrac{py}{q} = \dfrac{xq}{q}$$

$$\dfrac{py}{q} = x \text{ or } x = \dfrac{py}{q}$$

Evaluating Expressions

To *evaluate* an expression, just insert the value for the unknowns and do the arithmetic. *For example:*

Evaluate: $2x^2 + 3y + 6$ if $x = 2$ and $y = 9$

$$2(2^2) + 3(9) + 6 =$$
$$2(4) + 27 + 6 =$$
$$8 + 27 + 6 = 41$$

Monomials and Polynomials

A *monomial* is an algebraic expression that consists of only one term. For instance, $9x$, $4a^2$, and $3mpxz^2$ are all monomials.

A *polynomial* consists of two or more terms; $x + y$, $y^2 - x^2$, and $x^2 + 3x + 5y^2$ are all polynomials.

Adding and Subtracting Monomials

To *add or subtract monomials,* follow the same rules as with regular signed numbers, provided that the *terms are alike:*

$$\begin{array}{r} 15x^2yz \\ -18x^2yz \\ \hline -3x^2yz \end{array} \qquad 3x + 2x = 5x$$

Multiplying and Dividing Monomials

To *multiply monomials,* add the exponents of the same terms:

$$(x^3)(x^4) = x^7$$

$$(x^2y)(x^3y^2) = x^5y^3$$

$$-4(m^2n)(-3m^4n^3) = 12m^6n^4 \text{ (multiply numbers)}$$

To *divide monomials,* subtract the exponents of the like terms:

$$\frac{y^{15}}{y^4} = y^{11} \qquad \frac{x^5y^2}{x^3y} = x^2y \qquad \frac{36a^4b^6}{-9ab} = -4a^3b^5$$

Remember: x is the same as x^1.

Adding and Subtracting Polynomials

To *add or subtract polynomials,* just arrange like terms in columns and then add or subtract:

Add:

$$a^2 + ab + b^2$$
$$3a^2 + 4ab - 2b^2$$
$$\overline{4a^2 + 5ab - b^2}$$

Subtract:

$$a^2 + b^2$$
$$- 2a^2 - b^2$$ $\longrightarrow$ $$a^2 + b^2$$
$$+ -2a^2 + b^2$$
$$\overline{-a^2 + 2b^2}$$

Multiplying Polynomials

To *multiply polynomials,* multiply each term in one polynomial by each term in the other polynomial. Then simplify if necessary:

$(3x + a)(2x - 2a) =$

$$
\begin{array}{r}
2x - 2a \\
\times\, 3x + a \\
\hline
+\, 2ax - 2a^2 \\
6x^2 - 6ax \\
\hline
6x^2 - 4ax - 2a^2
\end{array}
\qquad
\text{similar to}
\qquad
\begin{array}{r}
23 \\
\times\, 19 \\
\hline
207 \\
23 \\
\hline
437
\end{array}
$$

Factoring

To *factor* means to find two or more quantities whose product equals the original quantity. There are three kinds of factoring:

A. *Factoring out a common factor*

Factor: $2y^3 - 6y$

1. Find the largest common monomial factor of each term.
2. Divide the original polynomial by this factor to obtain the second factor. The second factor will be a polynomial. *For example:*

$$2y^3 - 6y = 2y(y^2 - 3)$$
$$x^5 - 4x^3 + x^2 = x^2(x^3 - 4x + 1)$$

B. *Factoring the difference between 2 squares*

Factor: $x^2 - 144$

1. Find the square root of the first term and the square root of the second term.
2. Express your answer as the product of: the sum of the quantities from step 1, times the difference of those quantities. *For example:*

$$x^2 - 144 = (x + 12)(x - 12)$$
$$a^2 - b^2 = (a + b)(a - b)$$

Inequalities

An *inequality* is a statement in which the relationships are not equal. Instead of using an equal sign (=) as in an equation, we use > (greater than) and < (less than), or ≥ (greater than or equal to) and ≤ (less than or equal to).

When working with inequalities, treat them exactly like equations, EXCEPT: if you multiply or divide both sides by a negative number, you must *reverse* the direction of the sign. *For example:*

$$\text{Solve for x: } 2x + 4 > 6$$

$$\begin{array}{r} 2x + 4 > 6 \\ -4 - 4 \\ \hline 2x \quad\;\; > 2 \end{array}$$

$$\frac{2x}{2} > \frac{2}{2}$$

$$x > 1$$

Solve for x: $-7x > 14$ (divide by -7 and reverse the sign)

$$\frac{-7x}{-7} < \frac{14}{-7}$$

$$x < -2$$

$3x + 2 \geq 5x - 10$ becomes $-2x \geq -12$ by opposite operations.
Divide both sides by -2 and reverse the sign.

$$\frac{-2x}{-2} \leq \frac{-12}{-2}$$

$$x \leq 6$$

GEOMETRY

GEOMETRY DIAGNOSTIC TEST

Questions

1. Name any angle of this triangle three different ways.

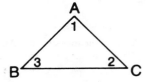

2. A(n)＿＿＿＿＿＿angle measures less than 90 degrees.

3. A(n)_____angle measures 90 degrees.

4. A(n)_____angle measures more than 90 degrees.

5. A(n) _____angle measures 180 degrees.

6. Two angles are complementary when their sum is _____.

7. Two angles are supplementary when their sum is _____.

8. In the diagram, find the measures of ∠a, ∠b, and ∠c.

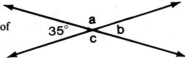

9. Lines that stay the same distance apart and never meet are called _____lines.

10. Lines that meet to form 90 degree angles are called_____lines.

11. A(n)_____triangle has three equal sides. Therefore, each interior angle measures_____.

Questions 12 and 13

12. In the triangle, $\overline{AC}$ must be smaller than_____inches.

13. In the triangle, which angle is smaller, ∠A or ∠C?

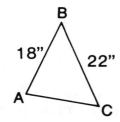

14. What is the measure of ∠ACD?

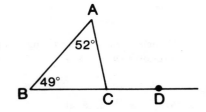

15. What is the length of $\overline{AC}$?

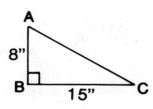

16. What is the length of $\overline{BC}$?

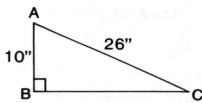

17. Name each of the following polygons:

(A) $\overline{AB} = \overline{BC} = \overline{AC}$
    $\angle A = \angle B = \angle C = 60°$

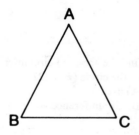

(B) $\overline{AB} = \overline{BC} = \overline{CD} = \overline{AD}$
    $\angle A = \angle B = \angle C = \angle D = 90°$

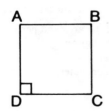

(C) $\overline{AB} \parallel \overline{DC}$
    $\overline{AB} = \overline{DC}$
    $\overline{AD} \parallel \overline{BC}$
    $\overline{AD} = \overline{BC}$
    $\angle A = \angle C$

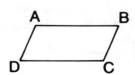

(D) $\overline{AB} = \overline{DC}$
$\overline{AD} = \overline{BC}$
$\angle A = \angle B = \angle C = \angle D = 90°$

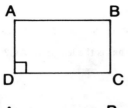

(E) $\overline{AB} \parallel \overline{DC}$

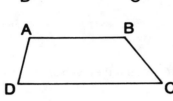

18. Fill in the blanks for circle R:
    (A) $\overline{RS}$ is called the _____.
    (B) $\overline{AB}$ is called the _____.
    (C) $\overline{CD}$ is called a _____.

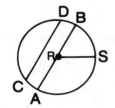

19. Find the area and circumference
    for the circle ($\pi \approx 22/7$):
    (A) area =
    (B) circumference =

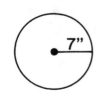

20. Find the area and perimeter
    of the figure:
    (A) area =
    (B) perimeter =

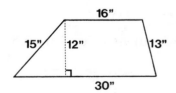

21. Find the area and perimeter of the
    figure (ABCD is a parallelogram):
    (A) area =
    (B) perimeter =

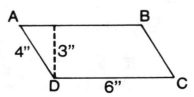

22. Find the volume of the figure
    if $V = (\pi r^2)\,h$
    (use 3.14 for π):

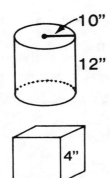

23. What is the surface area and
    volume of the cube?
    (A) surface area =
    (B) volume =

Answers

1. ∠3, ∠CBA, ∠ABC, ∠B
   ∠1, ∠BAC, ∠CAB, ∠A
   ∠2, ∠ACB, ∠BCA, ∠C

2. acute

3. right

4. obtuse

5. straight

6. 90°

7. 180°

8. a = 145°
   b = 35°
   c = 145°

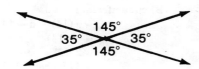

9. parallel

10. perpendicular

11. equilateral, 60°

12. 40 inches. Since $\overline{AB} + \overline{BC} = 40$ inches
    then $\overline{AC} < \overline{AB} + \overline{BC}$
    and $\overline{AC} < 40$ inches

13. ∠C must be the smaller angle, since it is opposite the shorter side $\overline{AB}$.

14. ∠ACD = 101°

15. $\overline{AC}$ = 17 inches

16. Since △ ABC is a right triangle, use the Pythagorean theorem:

$$a^2 + b^2 = c^2$$
$$10^2 + b^2 = 26^2$$
$$100 + b^2 = 676$$
$$b^2 = 576$$
$$b = 24''$$

17. (A) equilateral triangle   (D) rectangle
    (B) square   (E) trapezoid
    (C) parallelogram

18. (A) radius
    (B) diameter
    (C) chord

19. (A) area $= \pi r^2$
    $= \pi (7^2)$
    $= {}^{22}\!/_7 (7)(7)$
    $= 154$ square inches
    (B) circumference $= \pi d$
        $= \pi (14)$ $d = 14''$, since $r = 7''$
        $= {}^{22}\!/_7 (14)$
        $= 22(2)$
        $= 44$ inches

20. (A) area $= \frac{1}{2}(a + b)h$
        $= \frac{1}{2}(16 + 30)12$
        $= \frac{1}{2}(46)12$
        $= 23(12)$
        $= 276$ square inches
    (B) perimeter $= 16 + 13 + 30 + 15 = 74$ inches

21. (A) area $= bh$
        $= 6(3)$
        $= 18$ square inches

(B) perimeter = 6 + 4 + 6 + 4 = 20 inches

22. Volume = $(\pi r^2)h$
    = $(\pi \cdot 10^2)$ (12)
    = 3.14 (100) (12)
    = 314(12)
    = 3,768 cubic inches

23. **(A)** All six surfaces have an area of 4 × 4, or 16 square inches, since each surface is a square. Therefore, 16(6) = 96 square inches in the surface area.
    (B) Volume = side × side × side, or 4^3 = 64 cubic inches.

GEOMETRY REVIEW

Plane geometry is the study of shapes and figures in two dimensions (the plane).

Solid geometry is the study of shapes and figures in three dimensions.

A point is the most fundamental idea in geometry. It is represented by a dot and named by a capital letter.

Lines

● A straight *line* is the shortest distance between two points. It continues forever in both directions. A line consists of an infinite number of points. It is named by any two points on the line. The symbol ↔ written on top of the two letters is used to denote that line.

This is line AB:

It is written: $\overleftrightarrow{AB}$

A line may also be named by one small letter. The symbol would not be used.

This is line *l*:

● A *line segment* is a piece of a line. A line segment has two endpoints. It is named by its two endpoints. The symbol — written on top of the two letters is used to denote that line segment.

This is line segment CD:

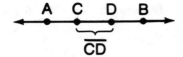

$$CD$$

It is written: $\overline{CD}$
Note that it is a piece of $\overleftrightarrow{AB}$.

- A *ray* has only one endpoint and continues forever in one direction. A ray could be thought of as a half-line. It is named by the letter of its endpoint and any other point on the ray. The symbol → written on top of the two letters is used to denote that ray.

This is ray AB:

It is written: $\overrightarrow{AB}$

This is ray BC:

It is written: $\overrightarrow{BC}$ or $\overleftarrow{CB}$
Note that the direction of the symbol is the direction of the ray.

Angles

- An *angle* is formed by two rays that start from the same point. That point is called the *vertex;* the rays are called the *sides* of the angle. An angle is measured in degrees. The degrees indicate the size of the angle, from one side to the other.

In the diagram, the angle is formed by rays $\overrightarrow{AB}$ and $\overrightarrow{AC}$. A is the vertex. $\overrightarrow{AB}$ and $\overrightarrow{AC}$ are the sides of the angle.

The symbol ∠ is used to denote an angle.

- An angle can be named in various ways:

  1. By the letter of the vertex—therefore, the angle above could be named ∠A.
  2. By the number (or small letter) in its interior—therefore, the angle above could be named ∠1.
  3. By the letters of the three points that formed it—therefore, the angle above could be named ∠BAC, or ∠CAB. The center letter is always the letter of the vertex.

Types of Angles

- *Adjacent angles* are any angles that share a common side and a common vertex.

In the diagram, ∠1 and ∠2 are adjacent angles.

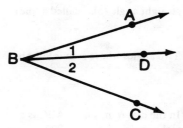

- A *right angle* has a measure of 90°. The symbol ∟ in the interior of an angle designates the fact that a right angle is formed.

In the diagram, ∠ABC is a right angle.

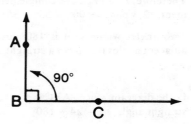

- Any angle whose measure is less than 90° is called an *acute angle*.

In the diagram, ∠b is acute.

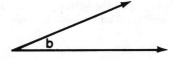

- Any angle whose measure is larger than 90°, but smaller than 180°, is called an *obtuse angle*.

In the diagram, ∠4 is an obtuse angle.

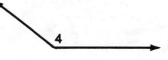

- A *straight angle* has a measure of 180°.

In the diagram, ∠BAC is a
straight angle (also called a line).

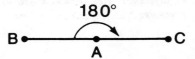

- Two angles whose sum is 90° are called *complementary angles*.

In the diagram, since ∠ABC is a
right angle, ∠1 + ∠2 = 90°.

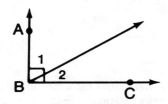

Therefore, ∠1 and ∠2 are complementary angles. If ∠1 = 55°, its complement, ∠2, would be: 90° − 55° = 35°.

- Two angles whose sum is 180° are called *supplementary angles*. Two
adjacent angles that form a straight line are supplementary.

In the diagram, since ∠ABC is a
straight angle, ∠3 + ∠4 = 180°.

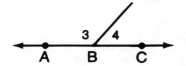

Therefore, ∠3 and ∠4 are supplementary angles. If ∠3 = 122°, its supple-
ment, ∠4, would be: 180° − 122° = 58°.

- A ray from the vertex of an angle that divides the angle into two equal
pieces is called an *angle bisector*.

In the diagram, $\overrightarrow{AB}$ is the angle
bisector of ∠CAD.

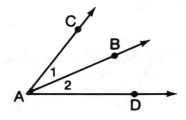

Therefore, ∠1 = ∠2.

- If two straight lines intersect, they do so at a point. Four angles are formed. Those angles opposite each other are called *vertical angles*. Those angles sharing a common side and a common vertex are, again, *adjacent angles*. Vertical angles are always equal.

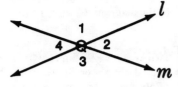

In the diagram, line *l* and line *m* intersect at point Q. $\angle 1$, $\angle 2$, $\angle 3$, and $\angle 4$ are formed.

$\angle 1$ and $\angle 3$ } are vertical
$\angle 2$ and $\angle 4$ } angles

$\angle 1$ and $\angle 2$ }
$\angle 2$ and $\angle 3$ } are adjacent
$\angle 3$ and $\angle 4$ } angles
$\angle 1$ and $\angle 4$ }

Therefore, $\begin{aligned}\angle 1 &= \angle 3\\ \angle 2 &= \angle 4\end{aligned}$

Types of Lines

- Two or more lines that cross each other at a point are called *intersecting lines*. That point would be on each of those lines.

In the diagram, lines *l* and *m* intersect at Q.

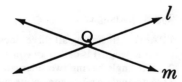

- Two lines that meet to form right angles (90°) are called *perpendicular lines*. The symbol ⊥ is used to denote perpendicular lines.

In the diagram, line *l* ⊥ line *m*.

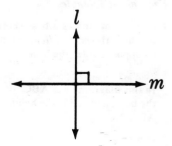

● Two or more lines that remain the same distance apart at all times are called *parallel lines*. Parallel lines never meet. The symbol ∥ is used to denote parallel lines.

In the diagram, *l* ∥ *m*.

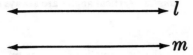

Polygons

● Closed shapes or figures with three or more sides are called *polygons*. (*Poly* means "many"; *gon* means "sides"; thus, *polygon* means "many sides.")

Triangles

● This section deals with those polygons having the fewest number of sides. A *triangle* is a three-sided polygon. It has three angles in its interior. The sum of these angles is *always* 180°. The symbol for triangle is △. A triangle is named by all three letters of its vertices.

This is △ ABC:

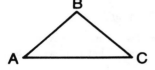

● Types of triangles:

1. A triangle having all three sides equal (meaning all three sides have the same length) is called an *equilateral triangle*.
2. A triangle having two sides equal is called an *isosceles triangle*.
3. A triangle having none of its sides equal is called a *scalene triangle*.
4. A triangle having a right (90°) angle in its interior is called a *right triangle*.

Facts about Triangles

● Every triangle has a base (bottom side) and a height (or altitude). Every height is the *perpendicular* (forms right angles) distance from a vertex to its opposite side (the base).

In this diagram of △ ABC, $\overline{BC}$ is the base, and $\overline{AE}$ is the height. $\overline{AE} \perp \overline{BC}$.

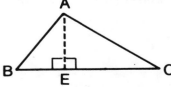

- Every triangle has a median. The median is the line segment drawn from a vertex to the midpoint of the opposite side.

In this diagram of △ ABC, E is the midpoint of $\overline{BC}$.

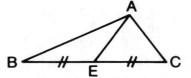

Therefore, $\overline{BE} = \overline{EC}$. $\overline{AE}$ is the median of ABC.

- In an equilateral triangle, since all three sides are equal, then all three angles will be equal; they are opposite equal sides. If all three angles are equal and their sum is 180°, the following must be true:

$$x + x + x = 180°$$
$$3x = 180°$$
$$x = 60°$$

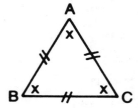

Every angle of an equilateral triangle always has a measure of 60°.

- In any triangle, the longest side is always opposite from the largest angle. Likewise, the shortest side is always opposite from the smallest angle. In a right triangle, the longest side will always be opposite from the right angle, as the right angle will be the largest angle in the triangle.

$\overline{AC}$ is the longest side of right △ ABC.

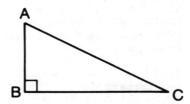

- The sum of the lengths of any two sides of a triangle must be larger than the length of the third side.

In the diagram of ABC:

$$\overline{AB} + \overline{BC} > \overline{AC}$$
$$\overline{AB} + \overline{AC} > \overline{BC}$$
$$\overline{AC} + \overline{BC} > \overline{AB}$$

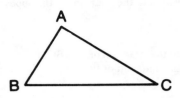

- If one side of a triangle is extended, the exterior angle formed by that extension is equal to the sum of the other two interior angles.

In the diagram of △ ABC, side BC is extended to D.

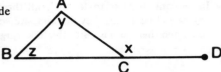

∠ACD is the exterior angle formed.
∠x = ∠y + ∠z

x = 82° + 41°
x = 123°

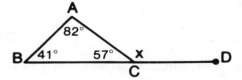

Pythagorean Theorem

- In any right triangle, the relationship between the lengths of the sides is stated by the Pythagorean theorem. The parts of a right triangle are:

∠C is the right angle.

The side opposite the right angle is called the *hypotenuse* (side c). (The hypotenuse will always be the longest side.)

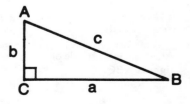

The other two sides are called the *legs* (sides a and b).

The three lengths a, b, and c will always be numbers such that:

$$a^2 + b^2 = c^2$$

For example:

If a = 3, b = 4, and c = 5,

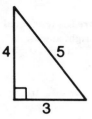

$$a^2 + b^2 = c^2$$
$$3^2 + 4^2 = 5^2$$
$$9 + 16 = 25$$
$$25 = 25$$

Therefore, 3-4-5 is called a Pythagorean triple. There are other values for a, b, and c that will always work. Some are: 1-1-$\sqrt{2}$, 5-12-13, and 8-15-17. Any multiple of one of these triples will also work. For example, using the 3-4-5: 6-8-10, 9-12-15, and 15-20-25 will also be Pythagorean triples.

- If perfect squares are known, the lengths of these sides can be determined easily. A knowledge of the use of algebraic equations can also be used to determine the lengths of the sides. *For example:*

$$a^2 + b^2 = c^2$$
$$x^2 + 10^2 = 15^2$$
$$x^2 + 100 = 225$$
$$x^2 = 125$$
$$x = \sqrt{125}$$
$$= \sqrt{25} \times \sqrt{5}$$
$$= 5\sqrt{5}$$

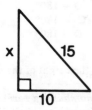

Quadrilaterals

- A polygon having four sides is called a *quadrilateral*. There are four angles in its interior. The sum of these interior angles will always be 360°. A quadrilateral is named by using the four letters of its vertices.

This is quadrilateral ABCD:

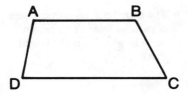

Types of Quadrilaterals

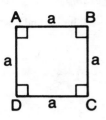

- The *square* has four equal sides and four right angles.

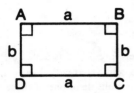

- The *rectangle* has opposite sides equal and four right angles.

- The *parallelogram* has opposite sides equal and parallel, opposite angles equal, and consecutive angles supplementary. Every parallelogram has a height.

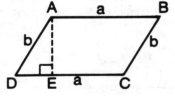

∠A − ∠C
∠B − ∠D
∠A + ∠B − 180°
∠A + ∠D − 180°
∠B + ∠C − 180°
∠C + ∠D − 180°

AE is the height of the parallelogram, $\overline{AB} \parallel \overline{CD}$, and $\overline{AD} \parallel \overline{BC}$.

- The *rhombus* is a parallelogram with four equal sides. A rhombus has a height. BE is the height.

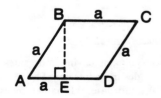

- The *trapezoid* has only one pair of parallel sides. A trapezoid has a height. AE is the height. $\overline{AB} \parallel \overline{DC}$.

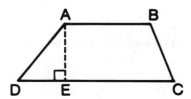

Other Polygons

- The *pentagon* is a five-sided polygon.
- The *hexagon* is a six-sided polygon.
- The *octagon* is an eight-sided polygon.
- The *nonagon* is a nine-sided polygon.
- The *decagon* is a ten-sided polygon.

Facts about Polygons

- *Regular* means all sides have the same length and all angles have the same measure. A regular three-sided polygon is the equilateral triangle. A regular four-sided polygon is the square. There are no other special names. Other polygons will just be described as regular, if they are. For example, a regular five-sided polygon is called a regular pentagon. A regular six-sided polygon is called a regular hexagon.

Perimeter

- *Perimeter* means the total distance all the way around the outside of any polygon. The perimeter of any polygon can be determined by adding up the lengths of all the sides. The total distance around will be the sum of all sides of the polygon. No special formulas are really necessary.

Area

Area (A) means the amount of space inside the polygon. The formulas for each area are as follows:

- Triangle: $A = \frac{1}{2}bh$

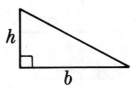   or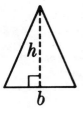

For example:
$A = \frac{1}{2}bh$
$A = \frac{1}{2}(24)(18) = 216$ sq in

- **Square or rectangle:** $A = lw$

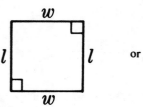

For example:

$A = l(w) = 4(4) = 16$ sq in

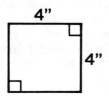

$A = l(w) = 12(5) = 60$ sq in

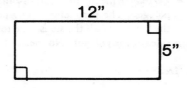

- **Parallelogram:** $A = bh$

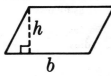

For example:
$A = b(h)$
$A = 10(5) = 50$ sq in

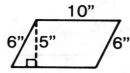

- **Trapezoid:** $A = \frac{1}{2}(a + b)h$

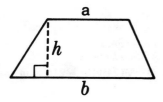

For example:
A = ½(a + b)*h*
A = ½(8 + 12)7
    = ½(20)7 = 70 sq in

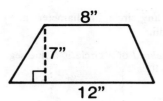

Circles

- A closed shape whose side is formed by one curved line all points of which are equidistant from the center point is called a *circle*. Circles are named by the letter of their center point.

This is circle M:

M is the center point, since it is the same distance away from any point on the circle.

Parts of a Circle

- The *radius* is the distance from the center to any point on the circle.

$\overline{MA}$ is a radius.
$\overline{MB}$ is a radius.

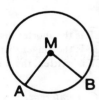

In any circle, all radii (plural) are the same length.

- The *diameter* of a circle is the distance across the circle, through the center.

$\overline{AB}$ is a diameter.
$\overline{CD}$ is a diameter.

In any circle, all diameters are the same length. Each diameter is two radii.

- A *chord* of a circle is a line segment whose end points lie on the circle itself.

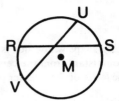

$\overline{RS}$ is a chord.
$\overline{UV}$ is a chord.

The diameter is the longest chord in any circle.

- An *arc* is the distance between any two points *on* the circle itself. An arc is a piece of the circle. The symbol ⌒ is used to denote an arc. It is written on top of the two endpoints that form the arc. Arcs are measured in degrees. There are 360° around the circle.

This is $\overset{\frown}{EF}$:

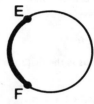

Minor $\overset{\frown}{EF}$ is the shorter distance between E and F.
Major $\overset{\frown}{EF}$ is the longer distance between E and F.
When $\overset{\frown}{EF}$ is written, the minor arc is assumed.

Area and Circumference

- *Circumference* is the distance around the circle. Since there are no sides to add up, a formula is needed. π (pi) is a Greek letter that represents a specific number. In fractional or decimal form, the commonly used approximation are: $\pi \simeq 3.14$ or $\pi \simeq {}^{22}/_7$. The formula for circumference is: $C = \pi d$ or $C = 2 \pi r$. *For example:*

In circle M, d = 8, since r = 4.

$C = \pi d$
$C = \pi (8)$
$C = 3.14(8)$
$C = 25.12$ inches

- The *area* of a circle can be determined by: $A = \pi r^2$. *For example:*

In circle M, r = 5, since d = 10.

$A = \pi(r^2)$
$A = \pi(5^2)$
$A = 3.14(25)$
$A = 78.5$ sq in

Volume

- In three dimensions there are different facts that can be determined about shapes. *Volume* is the capacity to hold. The formula for volume of each shape is different. The volume of any *prism* (a three-dimensional shape having many sides, but two bases) can be determined by: Volume (V) = (area of base) (height of prism).

Specifically for a rectangular solid:

$V = (lw)(h)$
$= lwh$

Specifically for a cylinder (circular bases):

$V = (\pi r^2)h$
$V = \pi r^2 h$

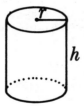

Volume is labeled "cubic" units.

Surface Area

- The *surface area* of a three-dimensional solid is the area of all of the surfaces that form the solid. Find the area of each surface, and then add up those areas. The surface area of a rectangular solid can be found by adding up the areas of all six surfaces. *For example:*

The surface area of this prism is:

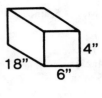

top	18 × 6 = 108
bottom	18 × 6 = 108
left side	6 × 4 = 24
right side	6 × 4 = 24
front	18 × 4 = 72
back	18 × 4 = 72

408 sq in

LITERATURE AND FINE ARTS REVIEW

The following pages are designed to give you a short, basic review of the major concepts and terms used on the NTE Literature and Fine Arts section. The glossaries provide short explanations for the main ideas in each field. Do not spend excessive time on any part of this review. *Do not attempt to memorize these lists.* Rather, use the glossaries to refresh your knowledge. When reviewing the terms, think about which terms are related or contrasted. Write your own comments after the terms; make helpful notes.

GLOSSARY OF TERMS IN LITERATURE

ALLEGORY: A narrative in which the characters and actions represent general concepts or moral qualities.

ALLITERATION: A series of words beginning with the same sound, as in "fifty fearless fighters."

BALLAD: A narrative song.

BLANK VERSE: Iambic pentameter without rhyme.

CLICHÉ: An expression which has been employed so often that it is overfamiliar.

DRAMA: A serious play of human conflict.

ELEGY: A formal poem lamenting someone dead.

EPIC: A long narrative poem about the deeds of a hero.

EPIGRAM: A brief and pointed poem.

EUPHEMISM: Soft words masking hard reality, as "he passed away" to relate death.

FREE VERSE: Verse lacking the discipline of meter.

GENRE: Type of style or subject.

HYPERBOLE: Exaggeration used for striking effect, like "as soft as the wind."

IRONY: The meaning is opposite to the literal meaning of the words.

MELODRAMA: A light play which interests the audience through action and tension.

METAPHOR: A figure of speech, as "my love is a red, red rose."

METER: The number of stressed syllables in a line of verse; *pentameter* has five feet or stresses.

ODE: A lyrical poem of high emotions.

PROSE: The ordinary language of speaking or writing, without the regular patterns of poetry.

REALISM: Writing conveying a sense of everyday life.
ROMANTICISM: Writing that creates an ideal or fanciful world.
SARCASM: Caustic words for the purpose of wounding another.
SATIRE: An attack on a person, custom, or institution, holding it up to ridicule or scorn by means of criticism and wit.
SONNET: A poem with fourteen lines of iambic pentameter.
SYMBOL: Something used to represent something else, as a bulldog for tenacity.
TRAGEDY: A play in which the hero's faults lead to catastrophe.

GLOSSARY OF TERMS IN ART

ABSTRACT: Nonrepresentational art, emphasizing colors, lines, and forms.
ATRIUM: The court of an ancient Roman residence.
CAPITAL: The upper part of a column, on which a lintel rests.
COLLAGE: An art work made by gluing together pieces of paper, photographs, cloth, and other materials.
CROSSING: In a cruciform church, the intersection of the nave and transept.
ENGRAVING: A print from a design incised into a metal surface.
FACADE: The front of a building.
FLYING BUTTRESS: A half-arch that supports the side of a building.
FRESCO: A wall painting on fresh plaster.
HUE: Color.
ICON: Sacred image or portrait, especially in a Greek church.
LINTEL: A horizontal beam spanning an opening.
LITHOGRAPH: A print from a design drawn on stone with a greasy pencil.
MEDIUM: The substance with which an artist works, as oil or watercolor.
MINARET: A slender tower on a mosque.
MOSAIC: A design made by assembling small pieces of glass or stone.
NAVE: The principal hall of a long church.
PERSPECTIVE: A geometric method for representing three-dimensional relations on a flat surface.
PRIMARY COLORS: Blue, red, and yellow; the other hues may be prepared by combining these.
RELIEF: Sculpted figures projecting from a background.
SARCOPHAGUS: A coffin made of stone.
STILL LIFE: A painting of nearby objects, like a vase of flowers.
TACTILE: Refers to the sense of touch.
TRACERY: Stonework decorating a window.
TRANSEPT: The arm of a cruciform church perpendicular to the nave.

VAULT: An arched roof.

WOODCUT: A print made from a wooden block into which a design has been engraved.

STYLES OF WESTERN ART

EGYPTIAN   4000 B.C.–1100 B.C.

GREEK   1100 B.C.–100 B.C.

ROMAN   100 B.C.–A.D. 400

MEDIEVAL   400–1400
    Early Medieval
    Romanesque
    Gothic

RENAISSANCE   1400–1600
    Early Renaissance
    High Renaissance
    Mannerist

BAROQUE   1600–1725

ROCOCO   1725–1775

NINETEENTH CENTURY   1775–1900
    Neoclassical
    Romanticist
    Realist or Naturalist
    Impressionist

TWENTIETH CENTURY   1900–2000
    Cubist
    Expressionist
    Abstract Expressionist
    Surrealist

GLOSSARY OF TERMS IN MUSIC

ALLEGRO: Fast tempo.

BRASSES: Wind instruments made of metal, including the trumpet, French horn, trombone, and tuba.

CHAMBER MUSIC: One to twenty performers.

CHORD: Several notes sounded together.
CLAVICHORD: A small predecessor of the piano.
CLEF: The symbol indicating the pitch of the notes.

treble clef (high) 𝄞   bass clef (low) 𝄢

DYNAMICS: The loudness of music.
HARMONY: Refers to the chordal aspect of music.
HARPSICHORD: Another predecessor of the piano, sounded by plucking the strings.
LARGO: Very slow tempo.
LENTO: Slow tempo.
LIED: German song.
LYRE: An ancient harp.
MASS: Music for a Catholic service.
MELODY: Concerns the sequence of notes.
MODERATO: Intermediate tempo.
MOTIF: A recurrent group of notes, as the four in Beethoven's Fifth Symphony.
MOVEMENT: A large section of a lengthy composition.
NOTE: A musical sound of specific pitch, as middle C.
OPUS: Work, usually identified by a number.
ORATORIO: A major orchestral piece with solo voices and chorus.
ORCHESTRA: A large group of instrument players, usually 75 to 90.
PERCUSSION: Instruments sounded by striking, as drums, cymbals, and chimes.
PITCH: The frequency of a sound wave.
POLYPHONY: Choral music with several simultaneous voice-lines.
PRESTO: Very fast tempo.
RHYTHM: Concerns the relative duration of the notes.
SCALE: A set of notes, from low to high in pitch.
SONATA: A work for one or two instruments.
STAFF: The five lines on which musical notes are written.
STRINGS: Violin, viola, cello, and double bass (bass viol).
SYMPHONY: A major orchestral composition.
TEMPO: The pace of the music.
TIMBRE: The characteristic sound of a voice or instrument.
TONE: A musical sound of a specific pitch.
WOODWINDS: Instruments originally made of wood, including the piccolo, flute, clarinet, oboe, English horn, bassoon, and saxophone

SCIENCE REVIEW

The following pages are designed to give you a basic review of the major concepts used on the NTE Science section. The science reviews provide explanations of the main ideas in each field, but many questions on the exam refer to modern everyday science with which you're probably familiar. *Do not spend excessive time on any one part of the review.* A working knowledge of test taking strategies is probably more important for this part of the test.

A glossary of scientific terms is also included. *Do not attempt to memorize these terms;* rather, use the glossary together with the reviews to provide a mini-course approach to the science areas. When reviewing the terms think about which terms are related or contrasted, like *atom* and *molecule.* Write your own comments after many of the terms; make helpful notes.

BIOLOGY REVIEW

BASIC CONCEPTS

BIOLOGY is the science of life. Life has astonishing variety, embracing bacteria and baboons, whales and walnuts, algae and alligators—yet all those life forms share some similar materials and processes. The complexity of life compels biologists to specialize in certain levels of life: organic molecules, cells, organs, individuals, species, and communities. Here are some important characteristics of most life forms. A living organism has a very complicated *organization* in which a series of *processes* takes place. Life *responds* to its environment, often with *movement.* An organism must *maintain* itself and *grow.* Finally, a plant or animal will produce new organisms much like itself; *reproduction* is the most universal process of life, explaining its survival and variety.

THE CELL is the smallest amount of living matter, a bit of organic material that is the unit of structure and function for all organisms. Cells range in size from the smallest speck visible through an excellent microscope to the yolk of the largest egg. Some tiny organisms (like bacteria) are one-celled, but all larger organisms are composed of many cells arrayed in tissues.

METABOLISM is the set of chemical reactions within protoplasm, the living material of the cell. The chemical constituents of protoplasm include water as well as organic and inorganic compounds. The organic molecules are proteins, carbohydrates, lipids, and nucleic acids. Proteins are both structural components and enzymes, organic catalysts that enable particular metabolic reactions to proceed; all proteins are built from simpler amino acids. Carbohydrates (starches and sugars) and lipids (fats) are energy sources for cellular processes. The two nucleic acids, deoxyribose nucleic acid (DNA) and ribose nucleic acid (RNA), are complex chained molecules with encoded instructions for metabolism; the chromosomes of the cell nucleus contain the DNA. Metabolic reactions involve assimilation, photosynthesis, digestion, and respiration. The result is to store chemical energy as adenosine triphosphate (ATP). During cellular work the ATP decomposes and yields energy.

MITOSIS is the process of cell division in which the nuclear material of the original cell is divided equally between the newer cells.

PLANTS may be divided into five broad groups. The more primitive groups are *algae* and *fungi;* these plants lack true roots, stems, and leaves. Algae range from a single cell to huge seaweeds; mostly they inhabit lakes and oceans. The fungi include molds, yeasts, and mushrooms. Fungi lack chlorophyll and thus are incapable of manufacturing food, so they are either parasites, preying on other living organisms, or saprophytes, existing on waste products and decaying organisms.

PHOTOSYNTHESIS is the process by which plants convert light into the chemical energy stored in foods. Chlorophyll, the green pigment within the leaf, is necessary to trap light energy for the photosynthetic reaction. In photosynthesis, carbon dioxide and water react to form sugar and oxygen.

ANIMALS cannot perform photosynthesis, and, therefore, derive their food from other organisms. Herbivores eat plants directly. Carnivores prey on other animals, but this food chain, too, ends in plants. Plants and animals are classified into *phyla* on the basis of their cells, tissues, organs, and overall organization. Each phylum is a major group of organisms.

THE SENSORY SYSTEM includes those specialized structures which initiate a nerve impulse after being affected by the environment. The eyes are the organs of vision. Light rays are refracted as they pass through the cornea, lens, and vitreous body to focus on the retina, where an image is formed. The optic nerve then carries impulses from the light-sensitive cells of the retina to the brain. The ear is the receptor of sound and the organ of balance. The seat of balance is in the semicircular canals within the inner ear. The receptors of taste are distributed on the upper surface of the tongue. Each taste bud detects one of the four primary tastes (salty, sweet, sour, and bitter); other taste sensations are combinations of the primary tastes.

THE NERVOUS SYSTEM is composed of the brain, spinal cord, and peripheral nerves which extend throughout the body.

THE DIGESTIVE SYSTEM includes the mouth, pharynx (throat), esophagus, stomach, small intestine, and large intestine. Other organs in this system are the salivary glands, liver, gallbladder, and pancreas. The enzymes contained in saliva, gastric juice, pancreatic juice, and intestinal fluids convert carbohydrates, fats, and proteins into molecules small enough to be absorbed into the blood. Simple sugars are absorbed as such and do not require digestion.

THE CIRCULATORY SYSTEM consists of the blood, the heart, and the blood vessels. The blood is composed of red cells, white cells, and platelets suspended in a watery medium called plasma. Red cells transport oxygen in combination with the iron pigment, hemoglobin.

REPRODUCTION in organisms may occur by either sexual or asexual processes. In asexual reproduction there is only one parent and simple mitotic divison produces the offspring; most protists, many plants, and a few primitive animals follow this reproductive strategy. Sexual reproduction involves two parents, as in all higher animals, except in the cases of self-fertilization in many flowering plants. The advanced plants and animals produce male and female sex cells by a special mode of cell division called meiosis.

NUCLEIC ACIDS store genetic messages and instruct the cell how to make the many proteins needed for life. Heredity has an elegant molecular basis. Nucleic acids are truly the secret of life. DNA in the chromosomes of the cell nucleus is a long molecule of two chains twisted into a double spiral or helix. Nitrogenous bases are attached to the chains in a special sequence that is a coded message, the instructions for life. The double chain permits the DNA to duplicate itself exactly during reproduction, retaining the original genetic message. The message contains the instructions necessary to build various proteins, many of which function as enzymes. Some RNA molecules carry the message from the DNA in the cell nucleus to the ribosomes in the cytoplasm, where protein assembly occurs.

GENES are the functional message units along the DNA chains within the chromosomes. One chromosome is composd of many genes, each of which determines or influences an inheritable trait.

EVOLUTION of life is indicated by the fact that fossil organisms in rock strata are different from modern organisms. As we go back in time, searching lower and older strata, the organisms diverge more and more from those living today. Yet the variation in life forms appears to be relatively continuous. For example, 60 million years ago horses were quite small and had four toes on each foot. As time passed, horses evolved through a series of larges sizes and fewer toes to today's large, single-toed creature. Other evidence for the evolution of life comes from the study of biogeography (the distribution of present-day species), embryology (the similarities among early developmental stages of animals), homology (structural similarities in various organisms), and biochemistry (chemical similarities in various organisms). Charles Darwin listed evidences for the progression of life in his book *The Origin of Species* (1859) and proposed that evolution proceeded by natural selection.

TAXONOMY is the classification and naming of organisms. Over 1,300,000 different species have been described, so it is essential to sort them systematically. The binomial nomenclature devised by the Swede Linnaeus (1735) gives each organism two names, the genus and species. For example, the dog is *Canis familiaris*. Genera are grouped into higher taxonomic levels, arranged in a hierarchy as shown in table 1. At the highest level are the three kingdoms: protists, plants, and animals. Organisms are classified into taxonomic groups by morphological similarities and genetic affinities.

TABLE 1

Kingdom
Phylum
Class
Order
Family
Genus
Species

GLOSSARY OF TERMS IN BIOLOGY

ADENOSINE TRIPHOSPHATE: A compound with energy-rich phosphate bonds involved in the transfer of energy in cellular metabolism; abbreviated ATP.

ADRENALIN: A hormone secreted by the adrenal medulla; also called epinephrine.

ALGAE: Simple plants containing chlorophyll.

AMINO ACID: An organic compound containing an amino and a carboxyl group; the building blocks of proteins.

AMPHIBIANS: Class of vertebrates capable of living both in water and on land. The larval forms have gills and the adults have lungs; includes frogs and toads.

ANTERIOR: Toward the forward end.

ANTIBIOTIC: A substance that destroys a microorganism or inhibits its growth.

ANTIBODY: A substance produced by the body to combat the injurious effect of a foreign substance (antigen).

ANTISEPTIC: A substance which kills bacteria.

AORTA: The main artery leaving the heart.

ARTERY: A blood vessel which carries blood away from the heart.

ASEXUAL: Reproduction in one individual, without the union of gametes.

BACTERIA: Unicellular organisms without a distinct nucleus and usually without chlorophyll.

BILE: A yellowish-green fluid secreted by the liver; aids in the digestion of fats.

BINOMIAL NOMENCLATURE: The international system of naming organisms with two names, the first generic and the second specific.

BOTANY: The science of plants.

CAPILLARY: The smallest blood vessel which carries blood between an artery and a vein.

CARBON CYCLE: The exchange of carbon between living things and their environment.

CARNIVORE: A flesh-eating animal.

CARTILAGE: A firm connective tissue, more flexible than bone.

CELL: The basic unit of organic structure and function.

CENTRAL NERVOUS SYSTEM: The brain and spinal cord.

CEREBELLUM: The part of the vertebrate brain which controls muscular coordination.

CEREBRUM: The upper part of the brain, where conscious mental processes occur.

CHLOROPHYLL: The green coloring matter in a plant; facilitates photosynthesis.

CHROMOSOME: A body in the cell nucleus; the bearer of genetic information.

CLASS: The main subdivision of a phylum.

COLD-BLOODED: An animal whose body temperature varies with the surroundings.

COLONY: A group of individuals of one species living together.

COMMUNITY: A group of individuals of many species living together.

CONIFER: A cone-bearing tree.

CORAL: A colonial marine coelenterate.

CORPUSCLE: A blood cell.

CROSS-POLLINATION: The transfer of pollen from one plant to a flower on another plant.

CRUSTACEANS: The class of arthropods with gills and two pairs of antennae; includes lobsters, crabs, barnacles, and crayfish.

DEOXYRIBOSE NUCLEIC ACID: The compound in the chromosomes that stores genetic information as a molecular code; abbreviated DNA.

DIGESTION: The breakdown of food for absorption.

DOMINANT: The one of two alternative genetic traits which is displayed in a heterozygous individual.

DORSAL: Toward the upper side; the back.

ECOLOGY: The study of relations between organisms and their environment.

EMBRYO: An organism in the early stages of development.

ENDOCRINE GLAND: A gland which secretes a hormone.

ENVIRONMENT: The conditions in which an organism lives.

ENZYME: A protein that serves as an organic catalyst for metabolic reactions.

EPIDERMIS: The outer layer of the skin.

EVOLUTION: The modification of life forms with the passage of time.

EXCRETION: The discharge of waste materials.

EXOSKELETON: A hard, jointed case outside the fleshy tissues of an animal.

FAMILY: The main subdivision of an order.

FOSSIL: Any naturally preserved remains of ancient life.

FRUIT: The mature ovary of a flower.

FUNGI: Plants that lack chlorophyll; molds, mushrooms, and yeasts.

GAMETE: A sex cell; an egg or sperm.

GENE: A unit of heredity located on the chromosome.

GENETICS: The study of inheritable characteristics.

GENUS: The main division of a family.

GERMINATION: The sprouting of a seed.

HEMOGLOBIN: The iron-bearing pigment of the red blood cells.

HERBIVORE: A plant-eating animal.

HEREDITY: The transmission of characteristics from parents to offspring.

HORMONE: A chemical substance that regulates body processes.

HYBRID: The offspring of genetically different parents.

INSECTS: A class of arthropods characterized by 3 body sections, 6 legs, and usually 4 wings.

INSULIN: A hormone produced by the pancreas, which regulates the body's utilization of sugar.

LIGAMENT: A fibrous band which supports an organ or connects two bones.

MAMMALS: A class of warm-blooded vertebrates possessing hair and feeding their young by means of mammary glands with milk.

MEIOSIS: The mode of cell division that produces gametes, each with one-half the number of chromosomes of the parent cell.

METABOLISM: The chemical processes within an organism.

METAMORPHOSIS: The change from a larval form to an adult form.

MITOSIS: Cell division with chromosome duplication, forming offspring cells with the same number of chromosomes as the parent cell; cell-splitting.

MUTATION: An inheritable change in a gene.

NATURAL SELECTION: The survival of the best-adapted organisms.

NERVOUS SYSTEM: The brain, spinal cord, and nerves.

NEURON: A nerve cell.

NUCLEUS: The central part of a cell, containing the chromosomes and controlling cellular activities.

ORDER: The main division of a class.

ORGAN: A group of cells or tissues functioning as a whole.

ORGANISM: A living plant or animal.

PARASITE: An organism that lives in or on another organism, deriving food at the expense of its host.

PASTEURIZATION: The killing of microorganisms in milk by heating to 145°F for 30 minutes.

PENICILLIN: An antibiotic drug obtained from molds.

PESTICIDE: A substance used to destroy plants or animals.

PHENOTYPE: Appearance of an organism, as opposed to its genetic constitution.

PHOTOSYNTHESIS: The production of carbohydrates by green plants in the presence of light.

PHYLUM: A major group of animals or plants; the main division of a kingdom.

PITUITARY: The endocrine gland located at the base of the brain, whose hormones regulate other glands.

PLANKTON: The microorganisms that live in the ocean.

PLASMA: The liquid part of the blood.

PLATELET: A particle in the blood which promotes clotting.

POLLEN: The mature microspores of seed plants.

POLLINATION: Fertilization by the transfer of pollen from an anther to a stigma.

POSTERIOR: Toward the hind end.

PREDATOR: An animal that lives by preying on other animals.

PROTEIN: An organic compound made up of amino acids.

PROTOPLASM: A general term for the living matter of the cell.

RECESSIVE: The one of two alternative genetic traits which is masked in a heterozygous individual.

REFLEX: A response to a stimulus.

REPTILES: The class of scaly vertebrates which includes the snakes, turtles, lizards, alligators, and crocodiles.

RESPIRATION: Biological oxidation.

RIBOSE NUCLEIC ACID: A substance in the cell with the function of making proteins; abbreviated RNA.

RIBOSOMES: Bodies in the cytoplasm concerned with protein synthesis.

SEXUAL: Reproduction involving the union of an egg and sperm.

SPECIES: A group of similar animals or plants, usually capable of interbreeding; the main division of a genus.

SPERM: A male gamete.

SPORE: An asexual reproductive cell found in fungi and ferns.

STAMEN: The organ of a flower that produces pollen.

SYMBIOSIS: The close living association of organisms of different species in which both benefit.

TAXONOMY: The classification of organisms.

TISSUE: A group of cells having the same structure and function.

TOXIN: A substance produced by an organism that is poisonous to another organism.

TRAIT: An inherited characteristic.

TROPISM: A growth movement in a plant in response to an environmental stimulus.

VACCINE: A fluid containing dead disease germs injected into an animal to produce immunity.

VEIN: A vessel conveying blood toward the heart.

VENTRAL: Toward the lower side.

VENTRICLE: A chamber from which blood leaves the heart.

VERTEBRATES: Chordates characterized by a well-developed brain, a backbone, and usually two pairs of limbs; includes the fishes, amphibians, reptiles, birds, and mammals.

VIRUS: A simple form of matter, on the borderline between inorganic chemicals and life; often infects higher organisms.

VITAMIN: An organic compound needed in small quantities for normal metabolism.

WARM-BLOODED: An animal with a constant body temperature.

YEAST: A fungus that causes fermentation; used in baking and brewing.

ZOOLOGY: The science of animals.

GEOLOGY REVIEW

BASIC CONCEPTS

GEOLOGY is the science that describes and interprets the earth. It classifies the materials that make up the earth, observes their shapes and distribution, and tries to discover the processes that caused the materials to be formed in that manner. Some major geological fields are geomorphology (landforms), petrology (rocks), stratigraphy (layered rocks), and paleontology (fossils).

THE EARTH'S STRUCTURE (see figure 1) has been inferred from its astronomical properties and seismic records of earthquake waves which

STRUCTURE OF THE EARTH

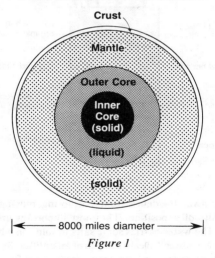

Figure 1

traveled through the interior of the earth. Temperature rises from the surface (20°C) to the center (3000°C) of the earth; this fact is essential to understanding geological processes. About 31% of the earth's mass is a dense core of iron and nickel metals, melted by the extremely high temperature of the center of the earth. Around that liquid core is the largest zone of the planet (68%), the mantle of crystalline silicates rich in magnesium, calcium, and iron. The very hot mantle is mainly solid, but local melting to magma (molten rock) is the source of volcanic eruptions. Above the mantle is the crust, which makes up less than 1% of the earth. This relatively thin zone (5–25 miles) contains the only rocks we can study, even in the deepest mines or drillholes.

MINERALS are natural chemical compounds which are the crystals that make up rocks.

WEATHERING is the destruction of bedrock by atmospheric action, with the generation of soil and loose, erodible debris. Most weathering involves chemical action by the air and water, which attack the minerals of the rocks.

SOIL PROFILE

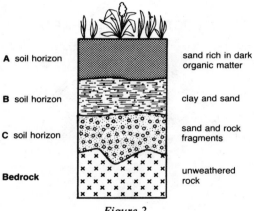

A soil horizon	sand rich in dark organic matter
B soil horizon	clay and sand
C soil horizon	sand and rock fragments
Bedrock	unweathered rock

Figure 2

EROSION carries away the debris from weathering, moving it downslope to a more stable site of deposition. The most important erosional agent is running water. The water carries some salts in solution while particles are transported in suspension. Stream erosion of an uplifted highland leads to a characteristic time-series of landforms, from youthful terrain with V-shaped valleys to mature terrain with rounded hills and broad valleys. Wind is a significant means of erosion in arid regions; fine particles are blown away to be deposited downwind as sand dunes. At high elevations and polar latitudes ice is present throughout the year, so glacial erosion may occur. Snow accumulates and its weight transforms it to ice, which oozes slowly downslope under the pressure of its own weight. Glacial ice is a remarkably effective agent of erosion, capable of carving out U-shaped valleys in mountains. During the Pleistocene Ice Age, which ended only about 12,000 years ago, great glacial sheets covered much of North America and deposited an irregular blanket of till (mud and boulder debris).

STRATA are the layers of sediment deposited in a quiet environment. Common sites of deposition are lakes, deltas at the mouths of rivers, beaches and sandbars along the coast, and (most importantly) the marine environment. Strata are commonly very extensive laterally and relatively thin vertically, like a blanket. An important geological rule is the law of original horizontality, which states that most sediments are deposited in beds which were originally horizontal, and any tilting is due to later earth movements. A second stratigraphic principle is the law of superposition; younger beds were originally deposited above older beds.

FOSSILS are traces of ancient life preserved in the strata as shells, footprints, and the like. Because life has evolved (changed) continually through geological history, the fossils in older strata differ from those found in more recent deposits. In fact, strata deposited during one geological period contain characteristic life forms different from those of any other period.

THE GEOLOGICAL TIME SCALE was a major achievement of stratigraphers, who used fossils to arrange strata in a standard order. More recently, geochemists have measured the amount of radioactive decay in minerals and calculated the time at which the rock formed. So the geological time scale in table 2 represents interpretations from fossils and radioactivity. The earth is believed to be about 5.6 billion years old. The fossiliferous strata record only the last 11% of earth's history. And human civilization has lasted only 10,000 years, a brief moment on the geological

TABLE 2

Geological Era	Beginning (years before present)	Duration (years)	Characteristic Life Forms
Cenozoic	70,000,000	70,000,000	mammals
Mesozoic	225,000,000	155,000,000	reptiles
Paleozoic	600,000,000	375,000,000	invertebrates
Precambrian	5,600,000,000	5,000,000,000	no life except algae

time scale. The immensity of geological time is the major discovery of geology. There has been ample time for very slow processes to produce large consequences.

OCEANS cover 70% of the earth's surface. The salts in seawater were dissolved during the weathering of bedrock. During one period or another, every portion of the continents has been depressed beneath sea level, and most of the strata seen in roadcuts throughout the United States are marine deposits. A typical cross section for the Atlantic Ocean would look like figure 3. The broad, shallow continental shelf collects much sediment from the continents. The mid-ocean ridge has frequent earthquakes and volcanic eruptions, so it is thought to be the site of upwelling of material from within the mantle.

THE ATLANTIC OCEAN

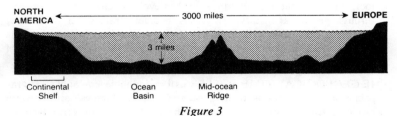

Figure 3

CONTINENTS may be divided into two zones. A shield area is a broad plain of Precambrian-age granite and gneiss, providing a stable core for the continent. Most of Canada is such a shield area. The second type of zone is one of recent upheaval, an orogenic (mountain-building) zone. Mountains occur in long, narrow belts, mostly along the edges of continents. On a map or globe, look at the western margins of South and North America to realize the edge-of-continent location of mountain ranges. Orogenic belts are sites of many earthquakes and volcanoes.

EARTH MOVEMENTS are the result of forces witnn the earth, where temperature and pressure differences lead to instability. The stress is particularly severe in orogenic zones, which are characterized by volcanism, metamorphism, deformation, and uplift. Two styles of rock deformation are faulting and folding as shown in figure 4.

NATURAL RESOURCES obtained from the earth may be classed as metal and fuel deposits. Most metals are obtained by mining ore minerals in open-pit or underground mines. Gold is the only metal to occur commonly in its native, metallic state.

STRUCTURES IN LAYERED ROCKS

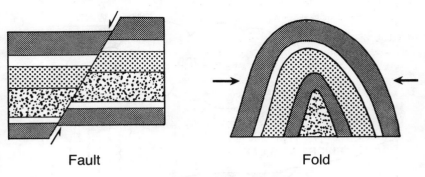

Fault   Fold

arrows show movements

Figure 4

METEOROLOGY is the science of the atmosphere and weather. The composition of air is shown in table 3. The amount of water vapor in the air depends on the prevailing temperature and the availability of water. The hydrologic cycle as shown in figure 5 links the processes. Water in the ocean is evaporated by the sun's energy. As the warm, moist air rises to altitudes of lower pressure, the air expands and cools. The cooling results in condensation of water vapor to minute droplets of liquid water, which make up visible clouds. The clouds may be blown inland and cool further, leading to precipitation of rain or snow. Much of such precipitation is drained by rivers (the process is termed *runoff*) into the ocean, but an important fraction seeps into porous soil and rocks. That groundwater percolates laterally through permeable materials until it too ultimately reaches the ocean.

TABLE 3

Gas		Percent
Nitrogen	N_2	78.08
Oxygen	O_2	20.95
Argon	Ar	0.93
Carbon dioxide	CO_2	0.03
Water vapor	H_2O	varies

THE HYDROLOGIC CYCLE

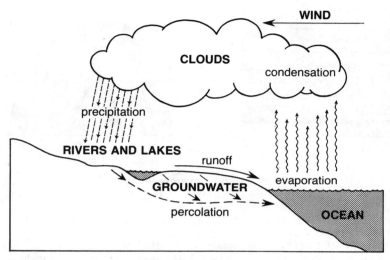

Figure 5

GLOSSARY OF TERMS IN GEOLOGY AND METEOROLOGY

ALTIMETER: An instrument for measuring altitude, commonly by means of air pressure.

ANEMOMETER: An instrument for measuring wind speed.

ARTESIAN WELL: A water well drilled into a confined aquifer with high water pressure which forces the water toward the surface.

ATMOSPHERIC PRESSURE: The pressure exerted by the weight of the air lying directly above the area; at sea level, about 15 pounds per square inch.

ATOLL: A coral reef enclosing a lagoon.

AURORA: The radiant emission from the upper atmosphere known as the northern lights in our continent.

BAROMETER: An instrument for measuring atmospheric pressure.

CAVERN: A large cave usually formed by the dissolving action of groundwater.

CLOUD: A collection of tiny water or ice droplets sufficiently numerous to be seen.

COAL: A rock composed of partly decayed and compressed plant material.

CONTINENTAL DRIFT: The hypothesis of continents moving laterally.

CONTINENTAL SHELF: The marine zone between the shore and the deep ocean basin.

CONTOUR: On a topographic map, a line connecting points of equal elevation. Hills are shown as concentric circles.

CORE: The center of the earth.

CRUST: The thin outer zone of the earth, above the mantle.

CYCLONE: A low-pressure area around which winds blow counterclockwise in the Northern Hemisphere.

DELTA: A triangular deposit of sediment at the mouth of a river.

DIASTROPHISM: A general term for large-scale earth movements.

DIVIDE: The ridge between areas draining into different river systems.

EPICENTER: The place on the earth's surface closest to the origin of an earthquake.

EROSION: The removal of rock debris by water, ice, and wind.

EVAPORATION: The process by which a liquid changes to a gas; specifically, when water changes to water vapor.

FAULT: A planar break in rock along which displacement has occurred.

FORMATION: A rock unit shown on a geological map.

FOSSIL: Preserved trace of ancient life.

FRONT: The boundary between two air masses of different temperatures; a common site for cloud formation and precipitation.

GEOTHERMAL ENERGY: Heat obtained from hot water or steam within the earth.

GEYSER: A hot spring which periodically erupts steam and hot water.

GLACIER: A body of permanent ice thick enough to slowly flow under its own weight.

GROUNDWATER: Subsurface water in the pores and cracks of soil and rocks.

HARDNESS: The relative resistance of a mineral to scratching, usually expressed on Mohs' scale of 1 (softest) to 10 (hardest).

HUMIDITY: The amount of water vapor in the air.

HURRICANE: A large, severe tropical storm having wind speeds exceeding 73 miles per hour.

IGNEOUS: Rock formed by the solidification of molten rock material.

LATITUDE: Location north or south of the equator, expressed in degrees.

LAVA: Molten rock at the surface of the earth, near a volcanic vent.

LONGITUDE: Location east or west of the prime meridian at Greenwich, England.

MAGMA: Molten rock within the earth.

MANTLE: The zone of the earth between the core and the crust.

MEANDER: A wide curve or bend in the course of a large, winding river.

METAMORPHIC: Rock formed by the transformation, under high temperature and pressure, of older sedimentary or igneous rock.

METAMORPHISM: The recrystallization of rock to new minerals or texture.

METEOROLOGY: The science of the atmosphere and weather.

MINERAL: A naturally occurring inorganic chemical compound.

MIRAGE: An optical illusion where the sky is seen in place of the land, which appears wet.

MORAINE: A ridge of rocks and mud deposited by a glacier.

ORE: A rock rich enough in an economically valuable mineral to be mined.

PALEONTOLOGY: The science of fossil life.

PERMAFROST: Ground that is frozen throughout the year.

PETROLEUM: A liquid fuel from the transformation of plant and animal remains.

PRECIPITATION: Any form of water, whether liquid or solid particles, that falls from the atmosphere; rain, sleet, snow, or hail.

RADIOMETRIC DATING: Determining geological age by measuring the amount of radioactive decay products in a rock or fossil.

RAINBOW: A circular arc of colored bands produced by the refraction and reflection of sunlight by a sheet of raindrops. The sun must be behind the observer.

RICHTER SCALE: A scale measuring earthquake magnitude.

SEAMOUNT: An underwater volcanic peak, commonly with a flat top.

SEDIMENTARY: Rock formed by deposition at the earth's surface.

SEISMIC: Refers to earthquakes.

SEISMOGRAPH: An instrument used to detect movements of the earth's crust.

SOIL: Broken and decomposed rock and humus.

STALACTITE: A cone of calcareous rock hanging from the roof of a cavern.

STALAGMITE: A pillar of calcareous rock rising from the floor of a cavern.

STRATA: Layers of sedimentary rock; singular is *stratum.*

STRATOSPHERE: The atmospheric shell above the troposphere; the stratosphere extends from 6 to 30 miles above the earth's surface.

THRUST: Horizontal movement of the crust.

THUNDERSTORM: A small storm with cumulonimbus clouds accompanied by lightning and thunder, rain, and gusty winds.

TILL: Rocks and mud deposited by a glacier.

TOPOGRAPHY: The shape of the earth's surface.

TORNADO: A violently rotating column of air extending as a funnel beneath a cumulonimbus cloud. The winds may attain a speed of 200 miles an hour.

TROPOSPHERE: The lowest 6 miles of the atmosphere, characterized by temperature decreasing with height.

VOLCANIC: Rock formed when lava reaches the surface.

WATERSHED: The area which drains into one river system.

WATER TABLE: The upper limit of groundwater, below which all pores in the rocks are filled with water.

WEATHERING: The physical and chemical destruction of rock by the atmosphere.

WIND DIRECTION: A wind is described by its source; for example, a north wind comes from the north and blows southward.

CHEMISTRY REVIEW

BASIC CONCEPTS

CHEMISTRY is the science of the substances which make up our world. Any tangible matter is chemical in its nature. Chemists study substances by measuring their properties and observing the changes they undergo. Matter is anything which occupies space and has mass. Matter may exist in the state of solid, liquid, or gas, depending on the prevailing temperature and pressure. Modern chemistry began when the Frenchman Lavoisier stated (1780) the law of conservation of mass: there is no gain or loss of mass in a chemical change. For example, when hydrogen reacts with oxygen to yield water, the water produced has precisely the same weight as the gases that reacted. Consequently, water can be considered to be built from the *elements* hydrogen and oxygen. Elements are the simplest chemical substances. Compounds (like water) are homogeneous substances of constant composition that have formed by chemical union of elements.

ATOMS are the smallest particles of chemical elements. The experimental fact that chemical compounds have fixed compositions led the Englishman John Dalton to propose (1805) that substances consist of small particles of matter, which he called atoms from the Greek word for indivisible. Later it was realized that chemical compounds must likewise have a smallest particle, the molecule. Water, for example, is made up of many molecules with the composition H_2O and the structure (arrangement) shown in figure 6. The straight lines denote bonds between atoms. One water molecule is built from two atoms of hydrogen and one atom of oxygen. The molecules of the gaseous elements hydrogen and oxygen are shown in figure 7. Each of these molecules is itself diatomic, with two atoms

WATER MOLECULE

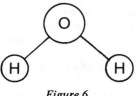

Figure 6

bonded together. Finally, we can diagram the reaction that produces water molecules. (See figure 8). The size of each box portrays the fact that the volume of gas is proportional to the number of molecules, rather than atoms. The chemical reaction is seen to be primarily a change in the bonding of atoms.

HYDROGEN MOLECULE   OXYGEN MOLECULE

Figure 7

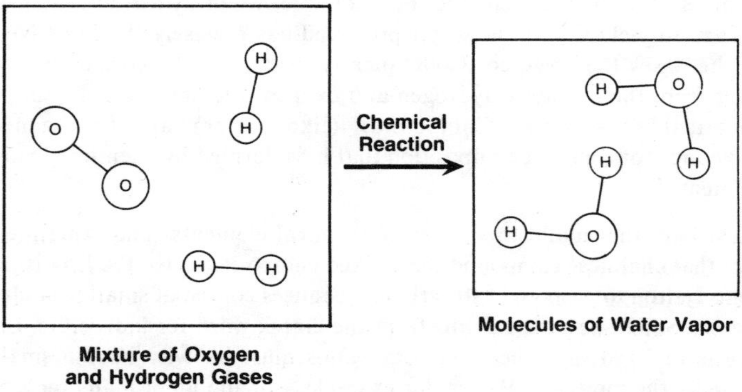

Chemical
Reaction

Molecules of Water Vapor

**Mixture of Oxygen
and Hydrogen Gases**

Figure 8

SUBATOMIC PARTICLES have been discovered as physicists learned how to split the supposedly indivisible atom. The three principal particles are listed in table 4. An atom has a small, dense nucleus composed of

TABLE 4

Particle	Charge	Mass
Proton	+1	1.007
Neutron	0	1.009
Electron	−1	0.001

protons and neutrons packed together. The nucleus is surrounded by a much larger cloud of electrons. Thus atomic weight is determined by the nucleus but the size of the atom is fixed by the electrons. *The number of protons establishes the chemical nature of an atom.* The number of neutrons is approximately equal to the number of protons, and the function of neutrons appears to be to stabilize the nucleus. The number of electrons precisely equals the number of protons for an electrically neutral atom.

CHEMICAL ELEMENTS may be assigned atomic numbers equal to the protons in their atoms. When elements are charted in order of increasing atomic number, a pattern of recurring physical and chemical properties is displayed. This periodic table of the chemical elements was first devised by the Russian Mendeleev (1869). Ninety-one elements occur naturally and another 13 have been made in the laboratory. Of these 104 elements, only the first 20 are shown in table 5. The elements increase in atomic number and atomic weight horizontally. Each vertical column contains a group of elements with similar chemical properties. Note that you need not have memorized these for the NTE.

COMPOUNDS are written as formulas with standard symbols for the chemical elements. The subscript following each symbol shows the number of atoms of that type in one molecule or formula unit of the compound; absence of a subscript implies one atom. Therefore a molecule of the gas ethylene (C_2H_4) has two atoms of carbon and four of hydrogen. The common mineral calcite ($CaCO_3$) has one calcium, one carbon, and three oxygen atoms per formula unit. Most compounds contain metallic and nonmetallic elements in proportions so that their valences sum to zero. Check again the abridged periodic table and note that hydrogen has a valence of $+1$ while oxygen is -2; consequently they combine in the proportion 2:1 as the formula H_2O denotes. Sodium ($+1$) combines with chlorine (-1) to yield NaCl, common table salt. The valence number summarizes the chemical behavior of each element. Metals have positive valence while nonmetals are negative. Note that in a formula the metallic symbol is written first.

TABLE 5

ABRIDGED PERIODIC TABLE OF THE CHEMICAL ELEMENTS

1 hydrogen H							2 helium He
3 lithium Li	4 beryllium Be	5 boron B	6 carbon C	7 nitrogen N	8 oxygen O	9 fluorine F	10 neon Ne
11 sodium Na	12 magnesium Mg	13 aluminum Al	14 silicon Si	15 phosphorous P	16 sulfur S	17 chlorine Cl	18 argon Ar
19 potassium K	20 calcium Ca						
$+1$	$+2$	$+3$	$+4, -4$	$+5, -3$	-2	-1	0

valence for each column

BONDS between atoms are electronic in origin. Electrically neutral atoms may share electrons to form a covalent bond, as in a hydrogen molecule. (See figure 9.) The electrons are in shells around the nuclear protons. Atoms which have an electrical charge are called *ions*. A positive ion has lost electrons (which have a charge of -1, remember) and a negative ion has gained electrons. Ions of different charge have a strong electrostatic attraction or ionic bond.

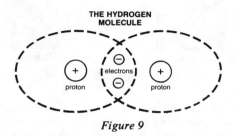

THE HYDROGEN MOLECULE

Figure 9

SOLIDS are characterized by their ability to retain their shape. They are relatively incompressible. Solids melt when heated and vaporize only slightly. All substances become solid if cooled sufficiently. Solids may be either crystalline or amorphous, depending on whether the arrangement of the atoms is regular or irregular.

LIQUIDS take on the shapes of their containers, yet cannot be compressed to any significant extent. The volume of a liquid is constant unless evaporation is occurring. Liquids crystallize when chilled sufficiently, while heat causes liquids to vaporize; boiling is very rapid vaporization. When evaporation occurs, some molecules in the liquid have gained enough energy to overcome the attractive forces exerted by the neighboring molecules and escape from the surface of the liquid to become gas. Thus the liquid state is intermediate between the solid and gaseous states, with regard to molecular motion and attractive forces between molecules.

GASES expand to fill any available space. A gas is a compressible fluid, with its volume determined by the pressure and temperature of the environment. The volume varies inversely with pressure, a relationship known as Boyle's law (see figure 10) and written

$$PV = k_1$$

where k_1 is a constant. Another relationship is Charles' law (see figure 10), that gas volume varies directly with temperature:

$$V = k_2 T$$

BOYLE'S LAW

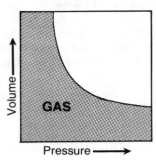

CHARLES' LAW

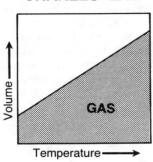

Figure 10

where k_2 is another constant, not equal to k_1. According to the kinetic molecular theory, gases are swarms of tiny molecules moving at a speed dependent on the temperature. Pressure is due to the molecular impacts on the walls of the container. The Italian physicist Avogadro proposed that equal numbers of molecules are contained in equal volumes of all gases, providing the pressure and temperature are identical. Experiments have found that 22.4 liters of gas at room temperature and pressure contain 6×10^{23} molecules, a value known as Avogadro's number.

WATER is the most familiar of all liquids. It is a major constituent of living creatures and our environment. Ordinary water, even rainwater, is impure, with dissolved salts and gases. It may be purified by distillation, where the water is boiled to vapor, which is condensed and collected. The particular *state* of water—liquid, solid, or gas—is determined by the pressure and temperature. (See figure 11.) The dashed line shows the behavior of water at room pressure (1 atmosphere), freezing at 0°C and boiling at 100°C. At other pressures, the freezing and boiling temperatures for liquid water differ from the familiar values.

A SOLUTION is a mixture of two or more substances, the proportions variable between wide limits. Most solutions have a liquid solvent containing a lesser amount of dissolved solute, either a solid, a gas, or another liquid. An aqueous solution has water as the solvent. The concentration of a solution expresses the amount of solute dissolved in a standard unit (usually 1 liter) of the solvent. The solubility of a substance is the maximum concentration of solute which a solution can hold. The solubility

STATES OF H₂O

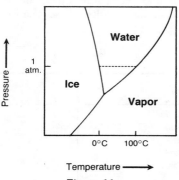

Figure 11

of solids commonly increases with higher temperature, while the solubility of gases decreases with higher temperature. Precipitation of a salt occurs when the solution becomes supersaturated in that salt, the concentration exceeding the solubility.

IONS form when compounds dissociate in solution to positive and negative particles. For example, magnesium fluoride (MgF_2) separates in solution to magnesium and fluorine ions:

$$\underset{salt}{MgF_2} \xrightarrow{H_2O} \underset{ions\ in\ solution}{Mg^{+2} + 2F^{-1}}$$

ACIDS AND BASES are solutions with unusual concentrations of either hydrogen or hydroxyl ions, such a solution being acidic or alkaline (basic). The familiar acids contain hydrogen which is loosely bound, while the bases are hydroxides of alkaline metals. (See table 6.) Acids and bases

TABLE 6

Acids	Hydrochloric	HCl
	Nitric	HNO_3
	Sulfuric	H_2SO_4
Bases	Sodium Hydroxide	NaOH
	Potassium Hydroxide	KOH
	Ammonium Hydroxide	NH_4OH

dissociate in aqueous solution and modify the concentration of hydrogen ions, which is measured as pH by litmus paper or other indicators. (See table 7.) The reaction of an acid with a base is called neutralization and releases some heat.

TABLE 7

Solution	pH
strong acid	1
weak acid	4
neutral	7
weak base	10
strong base	13

CHEMICAL REACTIONS show the number of molecules or formula units of the reactants and products. For example, nitrous oxide is a colorless, odorless gas which causes mild hysteria when breathed, hence the name *laughing gas;* it is prepared by heating ammonium nitrate crystals:

$$\underset{\substack{ammonium\\nitrate}}{\text{NH}_4\text{NO}_3} \xrightarrow{\text{heat}} \underset{\substack{water\\vapor}}{2\text{H}_2\text{O}} + \underset{\substack{nitrous\\oxide}}{\text{N}_2\text{O}}$$

Conditions necessary for the reaction to proceed—like heat, light, or catalyst—are shown alongside the reaction arrow, which always points from reactants to products. In our example, one molecule of ammonium nitrate yielded two molecules of water and one of nitrous oxide.

GLOSSARY OF TERMS IN CHEMISTRY

ACID: A compound which yields hydrogen ions in solution.

ALLOY: A metal composed of two or more metallic elements.

ANION: An ion with a negative charge; in electrolysis, an anion moves toward the anode.

ANODE: The positive electrode.

ATOM: The smallest particle of matter that cannot be subdivided by chemical reactions.

ATOMIC NUMBER: The number of protons in an atomic nucleus; the different chemical elements have different atomic numbers.

ATOMIC WEIGHT: The weight of an atom relative to a carbon atom; C^{12} = 12. The atomic weight is approximately the number of protons plus neutrons.

AVOGADRO'S NUMBER: 6×10^{23}, the number of molecules in a gram molecular weight of a substance.

BASE: A compound which yields hydroxyl (OH^-) ions in solution.

BOILING POINT: The temperature at which a liquid changes to a gas.

BOILING POINT ELEVATION: An increase in the boiling piont of a solvent, proportional to the amount of solute.

BOYLE'S LAW: The volume of a gas varies inversely with pressure.

CARBON DIOXIDE: CO_2 is a colorless, noncombustible gas under normal conditions.

CATALYST: A substance which accelerates a chemical reaction, without itself being a reactant.

CATHODE: The negative electrode.

CATION: An ion with positive charge; in electrolysis, a cation moves toward the cathode.

CHARLES' LAW: The volume of a gas varies directly with temperature.

COLLOID: A suspension of tiny particles in a fluid.

COMBUSTION: Rapid oxidation that releases heat and light.

COMPOUND: A substance formed by the chemical union of several chemical elements.

CONCENTRATION: The amount of dissolved material in a given amount of solution.

CONDENSATION: The liquefaction of a vapor.

CONSERVATION OF MASS: The law that there is no gain or loss of mass in a chemical reaction.

DECOMPOSITION: A chemical reaction in which a compound is broken down into simpler compounds or elements.

DENSITY: Mass per unit volume of a substance.

DIFFUSION: The mixing of different substances, commonly in a liquid or gas.

DISTILLATION: The process of purification in which an impure substance is heated to vapors, which are collected and condensed.

ELECTRODE: A charged pole of metal dipped into a liquid that conducts electricity.

ELECTRON: A negatively charged, subatomic particle; electrons form a cloud around the atomic nucleus. Electron movement constitutes electrical current.

ELECTROLYSIS: A chemical change brought about by an electric current; used to separate chemical elements.

ELECTROLYTE: A liquid that conducts electricity.

ELEMENT: A substance which cannot be decomposed to simpler substances.

EQUILIBRIUM: The point at which two opposing chemical reactions balance.

EVAPORATION: A change of state from a solid or liquid to a gas.

FREEZING POINT: The temperature at which a liquid changes to a solid.

FUSION: The melting of a solid to a liquid.

GROUP: A vertical column of elements in the periodic table; elements in one group have similar chemical properties.

HETEROGENEOUS: Describes a substance that is a mixture.

HYDROCARBONS: Compounds of carbon and hydrogen.

HYDROLYSIS: Chemical decomposition of a compound by reaction with water.

ION: A charged atom or group of atoms formed by the gain or loss of electrons.

IONIZATION: Adding or subtracting electrons from an atom.

ISOTOPE: Isotopes of an element have the same number of protons and show the same chemical behavior, but they differ in a number of nuclear neutrons and thus in atomic weight; isotopes may be stable or radioactive.

LITMUS: Paper that turns red in acid and blue in alkaline solution.

MELTING POINT: The temperature at which a solid changes to a liquid.

METHANE: The simplest hydrocarbon, a gas with the composition CH_4.

MISCIBLE: Capable of being mixed, referring to two liquids.

MIXTURE: Substances mixed without a chemical reaction; the substances can be in any proportion.

MOLE: Abbreviation for molecular weight.

MOLECULAR WEIGHT: The sum of the weights of the atoms in a compound.

MOLECULE: The smallest particle of a compound, composed of several bonded atoms.

NEUTRALIZATION: The chemical reaction of an acid and a base to form a salt and water.

NEUTRON: A subatomic particle of zero charge which occurs in the atomic nucleus.

NUCLEUS: The dense center of an atom, made up of protons and neutrons.

ORGANIC COMPOUND: A compound with interconnected carbon atoms.

OXIDATION: The addition of oxygen to a substance.

OXIDE: A compound of oxygen and another element.

PERIODIC LAW: The chemical and physical properties of the elements are periodic functions of their atomic numbers.

pH: A number indicating the concentration of hydrogen ions in a solution. A pH of 7 is neutral, less than 7 is acidic, and greater than 7 is alkaline.

POLYMER: A giant organic molecule, made by chaining together smaller units.

PRECIPITATE: A solid which separates from solution.

PROTON: A subatomic particle with a positive charge, occurring in the atomic nucleus.

REACTION: A chemical change of substance, from reactant(s) to product(s).

REDUCTION: The removal of some oxygen from a compound.

SALT: A solid compound composed of both metallic and nonmetallic elements.

SATURATED: Describes a solution which contains as much solute as possible.

SOLUTE: The substance dissolved in a solution.

SOLVENT: The pure liquid within a solution.

STATE OF MATTER: Solid, liquid, or gas.

SUBLIMATION: The change from a solid to a gas, without an intermediate liquid.

SYNTHESIS: The formation of a compound by combining elements or simpler compounds.

VALENCE: A number describing the combining power of an atom, the number of electrons it can gain or lose in combination with other atoms.

VAPOR: Gas.

VISCOSITY: The resistance of a liquid to flowage.

VOLATILITY: The ease of vaporization for a liquid or solid.

PHYSICS REVIEW

BASIC CONCEPTS

PHYSICS is the most basic and most general of the natural sciences. It covers subjects from matter to energy in the most general way. Physicists try to provide orderly explanations for natural events by formulating laws broad enough to explain all particular situations. Such laws are often suggested by regularities in experiments, but the clear logic and advanced mathematics used to construct physical formulas make physics the supremely theoretical science. The scientific method requires observation, conjecture, calculation, prediction, and testing. Successive scientific revolutions have taught us that today's laws are not certain, only more accurate than yesterday's laws.

MEASUREMENT is the beginning of scientific wisdom. The physicist's first reaction to a new idea is: Can it be measured? Can I describe it with numbers? Numerical data can be manipulated with many powerful mathematical tools, from arithmetic and geometry to statistics and differential equations. Physical quantities range from subatomic smallness to astronomic hugeness, so the numbers are conveniently expressed in *scientific notation*, in which any number is written in the form

$$N \times 10^P$$

where N is a number between 1 and 10, and P is a power of 10. The population of Brazil is about 130,000,000 and that number could be written as

$$1.3 \times 10^8$$

You should also be aware of the three basic units of the metric system. (See table 8.) A unit 1000 times the basic unit has the prefix *kilo*, so a kilometer equals 1000 meters. The prefix *milli* (as in millimeter) denotes a unit 1/1000 the basic unit.

TABLE 8

Quantity	Unit	Symbol	Approximation
Length	meter	m	1.1 yard
Volume	liter	l	1.1 quart
Mass	gram	g	1/30 ounce

MOTION is described by stating an object's position, velocity, and acceleration. Velocity is the rate of change of position with time. For example, an automobile that is 100 miles further along a highway at 3:00 than at 1:00 has an average velocity during that interval of

$$v = \frac{\Delta d}{\Delta t} = \frac{100}{2} = 50 \text{ miles/hour}$$

where the Δd represents change of distance and Δt is the change of time. Acceleration is the rate of change of velocity with time. If the automobile in our example had an initial velocity of 40 mph and a final velocity of 60 mph, then its average acceleration would be

$$a = \frac{\Delta v}{\Delta t} = \frac{20}{2} = 10 \text{ miles/hour/hour}$$

NEWTON'S LAWS relate the motion of an object to the forces acting upon it. The *law of inertia* asserts that, in the absence of any force, a body at rest will continue at rest while another body moving in a straight line will continue to move in that direction with uniform speed. Any change of speed or direction must be due to a force. The *law of acceleration* states that a body acted on by a force will undergo acceleration proportional to the force:

$$f = m \cdot a$$

where m is the mass of the object, the quantity of matter for that object. Table 9 lists masses for a range of objects. Newton's *law of reaction* says that for every action, there is an equal and opposite reaction.

TABLE 9

Representative Object	Mass in Grams
Electron	10^{-27}
Atom	10^{-23}
Amoeba	10^{-5}
Ant	10^{-2}
Human	10^{5}
Whale	10^{8}
Earth	10^{28}
Sun	10^{33}

GRAVITATION is familiar to us through weight, which is directly proportional to mass:

$$w = m \cdot g$$

where g is the acceleration due to gravity. The mass of an object is constant throughout the universe, but its weight varies with the object's position. Because the moon has a weaker gravitational field than the earth, an astronaut weighing 180 pounds here would weigh only 30 pounds there. Gravitational forces exist between all pairs of tangible objects, with the force being directly proportional to the product of their masses and inversely proportional to the square of the distance separating them. An astronaut weighs less on the moon because its mass is less than that of the earth. A balloon rising from the surface decreases in weight as it ascends and the distance from the earth increases.

ENERGY is the ability to perform work, to move objects. That ability can take several forms. The energy possessed by a moving object is called *kinetic* energy. An object in an unstable position has *potential* energy, for the position could be converted into movement. Let's consider a baseball thrown vertically upward. (See figure 12.) Its speed decreases upward because the acceleration of gravity is acting downward. The rising ball

CONSERVATION OF ENERGY

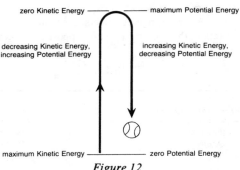

Figure 12

loses kinetic energy (slows down) as it gains potential energy (rises higher). At the peak of the ball's flight, the ball is instantaneously at rest, with no kinetic energy but maximum stored potential energy. As the ball falls, the potential energy is transformed into kinetic energy and the ball accelerates. *Thermal* energy also exists, for it has been shown that heat can be converted to motion, and motion can produce heat. Electricity and magnetism are still other forms of energy, for they can be converted into heat and motion. Notice that this key concept of energy is the abstract idea that there is something identical in motion, heat, and electricity, which appear so different to our senses. It is possible to define the various forms of energy so that their mathematical sum is constant. The law of conservation of energy states that energy can be neither created nor destroyed.

TEMPERATURE is a measure of the movement of the molecules in a substance. Heat is nothing else than kinetic energy on an atomic level. The basic temperature scale of science is the centigrade (or Celsius) scale (see table 10), on which water freezes at 0°C and boils at 100°C. At absolute zero, all molecular motion would cease. You should be able to convert our familiar Fahrenheit temperatures to centigrade or vice versa:

$$C = \frac{5}{9} (F - 32)$$
$$F = \frac{9}{5} C + 32$$

Just for practice, try to calculate the centigrade temperature equivalent to 50°F, then look at the answer in the footnote. The quantity of heat contained in a substance is measured in calories and must not be confused with temperature. At one temperature, a large mass of lead contains more heat than a smaller mass of lead. If those two pieces of lead had equal heat contents, the small mass would have a higher temperature than the larger mass.

TABLE 10

Temperature of Object in ° C

Absolute zero	−273
Oxygen freezes	−218
Oxygen liquifies	−183
Water freezes	0
Human body	37
Water boils	100
Wood fire	830
Iron melts	1535
Iron boils	3000

SOUND is produced by the mechanical disturbance of a gas, liquid, or solid. The disturbance consists of alternating zones of abundant and scarce molecules, and such zones travel as waves. (See figure 13.) In such waves, the molecules vibrate and collide with each other, thus passing on their

SOUND WAVES
IN A PIPE

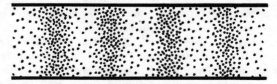

Figure 13

$$C = 5/9 (F - 32) = 5/9 (50 - 32) = 5/9 (18) = 10°C$$

kinetic energy without changing their average position. The speed of sound depends on the physical properties of the medium through which it travels. In air, sound travels at 740 miles per hour, while steel transmits sound 15 times faster. The intensity level of sound is commonly reported in decibels.

ELECTRICITY exists where the number of negative electrons does not precisely equal the number of positive protons. If we suspend small charged balls on nonconducting threads (see figure 14), we find that there are forces of repulsion between similar charges and attraction between

ELECTRIC FORCES

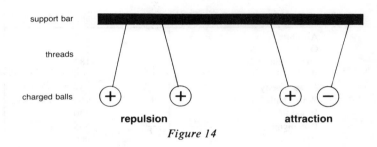

Figure 14

unlike charges. One type of electricity can neutralize the effect of the other type, so we regard the opposite charges as being due to an excess (−) or deficit (+) of *negative* electrons. Two bodies of opposite charge are said to have a difference of electrical potential, which is measured in volts. The chemical reaction in a battery produces a potential difference, and connecting the two poles through a conducting wire leads to the passage of an electric current, which is simply a flow of electrons.

MAGNETISM is displayed by permanent magnets and around electric currents. All of us have had the opportunity to study the interesting properties of permanent magnets, small bars or horseshoes of iron which have aligned internal structures induced by other magnets. The north pole of one magnet attracts the south pole of another, but like poles repel each other. Either pole can attract unmagnetized iron objects. Iron filings spread on a piece of paper above a bar magnet become arranged in a pattern which maps a magnetic *field* in the space around the magnet. (See figure 15.) The earth's magnetic field orients the iron needles of navigational compasses. An electric current also generates a magnetic field, demonstrating an intimate connection between electricity and magnetism.

Later work has united these phenomena and light, too, into electromagnetic radiation.

MAGNETIC FIELD
ABOVE A BAR MAGNET

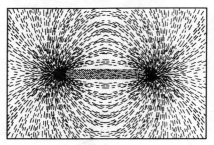

Figure 15

LIGHT seems to travel in perfectly straight lines as rays. The direction of a ray changes at the interface between two transparent materials, like air and water as depicted in figure 16. Notice that some of the light is

REFLECTION AND REFRACTION

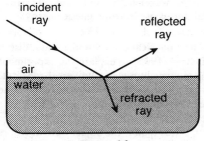

incident ray

reflected ray

air
water

refracted ray

Figure 16

reflected, the angle of reflection being equal to the angle of incidence. The portion of the light that crosses the boundary is, however, deflected in another direction, and the angle of refraction does not equal the angle of incidence. Other optical experiments are inconsistent with a simple ray theory and require that light travels as waves of electromagnetic energy. When white light (including sunlight) is refracted by a glass prism, it is separated into its component colors as a beautiful spectrum. (See figure 17.) Experiments have shown that the various colors travel at the uniform speed c:

$$c = 186,000 \text{ miles} / \text{second} = 3 \times 10^8 \text{ meters} / \text{second}$$

DISPERSION OF SUNLIGHT

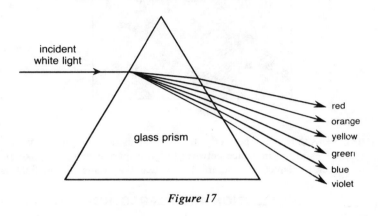

Figure 17

The colors differ in wavelength, and table 11 displays the relative wavelengths for all forms of electromagnetic energy.

RELATIVITY of basic physical concepts like mass, distance, and time was postulated by Einstein (1905) to explain the experimental discovery that the speed of light in a vacuum was a universal constant. The principle of relativity states that all the laws of physics have the same form despite the movement of the observer. An observer performing an experiment on an object moving relative to himself finds that the object's measured mass is greater and length is less than if the object were at rest relative to himself. These curious effects are significant only at incredibly high velocities and may be neglected for most purposes. Einstein's famous law for the conversion of mass to energy

$$E = mc^2$$

suggested that atomic reactions could release unprecedented quantities of energy.

TABLE 11
ELECTROMAGNETIC RADIATION

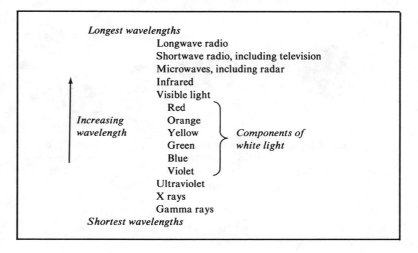

NUCLEAR ENERGY has been obtained by two different means, fission and fusion. Nuclear fission releases energy when a heavy nucleus splits into smaller fragments. (See figure 18. Black balls show neutrons, and white balls show protons.) Bombarding uranium with a neutron produces an unstable intermediate, which disintegrates to lighter nuclei with the conversion of 0.1% of the mass into energy. Nuclear fission is used in power plants and atomic bombs. The opposite process of nuclear fusion yields energy when very light nuclei unite to a heavier nucleus. (See figure 19.) A hydrogen bomb contains the two heavy isotopes of hydrogen, deuterium (H^2) and tritium (H^3) which unite to form helium nuclei and neutrons, with a conversion of 0.4% of the initial mass into energy. Stars (including the sun) derive their energy from nuclear fusion.

ASTRONOMY is the science of the heavens, from the moon to distant galaxies. In past cultures, men spent much more time outside than we do, and the recurring patterns of day and night, the seasons, eclipses, and the paths of the planets across the background of fixed stars led to the birth of science, an attempt to find order rather than mystery in our world. The ancient Greeks understood the cause of eclipses. A lunar eclipse darkens the moon as the earth passes between it and the sun, casting a shadow on

FISSION

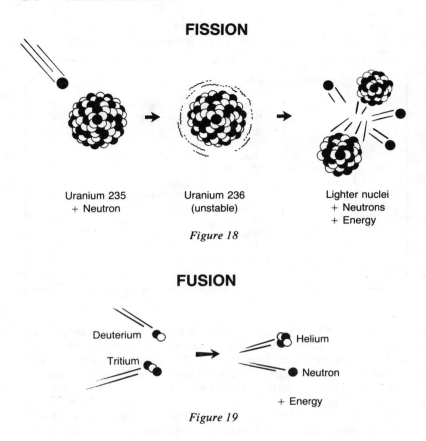

| Uranium 235
+ Neutron | Uranium 236
(unstable) | Lighter nuclei
+ Neutrons
+ Energy |

Figure 18

FUSION

Deuterium

Tritium

Helium

Neutron

+ Energy

Figure 19

the moon. (See figure 20.) A solar eclipse takes place when the moon passes between the earth and the sun, the moon blocking the sunlight for about 2 minutes for the most magnificent sight in astronomy. (See figure 21.) The first great triumph of modern science was when Copernicus (1543) realized that the earth was not at the center of the universe, but revolved around the sun yearly and rotated on its axis daily. Table 12 shows current data on the solar system. The earth is 93 million miles from the sun and has a radius of 4000 miles. From the table one can calculate that Jupiter, for example, is about 500 million miles from the sun and has a radius of about 44,000 miles; the mass of that giant planet is nearly three times that of all other planets combined.

LUNAR ECLIPSE

Figure 20

SOLAR ECLIPSE

Figure 21

TABLE 12

Planet	Distance* from Sun	Radius*	Mass*	Moons
Mercury	0.39	0.38	0.05	0
Venus	0.72	0.96	0.82	0
Earth	1.00	1.00	1.00	1
Mars	1.52	0.53	0.11	2
Asteroids	2.8	(thousands of small bodies)		
Jupiter	5.2	11.0	317.8	16
Saturn	9.5	9.2	95.1	18
Uranus	19.2	3.7	14.5	5
Neptune	30.1	3.5	17.2	2
Pluto	39.5	0.5	0.1(?)	1

*relative to Earth = 1

GLOSSARY OF TERMS IN PHYSICS AND ASTRONOMY

ABSOLUTE TEMPERATURE: Temperature expressed in degrees Kelvin (°K), which is zero at absolute zero; °K = °C + 273.

ABSOLUTE ZERO: The lowest possible temperature, equal to −459°F, −273°C, or 0°K.

ACCELERATION: The rate of change of velocity with time.

ALPHA PARTICLE: A positive particle composed of two protons and two neutrons, emitted during radioactive decay.

AMPERE: The unit of measurement of electric current.

ARCHIMEDES' PRINCIPLE: A body immersed in a fluid is lifted by a force equal to the weight of the fluid displaced by the body.

ASTEROID: A planetary fragment or minor planet. Most of the thousands of known asteroids are between the orbits of Mars and Jupiter. Ceres is the largest asteroid.

AXIS: A straight line around which a body rotates.

BETA PARTICLE: An electron emitted from an atomic nucleus during radioactive disintegration.

BUOYANCY: The upward force on an object immersed in a fluid.

CALORIE: The amount of heat required to raise the temperature of one gram of water 1°C.

CENTRIFUGAL FORCE: The apparent force deflecting a rotating mass radially outward.

CHAIN REACTION: Occurs when the fission of one atom causes the fission of other atoms.

CHARGE: The electrical state of matter, positive or negative.

COMET: A diffuse body which glows with a prominent tail when its orbit brings it near the sun.

CONDUCTION: Transfer of heat or electricity.

CONSERVATION OF ENERGY: Energy may be changed from one form to another, but it can't be created or destroyed.

CONSTELLATION: An apparent group of stars.

CORONA: A halo of glowing gases around the sun, visible only during a total solar eclipse.

CURRENT: A direct electric current (DC) flows in one direction, but an alternating current (AC) periodically reverses the direction of flow.

CYCLOTRON: A machine that accelerates atomic particles by means of an alternating electric field.

ECLIPTIC: The plane within which the planets orbit around the sun.

ELECTROMAGNETIC RADIATION: Energy traveling as a disturbance of electric and magnetic fields.

ENERGY: The ability to perform work. Kinetic energy is due to a body's motion, while potential energy is due to a body's position.

ESCAPE VELOCITY: The speed a rocket must reach in order to leave the earth's vicinity.

FIELD: The region where a force is felt.

FISSION: The splitting of an atomic nucleus into parts.

FLUID: A liquid or gas.

FOCUS: The place where an image is formed by a mirror or lens.

FORCE: A force causes a body to accelerate.

FREQUENCY: The number of vibrations of a wave per unit time.

FULCRUM: The support on which a lever pivots.

FUSION: Nuclear fusion is the union of atomic nuclei.

GALAXY: An astronomical system composed of billions of stars; the Milky Way is our galaxy.

GAMMA RAY: High-energy electromagnetic radiation emitted during radioactive disintegration.

GRAVITATION: The attraction of bodies because of their masses; an especially familiar case is the attraction between the earth and an object.

GROUND: A connection to the earth to dissipate an electric charge.

HALF-LIFE: The time required for the radioactivity of a substance to drop by one-half.

HEAT: Kinetic energy of molecular motion.

HYPOTHESIS: A tentative explanation of a phenomenon.

INERTIA: The ability of a body to resist acceleration, continuing either at rest or in motion with uniform velocity.

JUPITER: The fifth planet from the sun is the largest in the solar system, with a diameter eleven times that of the earth. Jupiter has sixteen known satellites, the largest being Ganymede.

LAW: A general statement about a group of related facts.

LENS: A transparent material shaped either concave or convex to refract light and form a magnified image.

LIGHT-YEAR: The distance light travels in one year.

MAGNETIC POLES: The ends of a bar magnet are referred to as the north and south poles.

MAGNITUDE: The apparent brightness of a star; a larger magnitude represents a dimmer star.

MARS: The fourth planet from the sun, with a diameter 53% that of the earth. Mars has two small satellites, Phobos and Deimos.

MASS: The quantity of matter; the measure of inertia.

MERCURY: The small planet closest to the sun, with a diameter 39% that of the earth.

METEOR: The streak of light produced by an interplanetary particle in its passage through the earth's atmosphere.

METEORITE: A rock from interplanetary space, found on the earth's surface.

MOMENTUM: The product of mass and velocity. The conservation of momentum is a fundamental law of nature.

NEBULA: A cloud of gas or dust in interstellar space.

NEPTUNE: The eighth planet from the sun, with a diameter nearly four times that of the earth. Neptune has two satellites, the largest being Triton.

NOVA: A star which suddenly becomes many times brighter than usual.

NUCLEUS: The central part of an atom, containing almost all of its mass; plural is *nuclei*.

ORBIT: The path of one celestial body around another.

PARALLAX: The apparent shift in position of an object viewed from two different points; used for range-finding by triangulation.

PAYLOAD: The load of explosives, instruments, or passengers carried by a rocket.

PENDULUM: A mass hanging on the end of a string or other support, which is free to swing.

PHOTON: A quantum or particle of light energy.

PLUTO: The ninth planet from the sun, discovered in 1930; Pluto has one satellite, Charon.

PRISM: A glass wedge used to disperse light.

RADIATION: Includes both electromagnetic waves and particles emitted during radioactive disintegration.

RADIOACTIVITY: Spontaneous decay of an atomic nucleus, with emission of alpha particles, beta particles, and gamma rays.

RADIO TELESCOPE: An electronic antenna that receives radio waves from outer space.

REFRACTION: The bending of a light ray or wavefront at the boundary between two substances.

REVOLUTION: The movement of a celestial body in its orbit. The earth takes $365\frac{1}{4}$ days to revolve around the sun.

ROTATION: The spinning of a body on its axis. One rotation of the earth requires 24 hours.

SATELLITE: A body orbiting around a planet.

SATURN: The sixth planet from the sun has very prominent rings and a diameter over nine times that of the earth. Saturn has eighteen known moons, the largest being Titan.

SCIENCE: Systematic and verifiable knowledge.

SPECTROSCOPE: An instrument that separates a beam of light into its component colors, usually for obtaining a chemical composition.

SPECTRUM: The visible spectrum is the band of colors seen when white light is dispersed. The electromagnetic spectrum is the total range of frequencies of electric and magnetic waves, including radio and light waves.

TEMPERATURE: Average kinetic energy of a group of molecules; determines the direction of heat flow.

TERMINAL VELOCITY: The final, constant speed of fall of a body in a fluid.

TIDE: The rising and falling of the ocean due to the gravitational attraction of the moon and sun.

URANUS: The seventh planet from the sun, with a diameter almost four times that of the earth. Uranus has five known satellites and a faint ring.

VELOCITY: The rate of change of position with time.

VENUS: The second planet from the sun is very nearly the same size as the earth and is cloaked by dense, hot clouds.

VOLT: Unit of measurement of electric potential.

WAVE: A disturbance that can travel.

WAVELENGTH: The distance from one wave crest to the next.

WEIGHT: A measure of the gravitational pull on an object.

WEIGHTLESSNESS: A condition that arises where accelerating forces precisely offset one another.

WORK: The product of force and distance.

X RAYS: Short electromagnetic waves that can penetrate solids.

ZENITH: The point directly overhead.

PROFESSIONAL KNOWLEDGE REVIEW

The following pages present a survey of major educational figures, concepts, philosophies, and terms. This section is meant to provide a simple overview of educational theory and practice. It is not meant to be memorized. Test emphasis has been on classroom management, methodology, evaluation, etc., and much less on history or identification of important educators.

Skim the survey before taking the first practice test, noting especially those names and concepts with which you are unfamiliar and those with which you had difficulty on the Mini-Test. After discovering your problem areas in Practice Test 1, return to the review to reinforce your knowledge and understanding. In addition, be sure to make full use of the explanations given in the answer sections following each practice test. These answers will provide you with an intensive review of important test areas.

SURVEY OF IMPORTANT PEOPLE AND IDEAS IN EDUCATION

Abelard	12th century	Wrote *Sic et Non* (Yea and Nay); popularized concept that constant questioning is first key to wisdom
Academies	18th century	Development of secular and practical education in colonial America; used English as basic language rather than Latin
Alternative schools	20th century	Nontraditional academic program
American Association for the Advancement of Education	1851	Established *Journal of American Education*
Apperception	19th century	New ideas are interpreted through those already learned; established by Herbart
Apprenticeship system	17th and 18th centuries	System of education designed for lower classes; informal method of teaching
Aquinas, St. Thomas	1225–1274	The greatest of the scholastics; *Summa Theologica*
Aristotle	384–322 B.C.	Educational philosophy stressed ethics, politics, and physics; education as a life activity
Bacon, Francis	1561–1626	*Novum organum* (new method); philosopher of scientific movement; stressed education as training of mental faculties; advocated inductive scientific method

Bailyn, Bernard	20th century	*Education and Forming of American Society* (1960); stressed that education can be a vehicle to change or control society; changing role of state and effect on education
Block grant	20th century	Federal or state aid given *in toto* with unspecified use but for educational purposes only
Bloom's taxonomy	20th century	Six major classes of learning: knowledge, comprehension, application, analysis, synthesis, and evaluation
Brown v. Board of Education	1954	Historic Supreme Court decision that declared "separate but equal" principle unconstitutional
Bruner, Jerome S.	20th century	*The Process of Education* (1960); theories strengthened the academic curriculum; advocated the early teaching of science and mathematics
Calvinistic education	16th and 17th centuries	Stressed rhetoric, grammar, classical subjects, and moral conduct; cornerstone of Puritan education
Categorical aid	20th century	Federal or state aid earmarked for a special aspect of the school curriculum
Cathedral schools	Middle Ages	Stressed seven liberal arts: grammar, rhetoric, logic, arithmetic, geometry, astronomy, and music
Charity schools	18th century	Started in France and England; move toward popular education
Classical languages		Latin, Greek

Term	Period	Description
Common school	19th century	School system designed to achieve popular education open to all members of the society
Conant, James	20th century	Stressed the democratic aspects of the comprehensive secondary school; *American High School Today* (1959)
Core curriculum	20th century	Correlated courses designed to promote a broad-field approach to the curriculum
Cremin, Lawrence	20th century	*Transformation in the School* (1964); definitive study of progressive-education movement
Curriculum		Appropriate subject matter and skills
Dame schools	17th century	Colonial practice of teaching children how to read in one's home while household chores were being performed
Darwin	1809–1882	*Origin of Species* (1859); theory of evolution; revolutionized educational thought
Department of Education, U.S.	19th century	Established in 1867; represented the growth of federal participation in education
Dewey, John	1859–1952	Applied philosophy to the practice of education; laboratory school at the University of Chicago was alternative to traditional education; *School and Society* (1899); *Democracy and Education* (1916)
Dialectic		Developed by Plato; discourse or discussion

ECE	20th century	Early childhood education programs designed for children below first grade
Elective system	19th and 20th centuries	Educational concept based on freedom of choice among subject areas
Émile	1762	Rousseau's chief work on education; developed child-centered theory of education
Empiricism	17th century	Emphasizing sensory experience as a true source of knowledge
Enlightenment, the age of	1700–1789	Intellectual movement that stressed rationalist, liberal, humanitarian trends of thought; emphasized study of man
Experimental schools	20th century	Developed by Dewey to further his educational philosophies; rejected regular education as failing to keep up with changes in an industrial society
Extracurricular activities		Activities beyond traditional subject areas; part of comprehensive high school
"Four quarter" plan	20th century	Utilize schools the entire year
Franklin, Benjamin	1706–1790	Developed academy in colonial America; started concept of popular education in America
Fundamentalism	19th and 20th centuries	Philosophy stressing theistic view; developed in response to new science; spiritual concept of man
Gary Plan	20th century	Attempt to incorporate the progressive ideas of Dewey into the public schools of Gary, Indiana

Term	Period	Description
Gestalt psychology	1920	Philosophy that stressed learner as whole organism; emphasized learning by insight rather than drill and repetition
GI Bill of Rights	1944	Federal support for education in the form of tuition, books, and supplies to enable armed forces personnel to continue their education
Glazer, William	20th century	*Schools without Failure* (1969); nongraded education
Guild schools	Middle Ages	Development of university system; societies of masters and students
Gymnasium	16th century	German center of classical learning
Heterogeneous grouping		Grouping without regard to ability levels
Higher education		Postsecondary education
Hobbes, Thomas	1588–1679	Materialist concept of human nature; stressed mathematics as key to the scientific method
Home economics	19th and 20th centuries	Example of vocational education; part of comprehensive high school
Homogeneous grouping		Ability-level grouping
Humanism	16th century	A Renaissance movement that focused on secular concerns and the revival of classics
Idealism	19th century	Influential theory that stressed nonsectarian reliance on spirituality

Industrial or vocational education	19th and 20th centuries	Response to industrial change in American society; manual, industrial, and commercial education
Intelligence tests	19th and 20th centuries	Developed by Binet to determine mental age and innate ability
Jefferson, Thomas	1743–1826	Influenced by Enlightenment; stressed practical school curriculum
Jesuit education	16th century	Catholic education formed in response to the Reformation
Junior college	19th and 20th centuries	Two-year college encompassing freshman and sophomore years
Kant, Immanuel	1724–1804	Espoused Rousseau's child-centered educational philosophy; called for public education
Kindergarten	19th century	Developed by Froebel; formal education to start at age of three or four
Lesson plan	20th century	To present objectives and content in a logical and systematic manner
Locke, John	1632–1704	Stressed necessity for individualization of education and comprehensive course of studies; government by consent of governed
Mann, Horace	1796–1859	Developed concept of a public, free, and compulsory education
Maslow, Abraham H.	20th century	*Toward a Psychology of Being;* role of choice in learning; children's choices are usually wise

Master's degree	Middle Ages to 20th century	Postgraduate degree; originally stressed completing the seven liberal arts
Memorizing		Educational theory based on training mental faculties by repetition
Morrill Act	1862	Federal aid to education in the form of land grants; land-grant colleges
Naturalism	18th century	Developed by Rousseau; stressed dignity of natural man
NDEA	1958	National Defense Educational Assistance Act. Financial aid to improve educational programs (especially science) in the United States.
NEA	19th and 20th centuries	National Education Association—national teachers' association
Neill, A. S.	20th century	*Summerhill* (1960); radical approach to education based on freedom of choice
Normal school, American	19th and 20th centuries	Curriculum designed to offer courses in professional education and teaching methods
Nursery schools	20th century	Preelementary education for two, three, or four year olds
Ordinances of 1785 and 1787	18th century	Initiated federal aid to education; land ordinances for western states
Parker, Francis	1837–1902	Father of progressive education; stressed learning experience

Pestalozzi, Johann	1746–1827	*How Gertrude Teaches Her Children;* stressed child-centered education
Phi Beta Kappa	1779	First intercollegiate fraternity in America
Piaget, Jean	20th century	Theories led to understanding the differing stages of child development
Plato	429–348 B.C.	*The Republic;* developed concept of ideal state; based on three classes: philosophers, soldiers, workers; elitist education controlled by state
Plessy v. Ferguson	1896	Established principle of "separate but equal"
Pragmatism	19th century	Philosophy that stressed that theories must be tested in practice to determine their consequences
Programmed instruction	20th century	Designed to provide self-paced, individualized instruction
PTA	20th century	Parent-Teacher Association
Puritans	17th century	Responsible for the development of public education in colonial America
Realism	Middle Ages	Reality consists of ideas independent of our sensory powers
Republic	4th century B.C.	Plato's educational philosophy; higher education only to those specifically suited for it
Rhetoric	4th century B.C.	Discourse; the study of composition; considered part of classical curriculum up to the 19th century

Rickover, H. G.	20th century	*American Education—A National Failure* (1964); criticized American system of education in favor of European system; stressed reform of public education
Rogers, Carl	20th century	Learning is "learning how to learn"
Rorschach test	20th century	A projective test that uses inkblots to elicit an unstructured response
Rousseau, Jean Jacques	1712–1778	Developed concept of a child-centered education; education in a natural state
Scholasticism	Middle Ages	Church's efforts to organize and systematize knowledge; attempt to reconcile faith and reason
Scopes Trial	1925	Legal contest between fundamentalist view of Bible and theory of evolution
Smith-Hughes Act	1917	Federal aid for vocational education in the secondary schools
Socrates	469–399 B.C.	Greek philosopher; "Socratic method" of dialogue through constant questioning and debate
Spencer, Herbert	1820–1903	Applied Darwin's theories of evolution to society; led to development of social sciences
Team teaching	20th century	Organizational pattern where two or more teachers plan, teach, and evaluate a part of the curriculum for the same group of students

Thorndike, Edward	1874–1949	Development of educational psychology; formulated stimulus-response (S-R) psychology
Three R's	19th century	Traditional education: reading, writing, and arithmetic
Transcendentalism	19th century	Stressed human spirit; reaction against materialism and industrialism
UNESCO	1945	United Nations Educational, Scientific, and Cultural Organization
Vernacular		Modern languages and literature

PART V: Practice-Review-Analyze-Practice

Two Full-Length Practice Tests with Complete Answers and Explanations

This section contains two full-length practice simulation NTE Core Battery examinations. The practice tests are followed by answers and complete explanations and analysis techniques. The format, levels of difficulty, question structure, and number of questions are similar to those on the actual NTE. The actual NTE is copyrighted and may not be duplicated, and these questions are not taken directly from the actual tests.

When taking these exams, try to simulate the test conditions by following the time allotments carefully. Remember the total testing time is 6 hours and each section is 30 minutes long. The tests are divided as follows:

Test of Communication Skills
    Section I: Listening
    Section II: Reading
    Section III: Writing—Multiple Choice
    Section IV: Writing—Essay

Test of General Knowledge
    Section I: Social Studies
    Section II: Mathematics
    Section III: Literature and Fine Arts
    Section IV: Science

Test of Professional Knowledge—Sections I, II, III, and IV

PRACTICE TEST 1

296

TEST OF COMMUNICATION SKILLS

SECTION I   **SECTION II**   **SECTION III**

SECTION I	SECTION II	SECTION III	
1 Ⓐ Ⓑ Ⓒ Ⓓ	1 Ⓐ Ⓑ Ⓒ Ⓓ Ⓔ	1 Ⓐ Ⓑ Ⓒ Ⓓ Ⓔ	31 Ⓐ Ⓑ Ⓒ Ⓓ Ⓔ
2 Ⓐ Ⓑ Ⓒ Ⓓ	2 Ⓐ Ⓑ Ⓒ Ⓓ Ⓔ	2 Ⓐ Ⓑ Ⓒ Ⓓ Ⓔ	32 Ⓐ Ⓑ Ⓒ Ⓓ Ⓔ
3 Ⓐ Ⓑ Ⓒ Ⓓ	3 Ⓐ Ⓑ Ⓒ Ⓓ Ⓔ	3 Ⓐ Ⓑ Ⓒ Ⓓ Ⓔ	33 Ⓐ Ⓑ Ⓒ Ⓓ Ⓔ
4 Ⓐ Ⓑ Ⓒ Ⓓ	4 Ⓐ Ⓑ Ⓒ Ⓓ Ⓔ	4 Ⓐ Ⓑ Ⓒ Ⓓ Ⓔ	34 Ⓐ Ⓑ Ⓒ Ⓓ Ⓔ
5 Ⓐ Ⓑ Ⓒ Ⓓ	5 Ⓐ Ⓑ Ⓒ Ⓓ Ⓔ	5 Ⓐ Ⓑ Ⓒ Ⓓ Ⓔ	35 Ⓐ Ⓑ Ⓒ Ⓓ Ⓔ
6 Ⓐ Ⓑ Ⓒ Ⓓ	6 Ⓐ Ⓑ Ⓒ Ⓓ Ⓔ	6 Ⓐ Ⓑ Ⓒ Ⓓ Ⓔ	36 Ⓐ Ⓑ Ⓒ Ⓓ Ⓔ
7 Ⓐ Ⓑ Ⓒ Ⓓ	7 Ⓐ Ⓑ Ⓒ Ⓓ Ⓔ	7 Ⓐ Ⓑ Ⓒ Ⓓ Ⓔ	37 Ⓐ Ⓑ Ⓒ Ⓓ Ⓔ
8 Ⓐ Ⓑ Ⓒ Ⓓ	8 Ⓐ Ⓑ Ⓒ Ⓓ Ⓔ	8 Ⓐ Ⓑ Ⓒ Ⓓ Ⓔ	38 Ⓐ Ⓑ Ⓒ Ⓓ Ⓔ
9 Ⓐ Ⓑ Ⓒ Ⓓ	9 Ⓐ Ⓑ Ⓒ Ⓓ Ⓔ	9 Ⓐ Ⓑ Ⓒ Ⓓ Ⓔ	39 Ⓐ Ⓑ Ⓒ Ⓓ Ⓔ
10 Ⓐ Ⓑ Ⓒ Ⓓ	10 Ⓐ Ⓑ Ⓒ Ⓓ Ⓔ	10 Ⓐ Ⓑ Ⓒ Ⓓ Ⓔ	40 Ⓐ Ⓑ Ⓒ Ⓓ Ⓔ
11 Ⓐ Ⓑ Ⓒ Ⓓ	11 Ⓐ Ⓑ Ⓒ Ⓓ Ⓔ	11 Ⓐ Ⓑ Ⓒ Ⓓ Ⓔ	41 Ⓐ Ⓑ Ⓒ Ⓓ Ⓔ
12 Ⓐ Ⓑ Ⓒ Ⓓ	12 Ⓐ Ⓑ Ⓒ Ⓓ Ⓔ	12 Ⓐ Ⓑ Ⓒ Ⓓ Ⓔ	42 Ⓐ Ⓑ Ⓒ Ⓓ Ⓔ
13 Ⓐ Ⓑ Ⓒ Ⓓ	13 Ⓐ Ⓑ Ⓒ Ⓓ Ⓔ	13 Ⓐ Ⓑ Ⓒ Ⓓ Ⓔ	43 Ⓐ Ⓑ Ⓒ Ⓓ Ⓔ
14 Ⓐ Ⓑ Ⓒ Ⓓ	14 Ⓐ Ⓑ Ⓒ Ⓓ Ⓔ	14 Ⓐ Ⓑ Ⓒ Ⓓ Ⓔ	44 Ⓐ Ⓑ Ⓒ Ⓓ Ⓔ
15 Ⓐ Ⓑ Ⓒ Ⓓ	15 Ⓐ Ⓑ Ⓒ Ⓓ Ⓔ	15 Ⓐ Ⓑ Ⓒ Ⓓ Ⓔ	45 Ⓐ Ⓑ Ⓒ Ⓓ Ⓔ
16 Ⓐ Ⓑ Ⓒ Ⓓ	16 Ⓐ Ⓑ Ⓒ Ⓓ Ⓔ	16 Ⓐ Ⓑ Ⓒ Ⓓ Ⓔ	
17 Ⓐ Ⓑ Ⓒ Ⓓ	17 Ⓐ Ⓑ Ⓒ Ⓓ Ⓔ	17 Ⓐ Ⓑ Ⓒ Ⓓ Ⓔ	
18 Ⓐ Ⓑ Ⓒ Ⓓ	18 Ⓐ Ⓑ Ⓒ Ⓓ Ⓔ	18 Ⓐ Ⓑ Ⓒ Ⓓ Ⓔ	
19 Ⓐ Ⓑ Ⓒ Ⓓ	19 Ⓐ Ⓑ Ⓒ Ⓓ Ⓔ	19 Ⓐ Ⓑ Ⓒ Ⓓ Ⓔ	
20 Ⓐ Ⓑ Ⓒ Ⓓ	20 Ⓐ Ⓑ Ⓒ Ⓓ Ⓔ	20 Ⓐ Ⓑ Ⓒ Ⓓ Ⓔ	
21 Ⓐ Ⓑ Ⓒ Ⓓ	21 Ⓐ Ⓑ Ⓒ Ⓓ Ⓔ	21 Ⓐ Ⓑ Ⓒ Ⓓ Ⓔ	
22 Ⓐ Ⓑ Ⓒ Ⓓ	22 Ⓐ Ⓑ Ⓒ Ⓓ Ⓔ	22 Ⓐ Ⓑ Ⓒ Ⓓ Ⓔ	
23 Ⓐ Ⓑ Ⓒ Ⓓ	23 Ⓐ Ⓑ Ⓒ Ⓓ Ⓔ	23 Ⓐ Ⓑ Ⓒ Ⓓ Ⓔ	
24 Ⓐ Ⓑ Ⓒ Ⓓ	24 Ⓐ Ⓑ Ⓒ Ⓓ Ⓔ	24 Ⓐ Ⓑ Ⓒ Ⓓ Ⓔ	
25 Ⓐ Ⓑ Ⓒ Ⓓ	25 Ⓐ Ⓑ Ⓒ Ⓓ Ⓔ	25 Ⓐ Ⓑ Ⓒ Ⓓ Ⓔ	
26 Ⓐ Ⓑ Ⓒ Ⓓ	26 Ⓐ Ⓑ Ⓒ Ⓓ Ⓔ	26 Ⓐ Ⓑ Ⓒ Ⓓ Ⓔ	
27 Ⓐ Ⓑ Ⓒ Ⓓ	27 Ⓐ Ⓑ Ⓒ Ⓓ Ⓔ	27 Ⓐ Ⓑ Ⓒ Ⓓ Ⓔ	
28 Ⓐ Ⓑ Ⓒ Ⓓ	28 Ⓐ Ⓑ Ⓒ Ⓓ Ⓔ	28 Ⓐ Ⓑ Ⓒ Ⓓ Ⓔ	
29 Ⓐ Ⓑ Ⓒ Ⓓ	29 Ⓐ Ⓑ Ⓒ Ⓓ Ⓔ	29 Ⓐ Ⓑ Ⓒ Ⓓ Ⓔ	
30 Ⓐ Ⓑ Ⓒ Ⓓ	30 Ⓐ Ⓑ Ⓒ Ⓓ Ⓔ	30 Ⓐ Ⓑ Ⓒ Ⓓ Ⓔ	
31 Ⓐ Ⓑ Ⓒ Ⓓ			
32 Ⓐ Ⓑ Ⓒ Ⓓ			

CUT HERE

ANSWER SHEET FOR PRACTICE TEST 1
(Remove This Sheet and Use It to Mark Your Answers)

TEST OF GENERAL KNOWLEDGE

SECTION I	SECTION II	SECTION III	SECTION IV

CUT HERE

SECTION I

1 Ⓐ Ⓑ Ⓒ Ⓓ Ⓔ
2 Ⓐ Ⓑ Ⓒ Ⓓ Ⓔ
3 Ⓐ Ⓑ Ⓒ Ⓓ Ⓔ
4 Ⓐ Ⓑ Ⓒ Ⓓ Ⓔ
5 Ⓐ Ⓑ Ⓒ Ⓓ Ⓔ
6 Ⓐ Ⓑ Ⓒ Ⓓ Ⓔ
7 Ⓐ Ⓑ Ⓒ Ⓓ Ⓔ
8 Ⓐ Ⓑ Ⓒ Ⓓ Ⓔ
9 Ⓐ Ⓑ Ⓒ Ⓓ Ⓔ
10 Ⓐ Ⓑ Ⓒ Ⓓ Ⓔ
11 Ⓐ Ⓑ Ⓒ Ⓓ Ⓔ
12 Ⓐ Ⓑ Ⓒ Ⓓ Ⓔ
13 Ⓐ Ⓑ Ⓒ Ⓓ Ⓔ
14 Ⓐ Ⓑ Ⓒ Ⓓ Ⓔ
15 Ⓐ Ⓑ Ⓒ Ⓓ Ⓔ
16 Ⓐ Ⓑ Ⓒ Ⓓ Ⓔ
17 Ⓐ Ⓑ Ⓒ Ⓓ Ⓔ
18 Ⓐ Ⓑ Ⓒ Ⓓ Ⓔ
19 Ⓐ Ⓑ Ⓒ Ⓓ Ⓔ
20 Ⓐ Ⓑ Ⓒ Ⓓ Ⓔ
21 Ⓐ Ⓑ Ⓒ Ⓓ Ⓔ
22 Ⓐ Ⓑ Ⓒ Ⓓ Ⓔ
23 Ⓐ Ⓑ Ⓒ Ⓓ Ⓔ
24 Ⓐ Ⓑ Ⓒ Ⓓ Ⓔ
25 Ⓐ Ⓑ Ⓒ Ⓓ Ⓔ
26 Ⓐ Ⓑ Ⓒ Ⓓ Ⓔ
27 Ⓐ Ⓑ Ⓒ Ⓓ Ⓔ
28 Ⓐ Ⓑ Ⓒ Ⓓ Ⓔ
29 Ⓐ Ⓑ Ⓒ Ⓓ Ⓔ
30 Ⓐ Ⓑ Ⓒ Ⓓ Ⓔ

SECTION II

1 Ⓐ Ⓑ Ⓒ Ⓓ Ⓔ
2 Ⓐ Ⓑ Ⓒ Ⓓ Ⓔ
3 Ⓐ Ⓑ Ⓒ Ⓓ Ⓔ
4 Ⓐ Ⓑ Ⓒ Ⓓ Ⓔ
5 Ⓐ Ⓑ Ⓒ Ⓓ Ⓔ
6 Ⓐ Ⓑ Ⓒ Ⓓ Ⓔ
7 Ⓐ Ⓑ Ⓒ Ⓓ Ⓔ
8 Ⓐ Ⓑ Ⓒ Ⓓ Ⓔ
9 Ⓐ Ⓑ Ⓒ Ⓓ Ⓔ
10 Ⓐ Ⓑ Ⓒ Ⓓ Ⓔ
11 Ⓐ Ⓑ Ⓒ Ⓓ Ⓔ
12 Ⓐ Ⓑ Ⓒ Ⓓ Ⓔ
13 Ⓐ Ⓑ Ⓒ Ⓓ Ⓔ
14 Ⓐ Ⓑ Ⓒ Ⓓ Ⓔ
15 Ⓐ Ⓑ Ⓒ Ⓓ Ⓔ
16 Ⓐ Ⓑ Ⓒ Ⓓ Ⓔ
17 Ⓐ Ⓑ Ⓒ Ⓓ Ⓔ
18 Ⓐ Ⓑ Ⓒ Ⓓ Ⓔ
19 Ⓐ Ⓑ Ⓒ Ⓓ Ⓔ
20 Ⓐ Ⓑ Ⓒ Ⓓ Ⓔ
21 Ⓐ Ⓑ Ⓒ Ⓓ Ⓔ
22 Ⓐ Ⓑ Ⓒ Ⓓ Ⓔ
23 Ⓐ Ⓑ Ⓒ Ⓓ Ⓔ
24 Ⓐ Ⓑ Ⓒ Ⓓ Ⓔ
25 Ⓐ Ⓑ Ⓒ Ⓓ Ⓔ

SECTION III

1 Ⓐ Ⓑ Ⓒ Ⓓ Ⓔ
2 Ⓐ Ⓑ Ⓒ Ⓓ Ⓔ
3 Ⓐ Ⓑ Ⓒ Ⓓ Ⓔ
4 Ⓐ Ⓑ Ⓒ Ⓓ Ⓔ
5 Ⓐ Ⓑ Ⓒ Ⓓ Ⓔ
6 Ⓐ Ⓑ Ⓒ Ⓓ Ⓔ
7 Ⓐ Ⓑ Ⓒ Ⓓ Ⓔ
8 Ⓐ Ⓑ Ⓒ Ⓓ Ⓔ
9 Ⓐ Ⓑ Ⓒ Ⓓ Ⓔ
10 Ⓐ Ⓑ Ⓒ Ⓓ Ⓔ
11 Ⓐ Ⓑ Ⓒ Ⓓ Ⓔ
12 Ⓐ Ⓑ Ⓒ Ⓓ Ⓔ
13 Ⓐ Ⓑ Ⓒ Ⓓ Ⓔ
14 Ⓐ Ⓑ Ⓒ Ⓓ Ⓔ
15 Ⓐ Ⓑ Ⓒ Ⓓ Ⓔ
16 Ⓐ Ⓑ Ⓒ Ⓓ Ⓔ
17 Ⓐ Ⓑ Ⓒ Ⓓ Ⓔ
18 Ⓐ Ⓑ Ⓒ Ⓓ Ⓔ
19 Ⓐ Ⓑ Ⓒ Ⓓ Ⓔ
20 Ⓐ Ⓑ Ⓒ Ⓓ Ⓔ
21 Ⓐ Ⓑ Ⓒ Ⓓ Ⓔ
22 Ⓐ Ⓑ Ⓒ Ⓓ Ⓔ
23 Ⓐ Ⓑ Ⓒ Ⓓ Ⓔ
24 Ⓐ Ⓑ Ⓒ Ⓓ Ⓔ
25 Ⓐ Ⓑ Ⓒ Ⓓ Ⓔ
26 Ⓐ Ⓑ Ⓒ Ⓓ Ⓔ
27 Ⓐ Ⓑ Ⓒ Ⓓ Ⓔ
28 Ⓐ Ⓑ Ⓒ Ⓓ Ⓔ
29 Ⓐ Ⓑ Ⓒ Ⓓ Ⓔ
30 Ⓐ Ⓑ Ⓒ Ⓓ Ⓔ
31 Ⓐ Ⓑ Ⓒ Ⓓ Ⓔ
32 Ⓐ Ⓑ Ⓒ Ⓓ Ⓔ
33 Ⓐ Ⓑ Ⓒ Ⓓ Ⓔ
34 Ⓐ Ⓑ Ⓒ Ⓓ Ⓔ
35 Ⓐ Ⓑ Ⓒ Ⓓ Ⓔ

SECTION IV

1 Ⓐ Ⓑ Ⓒ Ⓓ Ⓔ
2 Ⓐ Ⓑ Ⓒ Ⓓ Ⓔ
3 Ⓐ Ⓑ Ⓒ Ⓓ Ⓔ
4 Ⓐ Ⓑ Ⓒ Ⓓ Ⓔ
5 Ⓐ Ⓑ Ⓒ Ⓓ Ⓔ
6 Ⓐ Ⓑ Ⓒ Ⓓ Ⓔ
7 Ⓐ Ⓑ Ⓒ Ⓓ Ⓔ
8 Ⓐ Ⓑ Ⓒ Ⓓ Ⓔ
9 Ⓐ Ⓑ Ⓒ Ⓓ Ⓔ
10 Ⓐ Ⓑ Ⓒ Ⓓ Ⓔ
11 Ⓐ Ⓑ Ⓒ Ⓓ Ⓔ
12 Ⓐ Ⓑ Ⓒ Ⓓ Ⓔ
13 Ⓐ Ⓑ Ⓒ Ⓓ Ⓔ
14 Ⓐ Ⓑ Ⓒ Ⓓ Ⓔ
15 Ⓐ Ⓑ Ⓒ Ⓓ Ⓔ
16 Ⓐ Ⓑ Ⓒ Ⓓ Ⓔ
17 Ⓐ Ⓑ Ⓒ Ⓓ Ⓔ
18 Ⓐ Ⓑ Ⓒ Ⓓ Ⓔ
19 Ⓐ Ⓑ Ⓒ Ⓓ Ⓔ
20 Ⓐ Ⓑ Ⓒ Ⓓ Ⓔ
21 Ⓐ Ⓑ Ⓒ Ⓓ Ⓔ
22 Ⓐ Ⓑ Ⓒ Ⓓ Ⓔ
23 Ⓐ Ⓑ Ⓒ Ⓓ Ⓔ
24 Ⓐ Ⓑ Ⓒ Ⓓ Ⓔ
25 Ⓐ Ⓑ Ⓒ Ⓓ Ⓔ
26 Ⓐ Ⓑ Ⓒ Ⓓ Ⓔ
27 Ⓐ Ⓑ Ⓒ Ⓓ Ⓔ
28 Ⓐ Ⓑ Ⓒ Ⓓ Ⓔ
29 Ⓐ Ⓑ Ⓒ Ⓓ Ⓔ
30 Ⓐ Ⓑ Ⓒ Ⓓ Ⓔ

ANSWER SHEET FOR PRACTICE TEST 1
(Remove This Sheet and Use It to Mark Your Answers)

TEST OF PROFESSIONAL KNOWLEDGE

SECTION I	SECTION II	SECTION III	SECTION IV
1 Ⓐ Ⓑ Ⓒ Ⓓ Ⓔ	1 Ⓐ Ⓑ Ⓒ Ⓓ Ⓔ	1 Ⓐ Ⓑ Ⓒ Ⓓ Ⓔ	1 Ⓐ Ⓑ Ⓒ Ⓓ Ⓔ
2 Ⓐ Ⓑ Ⓒ Ⓓ Ⓔ	2 Ⓐ Ⓑ Ⓒ Ⓓ Ⓔ	2 Ⓐ Ⓑ Ⓒ Ⓓ Ⓔ	2 Ⓐ Ⓑ Ⓒ Ⓓ Ⓔ
3 Ⓐ Ⓑ Ⓒ Ⓓ Ⓔ	3 Ⓐ Ⓑ Ⓒ Ⓓ Ⓔ	3 Ⓐ Ⓑ Ⓒ Ⓓ Ⓔ	3 Ⓐ Ⓑ Ⓒ Ⓓ Ⓔ
4 Ⓐ Ⓑ Ⓒ Ⓓ Ⓔ	4 Ⓐ Ⓑ Ⓒ Ⓓ Ⓔ	4 Ⓐ Ⓑ Ⓒ Ⓓ Ⓔ	4 Ⓐ Ⓑ Ⓒ Ⓓ Ⓔ
5 Ⓐ Ⓑ Ⓒ Ⓓ Ⓔ	5 Ⓐ Ⓑ Ⓒ Ⓓ Ⓔ	5 Ⓐ Ⓑ Ⓒ Ⓓ Ⓔ	5 Ⓐ Ⓑ Ⓒ Ⓓ Ⓔ
6 Ⓐ Ⓑ Ⓒ Ⓓ Ⓔ	6 Ⓐ Ⓑ Ⓒ Ⓓ Ⓔ	6 Ⓐ Ⓑ Ⓒ Ⓓ Ⓔ	6 Ⓐ Ⓑ Ⓒ Ⓓ Ⓔ
7 Ⓐ Ⓑ Ⓒ Ⓓ Ⓔ	7 Ⓐ Ⓑ Ⓒ Ⓓ Ⓔ	7 Ⓐ Ⓑ Ⓒ Ⓓ Ⓔ	7 Ⓐ Ⓑ Ⓒ Ⓓ Ⓔ
8 Ⓐ Ⓑ Ⓒ Ⓓ Ⓔ	8 Ⓐ Ⓑ Ⓒ Ⓓ Ⓔ	8 Ⓐ Ⓑ Ⓒ Ⓓ Ⓔ	8 Ⓐ Ⓑ Ⓒ Ⓓ Ⓔ
9 Ⓐ Ⓑ Ⓒ Ⓓ Ⓔ	9 Ⓐ Ⓑ Ⓒ Ⓓ Ⓔ	9 Ⓐ Ⓑ Ⓒ Ⓓ Ⓔ	9 Ⓐ Ⓑ Ⓒ Ⓓ Ⓔ
10 Ⓐ Ⓑ Ⓒ Ⓓ Ⓔ	10 Ⓐ Ⓑ Ⓒ Ⓓ Ⓔ	10 Ⓐ Ⓑ Ⓒ Ⓓ Ⓔ	10 Ⓐ Ⓑ Ⓒ Ⓓ Ⓔ
11 Ⓐ Ⓑ Ⓒ Ⓓ Ⓔ	11 Ⓐ Ⓑ Ⓒ Ⓓ Ⓔ	11 Ⓐ Ⓑ Ⓒ Ⓓ Ⓔ	11 Ⓐ Ⓑ Ⓒ Ⓓ Ⓔ
12 Ⓐ Ⓑ Ⓒ Ⓓ Ⓔ	12 Ⓐ Ⓑ Ⓒ Ⓓ Ⓔ	12 Ⓐ Ⓑ Ⓒ Ⓓ Ⓔ	12 Ⓐ Ⓑ Ⓒ Ⓓ Ⓔ
13 Ⓐ Ⓑ Ⓒ Ⓓ Ⓔ	13 Ⓐ Ⓑ Ⓒ Ⓓ Ⓔ	13 Ⓐ Ⓑ Ⓒ Ⓓ Ⓔ	13 Ⓐ Ⓑ Ⓒ Ⓓ Ⓔ
14 Ⓐ Ⓑ Ⓒ Ⓓ Ⓔ	14 Ⓐ Ⓑ Ⓒ Ⓓ Ⓔ	14 Ⓐ Ⓑ Ⓒ Ⓓ Ⓔ	14 Ⓐ Ⓑ Ⓒ Ⓓ Ⓔ
15 Ⓐ Ⓑ Ⓒ Ⓓ Ⓔ	15 Ⓐ Ⓑ Ⓒ Ⓓ Ⓔ	15 Ⓐ Ⓑ Ⓒ Ⓓ Ⓔ	15 Ⓐ Ⓑ Ⓒ Ⓓ Ⓔ
16 Ⓐ Ⓑ Ⓒ Ⓓ Ⓔ	16 Ⓐ Ⓑ Ⓒ Ⓓ Ⓔ	16 Ⓐ Ⓑ Ⓒ Ⓓ Ⓔ	16 Ⓐ Ⓑ Ⓒ Ⓓ Ⓔ
17 Ⓐ Ⓑ Ⓒ Ⓓ Ⓔ	17 Ⓐ Ⓑ Ⓒ Ⓓ Ⓔ	17 Ⓐ Ⓑ Ⓒ Ⓓ Ⓔ	17 Ⓐ Ⓑ Ⓒ Ⓓ Ⓔ
18 Ⓐ Ⓑ Ⓒ Ⓓ Ⓔ	18 Ⓐ Ⓑ Ⓒ Ⓓ Ⓔ	18 Ⓐ Ⓑ Ⓒ Ⓓ Ⓔ	18 Ⓐ Ⓑ Ⓒ Ⓓ Ⓔ
19 Ⓐ Ⓑ Ⓒ Ⓓ Ⓔ	19 Ⓐ Ⓑ Ⓒ Ⓓ Ⓔ	19 Ⓐ Ⓑ Ⓒ Ⓓ Ⓔ	19 Ⓐ Ⓑ Ⓒ Ⓓ Ⓔ
20 Ⓐ Ⓑ Ⓒ Ⓓ Ⓔ	20 Ⓐ Ⓑ Ⓒ Ⓓ Ⓔ	20 Ⓐ Ⓑ Ⓒ Ⓓ Ⓔ	20 Ⓐ Ⓑ Ⓒ Ⓓ Ⓔ
21 Ⓐ Ⓑ Ⓒ Ⓓ Ⓔ	21 Ⓐ Ⓑ Ⓒ Ⓓ Ⓔ	21 Ⓐ Ⓑ Ⓒ Ⓓ Ⓔ	21 Ⓐ Ⓑ Ⓒ Ⓓ Ⓔ
22 Ⓐ Ⓑ Ⓒ Ⓓ Ⓔ	22 Ⓐ Ⓑ Ⓒ Ⓓ Ⓔ	22 Ⓐ Ⓑ Ⓒ Ⓓ Ⓔ	22 Ⓐ Ⓑ Ⓒ Ⓓ Ⓔ
23 Ⓐ Ⓑ Ⓒ Ⓓ Ⓔ	23 Ⓐ Ⓑ Ⓒ Ⓓ Ⓔ	23 Ⓐ Ⓑ Ⓒ Ⓓ Ⓔ	23 Ⓐ Ⓑ Ⓒ Ⓓ Ⓔ
24 Ⓐ Ⓑ Ⓒ Ⓓ Ⓔ	24 Ⓐ Ⓑ Ⓒ Ⓓ Ⓔ	24 Ⓐ Ⓑ Ⓒ Ⓓ Ⓔ	24 Ⓐ Ⓑ Ⓒ Ⓓ Ⓔ
25 Ⓐ Ⓑ Ⓒ Ⓓ Ⓔ	25 Ⓐ Ⓑ Ⓒ Ⓓ Ⓔ	25 Ⓐ Ⓑ Ⓒ Ⓓ Ⓔ	25 Ⓐ Ⓑ Ⓒ Ⓓ Ⓔ
26 Ⓐ Ⓑ Ⓒ Ⓓ Ⓔ	26 Ⓐ Ⓑ Ⓒ Ⓓ Ⓔ	26 Ⓐ Ⓑ Ⓒ Ⓓ Ⓔ	26 Ⓐ Ⓑ Ⓒ Ⓓ Ⓔ
27 Ⓐ Ⓑ Ⓒ Ⓓ Ⓔ	27 Ⓐ Ⓑ Ⓒ Ⓓ Ⓔ	27 Ⓐ Ⓑ Ⓒ Ⓓ Ⓔ	27 Ⓐ Ⓑ Ⓒ Ⓓ Ⓔ
28 Ⓐ Ⓑ Ⓒ Ⓓ Ⓔ	28 Ⓐ Ⓑ Ⓒ Ⓓ Ⓔ	28 Ⓐ Ⓑ Ⓒ Ⓓ Ⓔ	28 Ⓐ Ⓑ Ⓒ Ⓓ Ⓔ
29 Ⓐ Ⓑ Ⓒ Ⓓ Ⓔ	29 Ⓐ Ⓑ Ⓒ Ⓓ Ⓔ	29 Ⓐ Ⓑ Ⓒ Ⓓ Ⓔ	29 Ⓐ Ⓑ Ⓒ Ⓓ Ⓔ
30 Ⓐ Ⓑ Ⓒ Ⓓ Ⓔ	30 Ⓐ Ⓑ Ⓒ Ⓓ Ⓔ	30 Ⓐ Ⓑ Ⓒ Ⓓ Ⓔ	30 Ⓐ Ⓑ Ⓒ Ⓓ Ⓔ

CUT HERE

TEST OF COMMUNICATION SKILLS

SECTION I: LISTENING

Time: 30 Minutes for Three Parts
32 Questions

Cut out pages 299 through 303 as shown and give them to a friend to read aloud to you. (In the actual exam, a tape recorder will be used.) These pages contain the script of the listening questions, statements, conversations, and talks for Practice Test 1, Parts A, B, and C. Ask the reader to allow 10 to 15 seconds after each question for you to mark your answer. Turn to page 305 where you will find the answer choices for each of the questions. Read the directions before beginning each part of Section I.

Questions, Statements, Conversations, and Talks—Script

Part A: Questions and Statements

1. Who phoned you long-distance this morning?

2. More members of the city council will travel this year, after voting themselves an increased allowance for fact-finding tours.

3. Although she planned her day very carefully, unexpected problems caused her to accomplish little.

4. After winning their first two baseball games, the San Diego Padres lost three in a row.

5. Do you spend more time watching television or reading?

6. How much cash are you carrying in your purse?

7. Because of bad weather, the landscaper did not begin work on the yard until late Wednesday afternoon.

8. The area code for the city will change from 714 to 619 on March 1.

9. When on Saturday would you like to leave for the zoo?

10. The school day has been shortened this year, but the number of subjects covered each day has not been changed.

11. Just as she expected, Meg missed the bus and was forced to walk to work.

CUT HERE

12. Why were Shakespeare's sonnets all fourteen lines long?

Part B: Conversations

Questions 13 and 14 are based on the following conversation.

Man: Several of my students turn in blank pages whenever I give a writing assignment.

Woman: Perhaps you should let them write about whatever is on their minds instead of specifying a subject.

Man: No, that didn't work; many of them have told me that they have nothing on their minds.

13. Why does the woman think the students are not writing?

14. What conclusion could be drawn about the man?

Questions 15 and 16 are based on the following conversation.

Woman: If you don't like watching television, why don't you read a book instead?

Boy: I read all my books already.

Woman: Would you like me to buy you more books?

Boy: No, I'd rather watch television.

15. What conclusion can be drawn about the woman?

16. What conclusion can be drawn about the boy?

Questions 17 and 18 are based on the following conversation.

Ballet Fan: I don't understand why you spend so much money for baseball tickets.

Baseball Fan: I watch the players with the same concentration and pleasure that you watch the ballet, paying attention to the precision with which they run, leap, and turn.

Ballet Fan: Yes, but ballet is art and baseball is sport; isn't there a difference?

Baseball Fan: All the elements of great art are there on the ballfield: suspense, conflict, characters, and style.

17. How does the baseball fan try to convince the ballet fan of the significance of baseball?

18. We can conclude that the baseball fan's familiarity with art is which of the following?

Questions 19 and 20 are based on the following conversation.

Student: Dad, the university catalogue says I can declare my major anytime until the beginning of my junior year, but I've decided to declare a psychology major even though I'm only a freshman.

Father: All my friends in college used to think psychology majors were strange and avoided them like the plague.

Student: Don't you want me to major in psychology?

Father: I just don't want you to be unhappy, that's all.

19. Why doesn't the father support the student's decision to major in psychology?

20. We can characterize the student's decision to major in psychology with which of the following terms?

Part C: Talks

Questions 21, 22, and 23 refer to the following talk.

It has been proposed that legalized gambling is the solution to our current education crisis. A state lottery, we are told, will raise enough money to fatten up our education programs and improve the facilities and the instruction that each child receives. And a lottery, we are told, will cost us nothing. Really? A state lottery will cost us economic and moral integrity; while it makes money for education, a lottery will educate our citizens in squandering their earnings on a chance for big money and will teach our children that the way to get what you want is to appeal to the greed in people. Would any teacher be content knowing that his or her salary raise came from the pockets of hopeful but nearly destitute citizens betting their last dime on a chance for wealth? Would any child be content knowing that new schoolbooks are paid for not by those who care about education but by those who care about fattening their own wallets? We cannot tolerate the contradiction between the moral uses of lottery money and the immoral nature of the lottery itself. Legalized gambling is no foundation for education.

21. What is the major topic of this talk?

22. What does the speaker imply that citizens should do?

23. What assumption does the speaker make about poor people?

CUT HERE

Questions 24, 25, and 26 refer to the following talk.

More than two thousand years ago, Aristotle described how to make a good speech. First, he said, the speechmaker must know the subject fully and must be aware of the facts that support both sides of the issue. Second, the speechmaker must know the audience well and say things that will appeal to the audience's beliefs and interests. Third, the speechmaker must have an absolute command of style and grammar; vague and incorrect sentences simply will not do. Aristotle's advice still seems quite useful, not only for speakers but for writers as well. A poor writer is usually someone who gives information that is either incomplete or too one sided; who offends, bores, or confuses the audience; who produces sentences that cannot be called standard English by any stretch of the imagination. The question is whether such writers can become better, and if we turn to Aristotle, we learn the answer is *no*. He tells us that although someone with talent can be trained to become an excellent communicator, those who are not born with such talent must simply be content with their lot. He would agree that good writers are born and not made.

24. What would Aristotle *not* associate with good speechmaking?

25. According to the speaker, Aristotle would probably disagree with which of the following statements?

26. What does the speaker conclude about Aristotle?

Questions 27, 28, and 29 refer to the following talk.

Twenty years ago, thousands of little boys were buying thousands of G.I. Joe dolls, and "war" was still a popular kid's game. Then came the Vietnam War, and we decided that war toys taught little boys to grow up to be killers. G.I. Joe disappeared from the shelves along with the platoons of military accessories: machine guns, grenades, and the other replicas of modern weaponry. Well, the kids are battling it out again, here in the '80s. But this time their battlefield is not the sands of Iwo Jima or the rice fields of Cambodia; war has been transported to outer space, and G.I. Joe has been replaced by Luke Skywalker. Now the futuristic artillery of Star Wars fills toy stores and the merchants can never stock enough of it. It would seem that playing war will not disappear from the American scene, and it also seems that even if the kids should lose interest in shooting each other, their parents will not.

27. What is the main topic of this talk?

28. What is the speaker's position on whether war toys should be sold or not?

29. What does the speaker conclude about playing war?

Questions 30, 31, and 32 refer to the following talk.

We have all heard about the importance of a balanced diet and seen poster after poster illustrating the four basic food groups and advising us to eat something from each group every day. Medical research has shown that the lack of a balanced diet can cause any number of physical problems, from fatigue to headaches to cancer. But if we take a wider view, we realize that it is not the lack of a balanced diet that causes problems. A bad diet is the symptom of more deeply rooted social, cultural, and economic problems. When people don't eat right, it is often because they cannot afford to do so or because they have been so inundated with ads for fast food that they find convenience more attractive than good health. It may be because the stress of competing for success in school or at work has them seeking the comfort of candy bars, alcohol, and perhaps even drugs. Poverty, mass-marketing, and aggressive competition: these are the real causes of all the diet-related diseases. Putting posters of the four food groups in our classrooms will not begin to solve the real problems, which are too large to reduce to pictures on the wall.

30. What is the major topic of this talk?

31. What does the speaker conclude about posters illustrating the four food groups?

32. According to the speaker, what can a bad diet cause?

Answer Choices

Part A: Questions and Statements

DIRECTIONS

You will be faced with two kinds of problems. You must either answer a short question or understand a brief statement. Each question and each statement will be spoken one time. After you hear a question, you will read four answer choices; select the correct answer. After you hear a statement, you will read four sentences; select the sentence closest to the meaning of the statement or supported by the statement.

1. (A) He apologized for disturbing me in the middle of a workday.
   (B) He reversed the charges, but I still accepted the call.
   (C) My uncle, asking me to visit him this summer.
   (D) It concerned my summer vacation.

2. (A) The members of the city council travel too much.
   (B) Some of the travel this year by council members will consist of fact-finding tours.
   (C) No members of the city council traveled last year.
   (D) The membership of the city council has increased this year.

3. (A) She did not follow her planned schedule rigidly.
   (B) What she had planned to do was not important.
   (C) She planned to accomplish little.
   (D) Her days never turn out as planned.

4. (A) In the long run, the Padres will lose more than they win.
   (B) The Padres cannot win consistently.
   (C) The Padres are a terrible team.
   (D) The Padres lost more of their first five games than they won.

5. (A) I write more frequently than I switch on the TV.
   (B) I watch only news shows.
   (C) The television is on all day at my house.
   (D) I read for most of the day and almost never watch TV.

6. (A) I spent most of my cash at the movies last night.
   (B) None, but I have my checkbook and credit cards.
   (C) No, in a leather wallet in my back pocket.
   (D) I have $20 hidden in the drawer at home.

7. (A) The weather report for Thursday forecast good weather.
   (B) The landscaper never works in the morning.
   (C) The weather was bad earlier in the day on Wednesday.
   (D) Landscaping is hard work.

8. (A) Area codes outside the city will not change.
   (B) Until March 1, the area code will be 714.
   (C) A change in the area code is long overdue.
   (D) The quality of telephone service will improve after March 1.

9. (A) Why don't we leave in my car?
   (B) Why don't we leave at 9:00.
   (C) We should leave from your house.
   (D) I haven't been to the zoo in years.

10. (A) No new subjects have been added to the curriculum.
    (B) The subjects taught required less time last year.
    (C) Last year more time was probably spent covering each subject.
    (D) Last year teachers and students found themselves with extra time.

11. (A) Meg was not surprised when she missed the bus.
    (B) This is not the first time Meg has missed the bus.
    (C) Meg can reach work on time by walking.
    (D) Meg was looking forward to walking to work.

12. (A) It takes longer to read just one act of *Hamlet* than to read a sonnet.
    (B) Some contemporaries of Shakespeare wrote longer poems.
    (C) Shakespeare's life often influenced the content of the sonnets.
    (D) Shakespeare was following the conventional limitation on sonnet length.

PROCEED DIRECTLY TO PART B.

Part B: Conversations

DIRECTIONS

You will hear short conversations between two speakers. After each conversation, a third speaker will ask questions about what the two were discussing. The conversations and each question will be spoken only once. After you hear each question, choose the best of the four possible answers.

13. (A) They do not appreciate the value of learning to write.
    (B) They are more interested in thinking than in writing.
    (C) They have nothing to say about the assigned subject.
    (D) The man is incompetent.

14. (A) He gives assignments that no student could complete.
    (B) He is content to receive blank pages.
    (C) He has asked the students to write on their own thoughts.
    (D) He does not respect the woman's opinion.

15. (A) She offers to get the boy more books.
    (B) She does not enjoy watching television.
    (C) She does not value reading.
    (D) She has never understood the boy.

16. (A) The boy likes watching television more than he likes reading.
    (B) Libraries are not as interesting as television.
    (C) The boy will not watch television unless forced to read.
    (D) There are some things the boy dislikes more than reading.

17. (A) by drawing a comparison
    (B) by criticizing the arts
    (C) by ridiculing the ballet fan
    (D) by introducing statistical proof

18. (A) hostile   (C) substantial
    (B) negligible   (D) professional

19. (A) The father does not trust the student's judgment.
    (B) The father never studied psychology himself.
    (C) The father does not think psychology is an important subject.
    (D) The father presumes that the student will become unpopular.

20. (A) rebellious   (C) early
    (B) ignorant   (D) mistaken

PROCEED DIRECTLY TO PART C.

Part C: Talks

DIRECTIONS

You will hear several short talks, each followed by questions. When you hear a question, choose the best answer of the four printed in your test booklet. Remember that the talks and questions will be spoken only once, so you must listen carefully while you attempt to understand and remember what the speaker says.

21. (A) improved education
    (B) gambling among the poor
    (C) using a lottery to improve education
    (D) buying schoolbooks about gambling

22. (A) gamble cautiously
    (B) refuse to support a lottery
    (C) buy schoolbooks for students
    (D) support legalized gambling but not a lottery

23. (A) They will not use their money wisely.
    (B) They are not as poor as they seem.
    (C) They rarely win lotteries.
    (D) They do not have school-age children.

24. (A) a deep, resonant voice
    (B) good grammar
    (C) understanding of the audience's point of view
    (D) full information on the subject

25. (A) Confusing writing is not good writing.
    (B) Writing is not easy for everyone.
    (C) Correct grammar is part of good writing.
    (D) Anyone can learn to write.

26. (A) His advice is still useful today.
    (B) He knew nothing about writing.
    (C) He was a popular teacher.
    (D) He was born under a lucky star.

27. (A) the Vietnam War
    (B) the morality of war
    (C) playing war
    (D) the elimination of war

28. (A) War toys should be outlawed.
    (B) War toys should be sold.
    (C) Only mature children should own war toys.
    (D) The speaker has no definite position on this issue.

29. (A) In America, playing war will be popular in one form or another.
    (B) Playing war turns kids into real killers.
    (C) Only toymakers really approve of playing war.
    (D) Outside America, no one plays war.

30. (A) Posters allow people to eat poorly.
    (B) A bad diet is a symptom of social, cultural, and economic problems.
    (C) Poor people are not aware of the four food groups.
    (D) Alcohol contributes to a bad diet.

31. (A) They are not the solution to dietary problems.
    (B) They do not illustrate all the food groups.
    (C) They appeal only to wealthy people.
    (D) They are not based on medical research.

32. (A) cultural problems
    (B) social problems
    (C) economic problems
    (D) physical problems

STOP. IF YOU FINISH BEFORE TIME IS UP, CHECK YOUR WORK ON THIS SECTION ONLY. DO NOT WORK ON ANY OTHER SECTION OF THE TEST.

SECTION II: READING

Time: 30 Minutes
30 Questions

DIRECTIONS

A question or number of questions follow each of the statements or passages in this section. Using only the *stated* or *implied* information given in the statement or passage, answer the question or questions by choosing the *best* answer from among the choices given.

Sociology was present in an undeveloped stage at the dawn of civilization, since speculation about society and human interaction has been a subject of continual interest to mankind.

1. We may infer which of the following from the passage?
   (A) Modern sociologists must study the views of ancient civilizations.
   (B) Sociology has not developed since the dawn of civilization.
   (C) Ancient civilizations were curious about the nature of society and human interaction.
   (D) Ancient civilizations reached conclusions similar to those of modern sociologists.
   (E) Before the dawn of civilization, sociology was not a concern.

To *reify* human behavior is to reduce a complex of factors to a single characteristic. For instance, when a child misspells a word, the conclusion that he or she is "ignorant" does not account for the complex of factors other than ignorance that might result in incorrect spelling.

2. The author of this passage would disagree with each of the following statements *except*
   (A) those who cannot read poetry are illiterate
   (B) those who refuse to fly in airplanes are cowards
   (C) those who do not sing well are tone deaf
   (D) those who cannot jog regularly are lazy
   (E) those who answer incorrectly on a test should not be judged hastily

A boy who steals hubcaps is conforming quite often to the norms of his peer group but not to the norms of the adult community that sets the laws. However, when he grows up and enters the adult community, he will conform to adult laws.

3. Which of the following is an unstated assumption by the author of this passage?
   (A) Unlawful behavior is practiced only by youths.
   (B) Adults do not need hubcaps.
   (C) Conformity becomes irrelevant when one grows up.
   (D) Young people are not aware of adult laws.
   (E) Adults should not be trusted with establishing laws.

Questions 4, 5, and 6 refer to the following passage.

[1]Some things are known through the feelings rather than by thinking or sense perceptions. [2]It is not difficult to find examples in which this is true. [3]How do we know what happiness is or what is the meaning of falling in love? [4]How do we know whether an object is beautiful or what kind of actions meet with our approval or disapproval? [5]One's own attitudes or dispositions are not known by any reasoning process nor are they revealed through sense perceptions. [6]They are known only through immediate experience and this is what we mean by intuition. [7]How much is known through intuition and whether it is capable of revealing anything other than one's private or subjective experience are questions concerning which intuitionists differ among themselves.

4. Which of the following is one function of sentences 5 and 6?
   (A) to define intuition
   (B) to raise questions about intuition
   (C) to point out that many things are different
   (D) to supply the reader with an immediate experience
   (E) to further explain the meaning of love

5. Which of the following, if true, would most weaken the author's argument?
   (A) When determining beauty, people usually move through a series of logical propositions.
   (B) Intuitionists have points of view that are not always in agreement.
   (C) Many people surveyed said that their feelings of happiness could not be explained through any reasoning process.
   (D) Some people have been accused of having no feelings.
   (E) An intuitionist is someone who studies the nature and significance of intuition.

6. Which of the following is the author's main point?
   (A) Feelings are more trustworthy than reason.
   (B) Intuitionists have highly developed intuitions.
   (C) People without intuition never fall in love.
   (D) We do not know how we feel by using a reasoning process.
   (E) Private experience is the most important experience.

Enrollment growth in educational facilities can be seen in a few, rather dramatic statistics. While in 1920 only 27 percent of the population in the United States aged twenty-five to thirty-five years old had completed high school, by 1980 the comparable figure was about 85 percent. And in the period 1963–64, 93 percent of those fourteen to seventeen years old were enrolled in secondary schools; for 1982 the figure is 97 percent.

7. What is the point to which the author is probably leading?
   (A) The vast majority of young adults attend and complete secondary school these days.
   (B) Fewer secondary schools were in session fifty years ago.
   (C) Before 1920 only elderly people had completed high school, and they made up less than 27 percent of the polulation.
   (D) Three percent of the population is not enrolled in secondary schools.
   (E) One hundred percent of those fourteen to seventeen years old will be enrolled in secondary schools by 1990.

Questions 8 and 9 refer to the following passage.

The organization and control of education varies widely throughout the world. In some European countries, such as Great Britain, there exist dual systems—one for the general public and the other for an elite group destined for high positions in later life. In the United States, public education is dominant and, at least on the surface, there is little distinction between the class levels.

8. We may infer which of the following about "high positions" in the United States?
   (A) Members of the elite group in the United States exert no influence on public education.
   (B) Those in high positions are not advocates of public education.
   (C) They are not available to those educated in other countries, especially Great Britain.
   (D) They are filled by those educated in some European countries.
   (E) They are not officially reserved for an elite group and are available to the general public.

9. What does the author suggest by using the term *destined*?
(A) Educators in the United States do not believe in destiny.
(B) Those born into an elite group in other countries are expected to attain high positions.
(C) The chance for public education to gain a foothold in other countries is hopeless.
(D) Members of the elite group never attain high positions early in life.
(E) Members of the elite group attain high positions whether they are educated or not.

A universal purpose of education is to socialize the young, to teach them the manners and morals, ways and customs, traditions and beliefs of their society and culture. However, once one is thoroughly familiar with the conventions of one's culture, one may decide to rebel against the culture and create a "counterculture."

10. The author of this passage would probably agree with which of the following statements?
(A) Education is a waste of time.
(B) The rebels in society are always the most educated people.
(C) A well-educated person knows enough about society to criticize it.
(D) Rebels are the educators of tomorrow.
(E) In a counterculture there is no education.

Questions 11 and 12 refer to the following passage.

Education can function to aid an individual in his or her personal development. Attendance in college, for instance, can lead to an appreciation of "culture" in its more limited sense, such as a love for music, art, and literature. Also, education has been found to alter a person's values and attitudes, to increase tolerance toward minorities, raise political interest, and produce a greater concern for civil liberties.

11. If the author had written "education *does* function" instead of "education *can* function," we could characterize the tone as which of the following?
(A) absolute
(B) indecisive
(C) angry
(D) intolerant
(E) humorous

12. Which of the following statements would weaken the author's argument about the benefits of education?
   (A) Studies show that most people with advanced college degrees are politically apathetic.
   (B) As opportunities for public education have grown, so has voter registration.
   (C) Educated people usually command higher salaries than those who lack education.
   (D) A group of graduate students from Yale has devised a civic plan for upgrading slum areas.
   (E) The President has recently voiced support for improvements in education.

Simple lack of money is not the main reason for nonattendance at college, since a few studies show that even when assistance is made available through veterans' benefits, persons from lower-class backgrounds tend not to take advantage of existing opportunities.

13. The point of this passage might be summarized as follows:
   (A) Those who wish to attend college need more money.
   (B) Veterans are not interested in higher educaton.
   (C) Factors other than affordability may cause a person not to attend college.
   (D) More people are attending college without paying for it.
   (E) There are no existing opportunities for poor people to enjoy higher education.

Questions 14 through 17 refer to the following passage.

The elementary school teacher is responsible for making all children aware, early in their school careers, that there are two important types of writing. The first, practical writing, which answers practical needs, requires a quality of honesty, clearness, and expression in acceptable form. Such writing may take the form of reports, listings, captions, and plans made by a large group or an individual student. The second, personal writing, includes those experiences in which children are free to express their thoughts and ideas in unique ways. Even though such writing may be trivial at the outset, children may realize that the writing experience offers a secret weapon for expressing their innermost feelings.

Regardless of grade level taught, the elementary school teacher is responsible for careful and consistent guidance of each child toward improved legibility. Children must become cognizant of the fact that handwriting must be pleasing both to oneself and to the reader. Beautiful flourishes and creative appendages will no doubt be added as individual students experiment with a unique style, but these must be channeled into the creative realm. A social awareness of the writing situation—whether personal or practical—may soon become a routine matter.

14. Which of the following is an unstated assumption in the last sentence of the first paragraph?
   (A) The writing of adults is never trivial.
   (B) It is important to express one's innermost feelings.
   (C) Young writers will realize that their personal writing is trivial.
   (D) A child's writing may become a weapon to insult others.
   (E) Children are often unwilling to express their innermost feelings.

15. Which of the following titles best summarizes the content of the passage?
   (A) *Creativity and Writing*
   (B) *The Practical Uses of Writing*
   (C) *The Uses and Characteristics of Elementary School Writing*
   (D) *The Elementary School Teacher's Responsibility*
   (E) *Channeling Writing into the Creative Realm*

16. The content indicates that the passage would be most likely to appear in which of the following?
   (A) a textbook for young students of writing
   (B) a philosophical treatise on language
   (C) a textbook for education majors
   (D) a government pamphlet on American higher education
   (E) an essay on the social uses of writing

17. With the statement that personal writing *may be trivial at the outset*, the author implies which of the following?
   (A) Personal writing will become less trivial later on.
   (B) Most personal matters are trivial.
   (C) Students with the most personality will be most trivial.
   (D) Most of us are trivial without realizing it.
   (E) Trivia is valuable.

Questions 18, 19, and 20 refer to the following passage.

There are a variety of problems unique to the teacher role. In particular, the teacher must be both an instrumental and an expressive leader. The instrumental role involves keeping discipline and order, being task oriented and concerned with getting things done. The expressive role centers upon the establishment and maintenance of affectual bonds, group morale, emotionally sympathetic ties and understanding. Research shows that these roles are nearly always played by different persons, perhaps because of the incompatible demands they make.

18. The final sentence of the passage implies which of the following?
   (A) Teachers are necessarily schizophrenic.
   (B) Some teachers stress discipline and order, and others stress expressive characteristics such as group morale.
   (C) Teachers who value discipline and order will never be able to understand those who do not.
   (D) Teachers for whom group morale is important rarely get anything done.
   (E) Research has not found the perfect teacher yet.

19. The primary purpose of this passage is to
   (A) describe the variety of problems that teachers face
   (B) survey current research in education
   (C) boost the morale of teachers by praising their roles
   (D) stress that teachers are the victims of incompatible demands
   (E) briefly discuss two particular roles involved in teaching

20. From the first sentence, we may conclude which of the following?
   (A) Teachers have more problems than they can handle.
   (B) One problem may be stressing discipline and group morale at the same time.
   (C) There are problems that are not unique to teaching.
   (D) Only problems that are unique to teaching are worth discussing.
   (E) Unique teachers frequently encounter unique problems.

Questions 21 and 22 refer to the following passage.

Bureaucracy in the educational system has produced many problems. The administrative bureaucracy in schools has grown and therefore so has an emphasis on coordinated lesson plans, centralized authority, and obedience to administrative rules and regulations. However, many teachers cling to the concept that each teacher should "rule" his or her own classroom and are simply unwilling to submit to an authority they consider alien and unjustified.

21. Which of the following best summarizes the information in the passage?
    (A) Many teachers do not wish to know what other teachers are doing.
    (B) Growing bureaucracy in education is not favored by teachers who wish to remain independent.
    (C) Coordinated lesson plans may lead some teachers to resign.
    (D) Growing bureaucracy in education has produced more problems than it has solved.
    (E) Teachers wish to create mini-bureaucracies, little kingdoms in which each teacher dominates every aspect of classroom behavior and materials.

22. Which of the following is one of the meanings of *rule* as used in the passage?
    (A) Make the students respect the teacher as much as they would respect royalty.
    (B) Use a ruler to exercise discipline as was done many years ago in classrooms.
    (C) Make the students memorize a number of rules, which they must follow.
    (D) Create his or her own rules and regulations rather than those of the administration.
    (E) Give the students free rein, without subjecting them to the rules created by the administration.

Questions 23 and 24 are based on the following passage.

As education has become more complex, teachers have assumed the status of expert professionals who expect to be treated as such and not as public servants. As well-trained professionals, teachers are better aware of the needs of the students and proper techniques in teaching; however, these methods and ideas may be in stark contrast to what the general public thinks.

23. We may infer which of the following conclusions from the passage?
    (A) Students today are learning more than ever before because teachers know more than ever before.
    (B) Many teachers will not even listen to the opinions of parents or other nonteachers.
    (C) Teachers and parents may not agree about the needs of students and proper techniques in teaching.
    (D) Teachers do not agree among themselves about the needs of students and proper techniques in teaching.
    (E) If education becomes more simple, teachers will never again be treated with respect.

24. Which of the following may be inferred from the passage?
   (A) Teachers have not always held the status of expert professionals.
   (B) Teachers have become better aware of proper teaching techniques.
   (C) Beacause of their new status, teachers should receive higher salaries.
   (D) Students do not learn from people who are not well-trained professionals.
   (E) The needs of students have changed as education has become more complex.

Questions 25 and 26 refer to the following passage.

Being a high school dropout is a more serious problem today than in the past because of the rapid disappearance of unskilled occupations. The dropout's chances for unemployment and consequences of unemployment such as delinquency and mental illness are therefore quite high. Since most dropouts are from low income or low class backgrounds, efforts have been made to improve the education of the disadvantaged.

25. Which of the following is an assumption of the passage?
   (A) Some students are better off dropping out of school than enduring the sometimes unpleasant experience of education.
   (B) Most teachers find dropouts undesirable and will not try to help them seek employment.
   (C) Delinquency and mental illness are probably not suffered by most dropouts.
   (D) Those who drop out of school most likely qualify for only unskilled occupations.
   (E) Those from low income backgrounds are destined to drop out.

26. Which of the following is *not* mentioned by the author of this passage?
   (A) the kinds of efforts that have been made to improve the education of the disadvantaged
   (B) the seriousness of the dropout problem
   (C) the class backgrounds producing most dropouts
   (D) the consequences of unemployment
   (E) the dropout's chances for unemployment

Questions 27 and 28 are based on the following passage.

There is significant variation in mortality, a variation affected by race and sex. Women in the United States generally live for an average of six years longer than men. The causes of this difference between male and female mortality are uncertain, but the consequences can be described. For example, more and more property today is owned by women who have received the property through a husband's will.

27. Which of the following details, if true, would strengthen the statement made in the first sentence?
    (A) Some researchers have argued that men are beginning to live just as long as women.
    (B) Studies of mortality are often financed and supervised by insurance companies.
    (C) The retirement benefits granted to women are usually different from those granted to men.
    (D) Men usually lead more full lives than women even though they die younger.
    (E) Caucasian males live for an average of four years longer than Asian males.

28. The author of the passage would probably agree with which of the following?
    (A) Married women should prepare to live their final years as widows.
    (B) Married men should prepare to live their final years as widowers.
    (C) Children are unaffected by the variations in mortality rates.
    (D) Women who own property should be younger than they are.
    (E) As more women become more active in the work force, the average life span of women will decrease.

Questions 29 and 30 refer to the following passage.

A fad is a short-lived mannerism or trait which is trivial and often irrational. The reader may know of the popularity of hula hoops in the 1950s or the prevalence of stuffing as many persons as possible into a telephone booth during the early 1960s. Fads occur in the world of the superficial; although they may be very pervasive for a short while, they rapidly die out when their novelty wears thin or their utility as a device to enhance status disappears.

29. What is the primary purpose of the passage?
    (A) to argue for the elimination of fads
    (B) to criticize the popularity of hula hoops
    (C) to define and evaluate fads in general
    (D) to ridicule those who participate in fads
    (E) to popularize fads

30. According to the passage, which of the following characteristics does a fad lack?

(A) fun
(B) popularity
(C) permanence
(D) appeal
(E) superficiality

STOP. IF YOU FINISH BEFORE TIME IS UP, CHECK YOUR WORK ON THIS SECTION ONLY. DO NOT WORK ON ANY OTHER SECTION OF THE TEST.

SECTION III: WRITING—MULTIPLE CHOICE

Time: 30 Minutes for Both Parts
45 Questions

Part A: Usage (Suggested Time 10 Minutes, 25 Questions)

DIRECTIONS

Some of the following sentences are correct. Others contain problems in grammar, usage, sentence construction, punctuation, and wordiness. There is not more than one error in any sentence. If there is an error, it will be underlined and lettered. Find the one underlined part that must be changed to make the sentence correct and choose the corresponding letter on your answer sheet. Mark (E) if the sentence contains no error.

1. The invitation asked that I come to the birthday party at the
        A   B   C
   restaurant in formal dress. No error
             D   E

2. People who write letters frequently recount the same experience
         A   B   C
   to different people. No error
      D   E

3. The effect of the libraries campaign to encourage children's reading
              A   B
   has been overwhelmingly successful according to the fact-finding team.
     C   D
   No error
   E

4. The welfare of labor is conditioned by several factors unique to
       A   B   C
   the United States and occurring only in this country. No error
                     D   E

5. Howard and yourself will attend the conference on behalf of the entire
            A   B
   company and report the latest technological advances to us next week.
         C   D
   No error
   E

6. To <u>help</u> students understand and use the concepts of <u>science</u>, science
     A   B

educators <u>place</u> much emphasis on observation, discovery, and
            C

<u>the inquiry method.</u> <u>No error</u>
      D   E

7. The music <u>had scarcely</u> begun <u>than</u> the guests <u>started to fill</u> the dance
           A   B   C

floor, most of them gyrating <u>out of time</u> with the music. <u>No error</u>
                           D   E

8. The policeman spoke <u>calmly</u> and firmly to <u>we</u> <u>spectators</u> as he <u>directed</u>
                     A   B   C   D

the crowd out of the football stadium. <u>No error</u>
                              E

9. The theme of the works <u>demonstrated</u> a <u>recognition</u> yet a
                         A   B

<u>departure from</u> the past masters of epic poetry,
     C

<u>whose</u> characters were greater than life. <u>No error</u>
     D   E

10. <u>Either this afternoon</u> or tomorrow morning the state legislature
              A

<u>must</u> decide <u>whether</u> or not <u>to enact</u> a new tax cut. <u>No error</u>
   B   C   D   E

11. Techniques of waging war <u>have changed</u> <u>considerably</u> since
                             A   B

<u>"Black Jack"</u> Pershing and other <u>"World War I"</u> generals
      C   D

commanded the troops in battles such as Chateau Thierry
and Belleau Wood. <u>No error</u>
                E

12. The <u>scope</u> of the community-redevelopment project <u>has been</u> enlarged
       A   B

and <u>will</u> require a minimum of twenty-three new workers, <u>more or less.</u>
     C   D

<u>No error</u>
  E

13. <u>Yesterday</u> several members of the class <u>presented</u> opinion papers
     A   B

<u>based</u> on their research <u>and respective points of view.</u> <u>No error</u>
   C   D   E

14. Students who write formal term papers, even the most hardworking,
         A   B   C
   sometimes have difficulty with placement and order of footnotes.
                              D
   No error
   E

15. The arguments for rent control and the arguments against rent control
              A
   expressed by those in opposition to it did not convince the city council
                      B   C
   one way or another. No error
              D   E

16. When the home team players scored three baskets in the
                        A
   final two minutes of the game and allowed no offsetting
                          B
   points to the visiting team, they literally broke the back
              C   D
   of the opposition. No error
                      E

17. The brothers' testimony not only implicated the leaders of the group
        A   B   C
   but also their subordinates. No error
        D   E

18. The movie received an Oscar, a coveted award, for its extraordinary
            A   B   C
   achievement in special affects. No error
                      D   E

19. The cause of the accident being that the intoxicated driver lost
        A   B
   control of the wheel and veered into an oncoming truck. No error
              C   D   E

20. Today's teenagers, aged 13 to 19, usually don't like any music that is
                      A   B
   played by the Guy Lombardo Orchestra because the orchestra's
                              C
   arrangements make even new songs sound "old." No error
                  D   E

21. Rachel <u>Carson, a great American</u> writer and marine biologist,
                        A
    produced a series of books <u>that tells</u> what people are doing
                                B
    to the delicate balance of the <u>earth's life forms</u> on the land
                                            C
    and <u>in and near</u> the sea. <u>No error</u>
            D   E

22. Neither <u>Jim, the hunter, nor Charles, his guide,</u> wanted <u>their</u>
                            A   B
    midday meal <u>to be delayed</u> past one o'clock. <u>No error</u>
                        C   D   E

23. Charles hated to play <u>chess with</u> anyone <u>who</u> was <u>better</u> than <u>he.</u>
                                A   B   C   D
    <u>No error</u>
        E

24. <u>Recent studies</u> from Rutgers University <u>shows</u> that cancer is <u>more</u>
            A   B   C
    prevalent on the East Coast <u>than</u> on the West Coast. <u>No error</u>
                                    D   E

25. To keep <u>calm, to think</u> clearly, and <u>answering</u> all the <u>questions that</u>
                    A   B   C
    are easy for <u>him or her are</u> three goals of any effective and
                        D
    well-prepared test taker. <u>No error</u>
                                    E

PROCEED DIRECTLY TO THE SENTENCE CORRECTION QUESTIONS.

Part B: Sentence Correction (Suggested Time 20 Minutes, 20 Questions)

DIRECTIONS

Some part of each sentence below is underlined; sometimes the whole sentence is underlined. Five choices for rephrasing the underlined part follow each sentence; the first choice (A) repeats the original, and the other four are different. If choice (A) seems better than the alternatives, choose answer (A); if not, choose one of the others.

For each sentence, consider the requirements of standard written English. Your choice should be a correct and effective expression, not awkward or ambiguous. Focus on grammar, sentence structure, punctuation, wordiness, and word choice. If a choice changes the meaning of the original sentence, do not select it.

26. The school-age child faces a formidable task when during the first few years of classroom experiences he or she is expected to master the printed form of language.
   (A) he or she is expected to master the printed form of language.
   (B) he or she expects to master the printed form of language.
   (C) he or she faces expectations of mastering the printed form of language.
   (D) mastery of the printed form of language is expected of him or her.
   (E) mastery of print is expected by his or her teacher.

27. He came to the United States as a young man, he found a job as a coal miner.
   (A) man, he found
   (B) man and found
   (C) man and there he was able to find
   (D) man and then finding
   (E) man and had found

28. To a large degree, poetry, along with all the other arts, is a form of imitation.
   (A) poetry, along with all the other arts, is
   (B) poetry along with all the other arts is
   (C) poetry, along with all the other arts, are
   (D) poetry, and other arts, is
   (E) poetry and art are

29. Delegates to the political convention found difficulty to choose a candidate from among the few nominated.
   (A) difficulty to choose
   (B) it difficult in making the choice of
   (C) it difficult to choose
   (D) choosing difficult when selecting
   (E) making a choice difficult in selecting

30. Reading in any language can be viewed as a developmental task much the same as learning to walk, to cross the street independently, to care for one's possessions, or accepting responsibility for one's own decisions.
   (A) accepting responsibility for one's own decisions.
   (B) accepting one's own decisions responsibly.
   (C) to accept responsibility for one's own decisions.
   (D) accepting responsibility and making one's own decisions.
   (E) to make one's own decisions.

31. Sea forests of giant kelp, which fringe only one coastline in the Northern Hemisphere, <u>is native to shores</u> throughout the Southern Hemisphere.
    (A) is native to shores
    (B) is native to most shores
    (C) are native only in shores
    (D) are native
    (E) are native to shores

32. A <u>university's board of regents and alumni association are two separate entities,</u> each having specialized areas of responsibility and kinds of authority.
    (A) university's board of regents and alumni association are two separate entities
    (B) universitys board of regents and alumni association are separate entities
    (C) university's board of Regents and alumni Association are two separate entities
    (D) university's board of regents and alumni association is separate entities
    (E) university's board of regents and alumni association are entities

33. Like so many characters in Russian fiction, *Crime and Punishment* <u>exhibits</u> a behavior so foreign to the American temperament that many readers find the story rather incredible.
    (A) *Crime and Punishment* exhibits
    (B) those in *Crime and Punishment* exhibit
    (C) those in *Crime and Punishment* exhibits
    (D) often exhibiting
    (E) characterized by

34. *Don Quixote* provides a cross section of Spanish life, thought, and <u>portrays the feelings of many Spaniards</u> at the end of the chivalric age.
    (A) portrays the feelings of many Spaniards
    (B) portrayal of the feelings of many Spaniards
    (C) feelings portrayed by Spaniards
    (D) feelings
    (E) Spanish feelings

35. Hamlet, Prince of Denmark, thought several times of killing Claudius <u>and finally succeeding</u> in doing so.
    (A) and finally succeeding
    (B) that finally was successful
    (C) finally a successful attempt
    (D) being finally successful
    (E) and finally succeeded

36. The lamb <u>had laid on the hay beside its mother and had begun to nurse</u> <u>as soon as the boy had sat</u> the lantern on the table.

   (A) had laid on the hay beside its mother and had begun to nurse as soon as the boy had sat

   (B) had lain on the hay beside its mother and had begun to nurse as soon as the boy had set

   (C) had laid on the hay beside its mother and had begun to nurse as soon as the boy had set

   (D) had lain on the hay besides its mother and had begun to nurse as soon as the boy had set

   (E) had lain on the hay beside it's mother and had begun to nurse as soon as the boy had set

37. An infant, <u>whether lying alone in the crib or enjoying the company of</u> <u>adults, is consistently fascinated at</u> the movement of toes and fingers.

   (A) whether lying alone in the crib or enjoying the company of adults, is consistently fascinated at

   (B) alone or in company, is consistently fascinated at

   (C) whether lying alone in the crib or enjoying the company of adults, is constantly fascinated at

   (D) whether lying alone in the crib or enjoying the company of adults, is consistently fascinated by

   (E) lonely in the crib and enjoying the company of adults is consistently fascinated at

38. A policeman of proven valor, <u>the city council designated him</u> the "Outstanding Law Enforcement Officer of the Year."

   (A) the city council designated him

   (B) the city council's designating him

   (C) the city council will designate him

   (D) he designated the city council

   (E) he was designated by the city council

39. The supervisor asked, <u>"Bob have you checked with our office in Canton,</u> <u>Ohio, to see if it stocks slate, flagstone, and feather rock?"</u>

   (A) "Bob have you checked with our office in Canton, Ohio, to see if it stocks slate, flagstone, and feather rock?"

   (B) "Bob have you checked with our office in Canton, Ohio, to see if it stocks slate flagstone and feather rock?"

   (C) "Bob, have you checked with our office in Canton, Ohio to see if it stocks slate, flagstone, and feather rock?"

   (D) "Bob, have you checked with our office in Canton, Ohio, to see if it stocks slate, flagstone, and feather rock?"

   (E) Bob, have you checked with our office in Canton, Ohio, to see if it stocks slate, flagstone, and feather rock?

40. If the room would have been brighter, I would have been more
    successful in my search for the lost earrings.
    (A) If the room would have been brighter
    (B) If the room was brighter
    (C) If rooms were brighter
    (D) If the room could have been brighter
    (E) If the room had been brighter

41. After announcing that no notes could be used during the final exam, the
    instructor was compelled to fail two students because they used notes
    anyway.
    (A) two students because they used notes anyway.
    (B) two students because of their notes.
    (C) two students because of them using notes.
    (D) two students whose notes were used.
    (E) two students due to the use of their notes.

42. The respiratory membranes, through which exchange of gases occurs,
    are the linings of the lungs.
    (A) through which exchange of gases occurs
    (B) through which exchange of gas occurs
    (C) after gases are exchanged
    (D) occurs through the exchange of gases
    (E) through which gas is exchanged

43. Jeff is one of those who tends to resist any attempt at classification or
    regulation.
    (A) who tends to resist any attempt at
    (B) whose tendency to resist any attempt at
    (C) who tend to resist any attempt at
    (D) who tends to resist any attempt to
    (E) who tends to resistance of any attempt at

44. The amount of water in living cells vary, but it is usually 65 percent and
    in some organisms may be as high as 96 percent or more of the total
    substance.
    (A) The amount of water in living cells vary
    (B) The amount of water varies
    (C) The amount of water in cells vary
    (D) The amount of water in living cells varies
    (E) The amounts of water varies in living cells

45. The belief of ancient scientists was that maggots are generated from decaying bodies and filth and are not formed by reproduction.

   (A) The belief of ancient scientists was
   (B) The ancient scientists beliefs were
   (C) The ancient scientists believe
   (D) The belief of ancient scientists were
   (E) The ancient belief of scientists was

STOP. IF YOU FINISH BEFORE TIME IS UP, CHECK YOUR WORK ON THIS SECTION ONLY. DO NOT WORK ON ANY OTHER SECTION OF THE TEST. YOU MAY RETURN TO THE USAGE QUESTIONS IF TIME PERMITS.

SECTION IV: WRITING—ESSAY

Time: 30 Minutes
1 Essay

DIRECTIONS

In this section, you will have 30 minutes to plan and write an essay. You may use the bottom of this page to organize and plan your essay before you begin writing. You should plan your time wisely. Read the topic carefully to make sure that you are properly addressing the issue or situation. YOU MUST WRITE ON THE SPECIFIED TOPIC. AN ESSAY ON ANOTHER TOPIC WILL NOT BE ACCEPTABLE.

The essay question included in this section is designed to give you an opportunity to write clearly and effectively. Use specific examples whenever appropriate to aid in supporting your ideas. Keep in mind that the quality of your writing is much more important than the quantity.

Your essay is to be written on the special answer sheets provided. No other paper may be used. Your writing should be neat and legible. Because you have only a limited amount of space in which to write, please do NOT skip lines, do NOT write excessively large, and do NOT leave wide margins.

Remember, use the bottom of this page for any organizational notes you may wish to make.

Topic

Should there be any restriction on how many years a teacher may teach the same subject or the same grade level? Explain your answer and, if possible, use personal experiences.

FOR YOUR ESSAY, USE TWO SIDES OF AN 8½" BY 11" LINED SHEET OF PAPER.

TEST OF GENERAL KNOWLEDGE

SECTION I: SOCIAL STUDIES

Time: 30 Minutes
30 Questions

DIRECTIONS

Following each of the questions or statements below, select the choice that best answers the question or completes the statement.

1. Following the passage of the landmark Voting Rights Act of 1965, which of the following U.S. geographic areas showed the greatest increase in voter registration?
   (A) Northeast
   (B) Pacific Northwest
   (C) Southwest
   (D) Gulf States
   (E) Midwest

2 Psychologists believe that standard tests of intelligence are generally an inappropriate measure of black intelligence primarily because
   (A) intelligence tests seldom correlate with academic achievement
   (B) blacks in the North score higher on intelligence tests than do blacks in the South
   (C) intelligence tests reflect culturally acquired knowledge
   (D) creativity cannot be tested by standard tests of intelligence
   (E) intelligence is based solely on genetic makeup

3. In the twentieth century, which of the following forces of social change had the greatest impact upon the traditional American family?
   (A) socialization and stratification
   (B) immigration and migration
   (C) specialization and assimilation
   (D) social disorganization and integration
   (E) industrialization and urbanization

4. "Since 1803, the federal courts have exercised the power to interpret the Constitution and to declare acts of Congress or the President 'null and void.' " This statement describes a basic relationship among the three branches of the federal government that best exemplifies
(A) separation of power   (D) division of power
(B) checks and balances   (E) constitutional supremacy
(C) judicial review

5. For which of the following government positions is the holder required to be a natural-born citizen of the United States?
(A) President
(B) U.S. Supreme Court Chief Justice
(C) U.S. Senator
(D) none of these
(E) all of these

Questions 6 and 7 refer to the following graph.

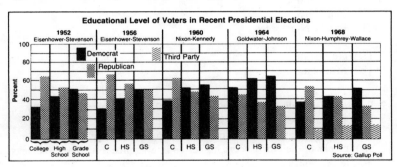

6. According to information presented in the graph individuals with a college education are more likely than individuals with a noncollege background to support
(A) a third party Presidential candidate
(B) a Democratic Presidential candidate
(C) a Republican Presidential candidate
(D) varies according to each election
(E) none of these

7. In which election did every group give greater support to the Democratic candidate?
(A) 1952   (B) 1956   (C) 1960   (D) 1964   (E) 1968

Questions 8 and 9 refer to the following map on which the letters A through E represent different countries in Europe.

8. Assuming no change in the current political climate, which country is least likely to become a member of the European Economic Community (Common Market)?

   (A) country A   (D) country D
   (B) country B   (E) country E
   (C) country C

9. Fear of being subordinated to a British-American domination of Europe led to this country's withdrawing from the NATO military alliance and forcing the organization to remove all military installations from its territory.

   (A) country A   (D) country D
   (B) country B   (E) country E
   (C) country C

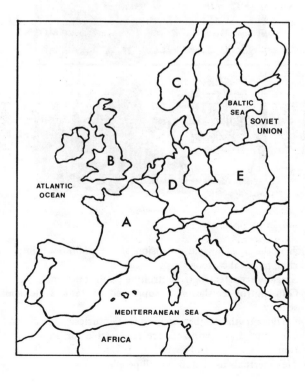

10. Two of the most obvious elements of American industrialization in the late nineteenth century were the increase in the labor force and its effects on the growth of urban areas. Which of the following was *not* associated with the industrialization of America?
    (A) the rise of cities
    (B) the trade-union movement
    (C) humanizing aspects of technological innovations
    (D) government protection of management through the use of court injunctions
    (E) the growth of the suburbs

Primitive Logic

11. Which is the most logical extension of the philosophy implied in the preceding political cartoon?
    (A) Slogans are effective in controlling public opinion.
    (B) Gun-control legislation is supported by radical elements in the society.
    (C) Obvious truths can be obscured for centuries.
    (D) Communist sympathizers are responsible for gun-control legislation.
    (E) Neanderthals used clubs to kill people.

Questions 12 and 13 are based on the following graph.

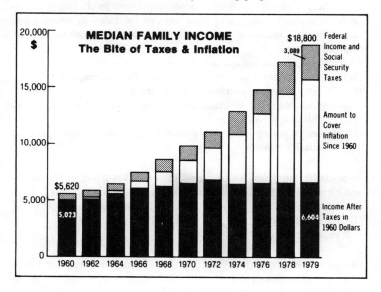

12. It can be inferred from the graph that
    (A) as the median family income increased, the percentage of federal taxes decreased
    (B) although the median family income has more than tripled since 1960, the actual income based on 1960 dollars has remained relatively constant
    (C) there is no correlation between actual income and the amount of federal taxes a family must pay
    (D) the amount of money necessary to cover inflation was greater in 1974 than in 1979
    (E) the estimated 1979 pretax income was lower than the actual amount of federal taxes for that year

13. Since 1960, the increase in federal taxes has been at a slower rate than that of the amount of total income.
    (A) definitely a true statement
    (B) possibly a true statement
    (C) definitely a false statement
    (D) possibly a false statement
    (E) insufficient information to determine the correct answer

14. "It is important to consider that the world population problem cannot be adequately resolved by simply producing more food. Increased food production cannot keep pace with current increases in world population." From the sentiment expressed in the quotation, it can be concluded that the author

   (A) favors government-sponsored research programs
   (B) opposes cooperative sharing of the world's food resources
   (C) favors a drastic reduction in the birthrate
   (D) opposes economic sanctions against countries that encourage over-production of food
   (E) favors a policy that allows food production to keep pace with population growth

15. In Socialist countries, which term best describes government takeover and ownership of the major industrial segments of an economy?

   (A) anarchy   (D) collectivization
   (B) nationalization   (E) kibbutzim
   (C) eminent domain

16. During the decade of the 1970s, the United States experienced a period of increased inflation. Which of the following groups benefit the *most* from long periods of increased inflation?

   (A) creditors
   (B) debtors
   (C) retirees on a fixed income
   (D) municipal employees
   (E) federal government employees

17. In 1982, Japan sold $20 billion more goods to the United States than it bought. At the same time, the dollar rose more than 50% against the yen. Which of the following would be the most likely economic impact of the foreign-exchange gap between the dollar and the yen?

   (A) American products would become cheaper in Japan.
   (B) Japanese products would become cheaper in the United States while boosting the cost of U.S. goods in Japan.
   (C) The American dollar would be undervalued in terms of the Japanese yen.
   (D) Japanese and American products at home and abroad would remain relatively unchanged.
   (E) The American-Japanese trade deficit would be significantly reduced.

18. Deferred gratification best characterizes which of the following?
    (A) the lower class
    (B) the middle class
    (C) the upper class
    (D) minority groups
    (E) industrial and agricultural workers

19. The federal government in the midst of inflationary pressures pursues a tight money policy. Which of the following would be the best method to accomplish this?
    (A) lower interest rates
    (B) lower bond prices
    (C) increase interest rates
    (D) decrease the discount rate
    (E) print additional currency

20. During the "return to normalcy" following the First World War, the United States consistently supported
    (A) military intervention in Latin America
    (B) isolationism
    (C) lowering protective tariffs
    (D) the League of Nations
    (E) the cancellation of European debts resulting from World War I

21. Which of the following famous black Americans is incorrectly paired with his area of expertise?
    (A) Langston Hughes—literature
    (B) Eldridge Cleaver—politics
    (C) Scott Joplin—music
    (D) Booker T. Washington—education
    (E) James Baldwin—sculpture

Election of 1868

CANDIDATES: 1868	ELECTORAL VOTE	POPULAR VOTE
REPUBLICAN Ulysses S. Grant	214	3,013,421
DEMOCRATIC Horatio Seymour	80	2,706,829
NOT VOTED	23	
	317	5,720,250

22. Of the choices given, which two states, according to the chart above, had the largest number of electoral votes in the 1868 election?
    (A) California and Massachusetts   (D) Pennsylvania and Ohio
    (B) Texas and Michigan   (E) New York and Virginia
    (C) New York and Florida

23. "To the States, respectively, or to the people, are reserved the powers not delegated to the United States by the Constitution nor prohibited by it to the States. Each state is a complete sovereignty within the sphere of its reserved powers. The government of the Union acting within the sphere of its delegated authority, is also a complete sovereignty." This statement most clearly exemplifies which of the following?
    (A) Federalism
    (B) separation of powers
    (C) checks and balances
    (D) government by the consent of the governed
    (E) enumerated state powers

24. Traditionally, in the United States, which of the following groups have most often been subject to stereotyping?
    (A) socioeconomic groups
    (B) national ethnic groups
    (C) political extremist groups
    (D) sexually deviant groups
    (E) subculture groups

Questions 25 and 26 refer to the map of the subcontinent of India. The letters A through E represent countries in that region.

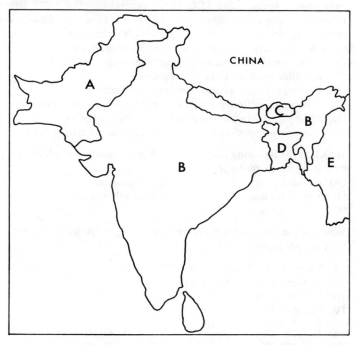

25. Which country does *not* have a Moslem or Buddhist religious majority?
    (A) country A
    (B) country B
    (C) country C
    (D) country D
    (E) country E

26. Which country, once called Bengal, gained independence in 1971 after fighting a bloody civil war with Pakistan?
    (A) country A
    (B) country B
    (C) country C
    (D) country D
    (E) country E

27. In 1936, the *Literary Digest* conducted a preelection poll which predicted that Alf Landon would defeat Franklin D. Roosevelt by a popular vote greater than 15%. In the general election, FDR defeated Landon by a popular vote majority of 24%. Which of the following is the primary criticism of newspaper polls which record the responses of readers who return questionnaires on political candidates?

(A) Newspapers frequently present the results of opinion polls as infallible predictors of public opinion.

(B) Newspaper polls have a direct effect on voter turnout.

(C) Newspaper polls are designed to produce a predetermined result.

(D) Newspaper polls are not based on random sampling.

(E) Newspaper polls are often paid for by political candidates.

28. Which of the following taxes would fall most heavily on individuals who earn less than $8,000 a year?

(A) a sales tax   (D) a gasoline tax
(B) a property tax   (E) an inheritance tax
(C) an income tax

29. Which of the following is the correct chronological order for the events in U.S. history listed below?

  I. League of Nations
 II. Tennessee Valley Authority
III. United Nations
 IV. Marshall Plan

(A) II, I, IV, III   (D) I, IV, II, III
(B) I, II, III, IV   (E) IV, I, II, III
(C) II, I, III, IV

30. "If Vietnam falls to communism, all of Southeast Asia will fall to communism." Which of the following best describes this statement?

(A) containment   (D) appeasement
(B) proliferation theory (E) liberation
(C) domino theory

STOP. IF YOU FINISH BEFORE TIME IS UP, CHECK YOUR WORK ON THIS SECTION ONLY. DO NOT WORK ANY OTHER SECTION OF THE TEST.

SECTION II: MATHEMATICS

Time: 30 Minutes
25 Questions

DIRECTIONS

Each of the mathematics questions or problems below is followed by five suggested answers. Select the best answer for each question.

1. The distance between two cities would be most suitably reported in
   (A) liters   (D) meters
   (B) kilograms   (E) millimeters
   (C) kilometers

2. A dress originally for sale at $80 was discounted 30%. Because it still didn't sell, it was discounted a further 20%. What was the price of the dress after the second discount?
   (A) $30   (B) $40   (C) $42.40   (D) $44.80   (E) $56

3. Average the numbers 10.2, 9.1, 8.7, 10.5, 8.8, and 9.4.
   (A) 9.45   (B) 9.5   (C) 9.55   (D) 9.6   (E) 9.65

Questions 4 and 5 refer to the following circle graph.

4. Approximately how many students received an unsatisfactory mark, below a C?
   (A) 4   (D) 10
   (B) 6   (E) 12
   (C) 8

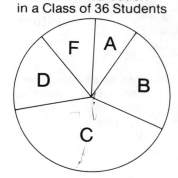

Grade Distribution
in a Class of 36 Students

5. Approximately what percentage of students obtained a B?
   (A) 8   (D) 35
   (B) 9   (E) 45
   (C) 22

6. How many integers between 2 and 99 are evenly divisible by 5?
   (A) 10   (B) 17   (C) 18   (D) 19   (E) 20

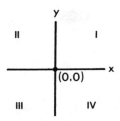

7. In the coordinate graph above, the point represented by $(-3,4)$ would be found in which quadrant?
   (A) I
   (B) II
   (C) III
   (D) IV
   (E) cannot be determined

8. Which is the largest of the following fractions?
   (A) 7/22   (B) 0.31   (C) 1/3   (D) 19/60   (E) 17/50

9. A nonstop passenger express left Chicago at 7:59 A.M. and arrived 412 miles away in Minneapolis at 3:05 P.M. Calculate the average (arithmetic mean) speed of the train.
   (A) 52 mph   (B) 54 mph   (C) 56 mph   (D) 58 mph
   (E) 60 mph

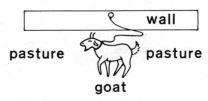

10. The diagram above shows a goat tied to a wall by a rope. The rope is too short to reach to either end of the wall. What is the shape of the pasture area on which the goat could graze?
    (A) circle
    (B) half circle
    (C) rectangle
    (D) square
    (E) triangle

11. $2/3 + 1/5 + 1/6 = ?$ can be most efficiently answered by
    (A) using a common denominator of 90
    (B) using a common denominator of 15
    (C) using a common denominator of 30
    (D) using the "invert and multiply" technique
    (E) multiplying denominators

12. Which of the following expressions could be used to demonstrate that multiplication can yield a product that is less than either of the numbers that are multiplied?
    (A) $(-1.652) \times (-0.001)$
    (B) $(-0.424) \times (0.8361)$
    (C) $(0.2175) \times (0.8917)$
    (D) $(0.4931) \times (2.4438)$
    (E) $(1.1522) \times (0.0363)$

13. Round off to the nearest tenth: 4,316.136
    (A) 4,320   (D) 4,316.14
    (B) 4,316.106   (E) 4,316.1
    (C) 4,316.13

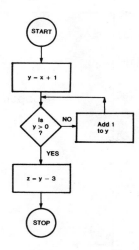

14. In the flow chart, if x = 3, then what is the value of z?
    (A) -1
    (B) 0
    (C) 1
    (D) 3
    (E) 6

15. Patricia has two dollars to purchase postage stamps of 17¢ and 1¢ denominations. What is the *fewest* number of stamps that she can buy with all of her money?
    (A) 15   (B) 18   (C) 21   (D) 24   (E) 27

16. If 3c = d, then c =
    (A) $3 + d$ (D) $1/3d$
    (B) $3d$ (E) $(1 + d)/3$
    (C) $d/3$

17. To find the total surface area in square meters of a rectangular solid whose length is 7 meters, width is 6 meters, and depth is 3 meters, one would use the following calculation:

(A) 7m × 6m × 3m

(B) 2(7m × 6m) + 2(6m × 3m) + 2(7m × 3m)

(C) 7m × 6m + 6m × 3m + 3m × 7m

(D) 7m × 6m × 3m × 2

(E) 7m × 3m × 2

Questions 18 and 19 refer to the following ratio-scale line graph.

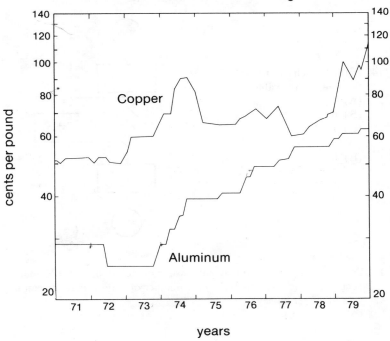

18. What was the lowest price for copper during this period?
    (A) 25¢   (B) 30¢   (C) 40¢   (D) 45¢   (E) 50¢

19. During how many calendar years did the market price of aluminum increase?

   (A) 4   (B) 5   (C) 6   (D) 7   (E) 8

20. On a map, 1 centimeter represents 35 kilometers. Two cities 245 kilometers apart would be separated on the map by how many centimeters?

   (A) 5   (B) 7   (C) 9   (D) 210   (E) 280

21. If ten dozen pencils cost $15, what is the cost of eight pencils?

   (A) $1   (B) $1.88   (C) $2.25   (D) $10   (E) $12

22. In the figure CF is perpendicular to BE. What is the measure of angle COD?

   (A) 26°
   (B) 34°
   (C) 36°
   (D) 46°
   (E) 64°

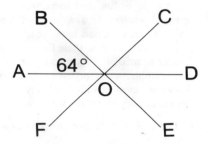

23. $5 - 2m - (m - 13) = m$. Solve for the value of m.

   (A) 2   (B) 4   (C) 4.5   (D) 6   (E) 9

24. For the first 3 spelling assignments during one month, Deborah averages 82. The next such assignment lowers her overall average to 78. What was her score on the fourth assignment?

   (A) 66   (B) 69   (C) 72   (D) 75   (E) 78

25. There is a fixed algebraic relation between two quantities, P and Q. The table on the right shows some correlations of the quantities. What is the value of Q if P equals −4?

   (A) −7
   (B) −6
   (C) 2
   (D) 9
   (E) 12

P	Q
3	−9
2	−6
1	−3
0	0
−1	3
−2	6

STOP. IF YOU FINISH BEFORE TIME IS UP, CHECK YOUR WORK ON THIS SECTION ONLY. DO NOT WORK ON ANY OTHER SECTION OF THE TEST.

SECTION III: LITERATURE AND FINE ARTS

Time: 30 Minutes
35 Questions

DIRECTIONS

Each of these questions or incomplete statements is followed by five possible answers or completions. Select the answer or completion that is best in each case.

We had a fine company of these river inspectors along this trip. There were eight or ten, and there was abundance of room for them in our great pilothouse. Two or three of them wore polished silk hats, elaborate shirt fronts, diamond breastpins, kid gloves, and patent leather boots. They were choice in their English, and bore themselves with a dignity proper to men of solid means and prodigious reputations as pilots. . . . I was a cipher in this august company, and felt subdued, not to say torpid. I was not even of sufficient consequence to assist at the wheel when it was necessary to put the tiller hard down in a hurry. . .

1. The author of the preceding passage has succeeded in conveying his own sense of
   - (A) adventure
   - (B) elegance
   - (C) history
   - (D) inferiority
   - (E) summer heat

2. *The Card Players* shown on the previous page is an impressionistic painting which depicts

   I. everyday life   II. impending crisis   III. irregular coloration

   (A) II only   (B) III only   (C) I and II   (D) I and III
   (E) II and III

Questions 3 and 4 refer to these statues.

I   II

3. Which of the following is true about sculptures I and II?
   (A) Both sculptures I and II consist of human forms, one having very pronounced angelic appendages, the other demonic in appearance.
   (B) Both sculptures I and II manifest great detail in the folds of their clothing.
   (C) The present appearance of both sculptures I and II indicates that the works, as they were originally created, were probably different in appearance.
   (D) While sculpture I has its right leg extended as though it were dancing, sculpture II has both arms and legs missing.
   (E) The positioning of sculpture II indicates that it is part of a larger sculpture utilizing several forms, whereas sculpture I represents a solitary figure.

4. Statue II probably portrays which of the following types of characters?
   (A) villainous   (B) unconscious   (C) loyal   (D) royal
   (E) part human

The dances of the American Indians were a form of folk art that also served an important purpose for the tribe. Seeking special favors from the gods, the dancers were careful to maintain dignity and precision in their performance and hopeful that their "prayers" would be answered.

5. According to the passage above, the dances of the American Indians could *not* be described as being
   (A) addressed to the gods
   (B) delightfully carefree
   (C) of religious significance
   (D) part of a supernatural ritual
   (E) very serious events

Questions 6 and 7 refer to this speech by Marcus Brutus in Shakespeare's play Julius Caesar.

> No, not an oath: if not the face of men,
> The sufferance of our souls, the time's abuse,—
> If these be motives weak, break off betimes,
> And every man hence to his idle bed;
> So let high-sighted tyranny range on,
> Till each man drop by lottery. But if these,
> As I am sure they do, bear fire enough
> To kindle cowards and to steel with valour
> The melting spirits of women, then, countrymen,
> What need we any spur but our own cause,
> To prick us to redress?

6. The word *fire* in the seventh line symbolizes
   (A) each man   (D) lottery
   (B) haughty tyranny   (E) suffering souls
   (C) important reasons

7. The purpose of Brutus's speech to the other conspirators against Caesar is to
   (A) argue against profane oaths
   (B) condemn both cowards and women
   (C) condemn both tyranny and lottery
   (D) declare that an oath is unnecessary
   (E) boast to his colleagues of his courage

8. One of the primary effects represented in this painting is
   (A) the sharp contrast between light and shadow
   (B) the threat of the prominent horizon
   (C) the discomfort of traveling on horseback
   (D) the desolation of an urban landscape
   (E) the threat of loose boulders on the hillside

9. The building in the photograph houses an important art collection. Why
   was the building most likely constructed in this particular style?
   (A) The building was constructed nearly two thousand years ago.
   (B) The columns and dome convey a sense of classical dignity.
   (C) The Italian architect was very familiar with similar buildings.
   (D) The spaces between the columns invite the public to enter.
   (E) The stonework keeps the art objects at a uniform temperature.

10. Charles Nordhoff and James Norman Hall wrote the set of historical novels *Mutiny on the Bounty, Men Against the Sea,* and *Pitcairn Island.* The latter two books continue the tale after the mutiny. Such a set of related novels is properly called

(A) an anthology   (D) an epic
(B) a ballad   (E) a trilogy
(C) a biography

Questions 11 to 13 refer to these five paintings of women.

A

B

C

D   E

11. Which of the five paintings has a religious theme?
    (A) A   (B) B   (C) C   (D) D   (E) E

12. Which of the five paintings is the work of an American artist?
    (A) A   (B) B   (C) C   (D) D   (E) E

13. Which of the following statements is true for the five paintings?
    (A) Paintings A and B have the models posed against a neutral
        landscape.
    (B) Paintings B and C are the most highly idealized of the five
        portraits.
    (C) Paintings C and D have pale skies to emphasize the hands of the
        women.
    (D) Paintings D and E are the most painstakingly realistic of the five
        works.
    (E) Paintings E and A have the model looking directly at the artist.

Doctor Marcus on his way
Touched this statue yesterday.
Now, although a god and clay,
Its funeral will be today.

14. The preceding epigram by Bernard Grebanier ridicules
   (A) bachelorhood
   (B) commercialized sculpture
   (C) the effectiveness of physicians
   (D) unpredictable fortune
   (E) the value of religion

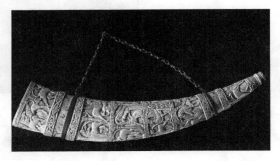

15. Above is a picture of a hollow ivory object covered with carved images of
    animals and Christianity. Which of the following statements does *not*
    apply to the object?
   (A) It was a very early example of abstract art.
   (B) It could have been owned by a church.
   (C) It was fashioned from an elephant tusk.
   (D) It shows that the culture was fond of hunting.
   (E) It was a cup for ceremonial drinking.

Questions 16, 17, and 18 refer to the following passage

   Hardly a man takes a half-hour's nap after dinner, but when he wakes
he holds up his head and asks, "What's the news?" as if the rest of
mankind had stood his sentinels. Some give directions to be waked every
half-hour, doubtless for no other purpose; and then, to pay for it, they tell
what they have dreamed. After a night's sleep the news is as indispensable as the breakfast. "Pray tell me anything new that has happened to a
man anywhere on this globe"—and he reads it over his coffee and rolls,
that a man had his eyes gouged out this morning on the Wachito River;
never dreaming while that he lives in the dark unfathomed mammoth
cave of this world, and has but the rudiment of an eye himself.

16. Which of the following best describes the content of the passage above?
    (A) a factual account of life in a small town
    (B) a survey of the various sources of news that are available to well-informed individuals
    (C) a warning against sleeping past the significant events of the day
    (D) a criticism of those who keep up with the news obsessively
    (E) an indictment of those who allow crime to take place while they sleep

17. Which of the following best characterizes the author's tone in the passage?
    (A) sleepy   (D) derisive
    (B) defensive   (E) plain
    (C) neutral

18. In the third line, the word *sentinels* refers to
    (A) those who guard the sleeper from harm
    (B) those willing to answer the sleeper's questions
    (C) those who keep track of the news for the sleeper
    (D) those who are out of the sleeper's control
    (E) those stationed at various points around the globe

19. One strong element of symmetry in this painting is the
    (A) arrangement of angels
    (B) expression in Mary's face
    (C) folds in Mary's apparel
    (D) position of the Christchild
    (E) size of the halos

Questions 20 throuth 23 refer to these excerpts from poems.

   (A) As fair art thou, my bonie lass,
        So deep in luve am I;
        And I will luve thee still, my dear,
        Till a' the seas gang dry.

   (B) For I loved that cook as a brother, I did,
        And the cook he worshipped me;
        But we'd both be blowed if we'd either be stowed
        In the other chap's hold, you see.

   (C) Had we but world enough, and time,
        This coyness, lady, were no crime.
        We would sit down, and think which way
        To walk, and pass our long love's day.

   (D) I will be open.   I think he never loved me:
        he loved the bright beaches, the little lips of foam
        that ride small waves, he loved the veer of gulls:
        he said with a gay mouth: I love you.   Grow to know me.

   (E) Sigh no more, ladies, sigh no more;
        Men were deceivers ever;
        One foot in sea, and one on shore,
        To one thing constant never.

20. Which of the poems is written in Scottish dialect?
    (A) A   (B) B   (C) C   (D) D   (E) E

21. Which of the poems does *not* have a regular rhythm?
    (A) A   (B) B   (C) C   (D) D   (E) E

22. Which of the poems is part of a humorous tale of cannibalism?
    (A) A   (B) B   (C) C   (D) D   (E) E

23. Which of the poems has the most modern style?
    (A) A   (B) B   (C) C   (D) D   (E) E

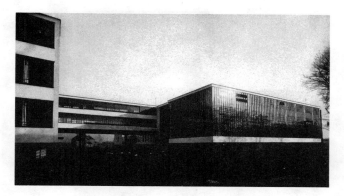

24. The group of buildings in the preceding picture constitute a residential school for architectural students to learn the fine arts, industrial crafts, and building design. The school buildings themselves fulfill all of the following functions except one. Which do they *not* fulfill?
   (A) The geometric design is well suited to modern materials and construction methods.
   (B) The glass walls bring the exterior world into intimate contact with the interior rooms.
   (C) They proclaim the usefulness and dominance of machines in our society.
   (D) They represent a standard of excellence to challenge the students.
   (E) They show that architectural beauty arises from ornamentation instead of basic structure.

   And at last, in its curved and imperceptible fall, the sun sank low, and from glowing white changed to a dull red without rays and without heat, as if about to go out suddenly, stricken to death by the touch of that gloom brooding over a crowd of men.

25. In the passage, the sun is characterized as a
   (A) blessing   (D) victor
   (B) life source   (E) curse
   (C) victim

26. The reason the preceding painting by Gilbert Stuart may be the most famous American portrait of all times is that
   (A) George Washington is our most beloved President
   (B) the identical portrait appears on the $5 bill
   (C) it is the model for copies by many other artists
   (D) Stuart was the most talented American painter
   (E) the unfinished nature of the work is unforgettable

27. Following are five sayings from *Poor Richard's Almanack* by Benjamin Franklin. Which of them implies that a person can't make friends by continually making sarcastic remarks?
   (A) Glass, china, and reputation are easily cracked and never well mended.
   (B) If a man could have half his wishes he would double his troubles.
   (C) The sleeping fox catches no poultry.
   (D) A spoonful of honey will catch more flies than a gallon of vinegar.
   (E) 'Tis hard for an empty bag to stand upright.

28. The wooden statue is a remarkable portrayal of a Buddhist priest at peace with himself and the world. That theme of peacefulness is conveyed by all of the following aspects *except*
   (A) the expression on the priest's face
   (B) the gestures made by the hands
   (C) the gigantic size to humble a viewer
   (D) the smooth folds in the garment
   (E) the sitting posture of the priest

... shaped, you might say, like a fat dragon standing up, and had two fine land-locked harbors, and a hill in the centre part marked "The Spy-glass." There were several additions of a later date; but, above all, three crosses of red ink...

29. The preceding lines from a popular novel describe a
   (A) coral island   (D) treasure map
   (B) golf course   (E) volcanic eruption
   (C) mythical kingdom

30. For the painting above, which of the following might represent the artist's theme?
    (A) the ecstasy of finally reaching Heaven
    (B) the fear of a war involving nuclear weapons
    (C) the hope of finding the Fountain of Youth
    (D) the joy of a simple, natural lifestyle
    (E) the preference for agricultural pursuits

Questions 31 and 32 refer to this stanza from a poem by Tennyson.

> Half a league, half a league,
> Half a league onward.
> All in the valley of Death
> Rode the six hundred.
> "Forward the Light Brigade!
> Charge for the guns!" he said.
> Into the valley of Death
> Rode the six hundred.

31. The word *league* is used as
    (A) a group of soldiers
    (B) an interval of time
    (C) a hesitation before battle
    (D) a promise of battle
    (E) a unit of distance

32. The phrase *six hundred* refers to
    (A) the forthcoming attack
    (B) the length of the valley
    (C) many cavalrymen
    (D) the number of guns
    (E) souls of those departed

33. The floors inside this modern building are continuous. There are no
    stairs, yet a visitor gradually shifts from level to level while walking
    around. Which of the following terms best expresses the basic plan
    uniting the building?
    (A) circular floors
    (B) concave lobby
    (C) convex balconies
    (D) radial hallways
    (E) spiral ramp

    The executioner's argument was that you couldn't cut off a head
unless there was a body to cut it off from. . .
    The King's argument was that anything that had a head could be
beheaded, and that you weren't to talk nonsense.
    The Queen's argument was that, if something wasn't done about it in
less than no time, she'd have everybody executed, all round.

34. The preceding discussion about the Cheshire Cat in *Alice in Wonderland*
    shows Lewis Carroll's delight in
    (A) compassion   (D) plot
    (B) logic   (E) terror
    (C) meter

35. The painting above shows a number of English citizens witnessing informal horse races in the countryside. What is the principal feature used by the artist to imply that this is a realistic view, rather than a carefully posed view?
    (A) Almost all the people are in energetic, unbalanced postures.
    (B) The background includes trees and houses unrelated to the subject.
    (C) The prominent carriage and horses are cut off at the margins.
    (D) The relatively unimportant sky occupies over half of the painting.
    (E) The umbrella and dog interfere with our view of the races.

STOP. IF YOU FINISH BEFORE TIME IS UP, CHECK YOUR WORK ON THIS SECTION ONLY. DO NOT WORK ON ANY OTHER SECTION OF THE TEST.

SECTION IV: SCIENCE

Time: 30 Minutes
30 Questions

DIRECTIONS

Each of the science questions is followed by five suggested answers. Select the best answer for each question.

1. A plugged drain in a bathtub may often be reopened simply by filling the tub with water. What physical process explains such unplugging of the drain?
   (A) The water molecules lubricate the drain and decrease friction holding the blockage.
   (B) To every action, like filling, there is an equal and opposite reaction, like draining.
   (C) The greater water depth in the tub produces a higher pressure against the blockage.
   (D) The increased volume of water ultimately allows most of the blockage to dissolve.
   (E) There is a chemical reaction between the water and the material stopping the drain.

2. Steel bridges are commonly painted to inhibit rusting. The fundamental purpose of the paint is to
   (A) enhance the cohesion of metallic atoms
   (B) keep oxygen away from iron
   (C) prevent dew from forming
   (D) seal mineral oils inside
   (E) shield the steel from corrosive salt

3. Of all our planet's environments, the desert may be most susceptible to destruction by human activities. Which of the following actions would be *least* harmful to the desert environment?
   (A) establishment of dude ranches and resorts
   (B) grazing by large herds of cattle or sheep
   (C) limiting the number of people entering an area
   (D) making much of the desert accessible by road
   (E) pumping up water for surface irrigation

4. Precipitation which has been poisoned by industrial pollutants is called
   (A) nuclear poison   (D) smog
   (B) radioactive waste   (E) ozone
   (C) acid rain

Food	Temperature (°F)	Time (min)
Gravy	260	90
Pork and beans	240	105
Corn	240	50
Tomatoes	212	34
Orange juice	145	15

5. The table above shows the temperatures and times necessary for safely processing several canned foods. For which of the following foods is the accompanying processing *not* shown to be safe?
   (A) corn at 240° for 75 minutes
   (B) gravy at 280° for 90 minutes
   (C) orange juice at 150° for 20 minutes
   (D) pork and beans at 285° for 90 minutes
   (E) tomatoes at 215° for 35 minutes

6. Plants are known to grow in particular directions governed by external features of the environment. The bending of a houseplant toward a window is a growth response to which external stimulus?
   (A) open air   (D) photosynthesis
   (B) gravity   (E) nitrogen
   (C) light

7. The forces that produce the earth's tides are due to
   (A) centrifugal forces of the rotating earth
   (B) continental drift
   (C) daily changes in temperature
   (D) the earth's magnetic field
   (E) the moon's mass

Questions 8 and 9 refer to the following passage.

The near-surface waters of the ocean teem with a rich variety of organisms. Most plentiful are one-celled plants, including algae, that transform solar energy into starches and sugars. Copepods are tiny, shrimp-like creatures that feed upon the plant life. Herring are small fish that nourish themselves on the copepods. Mackerel are large enough to eat herring but fall prey to yet larger sharks. These particular marine organisms form a typical food pyramid.

8. The food pyramid rises from the most common, independent organisms at the base upward to the least common, most dependent organisms at the top. Which of the five organisms would be at the top of our marine food pyramid?
   - (A) algae
   - (B) copepods
   - (C) herring
   - (D) mackerels
   - (E) sharks

9. Based on the concept of the food pyramid, which animal would be most numerous in shallow ocean waters?
   - (A) algae
   - (B) copepods
   - (C) herring
   - (D) mackerels
   - (E) sharks

10. The planet Mars appears to be a bright, reddish object in the night sky. What is the origin of the red light?
    - (A) radioactive dust
    - (B) reflected sunlight
    - (C) the two moons of Mars
    - (D) very hot deserts
    - (E) volcanic eruption

11. Which of the following cities would have the lowest mean temperature during July?
    - (A) Berlin
    - (B) Buenos Aires
    - (C) New Orleans
    - (D) Rome
    - (E) Toronto

12. All of the following would be considered conservation methods *except*
    - (A) putting a brick in the water fill-up part of your toilet
    - (B) using lower wattage light bulbs
    - (C) insulating your home
    - (D) driving within the speed limit
    - (E) watering your lawn during midday

13. Biologists define *symbiosis* as individuals from different species living together in intimate association, regardless of whether the association is beneficial, neutral, or harmful. All of the following pairs are examples of symbiosis *except*
    - (A) ants and aphids
    - (B) dogs and fleas
    - (C) foxes and chickens
    - (D) humans and tapeworms
    - (E) whales and barnacles

14. Both *momentum* and *kinetic energy* depend on the same two fundamental physical quantities. Identify those quantities from the following list.

    I. charge   III. temperature
    II. mass   IV. velocity

    (A) I and II   (D) II and IV
    (B) I and III   (E) III and IV
    (C) II and III

15. A marathon runner training at sea level may have difficulty running for a long period of time at a high altitude because
    (A) the ground is harder at high altitudes
    (B) the ground is steeper at high altitudes
    (C) the air is thicker at high altitudes
    (D) the pressure is lower at high altitudes
    (E) the humidity is lower at high altitudes

16. For which of the following elements is the commercial supply obtained otherwise than by mining?
    (A) copper   (D) nitrogen
    (B) iron   (E) silver
    (C) nickel

17. Major components of smog produced during combustion are hydrocarbons, carbon monoxide, and sulfur dioxide. Which of the following fuels used in electricity generating plants would *not* contribute to the smog problem?
    (A) coal   (D) natural gas
    (B) fuel oil   (E) uranium
    (C) garbage

18. Photosynthesis in plants does *not* require the availability of
    (A) carbon dioxide   (D) oxygen
    (B) chlorophyll   (E) water
    (C) light

19. pH is a measure of
    (A) the energy released by a chemical reaction
    (B) the pressure of gas
    (C) the solubility of a salt
    (D) the strength of an acid
    (E) physical properties of metals

Questions 20 and 21 refer to the following diagram.

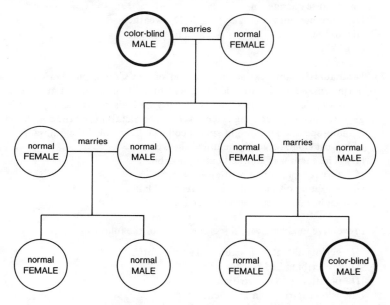

20. About one man in fifteen is color blind, and the preceding diagram shows the common pattern of inheritance. Which of these statements best describes the inheritance of color blindness?
    (A) A man derives his color blindness from his father's brother.
    (B) A man derives his color blindness from his father's father.
    (C) A man derives his color blindness from his mother's brother.
    (D) A man derives his color blindness from his mother's father.
    (E) A man derives his color blindness from his mother's mother.

21. On the diagram, who would you identify as being a hidden carrier of the gene for color blindness?
    (A) the daughter of a color-blind man
    (B) the grandaughter of a color-blind man
    (C) the grandson of a color-blind man
    (D) the son of a color-blind man
    (E) the wife of a color-blind man

22. Possibly the most significant biological danger of nuclear energy is that it can cause changes in

(A) chromosomes   (D) weather
(B) ozone   (E) weight
(C) skin

23. Dinosaurs became extinct at the end of the Cretaceous Period. The recent discovery of worldwide traces of metallic iridium in Late Cretaceous sedimentary rocks suggests to many geologists that the impact of a gigantic meteorite bearing traces of that rare metal caused the extinction of many species. How might such a collision have killed the dinosaurs?

(A) Dust clouds severely modified the weather.
(B) The earth was knocked out of its orbit.
(C) Great reptiles had brittle, weak bones.
(D) Iridium poisoned all major rivers and lakes.
(E) Unbearable heat burnt all the forests.

24. Preventive medicine would include which of the following?

I. getting a dental checkup every six months
II. prescribing bed rest for a cold
III. practicing good nutrition
IV. using aspirin for a headache

(A) I only   (D) I and III
(B) I and II   (E) I, II, III, and IV
(C) III only

25. Assuming that the data are equally accessible, which of the following types of data would be *least* useful in classifying the chemical elements into the familiar Periodic Table?

(A) the charge on each atom when a salt is dissolved
(B) the color of compounds formed by the elements
(C) the number of protons in each atom
(D) the reaction of each element with other elements
(E) the relative weights of the various atoms

26. Which of the following factors is *not* a significant nuisance or hazard for human exploration of the solar system?

(A) meteors   (D) temperatures
(B) psychological isolation (E) weightlessness
(C) relativity effects

27. Which of the following five choices is *not* essential for all known forms of life?

  (A) air
  (B) amino acids
  (C) carbon atoms
  (D) nucleic acids
  (E) water

28. A charcoal fire fanned by a brisk wind should yield mostly

  (A) carbon dioxide
  (B) carbon monoxide
  (C) graphite
  (D) oxygen
  (E) steam

29. In an experiment, the researcher ignites a flammable rag, places it into a metal cylindrical container with very thin sides, and after one minute tightly seals the lid. One hour later the sides of the container are observed to have partially collapsed inward. Which of the following would help to explain this result?

  (A) After one hour, the air pressure inside the container exceeded that outside the container.
  (B) The smoke generated by the flame was less dense than the air outside the container.
  (C) The heat from the burning rag forced some of the gases out of the container during the first minute.
  (D) The heat of combustion gradually weakened the mechanical strength of the metal sides of the container.
  (E) The sides of the container eventually became hot enough to force an inward contraction.

30. Scientists have discovered traces of pristane and phytane in the Soudan Iron Formation of northern Minnesota, a geological stratum known to be three billion years old. The two compounds are hydrocarbons believed to be made only by living organisms. Which of these statements is a valid deduction from that evidence?

  (A) Life has always required traces of iron for biochemical reactions.
  (B) Life has existed on earth for at least three billion years.
  (C) Primitive life forms could tolerate very cold weather.
  (D) Minnesota would be a promising target for petroleum exploration.
  (E) The pristane and phytane molecules are rich in iron.

STOP. IF YOU FINISH BEFORE TIME IS UP, CHECK YOUR WORK ON THIS SECTION ONLY. DO NOT WORK ON ANY OTHER SECTION OF THE TEST.

TEST OF PROFESSIONAL KNOWLEDGE

SECTION I

Time: 30 Minutes
30 Questions

DIRECTIONS

Following each of the questions or statements below, select the choice that best answers the question or completes the statement.

1. Which of the following is *not* generally considered a true statement regarding alternative schools?
   (A) They are vulnerable to budget cuts and understaffing.
   (B) They are often the target of bitter criticism from traditionalists.
   (C) They find it difficult to achieve the proper balance between structure and freedom.
   (D) They often have difficulty meeting legal and state requirements.
   (E) They are tied to the conventional school program.

2. Which of the following would *not* be characteristic of a mentally gifted child?
   (A) less mature both socially and physically than children of average ability
   (B) superior in mastery of school subjects
   (C) superior in moral attitudes as measured by either moral or trait tests to children of average ability
   (D) ability to read prior to entering the first grade
   (E) an IQ of 130 or higher

3. Aptitude tests attempt to predict the
   (A) level of efficiency of an individual
   (B) degree of achievement already attained by an individual
   (C) probable success in a specific field
   (D) an individual's capacity for improvement without training
   (E) an individual's general knowledge

4. The primary reason a school district would adopt a three-way conference between parent, teacher, and child as a method to evaluate student performance would be that
    (A) such conferences provide an opportunity to improve communication between the student, the parent, and the teacher
    (B) the child would be put in an adversary position
    (C) the conversations would mostly be between parent and child, not teacher and parent
    (D) the child would assume more self-responsibility, since the student is being made part of the evaluative process
    (E) such comments as "your teacher said" or "my child said" would largely be eliminated

5. Which of the following areas was generally ignored by educational psychologists in the period 1900–1960?
    (A) aptitude and achievement
    (B) motivational aspects of education
    (C) intellectual structure of class activities
    (D) testing and evaluation
    (E) the learning process

6. A school district applies for and receives a block grant from the federal government. This entitles the school district to
    (A) use the money for any specified program as determined by the state department of education
    (B) use the money for any educational purpose
    (C) hire library aides, lunch supervisors, and other classified personnel as long as the school district earmarked the money for that purpose
    (D) promote a teacher-retirement investment fund
    (E) use the money in compliance with the categorical nature of the federal aid

7. The best example of evaluation in an individualized education program would be
    (A) tests given at the end of unit
    (B) a written description of the pupil's performance
    (C) early diagnosis and ongoing feedback and guidance
    (D) tests that measure one person against another within a given class or group
    (E) a report card with a classified scale of letters A–F

8. In seventeenth-century colonial America the Puritan concept of education included all of the following *except* that
   (A) the classics were not incorporated into the curriculum
   (B) their basic educational philosophy stemmed directly from the religious orthodoxy of Calvinism
   (C) they believed that the child was a sinful version of an adult person
   (D) they favored education as a means to develop proper obedience and behavior
   (E) fear and discipline were the basis of their educational method

9. The terms *cues, prompts, frames, chains,* and *branches* refer to
   (A) team teaching
   (B) programmed learning materials
   (C) computer programming
   (D) sociodrama
   (E) lesson structuring

10. The major educational contribution of Heinrich Pestalozzi was
    (A) the development of a national system of education
    (B) the adaptation of the educational system to the nature of the child
    (C) to reverse the traditional view of discipline by insisting that discipline should never be harsh
    (D) understanding the connection between positive and negative reinforcement
    (E) to improve the effectiveness of school through the use of appropriate tests and materials

11. Some values and goals for science teaching could be

    I.   to give a practical grasp of scientific methodology
    II. to enable the student to criticize and to appreciate the effects of the sciences on society
    III. to understand science, its history, and present alternative prospects

    (A) I
    (B) II
    (C) I and II
    (D) II and III
    (E) I, II, and III

12. Good teaching requires that teachers are most alert to
    (A) public concerns about education
    (B) the sexual differences of students
    (C) the family backgrounds of students
    (D) poor behavior and use of immediate punishment
    (E) appropriate behavior and proper rewards

13. Understanding children's individual perceptions of their environment is fundamental in
    (A) diagnosing learning disabilities
    (B) psychomotor skills
    (C) influencing children's behavior and learning
    (D) judging learning aptitudes
    (E) judging learning abilities

14. According to the President's Council on Physical Fitness and Sports, the most urgent task facing physical education in the early years of the 1980s is
    (A) identifying physically underdeveloped children and finding remedies for their problems
    (B) providing a uniform standard of physical fitness testing
    (C) identifying students who demonstrate antisocial behavior, including poor sportsmanship
    (D) reducing the competitive nature of physical education programs
    (E) implementing a curriculum that provides for individual differences in physical education

15. Which of the following is the best example of a behavioral objective under which the criterion behavior is to occur?
    (A) Develop an understanding of why Johnny can't read.
    (B) Discuss the techniques of letter writing with the class on Monday.
    (C) The student must be able to correctly identify ten terms associated with the French Revolution in a period of 45 minutes.
    (D) Given a list of sentence fragments, the student must be able to construct an acceptable sentence.
    (E) Be able to complete a marathon race.

16. The Gary Plan (1907–1916) was considered the leading example of progressive education in the early twentieth century. Which of the following was *not* characteristic of the Gary Plan?
    (A) It was an all-year school.
    (B) It attempted to use the public schools to promote social progress.
    (C) It was organized as a miniature community.
    (D) The administration was responsible for maintaining school records.
    (E) The student participated in the industrial activity of the school.

17. Cultural bias in testing refers to the fact that
    (A) some cultures do better on tests than others
    (B) cultured people score higher on tests
    (C) test items are more familiar to some cultures
    (D) tests will show who is more cultured
    (E) tests are biased towards those who are more cultured

18. According to "child-oriented" play theorists, which of the following is *not* considered a factual statement regarding childhood play?
    (A) Play is children's means of interpreting the world around them.
    (B) Play is one of the most significant aspects of a child's life.
    (C) Play has its own intrinsic value and should not be confused with education.
    (D) Play is a natural process in a child's education.
    (E) Play involves a variety of complex behaviors.

19. In testing, a criterion is
    (A) a Greek word meaning validity
    (B) a standard against which answers can be measured
    (C) a group average
    (D) the basic content of the test
    (E) an answer sheet that is machine scored

20. Which of the following is the best example of a core curriculum?
    (A) building a computer from the knowledge gained in an extended-day electronics class
    (B) devising a course of study called "Social Responsibilities"
    (C) unifying the science curriculum by providing multigrade input
    (D) using teaching resources, textbooks, and teaching aids to plan a curriculum
    (E) correlating the English and social studies curriculums

21. Without provocation and without a search warrant, school officials entered a locked vehicle parked on the school grounds. The officials found a small amount of a controlled drug substance. Subsequently, the student owner of the car was suspended from school (based on the evidence found in the car). The school's actions violate which of the student's Fourth Amendment rights?
    (A) Students have a right to park private vehicles on public school grounds.
    (B) Students may bring small amounts of a controlled drug substance to a public school as long as the amount does not constitute a felony.
    (C) The student's suspension was based on illegally seized evidence.
    (D) The student's suspension violated constitutional safeguards protecting freedom of expression.
    (E) The student's suspension was unreasonable, since schools have a legal responsibility to inform a student population of a potential drug search.

22. A school board, reacting to news reports that teenage pregnancy is on the rise, considers adding a life-experience class to the science curriculum. It is acknowledged that such a class would probably facilitate open discussion on birth control. Before the board should authorize this program, they should
   (A) determine if there is a need for the curriculum change
   (B) conduct a district questionnaire on the changing sexual attitudes of teenagers
   (C) organize a citizens' advisory council made up of community leaders and interested people to gain support for such a program
   (D) abandon the plan because of its questionable legal basis
   (E) videotape a science discussion on human reproduction to determine if any misinformation is originating in the classroom

23. The *primary* educational value of a lesson plan is to
   (A) allow the teacher to evaluate the unit of study
   (B) facilitate the principle of continuous growth
   (C) prepare material in a logical and systematic manner
   (D) think out possible ways to teach
   (E) satisfy administrative requirements

24. A middle school social studies teacher plans to conduct a mock presidential election. The teacher thinks that the students' voting behavior will be directly influenced by their parents. He plans to send out a questionnaire to test this hypothesis. In order to insure proportional representation of boys and girls within each grade level, the teacher should use which type of sample?
   (A) random   (D) open end
   (B) stratified   (E) age and grade
   (C) population

25. An educational psychologist determined that students who achieve high academic marks in English have a more positive self-image than students who are below grade level in English. In the above case the independent variable is
   (A) students who show learning readiness
   (B) high academic achievement in English versus below-grade-level achievement in English
   (C) a more positive self-image
   (D) positive self-image and high academic achievement in English
   (E) the role of the educational psychologist

26. A seventh-grade science teacher is preparing to teach a state mandated sex education unit. In order to participate in the class, a signed parental consent form must be returned to the school by each student. A particular student in the class is very eager to participate in the program. However, based on a recent parent conference, the teacher strongly suspects that this student's parents will refuse to sign the consent form. The next day the student returns a signed consent form allowing participation in the class. Which of the following actions by the teacher would be considered professionally responsible?

(A) Allow the student to participate in the program, since the consent form meets the legal requirements for the class.

(B) Refuse to admit the student to the class, but provide library time for the student to research questions under discussion.

(C) Reprimand the student for forging a legal school document.

(D) Allow the student to remain in the class, but discuss with him or her why parental consent forms are important legal documents.

(E) Refuse to admit the student to the class until school contact is made with the parents, confirming their intentions.

27. John is an adolescent boy who often acts rebellious. As a normal adolescent, John probably demonstrates his rebellion by

(A) demanding more privileges and independence

(B) rejecting his religion

(C) completely rejecting his parents' advice

(D) fighting with other boys

(E) leaving home

28. A teacher isn't positive but suspects that a student is cheating on her eighth-grade final in history. The most appropriate teacher action would be to

(A) immediately take the exam from the student and send her to the office

(B) grade the exam and warn her that if it happens again she will fail the course

(C) announce loudly that all students must do their own work

(D) call the building supervisor and ask for school policy on suspected cheating

(E) wait for the end of the period and confront the student with the fact that you know she cheated

29. Which of the following are characteristic of Thorndike's laws of learning?

   I. Learning is governed by the influence of rewards. If you want someone to learn something, wait until the behavior occurs and then reward it.
   II. Punishment is effective in weakening habits.
   III. A learner must be ready to learn.
   IV. Learning depends on the consequences of behavior.
   V. Learners learn by trying one response after another.

   (A) I and V   (B) I, II, and III   (C) II, IV, and V
   (D) I, III, IV, and V (E) II and III

30. A study is said to have internal validity if
   (A) the results obtained would apply in the real world to other similar programs and approaches
   (B) the technique or approach that is being tested or evaluated is identifiable
   (C) the results are systematic and subject to research techniques
   (D) the outcome of the study is a function of the program rather than a result of causes not dealt with in the study
   (E) the researcher has used both independent and dependent variables

STOP. IF YOU FINISH BEFORE TIME IS UP, CHECK YOUR WORK ON THIS SECTION ONLY. DO NOT WORK ON ANY OTHER SECTION OF THE TEST.

SECTION II

Time: 30 Minutes
30 Questions

Following each of the questions or statements below, select the choice that best answers the question or completes the statement.

1. Which of the following statements is the best example of a null hypothesis?
   (A) Males are more likely to pursue an acting career than females.
   (B) Females are more likely to pursue an acting career than males.
   (C) Acting careers are related to the economic background of the participants.
   (D) There are more male actors than female actors.
   (E) Males and females are equally likely to pursue acting careers.

2. Which of the following definitions is considered operational?
   (A) high protective tariff—one in which the tariff rate is set at 25%
   (B) high protective tariff—one in which the tariff rate will definitely benefit the United States
   (C) high protective tariff—one in which the consumer will find the availability of domestic products greatly increased
   (D) high protective tariff—a historical method to solve an imbalance in trade
   (E) high protective tariff—one which is effective but not as effective as the nation needs

3. In which of the following cases are physical education programs an integral part of general education?

   I. Physical education programs provide standards for school attendance.
   II. Social abilities and interests are created along with self-evaluation.
   III. Physical education learning activities convey career information and career knowledge.
   IV. Physical education contributes to socially desirable behavior in interaction with others.
   V. Physical education develops awareness of how various recreational activities affect the environment.

   (A) I, II, and IV
   (B) II, IV, and V
   (C) all choices
   (D) II, III, and IV
   (E) II, III, IV, and V

4. A parameter is
   (A) a statistical characteristic of a population
   (B) a unit of measure in the metric system
   (C) the distance around a polygon
   (D) one standard deviation from the mean
   (E) a statistical byproduct of the normal curve

5. In 1969 Congress mandated a study of gifted education. The resulting Marland Report documented the fact that
   (A) the majority of school administrators were attending to the special needs of the gifted
   (B) the schools were inadequate in their efforts to serve the gifted
   (C) the average educational program provided individualized programs for the gifted
   (D) the Office of Education should have a greater voice in proposing educational policy for the gifted
   (E) state funding was sufficient to meet the needs of gifted education programs

6. A school administrator in a metropolitan school district is interested in finding out about the attitude of teachers toward students. A special area of concern is to determine teachers' attitudes toward minority students. The best method to obtain the desired information would be a
   (A) mandatory district-wide meeting in which the teachers would be free to discuss "any" minority problem experienced in the schools
   (B) voluntary questionnaire that uses a group of respondents who are part of the internal test population
   (C) questionnaire that gives the respondent a series of statements and asks him or her to rank order them in terms of the criteria being questioned
   (D) questionnaire that asks specific questions that deal with attitudes or beliefs teachers might have toward students
   (E) questionnaire that combines unstructured as well as structured methods of response

7. From the Middle Ages to the Renaissance, university lectures were generally given in
   (A) French
   (B) Latin
   (C) Italian
   (D) a combination of Latin and the European vernacular
   (E) Latin and Greek

8. During a junior high school math class, Karmela and Joan suddenly begin shouting and swearing at each other. After restoring order, the teacher calls the students involved in the verbal outburst to the side of the room and asks Karmela to explain what happened. The teacher also informs Joan that she will have equal time to explain her side of the story. At this point, the objective of this procedure is to

(A) determine who is at fault for the disruptive behavior
(B) determine each student's perception of the incident
(C) counsel the students about the impropriety of shouting and swearing
(D) allow the students to independently work out their own problems
(E) present the consequences of continued disruptive behavior

9. A teacher identifies a student as demonstrating a need to be seen by the school district psychologist. Which of the following actions by the teacher is most consistent with basic school district referral procedures?

(A) verbally informing the on-site administrator that a problem exists
(B) offering to participate in a district referral program
(C) mailing the district referral procedures to the parent
(D) stating in writing the reason for the referral and describing the behavior manifested by the student
(E) developing an individualized program to meet the needs of the referred student

10. The historic *Brown* v. *Board of Education* case (1954) ruled that

(A) mandatory prayer in the public schools violated the First Amendment
(B) free speech is guaranteed to student protest groups
(C) sex discrimination is a violation of the Fourteenth Amendment
(D) segregated schools are unconstitutional
(E) separate but equal facilities are protected by historical precedent

11. The educational philosophy of John Dewey was mainly responsible for

(A) the development of free public education
(B) the nation's first child-labor laws
(C) a return to traditional academic curriculum
(D) a curriculum that stressed learning by doing
(E) the growth of professional education and the American normal school

12. Which of the following is generally considered the most desirable first step in curriculum development?
   (A) Define the educational objectives.
   (B) Focus directly on the improvement of student learning experiences.
   (C) Identify limiting constraints.
   (D) Propose alternative objectives.
   (E) Initiate appropriate research.

13. Of the following choices, which one is the most accurate description of the first-year teachers' assessment of teacher-preparation programs?
   (A) Teacher-training programs are an adequate bridge between the theoretical teacher-training world and the actual experiences of everyday teaching.
   (B) Teacher-training programs are limited in the extent that they prepare one for the realities of teaching.
   (C) Teacher training provides the student teacher with adequate responsibility for the total classroom environment.
   (D) Teacher-training programs are effective in providing insight into disruptive students.
   (E) Instructional aspects of classroom life are more important than the need for precise classroom experience.

14. The main criticism from a teaching standpoint of an "open classroom" is that
   (A) administrators do not provide the necessary support staff conducive to an effective learning environment
   (B) students are not able to develop adequate self-awareness or inner growth
   (C) most students are not capable of making career-oriented decisions
   (D) the time commitment necessary in such an educational setting results in a tremendous physical and emotional drain
   (E) educating the "whole child" is inappropriate in inner-city schools

15. A state report assessing reading skills for junior high school students determined that comprehension and critical evaluation of content were the two most significant reading weaknesses. An English teacher would choose which of the following as the best method to improve comprehension for large groups?
   (A) reports that stress original thinking
   (B) library research projects
   (C) practice in learning to identify topic sentences
   (D) vocabulary enrichment to improve word recognition
   (E) practice in breaking up reading

16. The national movement toward competency-based education at the elementary level has resulted in all of the following *except*
    (A) that basic skills are usually restricted to math and reading
    (B) minimal tests for graduation
    (C) a general agreement on what constitutes basic skills
    (D) a list of the specific skills at each grade level for minimum competence
    (E) a performance-based objectives test

17. The best educational reason that teachers should incorporate behavioral objectives into daily planning is that
    (A) instruction can be based in terms of definable learned behavior
    (B) school boards can determine teaching efficiency
    (C) teaching is a goal-directed activity
    (D) objectives can be presented in a clear and precise manner
    (E) performance objectives enhance a student's previous experiences

18. Which of the following is the best example of terminal behavior?
    (A) the learner knows
    (B) the student will enjoy
    (C) the learner is able to recite
    (D) the pupil will appreciate
    (E) the student behaves

19. Class-management and discipline problems should take into consideration the thought that
    (A) the interests of the individual child are more important than the classroom as a whole
    (B) classroom discipline standards cannot change to meet the needs of any one person
    (C) class management is based on a teacher's ability to subordinate the interests of individual students
    (D) changing rules shows weakness on the part of teachers
    (E) proper functioning of the classroom and the individual interests of the child should be interrelated

20. The most important principle that a teacher should follow in initiating a program of positive reinforcement is to
    (A) punish negative behavior and reward positive behavior
    (B) provide regular opportunity for socially acceptable behavior
    (C) make sure the reward comes immediately after the appropriate behavior
    (D) provide peer approval and recognition
    (E) use secondary reinforcers as frequently as primary reinforcers

21. All of the following are correct statements regarding positive and negative reinforcement as they relate to behavior change in the classroom *except*
    (A) punishment tends to be more effective than rewards in controlling behavior
    (B) positive reinforcement refers to the rewarding of certain responses to specific stimuli
    (C) positive reinforcement strengthens desired behavior
    (D) punishment suppresses behavior but does not change it
    (E) social disapproval is a form of negative punishment

22. Which of the following governmental agencies would provide current information useful to a home economics teacher preparing a unit on nutrition?
    (A) Department of Commerce
    (B) Department of Agriculture
    (C) Department of Labor
    (D) National Academy of Sciences
    (E) Library of Congress

23. Who was the educational philosopher whose research on the method of growth and learning for young children produced the first kindergarten—"a garden where children could grow"?
    (A) Pestalozzi
    (B) Herbart
    (C) Dewey
    (D) Froebel
    (E) Rousseau

24. Which of the following would *not* be characteristic of a programmed text?
    (A) the immediate knowledge of results
    (B) individualized instruction
    (C) learning materials arranged in "large steps" that lead from one response to the next
    (D) bright students being unable to proceed at their own rate
    (E) a dialetic, question-based teaching

25. The number of scores falling within a given class interval is called the
    (A) mode
    (B) frequency
    (C) distribution
    (D) mean variation
    (E) standard deviation

26. The key to continuing community support for an instructional program is to
    (A) provide programs that enhance the learning experiences for gifted children
    (B) allow community participation in review boards that evaluate individual teacher effectiveness
    (C) develop a program responsive to changing needs of the community
    (D) rely on the media to improve the image of the schools
    (E) maintain an instructional program that stresses a traditional academic education

27. The main purpose in having an "open house" at the secondary level is to
    (A) encourage community support for controversial subjects
    (B) arrange for demonstrations and exhibits by the students
    (C) encourage citizens' advisory committees to support the instructional program
    (D) present the school programs to the community at large
    (E) provide a means for "on the spot" parent conferencing

28. A social studies teacher writes on the board, "The past is prologue." He then draws a parallel between the colonial boycott of tea and the U.S. boycott of the Olympics. The teacher, consciously or unconsciously, is following what established learning theory?
    (A) reinforcement   (D) transfer
    (B) relearning   (E) sensory learning
    (C) respondent conditioning

29. An eighth-grade student in social studies received a "fail" at the quarter grading period. The teacher requested a parent conference. During the conference the teacher indicated that Laurie's achievement in social studies is not acceptable. The teacher, in trying to make a point, compared Laurie's grades with other members in the class. Following these remarks an argument ensued between the parent and the teacher. Which of the following was a fundamental mistake that the teacher made in conducting the conference?
    (A) The teacher did not close the conference with a positive or constructive comment.
    (B) The teacher did not fully listen to the parent's complaints or criticisms concerning the teacher's grading policies.
    (C) The teacher's comments directed attention away from the problem at hand.
    (D) The teacher should never give advice unless it is asked for.
    (E) The teacher did not have prepared questions to use during the conference.

30. A school district decides to place a series of candy and soft-drink machines in its school buildings. The students are allowed access to the machines during lunch and all "free" periods. The teachers criticize district policy regarding the machines. Which of the following would be considered the most appropriate reason for the district to remove the machines?

(A) Teachers must have an effective voice in educational decision making.

(B) District educational objectives are being ignored regarding proper dental and health habits.

(C) The district does not have a financial investment in the machines.

(D) The state superintendent of public education indicates opposition to the machines.

(E) The students are allowed access to the machines during free periods.

STOP. IF YOU FINISH BEFORE TIME IS UP, CHECK YOUR WORK ON THIS SECTION ONLY. DO NOT WORK ON ANY OTHER SECTION OF THE TEST.

SECTION III

Time: 30 Minutes
30 Questions

DIRECTIONS

Following each of the questions or statements below, select the choice that best answers the question or completes the statement.

1. Historically, the Supreme Court claimed jurisdiction over specific areas of public school education by virtue of which of the following constitutional amendments?
   (A) First, Fourth, and Tenth
   (B) Eighth, Tenth, and Fourteenth
   (C) Fourth, Fourteenth, and Fifteenth
   (D) First, Fifth, and Fifteenth
   (E) First, Fourth, and Fourteenth

2. What is the main purpose for a supervisor to evaluate teacher effectiveness?
   (A) to determine the most effective teacher-pupil ratio
   (B) to evaluate and improve factors affecting learning
   (C) to satisfy state laws relating to teacher tenure
   (D) to assess the effectiveness of preset behavioral objectives
   (E) to gather information that must be kept on file in the superintendent's office

3. Which of the following problems are characteristic of evaluation procedures that rely on traditional evaluation techniques?
   I. cooperative attempt to solve a professional problem
   II. ambiguity of purpose
   III. evaluation that reflects the values of the school district
   IV. lack of definitive criteria
   V. rater bias

   (A) I, III, and IV   (D) III, IV, and V
   (B) all choices   (E) II, III, IV, and V
   (C) II, IV, and V

4. A teacher decides that the most appropriate form of mathematics instruction will be to divide her third-grade math class into several math groups. The most effective method to group the class would be on the basis of
   (A) chronological age
   (B) observation
   (C) standardized math tests
   (D) intelligence quotient (I.Q.)
   (E) peer group interaction

5. The most significant reason for the current interest in the "four quarter" plan at the elementary level is that
   (A) rising costs necessitate a creative solution to educational problems
   (B) voluntary summer school programs are ineffective in meeting individual needs
   (C) teacher scheduling would be more rigid and therefore more cost accountable
   (D) extracurricular and enrichment programs are being phased out of the regular curriculum
   (E) teacher salaries would become more competitive with private industry

6. Which of the following is generally considered the last step in program evaluation?
   (A) identifying the variables affecting the instructional program
   (B) analyzing collectable data
   (C) formulating a statement of desired outcomes
   (D) measuring desired outcomes
   (E) translating objectives into descriptive behavior

7. The largest percentage of a typical school budget goes for
   (A) maintenance of the physical plant
   (B) teacher salaries
   (C) classified and administrative salaries
   (D) books, supplies, and maintenance of the physical plant
   (E) new construction costs

8. Which of the following is true?
   (A) A test may be reliable even though it is not valid.
   (B) A reliable test is never valid.
   (C) A valid test is never reliable.
   (D) A reliable test is always valid.
   (E) none of these

9. Which of the following is most consistent with current educational thought concerning school and community participation?
   (A) Let the school district determine its own methods for citizen participation.
   (B) The community at large is not an active voice in evaluating educational programs.
   (C) Citizen involvement is the primary responsibility of the superintendent.
   (D) Improvement of school programs must rest with professional educators.
   (E) Citizen committees should first work with local PTA leadership before becoming an official voice in school decisions.

10. A student has a learning disability that is diagnosed as auditory association. Which of the following examples is characteristic of that problem?
    (A) The student cannot count to ten by rote.
    (B) The student does not know simple opposites.
    (C) The student has difficulty giving answers to simple math problems when they are spoken, but not when they are written.
    (D) The student cannot understand when someone is talking fast.
    (E) The student cannot define simple words.

11. How did the passage of the Morrill Act (1862) represent the changing objectives of American higher education?
    (A) Higher education was now accessible only to the rich and the well born.
    (B) New areas of inquiry such as science and law were elevated in importance.
    (C) It marked the first federal attempt to provide equal educational opportunity.
    (D) It foreshadowed the eventual demise of the private-university movement.
    (E) It represented an extension of public support and public control and therefore strengthened the concept of a state-university system.

12. The term *early childhood education* would most commonly describe
    (A) programs of formal schooling for children under six years of age or below first grade
    (B) programs of informal schooling for children under six years of age or below first grade
    (C) formal and informal programs for children in grades K–4
    (D) research and experimental programs for children in grades K–2
    (E) special education for children from disadvantaged areas

13. How do environment and intellectual factors correlate in teaching children how to talk?
    (A) They have little influence on the cognitive development necessary to produce speech.
    (B) They have a limited effect when all factors are considered in teaching children how to talk.
    (C) Environment is a greater factor than intelligence in teaching language patterns.
    (D) They have the greatest influence on children who are at least eight years old.
    (E) They are the key factors in language acquisition.

14. The *least* desirable practice of a teacher in dealing with small-group misbehavior in a class would be to
    (A) identify individuals who created problems and attend to them
    (B) stress class responsibility by creating a class assignment to compensate for the misbehavior
    (C) take time to analyze possible causes for the misbehavior
    (D) ask questions of the class concerning the incident
    (E) seek advice from another teacher

15. Which of the statements below is the most effective way of meeting individual needs in a classroom?
    (A) Set academic standards for the class and reward only those who meet them.
    (B) Isolate the slow learners from the rest of the class.
    (C) Allow the bright students to work independently so more time can be spent with students who are behind.
    (D) Reward students on the basis of participation in classroom activities.
    (E) Group children by abilities.

16. As age increases, the child's
    (A) reliance on physical action to express anger increases
    (B) behavior problems increase
    (C) family ties become less important
    (D) need to express anger increases
    (E) reliance on physical action to express anger decreases

17. Which of the following is usually considered the most important factor in a child's observable classroom behavior?
    (A) heredity   (D) sex
    (B) cultural background (E) self-concept
    (C) diet

18. Which of the following statements is *not* a proper reason for a supervised study period?
   (A) It allows students to explore topics in an independent fashion.
   (B) It allows the teacher time to prepare for the next period.
   (C) It provides an opportunity for students to use a variety of reference materials.
   (D) It allows students to work at a pace suited to their own abilities.
   (E) It helps to develop self-direction in learning.

19. In dealing with classroom misconduct, teachers tend to
   (A) plan long curative responses
   (B) respond to immediate causes
   (C) rely on the counseling staff
   (D) seek stronger punishment than parents would
   (E) respond to basic causes

20. A single parent complained to the school principal that the books available to her fifth-grade child did not contain any family style other than the two-parent family. She was more upset by the fact that her daughter overheard a teacher remark that without a father at home, children get into more trouble than the average child. The most appropriate action for the principal to take would be to
   (A) establish a committee of parents, teachers, and administrators to discuss the problem
   (B) request after-school supervision by the community recreation department for single-parent children
   (C) request in writing that the district textbook committee work on guidelines to improve the image of divorced families
   (D) provide inservice training for school personnel to make them more aware of problems associated with single-parent children
   (E) purchase library material that contains information to help children deal with divorce

21. Which of the following are *not* correctly matched?
   (A) Cremin—*The Transformation of the School*
   (B) Neill—*Summerhill*
   (C) Ginot—*Teacher and Child*
   (D) Dewey—*The Process of Education*
   (E) Piaget—*The Child's Conception of Space*

22. An eleventh-grade science teacher receives his class assignment for the first semester. He is told that one of his classes is grouped heterogeneously. Which of the following would *not* be an appropriate curricular response as it relates to the heterogeneous class?
    (A) programs to individualize assignments and tests
    (B) ability-achievement grouping within a class
    (C) a uniform academic program suitable for the science class as a whole
    (D) diagnostic and subjective tests to evaluate student performance
    (E) programs that are based on variations within the heterogeneous class

23. One standard deviation includes about _____ of the normal curve.
    (A) 10%   (D) 67%
    (B) 25%   (E) 75%
    (C) 50%

24. Admiral H. G. Rickover is most associated with which of the following educational reforms?
    (A) the setting of national standards through national examinations leading to national diplomas
    (B) the year-round school system
    (C) the use of teaching machines and computerized education to meet the challenge of modern society
    (D) making the schools more accountable by employing the cost-efficiency methods of modern business
    (E) flexible or modular scheduling incorporated into the comprehensive high school

25. The most valid educational argument in favor of a pass-fail grading system in senior high would be to
    (A) allow students who do not achieve in an academic course to take the course again
    (B) encourage superior students to work up to their capacity
    (C) eliminate the emphasis on memorization and therefore increase relevance
    (D) increase motivation, learning, and involvement in the educational process
    (E) allow academic standards to be lowered so that all students may participate in the educational process

26. A student in a fifth-grade science class demonstrates disruptive behavior by calling out answers. The teacher, through conferencing, has been able to make the student realize that he is calling out far too often. What would be the most appropriate teacher action to effectively change this behavior?

(A) extinguish the behavior by ignoring similar outbursts
(B) negatively reinforce the inappropriate behavior
(C) positively reinforce the calling-out behavior
(D) teach the child a lesson by sending him to the vice principal as soon as the inappropriate behavior is initiated
(E) positively reinforce a behavior that is "incompatible" with calling out

27. The best example of spontaneous recovery as it relates to classroom behavior is

(A) learning Italian grammar after finishing a course in French grammar
(B) receiving a teacher-developed "free-time" module for good behavior
(C) exhibiting a behavior pattern previously believed to be extinguished
(D) being able to comprehend subject matter originally thought to be too difficult
(E) testing one grade level higher after completing a remedial course in math

28. A junior high school student frequently doesn't dress for her physical education class. The teacher doesn't seem to be making much headway in convincing the student that her behavior is inappropriate. The teacher recognizes that this particular student is overweight and withdrawn. Which of the following would be most appropriate in trying to explain the student's behavior?

(A) The socioeconomic background of the student indicates that she is too poor to buy a new P.E. uniform.
(B) The student probably has a poor self-image.
(C) The student has experienced negative reinforcement in previous P.E. classes.
(D) The student is suffering from serious emotional problems and probably needs professional help.
(E) The problem isn't serious, since most junior high school girls don't like dressing for P.E.

29. Which of the following would be the most appropriate measure to protect a technical arts teacher from a lawsuit that claims teacher negligence?
   (A) Discuss all appropriate safety rules with the class.
   (B) Develop behavioral objectives that relate to specific safety practices.
   (C) Do not allow the use of any equipment until the individual students satisfactorily pass a safety test.
   (D) Insist that students who are not positive about the use of any part of the equipment immediately ask the teacher, and not other students, for assistance.
   (E) Analyze what might cause an accident and guard against it.

30. Jerome Bruner's thesis about children's learning capabilities is best summarized by which of the following statements?
   (A) Failing children will continue to fail if the teachers who work with them remind them of their failure.
   (B) Gifted children should be identified early and given early opportunities to challenge their powers and develop their talents to the fullest.
   (C) To impose anything by authority is wrong. Children should not do anything until they come to the opinion that it should be done.
   (D) Any subject can be taught in some intellectually honest form to any child at any stage of development.
   (E) The child is at the heart of the educative process, and the child-teacher relationship is critical.

STOP. IF YOU FINISH BEFORE TIME IS UP, CHECK YOUR WORK ON THIS SECTION ONLY. DO NOT WORK ON ANY OTHER SECTION OF THE TEST.

SECTION IV

Time: 30 Minutes
30 Questions

DIRECTIONS

Following each of the questions or statements below select the choice that best answers the question or completes the statement.

1. A teacher wants an eighth-grade class in social studies to understand the meaning of the Preamble to the Constitution. The most appropriate method to achieve this goal is to
   (A) assign individual library reports on the "founding fathers"
   (B) have the class recite key statements from the Preamble
   (C) have the class rewrite in their own words the key ideas embodied in the Preamble
   (D) assign extra recess time for the first ten students who can memorize the Preamble
   (E) show a filmstrip titled "How the Constitution Protects Individual Freedom"

2. If all of the following items in a U.S. government class were *equally* well learned, which would probably be best remembered?
   (A) Revolutions have occurred in modern European countries.
   (B) Some revolutions can be violent.
   (C) Revolutions may take many years to complete.
   (D) All revolutions are characterized by change.
   (E) Some revolutions have resulted in allowing women to vote.

3. Missy indicates to her friends that she hates science because there is too much memorization. However, on a test on the periodic table, Missy practices repeatedly until she is able to correctly identify all the elements in the periodic table. Given the above situation, which of the following motivation factors was most important to Missy?
   (A) peer-group pressure
   (B) intellectual curiosity
   (C) knowledge of results
   (D) intrinsic motivation
   (E) success

4. In general, the most important societal goal that influenced education in the decades of the 1960s and 1970s was
   (A) establishing minimum competency for high school graduation
   (B) providing parents with alternatives to public education
   (C) providing equal educational opportunity for the diverse elements of the U.S. population
   (D) incorporating traditional educational goals into the basic curriculum
   (E) initiating computer education competency as a high school graduation requirement

5. Of the following types of audiovisual equipment, which would be best suited to a classroom that is difficult to darken for the projection of visual material?
   (A) opaque projector   (D) overhead projector
   (B) motion pictures   (E) filmstrips
   (C) color materials

6. To be effective, team teaching should

   I. allow release time for teachers to plan and evaluate
   II. draw at random from the total teaching staff to secure impartiality
   III. orient students to the team-teaching organization
   IV. group students into many large-group activities
   V. have the support of the school administration

   (A) I and II   (D) I, III, IV, and V
   (B) I, II, and V   (E) I, II, IV, and V
   (C) I, III, and V

7. A fifth-grade student pushes other children during free play. The most appropriate first step in trying to eliminate this behavior would be to
   (A) negatively reinforce the inappropriate behavior
   (B) identify the behavior to be changed
   (C) isolate the child from the rest of the class
   (D) decide what constitutes positive and negative reinforcement
   (E) provide a means of immediate responsibility by appointing the student free-play monitor

8. According to Bloom's taxonomy of educational objectives, which of the following categories would represent the highest level of cognitive reasoning?
   (A) extrapolation   (D) evaluation
   (B) interpretation   (E) analysis of relationships
   (C) synthesis

9. Which of the following was the fundamental reason that John Dewey proposed a transformation of the public school system?
   (A) Dewey recognized that the intellectual motivation of the students was declining.
   (B) Dewey recognized that industrialism was destroying the home, shop, neighborhood, and church.
   (C) Dewey recognized that a traditional academic education did not serve the ideals of a democratic society.
   (D) Dewey recognized that there must be a dichotomy between freedom, self-government, and universal education.
   (E) Dewey recognized that change and innovation were essential ingredients of the progressive movement.

10. The basic reason for bringing professional people who are not full-time educators into the classroom setting is to
   (A) exemplify how education leads to important community positions
   (B) bring an element of reality into the academic curriculum
   (C) reinforce the principle that "presentation equals learning"
   (D) reinforce the educational theory that equates learning with the acquisition of specific skills
   (E) define the learning process as the legal responsibility of teachers and community leaders

11. Of the following, the statement that *least* characterizes the goal of effective thinking and action is that students should
   (A) be able to solve problems when faced by new and difficult issues
   (B) be able to properly organize resources in order to solve problems systematically
   (C) be able to problem solve with a minimum of teacher help
   (D) problem solve only after consultation with teachers
   (E) discover that they can learn and act outside of the classroom

12. Mr. Lohman's class includes a large number of students who are doing very poorly in their schoolwork. In reviewing their records, he finds that they have performed much better in the past. Mr. Lohman probably should
   (A) assume his students are having problems at home
   (B) discuss his problems with the school psychologist
   (C) attempt to transfer the underachieving students to another class
   (D) review the material he has taught with his students
   (E) examine the teaching methods he has used with these students to determine alternative teaching approaches

13. It is important that a teacher provide students with informative feedback
    (A) because teachers should not hide information from students
    (B) because of parental interest which leads to the questioning of the children
    (C) because students frequently are unable to evaluate the appropriateness of their own work or behavior without the help of others
    (D) that is not personal
    (E) that does not embarrass the school district

14. A longitudinal study
    (A) measures intelligence
    (B) measures height over a period of time
    (C) measures variables over a period of time
    (D) measures geographic variables
    (E) is rarely used in education

15. Which of the following is most consistent with current educational thought concerning the teaching of democratic beliefs in our classrooms?
    (A) The teaching of beliefs is best left to parents.
    (B) Democratic beliefs can be taught by assuring that we celebrate days honoring our nation's heros.
    (C) The teacher should lead the class in the flag salute daily.
    (D) Democratic beliefs can be taught based on respect for the worth of each individual and faith in the ability of people to govern themselves.
    (E) Democracy is the smoothest form of government and assures equality for all.

16. An academic testing program is important to a teacher because it can
    (A) provide motivation for most children
    (B) provide subjective information
    (C) provide information which can be used in determining a course of study for a child
    (D) identify teaching weaknesses
    (E) be used in judging educational materials

17. Recitation is best used to develop
    (A) leadership among brighter students
    (B) courtesy and socialization
    (C) oral English and presence in front of a group
    (D) posture
    (E) an appreciation for leadership potential

18. Which of the following situations would best fit a special education student who has been mainstreamed?
    (A) providing learning handicapped students educational materials consistent with appropriate grade levels
    (B) providing special education to students identified as handicapped
    (C) placing learning handicapped students in the least restrictive environment
    (D) teaching all special education students in regular classrooms
    (E) systematically reviewing each handicapped student's educational progress

19. When assigning individual or class projects to students, the work should *not* be
    (A) graded or otherwise evaluated
    (B) considered part of the curriculum
    (C) substituted for curriculum requirements
    (D) used to provide students with new experiences or knowledge
    (E) such that it does not require teacher input

20. In recent years, schools have become more aware of the importance of gross- and fine-motor efficiency
    (A) as an integral part of the science curriculum
    (B) when designing the physical education curriculum
    (C) in learning reading and writing
    (D) , and as a result, many teachers now assign a number of exercises to develop the thumb and forefinger
    (E) , and students low in such skills are required to see a physician

21. "The Constitution is a living document, since the rights of citizens are constantly being interpreted by the courts. Rights such as freedom of speech, press, and assembly are not absolute, but are subject to limitations imposed by the courts." Assuming this statement is going to be part of a teaching unit, which of the following best identifies the appropriate curriculum component?
    (A) unit objective   (D) material and resources
    (B) content   (E) lesson plan
    (C) activities

22. A second-grade reading instructor devised a reading scheme that depended heavily on individualized instruction as the primary focus in learning to read. Which of the following is the most legitimate criticism of an overemphasis on teaching reading through individualized instruction?

(A) Less verbal children will be hindered by individualized reading instruction.

(B) Evidence suggests that learning to read is an important social activity.

(C) Individualized reading hinders the "pretend" reader.

(D) Reading groups have been the traditional method of teaching reading.

(E) Individualized reading instruction depends on appropriate reading material.

23. A child in the third grade is suspected of stealing school property. Although the teacher has not caught the student in the act of stealing, she discusses the incident with the entire class, but does not mention any names. A major problem with this approach to correct inappropriate behavior is that

(A) peer pressure is inadequate in changing behavior patterns

(B) unpopular students might unjustly be accused of the behavior

(C) the teacher must act as the facilitator of the group discussion

(D) the guilty student might feel isolated from the group

(E) only trained school psychologists should attempt behavior modification

24. Modality has been characterized as the teaching approach of the 1980s. Which of the following is the best example of a class activity based on auditory modality?

(A) making a macrame art project

(B) the use of flash cards for math practice

(C) frequent "spelling bees"

(D) writing historical names and places

(E) math drill from worksheets

25. Which of the following is *least* consistent with the goals of bilingual education programs?

(A) Students can learn the same skills expected from English-speaking children.

(B) Students can maintain their native language and customs.

(C) Students have a better opportunity to learn related subjects if they understand the subject matter being taught.

(D) Fluency in the native language is a deterrent to learning a second language.

(E) Prereading skills in the native language are important in learning English.

26. Which of the following are federally guaranteed parental rights regarding the education of children identified as handicapped?

   I. A free appropriate public education must be provided by a local school system.
  II. Information related to a handicapped child's performance must be available to the parents.
 III. The privacy of all school records must be maintained.
  IV. Parents have the right to request a due process hearing when they disagree with the procedures for evaluating a handicapped child.

   (A) I and II only
   (B) II and III only
   (C) II, III, and IV
   (D) I, II, and III
   (E) I, II, III, and IV

27. A student in the primary grades has a tendency to reverse letters and symbols (for example, *b* for *d*, *p* for *q*) and also to reverse words and invert letters. The teacher should suggest that the student has a reading impairment referred to as
   (A) dysphasia
   (B) blending
   (C) auditory dyslexia
   (D) emotional blocking
   (E) visual dyslexia

28. Which of the following student actions is *not* protected by the First Amendment of the Constitution?
   (A) A student in a ninth-grade class refuses to stand or recite the Pledge of Allegiance.
   (B) Meeting in the cafeteria, a group of students peacefully publicizes a series of grievances.
   (C) A high school student wears an insignia protesting U.S. involvement in Central America.
   (D) During a campus rally a member of the student council incites students to leave the campus to protest an unfair administrative decision.
   (E) A student newspaper refers to the school board as *unfair and biased*.

29. Which of the following reasons for using coloring books in a primary classroom situation is *least* consistent with appropriate instructional objectives?

    (A) Coloring books can facilitate small motor coordination skills.
    (B) The use of coloring books can develop a sense of design.
    (C) Coloring books enable substitute teachers to maintain consistent discipline.
    (D) The use of coloring books can develop important concepts and generalizations in a variety of subjects.
    (E) Coloring books can provide detailed visual aids for science lessons.

30. Which of the following would *not* be considered a legitimate result of the use of assertive discipline in the classroom?

    (A) minimizing classroom conflict
    (B) minimizing student-teacher interaction
    (C) maximizing student learning opportunities
    (D) maximizing motivational aspects of learning
    (E) maximizing classroom management

STOP. IF YOU FINISH BEFORE TIME IS UP, CHECK YOUR WORK ON THIS SECTION ONLY. DO NOT WORK ON ANY OTHER SECTION OF THE TEST.

ANSWER KEY FOR PRACTICE TEST 1

Test of Communication Skills

Section I: Listening

Part A Questions and Statements		Part B Conversations	Part C Talks	
1. (C)	7. (C)	13. (C)	21. (C)	27. (C)
2. (B)	8. (B)	14. (C)	22. (B)	28. (D)
3. (A)	9. (B)	15. (A)	23. (A)	29. (A)
4. (D)	10. (C)	16. (A)	24. (A)	30. (B)
5. (D)	11. (A)	17. (A)	25. (D)	31. (A)
6. (B)	12. (D)	18. (C)	26. (A)	32. (D)
		19. (D)		
		20. (C)		

Section II: Reading

1. (C)	9. (B)	17. (A)	25. (D)
2. (E)	10. (C)	18. (B)	26. (A)
3. (A)	11. (A)	19. (E)	27. (E)
4. (A)	12. (A)	20. (C)	28. (A)
5. (A)	13. (C)	21. (B)	29. (C)
6. (D)	14. (B)	22. (D)	30. (C)
7. (A)	15. (C)	23. (C)	
8. (E)	16. (C)	24. (A)	

Section III: Writing—Multiple Choice

Part A: Usage		Part B: Sentence Correction	
1. (D)	14. (C)	26. (A)	39. (D)
2. (B)	15. (B)	27. (B)	40. (E)
3. (A)	16. (D)	28. (A)	41. (A)
4. (D)	17. (B)	29. (C)	42. (A)
5. (A)	18. (D)	30. (C)	43. (C)
6. (E)	19. (B)	31. (E)	44. (D)
7. (B)	20. (A)	32. (E)	45. (A)
8. (B)	21. (E)	33. (B)	
9. (B)	22. (B)	34. (D)	
10. (E)	23. (E)	35. (E)	
11. (D)	24. (B)	36. (B)	
12. (D)	25. (B)	37. (D)	
13. (D)		38. (E)	

Test of General Knowledge

Section I: Social Studies

1. (D)	9. (A)	17. (B)	25. (B)
2. (C)	10. (C)	18. (B)	26. (D)
3. (E)	11. (C)	19. (C)	27. (D)
4. (C)	12. (B)	20. (B)	28. (A)
5. (A)	13. (C)	21. (E)	29. (B)
6. (C)	14. (C)	22. (D)	30. (C)
7. (D)	15. (B)	23. (A)	
8. (E)	16. (B)	24. (B)	

Section II: Mathematics

1. (C)	8. (E)	14. (C)	20. (B)
2. (D)	9. (D)	15. (D)	21. (A)
3. (A)	10. (B)	16. (C)	22. (A)
4. (D)	11. (C)	17. (B)	23. (C)
5. (C)	12. (C)	18. (E)	24. (A)
6. (D)	13. (E)	19. (D)	25. (E)
7. (B)			

Section III: Literature and Fine Arts

1. (D)	10. (E)	19. (A)	28. (C)
2. (D)	11. (C)	20. (A)	29. (D)
3. (C)	12. (D)	21. (D)	30. (D)
4. (E)	13. (B)	22. (B)	31. (E)
5. (B)	14. (C)	23. (D)	32. (C)
6. (C)	15. (A)	24. (E)	33. (E)
7. (D)	16. (D)	25. (C)	34. (B)
8. (A)	17. (D)	26. (C)	35. (C)
9. (B)	18. (C)	27. (D)	

Section IV: Science

1. (C)	9. (B)	17. (E)	25. (B)
2. (B)	10. (B)	18. (D)	26. (C)
3. (C)	11. (B)	19. (D)	27. (A)
4. (C)	12. (E)	20. (D)	28. (A)
5. (D)	13. (C)	21. (A)	29. (C)
6. (C)	14. (D)	22. (A)	30. (B)
7. (E)	15. (D)	23. (A)	
8. (E)	16. (D)	24. (D)	

Test of Professional Knowledge

Section I

1. (E)	9. (B)	17. (C)	25. (B)
2. (A)	10. (B)	18. (C)	26. (E)
3. (C)	11. (E)	19. (B)	27. (A)
4. (A)	12. (E)	20. (E)	28. (C)
5. (C)	13. (C)	21. (C)	29. (D)
6. (B)	14. (A)	22. (C)	30. (D)
7. (C)	15. (C)	23. (C)	
8. (A)	16. (D)	24. (B)	

Section II

1. (E)	9. (D)	17. (A)	25. (B)
2. (A)	10. (D)	18. (C)	26. (C)
3. (E)	11. (D)	19. (E)	27. (D)
4. (A)	12. (A)	20. (C)	28. (D)
5. (B)	13. (B)	21. (A)	29. (C)
6. (E)	14. (D)	22. (B)	30. (B)
7. (B)	15. (E)	23. (D)	
8. (B)	16. (C)	24. (C)	

Section III

1. (E)	9. (A)	17. (E)	25. (D)
2. (B)	10. (B)	18. (B)	26. (E)
3. (E)	11. (E)	19. (B)	27. (C)
4. (C)	12. (A)	20. (D)	28. (B)
5. (A)	13. (E)	21. (D)	29. (C)
6. (D)	14. (B)	22. (C)	30. (D)
7. (B)	15. (E)	23. (D)	
8. (A)	16. (E)	24. (A)	

Section IV

1. (C)	9. (B)	17. (C)	25. (D)
2. (D)	10. (B)	18. (C)	26. (E)
3. (E)	11. (D)	19. (C)	27. (E)
4. (C)	12. (E)	20. (C)	28. (D)
5. (D)	13. (C)	21. (B)	29. (C)
6. (C)	14. (C)	22. (B)	30. (B)
7. (B)	15. (D)	23. (B)	
8. (D)	16. (C)	24. (C)	

SCORING PRACTICE TEST 1

To score Practice Test 1, total the number of correct responses for each of the three tests separately. Do not subtract any points for questions attempted but missed, as there is no penalty for guessing. The score for each test is then scaled from 600 to 690.

ANALYZING YOUR TEST RESULTS

The charts on the following pages should be used to carefully analyze your results and spot your strengths and weaknesses. The complete process of analyzing each subject area and each individual question should be completed for each Practice Test. These results should be reexamined for trends in types of error (repeated errors) or poor results in specific subject areas. THIS REEXAMINATION AND ANALYSIS IS OF TREMENDOUS IMPORTANCE FOR EFFECTIVE TEST PREPARATION.

PRACTICE TEST I GENERAL ANALYSIS SHEET

Test of Communication Skills

	Possible	Completed	Right	Wrong
Section I: Listening	32			
Section II: Reading	30			
Section III: Writing—Multiple Choice	45			
COMMUNICATION SKILLS TOTALS	107			

Test of General Knowledge

Section I: Social Studies	30			
Section II: Mathematics	25			
Section III: Literature and Fine Arts	35			
Section IV: Science	30			
GENERAL KNOWLEDGE TOTALS	120			

Test of Professional Knowledge

Section I	30			
Section II	30			
Section III	30			
Section IV	30			
PROFESSIONAL KNOWLEDGE TOTALS	120			

ANALYSIS—TALLY SHEET FOR QUESTIONS MISSED

One of the most important parts of test preparation is analyzing WHY you missed a question so that you can reduce the number of mistakes. Now that you have taken Practice Test I and corrected your answers, carefully tally your mistakes by marking in the proper column.

REASON FOR MISTAKE

	Total Missed	Simple Mistake	Misread Problem	Lack of Knowledge

Test of Communication Skills

	Total Missed	Simple Mistake	Misread Problem	Lack of Knowledge
Section I: Listening				
Section II: Reading				
Section III: Writing—Multiple Choice				
COMMUNICATION SKILLS TOTALS				

Test of General Knowledge

	Total Missed	Simple Mistake	Misread Problem	Lack of Knowledge
Section I: Social Studies				
Section II: Mathematics				
Section III: Literature and Fine Arts				
Section IV: Science				
GENERAL KNOWLEDGE TOTALS				

Test of Professional Knowledge

Section I				
Section II				
Section III				
Section IV				
PROFESSIONAL KNOWLEDGE TOTALS				

PRACTICE TEST 1 ESSAY CHECKLIST

Diagnosis/Prescription for Timed Writing Exercise

A good essay will:

_____ address the assignment
          be well focused
_____ be well organized
          smooth transitions between paragraphs
          coherent, unified
_____ be well developed
          contain specific examples to support points
_____ be grammatically sound (only minor flaws)
          correct sentence structure
          correct punctuation
          use of standard written English
_____ use language skillfully
          variety of sentence types
          variety of words
_____ be legible
          clear handwriting
          neat

COMPLETE ANSWERS AND EXPLANATIONS FOR PRACTICE TEST I

TEST OF COMMUNICATION SKILLS

SECTION I: LISTENING

Part A: Questions and Statements

1. (C) The question asks *who*, and choices (A), (B), and (D) answer *what* rather than *who*.

2. (B) Each of the other choices requires supporting information beyond what is stated in the sentence. The sentence explicitly connects travel with fact-finding tours.

3. (A) The statement says that unexpected problems disrupted her day and leads directly to the conclusion that *she did not follow her planned schedule rigidly*. Each of the other choices offers a conclusion not necessarily supported by the statement.

4. (D) Choice (D) restates the original sentence in different words. Each of the other choices gives an unsupported generalization or conclusion.

5. (D) The question askes about *time spent*, and the only choice that compares reading and watching TV in terms of time spent is (D). Choice (C) does not refer to *watching* television, only to the TV being on.

6. (B) The two choices which answer the question *how much* are (B) and (D), but (D) does not refer to the cash in the purse.

7. (C) If bad weather delayed the landscaper until late Wednesday, we may conclude that the weather was bad earlier Wednesday. Each of the other choices requires conclusions not supported by the statement.

8. (B) Each of the other choices requires conclusions not supported by the statement. If the area code will change from 714 on March 1, we may conclude that it will be 714 until March 1.

9. (B) The only choice which responds to the question *when* is (B); although this choice is itself a question, such a question is also an indirect answer.

10. (C) We may conclude from the statement that last year the school day was longer, which would mean that more time was probably spent covering each subject. (A) is not a necessary conclusion because the statement refers only to the *number* of subjects not to their nature; (B) contradicts the information in the statement; and (D), while possible, is not a necessary conclusion or as logical as Choice (C).

11. (A) The statement says that Meg *expected* to miss the bus; each of the other choices is not a conclusion that follows necessarily from the statement.

12. (D) Only this choice answers the question *why*, giving a reason for the length of Shakespeare's sonnets. The other choices refer to reading time, Shakespeare's contemporaries, and the content of the sonnets. All are irrelevant to the question.

Part B: Conversations

13. (C) The woman recommends that the man not specify a subject, implying that the students may have nothing to say about the subject. The content and tone of her statement in no way suggests that the man is incompetent (D).

14. (C) Choice (B) contradicts the man's expressed problem, and neither (A) nor (D) is supported by the conversation; when the man says *that didn't work,* he suggests that he has already asked the students to write on their own thoughts.

15. (A) The woman explicitly offers to get the boy more books when she says, *Would you like me to buy you more books?*

16. (A) The boy's statement that he would *rather watch television* suggests that he prefers watching television to reading. None of the other choices is supported by the conversation.

17. (A) The baseball fan compares baseball to ballet throughout the conversation and finally connects baseball with great art to stress its significance.

18. (C) The baseball fan's ability to compare baseball with art, and in particular to mention the *elements of great art,* allows us to conclude that the familiarity with art is substantial.

19. (D) The father refers to his own college experience and connects psychology majors with unpopularity. He does not criticize the student's judgment or the subject itself.

20. (C) The student says that the declaration of a major is earlier than required. Choice (D), mistaken, is a weaker choice because it represents the father's conclusion and is not necessarily accurate.

Part C: Talks

21. (C) Improved education (A) is a concern of the speaker but is not the specific topic of the talk. Gambling among the poor is mentioned but not discussed extensively enough to be called a major topic. Choice (D) is irrelevant.

22. (B) The speaker does not explicitly tell the listeners not to support a lottery but does give arguments against the lottery. The speaker neither implies nor expresses that citizens should directly buy schoolbooks for children (C).

23. (A) The speaker assumes that *destitute citizens betting their last dime* will participate in the lottery.

24. (A) The speaker does not specify, or even discuss, the type of voice associated with good speechmaking.

25. (D) The speaker stresses Aristotle's opinion that good communicators are born and not made. With this opinion, Aristotle would not agree that anyone can learn to write.

26. (A) The speaker explicitly states that Aristotle's advice *still seems quite useful* and supports this conclusion repeatedly by associating Aristotle's treatment of speechmaking with good writing.

27. (C) After describing war toys from the '60s and the '80s, the speaker concludes that *playing war will not disappear from the American scene*. The Vietnam War, the morality of war, and the elimination of war are touched upon, but none of these receives extensive discussion.

28. (D) The speaker describes the popularity of war toys and the '60s criticism of war toys but does not identifiably agree with that criticism. The speaker describes the phenomenon of playing war but does not take a position.

29. (A) By showing that war toys have become popular again in the '80s, the speaker stresses and illustrates the conclusion that playing war was, is, and will be a popular pastime.

30. (B) The speaker discusses a bad diet in terms of social, cultural, and economic problems; only choice (B) includes these terms and therefore

reflects the speaker's major concern: those factors that contribute to a bad diet. Choice (D) is a minor rather than major topic.

31. (A) The speaker mentions the four food groups at both the beginning and the end of the talk and concludes that dietary problems have roots that awareness of the four food groups does not address.

32. (D) According to the speaker, cultural, social, and economic problems cause a bad diet, and that bad diet causes physical problems. Remember to answer a question based on what the speaker says and not on what you may believe about the topic.

SECTION II: READING

1. (C) We are told that speculation about society has been of continual interest to humankind, even at the dawn of civilization. Choice (C) draws a conclusion warranted by this statement. Choices (B) and (E) contradict the passage, and (A) and (D) are not supported by the passage.

2. (E) Each of the choices except (E) reduces a human activity to a single word: illiterate (A), cowards (B), deaf (C), and lazy (D). The author would disagree with such reduction.

3. (A) The final sentence of the passage implies that no one in the adult community is unlawful and is therefore based on the assumption that unlawful behavior is practiced only by youths.

4. (A) Sentences 5 and 6 name and discuss those things (attitudes, dispositions) that are known *through the feelings* and then add that this is what is meant by *intuition.*

5. (A) The author associates the determination of beauty with intuition rather than with logic. This choice weakens that association. Choice (B) is explicitly stated in the passage, choice (E) is suggested, and neither weaken the argument; choice (C) might strengthen the passage; (D) is irrelevant.

6. (D) Each of the other choices is not supported by the information in the passage. Although the author speaks of private experience, it is not characterized as most important. For this reason, (E) is not a good choice.

7. (A) The modern figures given by the author contrast with the 27 percent figure of 1920 and show that secondary school participation is close to 100 percent these days.

8. (E) The passage contrasts Great Britain, in which high positions go to an elite group, with the United States. None of the other choices is supported by the expressed or implied information in the passage.

9. (B) *Destined* is used in its normal sense here to indicate those whose future is predetermined.

10. (C) The rebel is characterized as someone *thoroughly familiar* with the culture. Each of the other choices requires information beyond that given in the passage.

11. (A) *Can,* in this case, means *is able to,* leaving open the possibility that education may not function to aid an individual; *does* leaves open no such possibility and makes the statement absolute.

12. (A) The author states that education raises political interest. Choice (A) contradicts this particular assertion. Each of the other choices gives expressed or implied support for the author's argument.

13. (C) The passage questions *lack of money* as a primary factor; (C) reiterates this point. Choices (A), (B), and (D) are not supported by the passage, and (E) contradicts the passage.

14. (B) By stressing that writing may be used to express innermost feelings, the author reveals the assumption that innermost feelings are important.

15. (C) Each of the other choices refers to only part of the content of the passage. Choice (C) supplies the general terms (*uses and characteristics*) that encompass the details surveyed in the passage.

16. (C) Comments about the duties of the elementary school teacher signal that this passage is aimed at those interested in teaching, and (C) is the only choice that describes such an audience.

17. (A) By restricting the *trivial* stage of personal writing to the *outset,* the author implies that following the outset, writing will become less trivial. Each of the other choices draws a conclusion beyond the expressed or implied information in the passage.

18. (B) The final sentence says that different roles (instrumental and expressive) are played by different people. Choice (B) reinforces this distinction. Each of the other choices generalizes beyond the information in the passage.

19. (E) Choices (A), (B), and (C) are too general, and (D) inaccurately characterizes teachers as victims.

20. (C) By stating that some problems are *unique* to teaching, the author suggests that some problems are *not* unique to teaching.

21. (B) None of the other choices is supported by expressed or implied information in the passage.

22. (D) The passage speaks of resistance to the rules and regulations of the administration; those readers who resist are those who would "rule" their own classrooms, those who would create their own rules and regulations.

23. (C) The passage states that the ideas of teachers and those of the *general public* may be in contrast. Making the reasonable assumption that the general public includes parents leads us to choose (C).

24. (A) Suggesting that the status of expert professionals is a relatively recent development for teachers, the author implies that teachers have not always held such status. The new status has occurred *as education has become more complex.* Choice (B) is explicit rather than implicit information and therefore is not the best choice.

25. (D) The author mentions the disappearance of unskilled occupations in connection with the disadvantages of dropping out of school, thus revealing the assumption that dropouts qualify only for unskilled occupations. None of the other choices is supported by the passage.

26. (A) Although *efforts* are mentioned in the final sentence, the author does not describe the *kinds of* efforts made.

27. (E) This fact strengthens the author's inclusion of race as a factor in mortality. The passage does not develop this point about race, and this statement would do so and thus strengthen the passage.

28. (A) This choice is supported by the final sentence of the passage in particular. Choice (B) contradicts the passage, and the other choices are unsupported.

29. (C) The author discusses the nature of fads in general but does not criticize a particular fad or faddist. Although the attitude toward fads is negative, the author does not argue for the elimination of fads (A).

30. (C) The author explicitly states that fads are *short-lived.*

SECTION III: WRITING—MULTIPLE CHOICE

Part A: Usage

1. (D) *In formal dress* is a misplaced modifier that should be positioned near *come,* the word it modifies. Otherwise, the sentence seems to say that the restaurant is wearing formal dress.

2. (B) Because of the placement of the word *frequently* in this sentence, it is unclear whether the people *write letters* frequently or *recount* frequently. To solve the problem, the word *frequently* could be placed preceding the

word *write.* Using a comma between *letters* and *frequently* or between *frequently* and *recount* would be inappropriate because it would set off the subject from its verb.

3. (A) *Libraries* should be either *libraries'* (the plural possessive) or *library's* (the singular possessive), depending on the intent of the writer. *Children's* (B) is the correct formation of an irregular plural possessive (*woman's/women's—man's/men's—mouse's/mice's*) where the root word changes to form the plural. *Fact-finding* correctly hyphenates two words used as a single adjective *preceding* a noun ("She was a well-known author" *but* "The author was well known").

4. (D) *And occurring only in this country* repeats the meaning of *unique* and is therefore unnecessary.

5. (A) *You* is the correct pronoun in this sentence instead of *yourself. Yourself* is the reflexive form of the pronoun and is correct only in such structures as *You, yourself, must be there* (subject repeated for emphasis) and *You hurt yourself* (subject repeated as object).

6. (E) No error. *The inquiry method* (D) is parallel to *observation* and *discovery* (all nouns). Adding the article *the* and the adjective *inquiry* to the noun does not change the fact that it is parallel.

7. (B) *Than* is ungrammatical. *When* is correct after *had . . . begun,* introducing the adverb clause describing when the music began.

8. (B) *We* is the subjective form of the pronoun and is incorrect. *Us* is the correct pronoun in this case. By mentally removing the word *spectators* and rereading the sentence, you can "hear" this error.

9. (B) The correct idioms are *recognition of* and *departure from;* choice (C) is correct, but (B) must be completed with a different preposition— *recognition of yet a departure from . . . Demonstrated* is correct, as it refers to *theme,* not to *works. Whose* is correct—not *who's* (the contraction for *who is*).

10. (E) No error. This is the correct spelling of *whether* as opposed to *weather.*

11. (D) *World War I* should not be enclosed in quotation marks. It is the standard name for the war and is not used in any unusual way requiring that it be set off. (C) *"Black Jack"* is correctly enclosed in quotation marks to draw attention to the fact that it is not the general's real name but a nickname. *Have changed* (A) is plural to agree with the subject, *techniques,* and *considerably,* the adverb, is the correct form to modify the verb *have changed.*

12. (D) *More or less* contradicts the idea of *minimum* and should be eliminated for the sake of clarity.

13. (D) *Respective points of view* repeats the idea expressed earlier in the sentence by *opinion* and should be omitted to correct the redundancy error.

14. (C) The placement of *even the most hardworking* makes it seem that the phrase refers to *term papers* rather than to *students* (which it correctly modifies). The problem may be solved by moving the phrase to the beginning of the sentence. There should be no comma between *students* and *who* (A) because *who write formal term papers* is restrictive (not *all* students are discussed here). Have difficulty *with* (D) is the correct idiom.

15. (B) *Expressed by those in opposition to it* is redundant when used with *arguments against*. In this context it might even be construed as referring to both *arguments for* and *arguments against*, which would make the sentence nonsensical. The phrase should be eliminated.

16. (D) The word *literally* means *according to fact—free from exaggeration*. The home team did not actually break the backs of the opposing players. The word that is wanted in this context is *figuratively*, meaning *in a manner of speaking—characterized by a figure of speech*. There should be no comma between *game* and *and*. The comma after *team* correctly sets off the subordinate clause from the main clause.

17. (B) Structures such as *not only . . . but also, either . . . or*, and *neither . . . nor* must be followed by parallel elements. As the sentence stands, *not only* is followed by *implicated*, a verb, and *but also* is followed by *subordinates*, a noun. The sentence should read, *implicated not only the leaders . . . but also their subordinates. Leaders* (noun) is parallel to *subordinates* (noun). There would be no reason to assume that the plural possessive *brothers'* (A) is incorrect. The plural pronoun *their* (D) correctly refers to *leaders* (C).

18. (D) "Special *affects*" should be "special *effects*." *Affect* is a verb, meaning to act upon or influence. *Effect* is a noun meaning a distinct impression (as in this example) or a verb meaning to bring about.

19. (B) *Being* is ungrammatical and creates a sentence fragment. The word should be *was*.

20. (A) The word *teenager* is sufficient and *aged 13 to 19* is redundant and unnecessary.

21. (E) No error. The present tense is always used when referring to books; therefore, *tells* is correct. As *tells* refers to *a series* (singular) not to *books* (plural), the singular form of the verb is correct.

22. (B) The pronoun *their* must refer to either the *hunter* or the *guide*—not to both, so the plural form is incorrect. *Their* should be changed to *his. The hunter* and *his guide* are correctly set off by commas, as they are appositives—that is, they give additional descriptive but not essential information about Jim and Charles. The use of *neither* and *nor* is correct here.

23. (E) No error. The pronouns *I, he, she,* and *they* are correct following *than.*

24. (B) *Show* is correct here instead of *shows* to match the plural subject *studies.*

25. (B) *To answer* instead of *answering* is correct parallel structure in this sentence.

Part B: Sentence Correction

26. (A) None of the choices improves on the original wording.

27. (B) Choice (B) corrects the run-on sentence. Two independent clauses cannot be connected with only a comma. Choice (B) adds *and* and eliminates *he,* correcting the structural error in the original. Choice (C) changes the meaning by emphasizing where he got a job and lacks a necessary comma before *and.*

28. (A) Choice (A) is correct. *Along with all the other arts* should be set off by commas and *is* is the correct verb form to agree with *poetry,* a singular subject. Choice (E) changes the meaning of the original sentence.

29. (C) The phrase *difficulty to choose* is idiomatically incorrect. Choices (B) and (E) are wordy and awkward options, and choice (D) slightly changes the emphasis in the original sentence from *difficulty* to *choosing.* Choice (C) is the most direct wording. *Difficulty in choosing* would also be correct, but that is not given as an option.

30. (C) The original sentence lacks parallel structure. Choices (B) and (D) do not change *accepting* to the parallel verb form *to accept.* Choice (E) changes the meaning of the sentence. Choice (C) is correct and parallel to the three other verb phrases *to walk . . . , to cross . . . , and to care. . . .*

31. (E) The singular verb *is* needs to be plural to agree with *sea forests.* Choice (B) is singular. Although *are* is used in choices (C) and (D), (C) is idiomatically wrong, and (D) does not make sense. Choice (E) corrects the verb error and structurally fits with the rest of the original sentence.

32. (E) *Entities* means *independent, separate, or self-contained units.* To use *separate entities* is redundant. To use *two separate entities* is doubly redundant; it is obvious from the beginning of the sentence that there are two.

All choices except (E) contain one or both of these errors. In addition, choice (B) drops a necessary apostrophe in *university's*; choice (C) capitalizes *regents* and *association* (these are not the names of specific groups and need not be capitalized; however, if capitals were used, *board* and *alumni* would have to be included); and (D) introduces a verb error in the singular *is* referring to the plural subject.

33. (B) Characters cannot be compared to the novel *Crime and Punishment.* Choice (B) inserts *those,* which correctly words the comparison. Choices (D) and (E) create an incomplete sentence and leave out necessary information. *Exhibits* in choice (C) is singular and incorrect.

34. (D) Choices (A) and (B) are not parallel and contain the redundant phrase *of many Spaniards.* Choices (C) and (E) are also redundant because they include the words *Spaniards* and *Spanish.* Choice (D) is parallel and concise.

35. (E) Choice (E) is the most concise wording of the original idea. Choice (B) suggests that *Claudius* was *successful.* Choices (A) and (C) are ungrammatical, and (D) is wordy and awkward.

36. (B) The original sentence contains two errors in usage—it uses *laid* (put something down) instead of *lain* (reclined), the past participle of *lie,* and *sat* (assumed a sitting position) rather than *set* (put something down). Choice (B) corrects both of these errors. Choice (C) corrects only the second; choice (D) introduces an error in using *besides* (in addition to) instead of *beside* (next to); and choice (E) contains an error in *it's* (it is) rather than *its* (possessive pronoun).

37. (D) *Fascinated by* or *fascinated with* is idiomatic. *Fascinated at* is not. All choices except (D) retain this error. Choices (B) and (E) also unnecessarily change the meaning of the sentence, as does (C) in substituting *constantly* for *consistently.*

38. (E) The misplaced-modifier error is corrected in choice (E) by placing *he* close to the phrase *a policeman of proven valor.* Choice (D) changes the meaning of the original sentence.

39. (D) The comma must be used after *Bob* to set off the person addressed. Choice (D) is the only choice that provides this correction without adding other errors. Choice (B) leaves out the series commas after *slate* and *flagstone.* Choice (C) deletes the comma after *Ohio* (commas must be used to set off all elements in addresses and geographical locations). Choice (E) would be correct if it retained the quotation marks necessary in direct discourse.

40. (E) This is a verb-tense error; *would have* should be changed to *had*.

41. (A) The original sentence is correct. Choices (B), (D), and (E) are ambiguous; it is not clear *who* was using the notes. Choice (C) contains a grammar error; it uses *them* instead of *their*.

42. (A) The sentence is correct as it stands. Choices (B) and (E) imply that there is only one type of gas, choice (C) that the membranes become linings only after the exchange of gases, and choice (D) that the membranes are caused by the exchange.

43. (C) Following the construction *one of those who,* the verb must be plural, *tend* instead of *tends,* because the verb refers to *those* (plural) not to *one.* Only choice (C) supplies the verb *tend.* Choice (B) creates a sentence fragment; and choice (D) introduces an idiomatic error—*attempt to classification.*

44. (D) The subject *amount* does not agree with the verb *vary.* Choice (D) corrects this error without changing the meaning of the original sentence.

45. (A) The sentence is correct. Choices (B), (C), and (E) are grammatically correct but change the meaning slightly. Choice (D) contains a subject-verb error.

TEST OF GENERAL KNOWLEDGE

SECTION I: SOCIAL STUDIES

1. (D) The Gulf States include Texas, Louisiana, Mississippi, Alabama, and Florida. Historically, the Gulf States (in conjunction with the rest of the "solid South") discriminated against black voters. Literacy tests, poll taxes, fraud, and intimidation restricted black attempts to register and vote. The 1965 landmark Voting Rights Act virtually banned literacy tests as a prerequisite to voting and authorized the use of federal registrars to guarantee black voting rights. The impact of the Voting Rights Act was most evident in the South.

2. (C) Intelligence tests are culture weighted and often reflect a white, middle-class bias. Psychologists generally agree that intelligence is a combination of both innate ability and socioeconomic factors. Social class, regardless of race, strongly influences intelligence test scores. Children who are not part of the white, middle-class culture to which the tests are geared are at a disadvantage.

3. (E) During the twentieth century, the traditional American family underwent profound social changes. Industrialization and urbanization had the greatest impact upon the family structure. Rural America was rapidly replaced by an urban based industrial society. Some of the effects of this modernization on the family were: greater emphasis on child-centered values, increased acceptance of alternative life styles, steady increase in the divorce rate, redefinition of the status of women, and greater social, political, and economic equality for minorities.

4. (C) Judicial review refers to the power of the federal courts to interpret the Constitution and declare certain actions of the Congress and the President unconstitutional. Judicial review was not provided for in the Constitution but was exercised by the Supreme Court in *Marbury* vs. *Madison* (1803). Judicial review greatly expands the power of the federal courts in the United States. Note that the highest court in each of the states exercises similar power over the state legislatures.

5. (A) The only government positions that are restricted to a natural-born citizen of the United States are those of the President and Vice President (the Vice President must be qualified to be President). The

country's founders included this requirement to allay fears that a foreign power might gain control of the presidency.

6. (C) The facts or data in the chart support the hypothesis that college-educated voters are more likely to vote for the Republican Presidential candidate than are noncollege voters. In four of the five elections from 1952 to 1968 college-educated voters supported the Republican candidate (1964 was the exception).

7. (D) In the election of 1964 all groups supported the Democratic Party candidate.

8. (E) The European Economic Community (Common Market) was founded in 1958 and is made up of Western European countries. For Common Market members, all internal tariffs and trade barriers have been abolished so member nations can move goods freely within the EEC, while competing goods from nonmembers countries are heavily tariffed. Poland, choice (E), is part of the Communist bloc countries of Eastern Europe and at the present time it is highly unlikely that the Soviet Union would allow Western European goods to compete freely with goods of Eastern Europe.

9. (A) In 1966, Charles de Gaulle withdrew French forces from NATO and subsequently forced that organization to remove all of its military installations from French soil. By charting an independent economic and political course for France, de Gaulle envisioned a resurgent France leading the affairs of Europe.

10. (C) Technological innovations that accompanied the industrialization of America resulted in more efficient, labor-saving machinery. However, as machine replaced worker and factories grew larger, the labor-management relationship became increasingly more impersonal. The quality of urban life (slums, economic dislocation, alcoholism, insecurity) was a conspicuous reminder of the dehumanizing aspects of the industrialization of America.

11. (C) The question asks for most logical extension of the philosophy implied by the political cartoon. Choice (A) is not the best choice because the effectiveness of the slogan is not addressed. The best answer, choice (C), is based on the assumption that the cartoonist, in drawing a parallel between clubs and guns, is implying that obvious truths go unnoticed.

12. (B) The median family income has more than tripled since 1960; the 1960 income was $18,800. However, as can be seen in the section of the graph marked "Income After Taxes in 1960 Dollars," the actual income has remained relatively constant. Individuals are making more in actual dollars, but in terms of purchasing power, the increase has been negligible.

13. (C) The statement is definitely false, since the 1960 federal tax for a median family income was $597 (a pretax income of $5,620 less income after taxes of $5,023 equals a 1960 tax of $597). In 1979, the federal tax stood at $3,089 for the median family income of $18,800, or more than five times in the 1960 figure. The total income for the corresponding period was approximately three and a half times greater.

14. (C) One can arrive at the correct answer by a process of elimination. It is evident from the passage that the author does not favor increasing food production as a solution to the population problem. Choices (A), (B), and (E) indicate programs that would lead to increased food production, and choice (D) would simply not discourage food production. These choices should therefore be eliminated. Choice (C), however, would be a solution to the problem of overpopulation.

15. (B) Nationalization is government acquisition of business and industries that were previously privately owned. Collectivization, choice (D), is primarily associated with agricultural systems in which small family farms are formed into state-owned, collectivized farms. A kibbutz, choice (E), is a collective agricultural settlement characterized by common ownership of property. Individuals are not forced, as in collectives, to join a kibbutz.

16. (B) Debtors would benefit the most from continued inflation because they are paying back outstanding debts with dollars that are worth less than they were at the time the debt was incurred. Inflation refers to continual upward trend in the level of prices without any corresponding change in the quality of goods and services sold. Inflation, therefore, amounts to an arbitrary redistribution of income, away from creditors and fixed income recipients—those most affected by continuing inflation—and to debtors.

17. (B) A 50% rise in the dollar against the Japanese yen would make Japanese products significantly cheaper in the United States while boosting the cost of U.S. goods in Japan. In effect, the dollar would be *overvalued* in relationship to the yen. The impact of this overvaluation would further deteriorate the U.S. trade balance with Japan.

18. (B) Deferred gratification is primarily associated with the middle class. Deferred gratification is a behavior pattern that encourages postponing immediate wants so that long-range goals can be achieved. For example, middle-class persons continue their education in order to achieve future economic success. Choice (A) is incorrect, since the unstable economic environment of the lower class often makes long-term economic planning impractical.

19. (C) Tight money is a method to reduce inflation by increasing interest rates. When borrowing becomes more expensive, consumer demand is reduced. Choice (D), decreasing the discount rate, would put more money in circulation. Lowering the discount rate is considered when the economy is in a recession.

20. (B) The term *normalcy* reflected the mood of the country in the 1920s. It symbolized not only a return to the politics of the late nineteenth century but also the abandonment of the progressive reform zeal and foreign policies of the Wilson administration. Harding favored an isolationist foreign policy and rejected any foreign policy commitment that threatened the status quo.

21. (E) James Baldwin is not a sculptor. He is noted primarily for his novels.

22. (D) Pennsylvania had 26 electoral votes and Ohio had 21. The electoral vote of a state is equal to the number of votes a state has in Congress (House and Senate). Thus the most populous states will not only have greater representation in the House (which is based on population) but also in the electoral college. It should also be apparent that in 1868 the most populous states would be in the northeastern section of the United States.

23. (A) Federalism in practice divides the power of government between the states and federal government. The country's founders added the Tenth Amendment to the Constitution, often referred to as the "states' rights amendment," to further accomplish this goal.

24. (B) *Traditionally,* national ethnic groups (Poles, Italians, Jews, etc.) have most often been subject to sterotyping. A stereotype is a prejudiced thought that summarizes whatever is believed to be typical about a group. Stereotypes are always false to some degree. *Currently,* stereotypes are often associated with subculture groups such as homosexuals, right-wingers, etc.

25. (B) India has a Hindu population of approximately 84%. Based on 1983 statistics, the religious breakdown of the region is as follows: Bangladesh and Pakistan are predominantly Moslem; Bhutan and Burma are predominantly Buddhist. In Nepal (not marked with a letter) Hinduism is the dominant faith of approximately 90% of the population.

26. (D) Bangladesh, formerly East Pakistan, declared its independence from West Pakistan in 1971 following a nine-month bloody civil war. It called itself the new nation of Bangladesh (meaning "Bengal Nation").

27. (D) Newspaper polls are not based on random sampling. Since one has to purchase the paper to cast a "ballot," certain groups may be overrepresented or underrepresented.

28. (A) A regressive tax is one that is not related to one's overall ability to pay. The sales tax is regressive in that a higher percentage of income is taken from those with low incomes. Most necessities are subject to a general sales tax, and while poor individuals can choose not to operate a car, choice (D), they cannot avoid paying a sales tax. The income tax is considered a progressive tax in that the higher one's income, the greater the tax burden.

29. (B) The League of Nations was part of Wilson's Fourteen Points (1919). The United States did not join the League of Nations, since the Senate rejected the Treaty of Versailles. The Tennessee Valley Authority (1933) was a landmark legislative act passed during the Great Depression. The United Nations charter was approved in 1945. The Marshall Plan was approved by the United States in 1948. It was designed to aid in the economic reconstruction of Western Europe and to repulse possible Communist advances into Western Europe.

30. (C) The domino theory was based on the assumption that Indochina was a testing ground in the struggle against global communism. The theory implied that if the United States allowed Vietnam to fall to communism, all of Southeast Asia would fall to communism. The domino theory was a specific extension of the containment policy, choice (A), as it applied to Southeast Asia. The containment of communism was first implemented during the Truman administration.

SECTION II: MATHEMATICS

1. (C) A kilometer is the best unit of measurement, as it equals about five-eighths of a mile. Both the meter (D) and millimeter (E) are too short to be used for intercity distances. The liter (A) is a unit of volume; the kilogram (B) is a unit of mass.

2. (D) The two discounts do *not* equal one 50% discount. Do the problem in two steps. First, the 30% discount: $80 \times .30 = 24; $80 - $24 = 56. Second, the 20% discount: $56 \times .20 = 11.20; $56.00 - $11.20 = 44.80.

3. (A) To average a list of numbers, simply add all the numbers, and then divided the sum by the numbers of items you added. Remember to keep the decimal points aligned when adding:

$$10.2 + 9.1 + 8.7 + 10.5 + 8.8 + 9.4 = 56.7$$

Then $$56.7 \div 6 = 9.45$$

4. (D) Notice that on the pie chart, D and F together total slightly more than a quarter of the pie. One-fourth of 36 students would be 9; a little more than one-fourth would be 10.

5. (C) Slightly less than a quarter of the students, or approximately 22%, received a B.

6. (D) Any number ending with 0 or 5 is evenly divisible by 5. Thus, any ten consecutive integers have two values evenly divisible by 5, as in this example:

$$11, 12, 13, 14, \textcircled{15}, 16, 17, 18, 19, \textcircled{20}$$
$$\textit{divisible by 5}$$

The one hundred integers from 1 to 100 have $10 \times 2 = 20$ numbers evenly divisible by 5. However, the assigned range of 2 to 99 omits one evenly divisible number (100) and so contains exactly 19 integers evenly divisible by 5.

7. (B) Points plotted on a coordinate graph are expressed (x,y) where x indicates the distance forward or backward and y indicates the distance up or down. Thus, $(-3,4)$ means 3 "steps" back and then 4 "steps" up. This will place the point within quadrant II.

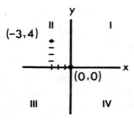

8. (E) Do not waste time converting all the fractions to decimal form. Instead, use the familiar fraction 1/3, choice (C), as your basis for comparison. Notice choices (A) 7/22, (B) 0.31, and (D) 19/60 are all slightly less than 1/3; therefore you need only compare 1/3 and 17/50.

This can be done by cross mutiplying as follows

$$\begin{array}{cc} 50 & \textcircled{51} \\ \dfrac{1}{3} & \dfrac{17}{50} \end{array}$$

Since 51 is greater than 50, 17/50 is greater than 1/3.

9. (D) Speed equals distance divided by time elapsed. The time elapsed was 7 hours and 6 minutes (check that you know how to figure that span) or 7.1 hours. The speed is $412/7.1 = 58$ miles per hour.

10. (B) The goat could graze over a half circle, where the length of the rope equals the radius. The question doesn't require that you write the formula, but the area of a half circle would be $\frac{1}{2}\pi r^2$, where r is the radius.

11. (C) To solve an addition problem containing fractions with different denominators, a common denominator must be found. Both 90 (choice A) and 30 (choice C) are common denominators, but only 30 is the *lowest* common denominator. Using 30 for the denominator eliminates the necessity of reducing your final answer and also minimizes the size of the numbers in your computations.

12. (C) In this type of problem, you should round the numbers off to save time. Let's do a few in sequence:

    (A) $(-1.6) \times (-0.001) = +0.0016$, greater than either number
    (B) $(-0.4) \times (0.8) = -0.32$, greater than the first number
    (C) $(0.2) \times (0.9) = +0.18$, less than either number

    Answer (C) is correct, so you should stop multiplying any more choices. Each math problem has only one right answer choice.

13. (E) The tenth place is the number immediately to the right of the decimal point. To round off the nearest tenth, check the hundredth place (two places to the right of the decimal point). If the hundredth number is a 5 or higher, round the tenth up to the next number. For instance, .36 would round to .4. If the hundredth is a 4 or lower, simply drop any places after the tenth place. For instance, .74356 would round to .7. Thus, 4,316.136 rounded to the nearest tenth is 4,316.1—which is answer choice (E).

14. (C) Plug in 3 for x:

15. (D) Patricia must buy as many 17¢ stamps as possible, which minimizes the number of 1¢ stamps obtained as "change" for her money. Dividing 200 by 17¢ gives 11.76. Therefore she can buy only 11 stamps of 17¢ denomination. That requires 11 × 17¢ = 187¢. That leaves 13¢ to buy 13 1¢ stamps. The total number is therefore 11 + 13 = 24 stamps.

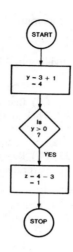

16. (C)

$$3c = d$$

$$\frac{3c}{3} = \frac{d}{3}$$

$$c = \frac{d}{3}$$

17. (B) To calculate total surface area of a rectangular solid, one must find the area of each of six faces. One face is 7m × 6m. Note that the face directly opposite that face also equals 7m × 6m. The same is true with the other two different faces. Therefore, each of the areas of the three different faces must be doubled and added together.

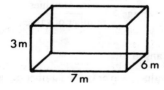

18. (E) The graph indicates that copper sold as low as 50¢ per pound during early 1971 and most of 1972.

19. (D) The price of aluminum rose from January to December of each year 1973 through 1979, which is 7 years.

20. (B)

$$\frac{245}{35} = 7 \text{ cm}$$

21. (A) Solve this by a proportion, knowing that ten dozen equals 120.

$$\frac{120}{15} = \frac{8}{c} \qquad (c = \text{cost of 8 pencils})$$

Cross multiplying gives

$$120c = 8 \times 15$$
$$120c = 120$$

Dividing by 120 gives

$$c = \$1$$

22. (A) Because CF is perpendicular to BE, angle BOC is a right angle. Then angle AOB + angle BOC = 154°. Therefore 180° − 154° = 26°

23. (C) Begin by multiplying through by the second minus sign to clear parentheses.

$$5 - 2m - (m - 13) = m$$
$$5 - 2m - m + 13 = m$$
$$18 - 3m = m$$
$$18 = 4m$$
$$\frac{18}{4} = m$$

$$m = 4.5$$

24. (A) The definition of the average, or mean, is

$$\text{average} = \frac{\text{sum of values}}{\text{number of values}}$$

which may be rearranged to

$$\text{sum of values} = \text{average} \times \text{number of values}$$

Using the latter relationship, the sum of Deborah's scores for the first three weeks was $82 \times 3 = 246$, while for the full four weeks it was $78 \times 4 = 312$. So on the last assignment she obtained $312 - 246 = 66$.

25. (E) It is first necessary to find the general relation between P and Q. If we ignore all negative signs, then Q is three times P. But since Q always has the opposite sign from P, the complete relation would be written

$$Q = -3P$$

and substituting in a value of -4 for P,

$$Q = -3(-4) = 12$$

SECTION III: LITERATURE AND FINE ARTS

1. (D) The author expresses his own sense of being inferior to the experienced river pilots. He describes himself as a "cipher," or zero, compared to them. He also says he "was not even of sufficient consequence to assist." Probably he was humbled both by their elegant clothes and their impressive reputations.

2. (D) *The Card Players* by Paul Cezanne illustrates two of the chief characteristics of impressionism. The subject is a slice of everyday life, not a heroic episode from remote antiquity. Also, the irregular coloration (see the blotchy coat of the man on the left) is a deliberate device to catch the real vagaries of lighting. Such works are meant to give the *impression* of the actual world.

3. (C) Both sculptures are missing parts, and it is quite obvious that the creators did not anticipate their sculptures' losing those parts.

4. (E) The wings clearly designate this statue as only part human. Each of the other choices is a possibility, but none of them is absolutely verified by the figure as given.

5. (B) The passage mentions the importance of maintaining dignity in the performance and implies that the dances had a serious purpose; *delightfully carefree* contradicts these characteristics. Each of the other choices is consistent with the information in the passage.

6. (C) The line means that the reasons are important enough *to kindle cowards*. The specific reasons Brutus gives for opposing Caesar are suffering, abuses, and tyranny.

7. (D) Both the first and last lines of Brutus's speech show that he is trying to convince his colleagues that an oath would be trivial. The speech opens with *No, not an oath* because their motives are strong, not weak. The speech closes by asserting that the cause is sufficient ground for their assassination plot.

8. (A) The contrast between light and shadow is very obvious. Choice (D) is incorrect because the painting shows a *rural* landscape of a barren countryside, but the term *urban* refers to a city.

9. (B) The building is an art museum and its style was selected to give the museum a very impressive sense of dignity. Until very recently, almost all public buildings were constructed in a Greek or Roman style for just that reason.

10. (E) Their three sea novels constitute a trilogy. Another trilogy of novels is by John Dos Passos: *The 42nd Parallel, Nineteen Nineteen,* and *The Big Money.* An anthology (A) is a collection of short works, generally by different authors. A ballad (B) is a poem to be sung. A biography (C) relates the life story of another person. An epic (D) is a long, narrative poem.

11. (C) The magnificent portrait of St. Catherine of Alexandria was painted by Raphael during the Italian Renaissance. As befits the sacred subject, St. Catherine is highly idealized. It is only since the Renaissance that art has shifted away from religious themes.

12. (D) The girl in the white dress was painted by the American artist James Whistler in 1862. All of the other women are portrayed with distinctively European clothes.

13. (B) The term *idealized* refers to an ethereal appearance, perfected beyond the natural look of this world. Of the five portraits, the earliest two, from the Renaissance, are the most idealized.

14. (C) An epigram is a brief poem which makes a witty point. Grebanier's epigram maliciously suggests that when a doctor touches something, it dies. The key words in the poem are *Doctor* and *funeral,* and they require the preceding interpretation. Choice (D) is too general to be the best choice.

15. (A) Abstract art does not have recognizable images. All of the other statements do apply to the sacred ivory cup. The animal images are consistent with a culture fond of hunting (D).

16. (D) The author gives an exaggerated description of people who virtually live for the news, thus strongly implying criticism of them.

17. (D) The author derides those who are obsessed with the news. Only this choice is consistent with the author's critical attitude and with the content of the passage.

18. (C) *Sentinels* are mentioned as those whom the sleeper expects to respond to his question *What's the news?* Choosing (B) would require a conclusion beyond the expressed or implied content of the passage.

19. (A) Symmetry is a balanced pattern. In the painting, the three angels on the left are the mirror images of the three angels on the right. Most art works contain some symmetrical features, although seldom is the symmetry so pronounced as in this painting. By the end of the Renaissance, artists were exploring the uses of *asymmetry* in their works.

20. (A) The lines are from "My Luve" by Robert Burns, a Scottish poet of the eighteenth century. Among the distinctive words in the poem are *bonie lass* (pretty girl), *luve* (love), *a'* (all), and *gang* (go). Other well-known poems by Burns include "John Anderson," "My Jo," and "Tam o' Shanter."

21. (D) A musical cadence, or "sing-song" effect, is obvious in each of the other choices. But (D) is arranged so that the rhythm is irregular and unpredictable.

22. (B) The second selection is from "The Yarn of the Nancy Bell" by W. S. Gilbert. The humorous poem tells how ten shipwrecked sailors had to eat one another to stay alive. In the quoted stanza, the surviving cook and narrator both resist the fate of becoming food for the other. Gilbert is famed for his comic operas, done in collaboration with Arthur Sullivan.

23. (D) The selection is from "Effort at Speech Between Two People" by Muriel Rukeyser, an American poet of this century. Some contemporary elements of her style are the lack of rhyme and the lines beginning with lower case letters. Note, too, the spaces which denote hesitation.

24. (E) The *Bauhaus* school buildings of Walter Gropius were among the earliest and best examples of modern design. They derive their stark beauty from the suitability of the glass-and-steel structures to the activities inside each building. The walls deliberately lack any ornaments or decorations.

25. (C) In the passage, the sun is described as *stricken to death,* a victim of the *touch of that gloom.* Obviously, what happens to the sun has a negative connotation in the passage, and only (C) and (E) are negative choices.

26. (C) Almost all of our familiar portraits of George Washington have been copied from this painting by Stuart, although many of them disguise their source by turning Washington's head in another direction. Choice (B) is wrong because the $5 bill features Abraham Lincoln; it is the $1 bill that has Washington.

27. (D) In the saying, *honey* symbolizes sweet words and *vinegar* stands for tart, caustic remarks. A few pleasant words will win more friends than many unpleasant remarks.

28. (C) Nothing in the photograph reveals the size of the statue. In fact, it is only 32 inches high. The size of the statue has little to do with the peacefulness it portrays.

29. (D) The passage describes a treasure map in Robert Louis Stevenson's novel *Treasure Island.* The first sentence says that the map of the island has a hill labeled *The Spy-glass.* The red crosses of the second sentence are locations of pirate gold, silver, and arms. Both sentences suggest a paper bearing writing.

30. (D) The French impressionist painter Paul Gauguin lived for several years in Tahiti. This painting shows native women splashing in the surf, a subject of many of his works. Clearly he appreciated the joy of people who had not yet been spoiled by civilization.

31. (E) A league is several miles long, and the first lines suggest the rhythmic gallop of the Light Brigade toward the guns at the end of the valley. This famous poem by Tennyson records the Battle of Balaclava in the Crimean War of 1854–56. British and French forces attacked the Russian Army.

32. (C) Over six hundred cavalrymen attacked the Russian guns and less than two hundred survived. You could deduce that the six hundred were troopers because the words are preceded by the word *rode*.

33. (E) A spiral ramp unites all the floors of this striking building, which contains a collection of art works. Visitors are lifted by elevator to the top floor, then gradually descend the spiral as they look at paintings and sculpture along the outer wall. However, a three-dimensional spiral is more properly called a *helix*.

34. (B) Lewis Carroll, whose real name was Charles Dodgson, was an English mathematician whose delight in logic led him to write humorous poems and novels which carry every point to a logical—and very funny—extreme. In the quoted passage, the three arguments make some sort of ridiculous sense. Among Carroll's nonsense poems are "Jabberwocky," "Father William," and "The Hunting of the Snark."

35. (C) The artist deliberately cut off the carriage and horses at the bottom and right margins. In this way, the realism of the scene is heightened. At first glance, it seems almost like a candid "snapshot" of the countryside rather than a carefully planned painting.

SECTION IV: SCIENCE

1. (C) The pressure exerted by a standing liquid is directly proportional to the depth of the liquid. For example, the pressure on the hull of a submarine increases as it dives deeper. So filling the bathtub increases the water pressure against the blockage in the drain.

2. (B) Common steel is composed of iron and a small amount of carbon. Rust is iron oxide, which forms when oxygen in the air combines with iron. Water only brings those two elements into intimate contact.

3. (C) To preserve the unspoiled desert from the activities of humans, it would be helpful to set some limit on the number of people who are allowed to enter a desert area. Choice (B) is wrong because the grazing destroys the sparse vegetation and any soil. Choice (E) would change the desert into irrigated farmland, possibly a desirable goal, but does not preserve the desert environment.

4. (C) *Acid rain* is the phrase recently coined describing the contaminated rainfall caused by noxious industrial pollutants and which endangers wildlife in North American waterways.

5. (D) Although the canning temperature for the pork and beans is more than adequate, the time of 90 minutes is less than that specified in the table.

6. (C) The plant grows toward the window in response to the sunlight coming from that direction. Such a growth response is called a *tropism*.

7. (E) Gravitational attraction by the moon (and to a much lesser extent, by the sun) causes tides, as the moon's mass attracts and distorts the earth and its oceans. You may remember that the height of tides corresponds to the lunar phase. The highest tides occur at new and full moon, when the sun's attraction is aligned with the moon's.

8. (E) The sharks would be at the top of the food pyramid. They are the largest meat-eaters described in the passage, and therefore would be the least common creatures. The algae, on the other hand, would provide the base of the entire pyramid.

9. (B) The most numerous creatures are toward the base of the pyramid. However, the algae at the base are *plants,* whereas the question specifies that it wants the most numerous *animal.* Such would be the copepod, which you know to be an animal since it is described as "shrimp-like."

10. (B) All planets are visible only by the sunlight reflected from them. Mars appears red because the other colors in sunlight tend to be absorbed by the Martian surface.

11. (B) The only city on the list in the Southern Hemisphere is Buenos Aires, Argentina. July is wintertime there and hence colder than any of the northern cities.

12. (E) Watering a lawn during the middle of the day would result in more evaporation of the water than if watering were to occur in the late afternoon or early morning. Thus (E) is not a conservation method.

13. (C) Foxes and chickens do not live together. In the examples of

432 ANSWERS AND EXPLANATIONS FOR PRACTICE TEST 1

symbiosis, notice that (A) is a beneficial association, (E) is basically neutral, and both (B) and (D) are harmful, parasitic associations.

14. (D) Momentum and kinetic energy (the energy of motion) are calculated from mass and velocity:

$$Momentum = mv$$
$$Kinetic\ energy = \frac{1}{2}mv^2$$

In those formulas, m represents mass and v represents velocity.

15. (D) The lower pressure at high altitudes means less oxygen enters the lungs with each breath. The lower supply of oxygen inhibits many of the metabolic reactions that provide energy for the runner.

16. (D) Nitrogen is obtained from air. Huge refrigeration plants cool air down to the temperature at which it condenses into a liquid. Because nitrogen and oxygen, the major components of air, have slightly different liquefaction points, they are readily separated during the process. The other four answer choices are all metals obtained from mines.

17. (E) The first four choices are all organic materials rich in carbon, and their combustion commonly yields some of the components of smog. The energy of uranium, however, is due to nuclear fission, during which the uranium nucleus splits apart; the fission produces smaller atomic nuclei and releases a large amount of energy. Since the nuclear fission is not a chemical process of combustion, it does not contribute to smog.

18. (D) Photosynthesis is the process by which green plants produce sugar, the reaction being:

$$6CO_2 + 6H_2O \xrightarrow{light\ and\ chlorophyll} C_6H_{12}O_6 + 6O_2$$

carbon dioxide + water → sugar + oxygen

19. (D) The strength of an acid or base is reported as a pH number. A neutral solution has a pH of 7, acids are less than 7, and bases are greater than 7.

20. (D) The diagram shows three generations, the color blindness occurring in the first and third. Consider the male at the lower right in the chart. His mother is on the next row up, and her father (the source of his color blindness) is on the top row.

21. (A) Color blindness is a sex-linked characteristic, for very few females manifest the problem. However, in the example of our diagram, the righthand female in the second generation must carry the gene for color blindness, because that is how her son in the lower right acquired his color blindness.

22. (A) A chromosome is the component within the nucleus of each cell that carries the genes controlling all the functions of life. This tiny, complex mechanism for inheritance is delicate enought to be disrupted by nuclear radiation. Without proper shielding, radiation can induce genetic mutations.

23. (A) If the impact generated immense quantities of dust, the opaque clouds might have blocked out solar radiation, abruptly lowering temperatures in the atmosphere. Note that the iridium is only *evidence* for meteoritic impact.

24. (D) Preventive medicine includes actions taken to lessen the risk of infection or disease. Regular dental checkups (I) and good nutrition (III) are two examples of preventive medicine.

25. (B) The color of compounds would not be too useful in arranging the elements in a meaningful pattern. All the other properties were actually used to create the familiar Periodic Table. Choice (C) is the most important of all, for the number of protons is unique for each element.

26. (C) Relativity effects are insignificant at the velocities of space flight in the foreseeable future. The other four factors are problems to solve. The temperature of interplanetary space is near absolute zero whereas high temperatures are generated by atmospheric friction during takeoff and reentry.

27. (A) Some bacteria are anaerobic, living without free oxygen. All forms of life require water for biochemical reactions, have proteins built of amino acids, and reproduce by means of nucleic acids—DNA or RNA. All organic molecules contain carbon atoms.

28. (A) The brisk wind would allow complete oxidation of the charcoal carbon to carbon dioxide. Carbon monoxide is the product of partial oxidation, where the oxygen supply is limited. Graphite is a crystalline variety of carbon, as is diamond.

29. (C) During the first minute when the container was unsealed, the heat caused the gases inside the container to expand, forcing much of those gases to leave the container. Then the researcher sealed the container, and the lack of oxygen soon extinguished the burning rag. As the hour passed, the container and its contents cooled. The contraction of the gases inside the container decreased the internal pressure to the point at which the greater external air pressure could crush the container.

30. (B) Since the two compounds were produced by life, and they are in rocks that are three billion years old, then life must have existed on earth for at least that period. Choice (D) is wrong because the hydrocarbons are detected only in trace amounts.

TEST OF PROFESSIONAL KNOWLEDGE

SECTION I

1. (E) Alternative schools make use of experimental programs, innovative curricula, and often controversial teaching techniques in providing a nontraditional educational program. All other choices are examples of current problems associated with alternative schools.

2. (A) Current evidence suggests that there is a marked tendency for children with superior IQs to be more mature both socially and physically than children of average ability. Choice (C) is incorrect, since educational research shows that gifted children measure superior in moral or trait tests when compared to children of average ability.

3. (C) Aptitude tests are designed to measure probable success in a specific field. Choices (A) and (B) refer to achievement tests.

4. (A) Of the choices given, *improved communication* would be the primary reason for *three-way conferences*. Choices (B) and (C) are potential problems associated with three-way conferences. Choices (D) and (E) are too narrow in scope to be considered the best answers.

5. (C) Prior to the 1960s, educational psychologists were primarily concerned with specific social, motivational, and aptitudinal aspects of learning. The intellectual structure of class activities and curriculum problems have been comprehensively studied only in the last two decades.

6. (B) A block grant is given *in toto* with unspecified use but for educational purposes only. Most federal or state aid is earmarked for some special aspect of the school program, choices (A), (C), and (E). Examples of categorical aid would be money for science education, vocational education, or education for the handicapped.

7. (C) Individualized learning necessitates that the teacher must measure growth in different ways. Evaluation must be an integral part of the teaching-learning process. *Ongoing feedback and guidance* directly involves the teacher in the evaluation process. Group methods of evaluation are inappropriate in individualized programs. Choice (B) is the second-best answer, but it doesn't specifically indicate that evaluation was an ongoing process.

8. (A) The influence of classical humanism was evident in Puritan educational thought and practice. Greek, Latin, and Hebrew became estab-

lished subjects in secondary schools and institutions of higher education. Puritan educational thought was consistent with the Calvinistic view that obedience and fear of God were necessary to obtain salvation, choices (B) and (E).

9. (B) The terms *cues, prompts, frames, chains,* and *branches* are associated with programed learning. Cues and prompts are hints to the correct response. Frames are the actual blocks of information or questions given at one time (one frame). Chains and branches are terms used in writing programed materials; they give the flow of the program.

10. (B) Pestalozzi (1746–1827) was influenced by Rousseau in adopting an educational philosophy based on the needs of the child. Pestalozzi recognized the dependence of the child on society for the development of effective personal growth. His most famous work was *Leonard and Gertrude* (1781).

11. (E) All of the choices, I, II, and III, would be excellent values and goals for teaching science.

12. (E) *Appropriate behavior and proper rewards* is the best choice. (A), (B), and (C) are not essential for *good teaching,* and (D) is not correct because punishment need not be immediate in many situations.

13. (C) The other responses have nothing to do with children's individual perceptions of their environment.

14. (A) According to standards set by the President's Council on Physical Fitness and Sports, one out of every six students in the United States is classified as physically underdeveloped. Identifying physically underdeveloped children and prescribing appropriate programs to remedy their problems is a fundamental and urgent task facing physical education.

15. (C) The criterion is the standard or test by which a behavior is evaluated. Choice (C) is the only objective stated in behavioral terms that indicates when the learning is to take place.

16. (D) The Gary Plan was a classic attempt to incorporate the progressive ideas of Dewey into the public schools of Gary, Indiana. As such, each school in the Gary system was organized as a "miniature community." The child participated in the industrial activity of the school, including the main responsibility for record keeping (D).

17. (C) Intelligence tests that give advantage to one group over another due to the experience of their culture are called culturally biased. For example, most popular tests today tend to favor urban over rural children because the tests were standardized on urban children. But including any

items that favor certain races, classes, or communities, or not balancing the test with equal numbers of such items, could be called cultural bias.

18. (C) Current educational research supports the fact that play is an effective means of learning. Play is a natural process in which children learn to interact with their environment. Effective use of play time and playground areas can enhance a child's physical development, as well as stimulate a child's creative thinking.

19. (B) A criterion is a standard against which answers can be measured. This is true by definition. The use of an appropriate criterion enables the researchers to determine if a test appears to measure what it is intended to measure. Therefore, the criterion of a test is that which you are trying to predict.

20. (E) In the core curriculum, broad fields of subjects are combined. In correlating English and social studies (for example, reading *Uncle Tom's Cabin* in a social studies class), a unified-studies approach can be adopted. In a core curriculum, the core class is usually scheduled for two or more of the regular class periods.

21. (C) Teachers and administrators cannot search vehicles, students, or lockers at random. For a search and seizure to be legal under the Fourth Amendment, it must be reasonable and be related to the school official's duties. The courts have held that school authorities may not search a student without provocation. However, school officials may do so when there is reason to believe, on the basis of *specific facts,* that a crime may have been committed. Depending on the amount, possession of an illegal drug can be classified as a misdemeanor or felony, choice (B). If the school officials were acting on information provided by a reliable source, the search and seizure would meet the legal requirements of the Fourth Amendment.

22. (C) Recommending the addition of a life-experience class is a legitimate prerogative of a school board. However, the community's stake in the school cannot be overlooked. Community support is essential if controversial classes are to be successful.

23. (C) A lesson plan is basically a tool for effective teaching. Its primary importance is to present objectives and content in a logical and systematic manner; as such, it is an integral part of the instructional process. The other choices are possible reasons for using a lesson plan, but choice (C) is the most comprehensive answer.

24. (B) In a stratified sample the elements being considered are proportional to their presence in the population. In the example the sample would have to be stratified by sex and grade.

25. (B) An independent variable is that factor which is measured, manipulated, or selected by the researcher to determine its relationship to other variables. The level of achievement will determine the type of self-image.

26. (E) Because of the delicate nature of the course and specifically because of previous home contact, the teacher should not allow the student to participate in the class until the school can confirm the parent's signature. Choice (B) is incorrect, since allowing library time to do parallel research might circumvent the parent's intentions.

27. (A) A normal adolescent would probably demonstrate rebellion by demanding more privileges and independence. The other choices are logical possibilities, but the most common sign of rebellion in an adolescent is stated in choice (A).

28. (C) This question basically involves teacher judgment. Since the teacher only *suspects* cheating, it would be inappropriate to accuse a student of an actual impropriety. By announcing that all students should do their own work, the teacher reinforces acceptable testing standards. Obviously, the appropriate response is determined by how positive the teacher is that cheating actually did take place.

29. (D) Edward Thorndike had a profound effect on American education. Thorndike's three laws of learning (the law of effect, the law of exercise, and the law of readiness) basically involved the use of rewards as a behavior modifier. Thorndike's research led him to the conclusion that punishment does *not* weaken a habit (statement II).

30. (D) Internal validity allows the researcher to increase the probability that what is studied is producing the attained outcome. Choice (A) is a definition of external validity.

SECTION II

1. (E) A *null hypothesis* is a negative, or "no difference," version of the original hypothesis. By stating a hypothesis in null terms (for example, "traditional teachers and nontraditional teachers are equally effective"), a researcher can reject the null hypothesis if the research indicates that the effectiveness of the two groups is not equal.

2. (A) An operational definition provides a variable with a specific methodology and a specific set of measuring devices or techniques. Operational definitions can apply to behavioral objectives—the outcome of the

desired learning is measured against a specific standard. Choice (C) is not statistically as measurable as choice (A).

3. (E) Statement I, *standards for school attendance,* is the only incorrect answer. It should be apparent that an effective physical education program develops social abilities and interests, facilitates self-evaluation, and contributes to a person's total lifestyle.

4. (A) One of the definitions of a parameter is *a statistical characteristic of a population.* You may have been able to eliminate choice (B) if you were familiar with the metric system. Choice (C) is referring to a perimeter and could also have been eliminated.

5. (B) Prior to the 1970s the gifted (making up approximately 5% of the school-age population) had been neglected. The Marland Report, the first federal attempt to determine the extent of gifted programs, was an indictment against the inadequate efforts to provide meaningful educational alternatives for the gifted. The Marland Report did result in the formation of the Office of the Gifted and Talented as part of the U.S. Office of Education.

6. (E) Questionnaires to determine how a person thinks often result in a potential response bias. The respondent might answer a question so as to be "shown in a good light." To maximize the validity of a questionnaire, the use of an unstructured response (a response that is open-ended or an interview-type question) as well as a structured response (ranking response or checklist response) often results in more meaningful information. Choice (A) would not provide an effective means to convert teacher information into data. Choices (B), (C), and (D) are limited in that bias would make validity questionable.

7. (B) Education from the early medieval period until the Renaissance was dominated by the church. Lectures were given in Latin, since it was considered the language of learning; Greek was not generally understood in the West and vernaculars did not contain scientific words.

8. (B) The goal of this procedure is to determine each child's perception of what happened. At this stage of managing classroom behavior each child's understanding of the incident is crucial—the facts at this stage are not important. By simply listening, the teacher sets the stage for follow-up objective questioning to help resolve the problem. In later stages of effective classroom management, the consequences for one's actions are spelled out by the teacher.

9. (D) Referral procedures must be completed in writing, stating the reason for the referral and describing the observed behavior manifested by

the student. A referral is a first step in implementing school district assessment procedures.

10. (D) In a 9 to 0 vote, the U.S. Supreme Court ruled that separate educational facilities are inherently unequal. The court used the equal-protection clause of the Fourteenth Amendment as the legal basis to desegregate the schools.

11. (D) John Dewey's philosophy of education was based on a belief that education was part of living. Dewey is closely associated with the develop-ment of progressive education in America. Dewey believed that "textbook" education limited a student's ability to think creatively. Dewey furthered the concept that learning by doing, especially in the form of projects, was the key to successful education.

12. (A) Defining educational objectives is the first step in curriculum development. The next step would be to decide what learning experiences will best achieve these objectives.

13. (B) Most teacher-education surveys point out that first year teachers, in assessing teacher-training programs, (1) cite the need for more field experience and (2) recognize the inherent limitations of teacher-preparation programs. Choices (A), (C), and (D) are refuted by research dealing with teacher training.

14. (D) The main criticism from a teaching standpoint is that teachers are often "burned out" in a relatively short period of time in trying to meet the challenges of an "open classroom." In short, open education requires the total commitment of the classroom teacher. Other conflicts associated with open classrooms are (1) the student's capacity to make decisions, (2) the relevancy for inner-city youth, (3) the cost factor including aides and teacher materials, and (4) the need for a low teacher-pupil ratio.

15. (E) Breaking up reading material (paragraphs, essays, etc.) into component parts is essentially a small-step progression. It enables students to develop an understanding of major concepts by first comprehending the meaning of individual sentences. Choice (C) enables a student to identify *only a part* of a paragraph and does not necessarily lead to a comprehension of the entire passage.

16. (C) The national movement towards competency-based education has resulted in many states compiling basic skills lists that students must master at each grade level. However, on a nationwide basis (1) there seems to be little agreement on what specifically constitutes minimum skills and (2) there is a danger that curriculum development will be geared to achieving competency in only one or two areas, for instance math and reading.

17. (A) Educators feel that clearly stated objectives will positively influence the instructional process. Behavioral objectives provide a method to verify results by stating outcomes in terms of student behavior—they therefore provide a basis for determining the extent of learner achievement. Performance objectives (E) have been criticized, since they may limit a student's response in trying to go beyond the scope of the original objective.

18. (C) A terminal behavior is one that describes a behavior in exact terms (identify, list, recite). A terminal behavior can be *measured*. It also describes how the learner will achieve the stated objectives. All other choices cannot be adequately measured.

19. (E) *Proper functioning of the classroom and the individual interests of the child should be interrelated.* This answer is the most comprehensive and states a basic concern of class management and discipline.

20. (C) Positive reinforcement is most effective in strengthening a desired behavior when the reward immediately follows the desired response. Choice (B) is an important factor in any reinforcement program, but in initiating a reinforcement schedule, the practical rule is: if you want students to learn something, wait until they do it and then reward them. Rewards tend to be more effective than punishment in controlling behavior (A).

21. (A) Rewards tend to be more effective than punishment in controlling student behavior. Negative reinforcement often is accompanied by emotional side effects, which often are the cause of continued learning disabilities. Rewards reinforce acceptable behavior, while punishment can result in the reinforcement of the deviant behavior.

22. (B) The Department of Agriculture is involved in sponsorship of 4H clubs and provides information on home economics and biology. The Department of Commerce (A) provides information on student age, sex, and geographic distribution.

23. (D) Friedrich Froebel (1782–1852) established the first kindergarten. Froebel believed that education would facilitate the spiritual growth of children. Froebel's theory that play is the characteristic method of learning and growth led to curricular advances that emphasized sensory stimulation.

24. (C) Programmed instruction is designed to provide self-paced, individualized instruction. Programmed texts are divided into a vast series of small steps, or segments, that are part of a larger response pattern. Choice (E) is incorrect, since programmed texts are a question-and-answer-based learning.

25. (B) The term *frequency* means the number of scores falling within a given class interval.

26. (C) The question calls for the key to continuing community support. A school is basically a "mirror of the community." As the community changes (housing patterns, declining enrollment, minority representation) the schools will reflect those changes. An effective educational program must foster the understanding and cooperation of all elements in the community at large.

27. (D) An "open house" enables a school district to present the school programs to the community. Effective open-house activities can further community participation in the educational process. Choices (A), (B), and (C) are not the primary function of an open house. An open house is an inappropriate time for parent conferencing (E).

28. (D) Transfer results when past learning helps one learn and remember something in the present. Transfer is best facilitated when generalizations help the student see similar elements in different situations. Respondent conditioning (C) refers to the environment acting on an organism. There is insufficient evidence to suggest that reinforcement (A) was used in the learning process.

29. (C) Avoid discussing other students during a parent conference. Such comments often result in an emotional reaction by the parent and can interfere with the purpose of the conference. There is insufficient evidence to suggest choices (A), (B), and (E). However, choices (A) and (B) are appropriate measures to improve parent conferencing.

30. (B) It is the schools' responsibility to promote personal, emotional, and social health. It should be apparent that the school district would be disregarding proper dental and health habits by installing *candy and soft-drink machines.* Choice (A) is an important principle, but it would not be the most appropriate reason for removing the machines.

SECTION III

1. (E) The Supreme Court, by virtue of the First Amendment, outlawed prayer in the public schools and defined student rights in cases involving free speech, dress regulations, and student newspapers. The Fourteenth Amendment ("due process" and "equal protection of the laws") was used to desegregate public education. The Fourth Amendment was interpreted to allow school officials to search school facilities and seize illegal contraband. The Fifth Amendment ("due process") and the Sixth Amendment (rights of the accused) have also been used in school cases.

2. (B) It is generally accepted among administrators that evaluation should be a cooperative effort to improve the quality of learning. Choice (D)

is a narrow method to evaluate teacher effectiveness. Many educational and noneducational factors can determine if preset objectives will be reached.

3. (E) The question asks for a characteristic problem associated with traditional evaluation techniques. Statement I is the only choice that is not considered a problem. All other statements are reflective of the *subjective* nature of traditional evaluation techniques.

4. (C) Standardized math tests establish a child's overall performance level and can help to identify specific areas that need further assessment. The use of standardized tests (math, reading, etc.) provide uniform criteria on which to base the makeup of a group. Observation, choice (B), is not as efficient or reliable as standardized tests in determining appropriate group makeup.

5. (A) The "four quarter" plan, or year-round school, is gaining support largely due to the financial implications of modern education. The year-round school can feasibly increase the utilization of school buildings by one-third and at the same time reduce new construction costs. A major incentive of the "four quarter" plan is to make teaching and learning more attractive. A possible problem with the year-round school is the difficulty of implementing extracurricular activities.

6. (D) The first step in program evaluation is normally to identify the behavioral objectives. One of the last steps involves measuring the desired outcomes.

7. (B) Teacher salaries account for approximately fifty percent of a school budget. Any major proposal designed to reduce educational expenditures will ultimately necessitate a cut in the teaching staff.

8. (A) A test is valid if it measures what it is intended to measure. A test is reliable if it is consistent. Therefore, a test may be consistent even though it does not measure what it is intended to measure.

9. (A) A major challenge of modern education is to determine how the schools can best involve diverse citizen groups directly in the educational process. The consensus today is to allow the individual school districts the latitude to develop their own programs to provide effective citizen participation. The primary responsibility for citizen involvement rests with the educational team—the superintendent, administrators, and teachers, not only the superintendent (C); the improvement of school programs is not the sole prerogative of professional educators (D).

10. (B) In auditory-association learning problems the student often has difficulty with opposites and is confused on temporal sequences. Choice (A)

is an example of an auditory-memory problem; choice (C) is an example of an auditory-reception problem; choice (D) is an example of an auditory-closure and sound-blending problem; choice (E) is an example of a verbal-expression problem.

11. (E) The Morrill Act (1862) extended the principle of federal support for public education, the earliest attempt being the Northwest Ordinance of 1787. The Morrill Act established land-grant colleges in each state and specified a curriculum based on agriculture and mechanical arts. Land-grant colleges often were a state's first institution of public higher education. Public support and public control strengthened the concept of the state-university system. The Civil Rights Act of 1875 was the first federal attempt to provide equal educational opportunity (C).

12. (A) By definition, Early Childhood Education programs (ECE) are designed for children below the first grade. ECE programs are formal programs and are primarily concerned with the care and development of preschool children. Research and experimental programs, Head Start programs, and daycare centers for children of working mothers are part of the ECE program. Some states include the early primary grades in their ECE programs.

13. (E) An open and stimulating environment as well as the child's intellectual ability are key factors in language development. It is important to consider that language development corresponds to a child's cognitive and physical age. At ages five and six a child's language patterns begin to resemble adult speech. There is no evidence to suggest that choice (C) is a correct statement.

14. (B) Punishing an entire class for the misbehavior of a few is inappropriate. Since a few students can so affect a class, the teacher may be giving the misbehaving few undue status. Resentment that develops may be directed against the teacher and not the misbehaving students.

15. (E) Grouping students by abilities is an effective way of meeting individual needs in a classroom. The other procedures may penalize students for not being able to work at the same level as some bright students. Choice (C) would not provide bright students with adequate direction unless properly organized and supervised.

16. (E) As age increases, reliance on physical action to express anger decreases. This statement is a generalization that is commonly accepted and reinforced through observation.

17. (E) Self-concept is the only response that is sufficiently comprehensive to answer the question of the most important factor. An adequate

self-concept is essential if a student is to relate well with others. A student's self-concept may be influenced by the other factors, choices (A) through (D).

18. (B) The study period should not be used by the teacher for preparation time. The teacher should be supervising the study period.

19. (B) Teachers tend to respond to immediate causes. The nature of being in a classroom requires that misbehavior is quickly dealt with so that the learning situation can continue.

20. (D) An inservice program enables a school district to provide up-to-date training in current educational problems. This approach has the best chance to modify teacher misconceptions regarding single-parent children. Choice (A) is too vague to deal with the specifics of the problem. Choices (B) and (E) would not necessarily improve teacher awareness of the problem, and choice (C) is too limited in scope to be an acceptable answer.

21. (D) Jerome S. Bruner's *Process of Education* (1960) theorized that the public schools were wasting precious years by postponing the teaching of many subjects on the ground that they were too difficult. Bruner's book had a profound influence on strengthening the academic portion of the curriculum.

22. (C) You are looking for an inappropriate response. A heterogeneous class has special needs. The teacher must take into consideration the fact that there are continuous variations within a particular group. Curricular options should provide for individual differences. Choice (C) is inappropriate, since a uniform program would not necessarily provide for individual differences. The other choices are consistent with programs designed to meet individual needs.

23. (D) About two-thirds (67%) of the normal curve falls within one standard deviation of the arithmetic mean.

24. (A) H. G. Rickover became a significant voice during the educational-reform zeal of the 1960s. His books *Education and Freedom* (1959) and *American Education—A National Failure* (1963) detailed the shortcomings of public education. His thesis was that U.S. educational standards are "quantitatively and qualitatively" inferior to the European system of education. Rickover advocated the adoption of many European educational features such as national standards of education and national examinations.

25. (D) Choice (D) is the most comprehensive answer. A pass–fail system encourages students to take interest-oriented courses, since the fear of failure is greatly reduced. Choice (A) is not a relevant reason to initiate a pass–fail grading system. Choices (B) and (C) would not necessarily follow.

Choice (E) is a generalization that is not supported by research on the academic standards of pass–fail courses.

26. (E) A teacher can achieve the appropriate behavior by positively reinforcing some behavior incompatible with the negative behavior of calling out. Consistent and immediate positive reinforcement for appropriate behavior will make that response more probable than the inappropriate behavior. Choice (A) is incorrect because only a new response will be extinguished by ignoring it. Negative reinforcement (B) is incorrect, since negative reinforcement can actually strengthen the undesirable behavior.

27. (C) Spontaneous recovery describes the recurrence of a behavior previously thought to be extinguished.

28. (B) A significant fact in interpreting this question is that the student is *overweight and withdrawn.* It should be apparent to the teacher that the student probably has a poor self-image. The teacher should use the P.E. class as a steppingstone to improve the student's self-image. Choices (A) and (C) are not supported by evidence in the example. Choice (D) is too extreme based on the demonstrated behavior.

29. (C) Of the examples given, choice (C) is the best method to protect the teacher from a lawsuit claiming negligence. This is the only example that specifically tests competency *before* the equipment is to be used by the students. Choice (D) does not indicate that the students have received instruction on the equipment.

30. (D) The statement is the thesis of Jerome Bruner's book *The Process of Education* (1960). Bruner advocated the early teaching of science, mathematics, social studies and literature. Choice (A) is associated with William Glazer; choice (C) is associated with A. S. Neill.

SECTION IV

1. (C) By stating the Preamble in their own words, the students must analyze and evaluate the passage. This is the only example that facilitates practice in determining the meaning of the Preamble. Simply reciting key statements (B) does not imply that the material is understood.

2. (D) Under the conditions set in the question, choice (D) would facilitate positive transfer and therefore would be the best remembered. In positive transfer something you have already learned aids the learning of new material. In choice (D) the generalization applies to *all* revolutions. If you know that all revolutions are characterized by change, the French, Russian, or *any* revolution will have that characteristic.

3. (E) Success is a significant variable in motivation. In the example, the negative feelings concerning memorization are outweighed by the need to succeed. Degree of difficulty is closely related to success. Missy became highly motivated because the goal was attainable. Knowledge of results (C) would not be the best answer, since Missy could be relatively positive of how she performed on the test without immediate feedback. Although peer-group pressure (A) is a powerful motivator, there is insufficient evidence to suggest this as the best answer. The lack of difficulty of the task would preclude (B) as an acceptable answer.

4. (C) Since 1960, a public commitment to treat the diverse elements of the U.S. population in an equitable manner has shaped educational policy. In short, providing equal educational opportunity has dominated current state and federal education guidelines. Legislated programs such as English as a Second Language (ESL), bilingual education, Individualized Education Programs (IEP), and special funding for inner-city schools are representative of a continuing effort to provide equal educational opportunity for all students.

5. (D) The overhead projector is sufficiently powerful to permit successful operation in a lighted room. The other equipment needs a darkened room to be viewed effectively.

6. (C) Team teaching, by definition, is an organizational pattern where two or more teachers plan, teach, evaluate, and replan a part of the curriculum for the same group of students. Statement II is incorrect, since the team members should embrace the basic philosophy of team teaching. Statement IV is incorrect, since effective team teaching is limited by large-group activities. A team group should be limited to twenty-five students or fewer.

7. (B) In applying reinforcement techniques to a learning situation, the first step is to identify the behavior to be changed. It is also necessary to identify the appropriate new behavior that should replace the inappropriate behavior. Choice (D) would be the second step. Punishment (C) will often result in negative side effects, and (E) might backfire, since the student is being rewarded for inappropriate behavior.

8. (D) Bloom's taxonomy contains six major classes: knowledge, comprehension, application, analysis, synthesis, and evaluation. Evaluation (the highest level) is defined as quantitative and qualitative judgments about the extent to which material and methods satisfy criteria. Evaluation is placed at the end of the taxonomy because it involves some combination of all other behaviors plus the addition of criteria and values.

9. (B) The progressive theories of John Dewey had a profound effect on public education. Dewey believed that education included the home, shop, neighborhood, church, and school. However, industrialization was destroying the educational functions of these institutions. Dewey believed that the public schools must be society's instrument for "shaping its own destiny." To do this the schools had to be transformed in order to serve the interests of democracy. Choices (A) and (C) are accurate statements but they are not comprehensive enough to be the acceptable answer.

10. (B) Bringing the real world into the classroom augments the curriculum and enhances the students' perspective of actual events. Choice (C) is incorrect, since there is no positive correlation that presentation equals learning. Choice (E) is incorrect. Teachers are ultimately responsible for education; "invited" community leaders are not legally responsible for the learning process.

11. (D) When teacher assistance is not needed, problem solving can and should be an independent action.

12. (E) Mr. Lohman should examine the teaching methods he has used with these students to determine alternative teaching approaches. Choices (B) and (C) are not adequate responses. Mr. Lohman can discuss his classroom problem with other teachers or his supervisor, or he can examine his own teaching methods as stated in choice (E). He can review the material he has taught with his students (D), but this does not address the problem of underachieving students in his class as does choice (E). Choice (A) is inadequate, since it is unlikely a "large number" of Mr. Lohman's students are having home problems.

13. (C) Students frequently are unable to evaluate the appropriateness of their own work or behavior without the help of others. All of the choices have some truth to them. Choice (C), however, needs no qualifications.

14. (C) Longitudinal studies, which are often expensive and time consuming, measure a variable repeatedly over many years.

15. (D) Democratic beliefs can be taught based on respect for the worth of each individual and faith in the ability of people to govern themselves. This choice best fits our society's definition of democracy and the beliefs it wishes to impart to our children.

16. (C) An academic testing program can provide information which can be used in determining a course of study for a child. The other choices would in themselves be misuses of academic tests.

17. (C) Recitation is best used to develop oral English and presence in front of a group. The other choices would not be good uses for recitation.

18. **(C)** *Mainstreaming* means that learning handicapped students must be placed in the least restrictive school environment to best provide for their educational needs. Placement is determined cooperatively by school administrators, parents, special education teachers, and in some cases, the student. Mainstreaming is an attempt to adequately serve learning handicapped children who need special education. Because of wide differences among special education pupils, the most appropriate and least restrictive environment could include part-time participation in regular classes. The Education of All Handicapped Children Act of 1975 (PL 94-142) is the appropriate federal statute governing mainstreaming.

19. **(C)** Projects should fall within the area of curriculum. They should be supervised and evaluated and hopefully allow students to discover new knowledge or experience.

20. **(C)** The schools have become more aware of the importance of gross- and fine-motor efficiency in learning reading and writing. The other choices are not true.

21. **(B)** Content includes the data (concepts, facts, generalizations) used in a teaching unit. However, only content that will directly contribute to achieving the teaching objectives should be selected. Teaching units are precise guides designed for a specific instructional plan. Content is only one part of an instructional program. The critical factor in any instructional program is to determine which resources are used with each activity, with what content, and with what objectives.

22. **(B)** Current educational research indicates that learning to read is an important social activity. An overemphasis on an individualized reading program can isolate a student, depriving the pupil of important peer-group support.

23. **(B)** When the actions of an unknown individual are discussed, unpopular students are often the subject of personal accusations and ridicule. The unpopular student, often at the bottom of the social acceptance scale, can easily become a scapegoat for the group. Choice (A) is not the best answer since peer pressure can act as an important catalyst to change inappropriate behavior. Choice (E) is incorrect since negative and positive reinforcement (the use of operant conditioning techniques) is an important aspect of classroom management.

24. **(C)** In an auditory classroom, instruction is mainly in the form of verbal discussion and lecture. Reading instruction in such classrooms is built on phonics and children participate in frequent "spelling bees." Choice (A) is an example of a kinesthetic classroom; choices (B), (D), and (E) are

examples of a visual classroom. Since children do not learn in the same manner, the use of different sensory modes facilitates learning.

25. (D) Developing fluency in a native language is definitely beneficial in learning a second language. Skills that are learned in the native language are transferable to skills necessary to learn a second language. The other choices are obvious goals of bilingual education.

26. (E) All choices are correct. Public Law 94-142 identifies and describes the procedures a school must use to inform parents of handicapped children of their rights and also to provide notice to such parents regarding evaluation procedures. PL 94-142 provides a specific sequence of events from referral to the formal evaluation of a child identified as handicapped. Under this law parents have the right to refuse to give permission, or revoke permission for the evaluation of their child. This is considered a "due process" safeguard for parents of handicapped children.

27. (E) The term *dyslexia* implies partial inability to read or to understand what one reads. Brain damage is usually associated with the condition. Visual dyslexic children demonstrate difficulty in learning and retaining the appearance of letters. Common problems are reversing of words and difficulty identifying changes in visual stimuli. *Dysphasia,* choice (A), implies the partial inability to comprehend the spoken word or to speak.

28. (D) Certain activities are not protected by the First Amendment. For instance, the federal courts have held that if an activity is classified as free speech, it is not protected by the First Amendment if the activity incites students to violate the law. Depending on the circumstances, First Amendment freedoms can include wearing buttons, badges, and other insignia, refusing to salute the flag, distributing literature, and *peacefully* demonstrating.

29. (C) Instructional objectives describe specific learning outcomes and also the terminal behavior of students who have achieved the objectives. Coloring books are valuable classroom tools that can provide motivational lessons in a variety of subjects. Although a substitute teacher's classroom discipline might benefit, choice (C) would hardly classify as an instructional objective.

30. (B) Assertive discipline is a method to improve classroom management techniques. It is an attempt to modify teacher behavior so that student-teacher confrontations can be dealt with effectively. As such, assertive discipline does not seek to minimize student-teacher interaction, but rather to broaden the base for such interaction. A key aspect of assertive discipline is to cooperatively specify rules and regulations and to define the consequences for atypical behavior.

PRACTICE TEST 2

ANSWER SHEET FOR PRACTICE TEST 2
TEST OF DATA INTERPRETATION SKILLS

SECTION I   SECTION II   SECTION III

452

ANSWER SHEET FOR PRACTICE TEST 2
(Remove This Sheet and Use It to Mark Your Answers)

TEST OF COMMUNICATION SKILLS

SECTION I	SECTION II	SECTION III

SECTION I

1 Ⓐ Ⓑ Ⓒ Ⓓ
2 Ⓐ Ⓑ Ⓒ Ⓓ
3 Ⓐ Ⓑ Ⓒ Ⓓ
4 Ⓐ Ⓑ Ⓒ Ⓓ
5 Ⓐ Ⓑ Ⓒ Ⓓ
6 Ⓐ Ⓑ Ⓒ Ⓓ
7 Ⓐ Ⓑ Ⓒ Ⓓ
8 Ⓐ Ⓑ Ⓒ Ⓓ
9 Ⓐ Ⓑ Ⓒ Ⓓ
10 Ⓐ Ⓑ Ⓒ Ⓓ
11 Ⓐ Ⓑ Ⓒ Ⓓ
12 Ⓐ Ⓑ Ⓒ Ⓓ
13 Ⓐ Ⓑ Ⓒ Ⓓ
14 Ⓐ Ⓑ Ⓒ Ⓓ
15 Ⓐ Ⓑ Ⓒ Ⓓ
16 Ⓐ Ⓑ Ⓒ Ⓓ
17 Ⓐ Ⓑ Ⓒ Ⓓ
18 Ⓐ Ⓑ Ⓒ Ⓓ
19 Ⓐ Ⓑ Ⓒ Ⓓ
20 Ⓐ Ⓑ Ⓒ Ⓓ
21 Ⓐ Ⓑ Ⓒ Ⓓ
22 Ⓐ Ⓑ Ⓒ Ⓓ
23 Ⓐ Ⓑ Ⓒ Ⓓ
24 Ⓐ Ⓑ Ⓒ Ⓓ
25 Ⓐ Ⓑ Ⓒ Ⓓ
26 Ⓐ Ⓑ Ⓒ Ⓓ
27 Ⓐ Ⓑ Ⓒ Ⓓ
28 Ⓐ Ⓑ Ⓒ Ⓓ
29 Ⓐ Ⓑ Ⓒ Ⓓ
30 Ⓐ Ⓑ Ⓒ Ⓓ
31 Ⓐ Ⓑ Ⓒ Ⓓ
32 Ⓐ Ⓑ Ⓒ Ⓓ

SECTION II

1 Ⓐ Ⓑ Ⓒ Ⓓ Ⓔ
2 Ⓐ Ⓑ Ⓒ Ⓓ Ⓔ
3 Ⓐ Ⓑ Ⓒ Ⓓ Ⓔ
4 Ⓐ Ⓑ Ⓒ Ⓓ Ⓔ
5 Ⓐ Ⓑ Ⓒ Ⓓ Ⓔ
6 Ⓐ Ⓑ Ⓒ Ⓓ Ⓔ
7 Ⓐ Ⓑ Ⓒ Ⓓ Ⓔ
8 Ⓐ Ⓑ Ⓒ Ⓓ Ⓔ
9 Ⓐ Ⓑ Ⓒ Ⓓ Ⓔ
10 Ⓐ Ⓑ Ⓒ Ⓓ Ⓔ
11 Ⓐ Ⓑ Ⓒ Ⓓ Ⓔ
12 Ⓐ Ⓑ Ⓒ Ⓓ Ⓔ
13 Ⓐ Ⓑ Ⓒ Ⓓ Ⓔ
14 Ⓐ Ⓑ Ⓒ Ⓓ Ⓔ
15 Ⓐ Ⓑ Ⓒ Ⓓ Ⓔ
16 Ⓐ Ⓑ Ⓒ Ⓓ Ⓔ
17 Ⓐ Ⓑ Ⓒ Ⓓ Ⓔ
18 Ⓐ Ⓑ Ⓒ Ⓓ Ⓔ
19 Ⓐ Ⓑ Ⓒ Ⓓ Ⓔ
20 Ⓐ Ⓑ Ⓒ Ⓓ Ⓔ
21 Ⓐ Ⓑ Ⓒ Ⓓ Ⓔ
22 Ⓐ Ⓑ Ⓒ Ⓓ Ⓔ
23 Ⓐ Ⓑ Ⓒ Ⓓ Ⓔ
24 Ⓐ Ⓑ Ⓒ Ⓓ Ⓔ
25 Ⓐ Ⓑ Ⓒ Ⓓ Ⓔ
26 Ⓐ Ⓑ Ⓒ Ⓓ Ⓔ
27 Ⓐ Ⓑ Ⓒ Ⓓ Ⓔ
28 Ⓐ Ⓑ Ⓒ Ⓓ Ⓔ
29 Ⓐ Ⓑ Ⓒ Ⓓ Ⓔ
30 Ⓐ Ⓑ Ⓒ Ⓓ Ⓔ
31 Ⓐ Ⓑ Ⓒ Ⓓ Ⓔ
32 Ⓐ Ⓑ Ⓒ Ⓓ Ⓔ

SECTION III

1 Ⓐ Ⓑ Ⓒ Ⓓ Ⓔ
2 Ⓐ Ⓑ Ⓒ Ⓓ Ⓔ
3 Ⓐ Ⓑ Ⓒ Ⓓ Ⓔ
4 Ⓐ Ⓑ Ⓒ Ⓓ Ⓔ
5 Ⓐ Ⓑ Ⓒ Ⓓ Ⓔ
6 Ⓐ Ⓑ Ⓒ Ⓓ Ⓔ
7 Ⓐ Ⓑ Ⓒ Ⓓ Ⓔ
8 Ⓐ Ⓑ Ⓒ Ⓓ Ⓔ
9 Ⓐ Ⓑ Ⓒ Ⓓ Ⓔ
10 Ⓐ Ⓑ Ⓒ Ⓓ Ⓔ
11 Ⓐ Ⓑ Ⓒ Ⓓ Ⓔ
12 Ⓐ Ⓑ Ⓒ Ⓓ Ⓔ
13 Ⓐ Ⓑ Ⓒ Ⓓ Ⓔ
14 Ⓐ Ⓑ Ⓒ Ⓓ Ⓔ
15 Ⓐ Ⓑ Ⓒ Ⓓ Ⓔ
16 Ⓐ Ⓑ Ⓒ Ⓓ Ⓔ
17 Ⓐ Ⓑ Ⓒ Ⓓ Ⓔ
18 Ⓐ Ⓑ Ⓒ Ⓓ Ⓔ
19 Ⓐ Ⓑ Ⓒ Ⓓ Ⓔ
20 Ⓐ Ⓑ Ⓒ Ⓓ Ⓔ
21 Ⓐ Ⓑ Ⓒ Ⓓ Ⓔ
22 Ⓐ Ⓑ Ⓒ Ⓓ Ⓔ
23 Ⓐ Ⓑ Ⓒ Ⓓ Ⓔ
24 Ⓐ Ⓑ Ⓒ Ⓓ Ⓔ
25 Ⓐ Ⓑ Ⓒ Ⓓ Ⓔ
26 Ⓐ Ⓑ Ⓒ Ⓓ Ⓔ
27 Ⓐ Ⓑ Ⓒ Ⓓ Ⓔ
28 Ⓐ Ⓑ Ⓒ Ⓓ Ⓔ
29 Ⓐ Ⓑ Ⓒ Ⓓ Ⓔ
30 Ⓐ Ⓑ Ⓒ Ⓓ Ⓔ

31 Ⓐ Ⓑ Ⓒ Ⓓ Ⓔ
32 Ⓐ Ⓑ Ⓒ Ⓓ Ⓔ
33 Ⓐ Ⓑ Ⓒ Ⓓ Ⓔ
34 Ⓐ Ⓑ Ⓒ Ⓓ Ⓔ
35 Ⓐ Ⓑ Ⓒ Ⓓ Ⓔ
36 Ⓐ Ⓑ Ⓒ Ⓓ Ⓔ
37 Ⓐ Ⓑ Ⓒ Ⓓ Ⓔ
38 Ⓐ Ⓑ Ⓒ Ⓓ Ⓔ
39 Ⓐ Ⓑ Ⓒ Ⓓ Ⓔ
40 Ⓐ Ⓑ Ⓒ Ⓓ Ⓔ
41 Ⓐ Ⓑ Ⓒ Ⓓ Ⓔ
42 Ⓐ Ⓑ Ⓒ Ⓓ Ⓔ
43 Ⓐ Ⓑ Ⓒ Ⓓ Ⓔ
44 Ⓐ Ⓑ Ⓒ Ⓓ Ⓔ
45 Ⓐ Ⓑ Ⓒ Ⓓ Ⓔ

CUT HERE

453

ANSWER SHEET FOR PRACTICE TEST 2
(Remove This Sheet and Use It to Mark Your Answers)

TEST OF GENERAL KNOWLEDGE

SECTION I	SECTION II	SECTION III	SECTION IV
1 Ⓐ Ⓑ Ⓒ Ⓓ Ⓔ	1 Ⓐ Ⓑ Ⓒ Ⓓ Ⓔ	1 Ⓐ Ⓑ Ⓒ Ⓓ Ⓔ	1 Ⓐ Ⓑ Ⓒ Ⓓ Ⓔ
2 Ⓐ Ⓑ Ⓒ Ⓓ Ⓔ	2 Ⓐ Ⓑ Ⓒ Ⓓ Ⓔ	2 Ⓐ Ⓑ Ⓒ Ⓓ Ⓔ	2 Ⓐ Ⓑ Ⓒ Ⓓ Ⓔ
3 Ⓐ Ⓑ Ⓒ Ⓓ Ⓔ	3 Ⓐ Ⓑ Ⓒ Ⓓ Ⓔ	3 Ⓐ Ⓑ Ⓒ Ⓓ Ⓔ	3 Ⓐ Ⓑ Ⓒ Ⓓ Ⓔ
4 Ⓐ Ⓑ Ⓒ Ⓓ Ⓔ	4 Ⓐ Ⓑ Ⓒ Ⓓ Ⓔ	4 Ⓐ Ⓑ Ⓒ Ⓓ Ⓔ	4 Ⓐ Ⓑ Ⓒ Ⓓ Ⓔ
5 Ⓐ Ⓑ Ⓒ Ⓓ Ⓔ	5 Ⓐ Ⓑ Ⓒ Ⓓ Ⓔ	5 Ⓐ Ⓑ Ⓒ Ⓓ Ⓔ	5 Ⓐ Ⓑ Ⓒ Ⓓ Ⓔ
6 Ⓐ Ⓑ Ⓒ Ⓓ Ⓔ	6 Ⓐ Ⓑ Ⓒ Ⓓ Ⓔ	6 Ⓐ Ⓑ Ⓒ Ⓓ Ⓔ	6 Ⓐ Ⓑ Ⓒ Ⓓ Ⓔ
7 Ⓐ Ⓑ Ⓒ Ⓓ Ⓔ	7 Ⓐ Ⓑ Ⓒ Ⓓ Ⓔ	7 Ⓐ Ⓑ Ⓒ Ⓓ Ⓔ	7 Ⓐ Ⓑ Ⓒ Ⓓ Ⓔ
8 Ⓐ Ⓑ Ⓒ Ⓓ Ⓔ	8 Ⓐ Ⓑ Ⓒ Ⓓ Ⓔ	8 Ⓐ Ⓑ Ⓒ Ⓓ Ⓔ	8 Ⓐ Ⓑ Ⓒ Ⓓ Ⓔ
9 Ⓐ Ⓑ Ⓒ Ⓓ Ⓔ	9 Ⓐ Ⓑ Ⓒ Ⓓ Ⓔ	9 Ⓐ Ⓑ Ⓒ Ⓓ Ⓔ	9 Ⓐ Ⓑ Ⓒ Ⓓ Ⓔ
10 Ⓐ Ⓑ Ⓒ Ⓓ Ⓔ	10 Ⓐ Ⓑ Ⓒ Ⓓ Ⓔ	10 Ⓐ Ⓑ Ⓒ Ⓓ Ⓔ	10 Ⓐ Ⓑ Ⓒ Ⓓ Ⓔ
11 Ⓐ Ⓑ Ⓒ Ⓓ Ⓔ	11 Ⓐ Ⓑ Ⓒ Ⓓ Ⓔ	11 Ⓐ Ⓑ Ⓒ Ⓓ Ⓔ	11 Ⓐ Ⓑ Ⓒ Ⓓ Ⓔ
12 Ⓐ Ⓑ Ⓒ Ⓓ Ⓔ	12 Ⓐ Ⓑ Ⓒ Ⓓ Ⓔ	12 Ⓐ Ⓑ Ⓒ Ⓓ Ⓔ	12 Ⓐ Ⓑ Ⓒ Ⓓ Ⓔ
13 Ⓐ Ⓑ Ⓒ Ⓓ Ⓔ	13 Ⓐ Ⓑ Ⓒ Ⓓ Ⓔ	13 Ⓐ Ⓑ Ⓒ Ⓓ Ⓔ	13 Ⓐ Ⓑ Ⓒ Ⓓ Ⓔ
14 Ⓐ Ⓑ Ⓒ Ⓓ Ⓔ	14 Ⓐ Ⓑ Ⓒ Ⓓ Ⓔ	14 Ⓐ Ⓑ Ⓒ Ⓓ Ⓔ	14 Ⓐ Ⓑ Ⓒ Ⓓ Ⓔ
15 Ⓐ Ⓑ Ⓒ Ⓓ Ⓔ	15 Ⓐ Ⓑ Ⓒ Ⓓ Ⓔ	15 Ⓐ Ⓑ Ⓒ Ⓓ Ⓔ	15 Ⓐ Ⓑ Ⓒ Ⓓ Ⓔ
16 Ⓐ Ⓑ Ⓒ Ⓓ Ⓔ	16 Ⓐ Ⓑ Ⓒ Ⓓ Ⓔ	16 Ⓐ Ⓑ Ⓒ Ⓓ Ⓔ	16 Ⓐ Ⓑ Ⓒ Ⓓ Ⓔ
17 Ⓐ Ⓑ Ⓒ Ⓓ Ⓔ	17 Ⓐ Ⓑ Ⓒ Ⓓ Ⓔ	17 Ⓐ Ⓑ Ⓒ Ⓓ Ⓔ	17 Ⓐ Ⓑ Ⓒ Ⓓ Ⓔ
18 Ⓐ Ⓑ Ⓒ Ⓓ Ⓔ	18 Ⓐ Ⓑ Ⓒ Ⓓ Ⓔ	18 Ⓐ Ⓑ Ⓒ Ⓓ Ⓔ	18 Ⓐ Ⓑ Ⓒ Ⓓ Ⓔ
19 Ⓐ Ⓑ Ⓒ Ⓓ Ⓔ	19 Ⓐ Ⓑ Ⓒ Ⓓ Ⓔ	19 Ⓐ Ⓑ Ⓒ Ⓓ Ⓔ	19 Ⓐ Ⓑ Ⓒ Ⓓ Ⓔ
20 Ⓐ Ⓑ Ⓒ Ⓓ Ⓔ	20 Ⓐ Ⓑ Ⓒ Ⓓ Ⓔ	20 Ⓐ Ⓑ Ⓒ Ⓓ Ⓔ	20 Ⓐ Ⓑ Ⓒ Ⓓ Ⓔ
21 Ⓐ Ⓑ Ⓒ Ⓓ Ⓔ	21 Ⓐ Ⓑ Ⓒ Ⓓ Ⓔ	21 Ⓐ Ⓑ Ⓒ Ⓓ Ⓔ	21 Ⓐ Ⓑ Ⓒ Ⓓ Ⓔ
22 Ⓐ Ⓑ Ⓒ Ⓓ Ⓔ	22 Ⓐ Ⓑ Ⓒ Ⓓ Ⓔ	22 Ⓐ Ⓑ Ⓒ Ⓓ Ⓔ	22 Ⓐ Ⓑ Ⓒ Ⓓ Ⓔ
23 Ⓐ Ⓑ Ⓒ Ⓓ Ⓔ	23 Ⓐ Ⓑ Ⓒ Ⓓ Ⓔ	23 Ⓐ Ⓑ Ⓒ Ⓓ Ⓔ	23 Ⓐ Ⓑ Ⓒ Ⓓ Ⓔ
24 Ⓐ Ⓑ Ⓒ Ⓓ Ⓔ	24 Ⓐ Ⓑ Ⓒ Ⓓ Ⓔ	24 Ⓐ Ⓑ Ⓒ Ⓓ Ⓔ	24 Ⓐ Ⓑ Ⓒ Ⓓ Ⓔ
25 Ⓐ Ⓑ Ⓒ Ⓓ Ⓔ	25 Ⓐ Ⓑ Ⓒ Ⓓ Ⓔ	25 Ⓐ Ⓑ Ⓒ Ⓓ Ⓔ	25 Ⓐ Ⓑ Ⓒ Ⓓ Ⓔ
26 Ⓐ Ⓑ Ⓒ Ⓓ Ⓔ		26 Ⓐ Ⓑ Ⓒ Ⓓ Ⓔ	26 Ⓐ Ⓑ Ⓒ Ⓓ Ⓔ
27 Ⓐ Ⓑ Ⓒ Ⓓ Ⓔ		27 Ⓐ Ⓑ Ⓒ Ⓓ Ⓔ	27 Ⓐ Ⓑ Ⓒ Ⓓ Ⓔ
28 Ⓐ Ⓑ Ⓒ Ⓓ Ⓔ		28 Ⓐ Ⓑ Ⓒ Ⓓ Ⓔ	28 Ⓐ Ⓑ Ⓒ Ⓓ Ⓔ
29 Ⓐ Ⓑ Ⓒ Ⓓ Ⓔ		29 Ⓐ Ⓑ Ⓒ Ⓓ Ⓔ	29 Ⓐ Ⓑ Ⓒ Ⓓ Ⓔ
30 Ⓐ Ⓑ Ⓒ Ⓓ Ⓔ		30 Ⓐ Ⓑ Ⓒ Ⓓ Ⓔ	30 Ⓐ Ⓑ Ⓒ Ⓓ Ⓔ
		31 Ⓐ Ⓑ Ⓒ Ⓓ Ⓔ	
		32 Ⓐ Ⓑ Ⓒ Ⓓ Ⓔ	
		33 Ⓐ Ⓑ Ⓒ Ⓓ Ⓔ	
		34 Ⓐ Ⓑ Ⓒ Ⓓ Ⓔ	
		35 Ⓐ Ⓑ Ⓒ Ⓓ Ⓔ	

454

ANSWER SHEET FOR PRACTICE TEST 2
(Remove This Sheet and Use It to Mark Your Answers)

TEST OF PROFESSIONAL KNOWLEDGE

SECTION I	SECTION II	SECTION III	SECTION IV
1 Ⓐ Ⓑ Ⓒ Ⓓ Ⓔ	1 Ⓐ Ⓑ Ⓒ Ⓓ Ⓔ	1 Ⓐ Ⓑ Ⓒ Ⓓ Ⓔ	1 Ⓐ Ⓑ Ⓒ Ⓓ Ⓔ
2 Ⓐ Ⓑ Ⓒ Ⓓ Ⓔ	2 Ⓐ Ⓑ Ⓒ Ⓓ Ⓔ	2 Ⓐ Ⓑ Ⓒ Ⓓ Ⓔ	2 Ⓐ Ⓑ Ⓒ Ⓓ Ⓔ
3 Ⓐ Ⓑ Ⓒ Ⓓ Ⓔ	3 Ⓐ Ⓑ Ⓒ Ⓓ Ⓔ	3 Ⓐ Ⓑ Ⓒ Ⓓ Ⓔ	3 Ⓐ Ⓑ Ⓒ Ⓓ Ⓔ
4 Ⓐ Ⓑ Ⓒ Ⓓ Ⓔ	4 Ⓐ Ⓑ Ⓒ Ⓓ Ⓔ	4 Ⓐ Ⓑ Ⓒ Ⓓ Ⓔ	4 Ⓐ Ⓑ Ⓒ Ⓓ Ⓔ
5 Ⓐ Ⓑ Ⓒ Ⓓ Ⓔ	5 Ⓐ Ⓑ Ⓒ Ⓓ Ⓔ	5 Ⓐ Ⓑ Ⓒ Ⓓ Ⓔ	5 Ⓐ Ⓑ Ⓒ Ⓓ Ⓔ
6 Ⓐ Ⓑ Ⓒ Ⓓ Ⓔ	6 Ⓐ Ⓑ Ⓒ Ⓓ Ⓔ	6 Ⓐ Ⓑ Ⓒ Ⓓ Ⓔ	6 Ⓐ Ⓑ Ⓒ Ⓓ Ⓔ
7 Ⓐ Ⓑ Ⓒ Ⓓ Ⓔ	7 Ⓐ Ⓑ Ⓒ Ⓓ Ⓔ	7 Ⓐ Ⓑ Ⓒ Ⓓ Ⓔ	7 Ⓐ Ⓑ Ⓒ Ⓓ Ⓔ
8 Ⓐ Ⓑ Ⓒ Ⓓ Ⓔ	8 Ⓐ Ⓑ Ⓒ Ⓓ Ⓔ	8 Ⓐ Ⓑ Ⓒ Ⓓ Ⓔ	8 Ⓐ Ⓑ Ⓒ Ⓓ Ⓔ
9 Ⓐ Ⓑ Ⓒ Ⓓ Ⓔ	9 Ⓐ Ⓑ Ⓒ Ⓓ Ⓔ	9 Ⓐ Ⓑ Ⓒ Ⓓ Ⓔ	9 Ⓐ Ⓑ Ⓒ Ⓓ Ⓔ
10 Ⓐ Ⓑ Ⓒ Ⓓ Ⓔ	10 Ⓐ Ⓑ Ⓒ Ⓓ Ⓔ	10 Ⓐ Ⓑ Ⓒ Ⓓ Ⓔ	10 Ⓐ Ⓑ Ⓒ Ⓓ Ⓔ
11 Ⓐ Ⓑ Ⓒ Ⓓ Ⓔ	11 Ⓐ Ⓑ Ⓒ Ⓓ Ⓔ	11 Ⓐ Ⓑ Ⓒ Ⓓ Ⓔ	11 Ⓐ Ⓑ Ⓒ Ⓓ Ⓔ
12 Ⓐ Ⓑ Ⓒ Ⓓ Ⓔ	12 Ⓐ Ⓑ Ⓒ Ⓓ Ⓔ	12 Ⓐ Ⓑ Ⓒ Ⓓ Ⓔ	12 Ⓐ Ⓑ Ⓒ Ⓓ Ⓔ
13 Ⓐ Ⓑ Ⓒ Ⓓ Ⓔ	13 Ⓐ Ⓑ Ⓒ Ⓓ Ⓔ	13 Ⓐ Ⓑ Ⓒ Ⓓ Ⓔ	13 Ⓐ Ⓑ Ⓒ Ⓓ Ⓔ
14 Ⓐ Ⓑ Ⓒ Ⓓ Ⓔ	14 Ⓐ Ⓑ Ⓒ Ⓓ Ⓔ	14 Ⓐ Ⓑ Ⓒ Ⓓ Ⓔ	14 Ⓐ Ⓑ Ⓒ Ⓓ Ⓔ
15 Ⓐ Ⓑ Ⓒ Ⓓ Ⓔ	15 Ⓐ Ⓑ Ⓒ Ⓓ Ⓔ	15 Ⓐ Ⓑ Ⓒ Ⓓ Ⓔ	15 Ⓐ Ⓑ Ⓒ Ⓓ Ⓔ
16 Ⓐ Ⓑ Ⓒ Ⓓ Ⓔ	16 Ⓐ Ⓑ Ⓒ Ⓓ Ⓔ	16 Ⓐ Ⓑ Ⓒ Ⓓ Ⓔ	16 Ⓐ Ⓑ Ⓒ Ⓓ Ⓔ
17 Ⓐ Ⓑ Ⓒ Ⓓ Ⓔ	17 Ⓐ Ⓑ Ⓒ Ⓓ Ⓔ	17 Ⓐ Ⓑ Ⓒ Ⓓ Ⓔ	17 Ⓐ Ⓑ Ⓒ Ⓓ Ⓔ
18 Ⓐ Ⓑ Ⓒ Ⓓ Ⓔ	18 Ⓐ Ⓑ Ⓒ Ⓓ Ⓔ	18 Ⓐ Ⓑ Ⓒ Ⓓ Ⓔ	18 Ⓐ Ⓑ Ⓒ Ⓓ Ⓔ
19 Ⓐ Ⓑ Ⓒ Ⓓ Ⓔ	19 Ⓐ Ⓑ Ⓒ Ⓓ Ⓔ	19 Ⓐ Ⓑ Ⓒ Ⓓ Ⓔ	19 Ⓐ Ⓑ Ⓒ Ⓓ Ⓔ
20 Ⓐ Ⓑ Ⓒ Ⓓ Ⓔ	20 Ⓐ Ⓑ Ⓒ Ⓓ Ⓔ	20 Ⓐ Ⓑ Ⓒ Ⓓ Ⓔ	20 Ⓐ Ⓑ Ⓒ Ⓓ Ⓔ
21 Ⓐ Ⓑ Ⓒ Ⓓ Ⓔ	21 Ⓐ Ⓑ Ⓒ Ⓓ Ⓔ	21 Ⓐ Ⓑ Ⓒ Ⓓ Ⓔ	21 Ⓐ Ⓑ Ⓒ Ⓓ Ⓔ
22 Ⓐ Ⓑ Ⓒ Ⓓ Ⓔ	22 Ⓐ Ⓑ Ⓒ Ⓓ Ⓔ	22 Ⓐ Ⓑ Ⓒ Ⓓ Ⓔ	22 Ⓐ Ⓑ Ⓒ Ⓓ Ⓔ
23 Ⓐ Ⓑ Ⓒ Ⓓ Ⓔ	23 Ⓐ Ⓑ Ⓒ Ⓓ Ⓔ	23 Ⓐ Ⓑ Ⓒ Ⓓ Ⓔ	23 Ⓐ Ⓑ Ⓒ Ⓓ Ⓔ
24 Ⓐ Ⓑ Ⓒ Ⓓ Ⓔ	24 Ⓐ Ⓑ Ⓒ Ⓓ Ⓔ	24 Ⓐ Ⓑ Ⓒ Ⓓ Ⓔ	24 Ⓐ Ⓑ Ⓒ Ⓓ Ⓔ
25 Ⓐ Ⓑ Ⓒ Ⓓ Ⓔ	25 Ⓐ Ⓑ Ⓒ Ⓓ Ⓔ	25 Ⓐ Ⓑ Ⓒ Ⓓ Ⓔ	25 Ⓐ Ⓑ Ⓒ Ⓓ Ⓔ
26 Ⓐ Ⓑ Ⓒ Ⓓ Ⓔ	26 Ⓐ Ⓑ Ⓒ Ⓓ Ⓔ	26 Ⓐ Ⓑ Ⓒ Ⓓ Ⓔ	26 Ⓐ Ⓑ Ⓒ Ⓓ Ⓔ
27 Ⓐ Ⓑ Ⓒ Ⓓ Ⓔ	27 Ⓐ Ⓑ Ⓒ Ⓓ Ⓔ	27 Ⓐ Ⓑ Ⓒ Ⓓ Ⓔ	27 Ⓐ Ⓑ Ⓒ Ⓓ Ⓔ
28 Ⓐ Ⓑ Ⓒ Ⓓ Ⓔ	28 Ⓐ Ⓑ Ⓒ Ⓓ Ⓔ	28 Ⓐ Ⓑ Ⓒ Ⓓ Ⓔ	28 Ⓐ Ⓑ Ⓒ Ⓓ Ⓔ
29 Ⓐ Ⓑ Ⓒ Ⓓ Ⓔ	29 Ⓐ Ⓑ Ⓒ Ⓓ Ⓔ	29 Ⓐ Ⓑ Ⓒ Ⓓ Ⓔ	29 Ⓐ Ⓑ Ⓒ Ⓓ Ⓔ
30 Ⓐ Ⓑ Ⓒ Ⓓ Ⓔ	30 Ⓐ Ⓑ Ⓒ Ⓓ Ⓔ	30 Ⓐ Ⓑ Ⓒ Ⓓ Ⓔ	30 Ⓐ Ⓑ Ⓒ Ⓓ Ⓔ

CUT HERE

TEST OF COMMUNICATION SKILLS

SECTION I: LISTENING

Time: 30 Minutes
32 Questions

Cut out pages 449 through 453 as shown and give them to a friend to read aloud to you. (In the actual exam, a tape recorder will be used.) These pages contain the script of the listening questions, statements, conversations, and talks for Practice Test 2, Parts A, B, and C. Ask the reader to allow 10 to 15 seconds after each question for you to mark your answer. Turn to page 455 where you will find the answer choices for each of the questions. Read the directions before beginning each part of Section I.

Questions, Statements, Conversations, and Talks—Script

Part A: Questions and Statements

1. How long will the state hiring freeze last?

2. As automobiles get smaller and more economical, they also become more dangerous.

3. The study of the past helps us to understand the present and improve the future.

4. After he quit smoking, Hal began to gain weight, so he decided to follow a plan for eating less.

5. Is admission to the museum free on Tuesday?

6. By closing five schools, the district will save enough money to upgrade facilities throughout the county.

7. Are video games just a temporary phenomenon?

8. One month after his automobile warranty expired, Dolph's transmission fell apart.

9. No televisions were sold last week, but ten have been sold this week because the price of each was reduced.

10. Have you finished last night's homework yet?

455

11. The citizens opposing the ballot proposal were disappointed at the outcome of the election.

12. The principal offered every teacher a lighter student load; at the same time he announced an increase in next year's salaries.

Part B: Conversations

Questions 13 and 14 are based on the following conversation.

Woman: I have been trying to reach you all morning, sir; the results of your tests are all very encouraging.

Man: Well, thanks for the news, doctor. I've been out of the office all morning, worried every minute that the news would be bad.

Woman: We would like to run one more test. Nothing to worry about. Could you be here at 9:00 tomorrow morning?

Man: Whatever you say.

13. The woman's profession is probably which of the following?

14. How are the two people probably speaking?

Questions 15 and 16 are based on the following conversation.

Boy: How do you spell *alfalfa*? Is it a-l-f-a-l-f-a?

Girl: Well, I just learned that *p-h* sounds like *f*, so you'd better spell it a-l-p-h-a-l-p-h-a.

Boy: That can't be right. Too many letters.

15. Which of the following assumptions is the girl making?

16. Which of the following assumptions is the boy making?

Questions 17 and 18 are based on the following conversation.

Woman: Tomorrow's meeting has been canceled because no one except Dodsworth can make it then.

Man: Yes, but Dodsworth cannot make it at any other time.

Woman: What happens if Dodsworth misses the meeting?

Man: Well, every meeting she has missed has turned into a fight.

17. The man implies that Dodsworth does what at the meeting?

18. What is one possible reason that the woman asks her question?

Questions 19 and 20 are based on the following conversation.

Man: Channel 8 has predicted my loss, so I'd better concede.

Woman: But Channel 12 has predicted your victory.

Man: Oh well, then conceding would make me look foolish.

Woman: Why don't we wait to hear Channel 4's prediction and then decide what to do?

19. What is it that the man may have won or lost?

20. What does neither speaker consider?

Part C: Talks

Questions 21, 22, and 23 refer to the following talk.

Learning may not be a matter of efficiency, but getting through school certainly is. Usually by the time students are juniors in college, they realize that getting A's depends upon disciplined study techniques. After suffering the pain of repeated academic failure, they realize that a simple matter of scheduling one's time, reviewing class notes regularly and systematically, and memorizing key terms and concepts can save hours of last-minute cramming and make anxiety a thing of the past. And they may also realize something far more important—that the efficient handling of their academic chores frees them to read and write leisurely, to wonder and speculate about the matters that mean most to them, to learn more about themselves and their world than is available in homework and tests.

21. What does the speaker encourage in this talk?

22. What does the speaker conclude about schoolwork?

23. What assumption does the speaker make about students?

Questions 24, 25, and 26 refer to the following talk.

Some people argue that a poem can mean anything you want it to mean. They look at it this way: Every reader is different and brings to every poem his or her own unique background and experience. For instance, as I read Randall Jarrell's poem about the death of an aerial gunner during World War II, I may conclude that the poem is about the horror of war and the ugliness of death. However, others have concluded that the poem praises courage and bravery in the face of death. In most cases, those who see the poem as an argument against war are those who were against war before they began reading, and those who see the poem as a glorification of courage were advocates of military courage and bravery before they began reading. In short, how you read a poem depends on the beliefs and attitudes you bring to it. A poem always means something but may not always mean the same thing to everyone.

24. What is the speaker's main point in this talk?

25. According to the speaker, what role do a person's beliefs and attitudes play in the reading of a poem?

26. What may we infer from this talk about readers who share similar beliefs and attitudes?

Questions 27, 28, and 29 refer to the following talk.

As our students get better at scoring high on objective tests, they get worse at reading, writing, and critical thinking. This is the major conclusion of the recent National Assessment of Educational Progress, which finds fault with the popular "back to basics" movement. For many, "back to basics" meant back to multiple-choice tests that reduce writing to the rules and regulations of grammar and reduce reading to finding the answers to the questions quickly. Students aiming at high scores on objective tests rarely practice any sustained writing, rarely read for pleasure, and rarely take the time to think long and carefully about a subject. Instead, these students pay attention to only the "data" that will help them to pass the test. And teachers concerned with their students' achieving higher test scores may teach only the data that will help them to pass objective tests. Consequently, a broader appreciation of reading, writing, and thinking is lost to our children.

27. What is the speaker's attitude toward objective tests?

28. How does the speaker support the conclusions about objective tests?

29. According to the speaker, which movement in education deserves criticism?

Questions 30, 31, and 32 refer to the following talk.

A national commission has concluded that education in this country is mediocre. And one of their major solutions to this problem is itself mediocre, if not worse. They say we should lengthen the school day and add days to the school year. And they say this without realizing that the quantity of time children spend in school does not improve the quality of their education. The only quantity that affects the quality of learning is the quantity of students each teacher must deal with. *That* quantity must be reduced so that each student receives more personal attention and so that teachers are not so exhausted from managing an overcrowded classroom that they cannot listen or respond well to their students. Let us increase the number of teachers in order to decrease the

CUT HERE

number of students per teacher, and let us not merely add more hours and days of overcrowded conditions.

30. What does the speaker recommend for improving the quality of education?

31. What does the speaker assume about the personal attention each student receives now?

32. What relationship does the speaker refer to throughout the talk?

CUT HERE

Answer Choices

Part A: Questions and Statements

DIRECTIONS

You will be faced with two kinds of problems. You must either answer a short question or understand a brief statement. Each question and each statement will be spoken one time. After you hear a question, you will read four answer choices; select the correct answer. After you hear a statement, you will read four sentences; select the sentence closest to the meaning of the statement or supported by the statement.

1. (A) Not all state agencies have frozen their hiring.
   (B) Protests against the freeze will have some effect.
   (C) The last freeze was two years ago.
   (D) The freeze will end this summer if the state budget is approved.

2. (A) Reckless drivers often purchase small cars.
   (B) The full-size automobiles are all safe.
   (C) A less expensive car isn't necessarily more safe.
   (D) Drivers concerned about their safety are rarely rich.

3. (A) Don't live in the past.
   (B) All our present problems have occurred in the past.
   (C) History is a worthwhile subject.
   (D) History should not be studied by everyone.

4. (A) Hal started a diet.
   (B) Hal feared the effects of smoking and overeating.
   (C) Hal began to exercise regularly.
   (D) Hal was in awful physical shape.

5. (A) Admission is higher for adults than for children.
   (B) Many of the exhibits are closed on Tuesday.
   (C) Children are free, but adults pay the regular price.
   (D) No one is admitted between 4:30 and 5:00 P.M.

6. (A) The five schools being closed cannot be upgraded.
   (B) More than five schools cannot be closed.
   (C) Countywide improvements will result from the closing of five schools.
   (D) Students will be transferred to other schools.

7. (A) They keep children from reading books.
   (B) Undoubtedly they are here to stay.
   (C) The competition among video game manufacturers is fierce.
   (D) Some people like them and some people don't.

8. (A) Dolph had not cared for his transmission properly.
   (B) The automobile warranty was a standard one.
   (C) The transmission failure was not under warranty when it occurred.
   (D) Dolph had experienced other problems with his automobile.

9. (A) Many people needed televisions this week.
   (B) Reduced prices attracted buyers.
   (C) No televisions were for sale last week.
   (D) Television was less popular in the past.

10. (A) I thought that it was very long.
    (B) I finished it an hour ago.
    (C) It was very difficult to understand.
    (D) The homework was a repeat from a previous assignment.

11. (A) The ballot proposal passed.
    (B) The ballot proposal was defeated.
    (C) No similar proposal had ever appeared on the ballot.
    (D) Very few citizens opposed the ballot proposal.

12. (A) No principal had ever made such an offer.
    (B) The teachers had demanded more money.
    (C) Fewer students have been attending school lately.
    (D) Next year salaries will rise and the student load will decrease.

PROCEED DIRECTLY TO PART B.

Part B: Conversations

DIRECTIONS

You will hear short conversations between two speakers. After each conversation, a third speaker will ask questions about what the two were discussing. The conversations and each question will be spoken only once. After you hear each question, choose the best of the four possible answers.

13. (A) nurse   (C) professor
    (B) scientist   (D) physician

14. (A) in person   (C) over the radio
    (B) by phone   (D) through an intercom

---

15. (A) Certain *f* sounds are spelled with *f*.
    (B) No *p-h* sounds are spelled with *f*.
    (C) All *f* sounds are spelled with *p-h*.
    (D) She knows nothing about spelling.

16. (A) The spelling of a word is related to how long it takes to pronounce it.
    (B) The girl's knowledge of spelling must be right.
    (C) Any spelling of *alfalfa* will do.
    (D) Correct spelling is a mystery.

17. (A) keeps everyone away
    (B) maintains order
    (C) keeps the proceedings lively
    (D) stays silent

18. (A) She has never been to one of the meetings being discussed without Dodsworth.
    (B) She does not know the purpose of the meeting.
    (C) She has no idea who Dodsworth is.
    (D) She will not attend a meeting without Dodsworth.

19. (A) a contract   (C) respect
    (B) a raffle   (D) an election

20. (A) the conflicting predictions
    (B) the wisdom of a concession speech
    (C) the actual results
    (D) the opinions of television stations

PROCEED DIRECTLY TO PART C.

Part C: Talks

DIRECTIONS

You will hear several shorts talks, each followed by questions. When you hear a question, choose the best answer of the four printed in your test booklet. Remember that the talks and questions will be spoken only once, so you must listen carefully while you attempt to understand and remember what the speaker says.

21. (A) less attention to schoolwork
    (B) a straight-A average
    (C) efficient study habits
    (D) homework and tests

22. (A) It does not offer students all there is to learn.
    (B) Good students can make it a thing of the past.
    (C) It becomes irrelevant once one enters college.
    (D) It should be done in a leisurely fashion.

23. (A) The best of them have photographic memories.
    (B) They never read and write except to complete a school assignment.
    (C) Most of them do not employ good study techniques through their high school years.
    (D) They rarely fail in school.

24. (A) People who argue about poetry are ignorant.
    (B) Randall Jarrell was a typical poet in that his poems weren't clear.
    (C) Poems about war are especially difficult to understand.
    (D) Different people derive different meanings from poetry.

25. (A) They complicate the meaning of the poem.
    (B) They contradict the meaning of the poem.
    (C) They determine the reader's concept of the meaning of the poem.
    (D) They must be more objective than they are.

26. (A) They will not find poetry meaningful.
    (B) They will not be understood by other readers.
    (C) They must change their beliefs before they can read poetry.
    (D) They may understand a poem in a similar way.

27. (A) neutral   (C) positive
    (B) objective   (D) negative

28. (A) by citing a national survey
    (B) by speculating based on intuition
    (C) by asking students what they think
    (D) by gathering statistics

29. (A) reading and writing   (C) data processing
    (B) back to basics   (D) critical thinking

30. (A) more teachers   (C) more money
    (B) more students   (D) more school days

31. (A) It is too late in the year.   (C) It will never change.
    (B) It is too early in the day.   (D) It is not enough.

32. (A) the relationship between quantity and quality
    (B) the relationship between problems and solutions
    (C) the relationship between parents and teachers
    (D) the relationship between length and number

STOP. IF YOU FINISH BEFORE TIME IS UP, CHECK YOUR WORK ON THIS SECTION ONLY. DO NOT WORK ON ANY OTHER SECTION OF THE TEST.

SECTION II: READING

Time: 30 Minutes
32 Questions

DIRECTIONS

A question or number of questions follow each of the statements or passages in this section. Using only the *stated* or *implied* information given in the statement or passage, answer the question or questions by choosing the *best* answer from among the choices given.

Questions 1, 2, and 3 refer to the following passage.

Art as experience is the view advocated by John Dewey (1859–1952). He is especially critical of the way in which art has so often been described as something that is separated from the common and ordinary experiences of everyday life. He holds that aesthetic values are possible in all walks of life and they are by no means confined to the objects located in museums or art galleries. In primitive societies art is associated with common objects such as domestic utensils and personal adornment. It is our task to restore the sense of continuity between aesthetic enjoyment and the common experiences of life. Art is a quality that permeates experiences and idealizes those activities which form a part of one's daily life. In characterizing art as experience he does not mean to imply that all experiences are works of art. Art is that particular kind of experience in which one finds unity, meaning, harmony, and fulfillment. It may occur in connection with almost any of life's activities. It may be the response which one makes to a sunset, looking at a flower, or even the eating of a delicious meal. It is the type of event that is indicated when one says, "That *was* an experience." The Greeks identified the good with grace, proportion, and harmony. For Dewey these same qualities are associated with art. Although art is not to be identified with either the intellectual or moral, it may be associated with either of them. The experience of thinking may have an aesthetic quality and the same is true of moral conduct.

1. According to this discussion of Dewey's ideas, which of the following might Dewey classify as an artist?
    (A) a barbarian
    (B) anyone who has an experience
    (C) a gourmet chef
    (D) all members of primitive societies
    (E) any description of a common experience

2. Which of the following titles suggests the broad definition of art advocated by Dewey?
    (A) *The Art of Nineteenth-Century Landscape Painting*
    (B) *The Art of Motorcycle Maintenance*
    (C) *The Art of Insignificant Experiences*
    (D) *The Art of Classical Chinese Sculpture*
    (E) *Art for the Elite*

3. We may infer which of the following from the final sentence?
    (A) Moral conduct and thinking usually have the same quality.
    (B) Thinking can never be separated from experience.
    (C) Those who exercise moral conduct are almost always thoughtful.
    (D) An "artistic" thinker finds unity, harmony, and fulfillment through thinking.
    (E) All thinkers are artists.

Much learning is formal, that is, deliberately transmitted by such agents as teachers or parents. For example, children are deliberately taught to respect the flag, be honest, and work hard. However, a great deal of learning is picked up unconsciously, the result of spontaneous and unplanned interaction. For example, a teenager's attitude and behavior toward the opposite sex is shaped by his or her interaction with other teenagers.

4. Which of the following would the author consider an example of informal learning?
    (A) At one time or another in all children's lives, their parents lecture them on the "value of a dollar."
    (B) "Sex education" is a class taught in most high schools these days.
    (C) Experience teaches us more about human relationships than any textbook.
    (D) Children in other countries are taught to respect the flag.
    (E) Teenagers who are inexperienced socially are often counseled by their older siblings.

The interpretations we make of the reactions of others are not always accurate, so we may have a more positive or negative self-image than is warranted by the actual opinions of others toward us.

5. What is the author's point in the above passage?
    (A) We always see ourselves just as others see us.
    (B) Others often form no opinion of our self-image.

(C) We do not always see ourselves as others see us.
(D) After learning what others think, we will be less likely to be ourselves.
(E) Our opinions of others are always figments of our imaginations.

Zuni or Hopi Indians believe that competition is socially unacceptable. I am dismayed by the possibility that if a Zuni or Hopi tribesman were watching the World Series he would react with disapproval rather than root for his favorite team.

6. Which of the following terms expresses the author's attitude toward the Zuni or Hopi belief about competition?
   (A) approval   (D) disapproval
   (B) hatred   (E) outrage
   (C) cheerfulness

Questions 7, 8, and 9 refer to the following passage.

[1]Although satisfaction is a very common term, it is difficult to define. [2]One can identify the cost of a sweater or a pair of shoes, but there are real problems in defining the magnitude of satisfaction derived from these goods. [3]In response to this problem, economists have developed the concept of utility, which means about the same thing as satisfaction and is quantitatively measured in terms of *utils*. [4]It is not assumed that consumers or the economist actually calculates the absolute number of utils derived from the purchase or use of goods, but it is assumed that consumers can specify the *relative* utility derived from goods. [5]That is, economists assume that the consumer can rank-order the utility that is obtained from all goods consumed. [6]Furthermore, it is assumed that the individual seeks to use his or her limited income in such a way that the satisfaction or utility derived from the consumption of any particular set of goods is maximized.

7. The author would agree with which of the following conclusions?
   (A) Certain products satisfy everyone equally.
   (B) A product worth one util to one person will be worth that much to most other people.
   (C) The amount of satisfaction one derives is tied to the relative utility of a product.
   (D) Individuals with limited income are usually more satisfied with a pair of shoes than with a sweater.
   (E) Before utility can be determined, a product must be purchased.

8. The second sentence provides which of the following?
   (A) supporting detail for the first sentence
   (B) evidence that contrasts with the argument of the first sentence
   (C) a new, general point
   (D) an evaluation of the argument in the first sentence
   (E) a deliberately unreasonable example

9. If the fourth sentence is true, which of the following must also be true?
   (A) In some countries, satisfaction is a mathematical constant.
   (B) I can specify the utility of my typewriter by comparing its value with that of other goods I possess.
   (C) Economists are full of assumptions about utility that are unfounded.
   (D) The utility of a sweater will never be comparable to that of a pair of shoes.
   (E) The more I wear my sweater, the less useful it becomes.

Questions 10 through 13 refer to the following passage.

The President of the United States is the most powerful official of any democratic state in the world. The President has been characterized by some writers as the most powerful official in the history of the world. And yet, the powers and prerogatives demanded of American Presidents have undoubtedly caused many of them to wring their hands in frustration, stalemated in the courses of action they deemed best for the nation and its people.

The authors of the United States Constitution were quite indefinite about what they considered to be the proper role of the President in the American government. Article II of the Constitution, which creates the presidency, is both brief and sketchy when compared with the length and detail of Article I, which created and circumscribed the legislative branch of government.

Because of the brevity of Article II, the great powers of the President of the United States grow less out of the Constitution than they do out of practice, precedent, and custom. Once a President exercises a power, that exercise has established a precedent which will serve as a source of power for future Presidents.

Those who wrote the United States Constitution created a presidency which is not duplicated by any governmental system in the world. The American presidency is unique in the assemblage of powers vested in a single leader, unique in the way the leader is chosen, and equally unique in the relationship between the leader and the legislative branch of government.

10. Which of the following is most likely the audience for this passage?
   (A) members of the United States Senate
   (B) teachers of American government
   (C) students of American government
   (D) candidates for the presidency
   (E) anyone interested in becoming a powerful official

11. We may infer which of the following from the author's comparison of Article II with Article I?
   (A) The authors of the Constitution had not thought carefully about the presidency.
   (B) The authors of the Constitution did not think that the President had a proper role.
   (C) The proper role of the legislative branch is explained more fully than that of the President.
   (D) The legislative branch is more important than the executive branch.
   (E) Many of the original authors of the Constitution were legislators.

12. If the information in paragraph 3 is true, which of the following must also be true?
   (A) President Johnson's decision to escalate the war in Vietnam may serve as a precedent for the current President if faced with a similar situation.
   (B) Anyone who makes an unprecedented decision has not sufficiently studied the political decisions of past American Presidents.
   (C) The power to make war and peace has changed from President to President.
   (D) Any President who is not familiar with the precedents set by former Presidents will almost never exercise any power at all.
   (E) Countries younger than the United States have accumulated fewer precedents.

13. Which of the following types of information would most strengthen the first paragraph of the passage?
   (A) the naming of those public servants other than Presidents who have had frustrating careers
   (B) a definition of what the author means by *history of the world*
   (C) the naming of which Presidents did not *wring their hands in frustration*
   (D) examples of Presidents *stalemated in the courses of action they deemed best for the nation and its people*
   (E) a clinical discussion of frustration

Peer pressure affects the members of a group to a marked degree, sometimes assuming dictatorial powers over the individual. For example, various studies have shown that brilliant students will actually work below their capacity when academic performance is devalued in their peer group.

14. The above passage supports which of the following statements?
    (A) One student who liked and respected his teacher ridiculed her whenever the other students did likewise.
    (B) Although the majority of students in a class decided to wear green on St. Patrick's Day, a number of their peers did not do so.
    (C) Students surveyed reported that they were only slightly influenced by what their classmates thought of them.
    (D) Each of the English teachers at Murphy Junior High uses the same textbook to teach the eighth-grade composition class.
    (E) Often, one student has tried to tell all of the other students what to think and believe.

Since the time of the Greek city-states, one position has been that education is the acquiring of an *ability* to think and reason, not merely the learning of information.

15. We may infer that the Greek teachers holding the position expressed above stressed which of the following for their students?
    (A) where knowledge could be found
    (B) how to think and reason
    (C) the names and dates of important historical events
    (D) the facts found in encyclopedias
    (E) the value of information

Henry George's solution to the uneven distribution of wealth in the United States was a single tax on land. In his book *Progress and Poverty* George argued that this one tax would not only create general prosperity but also make other taxes unnecessary.

16. Which of the following phrases describes the author's tone in this passage?
    (A) objectively descriptive   (D) openly angry
    (B) whimsically skeptical   (E) mildly scornful
    (C) cautiously curious

The philosophical system championed by William James and John Dewey was called pragmatism. This peculiarly American philosophy emphasized fact over theory. As James himself put it, "The true is the name of whatever proves itself to be good in the way of belief, and good, too, for definite, assignable reasons."

17. James would probably agree with which of the following statements?
   (A) The unexamined truth is the best truth.
   (B) Truth and justice are to be obeyed, not investigated.
   (C) The true cannot be determined.
   (D) Truth must be felt rather than believed and understood.
   (E) Whatever people believe with good reason and to good effect is true.

Questions 18 through 21 refer to the following passage.

Art as play is the theory which attempts to bridge the gap between eternal reality and the concrete activities of everyday life. It interprets artistic creation as a spontaneous activity that grows out of the surplus energy in the individual. Unlike labor, which involves stress, effort, and deprivation in order to achieve some particular end, play is a free and spontaneous expression of superfluous energy that is not performed as a means for something else. The instinctive character of the play impulse can be seen in the activities of the lower animals. After their physical needs have been satisfied the surplus energy which still remains finds an outlet in play. The same is true in the life of the small child and with variations it continues into the adult life. Art has its beginnings in this play impulse, and though it develops into something that is more than play, it still retains the element of spontaneity. The artist creates not from a sense of duty or simply for the sake of earning a living but because of an inner urge which will not allow the artist to do otherwise. It is not until the imagination has become regulated and controlled that the product of the play impulse becomes an aesthetic object. This is what happens when form takes possession of the material and imposes certain standards of taste on it. Sometimes the difference between play and art has been explained by saying that play is the activity of the "lower powers" of the organism, while art is the activity of the "higher powers."

18. Which of the following best summarizes the content of the passage?
   (A) Without a sense of duty, one cannot create art.
   (B) Play is an instinctive impulse which has a role in art
   (C) Playful artists exercise their lower powers only.
   (D) Most adults forget all about play.
   (E) Eternal reality has almost no connection with art.

19. The passage would probably appear in which of the following?
    (A) an editorial on the energy crisis
    (B) a book about the childhood of modern artists
    (C) an encyclopedia entry on art
    (D) a book on play activities for children
    (E) a magazine for artists

20. The author of the passage would agree with all of the following *except*
    (A) pure play is free and spontaneous
    (B) there is an element of playfulness in art
    (C) work and play are different activities
    (D) play and art are not the same
    (E) children at play are really young artists

21. What is an unstated assumption behind the second sentence, which defines art as play as a *spontaneous activity that grows out of the surplus energy in an individual?*
    (A) People with no energy left will not engage in art as play.
    (B) Individuals almost never engage in art as play.
    (C) A playful artist is always spontaneous.
    (D) Surplus energy produces nothing but art.
    (E) Devoting surplus energy to activities other than art is wrong.

Questions 22 through 26 refer to the following passage.

The question of teaching a foreign language in the elementary school continues to be sketchy and mildly controversial. Some proponents list two good reasons for the teaching of a foreign language: (1) because of America's present role in the world, more American children need to acquire culture, preferably through the medium of a foreign language, and (2) young children learn to speak foreign languages more easily, and with more accurate accent, than do older children or grownups.

The elementary school faces a number of problems with relation to the addition of foreign languages to the already crowded curriculum. The question of time and how to fit language instruction into the daily program is uppermost. Another question is that of who will teach it? The regular classroom teacher or a specialist?

At the present time television appears to have temporarily solved the problems of cost and the shortage of qualified teachers. However, the usual problem yet prevails. All too often, schools have started enthusiastically with foreign languages but have failed to carry on the work consistently for a sustained period of years. Typically, a foreign language program will begin in a school with great fanfare, only to be

found, upon another glance two years later, to have faded into a
memory.

22. We may infer which of the following from the third paragraph?
    (A) Children prefer television to learning.
    (B) Unqualified teachers prefer watching television to teaching.
    (C) Foreign language courses are taught on television.
    (D) Foreigners on television are often just as good as qualified teach-
        ers.
    (E) Foreign television programs help children to learn foreign lan-
        guages.

23. Which of the following would clarify point (1) in the first paragraph?
    (A) an explanation of *America's present role*
    (B) a description of the foreign language courses taught on television
    (C) a story about a grownup with a learning problem
    (D) an admission that many speakers of foreign languages are not
        cultured
    (E) speculation about whether teachers are cultured or not

24. Which of the following is an implied question that the author does *not*
    answer?
    (A) What are two reasons for teaching a foreign language?
    (B) Why do foreign language programs *fade* after two years?
    (C) What are some of the questions and problems related to adding
        foreign languages to the curriculum?
    (D) How many foreign languages should a child learn?
    (E) What of those children for whom the native language is "foreign"?

25. What is the most appropriate title for this passage?
    (A) *Foreign Languages: Their Cause and Cure*
    (B) *Problems in Elementary Schools*
    (C) *The Duties of the Classroom Teacher*
    (D) *Teaching a Foreign Language in the Elementary School*
    (E) *TV Learning: Will It Work?*

26. If point (2) in the first paragraph is true, which of the following must
    also be true?
    (A) A thirty-year-old will find it more difficult to learn a foreign
        language than will a six-year-old.
    (B) Younger children are more interested in foreign languages than are
        adults.
    (C) Young children cannot speak their native language easily.
    (D) Teachers cannot speak as well as their students.
    (E) Young children can learn to write in a foreign language more easily
        than adults.

Questions 27 through 32 refer to the following passage.

Nursery schools and kindergartens are prep schools for first grade. Right or wrong, this is the point of view of many parents, teachers, and administrators today. Perhaps the term *prep school* is inappropriate and distasteful. It denotes a certain kind of pressure—pressure on teachers to have preschool children at a certain point in reading when they enter first grade, pressure on parents to flit here and there in locating materials for home enrichment and wondering whom to believe among all the "authorities" (lay people and educators) on the teaching of reading.

This frenzy on the part of many parents and teachers has created a contagious frustration and concern about what is best for children in the long run versus hurried efforts to prepare them for a magical moment by September of a given year. It is as though we have to initiate a "crash program" in order to manufacture fifty tanks within thirty days or to train fifty recruits within six weeks. Why are we in such a hurry? What is so significantly important about being six years of age that was not of being three, four, or five years of age?

Can some kindergarteners read? Yes, a few may be reading quite early on their own initiative. Aren't American children as bright as children from other countries? If five-year-olds in Scotland are successful in learning to read, surely American children are as bright! When some American parents and teachers learn this sort of information they tend to initiate efforts to close the gap immediately.

27. What is the author's attitude toward pressuring children to learn to read before reaching kindergarten?
    (A) negative
    (B) optimistic
    (C) angry
    (D) hopeful
    (E) neutral

28. For what reason does the author use the term *frenzy* in the second paragraph?
    (A) to characterize scientifically the activities of parents and teachers
    (B) to stress the calm, careful attitude of parents and teachers
    (C) to suggest that the activities of parents and teachers are rushed
    (D) to give parents and teachers credit for their concern
    (E) to imply that parents and teachers are insecure about their own reading abilities

29. The analogy given in the second paragraph suggests a comparison between students and which of the following?
    (A) parents
    (B) war
    (C) soldiers
    (D) crash pilots
    (E) munitions experts

30. We may conclude that the author's point of view is opposed to the points of view of which of the following?
    (A) nursery school owners, students, and legislators
    (B) parents, teachers, and administrators
    (C) kindergarteners, recruits, and parents
    (D) readers, nonreaders, and writers
    (E) Americans, Scots, and Britons

31. What is the primary purpose of the passage?
    (A) to describe modern preschool programs
    (B) to argue against pressuring children to read early
    (C) to survey American educational practices
    (D) to compare American schools with Scottish schools
    (E) to praise progressive education

32. The structure of the final paragraph may be described as
    (A) question/answer
    (B) thesis/example
    (C) anecdote/conclusion
    (D) suggestion/statistics
    (E) topic/illustration

STOP. IF YOU FINISH BEFORE TIME IS UP, CHECK YOUR WORK ON THIS SECTION ONLY. DO NOT WORK ANY OTHER SECTION OF THE TEST.

SECTION III: WRITING—MULTIPLE CHOICE

Time: 30 Minutes for Both Parts
45 Questions

Part A: Usage (Suggested Time 10 Minutes, 25 Questions)

DIRECTIONS

Some of the following sentences are correct. Others contain problems in grammar, usage, sentence construction, punctuation, and wordiness. There is not more than one error in any sentence. If there is an error, it will be underlined and lettered. Find the one underlined part that must be changed to make the sentence correct and choose the corresponding letter on your answer sheet. Mark (E) if the sentence contains no error.

1. Some <u>symphonic arrangements</u> of the Beatles tunes <u>sound</u> more
   A   B
   <u>melodiously</u> than the original Beatles <u>band versions</u>. <u>No error</u>
   C   D   E

2. The scientist <u>reported</u> his latest laboratory findings <u>as to the</u>
   A   B
   <u>biochemical and physiological</u> causes of alcohol <u>addiction</u>. <u>No error</u>
   C   D   E

3. Black Americans were <u>legally enfranchised</u> by ratification of the
   A
   Fourteenth and Fifteenth <u>Amendments and by subsequent</u> acts of
   B
   <u>Congress, but enforcement</u> of their voting rights <u>has remained</u>
   C   D
   a continuing struggle. <u>No error</u>
   E

4. <u>Of the twelve teachers,</u> Mr. Feingold was the <u>more widely</u> respected
   A   B
   because of <u>his reputation</u> of fairness and consistency <u>in grading</u>
   C   D
   his students. <u>No error</u>
   E

5. After discussing the <u>depleted</u> treasury with <u>Mr. Taylor</u>, John felt
                    A   B

   that <u>he should have been</u> the one to head the committee's fundraising
             C

   drive <u>in November, 1980.</u> <u>No error</u>
          D   E

6. The rookie first <u>baseman, who</u> was a better player than most of the
                      A

   veterans, could <u>throw, catch,</u> and hit <u>more consistent</u> than any player
                B   C

   with <u>twice</u> the years of experience. <u>No error</u>
        D   E

7. "<u>Who</u> cares whether poor people <u>can take</u> care of themselves or
      A   B

   not?" <u>asked</u> the rich old <u>woman while</u> munching her caviar
         C   D

   dreamily. <u>No error</u>
             E

8. Hoping <u>to reserve</u> a room at an inexpensive <u>hotel Bill</u> phoned
           A   B

   many lodgings before he <u>concluded that</u> cheap accommodations
                     C

   were impossible to find. <u>No error</u>
     D   E

9. The Venus's-flytrap, a <u>well-known</u> carnivorous plant <u>that eats animals,</u>
                     A   B

   <u>responds</u> almost <u>instantaneously</u> to an entering insect. <u>No error</u>
     C   D   E

10. The <u>drama's</u> charm might be seen as <u>being comprised of</u> these
        A   B

    elements : an extraordinary leading <u>lady, an</u> exceptionally vivid
        C   D

    rendering by all players of the author's intent, and an exquisite
    set design. <u>No error</u>
              E

11. A major task of the reader of instructional materials in science <u>is</u>
                                                A

    to understand a <u>host</u> of details in <u>their</u> textbook that <u>lead</u> up
                B   C   D

    to generalizations or abstractions. <u>No error</u>
                              E

12. "It is a matter of <u>principal</u>," he <u>said</u>, "and I will not be
                            A   **B**

    <u>dissuaded from</u> the task at hand." <u>No error</u>
         C   **D**   **E**

13. With tears in their <u>eyes, the</u> mourners, <u>including the</u>
                       A   **B**

    widow of the late John T. Smith, <u>filed by</u> the <u>grave and</u> then
               B   **C**   **D**

    returned to their cars for the long journey home. <u>No error</u>
                                           E

14. <u>Unable</u> to keep a secret, he <u>announced</u> the <u>stupidity of his friend</u>
     A   **B**   **C**

    to <u>each and every member</u> of the class. <u>No error</u>
             D   **E**

15. <u>Either he meant to arrive at the business meeting</u> in time for the
                       A

    <u>chairman's</u> opening statement or the sales manager's <u>report ;</u>
        B   **C**

    in any <u>case ,</u> he missed both. <u>No error</u>
           D   **E**

16. The recitation of national <u>ills</u> <u>are not enough</u> to stem a regrettable
                             A   **B**

    <u>tendency toward</u> increased lobbying by self-interest groups, <u>which</u>
         C   **D**

    ignore the nation's larger concerns. <u>No error</u>
                            E

17. I must confess that it was <u>I</u> who <u>broke</u> the mirror, <u>not him,</u> the
                      A   **B**   **C**

    <u>person who</u> was blamed for it. <u>No error</u>
        D   **E**

18. The Greek <u>slave, Aesop,</u> had <u>the ability to</u> <u>translate</u> into memorable
               A   **B**   **C**

    stories the <u>idiosyncrasies ,</u> faults, and virtues of the people around him.
                   D

    <u>No error</u>
      E

19. In spite of <u>arguments to the contrary,</u> every bit of evidence submitted
                   A

    <u>infers</u> that the fire, <u>which</u> burned out of control, began in a highly
      B   **C**

    <u>inflammable</u> pile of kerosene-soaked rags. <u>No error</u>
        D   **E**

20. The typical plantation mansion <u>had</u> a high-columned <u>porch that</u> not
                                      A   B
    <u>only shaded</u> the first-floor rooms but gave the mansion an
          C
    appearance of <u>grandeur</u>. <u>No error</u>
                       D   E

21. Not one of the teacher's strict <u>recommendations concerning</u> punctuality
                                                   A
    was enforced vigorously <u>irregardless</u> of <u>the fact that</u> cases of tardiness
     B   C   D
    were increasing. <u>No error</u>
                          E

22. There <u>seems</u> to be no documented record <u>that</u> people accused of
                A   B
    witchcraft in seventeenth-century Salem were burned to
    <u>death however</u>, victims accused of being witches were hanged
           C
    after <u>being tried</u> and convicted. <u>No error</u>
               D   E

23. Sarah could <u>not</u> scarcely <u>believe</u> that her younger sister, who was
                  A   B
    habitually late, was <u>all ready</u> to leave when she <u>arrived</u> to
                              C   D
    pick her up. <u>No error</u>
                      E

24. <u>Increasingly insecure</u> and shy, the child <u>chose</u> <u>that of her mother</u>
              A   B   C
    rather than the help of any of her <u>friends</u>. <u>No error</u>
                                             D   E

25. If <u>one reads</u> the newspaper every day, you <u>will be surprised</u> at the
          A   B
    <u>improvement</u> in your <u>overall reading skills</u>. <u>No error</u>
          C   D   E

PROCEED DIRECTLY TO THE SENTENCE CORRECTION QUESTIONS.

Part B: Sentence Correction (Suggested Time 20 Minutes, 20 Questions)

DIRECTIONS

Some part of each sentence below is underlined; sometimes the whole
sentence is underlined. Five choices for rephrasing the underlined part follow
each sentence; the first choice (A) repeats the original, and the other four are

different. If choice (A) seems better than the alternatives, choose answer
(A); if not, choose one of the others.

For each sentence, consider the requirements of standard written English.
Your choice should be a correct and effective expression, not awkward or
ambiguous. Focus on grammar, sentence structure, punctuation, wordiness,
and word choice. If a choice changes the meaning of the original sentence, do
not select it.

26. Many professional-football fans feel Jim Plunkett is <u>the best quarter-
    back when compared to</u> Dan Fouts.
    (A) the best quarterback when compared to
    (B) a better quarterback than
    (C) one of the best quarterbacks when compared to
    (D) the best quarterback that compared to
    (E) the best quarterback compared to

27. Many college freshmen with poor writing skills <u>are liable from making
    careless grammar and punctuation errors</u>, but many writing instructors
    try to teach them to be more self-corrective.
    (A) are liable from making careless grammar and punctuation errors
    (B) are liable from making careless grammar and punctuation
        mistakes
    (C) are liable to make careless grammar and punctuation errors
    (D) are careless and liable to make grammar and punctuation errors
    (E) are liable for making careless grammar and punctuation errors

28. The mayor, in addition to the city council members, <u>are contemplating
    the rezoning</u> of a hundred acres of undeveloped land within the city
    limits.
    (A) are contemplating the rezoning
    (B) are contemplating rezoning
    (C) is contemplating over the rezoning
    (D) is contemplating the rezoning
    (E) all contemplate over the rezoning

29. Because of the accident <u>his insurance policy was canceled, his friends
    alienated, and his car abandoned.</u>
    (A) his insurance policy was canceled, his friends alienated, and his car
        abandoned.
    (B) his insurance policy canceled, friends alienated, and car aban-
        doned.
    (C) he canceled his insurance policy, alienated his friends, and aban-
        doned his car.
    (D) his insurance policy was canceled, his friends were alienated, and
        his car was abandoned.
    (E) his insurance policy, his friends, and his car were canceled, alien-
        ated, and abandoned respectively.

30. The ability to understand written English improves as <u>the skills of oral language increases.</u>
   (A) the skills of oral language increases.
   (B) oral language increases.
   (C) oral language increase.
   (D) the skills of oral language increase.
   (E) the skills improve oral language.

31. <u>To function well in the business world, requires that one be willing to spend long hours preparing materials for effective visual presentations.</u>
   (A) To function well in the business world, requires that one be willing to spend long hours preparing materials for effective visual presentations.
   (B) To function good in the business world requires that one be willing to spend long hours preparing materials for effective visual presentations.
   (C) To function well in the business world, requires that one be willing to spend long hours preparing materials for affective visual presentations.
   (D) To function well in the business world, requires that one be willing and able to spend long hours preparing materials for effective visual presentations.
   (E) To function well in the business world requires that one be willing to spend long hours preparing materials for effective visual presentations.

32. Taking an occasional respite between chapters or assignments is more desirable <u>than a long, continuous period of study.</u>
   (A) than a long, continuous period of study.
   (B) than a period of long, continuous study.
   (C) than a long period of continuous study.
   (D) than studying for a long, continuous period.
   (E) than a study period long and continuous.

33. The small seagoing craft was washed against the rocks <u>while the captain struggled to turn the wheel, and it foundered</u> with all on board.
   (A) while the captain struggled to turn the wheel, and it foundered
   (B) while the captain struggled to turn the wheel and it floundered
   (C) , while the captain struggled to turn the wheel and it foundered
   (D) because the captain struggled to turn the wheel, and it foundered
   (E) while the captain struggled to turn the wheel: and it foundered

34. Secularization of schools during the Renaissance is evidenced by school curricula that focused on the individual's place in society, de-emphasizing religious matters and became more interested in affairs of this world.
    (A) became more interested in affairs of this world.
    (B) had become more interested in affairs of this world.
    (C) became interested more in worldly affairs.
    (D) becoming more interested in affairs of this world.
    (E) interest in worldly affairs.

35. After many years of saving, worrying, and studying, she took great pride in being the first in her family to graduate college.
    (A) studying, she took great pride in being the first in her family to graduate college.
    (B) studying, she took great pride in being the first in her family to graduate from college.
    (C) study, she took great pride in being the first in her family to graduate from college.
    (D) studying, he or she took great pride in being the first family member to graduate college.
    (E) study, she took great pride in being the first in her family to be graduated from college.

36. Rolling the ball down the hill, the toddler did not see the bicycle and narrowly escaped being struck by it's front wheel.
    (A) the toddler did not see the bicycle and narrowly escaped being struck by it's front wheel.
    (B) the toddler did not see the bicycle and narrowly escaped being struck by it's front wheels.
    (C) the toddler did not see the bicycle and narrowly escaped being struck by its front wheel.
    (D) the bicycle was not seen by the toddler, and he narrowly escaped being struck by its front wheel.
    (E) the toddler did not see the bicycle and narrowly escaped being stricken by it's front wheel.

37. We trust your judgment implicitly, knowing that whoever you choose will do a fine job.
    (A) whoever you choose will do a fine job.
    (B) you will choose whoever will do a fine job.
    (C) whomever you choose will do a fine job.
    (D) you will choose whomever will do a fine job.
    (E) a fine job will be done by whomever you choose.

38. After having won first place in the regional finals, the talented twelve-year-old girl began working out for the national gymnastics competition.
    (A) After having won first place in the regional finals
    (B) Having won first place in the regional finals
    (C) To win first place in the regional finals
    (D) Soon after having won first place in the regional finals
    (E) After the regional finals

39. The board feels strongly that at this point in time there is no proven need for a new gymnasium floor or a repaved track.
    (A) The board feels strongly that at this point in time there is no proven need
    (B) The board feels strong that at this point in time there is no proven need
    (C) The board says strongly, that at this point in time there is no proven need
    (D) The board feels strongly that at present there is no proven need
    (E) There is a strong feeling that at this point in time there is no proved need

40. Less rainfall means less traffic accidents according to several experts on highway safety.
    (A) Less rainfall means less traffic accidents
    (B) A lack of rainfall means less traffic accidents
    (C) Less rainfall means the least traffic accidents
    (D) Less rainfall means fewer traffic accidents
    (E) Fewer rainfalls means less traffic accidents

41. My college professor used to say that "all it takes to successfully complete a graduate program is perseverance," but I'd add something else—the ability to manage on four hours of sleep a night.
    (A) say that "all it takes to successfully complete a graduate program is perseverance," but I'd add something else—
    (B) say that "all it takes to successfully complete a graduate program is perseverance", but I'd add something else—
    (C) say that all it takes to successfully complete a graduate program is perseverance, but I'd add something else—
    (D) say that all it takes to successfully complete a graduate program is perseverance but I'd add something else;
    (E) say that all it takes to successfully complete a graduate program is perseverance, but he added something else—

42. That all the people gathered here—parents, teachers, students—are interested in upgrading the quality of education in local schools, then we can begin drawing up a plan within the next few days.
   - (A) That all the people gathered here
   - (B) That all these people gathered here
   - (C) If all the people gathered here
   - (D) If all these people gathering here
   - (E) All the people gathered here

43. We are interested in your continued support; will you please fill out the enclosed questionnaire to let us know your opinions on these matters?
   - (A) We are interested in your continued support;
   - (B) Being interested in continued support,
   - (C) Because of your continued support,
   - (D) Your continued support is interesting;
   - (E) Interest in your continued support being what it is,

44. The salutation at the top of the letter said, "To whom it may concern."
   - (A) The salutation at the top of the letter said, "To whom it may concern."
   - (B) The salutation at the top of the letter said to whom it may concern.
   - (C) The salutation at the top of the letter introduced, "To whom it may concern."
   - (D) The salutation was, "To whom it may concern."
   - (E) The letter's salutation said, "To whom it may concern."

45. Henry Kissinger, the former Secretary of State, once called for a bipartisan agreement among the members of Congress whom, he realized, were divided on many issues.
   - (A) whom, he realized, were divided on many issues.
   - (B) who, he realized, were divided on many issues.
   - (C) who realized they were divided on many issues.
   - (D) being divided on many issues, he realized.
   - (E) whom nevertheless were divided on many issues.

STOP. IF YOU FINISH BEFORE TIME IS UP, CHECK YOUR WORK ON THIS SECTION ONLY. DO NOT WORK ON ANY OTHER SECTION OF THE TEST. YOU MAY RETURN TO THE USAGE QUESTIONS IF TIME PERMITS.

SECTION IV: WRITING—ESSAY

Time: 30 Minutes
1 Essay

DIRECTIONS

In this section, you will have 30 minutes to plan and write an essay. You may use the bottom of this page to organize and plan your essay before you begin writing. You should plan your time wisely. Read the topic carefully to make sure that you are properly addressing the issue or situation. YOU MUST WRITE ON THE SPECIFIED TOPIC. AN ESSAY ON ANOTHER TOPIC WILL NOT BE ACCEPTABLE.

The essay question included in this section is designed to give you an opportunity to write clearly and effectively. Use specific examples whenever appropriate to aid in supporting your ideas. Keep in mind that the quality of your writing is much more important than the quantity.

Your essay is to be written on the special answer sheets provided. No other paper may be used. Your writing should be neat and legible. Because you have only a limited amount of space in which to write, please do NOT skip lines, do NOT write excessively large, and do NOT leave wide margins.

Remember, use the bottom of this page for any organizational notes you may wish to make.

Topic

Some educators maintain that an all-male or all-female environment is beneficial to learning. Compare and contrast the advantages of such an academic environment to those of a coeducational atmosphere.

FOR YOUR ESSAY, USE TWO SIDES OF AN 8½" by 11" LINED SHEET OF PAPER.

TEST OF GENERAL KNOWLEDGE

SECTION I: SOCIAL STUDIES

Time: 30 Minutes
30 Questions

DIRECTIONS

Following each of the questions or statements below, select the choice that best answers the question or completes the statement.

1. Fact: Fewer people in the United States are in the childbearing years.
   Fact: The general population of the United States is becoming older.
   Which of the following statements is *not* a logical conclusion that one can draw from the above facts?
   (A) A greater percentage of national income will be spent on welfare for senior citizens.
   (B) The rate of growth of the general population may decline.
   (C) A "generation conflict" may develop between working adults and retired adults.
   (D) Retirement pensions will take a larger percentage of the total national income.
   (E) The senior population will resort to the "confrontation politics" of the 1960s to achieve political objectives.

2. A nation has an unfavorable balance of payments when
   (A) there is a decline in the Consumer Price Index
   (B) payments are not equal to receipts
   (C) prices in the exporting country are greater than prices in the importing country
   (D) imports are greater than exports
   (E) exports exceed imports

3. During a congressional election campaign, a candidate refers to his campaign workers as *dedicated professionals* but refers to the opponent's campaign workers as *scabs*. This practice is an example of which of the following propaganda devices?
   (A) card stacking   (D) glittering generality
   (B) bandwagon   (E) stereotyping
   (C) name calling

486

4. A lavish party is thrown by the nouveau riche in which luxury items are displayed in a highly visible manner. During the course of the party, many guests entertain by lighting expensive cigars with $20 bills. These actions are most clearly examples of
   (A) marginal adaptation
   (B) conspicuous consumption
   (C) benevolent despotism
   (D) infantile sensationalism
   (E) assimilation

5. "To maintain the strategic balance at its current levels would create a dangerous vulnerability for U.S. deterrent systems. A permanent imbalance would be codified between the sides. We prefer to approach the problem with an accent on reducing existing arsenals to an equal level of capability." The author of this passage is most clearly
   (A) a proponent of nuclear confrontation with the Soviet Union
   (B) an advocate of the proliferation of nuclear weapons
   (C) an opponent of nuclear freeze agreements
   (D) in agreement with the political thought of U.S. liberals
   (E) advocating Teddy Roosevelt's "Big Stick" political philosophy for current use

6. Fact: A crowd represents collective behavior.

   Which of the following is an *incorrect* statement in describing the characteristics of a crowd?

   (A) Suggestibility is heightened.
   (B) Behavior is more readily guided by emotion.
   (C) Members interact as unique individuals.
   (D) The phenomenon is temporary.
   (E) An element of anonymity is maintained.

7. "During the Korean War, General MacArthur referred to President Truman's foreign policy as 'prolonged indecision' and even indicated that Truman's restrictive military policies were, in effect, 'appeasement' to communism." The sentiment expressed in this statement eventually led to
   (A) a military victory in the Korean conflict
   (B) a military confrontation with the Soviet Union
   (C) the removal and subsequent dismissal of General MacArthur from the service
   (D) air strikes over mainland China
   (E) the United States threatening to withdraw from the United Nations

8. "Minorities in management positions increased from 11% to 12% last year, while minorities in clerical and secretarial positions jumped from 10% to 16%. The company's general goal is a 15% to 33% increase in these categories, as determined by the government." This statement represents a company's efforts to comply with which federal government mandated program?
   (A) federal sex discrimination standards
   (B) equal opportunity employment programs
   (C) affirmative action programs
   (D) desegregation programs
   (E) Title IX programs

9. Which of the following terms was *not* associated with the decade of the 1950s?
   (A) guns or butter   (D) the domino theory
   (B) containment   (E) global communism
   (C) brinkmanship

10. A school board member is a major stockholder in textbook company *A*. Without making this information public, the school board member recommends that the school board adopt a new social studies text published by company *A*. Such action on the part of the school board member would be an example of
    (A) unfair labor practices   (D) puritan ethic
    (B) conflict of interest   (E) capitalistic exploitation
    (C) civil service fraud

Questions 11 and 12 refer to the following map on which numbers 1 through 9 represent different countries in and around Central America.

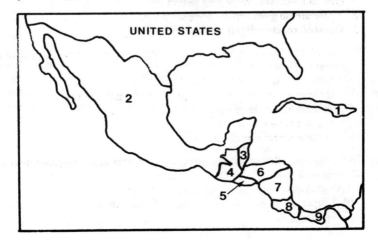

11. The United States accused which Central American area Communist country of supplying Soviet-made weapons to rebel forces attempting to take control of El Salvador?

   (A) 1   (B) 2   (C) 6   (D) 8   (E) 9

12. Historically, U.S. involvement in Central America was predicated on global considerations. In the year 2000, which Central American country will gain full control and sovereignty over a U.S. possession viewed as strategically important?

   (A) 1   (B) 4   (C) 5   (D) 8   (E) 9

13. Which of the following examples best represents functional illiteracy?
   (A) failure to graduate from high school
   (B) failure to pass a driving test
   (C) inability to read a *New York Times* book review
   (D) inability to pass a basic test of English skills
   (E) lowering the graduation requirements for high schools

14. A study revealed that following World War I racial incidents against blacks in the South increased in direct proportion to the drop in per capita income of poor whites. The term that best describes this situation is

   (A) economic determinism   (D) role determination
   (B) stereotyping   (E) scapegoating
   (C) self-fulfilling prophecy

15. Assume the following:

   1. A majority of the U.S. grain farmers produced an unusually large crop in a one-year recording period.
   2. There are no government price supports.
   3. Demand remains relatively constant.

   Which of the following statements would best represent the probable effect on farm income?
   (A) Income would tend to gradually increase.
   (B) Income would be subject to excess capital gains taxes.
   (C) Income would increase at a rapid rate.
   (D) Income would tend to fall.
   (E) Income would remain stable.

16. Which of the following countries is *not* a member of the Organization of Petroleum Exporting Countries (OPEC)?
   (A) Venezuela   (D) Turkey
   (B) Libya   (E) Saudi Arabia
   (C) Nigeria

A COMPARISON OF THREE STATE CONSTITUTIONS

	South Carolina	Pennsylvania	Massachusetts
	PRESIDENT	**COUNCIL**	**GOVERNOR**
Executive	2-year term, legislature elects, has full veto.	3-year term, voters elect.	1-year term, voters elect, $2/3$ vote can override veto.
Upper House	Life term, lower house elects.	None.	1-year term, voters elect.
Judges	Life term, legislature elects.	7-year term, appointed by council.	Life term, appointed by governor.
Voting Requirements	100 acres or £60 or pay 10 shillings in taxes.	Pay taxes.	£60 or £3 income from real estate yearly.
Eligibility to Hold Office	500 acres in parish or 500 acres and 10 slaves in county, or £1000.	Pay taxes.	Governor— £1000 real estate; Senator— £300 real estate or £600; Representative— £100 real estate or £200.

17. Which of the following conclusions can be drawn from the information provided in the chart?
    (A) Democracy was more a theory than a practicing principle.
    (B) The framers of the constitutions wanted to limit the power of the executive.
    (C) The legislative branch would maintain power.
    (D) both (A) and (B)
    (E) both (B) and (C)

18. If a bill is sent to the President prior to the last ten days of a legislative session and the President refuses to act on the bill, the bill
    (A) is subject to a pocket veto
    (B) automatically is sent back to Congress
    (C) may be overridden by a two-thirds vote in the House and Senate
    (D) becomes law without the President's signature
    (E) most likely was not opposed by the President's party

Questions 19 and 20 refer to the following population pyramid charts.

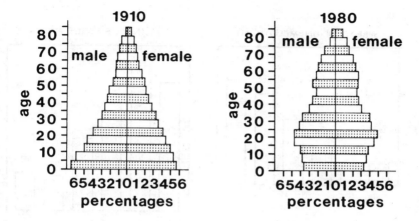

A population pyramid shows a frequency distribution by age and sex of a population at a given time.

19. According to information presented in the charts, which of the following is a true statement?
    (A) At every age group, the 1910 chart shows a greater number of males than females.
    (B) The proportion of the population 15 and under is smaller in 1980 than in the early twentieth century.
    (C) The center of population has shifted westward.
    (D) There are more middle-aged individuals in 1910 than in 1980.
    (E) As the country industrialized, the proportion of the population 65 and older declined.

20. It can be determined from information presented in the charts that
    (A) population pyramids are so called because the chart represents a pyramid with a narrow bottom and a narrow top
    (B) for the early twentieth century, the base of the pyramid reflects a small percentage of males and females at younger ages
    (C) the immigrant population steadily increased throughout the twentieth century
    (D) the amount of money spent on social welfare programs in the last quarter of the twentieth century is directly related to the increased age of the population
    (E) from 1910 to 1980, the proportion of young people decreased as the proportion of people over 65 increased

Questions 21 and 22 refer to the following charts.

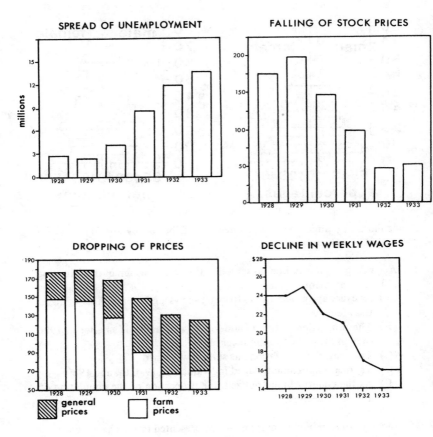

21. The year 1929 marked the statistical height of the American economy during the period covered in the charts. This statement is
    (A) definitely true
    (B) probably true
    (C) definitely false
    (D) probably false
    (E) cannot be determined from evidence presented in the chart

22. Based upon your knowledge of history and the data presented in the charts, which of the following is a true statement?
    (A) The unemployment rate had only a moderate effect on weekly wages.
    (B) The stock market crash was not a basic cause of the Great Depression.
    (C) Farm prices indicated that the agricultural section of the economy was substantially more affected by the depression than the economy as a whole.
    (D) Unemployment would have increased substantially if the U.S. had not abandoned the gold standard.
    (E) The increase in inflation was directly related to the rapid increase in the rate of unemployment.

23. In which of the following wars was the United States most appropriately labeled the *arsenal for democracy?*
    (A) American Revolution   (D) World War II
    (B) Mexican-American War   (E) Korean War
    (C) World War I

24. "The people's right to know is a cornerstone of the American legal system. However, media accounts of sensational criminal trials often result in prejudicial trial publicity." This statement most clearly represents a basic constitutional conflict between which of the following?
    (A) freedom of speech and the right to privacy
    (B) freedom of speech and the right to a fair trial
    (C) the right to an impartial jury and the equal protection of the law
    (D) freedom from cruel and unusual punishment and freedom of the press
    (E) the due process of the law and the legal requirement of being charged with a crime

25. In spite of increased government efforts, Soviet agriculture in the 1970s failed to meet projected quotas. Which of the following government programs could increase agricultural production without fundamentally changing the Soviet Union's orthodox agricultural policy?
    (A) giving individual factory managers the responsibility for determining national goals
    (B) allowing production quotas and budgets to be determined by each agricultural district
    (C) increasing the percentage of private farms now permitted
    (D) paying production-quota bonuses for the delivery of high-priority products
    (E) imposing government programs which restrict home consumption of grain products

26. If a city creates a zoning plan solely to exclude a minority from a particular parcel of land, the courts would most likely find the city in violation of
   (A) the Fourteenth Amendment—the equal protection of the law
   (B) affirmative action
   (C) the *Plessy* v. *Ferguson* case
   (D) the "due-process" clause of the Fifth Amendment
   (E) reverse discrimination

27. The world's population has created significant social problems. Which of the following is *not* a true statement regarding current world demographic characteristics?
   (A) China has the world's largest population.
   (B) In India, the government sponsored birth control programs have not been widely accepted.
   (C) Developing nations are characterized by low birth rates and high death rates.
   (D) Since the early 1900s, the percentage of elderly in the the U.S. population has increased.
   (E) The population of the world is unevenly distributed.

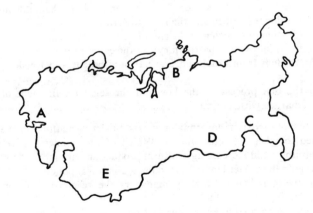

28. On the map above, the letters A through E represent different regions of the Soviet Union. The climate and vegetation of which region of the Soviet Union is most similar to the tundra region of North America?
   (A) A   (B) B   (C) C   (D) D   (E) E

Questions 29 and 30 refer to the following chart.

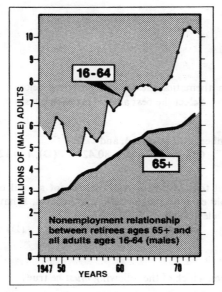

29. In which three-year period did adult male unemployment in the 16- to
    64-year-old range remain relatively constant?
    (A) 1949–1951   (D) 1956–1958
    (B) 1963–1965   (E) 1970–1973
    (C) 1965–1967

30. Which of the following statements is consistent with information
    presented in the chart?
    (A) As the 16- to 64-year-old unemployment figures show an increase,
        the 65+-year-old unemployment rate shows a decrease.
    (B) As the 16- to 64-year-old unemployment figures show a decrease,
        the 65+-year-old unemployment figures show an increase.
    (C) As the 16- to 64-year-old unemployment figures show an increase,
        the 65+-year-old unemployment figures show an increase.
    (D) The number of unemployed males age 16 to 64 years was much
        greater in 1950 than in 1973.
    (E) The adult male unemployment figures for 65+ years, showed
        greater variations than the 16- to 64-year-old unemployment fig-
        ures.

STOP. IF YOU FINISH BEFORE TIME IS UP, CHECK YOUR WORK ON THIS SECTION
ONLY. DO NOT WORK ON ANY OTHER SECTION OF THE TEST.

SECTION II: MATHEMATICS

Time: 30 Minutes
25 Questions

DIRECTIONS

Each of the mathematics questions or problems below is followed by five suggested answers. Select the best answer for each question.

1. Add the numbers 10.5, 122, 6.3, and 1.32.
   (A) 30.32   (B) 42.2   (C) 80.42   (D) 140.12   (E) 152

2. Ten identical television sets cost a merchant a total of $792 and the merchant sold each at a 40% markup of his cost. What was the selling price of one television set?
   (A) $82.37   (B) $83.20   (C) $110.88   (D) $119.20
   (E) $832

3. If $3x > 0$, then which of the following *must* be true?
   I. $x < 0$
   II. $1/x > 0$
   III. $-x < 0$

   (A) I only   (D) I and II
   (B) II only   (E) II and III
   (C) III only

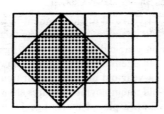

4. In the figure above, each small square represents an area of one square centimeter. What is the area of the large, shaded figure?
   (A) 6 sq cm   (D) $2\sqrt{2}$ sq cm
   (B) 8 sq cm   (E) $4\sqrt{2}$ sq cm
   (C) 10 sq cm

5. Which of the following algebraic expressions represents *six less than half of a quantity?*

(A) $6 - \dfrac{x}{2}$

(B) $\dfrac{6 - x}{2}$

(C) $6 - 2x$

(D) $(x - 6) \div 2$

(E) $\dfrac{x}{2} - 6$

6. Which value is closest to the square root of 4000?
   (A) 19   (B) 21   (C) 63   (D) 201   (E) 1999

Questions 7 and 8 refer to the following bar graph.

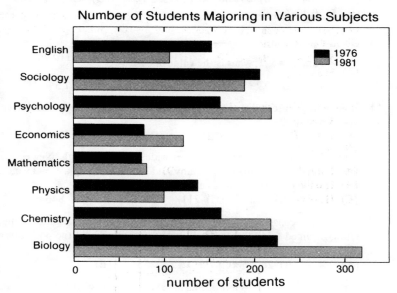

Number of Students Majoring in Various Subjects

7. The 1981 enrollment in psychology is approximately what percentage of the 1981 enrollment in biology?
   (A) 45   (B) 69   (C) 84   (D) 145   (E) 220

8. Which subject had the greatest percentage increase in students from 1976 to 1981?
   (A) biology
   (B) chemistry
   (C) economics
   (D) mathematics
   (E) psychology

9. If $2x + 16 = 1$, what is the value of $x + 7$?
   (A) -0.5 (B) -1.5 (C) 3.4   (D) 15   (E) 15.5

10. Mary is three years younger than half her mother's age, and Mary is 19 years old. How old is her mother?
    (A) 38   (B) 41   (C) 44   (D) 47   (E) 50

11. One pound of Green Demon grass seed is sufficient to plant 200 square feet. Approximately how many pounds of that seed are needed for a circular lawn, 50 feet across?
    (A) 4   (B) 10   (C) 20   (D) 22   (E) 40

12. What would be the quarterly interest received on a savings deposit of $2130 in an account yielding 8% annually?
    (A) $17.04   (B) $42.60   (C) $52.14   (D) $102.14
    (E) $170.40

13. Given the equation $\dfrac{2a - 6b}{5c - 1} = 4$
    If $a = 2$ and $b = -1$, what is the value of c?

    (A) 0.3   (B) 0.7   (C) 1.4   (D) 7.5   (E) 17.5

14. How many degrees does the minute hand of a clock sweep out during each 3 minutes?
    (A) 15   (B) 18   (C) 21   (D) 24   (E) 27

15. A small cabin is 15 feet long, 12 feet wide, and 9 feet high. Neglecting the door and any windows, how many square feet of fiberglass mat would be needed to insulate the walls and ceiling of the cabin?
    (A) 423   (B) 666   (C) 711   (D) 738   (E) 846

16. The last two censuses indicated that the population of Lonesome Spring, Utah, declined from 112 to 28. By what percentage did the population fall?
    (A) 25   (B) 28   (C) 72   (D) 75   (E) 84

17. R is to S as 3 is to 11. What is the approximate value of R when S equals 7?
    (A) 0.52   (B) 1.7   (C) 1.9   (D) 4.7   (E) 25.7

18. Which of the five lettered intervals on the preceding number line contains the *product* of -1.5 and -1.7?
    (A) A   (B) B   (C) C   (D) D   (E) E

Questions 19 and 20 refer to the following contour map.

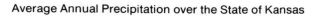

Average Annual Precipitation over the State of Kansas

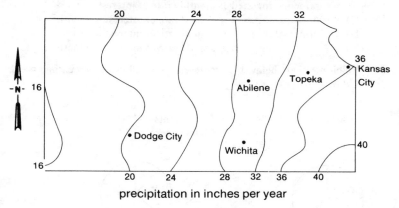

precipitation in inches per year

19. Which part of the state receives the most precipitation in a typical year?
    (A) central
    (B) northeastern
    (C) northwestern
    (D) southeastern
    (E) southwestern

20. Approximately how many more inches of precipitation does Abilene receive than does Dodge City during a typical year?
    (A) 9   (B) 11   (C) 15   (D) 19   (E) 29

21. A numerical series is 4, 7, 11, 16, 22, 29, _____. What number follows 29?
    (A) 8
    (B) 30
    (C) 36
    (D) 37
    (E) none of these

22. There are 24 girls in a class of 40. One-fourth of the girls have red hair, but none of the boys have red hair. What percent of the class has red hair?
    (A) 10   (B) 15   (C) 20   (D) 25   (E) 30

23. To find the amount of simple interest paid by a bank on a savings account, one would use the formula, where I = interest,
   (A) I = principal invested × annual rate of interest
   (B) I = principal invested × monthly rate of interest
   (C) I = principal invested × annual rate of interest × months
   (D) I = principal invested × annual rate of interest × years
   (E) I = principal invested × annual rate of interest × months × years

24. Which pie chart below best represents the following percentage breakdown?

75% adults
20% infants
5% teenagers

(A)

(D)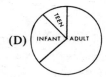

(B)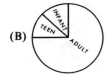

(E)

(C)

| 10 milligrams = 1 centigram |
| 100 centigrams = 1 gram |

25. How many milligrams are in 25 grams?
   (A) 25   (D) 25,000
   (B) 250   (E) 250,000
   (C) 2,500

STOP. IF YOU FINISH BEFORE TIME IS UP, CHECK YOUR WORK ON THIS SECTION ONLY. DO NOT WORK ON ANY OTHER SECTION OF THE TEST.

SECTION III: LITERATURE AND FINE ARTS

Time: 30 Minutes
35 Questions

DIRECTIONS

Each of these questions or incomplete statements is followed by five possible answers or completions. Select the answer or completion that is best in each case.

1. Which of the following characteristics of the painting above is most important in making it seem realistic?
   (A) the expressions of the two faces
   (B) the hairbrush on the edge of the table
   (C) the indistinct background
   (D) the positions of the arms
   (E) the rather ordinary clothing

He who possesses justice lays hold of her and she meets him as an honorable mother. With the bread of life and understanding she feeds him, and gives him the water of wholesome wisdom to drink.

2. From the preceding passage we may conclude that he who possesses justice also possesses which of these four items?

   I. honor
   II. nutrition

   III. understanding
   IV. wisdom

   (A) I and II
   (B) I and III
   (C) II and III

   (D) II and IV
   (E) III and IV

3. The beautiful vase above was made during the twelfth century. On which continent did the artist most likely live?

   (A) Africa
   (B) Asia
   (C) Europe

   (D) North America
   (E) South America

Questions 4 and 5 refer to these six lines from a poem by T. S. Eliot.

> For I have known them all already, known them all—
> Have known the evenings, mornings, afternoons,
> I have measured out my life with coffee spoons;
> I know the voices dying with a dying fall
> Beneath the music from a farther room.
> So how should I presume?

4. The last line is meant to rhyme with which preceding line?

   (A) line 1   (D) line 4
   (B) line 2   (E) line 5
   (C) line 3

5. What appears to be the theme of the poem?

   (A) futility   (D) politeness
   (B) curiosity   (E) sensuality
   (C) indignation

6. The painting above shows several ships at sea. The artist has used several components to suggest the awesome power of nature, including all of the following *except*

   (A) the flags on the nearest ship
   (B) the immense size of the waves
   (C) the insignificant size of the people
   (D) the tilt of the ships to the right
   (E) the wreckage in the foreground

Questions 7 and 8 refer to this passage from a novel by Joseph Conrad.

He might have been resigned to die but I suspect he wanted to die without added terrors, quietly, in a sort of peaceful trance. A certain readiness to perish is not so very rare, but it is seldom that you meet men whose souls, steeled in the impenetrable armour of resolution, are ready to fight a losing battle to the last; the desire of peace waxes stronger as hope declines, till at last it conquers the very desire of life

7. The passage reveals Conrad's acute interest in
   (A) esthetics   (D) politics
   (B) medicine   (E) psycology
   (C) nature

8. The passage occurs as part of the narration of
   (A) a black mass   (D) a hypnotic experiment
   (B) a boxing match   (E) a shipwreck
   (C) an election

9. Photographed above is the building housing an important collection of modern paintings and sculpture. Which of the following statements about the design of the building does *not* apply?
   (A) The building itself is a spectacular work of art.
   (B) One component is a cylinder that becomes larger with height.
   (C) The building attracts the general public to view the art collection.
   (D) The design lacks unity because it was developed by a committee.
   (E) The horizontal facade smoothly wraps around the end of the building.

10. Which would be the most appropriate title for the preceding painting by Bellini?
    (A) The City on the Hill   (D) Prayer in Springtime
    (B) Landscape with Two Figures   (E) The Temptation of Christ
    (C) Madonna of the Meadow

11. The sculpture above depicts which of the following?
    (A) a naturalist recording an unusual discovery
    (B) the prelude to a bloody human sacrifice
    (C) a ritual intended to create rain
    (D) a ruler offering cups of wine to a god
    (E) a zookeeper feeding a gigantic bird

Questions 12 through 15 refer to these excerpts from five poems.

> (A) A Monk ther was, a fair for the maistrye,
>   An out-rydere, that lovede venerye;
>   A manly man, to been an abbot able.
>   Ful many a deyntee hors hadde he in stable.

> (B) Go and catch a falling star,
>   Get with child a mandrake root,
>   Tell me where all past years are,
>   Or who cleft the devil's foot.

> (C) I am borne darkly, fearfully, afar;
>   Whilst burning through the inmost veil of Heaven,
>   The soul of Adonais, like a star,
>   Beacons from the abode where the Eternal are.

> (D) One by one he subdued his father's trees
>   By riding them down over and over again
>   Until he took the stiffness out of them,
>   And not one but hung limp, not one was left
>   For him to conquer.

> (E) 'Twas brillig, and the slithy toves
>   Did gyre and gimble in the wabe:
>   All mimsy were the borogroves,
>   And the mome raths outgrabe.

12. Which of the poems is a humorous fantasy?
    (A) A   (B) B   (C) C   (D) D   (E) E

13. Which poem was written during medieval times?
    (A) A   (B) B   (C) C   (D) D   (E) E

14. Which of the poems uses nature to symbolize the challenge of life?
    (A) A   (B) B   (C) C   (D) D   (E) E

15. Which poet is mourning another?
    (A) A   (B) B   (C) C   (D) D   (E) E

You see this creature with her kerbstone English: the English that will keep her in the gutter to the end of her days. Well, sir, in three months I could pass that girl off as a duchess at an ambassador's garden party. I could even get her a place as lady's maid or shop assistant, which requires better English. That's the sort of thing I do for commercial millionaires. And on the profits of it I do genuine scientific work in phonetics, and a little as a poet on Miltonic lines.

16. The preceding passage is taken from a
   (A) financial magazine   (D) scientific article
   (B) humorous play   (E) tactful sermon
   (C) popular song

Questions 17 through 19 refer to these five portrayals of men that follow.

17. Which of the five art works is a clay sculpture?
   (A) A   (B) B   (C) C   (D) D   (E) E

18. Which of the paintings uses geometric perspective to give an illusion of depth?
   (A) A   (B) B   (C) C   (D) D   (E) E

19. Which of the paintings has the most obvious brushstrokes?
   (A) A   (B) B   (C) C   (D) D   (E) E

A

B

C

D

E

There once was a young man named Cisco,
Whose favorite music was disco.
But no lady would chance
To join him in dance
'Cause the spectators would boo and hiss-co.

20. What is the rhyme scheme of the preceding limerick about Cisco?
(A) aabab (B) aabba (C) ababa (D) abbaa (E) abbab

21. The painting above has the title *Standing Figure*. When it was painted in 1908, it unveiled a revolutionary new type of art. Which of the following statements does *not* apply to that painting?
    (A) The painting emphasizes form and space.
    (B) The painting has a primitive power and crudity.
    (C) The painting is brilliantly imaginative.
    (D) The painting faithfully copies reality.
    (E) The painting relies on bold lines and colors.

"Maybe you don't," Smiley says. "Maybe you understand frogs and maybe you don't understand 'em; maybe you've had experience, and maybe you ain't only a amature, as it were. Anyways, I've got *my* opinion, and I'll resk forty dollars that he can outjump any frog in Calaveras County."

22. The slang and spelling errors in the preceding passage indicate which of the following?
    (A) The author is nearly illiterate.
    (B) The reader is made to feel comfortable.
    (C) The rustic setting is emphasized.
    (D) The story is centuries old.
    (E) The story was translated from German.

23. The photograph shows the
lobby of a hotel in
Brussels. Which of the
following statements does *not*
apply to the unusual
style of the hotel?
    (A) It is predominantly
        concerned with decoration.
    (B) It required the work of
        skilled craftsmen.
    (C) It shows much imagination
        and fantasy.
    (D) It uses plastic as the
        main material.
    (E) It was inspired by vines
        and flowers.

24. The *Mona Lisa* by Leonardo is
reproduced here. What
feature has made it
perhaps the most famous
painting in the world?
    (A) the ghostly landscape
    (B) the long, smooth hair
    (C) the shy, averted eyes
    (D) the subtle smile
    (E) the vivid colors

> O swallow, sister, O fair swift swallow,
>   Why wilt thou fly after spring to the south,
>   The soft south whither thine heart is set?

25. The preceding lines from "Itylus" by Algernon Swinburne display his
enthusiasm for
    (A) elegant beauty   (D) melodious rhyme
    (B) exaggerated humor   (E) repetitive sounds
    (C) friendly animals

26. Although one might initially think that
the pose of the figure is relaxed, upon realizing
that this is the marble statue of a bound slave one
must conclude that the figure is
    (A) asleep
    (B) exuberant
    (C) tortured
    (D) uncomfortable
    (E) victorious

27. This is the basic
floor plan for most
medieval cathedrals.
Which of the following
reasons explains why
that one plan was
followed so often?
    (A) It is dogmatic.
    (B) It is functional.
    (C) It is inexpensive.
    (D) It is symbolic.
    (E) It is unorthodox.

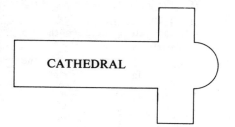

CATHEDRAL

In literature, a tragedy does not portray simple misfortune, but the
irresistible unrolling of destiny. Moreover, the tragic fall of the hero is
the consequence of his own character, or his "tragic flaws."

28. According to the above remarks on tragedy, which of the following is the
most promising theme around which to write a tragedy?
    (A) A woman forgets to mail invitations to a birthday party for her
        handicapped son.
    (B) Hoodlums overtake a terrified man in a dark alley after a chase
        through eerily deserted streets.
    (C) A man unknowingly marries his own sister after being warned by a
        fortune-teller against marriage.
    (D) A man notices that it is Friday the 13th and later that day is struck
        by a car as he is jogging.
    (E) A child who is too young to read finds a large can of rat poison on a
        basement shelf.

29. The painting shows a young couple waltzing on a French sidewalk. The artist has skillfully suggested that their love has elevated them above the ordinary. What aspect of the painting reveals that the young people are in love?

(A) the beautiful dress of the young lady
(B) the interest they have in their surroundings
(C) the jollity of the people at the table
(D) the mutual embrace of the two partners
(E) the shy expression on the man's face

When I heard the learn'd astronomer,
When the proofs, the figures, were ranged in columns before me,
When I was shown the charts and diagrams, to add, divide, and measure them,
When I sitting heard the astronomer where he lectured with much applause in the lecture room,
How soon unaccountable I became tired and sick,
Till rising and gliding out I wandered off by myself,
In the mystical moist night air, and from time to time,
Looked up in perfect silence at the stars.

30. What was the motivation for the poet who wrote the lines above?
(A) He felt inadequate to understand the calculations and proofs of astonomy.
(B) He preferred quiet, solitary study to the noisy applause sought by the lecturer.
(C) He realized that he would die before space travel became possible.
(D) He wanted to show that actual experience is far richer than any theory.
(E) He was saddened by the irreligious trends in modern science.

31. The photograph shows a
scale model for a glass
skyscraper that displays a
startling quality of lightness.
All of the following
features contribute to the
sense of lightness *except* the
   (A) many floors
   (B) pale colors
   (C) reflections
   (D) transparency
   (E) vertical lines

Questions 32 and 33 refer to the following passage by Ralph Waldo Emerson.

A foolish consistency is the hobgoblin of little minds, adored by little statesmen and philosophers and divines. With consistency a great soul has simply nothing to do. He may as well concern himself with his shadow on the wall. Speak what you think now in hard words, and tomorrow speak what tomorrow thinks in hard words again, though it contradict everything you said today. "Ah, so you shall be sure to be misunderstood." It is so bad, then, to be misunderstood? Pythagoras was misunderstood, and Socrates, and Jesus, and Luther, and Copernicus, and Galileo, and Newton, and every pure wise spirit that ever took flesh.

32. In the passage, the final phrase *took flesh* means
   (A) ate meat   (D) married
   (B) captured enemy soldiers   (E) was executed
   (C) lived

33. In the passage, Emerson uses Socrates and Copernicus, among others, as examples of people
   (A) of supreme consistency
   (B) sure to be misunderstood
   (C) who misunderstood others
   (D) who were adored
   (E) with great souls

Questions 34 and 35 refer to the following painting.

34. The artist who painted *An Interior with a Woman Drinking* (above) has characterized the major source of light as which of the following?
    (A) incandescent
    (B) heavenly
    (C) unnecessary
    (D) primitive
    (E) natural

35. Which part of the painting shows fine perspective?
    (A) the clothing of the people
    (B) the faces of the people
    (C) the floor and ceiling
    (D) the glass in the woman's hand
    (E) the tapestry on the back wall

STOP. IF YOU FINISH BEFORE TIME IS UP, CHECK YOUR WORK ON THIS SECTION ONLY. DO NOT WORK ON ANY OTHER SECTION OF THE TEST.

SECTION IV: SCIENCE

Time: 30 Minutes
30 Questions

DIRECTIONS

Each of the science questions is followed by five suggested answers. Select the best answer for each question.

1. In mammals, oxygen is carried to the body tissue by means of the
   (A) digestive tract
   (B) respiratory system
   (C) circulatory system
   (D) nervous system
   (E) reproductive system

2. Which of the following reactions would be classified as *nuclear* rather than chemical?

   I. the fusion of hydrogen atoms to helium inside stars
   II. the oxidation of sulfur atoms to sulfur dioxide
   III. the splitting of water molecules to hydrogen and oxygen

   (A) I only
   (B) II only
   (C) III only
   (D) I and II
   (E) II and III

3. You are probably aware that the time for an echo to return depends on the distance to the reflecting object. The same principle of timing a reflected signal is used to measure a variety of distances. Which of the following measurement techniques is *not* based on the reflection of signals?
   (A) acoustic measurement of ocean depth
   (B) radar detection of aircraft
   (C) seismic determination of geological structures
   (D) sonar finding of schools of fish
   (E) telescopic location of stars

4. The fact that ice floats atop water implies that the
   (A) atoms in ice are less dense than those in water
   (B) ice contains microscopic bubbles of air
   (C) molecules are closer in ice than water
   (D) molecules are closer in water than ice
   (E) water contracts upon freezing

5. Vertebrates are animals with an internal skeleton, a nerve cord, and bilateral symmetry. All of the following organisms are classified as vertebrates *except*

   (A) frog
   (B) human
   (C) lobster
   (D) pelican
   (E) shark

6. The Voyager II unmanned spacecraft was launched in 1977 on a "Grand Tour" of the outer solar system. Its trajectory was selected to visit in succession the planets Jupiter, Saturn, Uranus, and Neptune. Why was Venus omitted from the planetary tour?

   (A) The clouds of Venus would prevent photography.
   (B) Venus could be visited after passing Neptune.
   (C) Venus is too far away for Voyager to reach.
   (D) Venus is too near the sun for Voyager's path.
   (E) Venus shows no potential for supporting life.

Metal	Volume (cm³)	Mass (grams)
Beryllium	100	185
Calcium	100	155
Osmium	10	225
Titanium	10	45
Zinc	1	7

7. The preceding table shows the volume and mass for each of five metal pieces. Which metal piece has the lowest density?

   (A) beryllium
   (B) calcium
   (C) osmium
   (D) titanium
   (E) zinc

8. Which of the following substances decreases as grape juice ferments?

   (A) alcohol
   (B) CO_2
   (C) sugar
   (D) wine
   (E) yeast

9. Most of the dissolved material in salty lakes comes from

   (A) erosion of rocks
   (B) evaporation
   (C) industrial pollution
   (D) the ocean
   (E) the wind

10. The wave nature of light may be demonstrated by aiming two light beams to intersect each other. The evidence for waves is that
   (A) each beam is slightly deflected by the collision
   (B) the light beams collide and scatter the light
   (C) the two beams pass through each other without deflection
   (D) the light beams merge to produce one intermediate beam
   (E) the light spreads in all directions from the intersection

11. Vaccination has eradicated or limited several serious diseases, including smallpox, polio, and measles. Such an inoculation with infectious material prevents disease by
   (A) building up the immune system against all diseases
   (B) forming antibodies against that particular disease
   (C) infecting and killing the disease organisms
   (D) making the bloodstream too toxic for further infection
   (E) preventing reproduction of disease organisms

12. Desert plants have adapted to their harsh environment in many ways. Which of the following adaptations would *not* be used by desert plants?
   (A) Some plants grow quickly after a rainstorm, then go dormant.
   (B) Some plants have a resinous coating to minimize evaporation.
   (C) Some plants have abundant broad leaves to produce shade.
   (D) Some plants have thick, juicy leaves to store water.
   (E) Some plants have very deep roots to reach underground moisture.

13. Tuberculosis is *not* considered to be
   (A) bacterial   (D) infectious
   (B) chronic   (E) respiratory
   (C) hereditary

14. During the planning for the construction of a reservoir, engineers commonly do a cost/benefit analysis for the project, using about 75 years as the lifetime for the reservoir. Why do most reservoirs last only about 75 years?
   (A) They will be converted to meadows by the runaway growth of algae.
   (B) They will become steadily more polluted with industrial chemicals.
   (C) The concrete of the dam is progressively dissolved by the water.
   (D) They will gradually fill up with sediment brought in by streams.
   (E) They will very slowly evaporate until only salt flats remain.

15. Which of the following would contribute to a water shortage?

> I. lack of rainfall
> II. eroding of soil
> III. presence of mulch

(A) I only   (D) I and II
(B) II only   (E) I, II, and III
(C) III only

16. Of the following, the one factor that would *not* be considered a cause of environmental pollution would be
(A) increases in population and production
(B) industrial development
(C) changing standards of living
(D) leisure time
(E) conservation programs

17. Which *botanical community* would be found furthest north?
(A) coniferous forest   (D) permafrost
(B) deciduous forest   (E) tundra
(C) grassland

18. Metabolism and combustion are chemically similar, both resulting in oxidation of some compound. Which of the following foodstuffs would yield the most thermal energy if it were completely oxidized?
(A) two bananas
(B) a half-cup of flour
(C) a quarter-pound of ground beef
(D) a cup of ice cream
(E) a cup of sugar

19. When a cross of white flowers with red flowers leads to a next generation of only white flowers, the likeliest explanation is that
(A) insects consumed the red plants
(B) mutation has occurred
(C) sunlight bleached the flowers
(D) the red color is recessive
(E) the soil lacked iron

20. Glaciers demonstrate that
(A) rivers freeze during wintertime
(B) solids can flow slowly under pressure
(C) the earth's interior is cold
(D) the earth is colder than in the past
(E) the Ice Age is returning

Questions 21 and 22 refer to the following diagram of a very delicate balance with open cups suspended from the beam.

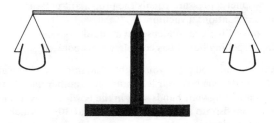

21. Which of these gases, if carefully injected from a rubber hose into the lefthand cup, would displace the air and cause the beam to tip downward to the left?

    (A) chlorine   (D) nitrogen
    (B) helium   (E) oxygen
    (C) hydrogen

22. Beginning the experiment again with both cups containing only air, what would happen if hydrogen gas were carefully injected into the righthand cup?

    (A) The beam would tip downward to the right due to the weight of the hydrogen.
    (B) The beam would tip downward to the left due to the weight of air in that cup.
    (C) The beam would remain horizontal as air would displace hydrogen from the open cup.
    (D) The beam would rise upward on the right due to the buoyancy of the hydrogen.
    (E) The beam would rise upward on the left because air is less dense than hydrogen.

23. A glass of cold water with many large ice cubes is allowed to stand for about ten minutes. After that period of equilibration, what happens to the water temperature during the next ten minutes as the ice cubes slowly become smaller?

    (A) The water temperature exceeds 32°F.
    (B) The water temperature falls.
    (C) The water temperature remains the same.
    (D) The water temperature rises.
    (E) The exact water temperature is unknown.

24. Sometimes aerosol cans "run out of propellant" before they are completely empty. The spraying action ceases when
    (A) all propellant has reacted with the other contents
    (B) atmospheric pressure equals the propellant pressure
    (C) the can contains a vacuum
    (D) the propelling gas condenses to a liquid
    (E) the propelling liquid has completely evaporated

25. In an experiment, you place your right hand into a bowl of water at 20°C. Simultaneously, you put your left hand into another bowl of water that is 40°C. After letting your hands soak in the bowls for several minutes, you place *both* hands into a third bowl of water at 30°C, which seems warm to your right hand and also cold to your left hand. Which is the best explanation for that result?
    (A) The change of temperatures temporarily confused the brain's interpretation.
    (B) Each hand finally reacted counter to the previous thermal action.
    (C) The left hand was warming the right hand, while the right hand was cooling the left hand.
    (D) The skin of each hand had become adapted to the earlier temperatures.
    (E) Temperatures were conducted through water so rapidly it seemed simultaneous.

26. The basic building blocks for proteins are
    (A) amino acids   (D) phosphates
    (B) carbohydrates   (E) vitamins
    (C) minerals

27. Polar explorers adrift on packs of sea ice can readily obtain drinkable water by melting chunks of ice. The fact that water derived from sea ice is pure enough to drink is evidence that
    (A) dissolved salts were excluded from the ice crystals
    (B) explorers need a large supply of fuel to heat the ice
    (C) no dangerous organisms survive at such low temperatures
    (D) polar oceans are not as salty as those nearer the equator
    (E) the seawater was boiled for a long time

28. The similar arrangement of bones within a person's arm and a whale's flipper suggests that
    (A) coincidences can occur
    (B) people evolved from fishes
    (C) people are meant to swim
    (D) people and whales have a common ancestor
    (E) similar tasks have led to similar structures

29. When completely immersed in water, a piece of glass
    - (A) appears bent by refraction
    - (B) appears to weigh less
    - (C) decreases in density
    - (D) increases in density
    - (E) increases its volume

30. The function of deoxyribose nucleic acid is to
    - (A) bond protons and neutrons
    - (B) digest food
    - (C) neutralize alkaline solutions
    - (D) prevent precipitation of salt in the ocean
    - (E) store genetic information

STOP. IF YOU FINISH BEFORE TIME IS UP, CHECK YOUR WORK ON THIS SECTION ONLY. DO NOT WORK ON ANY OTHER SECTION OF THE TEST.

TEST OF PROFESSIONAL KNOWLEDGE

SECTION I

Time: 30 Minutes
30 Questions

DIRECTIONS

Following each of the questions or statements below, select the choice that best answers the question or completes the statement.

1. A girl in Ms. Corman's class receives a poor grade on her report card in reading. Ms. Corman also sends a note home to the parents of the child that she is below grade level in reading and will have to work harder to catch up. The next day the parents come to the school and ask Ms. Corman to explain her comments and the child's grade. Which of the following is the most appropriate response to the questions?
   (A) Ms. Corman should ask the parents to see the principal.
   (B) Ms. Corman should inform the parents that their daughter should watch less television.
   (C) Ms. Corman should inform the parents that reading problems are common to low-income children and they should not worry.
   (D) Ms. Corman should explain how she reached her conclusions and what can be done to help the child improve.
   (E) Ms. Corman should explain that she is an experienced professional with knowledge of such things.

2. Mr. Scott examines his test questions after a test in order to determine the number of correct responses made by his students to each question. His survey method can be called
   (A) correlation   (D) frequency
   (B) finding the mean   (E) calculation
   (C) item analysis

3. Ms. Schultz attempted to teach sentence diagraming to a high school English class. At the end of the lesson none of her students were able to diagram sentences very well. The reason Ms. Shultz failed in her lesson is
   (A) probably because of a number of different factors
   (B) because the students weren't interested that day
   (C) because Ms. Shultz did not explain the significance of diagraming sentences
   (D) probably because diagraming sentences is irrelevant
   (E) because the students lacked the proper background for the lesson

522

4. In which of the following ways are states responsible for education?

    I. supervision of school district staff
    II. setting standards for teacher certification
    III. providing minimum standards with regard to school curriculum
    IV. providing standards with regard to school attendance
    V. providing supervision of local school board activities

    (A) I and V   (D) II, III, and IV
    (B) I, II, and V   (E) II, III, IV, and V
    (C) II and IV

5. Which of the following is the best reason for parent-teacher conferences?
    (A) to stress the importance of good citizenship
    (B) to share knowledge and the task of motivating the student
    (C) to allow the teacher to share knowledge of the student
    (D) to plan a child's future
    (E) to explain a child's standing in class

6. Achievement tests attempt to measure

    I. what an individual has learned
    II. the individual's present level of performance in academic learning
    III. the individual's learning potential

    (A) I   (D) II and III
    (B) II   (E) I, II, and III
    (C) I and II

7. Reinforcement tactics consist of both
    (A) positive and negative reinforcements
    (B) a great many repetitions of educational basics and discussion
    (C) reward and punishment
    (D) positive stimuli used at appropriate times and rewards
    (E) corporal punishment and positive stimuli

8. The goals of a school district's educational program are the primary responsibility of
    (A) the board of education   (D) the government
    (B) school district administrators   (E) teachers colleges
    (C) teachers and principals

9. Children with dyslexia are most likely to
    (A) come from low socioeconomic backgrounds   (D) be boys
    (B) come from broken homes   (E) be girls
    (C) be tall and clumsy

10. Social adjustment can be taught best
    (A) by setting clear standards for children
    (B) by giving children responsibility
    (C) by allowing the class to develop its own standards and relationships
    (D) within the context of group activities
    (E) through constant encouragement

11. When teachers employ modeling in their instruction, they are
    (A) presenting art lessons
    (B) seeking to modify the children's cognitive domain
    (C) acting without planning
    (D) attempting to help a child to learn by imitation
    (E) acting outside of the realm of accepted education

12. Some teachers do not favor parent conferencing. The best explanation of this is that
    (A) it may create conflicts between parents and teachers
    (B) it is not worth the time involved
    (C) a number of factors are involved having to do with individual teachers' abilities to relate to parents
    (D) it forces parents to become more involved with the school system
    (E) it creates anxiety among children

13. Which of the following is the most legitimate argument to support the maintenance of a free public education?
    (A) Public schools teach moral and ethical values.
    (B) Public schools provide the most effective means of teaching self-discipline.
    (C) Maintaining a free public school system is essential to a democratic society.
    (D) Public schools provide free lunch programs.
    (E) Public schools provide vocational and technical education.

14. The majority of cases of reading disability result from
    (A) brain damage
    (B) mental or neurological defects
    (C) lack of reading readiness when first exposed to reading instruction, uncorrected sensory problems, discouragement, emotional problems, and poor teaching
    (D) not properly teaching the child in kindergarten and first grade
    (E) experimental programs that create a diversity of teaching approaches, which confuse the child

15. Tests can most effectively be used by a teacher when given
    (A) to help the teacher understand statistical measures
    (B) upon completion of a unit
    (C) unexpectedly
    (D) to determine the final grades
    (E) without reviewing the material to be tested

16. About fifty percent of all children fall within the IQ range of
    (A) 80–90   (D) 50
    (B) 110–120   (E) 40–60
    (C) 90–110

17. When an irate parent makes an appointment to discuss a classroom problem with a teacher, the teacher's best response is to
    (A) listen to the parent's viewpoint before deciding the best response
    (B) firmly explain that the teacher is the authority in the classroom
    (C) inform the parent that he or she should see the principal
    (D) stress the need to obey rules and school regulations
    (E) require the parent's child be present at the meeting

18. Which of the following most clearly explains the content of the social studies curriculum?
    (A) History, the social sciences, and the experiences of students provide the areas from which the social studies curriculum is developed.
    (B) Human relationships form the basis for the social studies curriculum.
    (C) The curriculum is drawn from the study of various countries and cultures and the study of the United States.
    (D) Geography and citizenship are the basis of social science study.
    (E) Psychology, sociology, and values education determine content of the social studies curriculum.

19. Which of the following best states an important concept taught in developing cross-cultural and international understanding?
    (A) Beliefs, values, and customs are inherent in psychological makeup.
    (B) The institutions of family, school, and church are basically unchanging and found in all cultures.
    (C) Respect for individual dignity is most common in non-Communist countries.
    (D) People throughout the world are very different from each other.
    (E) Differences in ways of living are better understood when seen in the context of the values and customs that underlie them.

20. The psychology formulated by Thorndike, and later enlarged by B. F. Skinner, is known as
    - (A) IQ
    - (B) T-factor
    - (C) S-R
    - (D) Binet-Simon
    - (E) NEA

21. Mr. Kramer has taught for ten years yet admits that he often makes mistakes in interpreting the actions of his students. Which of the following statements provides the most probable explanation of Mr. Kramer's errors?
    - (A) He never asks other teachers for their advice.
    - (B) He should ask the students to explain their actions before coming to conclusions.
    - (C) He is probably not a very good teacher.
    - (D) He should spend more time seeking help from his principal and school psychologist.
    - (E) He often forgets that each student needs to be viewed individually.

22. Which of the following are considered to be integral parts of the teaching activity?

    I. organizing the physical conditions of the classroom
    II. getting the learners into a favorable attitude toward the subject or lesson to be learned
    III. evaluating what the pupil has learned
    IV. directing the learning activities of the pupils

    - (A) I, III, and IV
    - (B) II and IV
    - (C) II, III, and IV
    - (D) I, II, III, and IV
    - (E) III and IV

23. The philosophy that life and education should be interrelated and that schools should emulate life experiences as much as possible is most accurately credited to
    - (A) Dewey
    - (B) Hutchins
    - (C) Montessori
    - (D) Herbart
    - (E) Skinner

24. Which of the following is generally considered the *least* effective way to group for more individualization within a classroom?
    - (A) pupil age
    - (B) reading ability
    - (C) intelligence quotient
    - (D) interests
    - (E) placement tests

25. Basic to the formulation of educational goals
    (A) are our cultural values
    (B) are reading, writing, and arithmetic
    (C) is reading
    (D) are the guidelines provided by the federal government
    (E) are state guidelines

26. Which of the following are *not* principles of American education?

    I. Schools are free.
    II. Schools are not compulsory.
    III. Schools are universal.
    IV. Schools are supported and controlled by the public.
    V. Schools are sectarian.

    (A) I and V   (D) II and III
    (B) II and V   (E) II, III, and IV
    (C) III and V

27. In helping students to learn problem-solving approaches, the teacher should
    (A) guide and assist students when needed
    (B) tell students to select their own areas of study
    (C) keep the use of textbooks to a minimum
    (D) rarely allow students to solve problems without assistance
    (E) use programed instruction

28. An aversive condition is an event
    (A) encountered in health education
    (B) presented in science units
    (C) that creates no change in students
    (D) that arises in large groups
    (E) that causes the learner physical or mental discomfort

29. A course of study, or curriculum guide, is a document, usually prepared by the school district, that
    (A) carefully states educational objectives teachers should achieve during a school year
    (B) describes what is to be taught in particular courses at particular grade levels
    (C) describes the teaching units, lesson plans, and resource units to be used at each grade level throughout the school district
    (D) states the educational philosophy which guides curriculum
    (E) states books and other resources teachers should use in achieving the educational objectives of the school district

30. Which of the following (is) are *not* statistical measures of central tendency?

    I. median
   II. mode
  III. range
  IV. percentile
   V. mean

    (A) III   (D) III and IV
    (B) II and IV   (E) II
    (C) II, III, IV, and V

STOP. IF YOU FINISH BEFORE TIME IS UP, CHECK YOUR WORK ON THIS SECTION ONLY. DO NOT WORK ON ANY OTHER SECTION OF THE TEST.

SECTION II

Time: 30 Minutes
30 Questions

DIRECTIONS

Following each of the questions or statements below, select the choice that best answers the question or completes the statement.

1. Which of the following statements is most consistent with Jean Piaget's theories of intellectual development?
   (A) Piaget identifies basic stages in the intellectual development of children.
   (B) Intellectual development begins in the home as the result of environment.
   (C) Almost all children are capable of learning most mathematical concepts at the age of five.
   (D) Intellectual development occurs through the absorption of knowledge presented to us.
   (E) All-day kindergartens will raise the intellectual level of children.

2. During a P.E. basketball game an eleventh-grade student questioned a call made by a student referee. The P.E. teacher observed the incident and intervened. One of the male students loudly told the teacher to mind his own business. Which of the following actions by the teacher in response to the incident is *least* consistent with professional judgment and responsibility?
   (A) threatening to call the student's parents if the objectionable behavior does not stop
   (B) forcefully restraining the student in an attempt to take him to the office
   (C) in an agitated manner ordering student onlookers back to class
   (D) sending a student to find the on-site building administrator
   (E) calling another P.E. teacher over to help control the situation

3. A teaching unit is best described as
   (A) a plan of instruction covering a one-week to two-month span in time
   (B) an educational department or classroom in which teaching is coordinated
   (C) a series of lesson plans showing continuity
   (D) an instructional unit developed by the teacher
   (E) a plan of instruction organized around particular themes, problems, or skills

4. Ms. Jones is a new teacher. She has studied child development in school and wishes to apply her knowledge to her new job. Ms. Jones knows that
   (A) half of her students will be below the national average
   (B) since children grow at different rates, there cannot be individualized goals
   (C) that normal children do not differ in rates of intellectual growth
   (D) that children can differ in rate and quality of growth
   (E) all children can be above average

5. An agency that is best known for administering programs associated with research in education is
   (A) Parent-Teacher Association
   (B) American Medical Association
   (C) National Education Association
   (D) National Science Foundation
   (E) Smithsonian Institution

6. A teacher can tell that learning has taken place when
   (A) a correct response is given to a specific question
   (B) assignments are finished
   (C) a child seems self-assured at the end of a lesson and offers to help teach other children
   (D) correct responses are given a number of times in a variety of contexts
   (E) a child is able to work on assignments without further instruction

7. Which of the following is the most important factor in the success of grouping within a classroom?
   (A) the recess schedule
   (B) the number of students in a group
   (C) the flexibility of student assignments to the groups
   (D) the age range of the students within a group
   (E) the evaluation techniques used by teachers

8. Which of the following are true with regard to criterion-referenced instruction?
   I. Criterion-referenced instruction is more concerned with the results of instruction than with instructional procedures.
   II. Instructional materials are more likely based on teacher judgment than on performance data.
   III. The approach centers on the ability of the learner to perform specified criterion behaviors.

IV. The approach is "means" oriented.
V. The approach is "ends" oriented.

(A) II and IV

(D) I, III, and V

(B) I and II

(E) III and IV

(C) I, II, and IV

9. Which of the following statements is most accurate with regard to students' abilities to learn?
   (A) They are primarily determined by home environment.
   (B) They vary little throughout life.
   (C) They are primarily determined by cultural and socioeconomic factors.
   (D) They are determined by a combination of hereditary factors affected by environmental factors including the home and school.
   (E) They are primarily determined by genetic makeup and teachers' abilities to teach in a manner understood by the individual child.

10. In maintaining effective control in a classroom a teacher should
    (A) first of all, examine all points of view
    (B) discipline most severely those who start problems
    (C) keep lines of communication open with students who will talk about classroom problems
    (D) require the class members to police themselves if they wish to have special privileges.
    (E) first of all, attend to observable behavior

11. Which of the following best describes a lesson plan?
    (A) a plan of instruction for a class period
    (B) a plan of instruction covering the school year
    (C) a plan of instruction provided by school boards and administrators to guide a teacher's lessons
    (D) a document teachers regularly turn in to supervisors so that educational progress can be evaluated
    (E) a plan of learning signed by parents, teachers, and students

12. A subject-centered curriculum, in contrast to a child-centered curriculum,
    (A) emphasizes basic education
    (B) is oriented to the needs and values of a democratic society
    (C) requires stimulus mechanisms
    (D) emphasizes knowledge about the child
    (E) is built around student needs and interests

13. Transference is most likely to occur when
    (A) rules are memorized
    (B) learning is meaningful to the pupil
    (C) diagnostic tools have been used
    (D) routines are memorized
    (E) the teacher uses an individualized program

14. Children who purposely misbehave
    (A) do not like the teacher
    (B) believe their actions will eventually gain them attention
    (C) lack self-confidence
    (D) are not disciplined at home
    (E) must be isolated from classroom activity

15. Children at the primary level are best encouraged by
    (A) finding their assets or interests and involving them with these in
        mind
    (B) setting standards and pushing the children until they meet them
    (C) informing the children of their weaknesses in order to overcome
        them
    (D) telling the class to help those children who are behind
    (E) allowing the children to find their own level by themselves

16. During oral reading the teacher must keep in mind that
    (A) all children should use the same dialect
    (B) oral reading increases comprehension and recall better than silent
        reading
    (C) children do not enjoy reading aloud
    (D) this is the best method for determining good readers
    (E) understanding the pupils' difficulties is the important goal

17. For the beginner, learning to read mainly involves
    (A) learning to recognize printed symbols associated with sounds or
        words
    (B) shifting the focus of one's information-gathering process from the
        spoken to the printed form
    (C) reasoning
    (D) learning to coordinate hand-eye movements
    (E) a sensitizing of the visual process

18. The most positive factor of programmed instruction from the standpoint of teaching is that
    (A) it does not require teachers
    (B) it provides the student with immediate feedback
    (C) it is as effective and more economical than teachers
    (D) it frees the teacher to do things besides teaching
    (E) it is based on technological progress

19. Tests of general intelligence for children are usually expressed in
    (A) IQ scores
    (B) terms of children's intelligence quotients (CIQ)
    (C) scores usually lower than those of adults
    (D) terms of mental age (MA) and intelligence quotient (IQ)
    (E) terms of mental age (MA)

20. Which of the following should the teacher *not* do during parent-teacher conferences?
    (A) explain district, school, and classroom programs
    (B) put parents at ease
    (C) allow parents to express their feelings about their child's development
    (D) inform parents about the best ways to raise children
    (E) ask parents for their opinions

21. The current emphasis on inquiry in our classrooms is based on the assumption that
    (A) textbooks, as used by competent teachers, have the answers to student questions
    (B) students have more questions than answers
    (C) inquiry assures teacher involvement in the learning process
    (D) thinking is improved and learning takes place when students are actively involved in the teaching-learning process
    (E) knowledge is best displayed in a process involving intelligent questions and answers

22. When analyzing the test scores of groups it is preferable to compute the median as opposed to the mean when
    (A) accuracy is desired
    (B) the mean falls between actual test scores
    (C) achievement tests are not involved
    (D) properly trained psychologists are present
    (E) extreme scores would create a misleading average

23. In recent times team teaching has received a great deal of attention as an organizational scheme. Which of the following statements are true?

    I. There are many ways of structuring team teaching.
    II. Team teaching means a teacher will be teamed with teachers of equal or differentiated status and responsibilities.
    III. Team teachers usually work with the number of children we would find in a single normal classroom.
    IV. Team teaching insures fine results.
    V. Team teaching generally fosters greater individualization.

    (A) I, III, and V   (D) I, II, III, IV, and V
    (B) II, III, and IV   (E) I and IV
    (C) I, II, and V

24. The most accurate way to describe the American public school system would be in terms of
    (A) universal access to schooling
    (B) the number of students enrolled
    (C) state and local influence on schools
    (D) its being an institution reflecting American values and the American way of life
    (E) national objectives established by the federal government

25. An important element in Fernald's method which has produced very successful results with many severe reading-disability cases
    (A) is kinesthetic reinforcement
    (B) involves the use of basal readers beginning with preprimers
    (C) is the use of large groups of children numbering from thirty to forty
    (D) is the use of phonics
    (E) is the use of crawling to develop coordination

26. Which of the following is most consistent with current educational thought concerning school responsibility and student attitudes about learning?
    (A) The family is responsible for the learning attitudes of children.
    (B) Schools must take the responsibility for helping to influence the way children feel about learning.
    (C) Good classroom organization creates favorable learning attitudes.
    (D) Student attitudes are not a primary concern of schools.
    (E) Individualizing learning materials makes students responsible for learning attitudes.

27. The school curriculum's most difficult task is
   (A) meeting the needs of mentally gifted children
   (B) meeting the needs of individual children
   (C) changing society for the better
   (D) satisfying the general public
   (E) meeting the needs of children from low-income families

28. When discussing the cognitive domain we should understand that
   (A) cognitive objectives are more important that affective objectives
   (B) cognitive objectives are more difficult to measure and verify than affective objectives
   (C) knowledge, comprehension, and application are prerequisite to analysis, synthesis, and evaluation
   (D) analysis, synthesis, and evaluation are prerequisite to knowledge, comprehension, and application
   (E) objectivity does not fall within its realm

29. Audiovisual aids are most effectively used as a learning tool
   (A) to reward outstanding scholastic activity
   (B) as a stimulus to promote learning
   (C) to provide variety to the day
   (D) as part of a planned lesson
   (E) by quieting children and focusing their attention on a subject

30. Psychological testing should be performed by

   I. guidance counselors
   II. teachers
   III. aides
   IV. principals
   V. psychologists

   (A) V   (D) I, II, and V
   (B) I and V   (E) I, II, III, IV, and V
   (C) I, IV, and V

STOP. If you finish before time is up, check your work on this section only. Do not work on any other section of the test.

SECTION III

Time: 30 Minutes
30 Questions

DIRECTIONS

Following each of the questions or statements below, select the choice that best answers the question or completes the statement.

1. In establishing acceptable behavior in a classroom, the teacher should first of all
   (A) always follow through on threats of punishment
   (B) define limits of acceptable behavior and communicate these to the class members
   (C) attempt to isolate troublesome children before problems arise
   (D) allow children to define rules and punishments that will be enforced
   (E) realize that the students will gradually develop their own rules

2. It is important that the teacher recognize that he or she and a student have continual interaction
   (A) that should be carefully controlled
   (B) that is determined by curriculum set forth by the board of education
   (C) some of which is encouraging and some discouraging
   (D) governed primarily by the social background of the child
   (E) the quality of which is determined by the behavior standards of the school

3. Which of the following is usually considered the most useful in correcting a student's misbehavior?
   (A) providing the student with responsibility
   (B) criticizing the student
   (C) attempting to remove the causes of the misbehavior
   (D) transferring the student to another class
   (E) changing the classroom seating pattern

4. Which of the following concepts *least* reflects John Dewey's philosophy?
   (A) subject-centered education   (D) intrinsic motivation
   (B) learning by experiencing   (E) democracy
   (C) pragmatism

5. Which of the following is generally considered to be most essential to learning?
   - (A) motivation
   - (B) reading skills
   - (C) average intelligence
   - (D) good teaching
   - (E) parental support

6. Which of the following is the best example of proper anecdotal comments a teacher might make after observing a student?
   - (A) Parents will not cooperate. Sally is unhappy.
   - (B) Parents are very cooperative. Sally is happy.
   - (C) Sally completed her reading assignment early. She then drew pictures of horses for a few minutes before beginning her next assignment.
   - (D) Sally threw a temper tantrum. She must have serious home problems.
   - (E) Sally displayed signs of psychosis and schizophrenia throughout our music period today.

7. When a test measures what it intends to measure it is said to be
   - (A) valid
   - (B) standardized
   - (C) objective
   - (D) subjective
   - (E) reliable

8. Which of the following is *least* likely to be a part of a good drill exercise?
   - (A) time limits
   - (B) grades
   - (C) drill focus on student weaknesses
   - (D) well-understood drill material
   - (E) drill material involving a complex process that varies

9. The mother of an eight-year-old child visits the child's teacher and complains of frequent quarrels with the child's father. During these quarrels the father often threatens to beat the wife and child and has, on occasion, struck both. The appropriate action for the teacher is to
   - (A) contact the father to learn his side of the story
   - (B) sympathetically inform the mother that there is nothing the school can do to help
   - (C) refer the mother to the police department
   - (D) inform the principal as soon as possible to assure that proper agencies are contacted
   - (E) refer the problem to the principal, who is responsible for the child's welfare

10. What percentage of a distribution of students falls into the highest quartile?
    (A) 10   (B) 5   (C) 25   (D) 15   (E) 50

11. Learning transference increases most when the student
    (A) learns through a subject-centered curriculum
    (B) learns through a child-centered curriculum
    (C) understands the meaning of what has been learned
    (D) is right
    (E) is taught responsibility

12. When a teacher passes back corrected papers to a class and then discusses the correct answers, the teacher is probably doing this to
    (A) use time that should be spent on new lessons
    (B) provide students an opportunity to change incorrect answers
    (C) provide the students an opportunity to judge the adequacy of their responses
    (D) fulfill a need for repetition in the learning process
    (E) allow students to compare answers with each other so they can judge their class standing

13. If a student or parent complains about a report card grade, it is best for the teacher
    (A) not to raise the grade
    (B) to raise the grade
    (C) to refer the complaint to the principal
    (D) to review the student's records and explain how the grade was computed
    (E) reach a compromise

14. Which of the following best describes visual-motor-coordination problems?
    (A) The students will be clumsy or uncoordinated.
    (B) The learners will not be able to judge how far or near something is in relation to themselves.
    (C) The students will have difficulty in locating themselves spatially to their environment.
    (D) Learners will have difficulty in getting their eyes, hands, and thought processes to work together to achieve a given task.
    (E) The learners often cannot understand differences and sameness by category classification of objects presented visually.

15. Mr. Smith, a high school teacher, often invites successful community leaders to his class so that they can describe their activities to the students. When students show interest he praises them. Which of the following tactics is Mr. Smith using?
   (A) reinforcement
   (B) team teaching
   (C) modeling and reinforcement
   (D) contiguity
   (E) individualization

16. Betty is a student who has been transferred to a new school at midyear. Her parents inform the teacher that Betty is sensitive to criticism. In class, Betty does little work and constantly creates minor disturbances. The teacher's first step in seeking to correct the situation should be to
   (A) review the child's cumulative record
   (B) call Betty's parents in order to seek guidance
   (C) inform Betty's parents that her behavior is unacceptable and must be changed
   (D) report the child to a supervisor
   (E) discuss the problem with the school psychologist

17. A percentile is
   (A) a number indicating standing corresponding to a percentage of a group
   (B) the object of perception
   (C) the percentage of people who have received a given score on a standardized test
   (D) used in stating standard deviation
   (E) a way of expressing the number of questions answered correctly on a test

18. The major characteristics that are important in reading readiness are
   (A) age and general intelligence
   (B) age, sex, intelligence, visual and auditory perception, physical health and maturity, use of oral language, emotional and social adjustment, and interest
   (C) age, intelligence, visual and auditory perception, physical health and maturity, use of oral language, emotional and social adjustment, and interest
   (D) physical and emotional maturity
   (E) sex and a minimum mental age of six years

19. A disadvantage of programmed instructional material is that
    (A) the information is presented in small units
    (B) students may learn by memory and not understand the material
    (C) the information is presented sequentially
    (D) the questions reinforce learning
    (E) it makes teachers unnecessary

20. Ms. Jones attempts to draw every student into her classroom discussions.
    She probably does this because she understands the students' need
    (A) to get everything out into the open
    (B) to be creative
    (C) to show their oral abilities to the rest of the class
    (D) to show that they have done their homework
    (E) to feel significant and be a part of a larger group

21. Teachers' meetings are usually most effective when they
    (A) center on the problems of the school district
    (B) concern themselves with the problems of the PTA
    (C) center on topics or problems raised by teachers
    (D) are concerned with behavioral problems
    (E) have a preset time limit

22. The curriculum-development committee of a school district should
    (A) attempt to disregard the problems of individual schools so that a
        better general plan can be developed
    (B) provide supervision for the implementation of curriculum
    (C) strive to develop individual school planning
    (D) develop a unified curriculum for the school district
    (E) follow the directives of teacher representatives

23. Which of the following are good reasons to allow a free silent-reading
    period?

    I. It allows children to read material in which they are interested.
    II. It can positively affect the students' affective domain with regard to
        reading.
    III. It gives teachers the time to prepare for upcoming lessons.
    IV. It allows teachers to observe reading habits.
    V. It allows teachers time to correct papers.

    (A) I, II, and IV   (D) III, IV, and V
    (B) I, III, IV, and V   (E) III and V
    (C) IV and V

24. Effective teachers realize that each child needs to
    (A) feel accepted within the group
    (B) feel he or she is the most important person in the class
    (C) function independently of the group
    (D) function independently of the teacher
    (E) easily accomplish all of the assignments

25. Teaching machines are most effectively used
    (A) by slow learners
    (B) by gifted learners
    (C) to meet specific individual students' needs under the guidance of a
        teacher
    (D) to provide the teacher with more free time
    (E) under the guidance of classroom aides

26. Which of the following statements provides the best reason for use of
    dramatization in the classroom?
    (A) It enables students to learn cooperative self-expression.
    (B) It provides an opportunity for play within the classroom.
    (C) Children enjoy character portrayal.
    (D) It allows children to make moral statements to the class.
    (E) It allows the teacher to use psychodrama as a psychological tool.

27. Mary is an aggressive child who often fights with other children and
    appears to intentionally disrupt the classroom. Mary's teacher, Mr.
    Block, speaks to her parents about the situation. During the conference,
    the first thing Mr. Block should do is
    (A) attempt to understand and respond to the feelings of the parents
    (B) suggest alternative means of educating Mary
    (C) outline a program of behavior modification, which the parents can
        use to help Mary
    (D) suggest means of obtaining counseling for Mary
    (E) define the limits of school and parent responsibility

28. Reading comprehension is generally best demonstrated
    (A) by a student who has read a selection silently
    (B) by a student who has engaged in reading aloud to the class
    (C) by a student who has read aloud to the teacher
    (D) by a student who has read aloud to another student
    (E) in assignments asking the student to identify details from a selection
        read the previous day

29. Thinking ability can best be developed by
    (A) asking students to identify with characters in stories that ask moral questions
    (B) problem solving, critical and creative thinking, and related inquiry processes
    (C) obtaining a solid foundation of facts from which to work
    (D) asking students to concentrate on creative questioning of accepted ideas
    (E) creating situations in the classroom which approximate the kinds of problems students will face in the future

30. The curriculum of health education should
    (A) teach students about personal safety and hygiene
    (B) cure disease
    (C) lessen the need to regularly visit doctors
    (D) teach students how to care for each other when ill
    (E) teach students not to talk to strangers

STOP. IF YOU FINISH BEFORE TIME IS UP, CHECK YOUR WORK ON THIS SECTION ONLY. DO NOT WORK ON ANY OTHER SECTION OF THE TEST.

SECTION IV

Time: 30 Minutes
30 Questions

DIRECTIONS

Following each of the questions or statements below, select the choice that best answers the question or completes the statement.

1. Which of the following presents the best statement about the use of grades?
   (A) Grades should follow a strict curve.
   (B) Grades show be used as incentives.
   (C) Grades should reflect quality and quantity of performance.
   (D) Grades should not serve as communication with parents.
   (E) Grades should reward effort.

2. Which of the following would *not* be a goal of written composition?
   (A) It will develop self-expression.
   (B) It will develop an appreciation for group dynamics.
   (C) It will develop punctuation skills.
   (D) It will develop basic grammar skills.
   (E) It will develop the ability to share ideas with others.

3. The child who is most often referred for guidance counseling by a teacher is the child who is
   (A) an underachiever   (D) withdrawn
   (B) a slow learner   (E) mentally gifted
   (C) a behavior problem

4. Which statement is most valid concerning the quarrels of children?
   (A) Quarrels occur most often among girls.
   (B) Quarrels become less physical with increasing age.
   (C) Quarrels are usually solved physically.
   (D) Quarrels become more physical with increasing age.
   (E) Normal children rarely quarrel.

5. Which of the following statements best describes the proper teaching of the processes of arithmetic?
   (A) Understanding is more important than accuracy.
   (B) Rationalization is more important than memorizing processes.
   (C) Memorizing processes is more important than understanding application.
   (D) Process should become automatic through drill.
   (E) Specific application can be learned only through drill.

6. In teaching mathematics skills to children it is *least* important to the learning process that the teacher
   (A) provide a large number of problems for practice
   (B) show the students the systematic procedures necessary for problem solving
   (C) identify to the children the reasons they are missing problems
   (D) grade each problem and arrive at a total score
   (E) relate the math problems to everyday use

7. The social studies curriculum should include objectives that will help children learn to
   (A) consider multiple causes of events, evidence contrary to personal opinions, and the limits of generalization
   (B) express themselves clearly in written form
   (C) use the library and proper punctuation when doing reports
   (D) see good and bad in other cultures
   (E) use the insights of moral judgment in evaluating other peoples and cultures

8. The use of experiments or demonstrations in teaching science
   (A) is more valuable than teaching by lecturing
   (B) is more valuable than teaching through inquiry and discussion
   (C) is valuable if used in the context of a lesson that relates observation to other information
   (D) should be discouraged in elementary schools, since the concepts they encompass are difficult for young children
   (E) should be discouraged in elementary schools, since the time involved can be better used in discussion

9. In trying to point out a common error in a science experiment, Mr. Quider solicited responses from selected students in his class realizing that certain responses were more likely to be included than others. His sample of responses was
   (A) fair   (D) biased
   (B) consistent   (E) normal
   (C) favorable

10. Which of the following statements is generally most accurate with regard to slow learners?
    (A) They are best taught through visual experiences.
    (B) They learn faster outside of the school environment.
    (C) They are usually physically smaller than faster learners.
    (D) They are best motivated by tasks that require constant repetition.
    (E) They are as interested in being successful and gaining recognition as are faster learners.

11. Which of the following is stated as an affective objective?
    (A) After completing this unit, the teacher should be able to give two types of retention problems associated with learning disabled children.
    (B) After completing this unit, the teacher will be able to administer a diagnostic skills test.
    (C) After reading this unit, the teacher should have a greater sensitivity to the characteristics of learning disabled children.
    (D) After completing this unit, the teacher should be able to indicate a language problem characteristic of learning disabled children.
    (E) After reading this unit, the teacher should be able to write clear behavioral objectives related to learning disabled children.

12. Mr. Joseph calls the principal's office and reports that the drinking fountain next to his classroom is running over and students are slipping on the wet floor. Mr. Joseph is on his conference period and tells the office he has to prepare a test for his next class. A short time later, after returning to his classroom, Mr. Joseph allows a student without a pass to return a book to the library. The student slips on the wet floor and is injured. Subsequently the student sues the school district and Mr. Joseph. Legally, Mr. Joseph
    (A) is not negligent because he immediately informed the school of the hazardous situation
    (B) is not negligent because he remained at the fountain until the situation was resolved
    (C) is negligent because he allowed the student in the hall without an appropriate pass
    (D) is not negligent because he fulfilled his primary responsibility as a teacher by telling the office he had to prepare for his next class
    (E) is negligent because he did not take effective action to solve the problem

13. Which of the following was the most significant factor in the demise of the progressive-education movement in the 1950s?
    (A) the questioning of U.S. technological superiority
    (B) the proliferation of professional-education associations
    (C) the failure to attract popular support with slogans such as educating the "whole child"
    (D) lack of teacher commitment to make the progressive program succeed
    (E) the failure of the progressive movement to keep pace with the transformation of American society

14. The National Defense Education Act (NDEA) was passed in 1958. Which of the following was the catalyst for the passage of the act?
    (A) a desire to provide equal educational opportunity for all American citizens
    (B) a desire to counteract the Soviet Union's dominance in the space race
    (C) a desire to provide federal aid to disadvantaged school districts
    (D) a desire to provide individual stipends for students enrolled in agricultural and vocational education programs
    (E) a desire to provide federal aid to initiate local programs for the handicapped

15. In *Shaping Educational Policy*, James B. Conant made suggestions about how the policy-making process in education might be improved. Conant's educational recommendations called for
    (A) the administration of public education centralized at the national level
    (B) policy making at the national level to reflect the philosophy of the Department of Education
    (C) the strengthening of the federal Department of Education
    (D) massive federal aid to education in the form of open-ended educational grants
    (E) a "nationwide" educational policy derived from interstate consultation and planning

16. The radical approach that A. S. Neill suggested in *Summerhill* was
    (A) that the use of negative reinforcement can be an effective method to initiate long-lasting social change
    (B) that education was primarily emotional and not intellectual
    (C) a return to Rousseau's concept of a child-centered education without the use of force
    (D) an education that allowed the student to fulfill basic drives and motivations
    (E) that teachers are only facilitators of knowledge

17. Which of the following educators had the greatest impact on early-childhood education during the last two decades?
    (A) Bruner
    (B) Madlyn Hunter
    (C) B. F. Skinner
    (D) Piaget
    (E) Ginot

18. A landmark in the curricular development of the public school was formulated by Charles W. Eliot and the Committee of Ten (1893). The report proposed that
    (A) vocational education should be the cornerstone of the high school curriculum
    (B) the public high school should incorporate manual training into the curriculum
    (C) the high school curriculum should train students for the actual duties of life
    (D) the high school elective system should be confined to the nine traditional subject areas
    (E) the formal curriculum should be expanded to include cocurricular activities

19. An eleventh-grade American history teacher announces to his class that he is terminating the "traditional" approach to American history and, in its place, instituting a "U.S. Studies" program. Of the following, the main educational reason for instituting the change would be to
    (A) treat our national development as an isolated phenomenon
    (B) revise assumptions of national exclusiveness and reconsider flattering legends
    (C) foster an idealistic international view of the world
    (D) justify abandoning the memorization of dates and events
    (E) allow for individualization of instruction

20. Bill is continually out of his seat without permission and is frequently rude and discourteous. Which of the following disciplinary actions by a teacher is most consistent with establishing cooperation between home and school?
    (A) Sending a note home with the disruptive student, informing his parents of the need for firm and consistent discipline.
    (B) Assigning the student three consecutive days of detention, but providing one day off for good behavior if the boy's parents attend a parent conference.
    (C) Initiating phone contact in which the parent is apprised of the school performance involving disruptive behavior and detention.
    (D) Informing the parents of the disruptive nature of the inappropriate behavior and stating that unless the behavior stops, the student will be isolated from the class.
    (E) Devising a contract in which a daily progress report on the student's behavior is sent home and is signed by the teacher, parent, and student.

21. The current sixth-grade social studies unit is entitled "Understanding Central America." Ms. Romine believes that group activities can best facilitate studying the unit. Ms. Romine divides the class into six committees and assigns each committee the task of researching a specific Central American country. Which of the following reasons would be considered the most significant disadvantage of the pupil committee system?

   (A) The teacher has only a limited opportunity to be a facilitator of knowledge.
   (B) Committee reports often lack creativity and originality.
   (C) Committees are not conducive to informal discussion.
   (D) Committees spend an inordinate amount of time on research.
   (E) Group projects have been discredited by professional educators.

22. Which of the following would be considered prerequisites for organizing effective group activities in a high school class?

   I. Establish recognizable and understandable goals for group assignments.
   II. Establish a room environment that minimizes intergroup conflict.
   III. Determine the criteria to be used in selecting a group chairperson.
   IV. Determine the composition of each group through random selection.

   (A) I and II only   (D) I, II, and III
   (B) II, III, and IV   (E) I, II, III, and IV
   (C) I, III, and IV

23. Which of the following statements is most consistent with the educational purpose of continuous evaluation?

   (A) Continuous evaluation is the end product of the educational process.
   (B) Anecdotal records may be used in continuous evaluation procedures.
   (C) Continuous evaluation provides a diagnostic basis for discovering children's strengths and weaknesses.
   (D) Learning is more effective if students participate in evaluation.
   (E) Evaluation must be geared to the needs of the student if it is to be effective.

24. The main reason the National Education Association (NEA) has vigorously opposed the voucher plan is that

   (A) public schools have played a major role in instilling democratic beliefs in our children

(B) religious denominations would be entitled to a huge increase in tax dollars

(C) public control over the curriculum would be destroyed

(D) laws against sex discrimination could not be enforced in private schools

(E) the public schools would lose their traditional political, economic, and social base

25. Educational researchers have indicated that the greatest shortage of teachers in the decade of the 1980s will be in the fields of

(A) social science and science

(B) computer technology and physical education

(C) technical arts and math

(D) math and science

(E) foreign language and math

26. A student is disruptive by repeatedly talking out without being called on. The teacher seems to think that the disruptive behavior is constant. The most appropriate first step in developing a plan to modify the behavior would be to

(A) ignore the disruptive behavior to avoid reinforcing a negative set

(B) take a baseline data of the target behavior

(C) determine if the physical environment correlates with the undesirable behavior

(D) select and implement an appropriate modification technique

(E) modify the behavior through operative conditioning

27. Attempts to modify an elementary school child's atypical behavior have met with repeated failure. After consultation with the school administrator regarding the continued serious nature of the student's behavior, the teacher is authorized to administer corporal punishment. Which of the following describes the most appropriate professional and legal responsibilities regarding the use of reasonable corporal punishment?

(A) Corporal punishment should never be authorized.

(B) Verbal parental approval is necessary before corporal punishment may be administered.

(C) The on-site administrator has the final authority to authorize the use of corporal punishment.

(D) A teacher, vice-principal, principal, or any other certified or classified employee are the only individuals legally authorized to administer corporal punishment.

(E) The student's parent or guardian must give written approval for corporal punishment to be administered.

28. A school administrator authorizes a locker check in response to information that a drug ring is operating on campus. During the locker check a small amount of marijuana is discovered in a student's locker. The police are called on campus and subsequently a student is arrested. Which of the following examples meets the legal requirements of law enforcement officers operating on a school campus?

   (A) Law enforcement officers have to obtain the consent of school officials prior to placing a student in custody.

   (B) A school official must be present when law enforcement officials question a student.

   (C) A student cannot be removed from a school campus without first notifying the appropriate administrators who are legally responsible for the student.

   (D) Law enforcement officers can enter a school campus on their own discretion and school officials cannot in any way attempt to resist or obstruct them.

   (E) School security officers have jurisdiction over campus criminal activities.

29. The terms balance and posture, locomotion, contact and receipt, and body image and differentiation, would most closely be associated with

   (A) a perceptual-motor lab

   (B) characteristics of the learning disabled child

   (C) the development of temporal concepts

   (D) behavior modification

   (E) sequential development

30. Which of the following recommendations to improve the pay scale of classroom teachers would most often by opposed by teacher groups?

   (A) an across-the-board raise for all teachers regardless of rank on the salary schedule

   (B) a merit pay schedule

   (C) an additional stipend for department chairpersons who conduct seminars and give demonstrations to share expertise with colleagues

   (D) creating a limited number of "master teachers" entitling the recipient to receive additional money higher than regular teacher pay

   (E) initiating a pay scale that treats good and bad teachers exactly alike

STOP. IF YOU FINISH BEFORE TIME IS UP, CHECK YOUR WORK ON THIS SECTION ONLY. DO NOT WORK ON ANY OTHER SECTION OF THE TEST.

ANSWER KEY FOR PRACTICE TEST 2
Test of Communication Skills
Section I: Listening

Part A Questions and Statements	Part B Conversations	Part C Talks
1. (D)	13. (D)	21. (C)
2. (C)	14. (B)	22. (A)
3. (C)	15. (C)	23. (C)
4. (A)	16. (A)	24. (D)
5. (C)	17. (B)	25. (C)
6. (C)	18. (A)	26. (D)
7. (B)	19. (D)	27. (D)
8. (C)	20. (C)	28. (A)
9. (B)		29. (B)
10. (B)		30. (A)
11. (A)		31. (D)
12. (D)		32. (A)

Section II: Reading

1. (C)	9. (B)	17. (E)	25. (D)
2. (B)	10. (C)	18. (B)	26. (A)
3. (D)	11. (C)	19. (C)	27. (A)
4. (C)	12. (A)	20. (E)	28. (C)
5. (C)	13. (D)	21. (A)	29. (C)
6. (D)	14. (A	22. (C)	30. (B)
7. (C)	15. (B)	23. (A)	31. (B)
8. (A)	16. (A)	24. (B)	32. (A)

Section III: Writing—Multiple Choice

Part A: Usage		Part B: Sentence Correction	
1. (C)	14. (D)	26. (B)	37. (C)
2. (B)	15. (A)	27. (C)	38. (B)
3. (E)	16. (B)	28. (D)	39. (D)
4. (B)	17. (C)	29. (D)	40. (D)
5. (C)	18. (A)	30. (D)	41. (C)
6. (C)	19. (B)	31. (E)	42. (C)
7. (E)	20. (E)	32. (D)	43. (A)
8. (B)	21. (C)	33. (A)	44. (E)
9. (B)	22. (C)	34. (D)	45. (B)
10. (B)	23. (A)	35. (B)	
11. (C)	24. (C)	36. (C)	
12. (A)	25. (A)		
13. (B)			

Test of General Knowledge

Section I: Social Studies

1. (E)	9. (A)	17. (D)	25. (D)
2. (D)	10. (B)	18. (D)	26. (A)
3. (C)	11. (A)	19. (B)	27. (C)
4. (B)	12. (E)	20. (E)	28. (B)
5. (C)	13. (D)	21. (A)	29. (B)
6. (C)	14. (E)	22. (C)	30. (C)
7. (C)	15. (D)	23. (D)	
8. (C)	16. (D)	24. (B)	

Section II: Mathematics

1. (D)	8. (C)	14. (B)	20. (A)
2. (C)	9. (A)	15. (B)	21. (D)
3. (E)	10. (C)	16. (D)	22. (B)
4. (B)	11. (B)	17. (C)	23. (D)
5. (E)	12. (B)	18. (E)	24. (A)
6. (C)	13. (B)	19. (D)	25. (D)
7. (B)			

Section III: Literature and Fine Arts

1. (D)	10. (C)	19. (B)	28. (C)
2. (E)	11. (D)	20. (B)	29. (D)
3. (B)	12. (E)	21. (D)	30. (D)
4. (E)	13. (A)	22. (C)	31. (B)
5. (A)	14. (D)	23. (D)	32. (C)
6. (B)	15. (C)	24. (D)	33. (E)
7. (E)	16. (B)	25. (E)	34. (E)
8. (E)	17. (E)	26. (D)	35. (C)
9. (D)	18. (A)	27. (D)	

Section IV: Science

1. (C)	9. (A)	17. (E)	25. (D)
2. (A)	10. (C)	18. (E)	26. (A)
3. (E)	11. (B)	19. (D)	27. (A)
4. (D)	12. (C)	20. (B)	28. (D)
5. (C)	13. (C)	21. (A)	29. (B)
6. (D)	14. (D)	22. (C)	30. (E)
7. (B)	15. (D)	23. (C)	
8. (C)	16. (E)	24. (B)	

Test of Professional Knowledge

Section I

1. (D)	9. (D)	17. (A)	25. (A)
2. (C)	10. (D)	18. (A)	26. (B)
3. (A)	11. (D)	19. (E)	27. (A)
4. (D)	12. (C)	20. (C)	28. (E)
5. (B)	13. (C)	21. (E)	29. (B)
6. (C	14. (C)	22. (D)	30. (D)
7. (A)	15. (B)	23. (A)	
8. (A)	16. (C)	24. (A)	

Section II

1. (A)	9. (D)	17. (A)	25. (A)
2. (B)	10. (E)	18. (B)	26. (B)
3. (E)	11. (A)	19. (D)	27. (B)
4. (D)	12. (A)	20. (D)	28. (C)
5. (D)	13. (B)	21. (D)	29. (D)
6. (D)	14. (B)	22. (E)	30. (A)
7. (C)	15. (A)	23. (C)	
8. (D)	16. (E)	24. (D)	

Section III

1. (B)	9. (D)	17. (A)	25. (C)
2. (C)	10. (C)	18. (B)	26. (A)
3. (C)	11. (C)	19. (B)	27. (A)
4. (A)	12. (C)	20. (E)	28. (A)
5. (A)	13. (D)	21. (C)	29. (B)
6. (C)	14. (D)	22. (D)	30. (A)
7. (A)	15. (C)	23. (A)	
8. (E)	16. (A)	24. (A)	

Section IV

1. (C)	9. (D)	17. (D)	25. (D)
2. (B)	10. (E)	18. (D)	26. (B)
3. (C)	11. (C)	19. (B)	27. (E)
4. (B)	12. (E)	20. (E)	28. (D)
5. (D)	13. (E)	21. (B)	29. (A)
6. (D)	14. (B)	22. (D)	30. (B)
7. (A)	15. (E)	23. (C)	
8. (C)	16. (C)	24. (E)	

SCORING PRACTICE TEST 2

To score Practice Test 2, total the number of correct responses for each of the three tests separately. Do not subtract any points for questions attempted but missed, as there is no penalty for guessing. The score for each test is then scaled from 600 to 690.

ANALYZING YOUR TEST RESULTS

The charts on the following pages should be used to carefully analyze your results and spot your strengths and weaknesses. The complete process of analyzing each subject area and each individual question should be completed for each Practice Test. These results should be reexamined for trends in types of error (repeated errors) or poor results in specific subject areas. THIS REEXAMINATION AND ANALYSIS IS OF TREMENDOUS IMPORTANCE FOR EFFECTIVE TEST PREPARATION.

PRACTICE TEST 2 GENERAL ANALYSIS SHEET

Test of Communication Skills

	Possible	Completed	Right	Wrong
Section I: Listening	32			
Section II: Reading	32			
Section III: Writing—Multiple Choice	45			
COMMUNICATION SKILLS TOTALS	109			

Test of General Knowledge

Section I: Social Studies	30			
Section II: Mathematics	25			
Section III: Literature and Fine Arts	35			
Section IV: Science	30			
GENERAL KNOWLEDGE TOTALS	120			

Test of Professional Knowledge

Section I	30			
Section II	30			
Section III	30			
Section IV	30			
PROFESSIONAL KNOWLEDGE TOTALS	120			

ANALYSIS—TALLY SHEET FOR QUESTIONS MISSED

One of the most important parts of test preparation is analyzing WHY you missed a question so that you can reduce the number of mistakes. Now that you have taken the Practice Test I and corrected your answers, carefully tally your mistakes by marking in the proper column.

REASON FOR MISTAKE

	Total Missed	Simple Mistake	Misread Problem	Lack of Knowledge

Test of Communication Skills

	Total Missed	Simple Mistake	Misread Problem	Lack of Knowledge
Section I: Listening				
Section II: Reading				
Section III: Writing—Multiple Choice				
COMMUNICATION SKILLS TOTALS				

Test of General Knowledge

	Total Missed	Simple Mistake	Misread Problem	Lack of Knowledge
Section I: Social Studies				
Section II: Mathematics				
Section III: Literature and Fine Arts				
Section IV: Science				
GENERAL KNOWLEDGE TOTALS				

Test of Professional Knowledge

Section I				
Section II				
Section III				
Section IV				
PROFESSIONAL KNOWLEDGE TOTALS				

PRACTICE TEST 2 ESSAY CHECKLIST

Diagnosis/Prescription for Timed Writing Exercise

A good essay will:

_____ address the assignment
        be well focused
_____ be well organized
        smooth transitions between paragraphs
        coherent, unified
_____ be well developed
        contain specific examples to support points
_____ be grammatically sound (only minor flaws)
        correct sentence structure
        correct punctuation
        use of standard written English
_____ use language skillfully
        variety of sentence types
        variety of words
_____ be legible
        clear handwriting
        neat

COMPLETE ANSWERS AND EXPLANATIONS FOR PRACTICE TEST 2

TEST OF COMMUNICATION SKILLS

SECTION I: LISTENING

Part A: Questions and Statements

1. (D) Only this choice answers the question *how long;* the only other choice that refers to time is (C), but it refers to an irrelevant topic (*when* the last freeze was rather than *how long* the freeze will last).

2. (C) The statement connects danger with economical cars, and the only choice that maintains this connection is (C).

3. (C) The statement gives two reasons that history (the study of the past) is worthwhile and supports the generalization stated in choice (C).

4. (A) The statements mentions Hal's *plan for eating less,* and choice (A) mentions this plan again by using a synonymous term, *diet.* Each of the other conclusions does not necessarily follow from the statement.

5. (C) The only two choices that refer to admission price are (A) and (C); the only choice that answers *whether* the admission is free is choice (C).

6. (C) This choice rephrases the information given in the statement. Each of the other choices is a conclusion that does not necessarily follow.

7. (B) Only choice (B) answers the question of *whether* video games are temporary or not.

8. (C) We are told that the transmission fell apart *after* the warranty expired, and we therefore must conclude that the transmission was not under warranty.

9. (B) The statement connects reduction in prices with an increase in sales, and we must therefore conclude that reduced prices attracted buyers. Choice (A) is a possible conclusion but not one that necessarily follows from the statement.

10. (B) Only this choice responds to the question of *whether* the homework was finished or not.

11. (A) We must conclude that if those opposing the proposal were disappointed, the proposal passed. Choice (B) contradicts the statement, and (C) and (D) are irrelevant.

12. (D) This choice rephrases the information in the statement. Each of the other choices draws an unsupported conclusion.

Part B: Conversations

13. (D) The man refers to the woman as *doctor,* and we may reasonably conclude that the tests being discussed are medical tests.

14. (B) The man suggests that he is speaking from his office and has missed the doctor's communication because he has been out of the office. Given these rather obvious clues, we can conclude that they are probably speaking by phone.

15. (C) The girl replaces every *f* in alfalfa with *p-h,* thus suggesting her idea that all *f* sounds should be spelled with *p-h.* Choices (A) and (B) contradict the girl's words, and because she does give spelling advice, she does not assume that she knows nothing about spelling.

16. (A) Choices (B) and (C) are explicitly contradicted by the boy's response to the girl's spelling, and there is no evidence that he believes correct spelling to be a mystery. His final remark, *too many letters,* suggests that he associates the spelling of a word with its pronunciation.

17. (B) When Dodsworth misses a meeting, the meeting becomes a fight; therefore, we may infer that Dodsworth maintains order.

18. (A) The woman's question begins with *what happens* and suggests that she does not know what happens at such a meeting; in other words, she has never attended one of these meetings without Dodsworth. Choice (D) generalizes beyond the explicit or implicit information in the passage.

19. (D) The man refers twice to *conceding,* and this term often refers to admitting defeat in an election. Lost respect (C) may be indirectly tied to the election defeat but is not a strong answer.

20. (C) The speakers talk of television predictions but never of the actual results.

Part C: Talks

21. (C) The talk repeatedly stresses *disciplined study techniques.*

22. (A) At both the beginning and the end of the talk the speaker distinguishes between learning in a broad sense and doing well in school. Each of the other choices contradicts the speaker's belief that doing well in school is important.

23. (C) The speaker states that only when students are juniors in college do they recognize the importance of good study skills—thus implying that before that time (early college and high school) most students do not employ such skills.

24. (D) The speaker describes different reactions to a war poem to illustrate the general point that a poem *may not always mean the same thing to everyone.*

25. (C) The speaker stresses that the beliefs and attitudes of the reader will determine the personal meeting of the poem but does not criticize this fact. So (A), (B), and (D)—choices which imply criticism of subjective reading—should be eliminated.

26. (D) Since a reader's beliefs and attitudes can determine his or her understanding of a poem, we may infer that readers with similar beliefs and attitudes will understand a poem in similar ways. The talks suggests that different readers may hold different views of a poem but does not imply that the readers themselves will not understand *each other* as (B) suggests.

27. (D) The talk is an overall criticism of objective tests and their consequences.

28. (A) Early in the talk, the speaker cites the National Assessment of Educational Progress.

29. (B) The speaker associates the "back to basics" movement with the use of objective tests, which are soundly criticized in the talk. None of the other choices is a "movement," and none of them is mentioned in the talk.

30. (A) The speaker concludes by recommending that we *increase the number of teachers* but argues against more students (B) and more school days (D).

31. (D) In order to recommend an increase in the number of teachers and a reduced student-teacher ratio, the speaker must assume that students do not receive enough personal attention now. Choice (C) contradicts the speaker's inclination to recommend change.

32. (A) The speaker repeatedly and explicitly refers to the relationship between quantity and quality.

SECTION II: READING

1. **(C)** Each of the other choices contradicts the statement that art is a *particular kind of experience,* not just anything done by anyone. However, the passage does include dining as a possible artistic experience and thus suggests that a gourmet chef may be an artist.

2. **(B)** Choices (A), (D), and (E) restrict art to the sort of object found in a museum; (C) contradicts the idea that art is a *significant* experience. Choice (B) associates art with a particular experience of everyday life.

3. **(D)** Earlier in the passage, art is associated with unity, harmony, and fulfillment. We may infer that aesthetic thinking has these qualities.

4. **(C)** The author characterizes informal learning as that picked up unconsciously. Only Choice (C) is not deliberately taught.

5. **(C)** The author points out that our self-image may be different from the *actual opinions* of others.

6. **(D)** The author is *dismayed* by the Zuni and Hopi belief; however, the negative attitude is not so strong as to warrant choice (B) or (E).

7. **(C)** The author repeats in several ways that satisfaction is a relative quality tied to utility, which is also relative. Note that the term *relative* is stressed in the fourth sentence.

8. **(A)** Using the example of a sweater or pair of shoes, the second sentence supports the statement about how difficult satisfaction is to define.

9. **(B)** The fourth sentence says that relative utility can be specified; choice (B) makes this same point with a specific example.

10. **(C)** The passage offers a general description of certain aspects of American government, and those mentioned in choices (A), (B), and (D) would not need this general information. Choice (E) is too vague to be the best answer.

11. **(C)** Each of the other choices requires information beyond that given in the passage. The author stresses that Article I is lengthy and detailed, thus implying the it more fully explains the legislative branch.

12. **(A)** This choice is a particular example of a President exercising a power to perhaps establish a precedent.

13. **(D)** Choices (A), (B), and (E) are irrelevant to the points stressed in the first paragraph, and (C) might weaken the points made in the second sentence of that paragraph.

14. (A) This is an example of the sort of peer pressure described in the passage. Choices (B) and (C) contradict the passage; (D) and (E) are irrelevant.

15. (B) This is the only choice that stresses *ability* (how to).

16. (A) The author does not *judge* Henry George or his opinions on taxes; rather, the passage offers objective information.

17. (E) This choice paraphrases the quotation by James given in the passage; each of the other choices contradicts the pragmatist position that truth can be determined and understood (proved with *assignable reasons*).

18. (B) Each of the other choices contradicts information in the passage and all other choices are too specific to be regarded as summaries.

19. (C) The passage surveys general information, much in the manner of an encyclopedia entry. Each of the other choices suggests a specific focus that is not developed in the passage.

20. (E) To agree with choice (E), the author would have to admit that play is the same as art; however, it is explicitly stated that art is *something that is more than play*.

21. (A) To state that art as play grows out of surplus energy, one must assume that art as play requires energy and that those without energy will not engage in it.

22. (C) The paragraph states that television has solved the cost and teacher shortage problems, leading us to conclude that teaching is done on television. Each of the other choices is not supported by expressed or implied information in the passage.

23. (A) Each of the other choices is irrelevant to point (1); further explanation of *America's present role* would make the point clearer and more concrete. As it is, the meaning of *present role* is ambiguous.

24. (B) The author implies this question in the last sentence, but the passage ends before it is answered.

25. (D) The other choices are not specific enough to be appropriate titles for the passage.

26. (A) Point (2) is that young children learn to speak foreign languages more easily, and (A) is a specific illustration of this point.

27. (A) Throughout the passage, the author criticizes that attitude that hurries children to learn to read; however, the tone is not outright anger, so (C) is not the best choice.

28. (C) Choices (A), (B), and (D) suggest that the author has a positive attitude toward parents and teachers, and that attitude is contradicted by the clearly negative tone, expressed in negative terms such as *frenzy*. Choice (E) is irrelevent to the information in the passage. Only (C) reinforces the negative quality of *frenzy*.

29. (C) In the analogy, children are compared to *recruits*. Choice (E) is incorrect because the children are also compared to *tanks* but not to those who produce them.

30. (B) In the first paragraph, the author summarizes the point of view of *parents, teachers, and administrators* and goes on to criticize that viewpoint through the rest of the passage.

31. (B) The author develops a particular point of view; therefore, we cannot describe the passage's purpose in neutral terms such as *describe, survey,* or *compare* and must eliminate *praise* (E) because it suggests a positive viewpoint not shared by the author.

32. (A) This paragraph presents two questions and two answers and ends with a general conclusion. Therefore the choice that most accurately describes the structure of the passage is (A).

SECTION III: WRITING—MULTIPLE CHOICE

Part A: Usage

1. (C) *Melodious*, the adjective, is correct here to modify *tunes*. *Sound* is used here in the same sense as *seem*, rather than in the sense of "the bell sounded," meaning *made a sound*. Linking verbs of this kind may be followed by an adjective but not by an adverb.

2. (B) *About* or *regarding* or *concerning* would be correct. *As to* is nonstandard usage.

3. (E) No error. The comma after *Congress* correctly separates the two complete sentences.

4. (B) *Most widely* is the correct comparative form in this sentence because Mr. Feingold is being compared with several teachers. Were he being compared with only one other, *more* would be correct.

5. (C) While the verb form *should have been* is correct, referring to an event in the past, it is unclear to whom the pronoun *he* refers—Mr. Taylor or John. There are several methods that might be used to correct the ambiguity. For example, *him* could be substituted for *Mr. Taylor* and *Mr. Taylor* for *he* (if that is what is meant). Or a complete rewrite might be called for. *John*

was convinced that he should have been the one to head the committee's fundraising drive in November, 1980, especially after discussing the matter with Mr. Taylor.

6. **(C)** *More consistently,* the comparative adverb, is correct, modifying the verbs *throw, catch,* and *hit.*

7. **(E)** No error. The question mark is correctly placed. It applies only to the part of the sentence in quotation marks.

8. **(B)** A comma is needed after *hotel* to separate the introductory descriptive phrase from the rest of the sentence.

9. **(B)** *That eats animals* is redundant, repeating the meaning of *carnivorous,* and should be omitted. The words *well* and *known* are correctly joined by the hyphen when used as a modifier preceding the noun.

10. **(B)** *Being comprised of* is incorrect. It should be *comprising.* The word *comprise* means *to be composed of.* Thus, *being comprised of* would translate to *being composed of of.* The colon (C) correctly introduces the series.

11. **(C)** *Their* should be singular because it refers to *reader,* which is singular. *His or her* would be correct. To avoid the *his or her* construction, the sentence might be rewritten using the plural *readers;* however that is not given as an option.

12. **(A)** *Principal* is either a noun meaning the *administrator of a school* or an adjective meaning *main* or *primary.* What is required here is the noun *principle* meaning a *fundamental law* or *doctrine.* The use of quotation marks and commas is correct throughout.

13. **(B)** *Late* means *dead* and *widow* is the name for a woman whose husband *has died.* Using both words is repetitious. All other underlined portions are correct. The comma after *eyes* is correct to separate the introductory phrase from the rest of the sentence; *filed by* is acceptable idiom; and there is no need for punctuation separating the compound predicate *filed* and *returned.*

14. **(D)** *Each and every* is both a cliché and unnecessary repetition. Either *each* or *every* is correct but not both.

15. **(A)** There is confusion in meaning because of the placement of the word *either.* As the sentence stands, the reader expects a parallel structure to *to arrive,* and there is none. *He meant to arrive at the business meeting in time for either the chairman's opening statement or the sales manager's report* would be clearer, providing the parallel *statement or . . . report* closer to *either.*

16. (B) The verb in this sentence must agree with *recitation,* not with *ills.* Therefore it must be *is* instead of *are. Tendency toward* is the correct idiom, and *which* is properly used in referring to *groups.*

17. (C) *Not him* should be changed to *not he.* Substantives connected by a form of the verb *to be* must agree in case. You can identify this type of error by transposing the sentence. *It was I—I was it* (not *me was it*). *It was he—he was it* (not *him was it*).

18. (A) *Aesop* should not be set off with commas. It is restrictive— essential to the meaning of the sentence. The use of commas in this case suggests that Aesop was the only Greek slave in existence. Here is an example of correct use of such punctuation. *My sister, Jan, was born in October.* (I have one sister, and her name is Jan.) This is quite different from the following sentence. *My sister Jan was born in October.* (I have at least two sisters, and this particular sister was born in October.)

19. (B) *Infer* means to *surmise* or *judge from evidence.* The *evidence* could not do this. *Implies* is the correct word here, meaning *indicates* or *suggests. Inflammable* (or *flammable*—both are acceptable, meaning *readily set on fire*) is correct, not *inflammatory* (meaning *producing excitement*).

20. (E) No error.

21. (C) The correct word is *regardless.*

22. (C) A mark of punctuation must separate *death* and *however,* the break between the two complete sentences. *However* is a conjunctive adverb—such as *therefore, moreover,* and *nevertheless*—and the semicolon, rather than the comma, is the preferred mark of punctuation.

23. (A) *Not scarcely* is a double negative and incorrect. Either *not* or *scarcely* would be correct if used alone. *All ready* (the adjective form meaning *fully prepared*) is correct, rather than *already* (the adverb meaning *before now*).

24. (C) It is not clear to what *that* refers. The sentence might be rearranged in this way. . . . *the child chose the help of her mother rather than that of her friends. Chose,* choice (B), is the correct past tense of *choose.*

25. (A) To make the sentence consistent in point of view, *one reads* should be changed to *you read.*

Part B: Sentence Correction

26. (B) When you compare two items, *better* is correct. Choice (B) correctly words the comparison of the two quarterbacks. In addition, choice

(B), by deleting *when compared to,* is concise and less wordy.

27. (C) *Liable from* is idiomatically incorrect. Choice (C) corrects the error with *liable to,* meaning having a tendency to. Choice (D) changes the original meaning, and (E) suggests a legal meaning with *liable for,* a meaning not implied by the context of the original sentence.

28. (D) There is a subject-verb error here, which is corrected by choice (D). *Contemplating over* in choices (C) and (E) is idiomatically wrong. Phrases beginning with constructions such as *in addition to, as well as,* and *along with* affect the number of neither the subject nor the verb.

29. (D) The difficulty with the original sentence is that the verb *was* is being made to function with three separate elements, insurance policy, friends, and car. One can say *insurance policy was* and *car was* but not *friends was.* Choice (D) corrects the problem by using the proper form of the verb with each element. Choice (B) suggests that the policy, friends, and car are acting, which the original sentence does not suggest. Choice (C) suggests that *he* is acting, again something not suggested in the original. While choice (E) retains the intent of the orignal, it is extremely wordy and awkward.

30. (D) *Skills,* a plural noun, requires a plural verb, *increase.* Choices (B) and (E) change the meaning of the original sentence, and (C) has another subject-verb error.

31. (E) The phrase *to function well in the business world* acts as the subject of this sentence and, as such, should not be separated from its verb, *requires,* by the comma. Choice (B) removes the comma but introduces an error in using the adjective *good* rather than the adverb *well.* Choice (C) both retains the comma and introduces an error in using *affective* instead of *effective.* Choice (D) retains the comma and introduces a cliché in *willing and able.*

32. (D) You cannot compare *taking . . . respite* and a *period of study.* Choice (D) correctly words the comparison so that the sentence compares *taking* and *studying.*

33. (A) The sentence is correct as given. Choice (B) uses the word *floundered* (meaning *to move awkwardly*) for *foundered* (which in nautical terms means *to sink*) and removes the necessary comma separating the two complete sentences. Choice (C) adds a comma before *while,* changing its meaning from *at the same time* to the meaning of the conjunction *but* or *and* and drops the necessary comma. Choice (D) introduces a cause-and-effect relationship that the original does not suggest and (E) improperly uses a colon.

34. **(D)** The original sentence lacks parallel structure. Choice (D) corrects this error by using *becoming,* a verb form that is parallel with *de-emphasizing.*

35. **(B)** The correct idiom is *graduate from college,* not *graduate college.* Choices (C) and (E) both introduce an error in parallelism in that they substitute *study* for *studying. Study* is not parallel to *saving* and *worrying.* While the phrase *to be graduated from college* in choice (E) is accepted in informal English, it is not preferred in standard written English. There is no reason to add *he or she* (D) because the original sentence is speaking of a specific individual.

36. **(C)** *Its* is the possessive form. *It's* is the contraction for *it is.* Choice (B) retains the original error and adds another, the plural *wheels,* which would be inappropriate in speaking of a bicycle. Choice (D) introduces a misplaced modifier and suggests that the bicycle was rolling the ball down the hill. Choice (E) incorrectly uses *stricken* (which most commonly means *afflicted*) and also retains the original apostrophe error.

37. **(C)** This is a pronoun error. *Whoever* should be changed to *whomever.* Choices (D) and (E) change the original sentence unnecessarily and slightly alter its meaning.

38. **(B)** *After* is unnecessarily repetitious; it may be eliminated without damaging the clarity or meaning of the original sentence. Choices (C), (D), and (E) either change the meaning of the original or leave out necessary information.

39. **(D)** *At this point in time* is clichéd and awkward. It should be replaced with a direct and concise form such as *at present* or *now.* All other choices retain the cliché. In addition, choice (B) incorrectly uses the adjective *strong* rather than the adverb *strongly;* choice (C) changes the original meaning by inserting *says* in place of *feels* and introduces an error by using the comma before *that;* choice (E) leaves out necessary information and unnecessarily changes *proven* to *proved.* Both forms are correct.

40. **(D)** *Fewer* is used correctly to refer to items that are countable and *less* is used correctly to refer to items that are not countable. In this sentence, *less* belongs with *rainfall* and *fewer* belongs with *accidents.*

41. **(C)** Quotation marks should be used only in direct quotes. They would have been correct had the sentence read *used to say, "All it takes . . ."* Choice (B) retains the quotation marks and incorrectly places the comma outside of the end marks. If quotation marks are used, commas and periods always belong inside the end marks. Choices (D) and (E) delete the

quotation marks, but choice (D) both incorrectly uses a semicolon where a dash or comma is required and leaves out a necessary comma, and choice (E) changes the meaning of the original.

42. (C) The *then* following the comma indicates that this is an *if . . . then* construction.

43. (A) The sentence is correct as it stands. It is direct and does not confuse. The semicolon is the correct mark of punctuation to use between two complete sentences not connected by a conjunction. Choice (B) suggests that *you* are interested in *your continued support* rather than *we*. Choices (C) and (D) change the meaning of the original, and choice (E) is wordy and awkward and leaves the question of *whose* interest is being discussed.

44. (E) A salutation is, by definition, a greeting, and when used concerning a letter, means the greeting that comes before the body of the letter. The phase *at the top* is unnecessary because the word *salutation* carries that information. In addition to including that phrase, choice (B) does not use the quotation marks necessary in direct discourse and (C) changes the meaning of the original. Choice (D) is not the best choice because it leaves some doubt as to whether this was an oral or a written salutation.

45. (B) This sentence contains a pronoun error in the underlined portion. *Whom* should be changed to *who*. Choice (C) changes the meaning of the original sentence.

TEST OF GENERAL KNOWLEDGE

SECTION I: SOCIAL STUDIES

1. (E) It is highly unlikely that the senior sector of the population will embrace violent confrontation as a means to achieve political, social, and economic objectives. It is apparent, however, that as the population becomes progressively older, the political power of senior citizens will proportionately increase. Choice (B) is a logical conclusion, since the age composition of the general population affects the future birthrate. The rate of growth of the general population may decline based on the fact that fewer people are in the *childbearing* years.

2. (D) An unfavorable balance of payments or trade (a trade deficit) results when imports are greater than exports. The Consumer Price Index, choice (A), measures changes in the value of the dollar.

3. (C) *Name calling* is a propaganda device in which value-laden words are used to induce particular attitudes. In name calling, "loaded words" are used to make one reject an idea without examining appropriate evidence. *Glittering generality,* choice (D), is speech in vague but value-laden terms, such as *democratic* or *individual liberty*—the intention is to make one accept an idea without basis in fact.

4. (B) *Conspicuous consumption,* a term used by Thorstein Veblen (*The Theory of the Leisure Class*), describes the consumption of wealth, goods, and services primarily for the purpose of display. *Conspicuous consumption* implies that an individual can attain higher status when luxury goods are consumed in a highly visible manner.

5. (C) The passage clearly indicates sentiment against signing a nuclear freeze agreement with the Soviet Union. Under a nuclear freeze, the United States and the Soviet Union would agree to immediately halt the production, testing, and installation of new nuclear weapons systems. Opponents of a nuclear freeze argue that any agreement with the Soviets must not lock the United States into an inferior military position. Those who support an arms freeze indicate that unless immediate efforts are taken to reduce the arms race, a proliferation of nuclear weapons could end in a nuclear holocaust.

6. (C) There is a factor of impersonality in a crowd, since members do not interact with each other as unique individuals. The key characteristics of a crowd are suggestibility, anonymity, spontaneity, and invulnerability.

7. (C) President Truman, exercising his authority as Commander-in-Chief, recalled MacArthur from Korea (1951) and subsequently dismissed him from the service. Truman defended the dismissal by arguing that MacArthur's public criticism of presidential policy undermined the war effort and increase the risk of a confrontation with the Soviet Union. Although MacArthur favored air strikes over mainland China (D), Truman, in seeking to keep the Korean conflict a "limited war," never authorized such strikes.

8. (C) A mandated program is one designed to force compliance with a particular course of action. The passage implies that the company in question is meeting goals *as determined by the government*. Affirmative action programs are direct federal attempts to reverse the trend of previous discrimination against minorities. As such, guidelines are established to provide greater access for blacks, Mexican Americans, women, etc., to the job market.

9. (A) The term *guns or butter* was popularized during the Vietnam War years to indicate that limited tax dollars would not be used for both weapons and social welfare programs. The other choices are associated with the cold war philosophy of the 1950s. The *domino theory* was popularized during the Eisenhower administration.

10. (B) Conflict of interest can result from "insider" information. An individual, by the nature of his or her employment, is able to obtain information not available to the general public and, in turn, use that information for personal gain.

11. (A) Cuba. Fidel Castro established a Communist government in Cuba (1960). Since the early 1960s, Cuba has been supported militarily and economically by the Soviet Union. In the early 1960s, the United States charged Cuba with attempting to export Communist-style revolution to El Salvador by supplying military aid to Marxist guerrillas attempting to overthrow the American-supported Salvadoran government.

12. (E) In 1978, after thirteen years of discussion, the U.S. Senate ratified two treaties which will provide for the transfer of the Panama Canal to Panama by the year 2000. The second treaty, establishing neutrality in the Canal Zone, was not popular in the United States and passed the Senate with only one vote to spare over the needed two-thirds majority.

13. (D) An alarming percentage of high school graduates cannot understand a simple passage and cannot write a simple sentence or complete elementary math problems. The term that best describes this phenomenon is *functional illiteracy*. Choices (A) and (B) are incorrect, since there are many factors other than functional illiteracy that could cause the failure.

14. **(E)** By definition a *scapegoat* is one who is made to shoulder the blame for others or to suffer in their place. Scapegoating is *displaced aggression* against members of another group. Choice (A) is incorrect, since stereotyping does not necessarily imply displaced aggression.

15. **(D)** If a majority of farmers produce unusually large crops in a particular year, incomes would tend to fall. Overproduction increases supply, and assuming demand remains constant, the price of a crop tends to fall.

16. **(D)** Turkey ranks in the bottom 10% of the world's oil producers and is not a member of OPEC. The Organization of Petroleum Exporting Countries was formed in 1960 but reached world power after the 1973 Arab-Israeli war. OPEC was organized to coordinate programs and establish minimum prices for member nations. OPEC members include Algeria, Ecuador, Gabon, Indonesia, Iran, Iraq, Kuwait, Nigeria, Qatar, Saudi Arabia, the United Arab Emirates, Venezuela, and Libya.

17. **(D)** Both choices (A) and (B) can be inferred from information presented in the chart. In a democratic government, the people can rule themselves directly or indirectly through elected representatives. The chart indicates that not all people were allowed to participate in government. Although the new state constitutions were the beginning of democratic government, democracy was not yet a reality. The framers of the state constitutions were afraid of the potential ability of a powerful executive to restrict the rights of the people. Therefore, the term of office of the executive was limited, choice (B). This provided the people with a means to reevaluate the political leadership on a regular basis. With the exception of South Carolina, there is not evidence from the chart to support choice (C).

18. **(D)** If the President does not act on a submitted bill with ten days, that bill becomes a law without the President's signature. If a bill is sent to the President during the *last* ten days of a legislative session, the President does not act upon it, and Congress adjourns, the bill automatically dies instead of becoming law. This action is termed a pocket veto.

19. **(B)** The proportion of the population 15 and under is shown as smaller in the 1980 chart. *Proportion* refers to the distribution of the population. Choices (C) and (E) are not supported by information presented in the charts.

20. **(E)** Throughout the twentieth century, there has been a steady increase in the distribution of the population 65 and older. There are many factors to account for this, including a declining birth rate and increased longevity. Choice (C) is incorrect, since it is not possible to determine immigrant population growth from information presented in the charts.

Choice (D) is incorrect, since the charts do not deal with social welfare programs.

21. **(A)** A careful reading of the charts indicates that 1929 marked the statistical height of the U.S. economy during the period 1923–1933. The "bottom" fell out of the stock market in October of 1928, and by 1930 the economy was in the early stages of the depression. Among the causes of the depression were unequal distribution of income, overinvestment in industry, overspeculation in the stock market, and shortsighted government policies that failed to deal with the imbalance between farm and business income.

22. **(C)** Farm prices during the depression collapsed. In 1928 the farm price index stood at approximately 148. By 1932 the index had reached a low of approximately 64. This represented close to a 60% decrease in the farm price index in less than a four-year period. During the early 1930s the total farm production declined by only 6%, but the purchasing power of farmers declined by over 50% of that of a decade earlier.

23. **(D)** American industrial production was an indispensable factor in the defeat of the Axis powers. During World War II, America truly became the *arsenal for democracy*. The technological superiority of the U.S. wartime production doomed the Axis powers to defeat.

24. **(B)** The right to an impartial jury is an essential ingredient of a fair trial and is protected by the Sixth Amendment. In recent history the public's right to know, protected by the First Amendment (freedom of the press), has come in conflict with the Sixth Amendment right to a fair trial. Lawyers have argued successfully that in certain cases pretrial or regular trial publicity can jeopardize a defendant's right to an impartial jury. The courts are the final arbiters in maintaining a balance between First and Sixth Amendment freedoms.

25. **(D)** Paying production-quota bonuses as an incentive would not weaken Soviet control over agriculture. Choices (A), (B), and (C) would conflict with the basic Soviet dogma of a centrally planned economy. Soviet leadership does not want to increase the autonomy of the individual or the local district or authorize incentives that would lessen Soviet control over agriculture. Traditionally, the Soviets have used bonuses and promotions as incentives to achieve greater farm production. In this way, agricultural output can be increased without weakening central control.

26. **(A)** Only in recent decades has the Supreme Court reinterpreted the Fourteenth Amendment to make it an effective barrier against discrimination by states. The Fourteenth Amendement forbids states to deprive any person of the *due process of the law* or deny any person the *equal protection*

of the law. The due-process clause of the Fifth Amendment limits only the federal government.

27. (C) Demography is the study of human population. Undeveloped nations tend to have both high birth rates and high death rates. Recent improvements in technology and health care have had a profound effect in reducing the death rate. However, without a corresponding reduction in the birth rate to counterbalance a reduction in the death rate, a rapid increase in world population can result.

28. (B) The tundra is an area of permanently frozen ground and is characterized by treeless topography. The tundra zone lies at the high latitudes. it is a region of low winter temperatures and limited precipitation.

29. (B) 1963 to 1965 is the only three-year period in the choices given that shows a relatively constant unemployment rate. The number of unemployed males (16–64) for this period is approximately 7.75 million. Note that the broken line represents males in the 16 to 64 category. 1965 to 1967 (C) shows a slight drop.

30. (C) The 16- to 64-year-old unemployment rate fluctuates during the period under study while the 65+ unemployment rate shows a *marked increase* throughout the period. Therefore as the under-65 unemployment figures increase, so do the over-65 figures. It is important to realize that the entire issue of mandating retirement at age 65 or 70 is being tested in the courts. The argument against mandatory retirement is that "firing" a person from his job solely on the ground that he or she has reached some specified age is unreasonable and unfair.

SECTION II: MATHEMATICS

1. (D) The numbers must be aligned by their decimal points. You may also wish to add zeros.

$$
\begin{array}{r}
10.50 \\
122.00 \\
6.30 \\
\underline{1.32} \\
140.12
\end{array}
$$

Note that in this problem you could add only the numbers to the left of the decimal—10 + 122 + 6 + 1 = 139. Since the exact answer will be slightly more than this, choose (D), 140.12.

2. (C) Each televison set costs $792/10 = $79.20. Since there is a 40% markup, the selling price is 100% + 40%

$$\$79.20 + (40\% \text{ of } \$79.20) = \$79.20 + \$31.68 = \$110.88$$

Or you could have done it: $1.4 \times \$79.20 = \$110.88$. Notice that answers (A), (B), and (E) are not reasonable.

3. (E) If $3x > 0$, then x must be a positive number. Therefore, both statements II and III are true.

4. (B) The question may be most easily answered by counting the small squares and half-squares covered by the large, shaded square. Inside that figure are four complete squares and eight half-squares. Each small square equals one square centimeter. So the area of the large, shaded square is

$$4(1) + 8(\tfrac{1}{2}) = 8 \text{ sq cm}$$

5. (E) Let us use x to stand for the unknown quantity. Half of the quantity would then be written

$$\frac{x}{2}$$

"Six less" tells us to subtract six from the above:

$$\frac{x}{2} - 6$$

6. (C) This problem is most quickly solved by checking the answer choices. Since $20^2 = 400$, choices (A) and (B) are wrong. Choice (D) can also be rapidly eliminated, as $200^2 = 40,000$. But $63^2 = 3969$, close to 4000.

7. (B) The 1981 enrollment in psychology was approximately 220 and in biology was approximately 320. Thus, the psychology enrollment was 220/320 of the biology enrollment or slightly more than two-thirds. The answer must be (B). To obtain the precise percentage, you must divide 220 by 320.

$$320 \overline{\smash{\big)}\, 220.0000} = 68.75\%$$

$$.6875$$

8. (C) Economics enrollment increased from about 75 to 125, a rise of 50 students. To obtain the percentage increase, the change is divided by the starting figure: 50/75 = .67 or 67%. Note that although biology had an

increase of approximately 90 students, that was only about 40% of its 1976 enrollment.

9. **(A)** Let's first solve for x.

$$2x + 16 = 1$$
$$2x = -15 \text{ (subtracting 16 from each side)}$$
$$x = -7.5 \text{ (dividing each side by 2)}$$
Then $x + 7 = -7.5 + 7 = -0.5$

10. **(C)** Translate the statement into an equation, using the sumbol M for Mary's age and m for her mother's age. Were Mary three years older, she would be half her mother's age.

$$M + 3 = \tfrac{1}{2}m$$

Now substitute the fact that Mary is 19.

$$19 + 3 = \tfrac{1}{2}m$$
$$22 = \tfrac{1}{2}m$$
$$44 = m \qquad \text{(multiplying both sides by 2)}$$

11. **(B)** You must calculate the area of the circular lawn.

$$A = \pi r^2$$
$$\pi \simeq 3.14$$
$$A = 3.14 \times 25^2 \text{ (the radius is half the 50' diameter)}$$
$$A = 1963 \text{ square feet (rounded off)}$$

Each pound of seed plants 200 square feet, so P pounds are needed

$$P = 1963/200 \simeq 9.8 \text{ pounds or about 10 pounds}$$

12. **(B)** The annual interest is calculated by multiplying the principal invested (p) by the interest rate (r). The quarterly interest (i_Q) would be one-fourth the annual interest.

$$i_Q = \tfrac{1}{4}\,pr = 0.25 \times \$2130 \times 0.08 = \$42.60$$
$$\text{or}$$
$$\tfrac{1}{4} \times \$2130 \times .08 = \$2130 \times .02 = \$42.60$$

13. **(B)** Copy the equation.

$$\frac{2a - 6b}{5c - 1} = 4$$

Then substitute a = 2 and b = −1.

$$\frac{2(2) - 6(-1)}{5c - 1} = 4$$

$$\frac{4 + 6}{5c - 1} = 4$$

$$\frac{10}{5c - 1} = 4$$

$$10 = 4(5c - 1)$$

Now switch sides and divide by 4.

$$5c - 1 = 10/4 = 2.5$$
$$5c = 3.5$$
$$c = 0.7$$

14. **(B)** One complete revolution equals 360 degrees (thinking of the angle) and also 60 minutes (thinking of the time). Dividing those numbers, there are therefore 6 degrees per minute. In 3 minutes, the clock hand would travel $3 \times 6 = 18$ degrees.

15. **(B)** Mat must cover the ceiling, two end walls, and two side walls. The area of any rectangle is the product of its two dimensions. The area of the ceiling is $15 \times 12 = 180$, an end wall is $12 \times 9 = 108$, and a side wall is $15 \times 9 = 135$. So the insulation needed is

$$180 + 2(108) + 2(135) = 666 \text{ square feet}$$

16. **(D)** To find the percentage change (increase or decrease) use this formula:

$$\frac{\text{change}}{\text{starting point}} \times 100 = \text{percentage change}$$

$$\frac{84}{112} = 0.75 \times 100 = 75\%$$

17. **(C)** Set up the proportion.

$$\frac{R}{7} = \frac{3}{11}$$

Cross multiply. $11R = 3 \times 7$

$$11R = 21$$

Divide by 11. $R = 21/11 \simeq 1.9$

18. **(E)** The word *product* implies multiplication.

$$(-1.5) \times (-1.7) = +2.55$$

Notice that the product is positive because there is an even number of minus signs in the numbers being multiplied.

19. **(D)** The contours show that precipitation ranges from less than 16 inches in the southwest to over 40 inches in the southeast.

20. **(A)** Interpolating between the contours, you find that Abilene gets about $29\frac{1}{2}$ inches and Dodge City about $20\frac{1}{2}$ inches.

21. **(D)** Notice the change from one number to the next.

$$\underbrace{4 \quad}_{+3} \underbrace{7 \quad}_{+4} \underbrace{11 \quad}_{+5} \underbrace{16 \quad}_{+6} \underbrace{22 \quad}_{+7} 29$$

Thus, the next change will be $+8$. Adding 8 to the last number gives $29 + 8 = 37$.

22. **(B)** One-fourth of the 24 girls have red hair, so 6 girls (and no boys) have red hair. To express that as a percentage of the class, divide 6 by 40.

$$40 \overline{)6.00} = 15\%$$

with the quotient $.15$

23. **(D)** The formula to find simple interest is the amount invested (principal) times the annual rate of interest times the number (or part) of years the money was invested.

24. **(A)** Note that the adult portion of the "pie" is 75%, which may also be expressed as 3/4. The only choice in which adults are represented by 3/4 of the pie are choices (A) and (B). Note that in choice (B) teenagers and infants are represented as approximately equal. Only choice (A) represents adults, teenagers, and infants correctly.

25. **(D)** Since there are 10 milligrams in a centigram and 100 centigrams in a gram, to find the number of milligrams in 25 grams, multiply

$$10 \times 100 \times 25 = 25,000$$

There are 25,000 milligrams in 25 grams.

SECTION III: LITERATURE AND FINE ARTS

1. (D) The painting of a woman brushing the hair of a young lady is made much more realistic by the natural positions of the four arms during this activity. The painting appears candid and unposed. This style of art—the French Impressionism of the nineteenth century—used ordinary people and activities for its subject matter.

2. (E) The passage says that justice will then give him understanding and wisdom. The words dealing with eating and drinking are meant symbolically, not actually.

3. (B) The vase was made in Korea. Such delicate objects are often of Asian origin. One valuable clue is the bamboo plants on the right side of the vase. Also, in the twelfth century only Asia had such a high degree of civilization as the delicate vase reveals.

4. (E) The word *presume* rhymes only with *room*. Remember, for rhyme it is the pronunciation and not the spelling that matters.

5. (A) The lines are from Eliot's *The Love Song of J. Alfred Prufrock,* wherein he describes boredom with a world of pretence and futility. In the quoted lines, he states that he has done it all already, has tasted all that life offers: endless sessions of sipping coffee in drawing rooms.

6. (B) The waves do not seem particularly large. However, both the waving flags (A) and the tilting ships (D) reveal that a strong wind is blowing. The small scale of the people (C) also makes natural forces more impressive.

7. (E) As with most of Conrad's writing, these sentences show his fascination with morbid psychology. Some of the mental terms used in the passage are *resigned, trance, souls, desire,* and *hope.* Although many of Conrad's works concern the sea, this particular passage does not concern nature (C).

8. (E) You must consider the choices and passage carefully to answer this difficult question. In the passage, a man is perilously close to death, and the issue is whether he will resist or accept that fate. Of the answer choices, only a shipwreck (E) is a life-and-death event. The passage is from *Lord Jim,* a sea novel by Joseph Conrad in which the title character loses his self-respect in the crisis of the shipwreck.

9. (D) The fact that the building itself is such a spectacular work of art suggests that it is the work of one powerful mind, one architect with genius and audacity. No committee could have agreed on such a bold, unified design. In fact, the building is the Guggenheim Museum, designed by Frank Lloyd Wright.

10. (C) The painting is a typical religious theme from the Italian Renaissance. In the foreground are Mary and the Christchild; such works are called *Madonnas* (Italian for *mother*). In the background is a pastoral scene with cattle on a meadow.

11. (D) This sculpture from ancient Egypt shows a ruler offering two cups of wine to a god, represented by a gigantic falcon. The man's headdress shows that he is of the ruling class. The immense size of the bird shows it to be a symbol of the supernatural.

12. (E) The lines are the beginning of "Jabberwocky" by Lewis Carroll. In this most beloved of all nonsense poems, the words are literally meaningless. Two other nonsense poems by Carroll are "Father William" and "The Hunting of the Snark."

13. (A) The excerpt is from *The Canterbury Tales*, written by Geoffrey Chaucer in the fourteenth century in distinctive Middle English. The four lines describe a Monk who loved hunting, was capable of becoming an abbot, and owned many fine horses. *The Canterbury Tales* are told by a number of pilgrims and range, with life, from the sacred to the obscene.

14. (D) The lines are from "Birches" by Robert Frost, whose poems usually treat of the relationship of people to the countryside of New England. In the poem, the boy learns to face life and win—to ride the stiff trees until they are limp. As so often in poetry, the stated fact symbolizes something more profound and more general.

15. (C) This is part of Percy Bysshe Shelley's elegy to his fellow poet John Keats, who had just died. An elegy is an elevated expression of mourning. Shelley uses the Greek hero Adonais to represent Keats.

16. (B) The passage is from an amusing play, *Pygmalion* by George Bernard Shaw. Professor Higgins, an expert in phonetics, has noticed the Cockney slang of the flower girl Eliza and boasts to his friend of how greatly he could improve her speech. *Pygmalion* was made into *My Fair Lady*, a musical and movie; the latter starred Rex Harrison and Audrey Hepburn.

17. (E) This is an ancient Roman portrait-bust made from the type of clay called *terracotta*. The stern man is recorded so accurately because an initial model was made by placing wet plaster on his face.

18. (A) The straight lines of the window obey the laws of geometric perspective. Parallel lines seem to converge to a point in the distance, the "vanishing point." This technique gives a very convincing illusion of depth.

19. (B) This is a self-portrait by the Dutch artist Vincent van Gogh. The swirling brushstrokes in the background continue through into the lines of his coat. The skin and hair of his face are also made up of strong, separate

brushstrokes. The intense, passionate temperament of this famous painter is evident in his bold brushwork.

20. (B) Each letter of the rhyme scheme represents the sound ending one line. The first line is always denoted *a*. Our rhyme scheme is then *aabba* because lines 1, 2, and 5 have one sound, while lines 3 and 4 have a second sound. Note that the fifth line has an obviously forced ending to fulfill the *aabba* rhyme scheme of the typical limerick.

21. (D) The painting certainly does not faithfully copy reality. With a little imagination you can "see" a human figure molded from geometric parts. This painting by Picasso introduced the revolutionary style known as Cubism.

22. (C) The passage is from Mark Twain's hilarious story *The Notorious Jumping Frog of Calaveras County* in which the frog is filled with lead shot to prevent it from winning a jumping contest. Twain used colloquial language to enhance the rustic setting essential to the battle of wits between sharper and bumpkin.

23. (D) Slender rods of wrought iron are used to decorate the hotel lobby in this ornate architectural style known as Art Nouveau. This nineteenth-century style featured bizarre, curved ornaments inspired by vines and other plants.

24. (D) The astonishing popularity of the *Mona Lisa* comes mainly from her inscrutable smile. It is slight, it is enigmatic, and it seems to change as you study it. Answer choice (C) is wrong because her eyes are not averted to the side, but gaze directly at the viewer.

25. (E) The term for repeated consonants is *alliteration*. Notice *swift swallow, why wilt, soft south,* and *wither thine.* Each of these sounds occurs elsewhere in the lines too. The term *rhyme* (D) is usually used for similar sounds at the ends of lines.

26. (D) Knowing the title or subject of an artwork can sometimes affect our perception of it. Slavery has such a negative image that only answer choices (C) and (D) need be considered. However, there is no evidence of *torture*, so *uncomfortable* would be the best interpretation. This sculpture is *Bound Slave* by Michelangelo.

27. (D) The floor plan of the cathedral resembles a cross, the most powerful symbol of Christianity. Choice (A) is wrong because the cross-shaped plan was not a requirement. Although the functions (B) of religion could be conducted in such a cathedral, the symbolism was a more important factor in choosing between different designs.

28. (C) Only this choice sketches a situation which is not simple misfortune and which is connected with the hero's own character, that is, his stubborn disregard of the fortune-teller's advice.

29. (D) Their genuine affection is shown by their intimate embrace. The man's right hand pulls her toward him, while she holds him close with her left hand. The man's left hand is tightly squeezing her other hand. This painting of dancers by Pierre Renoir is a fine example of Impressionism, with fuzzy brushwork and an everyday subject.

30. (D) The poet clearly feels that the indoor lecture with calculations and diagrams is unimportant. So he walked outside and looked at the real stars, and no doubt this mystical dreamer thoroughly enjoyed a sense of glory from that actual experience. Incidentally, the poem is by Walt Whitman.

31. (B) The glass skyscraper really has no colors, for it is completely transparent. The repeated floors (A) and the vertical lines (E) both lend a strong sense of the building rising away from the earth. The reflections (C) from some of the glass surfaces also contribute to the lightness of the building.

32. (C) The last sentence of the essay states that every wise person that ever lived was misunderstood. For this type of question, which requires interpretation of a word or phrase, study most carefully the sentence containing the word or phrase. Do not be confused by the remainder of the passage.

33. (E) The second sentence of the passage mentions *great souls,* and examples of such people are provided in the final sentence. Choice (A) is incorrect because the intention of Emerson is to assert that great people are not necessarily consistent; consistency is for lesser mortals. Choice (B) is incorrect due to the word *sure.* The great are frequently misunderstood, not invariably misunderstood—else we should never recognize greatness.

34. (E) The light in the picture by Pieter de Hooch appears to be emanating from the windows and thus is characterized as sunlight, a natural source.

35. (C) Perspective is a geometric technique of giving the impression of depth to the picture. To accomplish that, the artist depicts parallel features as lines converging to a point on the background ("vanishing point"). Notice how the tiles of the floor and beams of the ceiling seem to converge toward the background, producing a three-dimensional effect.

SECTION IV: SCIENCE

1. (C) The blood, or circulatory, system is the body's way of moving oxygen from the lungs to tissues throughout the body. The same system also transports waste carbon dioxide from the tissues to the lungs.

2. (A) The temperature inside stars is so high that colliding hydrogen nuclei fuse together into larger helium nuclei, releasing an enormous amount of energy. The same process of nuclear fusion occurs in the explosion of a hydrogen bomb.

3. (E) The location of stars does not use reflected signals, for stars are so distant that it would take too long for a signal to return to an instrument on earth. It takes almost four years for light to travel one way from even the nearest star and many stars are thousands of times more distant.

4. (D) Since ice floats, the water must be denser. This is because the H_2O molecules are more closely packed in water than in ice. Choice (A) is incorrect because both substances have the same two types of atoms, hydrogen and oxygen.

5. (C) The lobster's shell serves as an *external* skeleton and so that animal is called an invertebrate. More precisely, it is classified as an arthropod, the phylum which also includes crabs, ants, and spiders.

6. (D) The orbit of Venus is closer to the sun than the earth's orbit. Voyager II was aimed to leave the earth and go away from the sun, visiting four planets of the *outer* solar system.

7. (B) Density is defined as mass divided by volume. For the five metal pieces, their densities are

Beryllium	1.85 grams per cubic centimeter
Calcium	1.55
Osmium	22.5
Titanium	4.5
Zinc	7.0

8. (C) Fermentation gradually converts the grape sugar to alcohol. Yeast cells conduct the fermentation, reproducing rapidly and evolving carbon dioxide.

$$\underset{\text{sugar}}{C_6H_{12}O_6} \rightarrow \underset{\text{alcohol}}{2C_2H_5OH} + \underset{\substack{\text{carbon} \\ \text{dioxide}}}{2CO_2}$$

9. (A) Weathering and erosion of the landscape produces salt dissolved in water. Such salts will become concentrated in lakes that lack outlets. Some, but not *most*, of the dissolved matter could come from processes (C) and (E).

The dissolved material cannot *come from* evaporation, which simply concentrates the dissolved salts.

10. (C) The fact that the light beams pass through each other and continue in their original directions is strong evidence that light is transmitted as waves. If light were particles, you would predict that the particles in the beams would collide, scattering the energy.

11. (B) The injected material stimulates the formation of antibodies to combat such disease material. The antibodies remain in the blood to act against any future infection of that particular disease.

12. (C) Desert plants are highly unlikely to have abundant broad leaves, for that would allow rapid evaporation of water from the leaves, making survival more difficult. The shade would not help the plant itself. The other four adaptive strategies are used by desert plants.

13. (C) Tuberculosis is a bacterial infection of the respiratory system, and a tubercular infection tends to persist (is chronic). The disease itself is not inherited, although a susceptibility to it may be.

14. (D) Reservoirs gradually fill up with sediment brought in by streams entering the man-made lake. Particles then settle in the still environment of the lake. Such sedimentation places a limit on the life of any reservoir.

15. (D) Both lack of rainfall and eroded soil (which causes runoff and hence wasted water) contribute to water shortage. Mulch, however, helps prevent evaporation and actually contributes to retaining water.

16. (E) Environmental pollution is a term that refers to the ways by which humans pollute their surroundings. Environmental pollution is best understood not as a single cause, but as a chain of events primarily associated with industrial development.

17. (E) Tundra is the sparse shrub-and-moss vegetation of high altitudes or the far north. Southward are the successive communities of conifers (evergreens), deciduous trees (which lose their leaves for the winter), and grasses. Permafrost is permanently frozen soil of the far north, not a community of plants.

18. (E) The metabolism of foods releases stored chemical energy, which is measured in *calories*. Of the five choices, the sugar has over 700 calories. All the other choices have 200 to 260 calories.

19. (D) Probably the whiteness is dominant in a gene and the redness is recessive, masked by the whiteness. Mutation is not a reasonable explanation because several flowers of each color must have been crossed and it is improbable the rare mutation could have occurred in every fertile seed.

20. (B) Glacial ice flows slowly as the snow and ice at higher elevation press downward. Glaciers are not frozen rivers but are solid year-round. Today's glaciers are residual from the Ice Age and may be shrinking. The earth becomes warmer at depth.

21. (A) Chlorine is the only gas on the list that is denser than air and would depress the lefthand cup. Even if you had forgotten the description of chlorine, you could have solved this question by eliminating the other four choices. Both helium and hydrogen are gases of low density, used to fill balloons. Nitrogen and oxygen are the major constituents of air, so neither is especially dense.

22. (C) Hydrogen is the least dense of all gases, so it would quickly escape upward as it was released into the open cup. Air would be in both cups and the beam would remain horizontal. You would need to seal one cup with hydrogen inside to see the end of the beam rise upward.

23. (C) As long as both ice and water are present in thermal equilibrium, they must be at the melting/freezing point, exactly 32°F. The water temperature could not be lower nor the ice temperature higher. An armchair experiment with a thermometer in a glass of ice and water will convince you that the temperature remains constant until all the ice has melted.

24. (B) A gaseous propellant stored at high pressure ejects a liquid, like paint or deodorant, in a fine spray. Depletion of the propellant leads to a fall in its pressure. Spraying ceases when that pressure has fallen as low as the atmosphere outside the can.

25. (D) The right hand had become adapted to 20°, so the later 30° seems warm. The left hand had become adapted to 40°, so the later 30° seems cold. You could do the experiment yourself to observe the contradictory sensations due to thermal adaptation.

26. (A) All organisms manufacture proteins from amino acids. Plants make all their amino acids from still simpler nutrients, but animals always depend on plants to supply some amino acids they cannot make themselves.

27. (A) Since the sea is very salty, it is somewhat surprising that the ice formed on the surface of the polar oceans contains almost no salts. As the water froze to ice crystals, the dissolved salts must have been prevented from entering the crystal structure.

28. (D) The proper inference is that human beings and whales have a common ancestor, the bone structure being inherited from some earlier mammal. The possibility that people evolved from fishes is not suggested by the human/whale similarity, for whales are not fishes but mammals.

29. (B) The force of buoyancy diminishes the apparent weight by the weight of water displaced by the glass object. The relation is known as

Archimedes' principle from the incident when that ancient Greek mathematician is said to have jumped out of his bath shouting "Eureka!" after he realized how to measure the purity of a crown. You know from swimming that submerged objects (including people) seem to weigh less.

30. (E) The compound DNA is the molecule which records genetic messages as a coded sequence of bases. It is found only in the chromosomes of cell nuclei and is duplicated during the cell-splitting of reproduction. The genetic information provides detailed control over the development and activity of cells and, hence, entire organisms.

TEST OF PROFESSIONAL KNOWLEDGE

SECTION I

1. (D) Ms. Corman should explain how she reached her conclusions and what can be done to help the child improve. Since the parents have asked for an explanation of their child's grades and the teacher's comments, the teacher should offer an explanation and advice. Choices (A) and (E) avoid the parents' questions. The premises for choices (B) and (C) are not stated in the question and the answers may be considered unnecessarily offensive.

2. (C) By examining the number of correct responses to an individual test question (item analysis) the teacher/researcher can (1) determine the difficulty of the test item, (2) evaluate the effectiveness of the teaching presentation, and (3) establish content validity.

3. (A) Choices (B) through (E) are key factors that might indicate why Ms. Schultz's class failed the assignment. However, the best choice is (A), since there is not enough information given in the question to lead to a specific answer.

4. (D) States do not provide supervision of individual school districts, statements I and V. They set minimum standards and provide certification, leaving the work of supervision to local communities.

5. (B) All of the choices may, in some way, enter into a parent-teacher conference. Choice (B) encompasses (C) and (E). The other choices are not adequate, since *good citizenship* talks are usually a minor part of a conference and planning a *child's future* is not the responsibility of a teacher.

6. (C) By definition, achievement tests attempt to measure what an individual has learned and the individual's present level of performance in academic learning. Learning potential is measured by aptitude tests.

7. (A) Reinforcement tactics consist of both positive and negative reinforcements. A negative reinforcement involves the removal of a negative stimulus. Choices (C) and (E) are incorrect, since *punishment* is not a reinforcement.

8. (A) The determination of a school district's goals lies with the elected representatives of the district, the board of education.

9. (D) Boys are more likely to be dyslexic than girls. This is statistically true. Dyslexia is a general term that refers to a broad range of reading disabilities.

10. (D) This is the best answer, since the learning activity of social adjustment can best be acted out, observed, and encouraged within the social context of a group. Choices (A), (B), and (E) state important ideas but lack the vehicles by which students can fully experience what they are learning.

11. (D) In modeling, behavior is learned by watching and imitating.

12. (C) You are looking for the best choice to explain why some teachers do not favor parent conferencing. Choice (A) is a possible answer. However, it is a specific explanation to a general problem. Choice (C) is broader in scope by suggesting that the explanation relates to a *number of factors.*

13. (C) A free public school system open to all segments of society is a cornerstone of our democratic system. Public education has strengthened America by effectively preparing students to live in our pluralistic society. Choice (A) is not the best answer, since private as well as public schools can effectively teach moral and ethical values.

14. (C) Choice (C), *lack of reading readiness when first exposed to reading instruction, uncorrected sensory problems, discouragement, emotional problems, and poor teaching,* encompasses most of the problems stated in the other choices.

15. (B) Tests should be used to determine the amount of learning which has taken place. This is best done upon the completion of a unit.

16. (C) The distribution of IQ scores for the general population centers around IQ 100 with higher and lower scores about equally common. Tests of mental maturity (Binet-Simon Intellectual Scale and California Tests of Mental Maturity) normally provide a verbal, a nonverbal, and a total IQ score. The goal of IQ tests is to predict intellectual and scholastic aptitude. Because of test question bias and socioeconomic and motivation factors, modern educators "downplay" the importance of IQ scores as predictors of general intelligence.

17. (A) The teacher should listen to the parent's viewpoint before deciding the best response. Parent interest and support should be encouraged. Not allowing parent input would discourage this, as would sending the parent to see the principal as in choice (C).

18. (A) History, the social sciences, and the experiences of students

provide the areas from which the social studies curriculum is developed. The other choices are not as complete as is (A).

19. (E) Differences in ways of living are better understood when seen in the context of the values and customs that underlie them. In teaching the understanding of other peoples, current popular thought assumes that all people are basically the same. Thus, choices (A) and (D) are incorrect. Choice (B) is incorrect, since institutions do change. Choice (C) shows a cultural bias, which does not lead to understanding.

20. (C) In the 1930s, B. F. Skinner extended the original learning studies of E. L. Thorndike. Skinner devised an apparatus that provides data on instrumental conditioning and has come to be called a "Skinner Box." It measures stimulus-response learning, or S-R.

21. (E) The question provides no statements that would lead to the other choices. Choice (E) is best, since it is a common problem among teachers (and people generally) that they forget to view people as individuals.

22. (D) All of these are integral parts of the teaching activity. As an information point, evaluation (III) is generally considered the most difficult process of curriculum planning. To be effective, evaluation must occur in conjunction with curriculum planning, since both are continuous processes.

23. (A) This philosophy is stated throughout Dewey's writings. Dewey's educational philosophy emphasized that learning and education were basically social in character. Dewey espoused an activities-based curriculum.

24. (A) The key to this question is the word *least*. Age and academic achievement, ability, and social development have very general correlations, which make grouping by age a poor choice. Although there is controversy concerning grouping by IQ, groupings of "mentally gifted minors" are common.

25. (A) Cultural values determine what we believe should be learned and therefore are basic to any decisions we make with regard to education.

26. (B) In this country public schooling is compulsory and nonsectarian. Public funds are constitutionally prohibited from being used to support or promote sectarian religious dogma in public or private schools.

27. (A) The teacher should guide and assist students when needed. The teacher must intervene in problem solving when needed so that the students will not become frustrated and be afraid to tackle problems by themselves.

28. (E) By definition, an aversive condition is an event that causes the learner physical or mental discomfort. Classroom examples of aversion

stimuli would include threatening behavior and the use of punishment and ridicule. Aversive stimuli are not considered conducive to effective learning.

29. (B) A curriculum guide, by definition, describes what is to be taught in particular courses at particular grade levels.

30. (D) The range (III) is the number representing the difference between the values of the largest and smallest scores in a distribution. The percentile (IV) is a number which represents the percent of scores that an individual raw score exceeds. Neither the range nor percentile specifically measures central tendency.

SECTION II

1. (A) Piaget identifies basic stages in the intellectual development of children. The ideas stated in the other choices do not belong to Piaget.

2. (B) Only in special circumstances is the use of physical force appropriate. Legally teachers are required to supervise students and to enforce rules and regulations necessary for their protection. However, the use of force should in no event exceed the amount of physical control *reasonably necessary* to maintain order and to protect the safety of students. The question does not provide sufficient information to justify physically restraining a student.

3. (E) Units are organized around topics or skills and can be as short or long as is necessary to cover the content. In choice (C) the word *continuity* is not as specific as the phrase *around particular themes, problems, or skills* in choice (E). Choice (C) also is not the proper answer because a unit may consist of one lesson plan. Choice (D) is not adequate because teaching units may come from textbooks and other sources and thus may not be developed by the teacher.

4. (D) Children can differ in rate and quality of growth. Choice (A) is possible but not necessarily true. Choice (B) reaches a conclusion that is not based on the premise. Choice (C) is not true and choice (E) is impossible.

5. (D) The National Science Foundation has long been known for giving grants for research in education as well as other areas. The Smithsonian Institution also gives many grants but is more closely associated with the technological development of the United States.

6. (D) A teacher can tell that learning has taken place when correct responses are given a number of times in a variety of contexts. In choices (B),

(C), and (E) the teacher has not asked the student to respond correctly. In choice (A) the student may guess the correct response.

7. (C) It is important that students can move from one group to another as their achievement level goes ahead or falls behind the rest of the group. Different teachers work better with different numbers of children in their groups and different teachers find different evaluation techniques most effective in determining grouping. Thus, choices (B) and (E) are not the best answers.

8. (D) Criterion referenced instruction is based on specific topics determined to be weak areas of students' knowledge. These areas are generally determined through item analysis of particular tests.

9. (D) They are determined by a combination of hereditary factors affected by environmental factors including the home and school. The issue of heredity versus environment is controversial. Choice (D) is the generally accepted opinion of modern times. Choice (B) is inadequate, since ability to learn varies due to many factors including readiness and the attitude of the learner.

10. (E) Teachers must respond to what they observe before they can consider the actions of choices (A), (B), (C), and (D).

11. (A) A lesson plan is basically a daily plan. Daily lesson plans often include objectives, content, materials, and a suggested time sequence. Choice (C) describes a course of study, and choice (E) describes a contract. It should be apparent that choice (D) is not the best definition for a lesson plan.

12. (A) The question asks for the one response that would differentiate a subject-centered curriculum from a child-centered curriculum. Only choice (A) is characteristic of a subject-centered curriculum—one that emphasizes traditional academic subjects. Choice (B) is characteristic of both types. Choices (D) and (E) are characteristic of a child-centered curriculum.

13. (B) If learning is meaningful, the student can see it in a larger context. Once seen in context, information is more easily used in another context.

14. (B) Children who purposely misbehave believe their actions will eventually gain them attention. Choices (A), (C), and (D) may be true, but there is not enough information in the question to reach any of these conclusions. Choice (E) could also be true in individual cases but cannot be applied to the general question involved.

15. (A) Encouragement can best be accomplished by helping children to

succeed in something they think important. This is most likely to occur if a teacher recognizes children's individual assets and helps them to use those assets to best advantage. Also, children will naturally pursue that in which they are interested.

16. (E) During oral reading understanding the pupil's difficulties is the important goal. Choice (A) is impractical and would probably be impossible to effect. Choices (B), (C), and (D) are not true.

17. (A) *Learning to recognize printed symbols associated with sounds or words* best fits a good definition of reading.

18. (B) Programed instruction provides the student with immediate feedback. Choices (A) and (C) are not true, and (D) and (E) are not as important as choice (B).

19. (D) Tests of general intelligence for children are usually expressed in terms of mental age and intelligence quotient. For example, on the Binet test, the intelligence quotient (IQ) of a child is simply a ratio of mental age over chronological age multiplied by 100. IQ = MA/CA × 100. Tests of mental maturity or intelligence tests are used to determine a child's mental age.

20. (D) Informing parents about the best ways to raise children is outside the areas of responsibility and expertise of teachers.

21. (D) Thinking is improved and learning takes place when students are actively involved in the teaching-learning process. This is the only choice that concentrates on what the *learner is gaining* from the inquiry process.

22. (E) Misrepresentative scores may be obtained by computing a mean when extreme scores are present.

23. (C) Statement III is not true; statement IV is not accurate, since team teaching may be effective or ineffective, depending on a number of variables.

24. (D) Choice (D) is the most comprehensive answer. Historically, a basic characteristic of American public education is that it reflects American democratic goals and purposes. Choices (A) and (C) are too limited in scope to be considered the best answer.

25. (A) Kinesthetic reinforcement is basically a multisensory approach to learning that culminates in the kinesthetic, or movement, process. A practical example would include the following steps in teaching a child to write the word *blue:* (1) say the word, (2) see the word, (3) write the word in the air in large, exaggerated letters, and (4) write the word on a paper. Note that steps (3) and (4) are examples of tactile stimulation.

26. (B) Schools must take the responsibility for helping to influence the way children feel about learning. This is the only answer that addresses the question and reflects current educational thought.

27. (B) Because of our schools' need to operate in classroom groupings, it is difficult to deal with individual needs. Notice that this question specifically deals with curriculum and not with other aspects of public education.

28. (C) One can arrive at the best answer through a process of elimination. Choice (A) can't be statistically determined; choice (B) is incorrect (cognitive objectives are more verifiable); choice (D) is incorrect (analysis, synthesis, and evaluation should follow knowledge, comprehension, and application); and choice (E) is incorrect. Assessing the cognitive domain is based on objective measurement. The cognitive domain includes objectives which deal with the development of intellectual abilities and skills.

29. (D) Audiovisual aids should be incorporated into lesson plans and should be used to help meet specific learning objectives.

30. (A) Psychologists, who are properly trained and possess the proper credentials to administer psychological testing, are the only ones who should do so.

SECTION III

1. (B) Defining limits of acceptable behavior and communicating these to the class members will provide children with standards that are necessary for classroom functioning.

2. (C) Student-teacher interaction can be both encouraging and discouraging. Choice (A) is improbable in a classroom setting. Choices (D) and (E) have some validity but are questionable as absolute statements.

3. (C) The most useful approach in correcting misbehavior is attempting to remove the causes of the misbehavior. The other choices are inadequate because they do not address the causes of the problem.

4. (A) The subject-centered education least reflects Dewey's philosophy; all other choices are characteristic of it. A subject-centered curriculum would emphasize "traditional" subjects, while Dewey advocated a practical, experience-based curriculum.

5. (A) Without proper motivation, active learning is difficult to achieve. Current educational research indicates that there is a high positive correlation between motivation and learning. In this example, choices (B) through (E) are less significant variables than motivation in successful learning.

6. (C) The other choices all are too subjective.

7. (A) By definition, an item is said to be valid when it measures what it is designed to measure. Reliability is defined as an indication of the consistency or stability of the test results.

8. (E) Complex processes that vary do not easily lend themselves to drill exercises.

9. (D) This kind of problem is handled by agencies other than schools. The principal will generally make the proper referrals himself or though the school district's representative to outside agencies. Attempting to mediate the problem is not part of the teacher's role and requires the authorized and trained personnel of other agencies. Failure to report the story to a principal may, in some states, cause the teacher to be legally liable.

10. (C) This is true by definition. The points in a distribution of scores divided into quarters is referred to as a quartile, meaning 25% in each quarter. The median point is called the second quartile (Q_2 or 50%).

11. (C) In order to properly use information in a new setting, it must be understood.

12. (C) It is important that students understand why their answers are right or wrong, and discussing correct answers provides an opportunity for students to gain this understanding.

13. (D) A teacher should keep grade records from which grades are computed. Grades should reflect student work and not be compromised by student or parent pressure. An explanation will usually clear up a problem and will head off referring a complaint to a principal.

14. (D) Learners will have difficulty in getting their eyes, hands, and thought processes to work together to achieve a given task. This answer is the most comprehensive and is true by definition. In students who demonstrate visual-motor-coordination problems, there is a lack of integration between vision and movement. This can result in gross-motor-coordination problems (the inability to develop skills involving natural movement) and fine-motor-coordination problems (the inability to make precise movements such as in writing).

15. (C) Community leaders are provided so that students can use them for modeling. Praise is used to reinforce student interest.

16. (A) Before a teacher takes action with regard to a particular child, the teacher should be aware of the child's school history and record. This is usually found in the cumulative record.

17. (A) A percentile is a number which represents the percent of scores that an individual raw score exceeds. The percentile allows the researcher to determine the relative standing of one score in relation to other scores. The percentile is determined by: (1) counting the number of scores which an individual score exceeds, (2) dividing this number by the total number of scores, and (3) multiplying by 100.

18. (B) This comprehensive answer lists all of the factors that most modern educators list as contributing to reading readiness.

19. (B) A disadvantage of programed instruction is that students may learn by memory and not understand the material. Choices (A), (C), and (D) are not disadvantages, and choice (E) is not true.

20. (E) All of the choices could be correct, but choice (E), the need to feel significant and be part of a larger group, is the best, since it speaks of the underlying motivations of the other answers.

21. (C) A meeting that centers on topics or problems raised by teachers is most valuable to teachers.

22. (D) The purpose of a curriculum-development committee is to develop a unified curriculum for the district under the direction of district supervisors. The problems of individual schools should be taken into consideration, but individual school planning and the implementation of curriculum is not the normal responsibility of curriculum committees.

23. (A) Silent-reading periods are not intended to provide teachers with extra time. Although teacher planning (III) and record keeping (V) may occur throughout a school day, the reasons for free silent-reading periods are not to provide more time for a teacher's nonteaching duties.

24. (A) Each child needs to feel accepted with the group. Choice (E) is not correct, since the child is not being challenged if he or she *easily* accomplishes all of the assignments. Although children should learn to function independently in many instances, choices (C) and (D) are not correct because the statements are absolute.

25. (C) A teaching machine is a mechanical device that makes use of programed materials. Programed instruction is useful in providing individualization of instruction. Choice (E) can be correct, but it is not as specific or comprehensive as choice (C).

26. (A) Dramatization provides an opportunity for students to learn cooperative self-expression. Choices (B), (C), and (D) are not, of themselves, educational. Choice (E) is not the best choice, since very few teachers are qualified to use psychodrama as a tool.

27. (A) An attempt should be made to understand and respond to the feelings of the parents. This should be done in order to facilitate communication. The other choices would be presumptive and inappropriate without an interchange of information and ideas.

28. (A) Silent reading enhances reading comprehension. Students tend to focus on words rather than meaning when reading aloud. Choice (E) requires memorization, not comprehension.

29. (B) Although all responses might lead to the development of thinking ability, choice (B) is the most comprehensive. Choices (A), (C), and (D) would not necessarily result in higher-level reasoning, and choice (E) is too narrow in scope to be considered the best answer.

30. (A) Health education should teach students about personal safety and hygiene. The other choices are not part of a health education curriculum.

SECTION IV

1. (C) Grades should reflect quality and quantity of performance. Grades should not be used as rewards or incentives, although they may be seen as such by students. Grades do communicate information to parents and students.

2. (B) Written composition is generally an individual effort and would not contribute to an appreciation for group dynamics.

3. (C) The child who is a behavior problem will most often be referred for counseling. The nature of the classroom environment requires that disruptive influences be dealt with so that the teaching process may continue. Other problems usually are not as pressing to a teacher and can often be more easily handled in a classroom.

4. (B) Quarrels become less physical with increasing age. This is the most accurate choice. Choice (C) is incorrect, since adults often solve children's quarrels, and it is questionable that quarrels end after physical action.

5. (D) Mathematical processes should be automatic in order to be functional. One must automatically know that $6 \times 6 = 36$. Rationalizing an answer is slow and makes application clumsy. Choices (A), (B), and (C) are value-laden, and choice (E) is inaccurate.

6. (D) Grading is not part of the learning process.

7. (A) Children should learn to consider multiple causes of events, evidence contrary to personal opinions, and the limits of generalization.

Choices (B) and (C) are language arts objectives, and (D) and (E) are subjective and moralistic.

8. (C) Experiments and demonstrations are valuable if used in the context of a lesson that relates observation to other information. In this way the experiment information reinforces or is reinforced by other teaching methods, and relationships are seen.

9. (D) When a certain response is more likely to be included than others, the sample is biased. Biased samples are not good indicators or predictors of the total picuture.

10. (E) Peer-group pressure and self-image are as important to slow learners as they are to more rapid learners. The other choices are not supported by educational research dealing with the motivation and learning potential of slow learners.

11. (C) Only choice (C) is stated as an affective objective. In the affective domain, objectives are stated as attitudes or personal values that should be inculcated in students. However, difficulty in evaluating desired outcomes is a major drawback associated with affective objectives. The other choices are stated as cognitive objectives. In the cognitive domain, objectives define a terminal behavior the teacher wants to measure. Cognitive objectives measure specific knowledge and generalizations, not attidues and values.

12. (E) Teachers can be held negligent in the performance of their duties if, after being apprised of a potentially hazardous situation, they do not take an appropriate course of action. Simply informing the school office does not relieve a teacher of legal responsibilities—the teacher must take effective action to alleviate the problem. In this case, the hazardous situation took precedence over Mr. Joseph's planning period (D). It should be apparent that the teacher didn't remain at the fountain until the situation was resolved (B). An appropriate action would have been to inform the office a second time that the situation was still hazardous.

13. (E) The failure of the progressive movement to adjust to the transformation of American society spelled its ultimate collapse. The progressive educational theories of the early 1900s were not conducive to an America that had entered the nuclear age.

14. (B) The NDEA was passed in response to the technological and scientific advances within the Soviet Union. It was hoped that a restructuring of our science programs (through direct federal aid) would provide the scientific leadership necessary to combat the Soviet Union's dominance in space.

15. (E) Conant suggested that to counterbalance the increasing role of the federal government in education, the states should form a compact. The compact would be a voluntary organization that would serve as a forum to review educational issues. Conant viewed interstate cooperation as a means to influence national educational policy. The other choices would promote increased federal control over education, an idea that Conant wished to discourage.

16. (C) Neill proposed a return to the eighteenth-century educational philosophy that espoused freedom, democracy, and self-determination. Neill reinstated the belief that children will learn best in an environment that is free of force. Choice (B) is incorrect, since Neill believed that education was both intellectual and emotional. Choice (D) is incorrect, since Neill strongly believed that freedom does not mean license.

17. (D) Jean Piaget's educational theories have led to a better understanding of the differing stages of child development. Piaget believed that there is an absolute continuity of all developmental processes. Each level of development is rooted in a previous phase and continues into the following one. The curricular implications of Piaget's theory included the concept that there are regular patterns in cognitive development, which are experienced by all children.

18. (D) 1900 marked a watershed in the history of American public education. In the decade that followed, Charles W. Eliot and the Committee of Ten (a committee of the National Education Assocation) recommended a dramatic change in the high school curriculum. Eliot stated that the public high schools were not preparing students for admission to college. To solve this problem Eliot proposed an elective system and uniform standards of instruction. The elective system was based on the equivalent value of the nine traditional academic courses. The other choices are characteristic of the progressive education movement.

19. (B) "U.S. Studies" implies a broader scope than the traditional U.S. history curriculum and is based on the belief that the United States is part of a global community. The curricular approach is to allow students to view U.S. history in the perspective of contemporary concerns. Choice (C) is incorrect, since the program is intended to view the United States in a world setting and not to foster idealistic internationalism.

20. (E) A daily progress report signed by the teacher, parent, and student provides the basis for effective home-school contact. Such contact also limits a student's potential to manipulate either teacher or parent with inaccurate information. To avoid needless confrontations, systematic records of student behavior should be available at all levels of home-school contact.

21. (B) Middle school group research reports can result in little more than verbatim accounts of reference material. As such, they lack originality. However, preparing appropriate instructional objectives and monitoring class activities can stimulate original thought. Gathering research, choice (D), is a legitimate aspect of committee assignments.

22. (D) In planning for effective group or committee work, the composition of the group is crucial. Randomly choosing group members insures that some groups will be poorly designed. Group dynamics must be considered in group and committee work. Personal observation, test scores, and peer relationships are key factors that a teacher must consider in selecting particular group members.

23. (C) Continuous evaluation provides a diagnostic basis on which to improve the learning process. Evaluation, if it is to be effective, must be a continuing activity that takes place at each stage of the learning process. It should be apparent that education cannot be measured solely in terms of end products, choice (A).

24. (E) The NEA is the national representative for teachers. A voucher plan or tax-credit plan would give tax benefits to parents who send their children to private schools. The NEA believes that the voucher plan would result in the proliferation of private and parochial schools to the detriment of the public school movement. Choice (E) encompasses the NEA's major concerns regarding a voucher system, especially the fear that the public schools would soon reflect only those students who could not afford a private education. Choices (A) and (B) are too limited to be the best answer.

25. (D) The President's Commission on Excellence (1983) stated that there is a dire shortage of math and science teachers in nearly all fifty states. The Commission also indicated that the quality of public education is *woefully inadequate*. Relatively low salaries contribute to the shortage of qualified math and science teachers. Also, financial and career incentives offered by industry have drawn off many top students who in earlier decades opted for a teaching career.

26. (B) Baseline data information provides the frequency of an undesirable behavior. The acquisition of baseline data is an important first step (after defining the target behavior) in modifying an undesirable behavior. Generally, data is gathered during specific observation periods in order to gain a representative sample of the child's behavior. Baseline data enable teachers to compare subsequent changes in the target behavior.

27. (E) For legal and professional reasons, a school district that has adopted a corporal punishment policy cannot administer such punishment

unless the student's parent or guardian has given written approval for such action. District notification of intent to administer corporal punishment should be in writing and in a language that is understandable to the parent. Choice (D) is incorrect, since certificated staff (not classified) have the legal authority to administer corporal punishment. It is important to note that if corporal punishment is found to be excessive, both the school district and the person administering the corporal punishment may be subject to civil action.

28. (D) Law enforcement officers have the legal power and responsibility to enter a school campus if a violation of the criminal code exists. In the performance of their duty, the police also have the right to question, and in extreme cases, to arrest students on school grounds. School administrators have no jurisdiction over the activities of law enforcement officers in the discharge of their duties on the school campus. If a student is arrested at school, the law enforcement personnel must give due consideration to the student's legal protections.

29. (A) Balance and posture, locomotion, contact and receipt, and body image and differentiation are terms associated with the perceptual-motor systems. Primary school age children who are assessed as lacking fundamental perceptual-motor abilities can be referred to a perceptual-motor specialist. Since motor activities can play a major role in intellectual development, perceptual-motor labs were established to allow children to develop competency in identifiable perceptual-motor deficiencies. Perceptual-motor deficits result primarily from brain dysfunction, peripheral nerve damage, and mental retardation.

30. (B) Merit pay has been consistently opposed by teacher groups for the following reasons: (1) it would undercut organizational bargaining power, (2) it would diminish job security, (3) teachers are afraid that administrators would not be fair judges of merit pay, (4) teacher groups are afraid that merit pay and favoritism would go hand-in-hand, (5) such a system would be hard to administer and might prove divisive. Teacher groups on the other hand have consistently favored maintaining tenure and the seniority system and raising all teacher salaries significantly. Supporters of merit pay argue that the current system is inadequate, since it treats good and bad teachers exactly alike.

FINAL PREPARATION: "The Final Touches"

1. Make sure that you are familiar with the testing center location and nearby parking facilities.
2. The last week of preparation should be spent on a general review of key concepts, test-taking strategies, and techniques.
3. Don't cram the night before the exam. It is a waste of time!
4. Arrive in plenty of time at the testing center.
5. Remember to bring the proper materials: identification, admission ticket, three or four sharpened Number 2 pencils, several ballpoint pens, an eraser, and a watch.
6. Start off crisply, working the questions you know first, and then coming back and trying to answer the others.
7. Try to eliminate one or more choices before you guess, but make sure you fill in all of the answers. There is no penalty for guessing.
8. Mark in reading passages, underline key words, write out important information, and make notations on diagrams. Take advantage of being permitted to write in the test booklet.
9. Make sure that you are answering "what is being asked" and that your answer is reasonable.
10. Cross out incorrect choices immediately, this will keep you from reconsidering a choice that you have already eliminated.
11. Using the TWO SUCCESSFUL OVERALL APPROACHES (p. 7) is the key to getting the questions right that you should get right—resulting in a good score on the NTE Core Battery.

Permission is gratefully acknowledged for the use of the following:

Photographs of paintings and sculpture from *Great Museums of the World—National Gallery London,* Newsweek, Inc. and Arnoldo Mondadori Editore, photographs by Kodansha, Ltd., © 1969 and *Great Museums of the World—Louvre Paris,* Newsweek, Inc. and Arnoldo Mondadori Editore, Photographs by Kodansha, Ltd., © 1967.

Cartoon by Frank Interlandi, © 1980 in the *Los Angeles News.*

Chart of state constitutions, map of the elections of 1868, and chart "Educational Level of Voters in Recent Presidential Elections" from *AMERICA! AMERICA!* by L. Joanne Buggey, Gerald A. Danzer, Charles L. Mitsakos, C. Frederick Risinger. Copyright © 1977 Scott, Foresman and Company. Reprinted by permission.

Graphs by James Francavilla titled "Median Family Income" © 1979, "Median Expenditures for Monthly Housing Expenses" © 1978, "World Oil Production" © 1980, "Nonemployment Relationship" © 1977, and "Real Gross National Product" © 1977 by the *Los Angeles Times.* Graph by Bob Allen titled "Distribution of Earned Degrees by Field of Study, 1974–75" © 1978 by the Los Angeles Times. Reprinted by permission.

Graph from *Hammond Almanac.* Courtesy of Hammond Incorporated.

Photographs of paintings and sculpture from the Museum of Fine Arts, Boston.

Architectural photographs from the Guggenheim Museum, New York.

Architectural photographs from the Museum of Modern Art, New York.

To understand great authors, you need to read between the lines.

Cliffs Complete Study Editions

The more you learn about the classics, the richer your enjoyment and the deeper your understanding become. These easy-to-use Complete Study editions contain everything a student or teacher needs to study works by Shakespeare or Chaucer. Each illustrated volume includes abundant biographical, historical and literary background information, including a bibliography to aid in selecting additional reading.

The three-column arrangement provides running commentary for the complete Cambridge edition of the Shakespeare plays, plus glossary entries explaining obscure Elizabethan words. The Chaucer titles contain running commentary, individual lines of the Middle English text, followed by literal translations in contemporary English, and glossaries.

Complete Study Editions
8½ × 11

Shakespeare	Qty.
1416-5 Hamlet	
1419-X Julius Caesar	
1425-4 King Henry IV, Part 1	
1422-X King Lear	
1428-9 Macbeth	
1431-9 Merchant of Venice	
1434-3 Othello	
1438-6 Romeo and Juliet	
1441-6 The Tempest	
1445-9 Twelfth Night	
Chaucer's Canterbury Tales	
1406-8 The Prologue	
1409-2 The Wife of Bath	

Prices subject to change without notice.

$6⁹⁵ each

Available at your booksellers, or send this form with your check or money order to **Cliffs Notes, Inc., P.O. Box 80728, Lincoln, NE 68501**
http://www.cliffs.com

☐ Money order ☐ Check payable to Cliffs Notes, Inc.

☐ Visa ☐ Mastercard Signature_____

Card no. _____ Exp. date_____

Signature _____

Name _____

Address _____

City _____

State _____ Zip _____

Cliffs NOTES INC.

Cliffs
Math Review
for
Standardized
Tests

**FOR ANYONE TAKING A
STANDARDIZED TEST
WITH MATH SECTIONS**

GMAT — SAT — NTE — GRE — State Teacher Credential Tests — PSAT — CBEST — ACT — PPST — GED
and many more!

Use your time efficiently with exactly the review material you need for standardized tests.

Provides insights and strategies for specific problem types, plus intensive review in the most needed basic skills in arithmetic, algebra, geometry, and word problems.

Includes hundreds of practice problems to reinforce learning at each step in a unique easy-to-use format.

Available at your local bookseller, or send in check or money order with the coupon below.

Cliffs Notes, Inc., P.O. Box 80728, Lincoln, NE 68501

- -

Cliffs Math Review
for Standardized Tests $8.95 _____

• *Price subject to change without notice*

Cliffs NOTES

P.O. Box 80728
Lincoln, NE 68501

Name _____

Address_____

City _____ State _____ Zip_____